AGE OF *Transition*

AGE OF *Transition*

READINGS IN CANADIAN SOCIAL HISTORY, 1800–1900

Norman Knowles

UNIVERSITY OF CALGARY

HARCOURT
BRACE
CANADA

Harcourt Brace & Company, Canada

Toronto Montreal Fort Worth New York Orlando
Philadelphia San Diego London Sydney Tokyo

Canadian Cataloguing in Publication Data

Main entry under title:

Age of transition: readings in Canadian social history,
    1800–1900

Includes bibliographical references.
ISBN 0-7747-3559-7

1. Canada — Social conditions — 19th century.   I. Knowles,
Norman James, 1963–   .

HN103.A46   1998   971.03   C97-930538-1

Senior Acquisitions Editor: Christopher Carson
Senior Developmental Editor: Laura Paterson Pratt
Supervising Editor: Semareh Al-Hillal
Production Co-ordinator: Carolyn McLarty, Sheila Barry

Copy Editor: Theresa Griffin
Permissions Editor: Martina van de Velde
Cover and Interior Design: Sonya V. Thursby/Opus House Incorporated
Typesetting and Assembly: IBEX Graphic Communications Inc.
Printing and Binding: Best Book Manufacturers, Inc.

Cover Art: Robert Harris, *A Meeting of the School Trustees* (1885). Reproduced by permission of the National Gallery of Canada, Ottawa.

This book was printed in Canada.

1 2 3 4 5   02 01 00 99 98

Preface

The nineteenth century was an age of economic growth and nation-building. It was also a period of startling and unsettling social changes. The articles contained in this reader explore the impact of many of these changes on the everyday lives of people, and the different strategies they adopted in order to survive in an increasingly complex society. The reader introduces students to many of the major themes and issues in social history: the role of class, gender, and ethnicity in shaping social behaviour and consciousness; the nature and sources of social inequality; the functions of the family; the impact of industrialization and urbanization; the process of state formation; the emergence of reform movements; and the significance of popular culture and religion in everyday life. Space limitations have meant that many topics could not be included in the reader; each of those selected, however, addresses a significant locus of change in Canadian society during the nineteenth century.

The articles include some of the most innovative recent scholarship as well as some well-known classics. An effort has been made to introduce students to a variety of methodologies and approaches. Care has been taken also to ensure that all regions of Canada are represented. The short introductions at the beginning of each section place the topics in their social and historical context, and call attention to debates in the historiography and particular issues raised in the articles. A set of questions follows each topic introduction to help facilitate reflection and discussion, and a list of suggested readings directs students to some of the most important works on the topic.

ACKNOWLEDGEMENTS

I am grateful to Chris Carson, Laura Paterson Pratt, Martina van de Velde, and Semareh Al-Hillal of Harcourt Brace for their support and assistance in preparing this reader, and to Theresa Griffin for her careful editing. Thanks are extended to David Marshall and Sarah Carter of the University of Calgary and Jean Barman of the University of British Columbia for their helpful suggestions on topics and readings. Constructive reviews were provided for Harcourt Brace by Donald Avery, University of Western Ontario; Gail G. Campbell, University of New Brunswick; Cecilia Danysk, Western Washington University; Alan Gordon, Queen's University; Susan Houston, York University; G.S. Kealey, Memorial University; Greg Marquis, St. Mary's University; Barry Moody, Acadia University; Eric Sager, University of Victoria; and Gerald Stortz, University of St. Jerome's College. Finally, I am indebted to all the authors who allowed their work to appear in this reader.

A NOTE FROM THE PUBLISHER

Thank you for selecting *Age of Transition: Readings in Canadian Social History, 1800–1900*, by Norman Knowles. The author and publisher have devoted considerable time to the careful development of this book. We appreciate your recognition of this effort and accomplishment.

We want to hear what you think about *Age of Transition*. Please take a few minutes to fill in the stamped reader reply card at the back of the book. Your comments and suggestions will be valuable to us as we prepare new editions and other books.

Contents

Introduction

The nineteenth century was an age of transition. Every era, of course, experiences change, but the scale and magnitude of the changes that transformed Canadian society during this period were unprecedented in their degree and magnitude. Until recently, historians of the period were preoccupied with Canada's political evolution and its economic growth and development. Their focus meant that many groups of people and many aspects of people's lives were overlooked. The rise of social history and its many subfields in the 1960s and 1970s, however, broadened the scope and subject matter of historical inquiry. Since its inception, social history has been concerned with the social processes and structures that shape society, the life experiences of ordinary people, and the manners and customs of everyday life. Social historians from the beginning have drawn upon the theories and techniques of other disciplines in the social sciences in making their own inquiry. Asking new questions about the past and equipped with new approaches and methodologies, they have rewritten the story of nineteenth-century Canada to include the experiences, values, and attitudes of people from all walks of life and backgrounds. Their work has promoted a deeper understanding of the social, economic, and political forces that shaped nineteenth-century Canada and a fuller appreciation of the diversity and complexity of Canadian society during this critical period.

At the beginning of the century, Canada consisted of seven disparate and largely undeveloped colonies inhabited by fewer than 350 000 persons. Most of these people lived along the waterways, which offered the only reliable means of transporting people and goods, and most of them made a living from the land or the sea. In 1800, the vast territories of the west were legally the domain of the Hudson's Bay Company but remained in the possession and control of the area's indigenous peoples. Natives played an essential role in the fur trade as trappers, provisioners, transporters, and interpreters. By 1900, however, Canada had become a vast transcontinental nation with a population of just over five million. Most Natives had been dispossessed of their lands and confined to reserves as a tide of immigrants occupied the west. Although many Canadians continued to earn a livelihood from the land, many others lived in cities and towns and worked in industry, commerce, and the professions. These changes altered the land and its people in a myriad of ways.

The tremendous growth in Canada's population during the nineteenth century was due to natural increase and to immigration. Prior to the outbreak of the War of

1812, most immigrants came from the United States. After the war, the majority of newcomers originated in the British Isles. Between 1815 and 1850 nearly a million persons arrived in British North America from England, Scotland, and Ireland. Many did not stay but simply passed through Canada on their way to the United States. Those who remained, however, provided the pool of labour essential for economic expansion. Later, during the century's final decade, tens of thousands of immigrants from continental Europe, Britain, and the United States began to pour onto the prairies. Over the course of the century, immigration significantly changed the ethnic make-up of Canada. Whereas in 1800 French Canadians made up 60 percent of the population, in 1901, French Canadians constituted less than a third. By that time, nearly 60 percent of the population was of British ancestry, and the remaining 15 percent of European or Asian background. Many of the newcomers to Canada throughout the nineteenth century encountered discrimination and even violence. Religious and cultural differences and the fear of economic competition gave rise to periodic outbursts of nativist sentiment.

During the early decades of the century, Canada was an overwhelmingly rural and agrarian society. Most farms were small, and scarcity, isolation, and back-breaking labour characterized the lives of many farmers. The rural family depended on the work of all its members. Women made a critical contribution to the economic viability of the household as home manufacturers and food producers and often brought in additional income by taking in boarders, laundry, and piecework or by working as teachers, midwives, and healers. Children were assigned chores at an early age. But over the course of the century, technology and the marketplace transformed rural life. Rural production was reorganized and mechanized so that commodities could be produced more efficiently for a growing market. Household manufacturing and subsistence farming were gradually displaced as agriculture became almost wholly commercial. By mid-century, rural families increasingly sold what they produced and bought what they needed. The pace of change accelerated during the final decades of the century. Farming became more specialized, mechanized, and dependent on international markets. Bankers and the middlemen who transported, stored, and sold farm produce became powerful players in the emerging business of agriculture. Many of these changes frustrated farmers and planted the seeds of agrarian protest.

Although a majority of Canadians continued to dwell in the countryside in 1900, more and more people moved to the cities and towns over the course of the nineteenth century. The growth of cities was one of the most dramatic and far-reaching developments of the period. In 1800, only Halifax, Montreal, and Quebec had a population of over 5000. A hundred years later, nearly four out of every ten Canadians lived in communities of 1000 or more people. The largest of these urban centres, Montreal, had a population of 328 000. The growing urban population came from both the countryside and abroad. The modernization of agriculture in the second half of the century forced many rural people to flock to the cities and towns in search of work, new opportunities, and the amenities of urban life. Attracted by the availability of work, large numbers of immigrants settled in the cities as well. By the end of the century, cities such as Montreal and Toronto had become thriving centres of commerce, industry, and transportation, and boasted grand mansions, impressive business and industrial buildings, imposing civic monuments, and whole neighbourhoods filled with substantial middle-class homes. They also contained crowded and unsanitary slums and suffered from a host of social problems such as disease, crime,

and juvenile delinquency. Such disparity made glaringly obvious a growing gap between rich and poor. But despite the miserable conditions in the slums, working-class families created a rich community life that helped to alleviate some of the dreariness of their physical surroundings.

The nineteenth century was a period of tremendous economic growth and change. Abundant natural resources, substantial population growth, a revolution in transportation, and rapid technological innovation combined to transform Canada from a pre-industrial to an industrial society by the century's end. Protected by mercantilist policies, the products of Canada's farms and forests found a secure market in Britain during the first half of the century. The export of these staples helped to create the wealth essential for industrialization. A growing population supplied the workers and consumers needed by industry. The revolution in transportation provided the greatest impetus for the growth of industry. At the start of the century, virtually all travel was by water. The few roads that existed in British North America were rough and often impassable. Transportation improved tremendously with the advent of the steamship and the construction of canals around the rapids of the St. Lawrence River and Niagara Falls. It was the coming of the railway at mid-century, however, that made the biggest contribution to the rise of industry. The railway facilitated the movement of goods, people, and information; decreased shipping costs; drew people into the domestic market; and stimulated agricultural expansion. The rails and engines needed by the railroads themselves laid the basis for the first large-scale industrial operations.

The gradual emergence after 1850 of a new industrial economy based on mass production for mass markets altered the scale and rhythms of work. At the beginning of the century, work was done by hand by skilled artisans in small shops located in or near the home. Artisans enjoyed considerable autonomy and controlled the pace of their own work. The craftsmen of the early part of the century belonged to their own associations and possessed a distinct set of values and attitudes. But in the second half of the century, work was increasingly done in large mechanized factories employing dozens if not hundreds of people. Workers were now closely supervised, and the pace of production was dictated by machines and the clock. Factory employees resisted these changes and organized to maintain their autonomy, values, and traditions. Most protest efforts, however, met with limited success. The law was used to prevent workers from organizing and withholding their labour, and the police and the militia were often used to intimidate them. Divisions between skilled and unskilled workers as well as ethnic and religious differences often hampered united action. From time to time, however, workers did succeed in coming together to defend their interests. The phenomenal rise of the Knights of Labor in the 1880s was the most impressive example of working-class solidarity, but smaller strikes and protests throughout the century testified to the existence of a distinct class culture and consciousness.

Industrialization had a considerable impact on family life. For the emerging middle class, the separation of work from the home and the creation of a consumer society significantly altered gender roles. An ideology of separate spheres emerged that emphasized women's maternal nature and domestic role and stressed men's responsibilities as breadwinners. Although the concept of domesticity seemed to confine women to their homes, it actually prompted women to assume a more active public role. As guardians of the home and morality, women became increasingly involved in religious, charitable, and reform organizations. Moreover, as gender roles

were reformulated, a new view of childhood emerged. Children ceased to be valued principally for their labour, as middle-class parents came to see childhood as a distinct period of character formation and preparation for adulthood. The size of families, too, declined significantly over the course of the century, as birth rates fell. Many middle-class couples chose to have fewer children now that their children's labour was no longer essential to the economic survival of the household. These changes, however, did not take place to the same extent in farm and working-class families, whose survival continued to depend on economic contributions from all their members. Working-class wives and mothers often took in piecework or were employed in sweatshops and factories. Male children worked in the streets as newsboys or scavengers, while female children cared for their siblings or worked as domestics.

The growth of cities and towns, the increase in the size of the professional and service sectors, and a shift in the nature of wealth away from land to capital resulted in the emergence of a new middle class in the nineteenth century. The rise of a commercial society in the first half of the century broke down old class barriers. By enterprise and initiative, people could break the ties binding them to the station to which they had been born. Status could now be gained, through the control of one's capital, the independence accompanying self-employment, and the authority conferred by expertise and specialized skills. The new middle class was characterized by a distinct set of cultural values that emphasized the individual, progress, reason, industry, respectability, self-control, achievement, and the family. But the final decades of the century witnessed the growth of an unease in the middle class. Fears of class polarization and social unrest along with changes in the middle-class workplace resulted in new efforts on the part of middle-class Canadians to defend their status and position.

The emergence of the middle class reflected the increasing prosperity of nineteenth-century Canada, but the country's wealth was not distributed equitably. Rural society was not as egalitarian or prosperous as is often assumed. Many rural families lived on marginally productive lands from which they could eke out only a bare subsistence. Population pressure, poor farming practices, soil exhaustion, pestilence, and variable markets forced many others to leave their farms. Some relocated to undeveloped areas of the Maritimes and the Canadas. Others went to the United States and, following Confederation, the Canadian west. Still others attempted to start life over again in the towns and cities. Low wages, injury, illness, and seasonal unemployment created considerable hardship and suffering among the urban working class as well. The poor, the maimed, and the unemployed, who often fell victim to charges of vagrancy or other crimes, filled the prisons and poorhouses of nineteenth-century Canada. In general, the search for land, work, and opportunity made nineteenth-century Canada an extremely fluid society. Census records reveal that few Canadians remained in the same locality for more than a decade. But if geographic mobility was great, social mobility appears to have been far more limited. The social and economic forces that transformed Canada in the nineteenth century generated great fortunes and new opportunities; they also resulted in appalling poverty and social misery.

A spirit of reform pervaded much of the nineteenth century. Disturbed by the social problems that accompanied urbanization and industrialization but buoyed by a strong faith in progress and their own ability to find solutions, middle-class Canadians organized to do battle against a host of perceived social ills. They formed societies to promote such ideals as temperance, moral purity, and women's rights and organized movements in support of public schools, libraries, parks, playgrounds, and

asylums for the mentally ill. But the solutions advocated by the reformers failed to address the structural sources of poverty and unemployment that were at the root of many social problems. This failure was due, in part, to the myth of the self-made man, which dominated middle-class thinking. It was widely believed in the nineteenth century that no individual need languish in the lower ranks of society, and that with industry, thrift, and sobriety any person could achieve success. It was assumed that one who was poor or unemployed yet able to work must be lazy, thriftless, and intemperate. Many reformers were convinced that the only effective way to combat pauperism and unemployment was to make war on the habits that brought poverty about and to inculcate the poor with the middle-class virtues of thrift, sobriety, hard work, and discipline. Working people, for their part, possessed a distinct culture, which enabled them to resist middle-class efforts to control their behaviour. Societies for social reform, moreover, were not the only organizations that nineteenth-century Canadians joined. An age of associations, the century witnessed the appearance of a myriad of social, occupational, ethnic, and religious societies. These associations performed a variety of functions, in offering their members support and assistance, opportunities for self-improvement, and a means of proclaiming their position and status. The church was another institution that occupied an important place in the lives of many people during the century. For women especially, the church provided opportunities for active involvement in the public sphere through reform and mission work.

The nineteenth century was a period of tremendous social transformation and upheaval in Canada, as older forms of behaviour and social organization were gradually displaced by new conventions and structures. These innovations significantly affected the relationships that existed between men and women, different classes, and various ethnic communities. The articles presented in this reader explore some of the responses of these different groups to the forces reshaping Canadian life during this critical period. The picture that emerges is of a complex and dynamic society struggling to adapt to the sweeping developments that were transforming Canada from a set of rural- and resource-based colonies into a modern urban and industrial nation.

TOPIC ONE
Aboriginal Peoples

A Native canoeist at
New Westminster, British
Columbia, around 1863.

The nineteenth century was a period of unprecedented change for Canada's aboriginal peoples. At the beginning of the century, many Natives enjoyed great influence and autonomy as vital economic partners and valued military allies of the European newcomers. The decline of the fur trade and the threat of American invasion, combined with increases in population, immigration, and settlement, pushed indigenous peoples to the margins of Canadian society. By the end of the century most Natives found themselves isolated on reserves and subject to government policies designed to destroy their identity and traditions. Throughout the century, however, Natives attempted to respond creatively to the challenge of change and actively to preserve their ways of life.

Only recently have historians begun to explore the response of the aboriginal peoples to the forces transforming Canadian society during the period. Prior to the 1970s, most Canadian history was preoccupied with the transplantation of European cultures to North American soil and the conquest of an "empty wilderness." Natives appeared as little more than background figures at the margins of society in much of this history. The rise of ethnohistory in the early 1970s did much to restore the place of indigenous peoples in the country's past. Drawing upon the findings and methodologies of archaeology and anthropology, ethnohistorians have offered new insights into the encounters between indigenous peoples and European fur traders, missionaries, settlers, and government officials. Natives no longer appear as passive objects swept aside by a European tide but as active and resourceful participants determined to maintain their ways of life and to defend their interests. In recent years, ethnohistorians have examined such diverse topics as the role of Native women in the fur trade, the formation of inter-racial families, Native spirituality, and the impact of residential schools and federal agricultural policies.

The articles that follow explore two understudied questions: the impact of landscape and environment on Native culture and identity and the participation of Native peoples in an emerging wage economy. In Article One, John Milloy examines the ways in which the buffalo shaped the social and spiritual worlds of the Plains Cree and contributed to their sense of territory. An appreciation of this sense of territory, Milloy maintains, is essential to an understanding of Plains Cree participation in the treaty making process of the 1870s. In Article Two, John Lutz analyzes the place of aboriginals in British Columbia following the decline of the fur trade. Challenging the long-standing view that Natives were peripheral to the economic development and industrialization of the province, Lutz demonstrates that Native workers played a vital role in the rise of new industries and the spread of capitalism.

QUESTIONS TO CONSIDER

1. How did the Plains Cree "bio-region" change in the nineteenth century? What impact did these changes have on the Plains Cree identity and way of life? How did the attitudes of the Plains Cree toward the land and its resources shape their understanding of the treaty making process?
2. How important was aboriginal labour to the British Columbia economy in the nineteenth century? Why and how did Native people join the paid labour force?
3. What are the limitations of traditional documentary sources in the study of ethnohistory? How can historians recover the Native voice and point of view?

SUGGESTED READINGS

Abel, Kerry. *Drum Songs: Glimpses of Dene History*. Montreal/Kingston: McGill-Queen's University Press, 1993.

Brown, Jennifer. *Strangers in Blood: Fur Trade Company Families in Indian Country*. Vancouver: University of British Columbia Press, 1980.

Carter, Sarah. *Lost Harvests: Prairie Indian Reserve Farmers and Government Policy*. Montreal/Kingston: McGill-Queen's University Press, 1990.

Fisher, Robin. *Contact and Conflict: Indian–European Relations in British Columbia, 1774–1890*. Vancouver: University of British Columbia Press, 1977.

Miller, J.R. *Skyscrapers Hide the Heavens: A History of Indian–White Relations in Canada*. Toronto: University of Toronto Press, 1989.

Ray, A.J. *Indians in the Fur Trade: Their Role as Trappers, Hunters, and Middlemen in the Lands Southwest of Hudson Bay, 1660–1870*. Toronto: University of Toronto Press, 1974.

Upton, Leslie F.S. *Micmacs and Colonists: Indian–White Relations in the Maritimes, 1713–1867*. Toronto: University of Toronto Press, 1979.

Van Kirk, Sylvia. *"Many Tender Ties": Women in Fur-Trade Society in Western Canada*. Winnipeg: Watson and Dwyer, 1980.

ONE

"Our Country": The Significance of the Buffalo Resource for a Plains Cree Sense of Territory

JOHN MILLOY

From late in the eighteenth century a Plains Cree culture flourished in the Old West — the land that today comprises the prairie provinces. It was a culture forged by the Cree experience in the fur trade, and by the rich resources of the parkland and plains regions. These historical and environmental elements in shaping the Cree community, giving in the 1790s a woodland people a new plains identity, refashioned Cree relationships with the land, with their creator, with other Native groups and with the newcomers — the white fur traders and the Métis. This culture, in its classic plains form, was to have a limited run, however, for from the 1850s onward the Plains Cree world, or bio-region (an ecology in an all-encompassing sense, combining the systems of nature with the social, political, economic, diplomatic and military systems of human communities), began to change. First a land of Indian nations and then one

Source: Excerpted from "'Our Country': The Significance of the Buffalo Resource for a Plains Cree Sense of Territory," in Kerry Abel and Jean Friesen, eds., *Aboriginal Resource Use in Canada: Historical and Legal Aspects* (Winnipeg: University of Manitoba Press, 1991), pp. 51–70. Reprinted by permission.

of a fur-trade society, the Old West was entering its last phase. The compact[1] among traders — Indian, white and Métis — that was the essence of fur-trade society was soon to be disrupted by the coming of the agents of a Canadian empire, by farmers, lumbermen and miners, and by their precursors — the treaty makers.

Irene Spry has charted the extensive change in this era. What she has termed "the great transformation"[2] was in fact "transition in western Canada from common property resources, to open access resources, and finally to private property. In essentials, it is the story of the tragedy of the disappearance of the commons on the prairies after 1870."[3] As Spry and many others have noted, the pivotal event in this transition was the failure of the fundamental plains resource — the buffalo. This event created a severe internal dislocation, which undercut the lives of Westerners, destroying traditional resource, land and inter-group relations, and it was a major step in preparing the West for Canadian colonization. In the last quarter of the nineteenth century, during the initial process of colonization that was achieved through treaties, the creation of Manitoba, territorial government, the North West Mounted Police and the building of the infrastructure of a settler-capitalist society, the prairie map was redrawn with the communal traditions and Aboriginal rights of Native nations replaced by the property rights of white individuals, the powers of often-distant corporations and the jurisdictional prerogative of the federal government over land and resources.

The Plains Cree were not, of course, excepted from this crisis and the subsequent process of colonization. For them, too, the transformation was dramatic, its consequences profound. Despite its melodramatic air, Major Butler's survey of the West in 1871 gave a sense of the fundamental break with the past that characterized Spry's "great transformation." He wrote: "There is not a sound in the air or on the earth; on every side lie spread the relics of a great fight waged by man against the brute creation; all is silent and deserted — the Indian and buffalo gone the settler not yet come."[4] The Cree were alienated from their land as they had known it and had been nurtured by it. Sweet Grass, one of the leading and most respected Plains Cree chiefs, informed Chief Factor W.J. Christie in the year of Butler's description: "Our country is no longer able to support us."[5] Hunting forays had to be made outside Cree land where buffalo herds still existed, westward into Blackfoot territory in southern Alberta and southward to the Missouri River country of the Cheyenne, Arapaho and Gros Ventre. By the middle of the next decade these desperate measures had failed and the harsh reality of starvation faced all.

Despite the catastrophic nature of the great transformation, it would be wrong to assume that the Cree, or any of the western tribes, were wholly disarmed by these changes. Indeed, before the Plains Cree found themselves in a world beyond manipulation, a world of marginalization, reserve isolation and government administration, they reacted in many creative ways to the buffalo-resource crisis. A rather significant one was an attempt, in Spry's phrasing, to restrict open access by diplomatic and military action. As a result, what Sweet Grass called "our country" was to become, to Plains Cree tribesmen and women at least, increasingly and exclusively, Cree land. What developed from, or more probably what was revealed by, the buffalo crisis after 1850 was a fully articulated definition of "our country." To a Plains Cree identity and to a Plains Cree sense of territory formed in the era of buffalo plenty from 1790 to 1850 — to those interlocking constructs of self and place bounded by ecological, social, spiritual and political dimensions — was added, in the period after 1850, a new economic dimension. By 1870, as a result of the scarcity of the buffalo resource, and as a consequence of the Plains Cree's adaptation to and manipulation of that fluctuating resource situation within the plains bio-region, a clear Plains Cree sense of territory had evolved, which linked identity with a proprietary relationship to land and resources.

The development of a Plains Cree sense of self and place, linked to a particular rhythm of land and resource use, became apparent in the 1790s. In that decade traders noted, sorrowfully, that many of the Saskatchewan River Cree, formerly the most energetic beaver hunters, were now a "useless set of lazy indolent fellows a mear nuisance to us; . . . they are generally to be found in large Camps, Winter, and Summer, where they remain Idle throughout the year."[6] Lazy, indolent, idle fellows — a sure sign that they were no longer prime beaver hunters but had become plains provisioners and were determined to hold to that course. In 1795, the Hudson's Bay Company (HBC) opened Edmonton House in an area still rich in beaver and otter, hoping to entice the Cree back to their former role. It was to no avail. The trader, James Bird, reported to his superiors: "I am sorry to inform you that we are utterly disappointed in our hopes that building here near the beaver ground would occasion the Indians hunting Beaver; . . . all without exception are tenting in the plains killing Buffalo."[7]

This new plains-based trade activity — buffalo provisioning — meant that the cycle of Cree life was no longer determined, in the main, by the canoe-bound middleman entrepreneurship that had, in the early days of the trade, taken many on an annual round from York Factory to a South Saskatchewan rendezvous with the Blackfoot and back. Now Plains Cree life, character and culture were formed on a north–south, horse-powered cycle that moved them through the buffalo country.

This formative country encompassed not only the plains but the parklands as well. These were, in turn, parts of a larger and again more complex ecology comprising, from north to south, woodland, parkland and grassland zones. This three-part region was shared, from earliest days through to treaty time, by Native groups of diverse types. The central parkland zone contained the widest range of food resources and thus was attractive to and exploited by all, particularly in winter. In addition, the separate seasonal cyclic variations in food supplies in the woodland, parkland and plains habitats were complementary. Woodland summer plenty, marked by an abundance of fish and wildfowl, was followed by mid-winter scarcities that brought the threat of starvation.

Parkland winter resources, with the retreat of the buffalo seeking shelter from storms out on the plains, were plentiful just when woodland resources were scarce. The grassland cycle was much like that of the woodland, with summers of plenty followed by chilling and barren winters. These complementary, interlocking zones drew plains and woodland bands across the wider area exploiting at least two, but sometimes three, zones seasonally.

This pattern of multi-zone resource exploitation held for Plains Cree bands throughout the historic period. Spring saw them move out onto the plains where they spent the summer hunting buffalo. In autumn, they returned to the protection of the parkland. This annual cycle brought them the widest, most well-stocked pantry: 15 types of fowl, 26 animals, fish, berries, prairie turnips and various roots.

In terms of the evolution of a plains variant of Cree culture in the last decade of the eighteenth century, it is important to be cautious when ascribing a value to the formative power of this plains-parkland ecology for, clearly, the buffalo country supported more than one manner of living. Woodland and plains people inhabited a common place but were not, therefore, forced into a narrow, common life pattern. There was, literally, room for variation, room for human choice, for a variety of survival strategies that sprang not solely from ecological factors but from historical and psychological factors as well. Thus even amongst those who seemed to make the same choices — the Blackfoot, Cree and Assiniboine — there were notable differences in social structure and customs, and there were marked differences between them and plains agriculturalists: the Mandan and Métis, for example. Indeed, even within plains groups there was not a single uniform pattern as much as there was a majority one. There were those Plains Cree who, as late as the 1860s, showed a greater propensity for the woodlands than others. Those, Hugh Dempsey has written, "never completely abandoned their woodland ways and were content to live off fish and small game during the cold weather. Others in the camp were pure plains men who would disdain to eat moose or deer and considered buffalo to be the only proper food for an Indian."[8] Even though at the end of the eighteenth century there was a separation of the western Cree population into woodlands and plains groups in the Saskatchewan and Red River areas, there continued to be, thereafter, a margin of cultural overlap based to a degree upon the common resource pool of the woodland-parkland-grassland ecology, but more so upon the maintenance of historical continuity through cross-cultural connections, trade and inter-marriage, for example. Big Bear's father, Black Powder, the leader of a mixed Cree-Ojibwa band, is an interesting example of how blurred the line between woodland and plains culture could be.

Black Power was "a wanderer; one day he would turn up at Edmonton house, and two months later he would be in his skin lodge in the Eagle Hills. Spring might find him in his bark canoe, bringing furs from his winter catch, but in the autumn he could be astride his best buffalo runner, acting as though he had spent his whole life on the Plains."[9] Big Bear himself was not as bi-cultural as his father and others, but he was known for his magical powers — a sure sign of his woodland ancestry.[10] Indeed, many aspects of Plains Cree material culture, such as beadwork designs, tipi decorations and burial customs, all underscore a persistent woodland heritage.

From other perspectives, however, the two cultures — Cree and Plains Cree — existed in separate contexts, in different social, economic, political and spiritual worlds. Increasingly over the period, despite the margin of overlap, despite the "intercourse and blending of different nations, most of the superstitions and customs peculiar to each one are still maintained and practised."[11] There was considerable cultural divergence. For the Plains Cree, this was rooted in the use of horses and in the heavy emphasis on buffalo within their survival strategy.

Plains people were buffalo people. Their existence and that of the herds were inextricably intertwined. Buffalo is, one trader commented, "the only object they have in view."[12] It was life. The missionary John McDougall recorded a remarkable conversation he had, again in the year 1871, with an old Cree man: "Where are you going was my next question? Travelling for life replied the old man. Where will you find it? I again asked and back came the answer, Look yonder my grandchild; do you see a blue range of hills far away; . . . there is life said the old man, there are my people, there are buffalo, these are life to me."[13] McDougall agreed that the Cree "lived and had their physical being in the buffalo."[14] The herds provided nearly every requirement — food, skins for shelter and clothing, bones and sinews for tools. The buffalo not only provided the hardware but were instrumental in the formulation of the cultural software as well.

It was the process of becoming a buffalo people and its consequences that, from the 1790s, defined Cree identity and shaped their place in the region, in that different social, political and economic and spiritual world from the one inhabited by their woodland relatives. Three elements of that process — three of the many ramifications of cultural transformation, and especially of the growing reliance on the herds — would seem particularly important not only for understanding aspects of Cree identity, of their plains culture, but also in attempting to understand the Plains Cree relationship to land and resources and from that their sense of territory. These three elements of Plains Cree cultural software are those of social formation, cosmology and boundaries.

First, with regard to social formation, it would seem obvious that the richness of the buffalo resource, in terms of both its utility and its vastness, facilitated the permanent, yet supple, basic kinship network that was the Plains band, and the social relations, customs and political systems that served the need for order and stability in a community that was now larger than the typical band of the woodland environment. Furthermore, the resource supported band gatherings, tribal meetings, for the summer Thirst Dance, for example, that were the site of exogamous family formation and of unifying ritual that served to stretch identity past family and band. Thus the kinship network was extended to at least a multi-band organization within the nation. Hence, for example, one belonged to a particular family in Loud Voice's band of the Calling River people (a group of bands) of the downstream division (composed of the Willow, Calling River, Prairie, House, Rabbitskins and Touchwood peoples) of the Plains Cree nation. Therefore, one had relations, a welcome and thus a place in all those units of Plains Cree life. Because of this extended network, the plains tribe may have been able to function, in some degree, as an active and conscious political entity, rather than being, as it is in the minds of some scholars, merely the outer limits of ethnic and linguistic identity.[15]

Sweet Grass's use of the word "our" in "our country" had this larger social connotation. There was a reality for the individual of band and tribal experience. Thus "our country" was in part a set of distinct, self-contained, parkland-plains, band-associated ranges, sub-sets of a people's territory and a regional division. It was also a collective tribal range, or homeland, to which individuals, families and bands had unrestricted access.

The second element is of all three the most intriguing, the most problematic and potentially the most instructive, in terms of identity and sense of territory. This is the effect of the buffalo resource on Plains Cree cosmology. The Plains Cree inherited, naturally, a woodland theology. Aspects of it persisted after the process of cultural reformulation. Both Plains and Woodland Cree held to a belief in a single creator of a world that was, David Thompson relates, "alive"[16] though many "cannot define what kind of life it is but say, if it was not alive it could not give life to other things and to animated creatures."[17] There was, however, considerable and very significant divergence. Most critical were the changes that characterized the relationship of humans to those "animated creatures" — changes reflected in hunting observances.

Within the general cosmology of the hunter-gatherers of the subarctic, it was believed that the Creator had placed all living creatures under the care of lesser but more immediate spiritual beings known as game bosses who allowed animal-tribe members to be taken by humans only within the context of a reciprocal relationship of respect. That relationship was one, Calvin Martin has explained, of "mutual courtesy:

intelligent animal beings had contracted long ago not to abuse one another."[18] Hunting was, in the main, a "holy occupation . . . conducted and controlled by spiritual rules."[19] While whites looked to their hardware, to hunting technology, the Indians relied upon prescribed ritual, upon "dreaming, divination, singing, drumming, sweating and other forms of hunting magic"[20] before the hunt and the careful observance of "taboos which governed the disposal of the remains"[21] of the animal after the hunt was concluded.

David Mandelbaum, the anthropological expert on the Plains Cree, places Woodland Cree beliefs within this general cosmological set. Hunting was essentially "a religious practise . . . directed toward a magical control of game in order to procure a stable supply of food"[22] in a world where mid-winter starvation was not an uncommon occurrence. Training as a hunter had as much to do with what might be termed "spiritual woodcraft," or "learning the spiritual rules," as with any other knowledge.

It appears that the Plains Cree modified radically those rules, rituals and practices. Life was still full of magic, and the world was populated by spirits in contact with humans, and invited by humans to be involved in their affairs. Paul Kane, the artist, recorded in his journal what was a quite typical invocation of the pipe ceremony. The pipestem carrier "called on the Great Spirit to give them success in war, to enable them to take many scalps, and set their enemies asleep whilst they carried off their horses; that their wives might continue virtuous and never grow old. He then turned the stem to the earth after blowing another puff of smoke and called upon the earth to produce an abundance of buffalo and roots for the coming season."[23] And, indeed, according to the Cree, the Creator did intervene, if not always in the most positive manner. Kane wrote of a Cree war party beset by illness: "This was considered by some of their great men a judgement upon them from the Great Spirit for some previous misconduct, and they, therefore, returned home without having accomplished anything."[24]

Nevertheless, despite the persistence of spirit power, as the object of supplication and even as an historical explanation, there was significant change in Cree cosmology here. The over-riding influence of the spirit-animal-human relationship that constituted the essence of woodland cosmology was greatly diminished as the Cree moved into a plains lifestyle.

Again the cause of this change was the buffalo resource. Its vastness reduced the anxiety of the woodland hunt and thus the need for hunting magic and the importance of the spirit pantheon. The woodland concept of an afterlife was significantly, Thompson pointed out, a place where "the sun is always bright and the animals plenty,"[25] which, Daniel Harmon explained, they would be able "to take with little or no trouble."[26] The plains approximated such a heaven — a land of buffalo easy to take. Mandelbaum's informant, Fine Day, recalled: "We depended mainly on the buffalo. This was because anyone could kill a buffalo but it took a great hunter to get a moose or elk."[27] The ease of the hunt, greatly facilitated by horses combined with dead-falls and surrounds, dispelled what Mandelbaum has characterized as "the almost frenzied attempt to secure magical control over game animals that occurs"[28] in a woodland environment. As non-buffalo food sources (moose and elk, for example) dwindled in importance, so did their spirits, their keepers or bosses, and the need to propitiate them. Hunting rituals fell into disuse, or were, Mandelbaum claimed, "loosely observed and counted for little."[29] Additionally, no new plains-associated rituals were created and, most critically, none was originated with respect to plains-style buffalo hunting, notably the rush on horseback. In fact, in this most classic form of plains hunting, success was guaranteed not through the agency of a manito but by the activity of a secular body, the soldier's lodge,[30] which organized the hunt and brought discipline to the hunters. Symbolic of the relative decline of the importance of the metaphysical in the hunting sector and the promise of secular governance in plains communities, the spiritual taboos were now replaced by civil regulations and retribution, for violations came not in some "medicine" form from the game boss, but from the soldiers who could appropriate the offender's horses and hunting equipment and even destroy the hunter's tipi. Finally, no taboos regarding the disposal of buffalo remains seem to have been observed.

Only with respect to buffalo pounding, a parkland activity and a woodland cultural memory, did hunting ritual continue. The persistence was, indeed, remarkable. The fur trader J. Macdonnell described the central figure of a Cree and Assiniboine pound around 1797 who

> . . . lights a pipe & offers the end to the Buffaloes or to some old Bull amongst them who he takes for the father or chief of the Band whom he harangues sometimes to that effect. After thanking the master of life for sending them food for themselves and their children. . . . My grandfather we are glad to see you, & happy to find that you are not come in a shameful manner for you have brought plenty of your young men with you; be not angry at us; tho' we're obliged to destroy you to make ourselves live.[31]

Over half a century later, Paul Kane encountered the same spiritual elements when he visited a Cree pound near Fort Edmonton. There again was a man "with a medicine pipe stem in his hand, which he waves continually chanting a sort of prayer to the Great Spirit, the burden of which is that the buffaloes may be numerous and fat."[32]

It is possible to argue from the above that nothing had changed, that, with regard to that particular form of hunting, the propitiation of the buffalo game boss was still the central fact of Cree strategy. However, given the references to the Great Spirit, it is more likely that even the buffalo-pounding rituals are traits of a new plains tradition, or that the persistence of those traits is to be explained by the fact that the ritual is so consistent with the principles of the new tradition. The effect of the buffalo resource, seen in the creation of a larger and more permanent band community and in the reduction of hunting rituals generally and thus the influence of lesser spirits, promoted these principles in the form of a cosmology more clearly and exclusively balanced on an axis between the Creator, that human community and its individual members. Mandelbaum states unequivocally that "the great emphasis in Plains Cree religious activity is upon securing long life for the people."[33] This concern for the health of the people — and health is to be understood in its widest meaning to include a concern for a good life and for the welfare of the needy — was the prime determinant of individual and community action on both the spiritual and the secular levels.

In terms of the secular world, Cree men followed well-defined paths of life which, through proscribed behaviour, promised the rewards of increased status. From the lowest rank, Worthy Youngman, the ambitious warrior, could aspire to become a chief. But this quest for status, conducted by amassing a war record and wealth, brought responsibilities to the community. To the criterion of a war record and wealth was added the duty of liberality, a duty that was carefully defined by the community in terms of the individual's growing ability to bear the burden or a duty carefully calculated by the individual in terms of his growing pretensions to increasing his status beyond that of his competitors. At every status level there were social responsibilities. Chiefs had to distribute food to the aged and poor, and members of the solders' lodge were pledged to respond to requests for assistance from the less well-off in the band. As well, there were social occasions such as the give-away dance and the sitting-up-until-morning ceremony that were mechanisms to reward gift giving with enhanced status and to facilitate the redistribution of property as part of a social-welfare net. In this process of establishing social rank, the individual's mobility was tied firmly to the discharge of a welfare function.[34]

Contact with the world of the sacred was directly linked to this system of social relations. The general set of Plains Cree band and tribal rituals stressed the direct spirit empowering of the individual to face and overcome the challenges of plains life in service to the people. That service took the form of liberality and leadership. It was this search for empowerment, seen most classically in the vision quest through which a young man or woman acquired *pawakan* (spirit helper) or medicine, a gift such as the ability to construct a buffalo pound, that formed the core of the ritual cycles and the vowed ceremonies of Plains Cree life, the most important of these being the Sun, or Thirst, Dance. Through these ceremonies and by such as the "pity-me prayers,"[35] which were direct supplications to the Great Spirit for aid, the individual, the community and the Creator were fused in a theology of considerable social dynamism.

It is in the context of the centrality of this utilitarian relationship between the Creator and humans that land and buffalo might be placed within Plains Cree cosmology. Clearly, plains people stood in a different relationship to the buffalo than woodland people did to the animals of their environment. That plains relationship, shorn of its spirit intermediaries, was to a degree secularized, and may even have been proprietary. While the evidence for this conjecture is not plentiful and may be plagued by translation difficulties, what exists is suggestive. One of the most useful pieces of evidence is a lecture delivered by a Cree chief to the famous tourists Milton and Cheadle:

> In your land you are, I know, great chiefs. You have abundance of blankets, and powder and shot as much as you can desire. But there is one thing that you lack — you have no buffalo, and you come here to seek them. I am a great chief also. But the Great Spirit has not dealt with us alike. You he has endowed with various riches, while to me he has given the buffalo alone, why should you visit this country to destroy the only good thing I possess.[36]

This is not only good rhetoric but also most helpful information for an understanding of Cree cosmology. Our buffalo, and perhaps the terms "our land" and "our country" that appear continually in Cree speeches through to the treaty of 1876 and thereafter, were something the Cree "possessed." They had been given them "here," that is, on their land, in "our country," just as the English had been "endowed with various riches" by the Creator "in your land." The Cree had the buffalo as a gift from the Creator to be used "to secure health and long life for the people"[37] and, therefore, as a spiritual gift, as are all things that belong to an "us" exclusive of others not of our community; not, for example, of a particular band, people or division of the Plains Cree.

There may have been much more to this, however. The Cree may have perceived the buffalo and the land as not merely gifts. Mandelbaum claims with certainty that the Cree prayer formula "said or implied that the Powers were obliged to fulfill their contractual obligations"[38] by the very fact that the Cree had done their part by faithfully enacting the rituals and vowed ceremonies and, in particular, by voicing the pity-me prayers. There may have been, therefore, the supposition by the Plains Cree of a guaranteed reciprocity with the Creator that constituted a Cree right to Cree land and the buffalo resource, a reciprocity that might be most appropriately termed, as the contemporary Cree do, a sacred right.

It might be interesting to consider, if only as an aside, the extent to which Cree statements of rights to land and resources, made plainly in the 1870s and 1880s in political terms, came originally from such concepts as are contained in the Milton-Cheadle statement and from theological roots. If hunting can be said to be a spiritual occupation, can politics have been rooted in the spiritual as well? There may be considerable evidence that this was, indeed, the case. The pity-me prayer, for example, became an element in the political strategy that the Cree employed to deal with the treaty makers. The prayers were an attempt to co-opt the Queen's representative into a supportive relationship to bring him to assume the role played by the other great power — the Creator. In 1875, Sweet Grass, in advance of the treaty negotiations, sent a message clearly based on the prayer formula to Governor Archibald, the Great Father: "Our country is getting ruined of fur bearing animals, hitherto our sole support, and now we are poor and want help — we want you to pity us."[39] Short Tail, another Cree chief, sent along his message at the same time and in the same form: "My brother, this is coming very close. I look upon you as if I see you; I want you to pity me, and I want help to cultivate the ground for myself and descendants."[40]

The last of the three factors to be considered is concerned with the establishment of boundaries to "our country." The boundaries of Aboriginal homelands were not sharply drawn geographic lines but a combination of ranges, approximate lines and states of relationships among tribes in a given region. Here again the major determinant was the reliance on the buffalo resource and the fact of horse ownership as the primary status register. Among the results of these changes in the period after 1790 was the development of a set of plains-based inter-tribal trade, diplomatic and military systems that established particular geo-political areas within Aboriginal boundaries and governed access to those areas, to the land and resources, until the final crisis era, after 1850, produced changes again.

In the case of the Plains Cree, the factors connected to the social and economic transformation of culture in the 1790s forged an unyielding western boundary. The disappearance of their middleman role, their abandonment of beaver trapping, and the move into provisioning posts as they were established throughout the Saskatchewan and Red River regions and, particularly, the focus on the acquisition of horses resulted in a failure of the historic Blackfoot-Cree alliance and a state of almost unrelieved hostility from about 1810 to 1870 along an approximate line running from Edmonton through the Elbow of the South Saskatchewan to the junction of the Yellowstone and Missouri rivers.[41]

In the south and east, however, the situation remained fluid throughout the first half of the century (the era of the horse wars),[42] and the Cree could manage access. They did manage it well, by juggling their military and/or trade value to gain entrance to horse markets.

Throughout the period of classic Plains Cree culture, coincidental with the era of buffalo plenty, the nature of boundaries, then — whether access was open or closed, whether resources were shared or not shared with a particular group — was determined, in the main, by a group's relation to horse trading. For example, there was a positive relationship, with Cree land and resources open, with the Mandan-Hidatsa agriculturalists, who controlled a rich horse market, until about 1815 when Cree fur-trade profits were extensively undercut by the spread of posts in the southern Manitoba area and they were replaced as the primary suppliers of white technology in the villages. Thereafter, the Cree were shut out of the Mandan system. Allowed to remain in were old allies, the Métis, who had assisted in protecting the villages with their valuable agricultural produce and their connection with southern and western horse suppliers. In the central-southern quarter, access was governed in the 1840s through a formal Cree-Assiniboine-Crow treaty that linked resource sharing, trade in horses and other items with joint campaigns against the Blackfoot.[43]

Within those boundaries, Cree land was land for the Cree with the understanding that resources would be shared with Cree allies, such as the Assiniboine, and with trade partners — for a small fee. The territory was, as Harmon noted, to be defended against poachers and trespassers, those beyond the boundaries, those whom the Cree called, significantly, "outside men."[44] Alliance, war and trade protected the Plains Cree and their homeland and regulated access to the resources that the Great Master of Life had given them.

By 1850 the Cree were a fully established plains nation. A sense of what constituted Cree country, their relationship to it, and the relationship of reciprocal responsibility among the individual, the community and the Great Spirit in that homeland had been defined from ecological, social, spiritual and political (military, diplomatic and trade) perspectives. In the next two decades, owing to the tragic decline of the buffalo resource, the Cree would undergo further, and in some respects significant, changes in all these areas.

It is not necessary here to rehearse the well-known events surrounding the resource failure. Before discussing its effects, it is sufficient to note only two things. First, the decline became obvious to western observers by 1850. The missionary De Smet wrote, gloomily, in the fall of 1846: "The plains where the buffalo graze are becoming more and more a desert, and at every season's hunt the different Indian tribes find themselves closer together. It is probably that the plains of the Yellowstone and Missouri and as far as the forks of the Saskatchewan . . . will be within the next dozen years the last retreat of the buffalo."[45] Second, the decline can be traced to the fact that buffalo became, in the 1830s, a fur-trade commodity — a prime fur. Buffalo became beaver, in fur-trade terms, and the sorrowful tale of over hunting and depletion was to be retold on the plains. The dramatic change in the buffalo resource was felt, undoubtedly, throughout Cree culture. The switch to a rich resource base in the 1790s had produced a range of developments; scarcity was to produce others.

In the area of social formation it is possible, as O. Lewis postulates for the Blackfoot, that participation in the resource commercialization after 1830 caused the first gradations of class to appear in the community.[46] Families became factories, Lewis argues. Marriage became a labour contract as more women were needed to produce robes. A. Klein, in his more recent study, agrees, and notes, furthermore, that the egalitarian character of gender relations was shattered and women's role debased by this new relationship with the buffalo herds.[47]

It was wealth, in horses, acquired by theft, trade or purchase with buffalo-robe profits, that financed the creation of the family factory. The largest of those factories garnered such wealth that even the continued operation of a social system designed to mediate difference through redistribution could not iron out the humps of wealth differentials. For the Plains Cree, though more research needs to be done, there is some evidence of differences in tipi size within bands and of a lowering of the marriage age for females — two of Lewis's prime indicators for incipient class development.[48]

A second socio-economic reaction to buffalo resource depletion was the beginning of a substantial move into agriculture on the part of the Plains Cree. Sarah Carter's recent work charts the extensiveness of this development, though the consequences of it in cultural terms are yet to be ascertained.[49]

With regard to spirituality, it is conceivable that the growing scarcity of buffalo created a new interest in woodland hunting magic. Access to such magic was always possible when woodland and plains people met in the parklands. No doubt, the anxiety of the hunt returned, and with it the precondition for a spiritual strategy. That anxiety may be sensed in those pity-me treaty prayers that give witness to the wrenching change: "long ago it was good when we first were made. I wish the same were back again."[50] Fine Day related that two Cree bands strove to make it so; they tried to buy a buffalo-calling dance from some "outside men," but were unsuccessful because the owners "were afraid that we might get too many buffalo if we danced that dance."[51] The subject is so ephemeral and the period so short that it is difficult to gauge whether any new spiritual pattern was emerging before the whole process was obviated by reserve life. Clearly, however, many of the old rituals and much of the old theology survived the disappearance of the buffalo, as the continuation of sun dancing well into the twentieth century witnesses.

It is much easier to make judgements on the effect of the drastic reduction of the herds on the issues of boundaries and resource control and therefore on the nature of Plains Cree external affairs. Here the Cree reacted first by trying to restrict the access of those they perceived to be the major threats — white and Métis. They, indeed, Isaac Cowie recorded, "resented the intrusion of the half breed and whites on the plains for hunting purposes."[52]

The Métis may well have been seen, in relation to others, as a growing and, therefore, the most pressing threat. The size of the Métis hunts leaving Red River did increase over the period,[53] and Métis settlement within Cree territory in the Saskatchewan region increased also. The Métis hunts were viewed by the Plains Cree "with feelings of jealousy and enmity"[54] and reports circulated of "detached parties and stragglers"[55] being attacked and of fire being used by the Cree to "drive the game beyond their reach."[56] The most famous, and perhaps the most significant, clash was between Big Bear and Gabriel Dumont, in which the chief, though willing to share the resource, insisted he and not the Métis control and organize the hunt in Cree land.[57]

The Métis were not the only concern of the Cree. Whites generally, and the HBC, despite the fact that the Company's interest in robes was not as strong as that of the American Fur Company, were increasingly seen not only as outsiders but also as a central part of the resource problem. H.Y. Hind reported that a Cree council had "strong objections against the Hudson's Bay Company encroaching upon the prairies and driving away the buffalo."[58] The Company, the Cree realized, was not a benign presence. Some chiefs, "although they acknowledged the value of firearms, . . . thought they were better off in olden times when they had only bows and spears and wild animals were numerous."[59] They understood well the destructive forces of the trade. This was a radical departure from the historic perception of a Cree–white partnership of interests. In separate councils, those chiefs decided to shut the country down. "They would not permit either whiteman or half-breeds to hunt in their country or travel through it."[60]

It was not the intention of the chiefs, however, to isolate the country, to separate themselves, their land and their resources from the outside world. The external connections were to be maintained. Those connections were, and would continue to be, even long after the buffalo were gone, through the treaty days and in the reserve era, an essential part of Cree survival strategy. The chiefs therefore added an important rider to the hunting-travelling prohibition. Neither the Métis nor whites were to be allowed into the country except "for the purpose of trading for their dried meat, pemmican, skins and robes."[61] Others received the same message. Access was closed, but the trade was to remain open. A sealed country was not only an attempt to harbour a dwindling resource, but also a policy to deal with that resource as a now-valuable commercial commodity. To this end the Cree insisted that they had the primary economic right on their land, the right to benefit from the Creator's gift, from, as Milton and Cheadle had been told, "the only good thing I possess."[62] No one should come and take it without regard for that Cree right; no one should take it "simply for your own pleasure."[63] Some talked, additionally, of hunting fines, some of tolls for passage.[64]

None of this, even if the Cree had been able to shut the strangers out and enforce their rights, could have succeeded. By 1870 the buffalo were nearly gone and the Cree threw themselves into a desperate attempt to batter their way into Blackfoot country to locate the last of the herds. Behind them, to the east, their land was almost barren. Across it lay the shadow of the coming era — that of the treaty makers.

From this initial survey of the nature of, and the extent to which, a Plains Cree sense of territory evolved in relation to the buffalo resource, only preliminary conclusions or speculations can be made. But they are useful, nevertheless, in themselves, and as pointers for work on the Plains Cree–Canadian treaties.

The Cree meaning of "our" may well have been, in the 1870s, much closer in some respects to the European concept than is normally thought. Both were exclusive and, as with European territorial boundaries and identity in the age of the development of national consciousness, Cree boundaries became rigidly and aggressively defined and maintained in the decades after 1850. The Cree laid a presumptive claim to buffalo as the most fundamental national resource. It was not only a claim to own and use, internally, for the sake of bands and the tribe in accordance with particular social regulations that guaranteed order and general welfare, but also a commercial claim stating the right to organize the exploitation of, and to profit from, the resource in clear economic terms, terms understood by both cultures, cultures that had been involved in a trading relationship for over two centuries.

The Milton-Cheadle statement, and similar statements made during the treaty negotiations about land and resources (and here can be included other resources mentioned by the Cree in negotiating sessions with the government, such as timber), can best be understood in that commercial-claim context.

Throughout their plains experience, the ideas of land, resources and treaties had always been linked in Cree minds. The idea of land without resources was inconceivable. The function of land, of "our country," was, Sweet Grass stated, "to support us."[65] In terms of the relationship of the Cree to land, resources and outsiders, the Cree had normally arranged sharing (an element in international relations useful to themselves and to their ends) through treaties. These diplomatic devices set access to the land on Cree terms — that is, for the use of the resources, for timber, buffalo, water and, perhaps, as they became more involved in it themselves, for agricultural purposes, without changing the nature of the boundaries of the homeland or disturbing its national character. Agreements had been made on those grounds with the Blackfoot, the Mandan-Hidatsa and the Crow. The Queen's treaty makers may have been, therefore, just another set of outsiders looking for a deal with something valuable to offer in exchange.

Finally, it is undeniable that the key element for further consideration regarding Plains Cree history in general, and the treaties, was the pervasive influence of the sacred on the secular lives of the Cree.

It is clear that their pretensions to an exclusive right to their country and its resources, claims that underlay their nationality and their national behaviour, their economic and political dealings with outsiders, as outlined above, were founded in the belief that their land was a gift from the Creator. In turn, the gift was a sign of the Great Spirit's stewardship of the Plains Cree people and, from the treaties into modern times, that covenant has been the moral imperative underpinning their own claims to stewardship of the land. In Cree minds, the circle connecting the people, the land and the Creator has not been broken.

In addition, the Creator was seen to move in an open way in the lives of the people, in band and tribal affairs. The Great Spirit in many forms could be brought on side through the prayers and rituals. Secular life had a strong spiritual dynamic and events could be influenced and understood in spiritual terms. The creation of the world and human beings, the facts of life and death, the causes of natural events, the flow of personal fortunes, the disappearance of the buffalo all have a spiritual explanation. In the form of Old Man, Coyote and Spider, the Creator's stories told of these things, and still do.

The treaty negotiations, though they had a clear resource-management purpose, were also cast in that spiritual mold. Sweet Grass and others prayed for a treaty, and when Sweet Grass turned to explain to Big Bear why he had signed, he did so in spiritual terms: "My friend, you see the representative of the Queen here, who do you suppose to be the maker of it [the treaty]. I think the Great Spirit put it in their hearts to come to our help."[66] The treaty was an answer to his prayer sent to the governor some years previously. When the treaty was made and after the governor gave his farewell, "the Indians responded by loud ejaculations of satisfaction, and the chiefs and councillors, commencing with Sweet Grass, each shook hands with the governor, and addressed him in words of parting, elevating his hand as they grasped it, to Heaven, and invoking the blessings of the Great Spirit."[67] The people were blessed, and so too was the treaty.

NOTES

....

1. J.E. Foster, "Indian-White Relations in the Prairie West during the Fur Trade Period — A Compact," in *The Spirit of the Alberta Indian Treaties*, ed. R. Price (Montreal: Institute for Research on Public Policy, 1987).

2. I. Spry, "The Great Transformation: The Disappearance of the Commons in Western Canada," in *Man and Nature on the Prairies*, ed. R. Allan (Regina: 1976), 21.

3. Ibid.

4. Major W.F. Butler, *The Great Lone Land* (London: S. Law, Marston and Rivington, 1881), 217.

5. A. Morris, *The Treaties of Canada with the Indian of Manitoba and the North-West Territories* (Toronto: Belfords, Clarke, 1889), 171.

6. National Archives of Canada (NAC), MG19 A13, Henry's Journey, 765.

7. NAC, Hudson's Bay Company Papers, Setting River Post Journal Reel M131, 8 January 1799.

8. H.A. Dempsey, *Big Bear* (Vancouver, Toronto: Douglas and McIntyre, 1984), 36–37.

9. Ibid., 11.

10. Ibid., 19–20.

11. H.Y. Hind, *Narrative of the Canadian Red River Exploring Expedition of 1857 and of the Assiniboine and Saskatchewan Exploring Expeditions of 1858*. (Edmonton: M.G. Hurtig, 1971), 122.

12. NAC, MG19 A13, Henry's Journey, 765.

13. J. McDougall, *In the Days of the Red River Rebellion* (Toronto: William Briggs, 1911), 161.

14. Ibid.

15. See, for example, S.R. Sharrock, "Cree-Assiniboine, and Assiniboines: Inter-Ethnic Social Organization on the Far Northern Plains," in *Ethnology* 21 (1974).

16. J.B. Tyrrell, ed., *David Thompson's Narrative* (New York: Greenwood Press, 1968), 84.

17. Ibid.

18. C. Martin, "The War between Indians and Animals," in *Indians, Animals and the Fur Trade*, ed. S. Krech (Athens: The University of Georgia Press, 1981), 15.

19. C. Martin, "The European Impact on the Culture of a Northeastern Algonquian Tribe: An Ecological Interpretation," in *Out of the Background*, ed. R. Fisher and K. Coates (Toronto: Copp Clark Pitman, 1988), 72.

20. C. Martin, *Keepers of the Game* (Berkeley: University of California Press, 1978), 121.

21. Martin, "The European Impact on the Culture of a Northeastern Algonkian Tribe," 73.

22. D.G. Mandelbaum, *The Plains Cree* (Regina: Canadian Plains Research Centre, 1979), 308.

23. P. Kane, *Wanderings of an Artist* (Edmonton: M.G. Hurtig, 1968), 282.

24. Ibid., 284.

25. Tyrrell, *David Thompson's Narrative*, 84.

26. W.K. Lamb, *Sixteen Years in the Indian Country, the Journal of Daniel Williams Harmon 1800–1816* (Toronto: MacMillan, 1951), 229.

27. Mandelbaum, *The Plains Cree*, 68.

28. Ibid., 309.

29. Ibid., 308.

30. Ibid., 115.

31. "John Macdonnell's Red River," in *Early Fur Trade on the Northern Plains*, ed. W.R. Wood and T.D. Thiessen (Norman: University of Oklahoma Press, 1985), 91.

32. Kane, *Wanderings of an Artist*, 80.

33. Mandelbaum, *The Plains Cree*, 308.

34. J. Milloy, *The Plains Cree: Trade, Diplomacy and War, 1790 to 1870* (Winnipeg: University of Manitoba Press, 1988), chapter 7.

35. Mandelbaum, *The Plains Cree*, 231.

36. Viscount Milton and W.B. Cheadle, *The North-West Passage by Land* (Toronto: Coles Publishing, 1970), 66.

37. Mandelbaum, *The Plains Cree*, 308.

38. Ibid., 231.
39. Morris, *The Treaties of Canada*, 171.
40. Ibid.
41. Milloy, *The Plains Cree*, 31–40.
42. Ibid., 103–118.
43. B. Mishkin, *Rank and Warfare among the Plains Indians* (Seattle: University of Washington Press, 1940), 60.
44. Lamb, *Sixteen Years in the Indian Country*, 103.
45. H.M. Chittenden and A.T. Richardson, *Father De Smet's Life and Travels among the North American Indians* (New York: Francis Harper, 1905), 948.
46. O. Lewis, *The Effects of White Contact upon Blackfoot Culture with Special Reference to the Role of the Fur Trade* (New York: J.J. Augustin, 1942).
47. A. Klein, "The Political Economy of Gender: A 19th Century Plains Indian Case Study," in *The Hidden Half*, ed. G. Albers and B. Medicine (University Press of America, 1978).
48. J. McDougall, *Saddle, Sled and Snowshoe: Pioneering on the Saskatchewan in the Sixties* (Toronto: Ryerson Press, n.d.), 92.
49. Sarah Carter, *Lost Harvests* (Montreal: McGill-Queen's University Press, 1990).
50. Morris, *The Treaties of Canada*, 215.
51. Mandelbaum, *The Plains Cree*, 68.
52. I. Cowie, *The Company of Adventurers: A Narrative of Seven Years in the Service of the Hudson's Bay Company During 1867–1874* (Toronto: William Briggs, 1913), 302.
53. Hind, *Narrative*, 110.
54. J. McLean, *Notes of a Twenty-five Years Service in the Hudson's Bay Territory* (London: Richard Bentley, 1840), 302.
55. Ibid.
56. Ibid.
57. Dempsey, *Big Bear*, 54-55.
58. Hind, *Narrative*, 360.
59. Ibid.
60. Ibid., 334.
61. Ibid.
62. Milton and Cheadle, *The North-West Passage by Land*, 66.
63. Ibid.
64. Spry, *The Great Transformation*, 44.
65. Morris, *The Treaties of Canada*, 171.
66. Ibid., 239.
67. Ibid., 242.

TWO

After the Fur Trade: The Aboriginal Labouring Class of British Columbia, 1849–1890

JOHN LUTZ

A boriginal history is usually considered in isolation from mainstream Canadian history as though it were about aboriginal people and nobody else. But the major issues of native studies — such as the appropriation of aboriginal land and resources, the denial of citizenship rights to a large segment of the Canadian population, the conditions under which aboriginal people would agree to trap, hunt or do wage-work for a capitalist economy — are major issues of national development and central to Canadian history.

This paper takes up questions about aboriginal wage labour and applies them to a forty-year period on the west coast of North America from the creation of the Colony of Vancouver Island in 1849, through the gold rushes, the founding of the giant export sawmills, Confederation, the development and spread of the salmon canning industry, to just past the completion of the Canadian Pacific Railway in 1885, an event which tied the province of British Columbia to the North American continental economy. Throughout this period aboriginal people in British Columbia comprised the majority of the population. Despite introduced diseases which reduced the aboriginal population by approximately two thirds, when British Columbia entered Confederation in 1871 it was in many important respects an "aboriginal province" — there were three times as many aboriginal people as all the non-aboriginals taken together.

Although one might suppose historians would have turned their attention to the majority before beginning to examine minority groups, in British Columbia historiography the reverse has happened: only a few historians, notably Robin Fisher and Rolf Knight, have given their attention to the majority population in this era.[1] Most general accounts follow Fisher's pioneering work on aboriginal–non-aboriginal relations which argued that aboriginal peoples retained control of their lives during the fur trade, and had considerable influence over the trade itself. Fisher states that, with the gold rush, the colonies which comprise modern British Columbia changed from "colonies of exploitation, which made use of indigenous manpower, to colonies of settlement, where the Indians became, at best, irrelevant."[2] By contrast, this paper argues that aboriginal people were not made irrelevant by the coming of settlement. In fact, they were the main labour force of the early settlement era, essential to the capitalist development of British Columbia. With other recent scholarship, this paper takes a step towards rediscovering the largest component of British Columbia's early

Source: "After the Fur Trade: The Aboriginal Labouring Class of British Columbia, 1849–1890," *Journal of the Canadian Historical Association* (1992): 69–93. Reprinted by permission.

labouring class, and highlighting one element — paid work — of the lives of the majority aboriginal population.[3]

Even in the 1860s opinion among white notables was divided about the usefulness and importance of aboriginal people to the British Columbia economy. While Charles Forbes' 1862 guide to Vancouver Island argued resolutely that "their labour cannot be depended on, and with one or two slight exceptions at present forms no point of consideration in the labour market," and A.A. Harvey described aboriginal people as "valueless in the labour market,"[4] in his 1871 report on British Columbia the federal minister of public works observed that "the Indians have been, and still are, and will long continue an important population for [British] Columbia, in the capacity of guides, porters and labourers."[5]

Who was right? Were aboriginal people "valueless in the labour market" or "an important population of . . . labourers"? How important was their labour to British Columbia's nineteenth century economy? How important was wage and contract labour to the aboriginal economy? What motivated aboriginal people to join the early paid labour force?[6] Who, and how many, were recruited? Based on a varied sample of aboriginal voices captured in biographies, ethnographies and letters to government and church officials, as well as the correspondence of colonial officials, fur traders, missionaries and travellers together with the records of the Department of Indian Affairs, this paper not only attempts to answer these questions, but in doing so provides a fresh perspective from which to view the early years of capitalist development in British Columbia.

LABOURERS OF THE ABORIGINAL PROVINCE

Of the 34,600 or so inhabitants of the Colony of Vancouver Island and its adjacent islands and shores in 1855, all but 774 were aboriginal. Outside the colony there were probably an additional 25,000–30,000 aboriginal people living in the remainder of what became British Columbia. This vast population was extremely heterogeneous, both culturally and historically. It was comprised of ten distinct nations or ethnic groups, speaking twenty-six distinct, and largely mutually unintelligible, languages. Each nation had its own customary laws that defined property rights and social and gender relations, and by 1849 each village had its own history of relationships with non-aboriginal people or their trade goods.[7]

Victoria, the west coast headquarters for the Hudson's Bay Company (HBC), became the capital when the colony was established in 1849. As the largest community of non-aboriginal people north of Oregon, it became "the great emporium" for aboriginal people from all over the Pacific Northwest, from Russian America (Alaska) down. The mass migrations to Victoria began in the summer of 1853, when Governor Douglas reported a gathering of 3,000 "Indians" at a potlatch hosted by the local Songhees people living across the harbour.[8] The next year aboriginal people from "all parts of the mainland coast south of Cape Spencer, in north latitude 59 degrees" dropped in on Victoria itself. Annually, from 1853 through the 1880s, 2,000–4,000 aboriginal people canoed their way to Victoria to trade or spend part of the year, travelling as far as 800 miles to do so.

Why did thousands of aboriginal people, between 5 and 10 per cent of the whole aboriginal population north of Puget Sound, paddle so far to visit a community that in 1855 numbered only 232?[9] Trading was undoubtedly a major attraction — the variety in Victoria was greater, alcohol was more easily available, and the prices of goods were perhaps better than at closer trading posts; and in the beginning at least curiosity to see this alien community was, no doubt, another factor.

There was nevertheless a third and key reason why aboriginal people returned year after year. As Governor Douglas explained in his dispatches to the Colonial Office, he was not unduly alarmed about being out-numbered ten-to-one during these seasonal visits by "ignorant and barbarous people. . . . For the object of the Indians in visiting this place is not to make War upon the White man, but to benefit by his presence, by selling their Furs and other commodities."[10]

One of the commodities aboriginal people sold was labour, a practice well established as early as 1853, when Douglas had reported that "a great part of the agricultural labour of the colony, is at present performed by means of the Natives, who though less skilled and industrious than the white men, work at a comparatively much cheaper rate, so that on the whole, they are exceedingly useful to the colonists."[11] Indeed, nearly all early accounts mention the hiring of aboriginal labour. The first *bona fide* colonist, W.C. Grant, hired aboriginal people on his farm and reported in 1853 that "with the proper superintendence [they] are capable of being made very useful. They all live by fishing but take kindly to any kind of rough agricultural employment, though their labour is not to be depended on for any continuous period." Similarly, colonist J.S. Helmcken used Indians "chiefly from the north" to clear land for his home, while the colony itself paid "scores of Indians" in HBC blankets to clear the land around the surveyors office and to build roads. The Puget Sound Agriculture Company also hired aboriginal labour on their farms, and by 1857 missionary William Duncan observed that around Victoria "most of the Farm Servants employed here . . . are Chimsyan (Tsimshian) Indians — and they all give them a good character."[12]

The issue of wage labour was raised formally when, at the start of his 1856 seasonal visit, Douglas called the chiefs together and "spoke to them seriously on the subject of their relations with the whites, and their duties to the public, and after exacting a pledge for the good behaviour of their respective Tribes, *I gave them permission to hire themselves out as labourers to the white settlers, and for the public works in progress*." He reported at the end of August that "the greater number of those people have lately departed with their earnings to their distant homes, and will not return to Vancouver's Island, before the spring of 1856; those who still remain about the settlements will spend the winter here. . . ."[13]

Although the economies of the aboriginal peoples varied from the coast to the Interior and even within these divisions, generally they were based on a seasonal migration cycle from permanent winter villages to harvesting sites for fishing in the fall, hunting and trapping in winter and harvesting roots and berries in the summer. From 1853 onwards, however, a spring and summer visit to Victoria became a part of the seasonal cycle, and those who could not find work in Victoria often continued south into the American territory of Puget Sound. John Fornsby, a Coast Salish living in Puget Sound, first saw these "Northern Indians" when 40–50 of them came to work at a Puget Sound sawmill around 1858, while James Swan wrote from Port Townsend that the Northern Indians "yearly come to Victoria and whenever they get a chance, come over here to work — the men at our mills or among the farmers, where they prove themselves faithful and efficient; and the women, by their cleanly habits, their bright dresses and hoop skirts . . . winning the hearts or purses of the bachelors."[14] Others, who did not join the migration, found work closer to their own villages in the expanding activities of the Hudson's Bay Company posts, cutting shingles and spars, picking cranberries, harvesting ice, as well as gardening, fishing, preserving food and doing general construction.[15]

While the summer migrants from the north worked on the farms and public works, some of the local Songhees people became established in year-round employment in the homes of the better-off colonists as servants and cooks. Reverend Staines wrote in 1852 that his Indian servant procured meat each day by trading with other Indians, and that he was teaching his Indian cook how to prepare beef, mutton and venison. Other aboriginal people supplied venison, partridges, salmon, potatoes and berries to the colonists, as well as shingles, lathes, mats and baskets.[16]

With the 1858 gold rush and the consequent growth of Victoria came even more opportunities for work, and by 1860 whole villages might be deserted for the capital. Making for the Queen Charlotte islands in the *Alert*, James Cooper met the entire population of Masset heading for Victoria. At Skidegate, meanwhile, Chief "Estercana" asked the officials to "tell Mr Douglas and the man-of-war to send my people home; I wanted to build a house this summer [but] nearly all my people are away at Victoria."[17] That summer, the governor reported over 4,000 visiting Indians at Victoria, double the number of non-aboriginal inhabitants in the town.[18] Despite the large gold-induced increase in the non-aboriginal population, Douglas was still not concerned about its relations with the majority. "When not under the influence of intoxication," he told the Colonial Office in 1860, "[the aboriginal people] are quiet and well conducted, make good servants and by them is executed a large proportion of the menial, agricultural, and shipping labour of the Colony. Besides their value as labourers they are of value commercially as consumers of food and clothing. . . ."[19] He was not alone in his view. The San Francisco *Times*, for example, described the Indians around gold-rush Victoria as "industrious," which "alone establishes their superiority to the California aborigines."[20] Moreover, it was not just Victoria that felt their presence, as aboriginal people were also relocating seasonally, or even for several years, to the gold-mining communities of Fort Hope, Lytton, Yale, and New Westminster, the capital of the new colony of British Columbia.[21]

Despite claims by historians, aboriginal people were not made redundant by the influx of non-aboriginals to the gold fields, just less visible in the increasingly polyglot society of the colonies. Nor had they been bystanders as gold and coal became focal points of the economy of the Pacific Northwest between the 1840s and 1880s: in both cases, aboriginal people were the discoverers and the first miners, and they continued to work the mines throughout the century.

Coal was first discovered by aboriginal people on northern Vancouver Island. In 1846 the Royal Navy vessel *Cormorant* stopped there and "with the assistance of the Indians they collected about 60 tons."[22] The Kwakwaka'wakw (Kwakiutl) at this site told the HBC that "they would not permit us to work the coal as they were valuable to them, but that they would labor in the mines themselves and sell to us the produce of their exertions."[23] Between 1849, when the HBC established Fort Rupert at the coal mines, and 1851, when the seam was exhausted, the Kwakwaka'wakw people mined 3,650 tons of coal for which they were paid the handsome price of "one blanket 2½ pt.s or equivalent in Grey Cotton for every two tons delivered at the Fort."[24]

Starting in 1852, the Fort Rupert experience was repeated in Nanaimo after trader Joe McKay and then Governor Douglas were led to various seams of coal by the local people. Douglas sent the HBC's *Cadboro* to the spot "and succeeded in procuring, with the assistance of Indians, about 50 tons of coal in one day." "The natives," he reported, "who are now indefatigable in their researches for Coal, lately discovered a magnificent seam over six feet in depth. . . . Such places are left entirely to the Indians, who work, with a surprising degree of industry, and dispose of the coal to the Agents of the Hudson's Bay Company for clothing and other articles of European manufacture."[25]

With the removal of the surface coal and the need to dig shafts and use pumps, the Hudson's Bay Company brought skilled miners from Great Britain. However, as Douglas noted in 1857, aboriginal people remained crucial to the underground operations:

> The want of Indian labor is certainly a great inconvenience for the miners but really they must learn to be independent of Indians for our work will otherwise be subject to continual stoppage.[26]

In the 1850s the coal mines regularly stopped production when the local people went to their seasonal fisheries, potlatched or were attacked by illness. Although partly displaced by Chinese labour in the various coal mines that subsequently sank shafts around Nanaimo, in 1877 it was noted that "the Nanaimo Indians . . . have hitherto been chiefly employed about the coal mines as labourers." In 1882 the Indian agent overseeing Nanaimo noted that the aboriginal people there "find constant employment at the coal mines and wharves," and in 1888 that "many Indians are again working at the coal mines at Nanaimo, taking the place of the Chinese; the fear of accident by explosions deterred them for some time, but now the high wages paid has attracted them again to the mines."[27]

Gold, meanwhile, was first offered to the HBC in trade by the Haidas of the Queen Charlotte Islands in 1851, and in the mid-1850s by the Interior Salish of the Fraser and Thompson valleys. In both cases white men were "obstructed by the natives in all their attempts to search for gold," and "when [the whites] did succeed in removing the surface and excavating to the depth of the auriferous stratum, they were quietly hustled and crowded by the natives who . . . proceeded to reap the fruits of their labours."[28] In 1858, however, some 30,000 non-aboriginals surged into the Fraser valley and up the Thompson, completely overwhelming the few thousand aboriginal inhabitants, who continued to work alongside them. In 1858 James Moore reported that the "whole tribe of Yale Indians moved down from Yale and camped on Hill's bar, about three hundred men, women and children, and they also commenced to wash for gold," and Governor Douglas reported that "it is impossible to get Indian labor at present, as they are all busy mining, and make between two and three dollars a day each man."[29]

Within the decade the gold rushes had passed and while most of the aliens had abandoned the diggings, aboriginal people continued to include gold mining as part of their modified seasonal cycle. In 1871 Alfred Selwyn of the Geological Survey of Canada remarked that "nearly all the Indians of the Fraser above Yale have now become gold washers. They return to the same spot on the river year after year, at the season of lowest water, to wash the sands, and, it is asserted, can almost always earn for a day's labour from one to two dollar's worth of gold." The next year the Victoria Colonist reported that "from $15,000–$20,000 is annually contributed to the wealth of the Province by mining on the Thompson and Fraser Rivers, which is carried on almost exclusively by the Natives at low water."[30] The Indian agents and the mining department regularly recorded the bands along the Fraser and Thompson panning gold into the twentieth century.[31] In addition to mining, many bands along the Fraser, Thompson and Nicola rivers took up packing supplies as a vocation. Chief Justice Begbie, who travelled this circuit, recalled that "no supplies were taken in [to the gold districts] except by Indians. . . . Without them . . . the country could not have been entered or supplied in 1858–1860."[32]

Besides mining and packing, the aboriginal people of the southern Interior took up farming on their own behalf and worked as farm labour for others. In 1874 the Catholic missionary C.J. Grandidier wrote from Kamloops that "The Indians in this part of the country are now quite awake to the necessity of working, of following the examples of the whites, they look to the future and are afraid for their children's sake if they do not work." Acting on behalf of the people of the Fraser valley Alexis, chief of Cheam, asked the Indian agent for advance warning if he visited "in order to unite our people who are now a little dispersed as they are working for the whites."[33] "Every Indian . . . who could and would work — and they were numerous," the provincial attorney general recalled in 1875,

> was employed in almost every branch of industrial and domestic life, at wages which would appear excessively high in England or in Canada. From becoming labourers, some of the Natives . . . engaged on their own account in stock breeding, in river boating, and in "packing," as it is termed, as carriers of merchandise by land and water; while others followed fishing and hunting with more vigour than formerly to supply the wants of the incoming population. The Government frequently employed those living in the interior as police, labourers, servants, and as messengers entrusted with errands of importance.[34]

Did they also engage in more industrial pursuits? Martin Robin has argued that "it was not merely the shrinking numbers . . . which accounted for the low participation of the Indians in the new industrial system. By inclination and habit, the Indian did not fit the industrial mould. His customary and casual and seasonal work schedule hardly prepared him for the discipline, pace and rhythm of industrial employment."[35] Yet the evidence shows aboriginal people were among the region's first factory workers.

The "modern" factory arrived on Vancouver Island in 1861 when Captain Stamp commenced operation of the largest sawmill on the west coast of North America, a steam-powered facility that cost $120,000 to build and was eventually capable of cutting 100,000 feet of lumber a day. For the Tseshaht people of the Alberni Inlet, where the mill was located, the industrial revolution arrived at the end of a cannon. When the white labourers arrived to set up the mill they chose the site where the local people were camped. The mill's operators were satisfied that they had "bought" the site from the local people for "Some 50 blankets, muskets, molasses and food, trinkets etc . . .," but the Tseshaht clearly had a different view of the transaction than the mill owners — they refused to leave. They were introduced to capitalist property relations when the mill managers trained their cannons on them.[36] Ultimately they agreed to move, and when they returned to the mill site it was as workers. The mill manager subsequently recorded that when he "first employed Indians at Alberni, the price of their labour was two blankets and rations of bisquits and molasses for a month's work for each man, if he worked the whole time." One source reports that over its

operation, the mill paid out close to $30,000 in wages, and a considerable portion of that was likely paid to the local Tseshaht people.[37]

Two more giant export sawmills were established on Burrard Inlet between 1863 and 1867. Both rivalled the Alberni mill in size, but unlike their predecessor, they continued to operate into the next century. Together, these mills were the largest industrial operations in the colonies, each employing 75–100 mill hands, exclusive of loggers and longshoremen.[38] As with other settlements around the colonies, whole aboriginal communities relocated to the sawmills, and in Burrard Inlet, most of the workers inside and outside the factory were aboriginal.

"While Europeans or at least Whites fill the responsible posts," geologist George Dawson observed in 1875, "Indians [Squa'mich], Chinamen, Negroes & Mulattoes & Half breeds & Mongrels of every pedigree abound." That year George Walkem, attorney general of British Columbia, wrote that "our lumber mills alone pay about 130 Indian employés over $40,000 annually. Each individual receives from $20 to $30 per month and board." Recalling this period R.H. Alexander wrote: "Our mill hands were largely composed of runaway sailors and Indians and I have known the mill to shut down for several days because all the hands were engaged in an interesting poker game." By 1877 the Indian commissioner for the province found it "difficult to imagine" what "indeed in any part of the Province . . . the miner, the trader and the farmer, the manufacturer, the coast navigator, or almost any other vocation would do without the assistance of the Indian element."[39]

Inquiring into the income of the Musqueem band that worked in the Burrard Inlet the Indian Reserve Commission reported in 1877 that from the "saw mills and other concomitant interests . . . a sum variously computed at from $80,000 to $100,000 finds its way annually into the hands of the natives. The mill owners, too, and the shipping frequenting the mills, are benefitting by a corresponding degree, by having a local source of labour constantly available." The Indian commissioner remarked that in 1881 aboriginal sawmill workers were preferred to whites, and workers of both races earned up to $2.50 per day.[40]

At the same time sawmills in Puget Sound, Washington Territory, employed hundreds of British Columbia aboriginal people. William Pierce, a Tsimshian from Port Simpson, remarked that in the mid-1870s his co-workers in a Puget Sound sawmill included Haida from the Queen Charlottes, Tsimshian from the north coast and Nass and Skeena rivers, as well as Bella Bella, Bella Coola, Kitamaat and Kwakwaka'wakw from the central coast and Tlingit from Alaska.[41] A decade later, one of these migrants, Charles Nowell, a seventeen year old Kwakwaka'wakw from Fort Rupert recalled arriving in Vancouver after returning empty-handed from seeking work in Washington State:

> . . . I was dead broke, and went over to North Vancouver in a small canoe to the sawmill and asked the manager if he could give me a job. He told me I could be a fireman in the sawmill. I says, "I never did it before, but I will try and do my best." He says there is another Indian there who has been working there for two years and will tell me what to do.[42]

As Nowell's reference to "firemen" suggests, these mills were large factories operated by steam power. Morley Roberts worked alongside the crew of "Indians, half-breeds and Chinamen" at a New Westminster sawmill in the 1880s and his description leaves no doubt that sawmill work was among the most "industrial" in British Columbia.[43]

Some aboriginal people moved into skilled jobs but the majority of the aboriginal workers, like the non-aboriginals, were unskilled. Many aboriginal people, including the entire male population of the Sechelt band on the Sunshine Coast north of Burrard Inlet, cut wood for the mills. In addition to working for the big export mills, aboriginal people worked and ran several smaller sawmills that were scattered throughout the province, many of them first established by missionaries in order to encourage aboriginal people to adopt capitalist-Christian ethics. Not only was sawmill labour predominantly aboriginal but so were the longshoremen and -women.[44]

While the sawmills of Burrard Inlet were getting into full swing, the second major factory-based industry — salmon-canning — was in its infancy. First attempted in 1867, it was not until 1870 that continuous production started. Within a decade, however, the canneries were large, modern factories employing hundreds of people and using steam boilers and retorts to heat and cook the salmon and to seal the cans.[45] The early canneries relied almost exclusively on aboriginal men to do the fishing and a workforce comprised of aboriginal women and Chinese men to do most of the canning. Like the big export sawmills, they were frequently located in coastal inlets, remote from white settlement but in, or close to, aboriginal communities. One estimate suggested that the eleven canneries operating on the Fraser River in 1883 employed 1,000–1,200 aboriginal fishermen plus hundreds of aboriginal women to process the fish.[46]

By 1885 a crude estimate based on the reports of the Indian agents suggests that of the 28,000 aboriginal people in British Columbia in 1885, over 85 per cent belonged to bands that earned substantial incomes through paid labour. The remaining 15 per cent, although not wage labourers, participated to a lesser degree in the economy as fur traders.[47] More telling than the numbers are the accounts of whole villages being emptied by aboriginal people engaged in paid work. One surveyor reported, for example, that he did not know where to lay out a reserve because all the Haida were away at the canneries or the mills, while an ethnographer from the Berlin Museum was unable to trade artifacts in villages emptied by all who were mobile. One of the most interesting accounts is by Sayach'apis, a Nuu-cha-nulth, whose invitations to a potlatch in the mid-1880s were spurned by the Songhees, the Saanich, the Cowichan and the Hikwihltaah: "You are too late," they told him; "we are going to the hop fields," to harvest the crop.[48]

Twenty-five years after the gold rush, aboriginal people had not been marginalized — rather they remained at the centre of the transformed, capitalist, economic activity. "Almost all the labour of the province is done by Indians and Chinese, the federal minister of justice reported in 1883."

All the steamboats in which we travelled were manned by Indians — the Stevedores and longshoremen and the labourers you find about the streets are for the most part Indians. All the fishing for the canneries is done by them and in all these occupations they compare favourably with the labouring classes elsewhere. . . . They get good wages, frequently $2.00 a day and over. . . .[49]

"The stranger coming for the first time to Victoria is startled by the great number of Indians living in this town," wrote ethnologist Franz Boas in 1886. "We meet them everywhere. They dress mostly in European fashion. The men are dock workers, craftsmen or fish vendors; the women are washerwomen or working women. . . . Certain Indian tribes have already become indispensable on the labour market and without them the province would suffer great economic damage."[50] Moreover, Chinook, the *lingua franca* of the fur trade, and not English, was the language of the canneries, the docks, the sawmills, the hop-fields and many other sites where large amounts of labour were performed.[51] At no time since have aboriginal people been so central to the province-wide capitalist economy than in the early 1880s, though they continued to be vital to specific industries long after.

RECRUITMENT AND COMPOSITION OF THE ABORIGINAL WORKFORCE

There is virtually no information on how aboriginal people were recruited into the pre-industrial labour force for agriculture and public works, or the manifold handicraft industries sponsored by the Hudson's Bay Company and others. It seems clear, however, that with aboriginal labour abundant in and around the settlements of British Columbia, recruitment was not difficult. Moreover, in addition to the nearby bands, often whole communities moved to white settlements, some seasonally and others permanently, to trade and work. The slim evidence available suggests that, in this period, chiefs acted as labour brokers for their local groups. As we have seen, Governor Douglas held chiefs responsible for the behaviour of those of their people who hired themselves out, and the Fort Rupert journals record that chiefs were paid at the same rate as labourers, to supervise. Similarly, sealing schooners would negotiate with chiefs to bring a whole crew from a single village.[52]

Recruitment became more of an issue with the advent of large sawmills and canneries — the factories — because they demanded an unfamiliar work discipline. For one thing, it was critically important to have a large, regular workforce gathered at a single site for extended, and in the case of the salmon canneries, very precise periods; for another, everyone had to start and end work at the same time. In retrospect, however, it should come as no surprise that aboriginal people were recruited and employed in these factories in large numbers. They dominated the population and either lived close to the new industrial sites (since the canneries, especially, located specifically to take advantage of aboriginal labour) or had their own means of transport to and from them. In addition, aboriginal people, under some circumstances, could be paid less than "White" labour.

Yet little is known about the different methods used to bring aboriginal people into the factories or how they made the transition to factory labour discipline. At the beginning of the industrial era, chiefs were still relied upon as labour agents. We know, for example, that white recruiters visited the Sliammon chiefs on the Sunshine Coast in 1882 and told them that their people would earn $3 a day at the Fraser River canneries.[53] Evidence from the early twentieth century shows that canneries employed "Indian bosses" who would be given cash advances for themselves and others, and who would be responsible for getting a specified number of fishermen and inside workers, particularly women, to come to individual canneries. Employers also used Indian agents as informal recruiters, and large hop growers would send agents to visit bands and sign up workers in advance of the season.[54] However, it would seem from Charles Nowell's experience with the Burrard Inlet sawmill that as the number of industrial sites increased, local groups tended less to act as units; instead, individuals began to take control of their own labour and sell it independent of "Indian bosses."[55] By the late 1880s, it was common for aboriginal women to be hired by Chinese labour contractors in the canneries on the Fraser and Skeena Rivers.[56] Whether as individuals or groups, Alfred Niblack noted in October 1886, aboriginal people were aggressive and creative about finding work:

> It was just at the end of the hop-picking season around Puget Sound, and hundreds of Indians were coming into Port Townsend en route to their villages to the north. A party of Young Haida stopped, and one of their number telegraphed over to Whidbey Island to offer the services of the party to a farmer to dig potatoes for him. In view of the glut in the labour market, due to the presence of so many idle Indians just then, this clever bit of enterprise . . . secured them the job ahead of their rivals.[57]

The incorporation of aboriginal people into the capitalist labour force was a spatially discontinuous process that did not affect all aboriginal groups simultaneously or in the same way. Industry did not spread out gradually from the central settlements of Victoria, New Westminster and Nanaimo; rather it arrived suddenly on inlets far removed from settlement. Moreover, many aboriginal groups opted to travel long distances to obtain employment while their neighbours did not. Those aboriginal groups that had previous exposure to working with or for non-aboriginal people were the first to take up the long migrations to find wage labour in the south.[58]

Participation also varied across generations and gender. Overall, the industrial workplace favoured younger people; agriculture, on the other hand, did not discriminate between young and old or between men and women.[59] The contrast was captured by William Lomas, the Cowichan Indian agent: "All the younger men can find employment on farms or at the sawmills and canneries, and many families are about to leave for the hop fields of Washington Territory. . . ." The elderly he saw were not faring so well:

> The very old people who formerly lived entirely on fish, berries and roots, suffer a great deal through the settling up of the country. . . . With the younger men, the loss of these kinds of foods is more than compensated by the good wages that they earn, which supplement what they produce on their allotments; but this mode of life does away with their old customs of laying in a supply of dried meat, fish and berries for winter use, and thus the old people again suffer, for Indians are often generous with the food they have taken in the chase, but begrudge what they have paid money for.[60]

The British Columbia aboriginal societies had their own gender-based divisions of labour which were largely appropriated into the canneries.[61] Although, generally speaking, native men would fish and women would mend nets and work in the canneries, some women also fished with their husbands (the boats required a puller and a fisher)[62] and some, particularly older, men would mend nets and work inside. The infirm would look after the infants, while even young children had work in the canneries cleaning cans. In peak cannery periods, every possible person would be brought in to work and infants were placed in a corner where they could be watched.[63]

The traditional division of labour between male hunters and female processors of the catch was generally carried over into the capitalist economy of the sealing industry as well. When the local seals were hunted-out and schooners called at west coast villages to pick up crews, as many as 870 aboriginal people were hired, most of them men, although women were sometimes employed as boat-handlers. On the other hand, "the Indian women and children are always the most eager to go to the hop fields, where they always earn considerable sums of money, and, among these Indians, the wife's purse is generally entirely separate from the husband's."[64]

In some cases, however, aboriginal gender divisions of labour could not be grafted directly onto the capitalist economy. Were women or men better suited to work on steamships, in sawmills, or to sell food in the street markets? In the era 1849–90, both men and women worked at non-industrial occupations such as gold mining, farming, agricultural labour, rendering oil and loading coal. With regard to the service trades, men are more often mentioned as cutting and selling firewood while women are commonly recorded as bringing fish and game to urban markets. In urban areas women did domestic work such as washing clothes, taking in ironing and cleaning house,[65] and they were also employed to make fishnets.[66] Prostitution was an additional source of income for hundreds of aboriginal women from the late-1850s through the 1880s.[67] But in keeping with the gender divisions of labour prevalent in capitalist society, I have found no mention of aboriginal women being employed in the sawmills, in coal mines, and on railroad crews.

The effect on aboriginal social and familial relationships of different participation rates by age and gender deserves more scholarly attention. The one study that has been done, of the Carrier people of the Chilcotin, where there was more demand for males in wage-occupations, shows that aboriginal women carried on and even enlarged their role as providers for households in the subsistence economy. Among the Carrier people, this had the effect of increasing the social status and power of women.[68] Among the coastal people women were gaining more prominence as "title holders" or "chiefs." Further research may reveal whether this was due to depopulation, their new incomes, their increased role as providers of subsistence or other factors.

WHY DID ABORIGINAL PEOPLE WORK FOR WAGES?

It is noteworthy in itself that aboriginal people in British Columbia chose, in large numbers, to work for pay. Indeed, in 1852, one of the HBC agents wondered if they could get the west coast people interested in any work besides fishing:

> when they can get all their wants and even a superfluity by a course congenial to them (fishing), it would be erroneous to suppose that they may be easily persuaded to follow an occupation they dislike and which is less remunerative, merely to gratify our will.[69]

Certainly in the 1840s and 1850s there was no pressure on the traditional resource base or subsistence economy which had sustained them for eons.[70] Even by the 1870s and the beginning of truly industrial labour, only a few of the aboriginal groups on southern Vancouver Island and in the Fraser and Thompson valleys were finding their traditional resource-base eroded to the point that they could not have reverted to a totally subsistence economy if such was their preference. Nor did evangelism have a significant impact until the 1860s and then only in a few locations, by which time church representatives were merely reinforcing an existing desire to participate in wage labour.

Prior to the wide-scale opportunities for wage labour most of the people of the west coast participated in the fur trade for reasons which, according to the "enrichment thesis," were broadly based in their own culture's traditions. Moreover, the new wealth generated by the fur trade, the relocation of bands to common sites around forts, and population decimation from disease and firearms led to an enrichment of cultural activities, including, on the west coast, the potlatch.[71] "The arts and crafts, trade and technology, social and ceremonial life were all brought to new peaks of development. The climax of Indian culture was reached well after the arrival of the white man on the scene."[72]

Potlatch is a word in the Chinook jargon that refers to the different ceremonies among many nations of the Pacific Northwest that included feasting, dancing and the giving of gifts to all in attendance. The potlatch was a central feature of the lives and economy of, especially, the coastal Indians. It was only through potlatches that one's hereditary status and rights to resources, property (including songs and dances) and names could be claimed and maintained. The more guests and the more gifts, the higher the relative status of the person giving the potlatch. High-status recipients of potlatch gifts were expected to reciprocate with potlatches in order to maintain their own relative position, and to protect their claims to traditional prerogatives.[73] All the evidence suggests that the fur trade intensified potlatching, and along with it the carving of totems and masks, the weaving of blankets and all the other arts that were associated with the ceremony.[74]

Because of the cultural necessity to periodically distribute valuable gifts in a potlatch, the west coast people were a natural trading market. They had uses for property, possessions and wealth which, while very different from those of the traders themselves, were nevertheless complementary. The traditional potlatch goods were valuable precisely because they were rare, or because they took much time and laborious effort to make. "On the other hand, the intrusive white civilization offered its goods for things that were relatively abundant": fur, fish and unskilled labour.[75] Manufactured blankets and other mass-produced goods were substituted as potlatch goods for locally made, hand-produced items.

With some exceptions, aboriginal people welcomed the arrival of traders on boats and the establishment of trading posts in their territories. They were equally jealous of trading posts in their rival's territories, or territories that they considered their hinterland.[76] Thus, in the seventy years prior to 1849, and since the first direct trading with Europeans, the society of the aboriginal people had changed so that trade with the foreigners had become an integral and largely welcome part of their culture.[77]

It appears that the same cultural forces that drew aboriginal people into the fur trade continued to operate and draw them into the wage and industrial labour force. Aboriginal people permitted, if not welcomed, initial non-aboriginal expansion into their territories to take advantage of the wealth-generating potential that the aliens offered. In 1843 the Songhees people helped the HBC build Fort Victoria.[78] In the 1850s the Haida and the Cowichan both appealed to Governor Douglas to establish a settlement among them that they might find work.[79] When he first visited them in 1881, although their village was still suffering from an unprovoked attack by the Royal Navy, the Kitamaats asked Indian commissioner Powell if he would establish a sawmill in their community.[80] Even in the 1880s, when Port Simpson Tsimshian people refused to accept an Indian agent, refused to be administered under the Indian act and prevented surveyors from assigning reserves, they permitted salmon canneries into

their territory. Different bands of Kwakwaka'wakw refused to allow a priest into their village, yet they too permitted the canneries, sawmills and logging camps.

Aboriginal people apparently found that these new forms of work could be used like the fur trade, to enhance their position in their own society. In 1853, for example, using the wealth they had accumulated from working around Victoria, the Songhees people hosted a potlatch. Three thousand aboriginal people, perhaps a tenth of the population of the entire coastal area, attended this feast.[81] Once Victoria, the wealth of the Songhees and the opportunities for work had been seen, the steady flow of thousands of coastal people to Victoria started the following season. Wage-work became another adaptation of the seasonal subsistence round that had already been modified to include an extended trapping season, when furs were the easiest route to accumulation.

White employers, government officials and missionaries noticed that aboriginal people worked to be able to potlatch. But the non-aboriginal immigrants could not reconcile their own work ethic with the motivations that led aboriginal people into the workforce. The Indian agent for Fraser valley, James Lenihan, expressed his confusion this way:

> The Indians generally have views peculiar to the country as to the value of money. One band, numbering about fifteen families, applied to me in the spring for some agricultural implements and seeds. I questioned the Chief respecting a "potlatche" which he had held the previous winter, and ascertained that he himself and two of his headmen had given away in presents to their friends, 134 sacks of flour, 140 pairs of blankets, together with a quantity of apples and provisions, amounting in value to about $700, for all of which they had paid in cash out of their earnings as labourers, fishermen and hunters.[82]

George Grant, who accompanied Sanford Fleming on his cross-country inspection of possible routes for the CPR, exhibited his puzzlement in describing the aboriginal workforce at the Moodyville sawmill on Burrard Inlet in 1872:

> The aborigines work well till they save enough money to live on for some time, and then they go up to the boss and frankly say that they are lazy and do not want to work longer. . . . Another habit of the richer ones, which to the Anglo-saxon mind borders on insanity, is that of giving universal backshish or gifts to the whole tribe, without expecting any return save an increased popularity that may lead to their election as Tyhees or chiefs when vacancies occur.

Of particular interest was the story of "big George," who had

> worked industriously at the mill for years until he had saved $2,000. Instead of putting this in a Savings Bank, he had spent it all on stores for a grand 'Potlatch'. . . . Nearly a thousand assembled; the festivities lasted a week; and everyone got something, either a blanket, musket, bag of flour, box of apples, or tea and sugar. When the fun was over, "big George," now penniless, returned to the mill to carry slabs at $20 a month.

Similar comments can be found scattered throughout the accounts of missionaries, government agents and travellers.[83]

Aboriginal accounts confirm that income from wage-work was used to enhance the prestige of the labourers. Charley Nowell recollected that during 1870–76 his brother had regular employment as a cook. "That's why my brother was the richest of all the Indians at Fort Rupert. Every payday he used to be paid with trade — in blankets. . . . When the people of Fort Rupert know that my brother is paid, they come and borrow blankets from him. . . . My brother keeps on loaning until he has got enough (principal and interest) to collect and give a potlatch."[84]

In addition to accumulating wealth for potlatching, many aboriginal groups had other traditional uses for wealth. James Sewid, Kwakwaka'wakw, told the story of his great-grandfather who trapped for several winters in order to hold a potlatch needed to recruit a war party to revenge his son's life. Northern men especially paid a substantial bride price to the families of their future wives. Shamans were paid to cure illness, and compensation was often demanded as restitution for intentional or unintentional killing or wounding of another.[85]

Helen Codere, who has made an intensive study of the Kwakwaka'wakw, has noted that while fur-trade wealth increased the frequency of potlatches, wage labour increased the number of guests and the wealth distributed to an even greater extent, and to her the years between 1849 and 1921 could justifiably be called "the potlatch period."[86] Her conclusions are borne out by Kwawkewlth (Kwakwaka'wakw) district Indian agent George Blenkinsop's 1881 observation that potlatches, "of late years, increased to a very great extent." He explained that among the Kwakwaka'wakw "the custom was formerly almost entirely confined to the recognised chiefs, but that of late years it has extended to the people generally, and become very much commoner than before. . . . [The Potlatch] has spread to all classes of the community and become the recognised mode of attaining social rank and respect."[87] Codere charted the increases in the number of blankets given at Kwakwaka'wakw potlatches going back over a century, numbers which were well remembered by her informants owing to the importance of establishing relative prestige levels. The number of blankets distributed at the greatest single potlatch in the following twenty year periods gives an indication of the striking increase in wealth available and distributed: 1829–48: 320 blankets; 1849–69: 9,000 blankets; 1870–89: 7,000 blankets; 1890–1909: 19,000 blankets; 1910–29: 14,000 blankets; 1930–49: 33,000 blankets. The first memories of Billy Assu, a Kwakwaka'wakw from Cape Mudge, were of his father's 1911 potlatch: "My father worked for the money to give that potlatch for many years. He gave away goods and money to the value of more than $10,000."[88]

The same phenomena appeared to be drawing other aboriginal groups into the paid labour force. In 1881 Cowichan Indian agent Lomas predicted that a significant proportion of the $15,000 earned by the Cowichan people at the canneries that season would be given away at potlatches. Similarly, in 1884 a delegation of Nuu-chah-nulth chiefs explained that they worked for their money "and like to spend it as we please, in gathering our friends together; now whenever we travel we find friends; the 'potlatch' does that." Among the Haida the number of new totems being raised with the accompanying ceremonies reached its peak in the period 1860–76. Writing generally of this period missionary William Pierce, a converted Tsimshian, wrote: "In these days, any man of a common order may give a potlatch if he is rich enough."[89] In short, it would appear that aboriginal people were not just servants of industry but also made industrialization serve their interests as well.[90]

However, the fact that aboriginal people had their own reasons for working for wages and chose when they would both enter and leave the labour force was a source of constant frustration to white employers. Indeed, the fact that aboriginal peoples had their own agendas probably accounts for the schizophrenic comments of white employers who spoke about them as "indispensable" while condemning their "unreliability" and "laziness."

Like most other groups outside the urban area, the Kwakwaka'wakw, for example, "continued to earn their own subsistence, which meant that earnings could go to the purchase of manufactured goods. Since they required only a limited amount of manufactured goods for consumption needs and since they did not hoard, any surplus could be and was used in potlatching."[91] Because of their subsistence cycle, winter was the main ceremonial season — and few aboriginal people were willing to work year-round and miss the winter festivities. In the beginning this was not a problem in labour-intensive activities like fishing, canning, harvesting and logging, which were not conducted in the winter. Increasingly, however, the sawmills, the railways, the steamboats and other large employers were anxious to have a year-round and stable labour force so that seasonal labour, the choice of large numbers of aboriginal people, was becoming less compatible with the demands of capitalism.

It is no coincidence, then, that the federal government passed a law banning potlatch in 1884, just as aboriginal peoples reached their peak importance in the economy. Although the potlatch had drawn many aboriginal people into paid labour, by the mid-1880s it was inconsistent with the "stable" habits of industry that both missionaries and government agents saw as essential to the development of a Christian capitalist society. Seeing the potlatch as a bulwark which enabled the aboriginal people to resist acculturation since the seasonal cycle kept them mobile and away from schools and churches, missionaries and the Indian agents argued that it kept aboriginal people poor and militated against the accumulation of individual dwellings, land holdings and private property.

Although the law proved ineffectual, and was not successfully enforced until 1908, it did provide government agents and missionaries with powerful suasion against potlatching.[92] Some of the bands responded to government pressure, others that had been christianized gave up the institution at the insistence of their ministers;[93] some bands in urban areas seemed to be slowly adopting the more individualistic and acquisitive ideals of the new majority. So, despite the ineffective laws, the 1880s were also the climax years of the potlatch along the coast generally.[94] Ironically, the very cultural imperative that had brought aboriginal people into the workforce was outlawed because, due to changing circumstances, it was no longer sufficiently compatible with the requirements of capitalism.

CONCLUSION

In the period 1849–90 the connections to the capitalist economy varied widely among the many nations and linguistic groups that comprised the aboriginal people of present-day British Columbia. Depending on particular circumstances, integration into the paid labour force also had different effects on the social relations between men and women, youth and elderly, and nobles and commoners. Some patterns are nevertheless emerging as research in these areas moves ahead. West coast aboriginal people joined the international economy when Captain Cook first traded sea otter pelts with the natives of Yuquat (Nootka) in 1778, but their relationship to the economy changed dramatically in the mid-nineteenth century. Before the 1850s they were largely hunters, fishermen, trappers and gatherers who exchanged the products of the land for products of the European market. By 1890, however, the industrial revolution having arrived on many of their inlets, bays and rivers, most aboriginal people were trading their labour for wages.

Aboriginal people were central, not marginal, to the development of new industries and the spread of capitalism in the province-to-be. Coal would not have been mined in British Columbia in the 1840s and 50s, export sawmills would not have been able to function in the 1860s and 70s, canneries would not have had a fishing fleet, or the necessary processors, in the 1870s and 80s without the widespread participation of aboriginal people. The gold rush may have diverted the attention of historians, but it did not divert aboriginal people from the economy. It was the aboriginal workforce that allowed the creation of a capitalist regional economy based on fur trade, then coal mining, sawmilling and salmon canning. This was the regional economy that kept the Hudson's Bay Company on the Pacific coast, persuaded Britain that the establishment of colonies could be profitable as well as strategic and ultimately ensured that British Columbia would be *British* Columbia.

While the capitalist economy needed the vast pool of aboriginal labour, aboriginal people used the capitalist economy for their own cultural purposes. Wage labour was one juncture where the potlatch system and capitalism were curiously complementary. Aboriginal people fitted seasonal paid work into their own economic cycle and, in the era described, were able to maintain a level of control over their participation in both. However, the compatibility of capitalism and the aboriginal economy was breaking down by 1884, when the anti-potlatch laws were passed by the federal government: eager to participate in seasonal wage activities from spring to fall, aboriginal people were less interested in participating in the year-round employment that the economy was increasingly demanding.

By the taking of the census of 1891, British Columbia was no longer an "aboriginal province." Aboriginal populations had nearly reached their nadir and alternative pools of labour were becoming available. Since then, although aboriginal people have not comprised the majority of the labour force, they have been consistently important in key sectors, namely fishing, canning and agricultural sectors. In this way, as well as others, the aboriginal and non-aboriginal histories of British Columbia are still inextricably linked.

NOTES

1. Robin Fisher, *Contact and Conflict: Indian European Relations in British Columbia, 1774–1890* (Vancouver, 1977); Rolf Knight, *Indians at Work: An Informal History of Native Indian Labour in British Columbia, 1858–1930* (Vancouver, 1978).

2. Fisher, *Contact and Conflict*, 96, 109, 111. For other statements along these lines see David McNally, "Political Economy Without a Working Class," *Labour/Le Travail* 25 (Spring 1990): 220n; Paul Phillips, "Confederation and the Economy of British Columbia," in W. George Shelton, ed., *British Columbia and Confederation* (Victoria, 1967), 59; Martin Robin, *The Rush for the Spoils: The Company Province 1871–1933* (Toronto, 1972), 30.

3. Alicja Muszynski, "Major Processors to 1940 and the Early Labour Force: Historical Notes," in Patricia Marchak et al., eds., *UnCommon Property: The Fishing and Fish Processing Industries in British Columbia* (Agincourt, Ont., 1987), 46–65; Richard Mackie, "Colonial Land, Indian Labour and Company Capital: The Economy of Vancouver Island, 1849–1858" (MA thesis, University of Victoria, 1985); James K. Burrows, "'A Much

Needed Class of Labour': The Economy and Income of the Southern Interior Plateau Indians, 1897–1910," *BC Studies* 71 (1986): 27–46.

4. Charles Forbes, *Vancouver Island, its Resources and Capabilities as a Colony* (London, 1862), 25; A.A. Harvey, *A Statistical Account of British Columbia* (Ottawa, 1867), 9.

5. H.L. Langevin, *British Columbia: Report of the Hon. H.L. Langevin* (Ottawa, 1872), 28; A.C. Anderson, *Dominion on the West* (Victoria, 1872), 80.

6. For simplicity's sake, I have combined in the term "paid labour" wage-work (whether paid in kind, scrip, or cash), piece work, and independent commodity production (hand logging for example), although each system produced its own set of social relations.

7. For an introduction see William C. Sturtuvant, *Handbook of North American Indians* (Washington, D.C.), vols. 4, 6, 7.

8. The Songhees, a band of the Coast Salish, were an amalgamation of several nearby villages that relocated to a site across the harbour from Fort Victoria after the latter was founded in 1843.

9. Great Britain. Colonial Office, Original Correspondence, Vancouver Island, 1846–67, (CO)305/6, 10048, Governor James Douglas to Russell, 21 August 1855. Colonial Office correspondence (with a CO number) cited here was made available to me by James Hendrickson from his unpublished manuscript "Vancouver Island: Colonial Correspondence Dispatches."

10. CO 305/14, 9267, Douglas to Colonial Office, 8 August 1860.

11. CO 305/4, 9499, Douglas to Newcastle, 28 July 1853.

12. The Tsimshian were from the Skeena River area around Fort Simpson; William Duncan, "Journal," 11 July 1857, cited in Jean Usher, *William Duncan of Metlakatla: A Victorian Missionary in British Columbia* (Ottawa, 1974), 40; W.C. Grant in William Grew Hazlitt, *British Columbia and Vancouver Island* (London, 1858), 179; Dorothy B. Smith, The *Reminiscences of Doctor John Sebastian Helmcken* (Vancouver, 1975), 134.

13. CO 305/6, 10048, Douglas to Lord Russell, 21 August 1855; CO 305/4, 12345, Douglas to Newcastle, 24 October 1853, emphasis mine.

14. June Collins, "John Fornsby: The Personal Document of A Coast Salish Indian," in Marian Smith, ed., *Indians in the Urban Northwest* (New York, 1949), 301; "Northern Indians," San Francisco *Evening Bulletin* (October 4, 1860) reprinted in James Swan, *Almost Out of This World* (Tacoma, 1971), 99; CO 305/7, 3963, Douglas to Sir George Grey, 1 March 1856; and CO 305/7 5814, 10 April 1856.

15. Mackie, "Colonial Land, Indian Labour."

16. CO 305/3, Rev. R.J. Staines to Thomas Boys, 6 July 1852; Smith, *Reminiscences*, 134; CO/305/3 Douglas to Earl Grey, 31 October 1851.

17. British Columbia Archives and Record Services (BCARS), Colonial Correspondence, F347/26a, James Cooper, "Report by the Harbor Master at Esquimalt to the Acting Colonial Secretary"; Usher, *William Duncan of Metlakatla*, 58.

18. CO 305/14, 9267, Douglas to Colonial Office, 8 August 1860.

19. CO 305/14, 8319, Douglas to Colonial Office, 7 July 1860. One major change during the gold rush was that aboriginal labour was increasingly being paid in cash instead of goods. Previously the goods most sought after as pay were blankets, which were commonly used as "potlatch" gifts.

20. San Francisco *Times* (August 27, 1858) in Hazlitt, *British Columbia*, 208, 215. See also Robin Fisher, "Joseph Trutch and the Indian Land Policy," in W.P. Ward and R.A.J. McDonald, eds., *British Columbia: Historical Readings* (Vancouver, 1981), 155; Sophia Cracroft, *Lady Franklin Visits the Pacific Northwest: February to April 1861 and April to July 1870* (Victoria, 1974), 79.

21. Cracroft estimates 1,000 aboriginal people living at Yale in 1861 and mentions that some were engaged as servants, *Lady Franklin*, 53–3; at Lytton, the population of 250 was 80 per cent aboriginal and "the Indians . . . very industrious and peaceable. Their chief employment is gold mining and packing supplies to and from the interior with their

own horses of which they have in great numbers," *Lovell's Gazetteer 1870–3*, 181; Fisher, *Contact and Conflict*, 111.

22. James Douglas to the Governor and Committee of the Hudson's Bay Company, 7 December 1846, in Hartwell Bowsfield, *Fort Victoria Letters 1846–1851* (Winnipeg, 1979), 4.

23. E.E. Rich, ed., *The Letters of John McLoughlin from Fort Vancouver . . ., 1825–1838* (Winnipeg, 1941), 335.

24. The reference is to a blanket of 2½ points specifying a particular quality of blanket. Douglas to the Governor and Committee, 3 September 1849, 3 April and 16 November 1850 in Bowsfield, *Fort Victoria Letters*, 46, 84, 132; William Burrill, "Class Conflict and Colonialism: The Coal Miners of Vancouver Island During the Hudson's Bay Company Era, 1848–1862" (MA thesis, University of Victoria, 1987), 54.

25. CO 305/3, 10199, Douglas to Pakington, 28 August 1852; also CO 305/3, 933, 11 November 1852.

26. Douglas to Stuart, 22 August 1857, in Burrill, "Class Conflict," 127.

27. Canada. Parliament, House of Commons, *Sessional Papers*, (hereafter Canada, *SP*) 1878, 8, 1x; 1883, 54; 1889, 13, 100–102. The 1877 annual report of the B.C. minister of mines records 51 Indians working as coal-miners in the Nanaimo plus an unrecorded number working as miner's helpers. These annual reports show some aboriginal people working in the coal mines into the twentieth century. British Columbia. Legislative Assembly, *Sessional Papers*, (hereafter BC, *SP*) 1877, 617.

28. Quote from CO 305/3, 3742, Douglas to Earl Grey, 29 January 1852; CO 305/3, 9263, Staines to Boys, 6 July 1852; CO 305/3, Douglas to Earl Grey, 31 October 1851; CO 305/3, 8866, Captain A.L. Kuper to Admiralty, 20 July 1852; CO 305/9, 5180, Douglas to Labouchere, 6 April 1858.

29. James Douglas, in T.A. Rickard, "Indian Participation in the Gold Discoveries," *British Columbia Historical Quarterly* 2 (1938): 13 and *British Columbia Historical Quarterly* 3 (1938): 218. There are other estimates of between 200 and 500 aboriginal people mining at Hill's Bar compared to 50–60 white miners in Hazlitt, *British Columbia and Vancouver Island*, 137.

30. Alfred C. Selwyn, "Journal and Report of Preliminary Explorations in British Columbia," *Report of Progress for 1871–72* (Ottawa, 1872), 56; Victoria *Colonist* (26 November 1872).

31. Canada, *SP* 1886, 4, 87–92; BC, *SP* 1900, 724.

32. M.B. Begbie in Langevin, *British Columbia*, 27.

33. Canada. National Archives (NA), RG10, Department of Indian Affairs, Vol. 1001, items 82, 186, C.J. Grandidier to I.W. Powell, 2 July 1874 and Alexis to James Lenihan, 5 September 1875.

34. BC, *SP* 1875, George Walkem, "Report of the Government of British Columbia on the Subject of Indian Reserves," 3.

35. Robin, *The Rush for the Spoils*, 30.

36. BCARS, Colonial Correspondence, File 107/5, W.E. Banfield to the Colonial Secretary, 6 September 1860, from Lorne Hammond, unpublished manuscript on W.E. Banfield; James Morton, *The Enterprising Mr. Moody and the Bumptious Captain Stamp* (Vancouver, 1977), 22–23; H.C. Langely, *Pacific Coast Directory for 1867* (San Francisco, 1867), 158.

37. G.M. Sproat, *Scenes and Studies of Savage Life* (London, 1868, reprinted in Victoria, 1989), 40; G.W. Taylor, *Timber, History of the Forest Industry in B.C.* (Vancouver, 1975), 23.

38. Morton, *Enterprising Mr. Moody*, 33–37, 59; Taylor, Timber, 38.

39. Douglas Cole and Bradley Lockner, eds., *The Journals of George M. Dawson: British Columbia, 1875–78* (Vancouver, 1989), 115; R.H. Alexander, "Reminiscences of the Early Days of British Columbia, Address to the Canadian Club of Vancouver," *Proceedings of the Canadian Club of Vancouver 1906–1911* (Vancouver, 1911), 111; Walkem, "Report of the Government of British Columbia," 3; James Lenihan, Canada, *SP* 1876, 56; Powell in Canada, *SP* 1877, 33–34.

40. Canada, *SP* 1877, 8, "Report of the Indian Reserve Commissioners," lii; Powell in Canada, *SP* 1884, 107.

41. J.P. Hicks, ed., *From Potlatch to Pulpit: The Autobiography of W.H. Pierce* (Vancouver, 1933), 15. In 1876 "Hundreds and sometimes thousands of northern Indians congregate every spring" to trade and work at Puget Sound mills, according to J.G. Swan, "The Haida Indians of Queen Charlotte's Islands, British Columbia," *Smithsonian Contributions to Knowledge XXI* (1876): 2, 8.

42. Nowell found working as a fireman too hot so he switched to loading lumber onto the ships, for $2 a day, then became a tally man for $7.50 per day. Clellan Ford, *Smoke from Their Fires: The Life of a Kwakiutl Chief* (Hamdon, Conn., 1968), 134.

43. Morley Roberts, *The Western Avernus or Toil and Travel in Further North America* (London, 1887), 181–82.

44. In 1876 the 55 men of the Sechelt band cut 1,300,000 cubic feet of saw logs for the mills for which they received $3 per thousand, the same rate paid to white loggers: Canada, *SP* 1878, 8, "Report of the Indian Reserve Commissioners," lix; Knight, *Indians at Work*, 114, 123–24. Missionary William Duncan established a sawmill and a soap factory at Metlakatla by 1871. Other mission-mills followed at Alert Bay, Glen Vowell, Hartley Bay and Kispiox. A description of the latter can be found in Hicks, *From Potlatch to Pulpit*, 69–70.

45. Duncan Stacey, *Sockeye & Tinplate: Technological Change in the Fraser Canning Industry, 1871–1912* (Victoria, 1982).

46. "Salmon Pack for 1883, Fraser River Canneries," *Resources of British Columbia* 1 (1883): 4; aboriginal cannery labour has been considered in some detail by Muszynski and Knight.

47. This estimate subtracts the population figures of the Indian Affairs census for the bands listed as living primarily or exclusively on trapping, hunting and fishing, from the total aboriginal population. The bands subtracted are 239 people in Chilcotin, 600 on the coast, 300 of Kootenays and 2,000 for tribes not visited. See Wilson Duff, *The Indian History of British Columbia: The Impact of the White Man* (Victoria, 1965), 35–40 for estimates of tribes not visited.

48. J.A. Jacobsen, *Alaskan Voyage, 1881–83: An Expedition to the Northwest Coast of America*, translated from the German text of Adrian Woldt by Erna Gunther (Chicago, 1977), 13 and passim; Canada, *SP* 1888, 13, 109, 157–58; Edward Sapir, *Nootka Texts* (Philadelphia, 1939).

49. BCARS, A/E/Or3/C15, Alexander Campbell, "Report on the Indians of British Columbia to the Superintendent General of Indian Affairs," 19 October 1883.

50. R.P. Rohner, *The Ethnography of Franz Boas* (Chicago, 1969), 6, 9; Ernst von Hesse-Wartegg, "A visit to the Anglo-Saxon antipodes (Chapter XVIII of *Curiosa aus der Neuen Welt*, 1893, translated by John Maass)," *BC Studies* 50 (1981): 38; Jacobsen, *Alaskan Voyage*, 5.

51. Chinook was made up of words from aboriginal languages, French and English. A provincial business directory for 1877/78 published a Chinook-English, English-Chinook dictionary for the benefit of its readers: see T.N. Hibben, *Guide to the Province of British Columbia for 1877–78* (Victoria, 1877), 222–49. Franz Boas noted in 1889 that it was impossible for someone to get around British Columbia outside the major cities without knowledge of the language. See Rohner, *Ethnography*, 9 and BCARS, Add. Mss. 2305, Alfred Carmichael, "Account of a Season's Work at a Salmon Cannery, Windsor Cannery, Aberdeen, Skeena," ca. 1885, which records the widespread use of Chinook in the Skeena canneries in the mid-1880s.

52. Fort Rupert *Post Journal*, 22 November 1849 in Burrill, "Class Conflict," 34: for the sealing industry see C.E. Crockford, "Changing Economic Activities of the Nuu-chah-nulth of Vancouver Island, 1840–1920" (Hon. thesis, University of Victoria, 1991), 58.

53. Although they went, they did not like canning. The elders "did not like to expose their

young men and women to the temptations of city life"; thus few Sliammon people returned the next year, Canada, *SP* 1883, 61.

54. NA, RG10, Vol. 1349, items 85, 255, 290, 483, 501.

55. Clellan, *Smoke from Their Fires*, 134.

56. Canner F.L. Lord told the B.C. Fishery Commission in 1892 that Chinese contractors hired the native women and "of course these Chinamen pay the klootchmen" in BC, *SP* 1893, 178: "When the fishing commences the boss chinaman hires Indians to clean the fish and their squaws to fill the cans," according to Carmichael, "Account of a Season's Work."

57. A.P. Niblack, "The Coast Indians of Southern Alaska and Northern British Columbia," U.S. National Museum *Annual Report* (1888): 339.

58. The Tsimshian that lived around the HBC post at Fort Simpson went to Victoria before other Tsimshian groups not living at the fort. Similarly it was the Fort Rupert Kwak-waka'wakw, and the southern Haida around Skidegate (who had exposure to white miners and whalers in addition to itinerant sea-borne fur-traders), that were the first of their respective "nations" to begin labour migration. For the Fort Rupert people see Philip Drucker and R.F. Heizer, *To Make My Name Good: A Re-examination of the Southern Kwakiutl Potlatch* (Berkeley, 1976), 215; for the Haida see J.H. Van Den Brink, *The Haida Indians: Cultural Change Mainly Between 1876–1970* (Leiden, 1974), 51.

59. Jacobsen, *Alaskan Voyage*, 13.

60. Lomas in Canada, *SP* 1888, 13, 105.

61. Jo-Anne Fiske, "Fishing Is Women's Business: Changing Economic Roles of Carrier Women and Men," 186–97 and Lorraine Littlefield "Women Traders in the Fur Trade," 173–83, both in Bruce Alden Cox, ed., *Native People, Native Lands: Canadian Indians, Inuit and Metis* (Ottawa, 1988): Marjorie Mitchell and Anna Franklin, "When You Don't Know the Language, Listen to the Silence: An Historical Overview of Native Women in B.C.," in P.E. Roy, ed., *A History of British Columbia: Selected Readings* (Toronto, 1989), 49–68.

62. Canada, *SP* 1883, 60 records an aboriginal husband and wife fishing team, the wife pulling the boat and the husband handling the net and making $240 in 14 days.

63. Carmichael, "Account of a Season's Work."

64. Canada, *SP* 1887, 5, 92; 1888, 13, 105. In 1913 Indian agent Charles Cox reported that Nuu-chah-nulth men and women keep their incomes separate, in Royal Commission on Pelagic Sealing, Victoria, Indian Claims, December 1913, Vol. 8, 135, in Crockford, "Changing Economic Activities," 43. The Department of Fisheries Annual Reports in Canada, *Sessional Papers*, record the number of aboriginal people involved in pelagic sealing, 1882–1910.

65. Canada, *SP* 1888, 13, 106; Cracroft, *Lady Franklin*, 79. W.F. Tolmie wrote in 1883 that the aboriginal women in Victoria worked "as washerwomen, seamstresses and laundresses, earn much and spend it all in the city," BCARS A/E/Or3/C15.

66. Canada, *SP* 1884, 106; Carmichael, "Account of a Season's Work"; Indian women "knit" nets that "will average from 120–150 fathoms [long and 16 and a half feet deep], at the cost of one dollar per fathom," *Resources of British Columbia* 1 (December 1, 1883).

67. By 1865 the Victoria police were writing the Colonial Secretary that some 200 Indian prostitutes lived "in filthy shanties owned by Chinese and rented . . . at four to five dollars a month," in Peter Baskerville, *Beyond the Island, An Illustrated History of Victoria* (Windsor, Ont., 1986), 39–44. For the 1880s see John A. Macdonald, Canada, *SP* 1885, lix. For an aboriginal account of prostitution, see Franz Boas, *Contributions to the Ethnography of the Kwakiutl* (New York, 1925), 93–94.

68. Fiske, "Fishing Is Women's Business," 186–97.

69. J.M. Yale, 1852 in Mackie, "Colonial Land, Indian Labour," 89.

70. J.A. McDonald, "Images of the Nineteenth-Century Economy of the Tsimshian," in M. Seguin, ed., *The Tsimshian: Images of the Past: Views for the Present* (Vancouver, 1984), 49.

71. Philip Drucker, *Cultures of the North Pacific Coast* (New York, 1965), 129; Fisher, *Contact and Conflict*, 47–48.

72. Duff, *Indian History of B.C.*, 55.

73. There is an enormous ethnographic literature on the potlatch; a good bibliography can be found in D. Cole and I. Chaikin, *An Iron Hand upon the People* (Vancouver, 1990), 213–23.

74. Fisher, *Contact and Conflict; Duff, Indian History of B.C.*; Cole and Chaikin, *An Iron Hand*; Helen Codere, *Fighting with Property: A Study of Kwakiutl Potlatching and Warfare, 1792–1930* (Seattle, 1966).

75. Drucker and Heizer, *To Make My Name Good*, 15.

76. Fisher, *Contact and Conflict*, 27–49.

77. This is particularly true of the west coast people and, to a lesser extent, those of the Interior.

78. Thomas Lowe, Victoria *Colonist* (29 October 1897); Paul Kane, *Wanderings of an Artist* (Edmonton, 1968), 145.

79. CO 305/4, 12345, Douglas to Colonial Secretary, 24 October 1853; Margaret Ormsby states that when the Haidas were unable to mine gold on the Queen Charlotte Islands for lack of tools they offered to sell their rights if the HBC would form an establishment, Bowsfield, *Fort Victoria Letters*, xci.

80. Canada, *SP* 1881, 5, 143. This was also the wish of the Kincolith people of the Nass River, NA, RG10, Vol. 11007, W.H. Collinson to the Reserve Commissioner, 10 October 1887.

81. CO 305/4, 12345, Douglas to Newcastle, 24 October 1853.

82. Lenihan says that on reasoning with the chief he agreed to discontinue the potlatch and was given $80 in seeds, Canada, *SP* 1877, 38.

83. George M. Grant, *Ocean to Ocean: Sir Sanford Fleming's Expedition through Canada in 1872* (Toronto, 1873), 319–20; Knight has a similar story from a completely different source that seems to describe a response to big George's potlatch by a rival, *Indians at Work*, 114; Capt. C.E. Barrett-Leonard, *Travels in British Columbia With the Narrative of A Yacht Voyage Round Vancouver's Island* (London, 1862), 60.

84. Ford, *Smoke from Their Fires*, 54–55.

85. James Sewid, *Guest Never Leave Hungary: The Autobiography of a Kwakiutl Indian*, ed. James Spradley (Kingston, 1989), 27; Victoria Wyatt, "Alaskan Indian Wage Earners in the 19th Century," *Pacific Northwest Quarterly* 78 (1987): 43–49.

86. "The Kwakiutl had a potential demand for European goods in excess of any practical utility the goods might have possessed. This can be seen both as a stimulus to the Kwakiutl integration in their new economy and as a direct stimulus to the potlatch," Codere, *Fighting with Property*, 126.

87. George Blenkinsop, Indian Agent and Rev. A.J. Hall cited in G.M. Dawson, "Notes and Observations on the Kwakiool People of Vancouver Island and Adjacent Coasts made during the Summer of 1885," *Transactions of the Royal Society of Canada*, Section 2 (1887): 17.

88. Codere, *Fighting with Property*, 124; Harry Assu with Joy Inglis, *Assu of Cape Mudge: Recollections of a Coastal Indian Chief* (Vancouver, 1989), 39.

89. Canada, *SP* 1882, 160, 170; Canada, *SP* 1885, 3, 101; Brink, *The Haida Indians*, 42; Hinks, *From Potlatch to Pulpit*, 126.

90. Another indication of this is that traditional raiding of enemies was performed en route to and from their seasonal wage labour until the early 1860s; see for example CO 305/7, 9708, Douglas to Labouchere, 26 August 1856; CO 305/8, 7950, 13 June 1857; CO 305/10, 6949, 25 July 1859.

91. Codere, *Fighting with Property*, 126.

92. Cole and Chaikin, *An Iron Hand*, 19–20.

93. With the acceptance of Christianity "modified potlatching" continued in some places, but the new Christians also had new imperatives to work. New houses built with milled lumber, nails, and glass windows, as well as new standards for clothing, contributions to build a church or purchase musical instruments, etc., all demanded cash incomes.

94. Although the Kwakwaka'wakw proved an exception in this regard.

TOPIC TWO
Rural Life and Society

The Habitant Farm, *Cornelius Krieghoff's 1857 painting, depicts the spartan conditions of rural life in nineteenth-century Canada and the essential contributions made to the rural household by all its members.*

Nineteenth-century Canada has frequently been portrayed as an idyllic, pastoral society peopled predominantly by independent, hard-working, and self-sufficient farmers. The robust pioneers who cleared the Upper Canadian wilderness and the hardy settlers who broke sod on the prairies occupy an important place in the Canadian imagination, and have often been credited with planting the seeds of future progress and prosperity. Canada was in fact a largely rural society throughout the nineteenth century — despite the growth of towns and cities, six out of every ten Canadians still lived in the countryside in 1901.

The mythic images of the independent, prosperous, self-made yeomen that surround the nineteenth-century farmer, however, bear little resemblance to the realities of rural society. Interdependence, inequality, isolation, monotony, joyless labour, and grinding poverty were the norms of rural living for many in nineteenth-century Canada. The tendency to romanticize the agrarian way of life originated in the nineteenth century itself and was largely a reaction to the unsettling changes produced by urbanization and industrialization. Disturbed by the pace of economic and technological change, and the social tensions and problems that followed, many nineteenth-century Canadians idealized agrarian society and longed to return to a simpler rural past. Such sentiments concealed the darker side of rural life. The essays that follow move beyond the mythology surrounding much of our rural past and examine the difficult circumstances that often confronted rural people and the strategies adapted by farm families to survive in a changing world. In Article Three, Cole Harris looks at the chronic poverty that afflicted French-Canadian settlers who had migrated to the seigneurie of Petite-Nation in the Ottawa Valley. In Article Four, Royden K. Loewen compares the efforts of two distinct Mennonite communities to maintain their rural way of life and ethnic identity in the face of changing social and economic conditions.

QUESTIONS TO CONSIDER

1. Why did French Canadians migrate to seigneuries such as Petite-Nation? What were the main characteristics of the habitant economy? How does Harris explain the grinding poverty experienced by the settlers of Petite-Nation?
2. In what ways are the Mennonite communities described by Loewen similar and dissimilar? How did the "informal everyday interactions of rural life" shape these communities?
3. The authors of both articles suggest that culture played an important role in shaping rural society. What are the strengths and weaknesses of their respective uses of culture as an explanatory concept?

SUGGESTED READINGS

Akenson, Donald H., ed. *Canadian Papers in Rural History*. Vols. 1–8. Gananoque: Langdale Press, 1978–93.

Bennett, John W., and Seena B. Kohl. *Settling the Canadian and American West, 1890–1915*. Lincoln: University of Nebraska Press, 1995.

Bitterman, Rusty, et al. "Of Inequality and Interdependence in the Nova Scotian Countryside, 1850–70." *Canadian Historical Review*, 74, 1 (1993): 1–43.

Breen, David H. *The Canadian West and the Ranching Frontier, 1874–1924*. Toronto: University of Toronto Press, 1982.

Courville, Serge, and Normand Sequin. *Rural Life in Nineteenth-Century Quebec*. Ottawa: Canadian Historical Association, 1989.

Gagan, David. *Hopeful Travellers: Families, Land, and Social Change in Mid-Victorian Peel County, Canada West*. Toronto: University of Toronto Press, 1981.

Graham, W.H. *Greenbank: Country Matters in Nineteenth-Century Ontario*. Toronto: Broadview Press, 1988.

Greer, Allan. *Peasant, Lord, and Merchant: Rural Society in Three Quebec Parishes*. Toronto: University of Toronto Press, 1985.

Little, J.I. *Crofters and Habitants: Settler Society, Economy, and Culture in a Quebec Township, 1848–1881*. Kingston/Montreal: McGill-Queen's University Press, 1991.

MacCallum, John. *Unequal Beginnings: Agriculture and Economic Development in Quebec and Ontario until 1870*. Toronto: University of Toronto Press, 1980.

Silverman, Eliane Leslau. *The Last Best West: Women on the Alberta Frontier, 1880–1930*. Montreal: Eden Press, 1984.

THREE

Of Poverty and Helplessness in Petite-Nation

COLE HARRIS

During the three hundred and fifty years of white settlement along the lower St. Lawrence River there have been three major migrations of French-speaking people: the first bringing some 10,000 Frenchmen across the Atlantic before 1760; the second, beginning shortly before 1820, taking French Canadians to the Eastern Townships, to New England, or to the Canadian Shield; and the third, following closely on the second, gradually urbanizing French-Canadian society. Each of these migrations was predominantly a movement of poor people, and each characteristically involved individuals or nuclear families rather than groups or communities. Their results, however, have been vastly different. The first created a modestly prosperous base of agricultural settlement along the lower St. Lawrence. The third has brought French Canadians into the technological orbit of the modern world. But the second, especially when it turned north to the Canadian Shield, led to poverty as acute as that of any Negro sharecropper in the American South, and then, often within a generation or two, to land abandonment and migration to the cities. The magnitude of the third migration was partly a product of the failure of the second, and this failure still echoes through contemporary Quebec.

This paper deals with the French-Canadian migration to and settlement in the seigneurie of Petite-Nation, a small segment of the Quebec rim of the Canadian Shield

Source: "Of Poverty and Helplessness in Petite-Nation," *Canadian Historical Review*, 52, 1 (March 1971): 23–50. Reprinted by permission.

some forty miles east of Ottawa. It describes the coming of French Canadians to Petite-Nation and their way of life there before approximately 1860, then considers the reasons for the extreme poverty and the institutional weakness which were, perhaps, the dominant characteristics of French-Canadian life in the seigneurie. Although in most general respects the habitant economy and society of Petite-Nation were reproduced throughout the Shield fringe of southern Quebec, there is some justification for a close look at this particular place. It belonged to Louis-Joseph Papineau, the leading French-Canadian nationalist of his day and a man who believed, at least in his later years, that the seigneurial system and a rural life were central to the cultural survival of French Canada; and it can be studied in detail in the voluminous Papineau Papers in the Quebec Provincial Archives. This paper considers the ordinary French-Canadian inhabitants of Petite-Nation.

THE OCCUPATION OF PETITE-NATION

Although the penetration of the Shield for agricultural purposes had begun as early as the 1730s,[1] it gained little momentum until well into the nineteenth century. By 1820 a great many *rotures* in the older seigneuries had been subdivided until they produced a minimum subsistence living. French-Canadian agriculture, inflexible, uncompetitive, and largely subsistent, was incapable of supporting a growing population. Some of the young French Canadians whom the land could no longer support moved to the local village, finding there a way point, a time and a place of transition between the closely knit society of kin and *côte* and a new life among strangers. Others moved directly from the parental roture to a destination outside the St. Lawrence lowland. Whether from farm or village, French Canadians left the parish of their birth as individuals or in nuclear families, those going into the Shield travelling a relatively short distance from the adjacent lowland. Habitants settling in Petite-Nation before 1820 had come from the Island of Montreal, Ile Jésus, and the surrounding mainland seigneuries. Most later settlers came from a scattering of parishes in the lower Ottawa Valley.[2] A few of the earliest settlers had been brought to Petite-Nation by the seigneur,[3] a few others had scouted out the land and brought some capital to their destination,[4] but the great majority came unassisted and penniless. They had heard that there were jobs and land up the Ottawa Valley, they had set out with no specific place in mind, had perhaps worked here and there, and arrived, almost by chance, in Petite-Nation.[5]

Petite-Nation was a tract of land approximately fifteen miles a side and bounded on the south by the Ottawa River. Barely a tenth of the seigneurie lay in the Ottawa River plain; the rest, in the hilly southern fringe of the Canadian Shield.[6] Only approximately a third of the land was at all suited to agriculture, the rest being too rough, too swampy, or its soils too thin and acidic. The best soils, although they were hardly good even by the standard of those in Quebec, had developed on the marine clays of the lowland or on alluvial material in the north–south valleys in the Shield that once had been glacial spillways. The forest cover of this abrupt, knobby land was a typical segment of the mixed Laurentian forest:[7] white, red, and jack pine, fir, and white spruce predominated in rocky, excessively drained areas; black spruce, cedar, and larch dominated the bogs; and a beech-maple-birch association that included white ash, red oak, poplar, and a few coniferous species was common on more moderate sites. The climate was considerably more severe than at Montreal. Along the

Ottawa River the average frost-free period was 125 days and was less than 115 days along the northern border of the seigneurie. The climatic limit of wheat cultivation crossed Petite-Nation along the boundary between the Shield and the lowland.

The white settlement of this tract of land began in 1807 or 1808 when Joseph Papineau, then seigneur of Petite-Nation, contracted to cut a small quantity of squared timber,[8] and brought some twenty French-Canadian woodcutters to the seigneurie.[9] Early in 1809 he sold two-fifths of his seigneurie for £7220 to a Boston timber merchant, Robert Fletcher,[10] who in March of that year arrived in Petite-Nation with 160 well-provisioned New Englanders.[11] Within a year Fletcher defaulted on payments, committed suicide,[12] and his portion of the seigneurie reverted to Joseph Papineau. In 1817 when Joseph Papineau sold the entire seigneurie — mills, domain, back *cens et rentes*, and unconceded land — to Louis-Joseph Papineau,[13] his eldest surviving son, there were perhaps three hundred people there, a third of them the remnants of Fletcher's New Englanders, and almost all the rest French Canadians. One of the latter was Denis-Benjamin Papineau, younger brother of Louis-Joseph, a resident of Petite-Nation since 1808 and seigneurial agent for his brother until the late 1840s. For some twenty years after Louis-Joseph purchased the seigneurie, only a few settlers trickled into Petite-Nation each year: in 1828 there were 517 people,[14] in 1842 only 1368.[15] In the 1840s the rate of immigration increased sharply as population pressure in the older settlements dislodged a steadily larger number of French Canadians, and declined again in the 1850s when almost all the cultivable land in Petite-Nation had been taken up. Over 3000 people lived in the seigneurie in 1851, and some 4000 a decade later.[16] By this date five-sixths of the population was French Canadian.

Settlers in Petite-Nation, as in all other Canadian seigneuries, acquired a *roture* (a farm lot or, legally, the final form of land concession within the seigneurial system) which they held from the seigneur. Joseph Papineau had made forty such concessions before 1817,[17] and by the mid-1850s the rotures had been conceded, most of them by Denis-Benjamin Papineau. The Papineaus adopted without modification the cadastral system of the St. Lawrence lowland, conceding land in long lots laid out, as far as the interrupted terrain of Petite-Nation permitted, in côtes (or *rangs*) along the Ottawa River and its tributaries.[18] They charged surveying to the *censitaires*, which meant that it was usually inadequately done,[19] and they expected the censitaires to build their own roads.[20]

There is no evidence that the Papineaus withheld rotures from prospective censitaires while Petite-Nation was still a sparsely settled seigneurie. They were well aware, however, that some rotures were better than others and that it was advantageous to establish responsible settlers in new areas. From time to time Louis-Joseph wrote from Montreal to his brother in the seigneurie with instructions about the settlement of specific rotures.[21] By the late 1840s rotures were becoming scarce — almost invariably there were several applications for each new lot available[22] — and Louis-Joseph, who had returned from exile in France and spent much of his time in the seigneurie, granted land more cautiously. His prejudices ran strongly against English-speaking applicants — "foreign squatters . . . infinitely less satisfactory than our Canadians"[23] — partly because they were wont to cut his timber. In 1848 he began withholding formal title to any new roture until the settler had cleared six arpents (1 arpent equals approximately 5/6ths of an acre). Each applicant was informed that until that time he was a tenant, not a censitaire,[24] a procedure that was unheard of during the French regime when seigneurs were required to grant unconceded rotures to any applicant for them.[25] One habitant, wrote Louis-Joseph, "had the insolence to tell me that I was obliged to grant him land."[26] He also required anyone taking an abandoned roture to pay all the back cens et rentes.[27] As the back dues frequently equalled the value of the land, this was, in effect, a sale.

In Petite-Nation, as in most other seigneuries in the nineteenth century, roture contracts were standardized, printed forms with blanks left for the addition in long-hand of information about the particular censitaire and roture. Joseph Papineau had prepared the original contract, and when these forms ran out Louis-Joseph ordered a second and almost identical printing.[28] Apart from their printed form and much greater consistency, these contracts differed in two principal respects from any drawn up during the French regime: they increased the seigneur's access to timber, and they stipulated a higher cens et rente. To achieve the former purpose, roture contracts in Petite-Nation permitted the seigneur to cut oak and pine for profit on the roture and forbade the censitaire to do so. They allowed the seigneur to confiscate up to six arpents for the construction of a mill, and prevented the censitaire from building either a saw or a grist mill without the seigneur's written consent. Before 1760 many seigneurs had the right to cut timber on their censitaires' rotures for the construction of the banal mill or the seigneurial manor, but they never had the right to cut oak and pine there commercially.[29] Some contracts had given the seigneur power to confiscate an arpent or two, but not more, for a mill. Although the seigneur always had first claim to the grist mill banality, roture contracts had never forbidden the censitaires to build grist mills.[30] Sawmilling had not been a banal right, and during the French regime any censitaire had been allowed to build a sawmill provided that, in so doing, he did not interfere with the operation of the seigneur's grist mill. In Petite-Nation all of this had been changed, with the result that rights to all important forests on conceded as well as on unconceded land, and to the milling of timber, rested entirely with the seigneur.

The rotures granted by Joseph Papineau before 1817 and by his son thereafter paid an annual cens et rente of one *minot* of wheat (1 minot equals 1.07 bushels) and two *livres tournois* for each thirty arpents, a rate which was a third higher than the highest rate consistently charged during the French regime.[31] For a roture in Petite-Nation the annual charge was six and two-thirds minots of wheat plus thirteen livres, six sols, eight deniers (approximately $2.50 Halifax).[32] The Papineaus charged in wheat rather than in capons because the price of wheat was more tuned to inflation.[33] In Montreal in the first half of the nineteenth century, the average price of wheat was between five and six livres a minot, twice the average price a century earlier.[34] In 1813 wheat sold in Petite-Nation at fourteen livres ($2.58) a minot, and the cens et rentes for that year were calculated on this basis. These prices could almost quadruple a cens et rente: at two and one-half livres a minot a roture of 200 arpents paid thirty livres ($5.50) a year, at six livres a minot it paid just over fifty-three livres ($9.70), and at fourteen livres a minot it paid more than 106 livres ($19.40). Because wheat rarely ripened on Shield lots in Petite-Nation, and was a subsistence crop on lowland farms, cens et rentes were usually paid in the cash equivalent of the minots of wheat owned.[35]

After acquiring land on these terms, a settler usually built a tiny log cabin and cleared a little land. Most of the first cabins were shanties of perhaps ten to twelve feet long, with a one slope roof, a dirt floor, and a chimney usually made of short green rounds heavily chinked with clay. In a few years a settler might build another, larger cabin, some fourteen to eighteen feet long, with gable ends, a stone chimney, and a plank floor. Most of these buildings were of *pièce-sur-pièce* construction (squared logs laid horizontally and pegged to vertical timbers at the corners and at intervals along the walls), but some were made of round logs cross-notched at the corners,[36] and a few were frame. By the 1840s a cabin was typically in a clearing of some ten arpents.[37]

THE HABITANT ECONOMY

The occupations of working men and boys in Petite-Nation in 1851 are given in Table 3.1. At this date more than 90 per cent of the working French-Canadian men in Petite-Nation gave their occupation to the census enumerator as farmer, labourer, or river man. Most of the remainder described themselves as artisans or tradesmen, and only sixteen, some of them members of the Papineau family, as merchants, clerks, or professionals. Of those describing themselves as farmers, the great majority were heads of households, married men with several offspring. The labourers and river men were largely youths, some of them only twelve or thirteen years of age, who still lived on the parental roture, and many of the tradesmen listed in the first column were boys working with their fathers. Some men gave two occupations — cultivateur et menuisier, négociant et cultivateur — and many of those describing themselves only as farmers must also have worked intermittently in the logging camps.

Although the nominal census indicates that farming was the dominant occupation in Petite-Nation in 1851, agriculture had developed slowly in a rocky seigneurie that had been first settled for its timber. In the first years both Joseph Papineau and Louis-Joseph had sent biscuit and pork from Montreal,[38] and Denis-Benjamin, who doubted that agriculture was climatically possible in Petite-Nation, had imported wheat.[39] Only by the 1820s were the logging camps supplied locally and most settlers self-sufficient in basic foods. Even in 1842, when the first agricultural census was taken in Petite-Nation, virtually all habitant farms were subsistence operations on a few arpents of cleared land. The habitants were not selling produce to the lumber camps, which were supplied almost entirely by a handful of large farms. Table 3.2 gives examples of both subsistence and commercial farm types. In 1842 there were six large commercial farms in Petite-Nation. One of them (farm 3 in Table 3.2) belonged to Denis-Benjamin Papineau, the other five to English-speaking settlers, among them Alanson Cooke, the sawmill operator, and Stephen Tucker, the timber merchant. Between the commercial and subsistence farm types illustrated in Table 3.2 there were a few semi-commercial operations, and of these three belonged to French Canadians.

By 1861 there were twenty-five commercial farms in Petite-Nation, a quarter of them held by French Canadians. Farms 1 and 2 in Table 3.2 still describe characteristic habitant farms except that by 1861 there were likely to be fifteen to twenty cleared arpents and corresponding increases in crop acreage and livestock. Without manuring or adequate crop rotation, seed-yield ratios on the thin soils of Petite-Nation were extremely low, probably not higher than 1:6 for wheat or 1:12 for oats.[40] Livestock were scrub animals that browsed or grazed in the bush for most of the year. Such a farm rarely produced a marketable surplus. With clearing proceeding at an average rate per farm of well under one arpent a year, and with women and children doing much of the farm work, it required no more than a man's part-time attention.

The farmers and farmers' sons who sought off-the-farm employment usually worked in the sawmills or logging camps, thereby providing most of the labour for the Papineaus or the English-speaking timber merchants who controlled the forests. Joseph Papineau and his son Denis-Benjamin had managed the earliest sawmills, but

TABLE 3.1 *Occupations of Working Males in Petite-Nation, 1851*

Occupation	All Male Residents[a]		All Heads of Households[b]	
	Fr. Can.	*Others*	*Fr. Can.*	*Others*
Farmer	384	67	344	52
Labourer[c]	287	30	46	1
River man[d]	40	7	2	
Carpenter or joiner	22	2	14	2
Blacksmith	12	4	6	1
Woodcutter	1			
Fisherman	2		2	
Baker	1	1	1	
Mason	4		3	
Sawyer		1		1
Tanner	4		1	
Cooper	6	1	4	1
Tinsmith	1		1	
Painter	1		1	
Carter	1		1	
Saddler	2	1	1	
Miller	2		1	
Shake maker	3		2	
Sextant	2		2	
Bourgeois		1		1
Innkeeper		2		1
Merchant	7	8	7	6
Doctor	1	1		1
Clerk	5	6	4	1
Priest or minister		2[e]		1
Bailiff		1		1
Clerk of the JP		1		1
Clerk of the court	1		1	
Notary	1		1	
Surveyor	1		1	

[a] THIS COLUMN INCLUDES ALL MALE RESIDENTS OF PETITE-NATION UNDER SEVENTY YEARS OF AGE FOR WHOM AN OCCUPATION IS LISTED IN THE CENSUS.

[b] THIS COLUMN INCLUDES ALL MARRIED MEN AND WIDOWERS UNDER SEVENTY YEARS OF AGE FOR WHOM AN OCCUPATION IS LISTED IN THE CENSUS.

[c] INCLUDING *JOURNALIERS* AND *ENGAGÉS*.

[d] IN FRENCH, *VOYAGEURS*. SOME OF THIS GROUP MAY HAVE BEEN HIRED ON THE RIVER BOATS, BUT MOST MUST HAVE HAD SOME CONNECTION WITH THE TIMBER DRIVES.

[e] COMPRISING A BELGIAN PRIEST AS WELL AS A METHODIST MINISTER.

Source: Based on PAC, nominal census of Petite-Nation, Nominal Census, 1851, reels C-1131 and C-1132.

TABLE 3.2 *Farm Types in Petite-Nation, 1842*

	Held	Cleared	In wheat	Barley	Rye	Oats	Peas	Potatoes	Meadow & pasture	Other	Cattle	Horses	Sheep	Pigs
									Arpents				Number of	
Subsistence farms														
1/	100	7	2	1		2		1		1	1		1	3
2/	120	7	1	¼	1	2½	1	1			2			2
Commercial farms														
3/	1229	320	1			10	3	1	300	5	36	7	57	12
4/	90	40	1					2	37		36	2	18	5

Source: Derived from examples in PAC, nominal census of Petite-Nation, Nominal Census, 1842, reel C-729.

when Louis-Joseph acquired the seigneurie he leased the mill rights in the western half of it to Thomas Mears, a timber merchant from Hawkesbury.[41] Peter McGill, nephew and heir of the director of the Bank of Montreal, took over the lease in 1834, but the mills were managed by Alanson Cooke, son of one of the early settlers from New England.[42] In 1854 Louis-Joseph sold the mills and timber rights for ten years in the western half of the seigneurie to Gilmour and Company, a firm of Scottish origin then based in Liverpool, and with British North American operations on the St. John and Miramichi rivers as well as the Ottawa. Besides these mills, Asa Cooke, father of Alanson, operated a small mill in the first range;[43] and in the eastern part of the seigneurie another New Englander, Stephen Tucker, held a concession to cut and square timber.[44] A few habitants cut firewood for the steamers on the Ottawa River,[45] and others made potash. There were fourteen asheries in Petite-Nation in 1842, eight of them belonging to French Canadians. In 1851 there were thirty-nine asheries, two-thirds of them in the hands of habitants. These were part-time, family operations each producing three to five barrels of ash a year.[46]

The number and the aggregate income of the men employed in the forests and mills of Petite-Nation cannot be determined exactly.[47] Although most of the labourers and some of the farmers listed in Table 3.1 worked intermittently in forest industries, the census enumerator noted that only thirty to forty men were employed in Alanson Cooke's mill and another ten at his father's in 1851, and did not list the number of men cutting or squaring timber.[48] In 1861 Gilmour and Company employed 147 men in Petite-Nation, and Stephen Tucker employed sixty.[49] Certainly, during the 1850s there were sawmill jobs for perhaps half the year for not more than fifty to sixty men, jobs in the lumber camps for four or five winter months for not more than another 150 to 200, and jobs in the spring timber drives for perhaps fifty.[50] Seeking these jobs were the great majority of able-bodied French Canadians in Petite-Nation. At any given time most of them were unemployed or were engaged in work around the farm that brought almost no cash return. In these conditions wages were extremely low. Mill hands earned $12 to $14 a month in 1861, and wages had been even lower.[51] While some French Canadians earned as much as $100 a year in the forest industries, a great many more earned far less. In the 1850s sawmill and forest jobs could not have brought more than $20,000 in cash or credit into the seigneurie each year.[52]

Among the approximately 1300 people in Petite-Nation in 1842 there were only twelve artisans and tradesmen, nine of them French Canadians.[53] The two merchants then in the seigneurie were English-speaking. In the next decade the population almost trebled, and the number of artisans and tradesmen increased to the point shown in Table 3.1. As along the lower St. Lawrence at the same time, the number of tradesmen was essentially a reflection of poverty. With not enough work available in the forests, and little good farm land, several men would turn to carpentry, for example, when there was the opportunity. Of the handful of French-Canadian merchants and professionals in Petite-Nation in 1851, the doctor was a Papineau; the notary, Francis Samuel MacKay, was the son of an immigrant Scot and a French Canadian; the clerk of the lower court was another Papineau; and the eight French-Canadian merchants were small shopkeepers.

Essentially, then, the habitants in Petite-Nation were farmers, loggers, or sawmill hands. Farming was a subsistence activity that attracted few young men who competed for scarce jobs in the forests or mills. When the family depended entirely on farming, as frequently was the case, its annual cash income can rarely have exceeded $25, and often must have been virtually nothing. When the father worked on his roture and one or two unmarried sons had some work in the lumber camps, the family income would likely have been between $50 and $150 a year. In a few cases, as when the father was employed in the sawmill or had a trade, and two or three unmarried sons worked through the winter in the forests, the family income would have exceeded $200. Almost certainly, however, the gross annual income of most habitant families in Petite-Nation was between $50 and $150 a year.

Arriving without capital in Petite-Nation, taking out a roture that only slowly became a subsistence farm, finding intermittent and poorly paid work in the sawmills or logging camps, and facing payments for basic supplies and for land, almost all habitants in Petite-Nation quickly found themselves in debt. By 1822 the holders of forty-eight rotures in Petite-Nation owed Louis-Joseph over 11,000 livres ($2017).[54] In 1832 only ten lots, several of them belonging to the Papineaus, were free of debt, fifty-one lots each owed more than five hundred livres ($92), and five owed over 1000 livres.[55] Indebtedness had become a chronic condition, most of the habitants owing their seigneur a sum that was approximately equivalent to the value of a man's labour for six months in the sawmill. Many habitants had tried to reduce their debt by subdividing their rotures — as early as 1822 a third of the sixty-six rotures along the river had been broken up[56] — but after a few years even these fractions were likely to owe several hundred livres. Others attempted to escape from debt by selling their rotures, but the seigneur could exercise his *droit de retrait* in these sales, taking over the roture by paying his former censitaire the difference, if any, between the sale price and the debt.[57]

In the twelve years from 1825 to 1836 Denis-Benjamin Papineau collected just over 19,000 livres ($3480) from the censitaires in Petite-Nation.[58] As the cens et rentes accumulating during this period amounted to 55,000 livres ($10,080), and the *lods et ventes* to some 20,000 livres ($3670), he collected each year about a quarter of the annual dues. At least 20,000 livres were also owing for the years before 1825. Louis-Joseph had made several short visits to the seigneurie partly with the hope of collecting more of his debts, but found his censitaires no more able to pay him than his brother. He could sue his debtors but, although he blustered and threatened, in these years he rarely did so. Restraining him was the high cost and inconvenience of court action,[59] the advice of his brother Denis-Benjamin,[60] and undoubtedly, also, Papineau's recognition of the plight of his censitaires.[61]

When Louis-Joseph returned to Canada in 1845 after eight years in exile, he began to manage his seigneurie much more rigorously. He was no longer as involved in politics and had more time for his own affairs, he was more cantankerous, more concerned about his own rights; and he was planning to build an expensive manor house, a project that depended entirely on the collection of debts.[62] In letter after letter Louis-Joseph railed against his brother for allowing "ces animaux" (the censitaires) to fall so heavily into debt,[63] against the high cost of justice, against the sheriff ("maudite invention anglaise comme tant d'autres") for pocketing a commission on the sale of rotures. He could also write: "We will threaten court action and we will sue a few people, but in such a new area there is really so much poverty that I feel more repugnance in suing than they do in paying. Lack of foresight, ignorance, the tendency to become indebted to the merchants are the common failings of all the habitants without exception, but a few have acted out of ill will . . . which it is certainly necessary to rectify."[64] When a censitaire lost his roture after court action, it was sold by public auction, usually to the seigneur. As Louis-Joseph pointed out to his brother, "the certainty that the creditor is owed as much as the land is worth and that the debtor has not and never will have other means to pay means that the creditor is in reality the proprietor."[65]

Most habitants in Petite-Nation were also indebted to at least one merchant. At first Denis-Benjamin had acted as merchant, but he was neither particularly astute nor demanding, which may explain why, around 1830, the New Englander Stephen Tucker became the principal, and for a time the only, merchant in Petite-Nation. Tucker was a Baptist, a man, according to Denis-Benjamin, "so filled with the missionary spirit that he has promised up to $40.00 to any of our poor Canadians who will agree to join his sect."[66] Some years later he was still described as the most fanatical Protestant in Petite-Nation; nevertheless the Papineaus and a great many habitants bought from him. Of 145 *obligations* (statements of indebtedness) drawn up between 1837 and 1845 in Petite-Nation by the notary André-Benjamin Papineau, ninety-one recorded debts to the seigneur, and forty-nine debts to Stephen Tucker.[67] By the mid-1850s Tucker owned forty-four rotures,[68] almost all of them confiscated from his debtors.

Stephen Tucker and Louis-Joseph Papineau disliked each other intensely, and in the late forties and fifties when Louis-Joseph lived in the seigneurie, disputes between them were frequent. On one occasion, when the value of many rotures would not cover the debts owed to the two creditors and Tucker complained bitterly about prospective losses, Louis-Joseph, who, as seigneur, had prior claim, replied icily: "You forget the high credit prices of goods; the interest charges on back accounts, and what you have received from many when I had the right of being paid before you. If you advanced too much with too many, it was your choice."[69] From the habitants' point of view both men were creditors to whom their farms were vulnerable, but Tucker who combined economic and religious coercion and was usually the more insistent must have been the more feared.

THE HABITANT SOCIETY

By the 1820s French-Canadian society in most of the older parishes and seigneuries of the St. Lawrence lowland had sealed itself from outsiders; not only were there few if any non-French Canadians in many parishes, but as time went on there were fewer French Canadians who had not been born in the immediate vicinity. These areas exported many of their young while, with almost no immigration, the people who remained formed an increasingly consanguineous population. Petite-Nation, in contrast, was being settled and it attracted different people: French Canadians from many parishes and seigneuries, New Englanders, Englishmen, Irishmen, and some English-speaking people of Canadian birth. In several cases Catholic Irishmen and French-Canadian girls married in Petite-Nation, and the progeny of these matches were assimilated quickly into French-Canadian society.[70] At least three Protestants in Petite-Nation had also married French Canadians.[71] For the most part, however, the two groups kept to themselves socially. In 1842 forty-seven of the fifty-three English-speaking families in Petite-Nation had such a family in an adjacent lot, while 205 of 208 French-Canadian families lived next to a French-Canadian household.[72] In 1861 the interior parish in Petite-Nation was overwhelmingly French Canadian (with only four Irish by birth and 1489 Catholics against forty-five Protestants), where most English-speaking people lived on the Ottawa Valley plain towards the western corner of the seigneurie (in the parish of Ste-Angélique, with 1007 French Canadians against 545 others). By this date there were three tiny villages in the seigneurie, and only in one of them, Papineauville in the parish of Ste-Angélique, were French- and English-speaking people in Petite-Nation likely to live close together. The habitants encountered the English-speaking settlers as employers, as merchants, as creditors, occasionally as co-workers, but rarely in the ordinary social round of their lives.

The social importance of nuclear family, nearest neighbour, and côte in habitant life in Petite-Nation was not different, as far as can be ascertained, from that in the older settlements of the St. Lawrence lowland. However, migration into the Shield had weakened drastically the importance of kin group and parish. Not only had settlers in Petite-Nation come as individuals but they had come recently and in relatively large numbers. At mid century most adults were still immigrants and, because of the speed of settlement, many of their sons had not found land close to the parental roture. Table 3.3, which compares the kin affiliations in Petite-Nation with those in Lotbinière, a long-settled seigneurie on the south shore of the St. Lawrence some forty miles east of Quebec City, illustrates the effect of migration on the kin groups. The French Canadians who straggled up the Ottawa Valley had left a web of blood ties which they could not quickly recreate. Habitants in Petite-Nation were far less likely to have a relative as nearest neighbour, or even a relative in the same côte, than were habitants in the older seigneuries. Where kin groups existed in Petite-Nation, they rarely extended beyond sibling and parent-child relationships.

In many ways the parish in Petite-Nation resembled the parishes along the lower St. Lawrence in the late seventeenth and early eighteenth centuries.[73] For many years the seigneurie was visited briefly twice a year by a missionary priest who arrived in January on snowshoes and in June by canoe.[74] The first resident priest, an Irishman, was appointed in 1828 and stayed three years, his successor stayed for two years, and in 1833 the parish reverted to the missionary system.[75] In 1835 the Bishop appointed another priest who, in turn, soon begged to be relieved. When in 1838 the Bishop acquiesced, Petite-Nation was left without a resident priest for another four years. In this interval missionaries continued to visit the parish twice a year, but these were short visits, their essential purposes to baptise babies and to say mass for the dead.

TABLE 3.3 *Surnames in the Seigneuries of Petite-Nation and Lotbinière, 1842*

	Petite-Nation	Lotbinière
No. of families	267	458
No. of different surnames	143	126
Percent of families with the most common surname	3	12
Percent of families with one of the ten most common surnames	9	43
Percent of families with unique surname	33	14

Source: PAC, Nominal censuses of Petite-Nation and Lotbinière, Nominal Census, 1842, reels C-729 and C-730.

For the most part, Catholics in Petite-Nation were left alone, and exposed, as one missionary priest put it, "to fatal communications with methodists and baptists."[76] In 1841 the bishop established yet another priest, and this man stayed until 1849 when, amid bitter factional quarrels over the school tax and the location of a new church, he left for a newly constructed chapel and presbytery in the interior of the seigneurie.[77] The Bishop attempted to placate the feuding parties by dividing Petite-Nation into three parishes,[78] but for several more years the two parishes along the river were visited irregularly by their former curé or by the curé from l'Orignal, a seigneurie twenty miles away.

Priests did not stay in Petite-Nation because their financial support was inadequate. They could not have lived on the tithe (in Canada one twenty-sixth of the grain harvest) had it been paid regularly, and agreed to come only after the habitants had subscribed a sum for their maintenance. Yet, whatever the financial arrangements, priests in Petite-Nation were rarely paid. The first complained that he was reduced to "scratching among the stumps"[79] for a living, another that he paid out twice what he received from the habitants and was indebted to the merchant.[80] On one occasion the habitants agreed to tithe in potatoes,[81] but when the new priest arrived in a buggy pulled by two horses, the habitants decided that he was rich and refused to pay either tithe or subscription. The priest explained to his bishop that the buggy was old and had cost only a few dollars. "The mistake," he wrote, "is that I had it varnished, and that gives an appearance of luxury."[82] There were some who doubted that the habitants wanted a priest. One priest noted bitterly that the habitants could support several taverns,[83] and in 1833 the bishop informed Denis-Benjamin that "experience has proved that the habitants could not or *would not* pay even half of what they owed without being forced by law."[84] The priests had attempted to curtail the heavy drinking[85] and some adulterous behaviour in Petite-Nation, and this may have led to a reaction against them; but in the light of many meetings to petition for a priest, the number of times that funds were subscribed for his support, and the bitter rows over the location of a church, it is clear that most habitants wanted to have a resident priest but that he was a luxury they could hardly afford.

After 1840 a number of civil functions, notably the assessment and collection of taxes and the maintenance of roads and schools, were organized within the parish.[86] These civil functions were open to all parish residents, whatever their religious affiliations (the parish corresponding in this sense to the township in Ontario), and in Petite-Nation most responsible parish positions were held either by members of the

Papineau family or by New Englanders. Illiteracy alone disqualified almost all the habitants. New Englanders had established a school in Petite-Nation in 1820, but only two French Canadians (one of them Denis-Benjamin) sent their children to it. The habitants saw no need for formal education, and most of the effort to create schools had to come from outside the seigneurie.[87] The first major initiative in this direction came with the Common School Act of 1841,[88] which provided for the election of five school commissioners in each parish, for the division of parishes into school districts, for an assessment of £50 ($200) on the inhabitants of each district for the building of a school, and for a monthly fee of one shilling and three pence for each child at school. These were heavy charges on a poverty-stricken people who attached no value to formal schooling.[89] Then, when three of the first five school commissioners were English-speaking (elected because the New Englanders had attended the organizational meeting in greater number), the priest began preaching that the three English-speaking school commissioners were agents of religious and cultural assimilation.[90] In these circumstances schools were slowly built and then were often closed for want of pupils. The School Act was modified in 1846 to provide more operating revenue from property taxes whether or not parents sent their children to school.[91] Even so, Denis-Benjamin estimated in 1851 that not one French Canadian in thirty in Petite-Nation was literate.[92] The habitants usually became viewers of ditches and fences, the New Englanders the tax assessors and collectors.[93]

Although the seigneur or his agent was a powerful presence in Petite-Nation, the seigneurie itself was not a social unit. All censitaires had acquired land from the Papineaus; all paid, or were supposed to pay, annual charges for their land; almost all were in debt to the seigneur. This, coupled with Louis-Joseph's fame, his sense of himself as a leader, his excellent education and meticulous knowledge of Canadian civil law and, after 1849, his mansion at Montebello, which was by far the finest residence that most habitants in Petite-Nation had ever seen, made him an awe-inspiring figure in the seigneurie. Louis-Joseph liked to think of himself as the leader of a flock,[94] but the habitants undoubtedly viewed him with fear. He was a force in rural life as seigneurs had not been during the French regime, but not the focus of a rural society. As during the French regime, seigneurial boundaries were irrelevant to social patterns.

Until Louis-Joseph settled at Montebello, Denis-Benjamin Papineau, Stephen Tucker, and the two Cookes had been the most powerful men in the seigneurie. At one time or another each was a justice of the peace. In 1840 Denis-Benjamin was elected unanimously to represent Petite-Nation in the newly formed District Council; four years later he was succeeded by Alanson Cooke. In 1842 Denis-Benjamin was elected to the Legislative Assembly. His son was parish clerk and, at times, surveyor of roads in Petite-Nation, and for several years Stephen Tucker was the tax collector. Several prosperous farmers and merchants, all of them English-speaking, were fringe members of the elite.[95] The position of all this group rested, finally, on economic power. Denis-Benjamin's authority depended on his position as seigneurial agent, Tucker's on his role as employer and creditor, the Cookes' on the many jobs they controlled in the sawmills. The habitants elected these men to the District Council, to the Legislative Assembly, or to a local parish office because their livelihood, however meagre, was controlled by them. Moreover, the elite were the only men in the seigneurie who met the property qualification of £300 ($1200) for such public offices as district councillor or justice of the peace.

PETITE-NATION IN 1860

By 1860 parts of Petite-Nation had been settled for more than fifty years. The Ottawa Valley plain was cleared, long lots were conceded across it, and much of the land was farmed. Farm houses stretched in côtes along the river, and two small villages, Montebello and Papineauville, had taken shape towards opposite ends of this line. In the Shield, the patterns of clearing and settlement were much more irregular, but most of the fertile pockets in the valleys were farmed. In the largest of these valleys, the village of St-André Avellin contained a church, a number of stores, and even a few streets laid out, but still largely unoccupied, at right angles to the main road. North and west from St-André Avellin, where côtes had been settled in the previous two decades, there were still many shanties in tiny clearings amid the bush that was the aftermath of logging. Still farther north, pine and spruce were being cut and floated down the Petite-Nation River to Gilmour and Company's sawmill. In all, some 4000 people lived in Petite-Nation. Rough as in many respects it was, with stumps in many fields and the slash of recent logging almost everywhere, a settled place had emerged where just over fifty years before there had been only forest.

In this place there were three principal groups of people, and three landscapes associated with their different lives. In the manor he had built in 1848 and 1849 at Montebello lived Louis-Joseph Papineau and as many of his immediate family as he could entice away from Montreal.[96] His was one of the finest country houses in Lower Canada, its main unit forty by sixty feet and twenty-four feet high,[97] and its architectural inspiration an amalgam of ideas that Louis-Joseph had brought back from France. The house was sheltered by a row of towering pines, and overlooked a spacious garden to the river. In the village of Montebello just outside the gate to his domain, Louis-Joseph had considerably widened the through road from Montreal to Hull, and had lined the streets with trees, naming each street after its particular tree: rue des cèdres, rue des érables, rue des pins, rue des ormes, rue des sapins.[98] Several miles to the west in the village of Papineauville and its surrounding farms lived Denis-Benjamin Papineau and a group of prosperous New Englanders. Most of their houses were white clapboard in the New England style, or the brick or frame buildings with italianate trim that were becoming common in Ontario. Their large, well-managed farms produced oats, potatoes, hay, oxen, and meat for the logging camps, and their stores in Papineauville supplied settlers in much of the seigneurie. Throughout most of the rest of the coastal plain and in the cultivable valleys of the Shield were the tiny log houses, the barns, the fields, and the côtes of the French-Canadian habitant. However imperfectly, three traditions had emerged in the human landscape of Petite-Nation: that of the aristocrat,[99] that of the Yankee trader, and that of the habitant community of the lower St. Lawrence.

Underlying and shaping the habitant landscape in Petite-Nation were the two essential characteristics of French-Canadian life in Petite-Nation, its poverty and its weak institutions. The habitants faced the world individually or in nuclear families feebly supported by nearest neighbour or côte. The seigneur was a creditor not a leader, the parish priest was more often absent than not, the kin group was barely forming, and the local government was dominated by those who controlled the habitants' livelihood. Paradoxically, the New Englanders, who valued self-reliance, created more institutional support in Petite-Nation for their way of life than did the habitants, who tended to value community. To conclude this paper it is necessary to consider why this was so.

An explanation for the character of French-Canadian settlement in the Shield lies only partly in nineteenth-century Quebec, and even less in the physical character of the Canadian Shield or the commercial ascendancy of the English. The same soils on which French Canadians scratched out a living also supported large and prosperous farms. The forests in which the habitants worked for a pittance made the fortunes of others. English-speaking timber merchants exploited the habitants. So did Louis-Joseph Papineau. The Papineau manor at Montebello, Stephen Tucker's forty-four rotures confiscated from debtors, and the profits of the Mears, the McGills, and the Gilmours who built and operated the sawmills in Petite-Nation all rested on a poor habitant population. Seigneur and lumberman profited from the situation in Petite-Nation, but neither had created it. Rather, to understand the habitant landscape and society in Petite-Nation is to understand the evolving character of French-Canadian rural society over the previous century and a half.

What apparently had happened was this.[100] The few emigrants who crossed the Atlantic to the lower St. Lawrence in the seventeenth and early eighteenth centuries were, for the most part, poor and dispossessed people who had only a toehold in French society before they crossed the Atlantic. Among them were approximately 1000 girls from Paris poorhouses, 2000 petty criminals (mostly salt smugglers), over 3000 ordinary soldiers most of whom had been pressed into service, and perhaps 4000 engagés who came largely from the same group of landless labourers and un-employed as the soldiers. Many of the engagés were young, merely boys according to the intendants, and not very robust. These people came as individuals or within the type of temporary social structure — that of a poorhouse, a prison, or an army — in which they had never intended to spend their lives, and which was irrelevant to the settlement of Canada. Along the lower St. Lawrence they found an abundance of land that, when cleared, yielded a higher standard of living than that of most French peasants. They found an opportunity to settle along the river, away from official eyes, and in a setting where their lives could not be controlled. And they found in the untrammelled life of the fur trade contact with largely nomadic Algonkian Indians whose rhetoric, courage, and apparent lack of regime they admired and emulated.

Out of this emerged a habitant population characterized by bravado, insouciance, and a considerable disdain for authority. The habitants lived boisterously, spending their income, enjoying the independence and modest prosperity of their lives in the côtes, and, perhaps too, the Indian girls along the upper Ottawa; a style of life that grew partly out of their French background but probably more out of the opportunities of a new land. They had brought few institutions with them, and need-ed few in Canada. The Canadian seigneurie was neither a social nor an economic unit, the parish was only slowly emerging as a social unit at the end of the French regime. The village was almost absent; collective open-field agriculture never appeared. The côte did become a loose rural neighbourhood, as time went on neighbours were frequently kin, and, after perhaps the earliest years, the nuclear family was always important. In the background was the colonial government, eager to promote the settlement of the colony, paternalistic, tending to side with the habitants in disputes with the seigneurs. The government could not impose itself on the habitants, but it could offer certain services — inexpensive regional courts, for example, or the right of free appeal to the intendant. In operating hospitals, orphanages, and poorhouses, the religious orders did the same. Such support only increased the independence of the habitants who were not forced to compensate for an oppressive officialdom by a tighter social organization at the local level.

In the century after the Conquest, this way of life had slowly changed. Habitant mobility was constrained by the declining relative importance of the fur trade and, after 1821, by its loss to Hudson Bay; by English-speaking settlement in Upper Canada; and by growing population pressure along the St. Lawrence lowland. Farm land was becoming scarce as the seigneurial lands filled up, the value of land rose, and that of labour gradually fell. Seigneurs found their revenues rising, and close seigneurial management a paying proposition. They kept accounts regularly, insisted on payment of debts, and began to build sizeable manors throughout the lower St. Lawrence. Without an intendant to interfere, they often increased their cens et rentes[101] (indeed, they interpreted the seigneurial system to the English), and as alternative land became scarcer, the habitants had no alternative but to accept these charges. A situation which once had favoured the censitaire had turned to favour the seigneur.

At the same time French Canadians were losing control of commerce to more single-minded and better-connected Englishmen, Scots, and New Englanders. A government which had never controlled but had often supported the habitants during the French regime was taken over by an alien people with a different language, religion, and values. This was no longer a government to turn to as the habitants had turned to the courts and the intendant during the French regime. For a time the Conquest connected French Canada to a larger market for its agricultural products, but not to the larger world of social and intellectual change. It shielded French Canadians from the full impact of the French Revolution, for which most of them were thankful, and it filtered the late eighteenth- and nineteenth-century world through the eyes of the English-speaking merchant, the colonial administrator, or, especially in the nineteenth century, the parish priest. The fragment of France which had crossed the Atlantic to settle the côtes of the lower St. Lawrence and become the largely illiterate habitant population of the French regime, had been poorly connected before 1760 to contending French values and ideologies, and the long-term effect of the Conquest had been to prolong its isolation.

In this situation, French-Canadian life had become increasingly rural. Before 1760, 20 to 25 per cent of the people along the lower St. Lawrence were townsmen, but by 1815 only 5 per cent of the French Canadians. The central business districts and the upper class residential areas of Montreal and Quebec were overwhelmingly English-speaking. French-Canadian seigneurs who once had lived in the towns now lived in their seigneuries. In this rural introversion there were two deep ironies. French Canadians were turning to a rural life at a time when, for the ordinary habitant on the ordinary roture, such a life meant subsistence farming, poverty, debt, and, eventually, the departure of most of his children. Then, too, many of them gloried in an image of the French regime, of a rural way of life before the coming of the English built around seigneurie, parish, and Coutume de Paris,[102] without understanding that in the vastly different conditions of the French regime these institutions had been extremely weak. Economically and institutionally, the rural core around which French Canada had folded was hollow.

All that could be done was to make the most of what they had. The parish, which slowly had been gaining strength after the decision taken in 1722 to establish resident priests, gradually became more vital after the Conquest, and would have developed more rapidly had there not been a serious shortage of priests.[103] The extended family or kin group enlarged and probably strengthened and, with less rural mobility within its seigneurial lowlands, the côte and nuclear family may have strengthened as well. The Coutume de Paris, with its emphasis on family rather than on individual rights, and its protective view of landholding that became more relevant to the lower St. Lawrence as the population increased, became an essential prop, in many nationalist minds, of French-Canadian life. The seigneurial system, although neither a social nor an economic unit of habitant life, had become profitable for the seigneurs, most of whom insisted that the survival of French Canada depended on the survival of the system. These institutions, particularly the kin group and the côte, provided a measure of stability, but they did not provide an institutional framework for change, especially as parish priest and seigneur usually defended the status quo. French-Canadian society had achieved some strength in rural isolation, in closely knit, interrelated communities, and in a retrospective outlook, but had not the ability to cope with change, least of all with the internal problem of population pressure.

When young French Canadians were pushed out of the St. Lawrence lowland, they left in much the condition in which their forebears, a century and a half before, had crossed the Atlantic. They were young, illiterate, often destitute and, in the sense that they were not part of groups bound by ties of blood and tradition, alone. Immigrants in the late seventeenth century had found an abundance of agricultural land and a heady outlet in the fur trade. The many more French Canadians who settled in the Shield found a far more meagre agricultural land and lumber camps and sawmills operated by another people. In this setting, they had no defense against what they became, subsistence farmers and underpaid labourers. When their children or grandchildren left for the cities, they too left as their predecessors had come to the Shield. The years in the Shield had availed French Canadians nothing but poverty and some lag in the adjustment to changed conditions.

Finally, the tragedy of French-Canadian settlement in Petite-Nation lay perhaps less in poverty than in the habitants' inability to maintain a distinctive way of life. The values of the closely knit, rural communities of the lower St. Lawrence were neither those of an aristocrat such as Louis-Joseph Papineau, nor of liberals such as Stephen Tucker or Alanson Cooke. The habitants' outlook was more collective than that of the New Englanders, more egalitarian than that of Louis-Joseph Papineau. But communities such as those along the lower St. Lawrence in the nineteenth century depended on isolation and internal stability. When either is removed they are likely to be undermined, as they were for the habitants in Petite-Nation who stood almost alone to face a changing world.

NOTES

1. In St-Féréol behind the present settlement of Ste-Anne de Beaupré after the Séminaire de Québec had conceded all the land along the côte de Beaupré.
2. See Michel Chamberland, *Histoire de Montebello, 1815–1928* (Montréal 1929), chap. 7, for a description of early immigration to Petite-Nation.
3. Ibid., pp. 58–9.
4. See, for example, J. Papineau à son fils Benjamin, Ile Jésus, mai 1824, *Rapport de l'Archiviste de la province de Québec* [RAPQ], 1951–2, pp. 194–6; and a letter of 9 Feb. 1826, ibid., p. 231.

5. This process is described here and there in the Denis-Benjamin Papineau correspondence. See, for example, Denis-Benjamin Papineau à Louis-Joseph Papineau, fév. 1836, Archives de la province de Québec [APQ], Archives Personnelles [AP], P, 5, 29.
6. The physical geography of Petite-Nation is well surveyed in Paul G. Lajoie, *Etude pédologique des comtés de Hull, Labelle, et Papineau* (Ottawa 1968), pp. 14–31.
7. A detailed description of the forest in Petite-Nation before very much of the seigneurie had been cleared is in Joseph Bouchette's Field Book of the Line between the Seigniory of La Petite-Nation and the Augmentation of Grenville, beginning 1 Oct. 1826, APQ, AP, P, 5, 48.
8. Joseph Papineau à son fils Benjamin, Montréal, 22 juil. 1809, RAPQ, 1951–2, p. 173. Joseph Papineau does not give the date of the contract in this letter, but apparently it was made in the previous year or two.
9. Chamberland, *Histoire de Montebello*, pp. 58–9.
10. Vente de partie de la Seigneurie de Petite-Nation par J. Papineau, Ecr. à Robert Fletcher, Ecr., 17 jan. 1809, APQ, AP, P, 5.
11. *La Gazette de Québec*, 9 mars 1809, no 2289.
12. This account of Fletcher's death is given by Judge Augustin C. Papineau in a short history of Petite-Nation written in 1912. Copy of original manuscript by J.T. Beaudry, Oct. 1819, APQ, AP, P, 5.
13. Vente par Joseph Papineau à Louis-Joseph Papineau, 2 mai 1817, APQ, AP, P, 5, 46. In this case the sale was for £5000.
14. Lettre de D-B. Papineau à Mgr Lartigue, Petite-Nation, 25 fév. 1828, APQ, AP, P, 5, 29; Chamberland, *Histoire de Montebello*, pp. 79–81 gives 512 people in 1825.
15. Public Archives of Canada [PAC], nominal census of Petite-Nation, Nominal Census, 1842, reel C-729.
16. Ibid., 1851, reels C-1131 and 1132; 1861, reel C-1304.
17. Tableau de la Censive de la Petite-Nation, 1818, APQ, AP, P, 5, 48.
18. J-B.N. Papineau, son of Denis-Benjamin, pointed out in 1852 that rotures in Petite-Nation had been laid out "along the course of the Ottawa River or the Petite-Nation River and its tributaries so that the rivers can be used for roads until such time as the censitaires are able to build them." Nominal census of Petite-Nation, 1851, remarks of enumerator on back of page 131, 6 March 1852, reel 1132. See also Instructions de Denis-Benjamin Papineau sur l'arpentage, 1839, APQ, AP, P, 5, 46.
19. With inadequate surveying there was always a good deal of confusion about property lines, particularly in the irregular pockets of cultivable land in the Shield for which the cadastral system of long lot and côte was quite ill suited.
20. During the French regime seigneurs had been expected to build and the censitaires to maintain the roads. The title to Petite-Nation, however, did not specify the seigneur's responsibility to build roads, and there is no indication that the Papineaus built any roads in Petite-Nation other than a few short roads to mills.
21. Louis-Joseph Papineau à Benjamin Papineau, Montréal, 22 nov. 1829, APQ, AP, P, 5, 5 (folder 153a); and also Joseph Papineau à son fils Benjamin, Ile Jésus, mai 1824, RAPQ, 1951–2, pp. 194–6.
22. Louis-Joseph Papineau à Alanson Cooke, Petite-Nation, 22 oct. 1850, APQ, AP, P, 5, 48 (bundle Alanson Cooke).
23. Louis-Joseph Papineau à Benjamin Papineau, 23 oct. 1848, APQ, AP, P, 5, 5 (folder 185).
24. Louis-Joseph Papineau à Benjamin Papineau, 11 oct. 1848, ibid. (folder 184).
25. The legal position in this regard of the seigneur during the French regime is discussed in R.C. Harris, *The Seigneurial System in Early Canada: A Geographical Study* (Madison 1966), pp. 106–8.
26. Louis-Joseph Papineau à Benjamin Papineau, Petite-Nation, 22 oct. 1850, APQ, AP, P, 5, 5 (folder 203). The title deed to the seigneurie of Petite-Nation, unlike most others, did

not specify that the seigneur was required to sub-grant land, but it is doubtful that an intendant during the French regime would have permitted Louis-Joseph to grant land as he did.

27. Louis-Joseph Papineau à Benjamin Papineau, 11 oct. 1848, ibid. (folder 184).

28. For an example of a roture contract in Petite-Nation see Concession de roture no 2, côte du Moulin . . . à Alanson Cooke, 20 oct. 1846, APQ, AP, P, 5, 51.

29. In many seigneurial titles, even the seigneur had been forbidden to cut oak anywhere on the seigneurie.

30. Indeed, by an Arrêt du Conseil d'Etat of 4 June 1686, seigneurs during the French regime could lose their banal right if they did not put up a grist mill within a year.

31. Harris, *The Seigneurial System*, pp. 63–9, 78.

32. All dollar values are given in Halifax dollars, such a dollar being worth 5 English shillings, and approximately 5 and one-half livres tournois. Thus one livre tournois was worth approximately 18 cents Halifax currency.

33. Louis-Joseph was fully aware that seigneurs who fixed their charges in money payments were not likely to prosper in the long run from their holdings. He discusses this matter at some length in Tableau statistique des Seigneuries, circa 1851, APQ, AP, P, 5, 55.

34. A graph of wheat prices during the French regime is in J. Hamelin, *Economie et société en Nouvelle France* (Québec 1960), p. 61, and a similar graph for the later period is in Fernand Ouellet, *Histoire économique et sociale du Québec, 1760–1850* (Montréal 1966), p. 603.

35. In the seigneurial account books the charge for each year was always listed in livres rather than in minots, and depended on the price of wheat in that year. It was not possible for a censitaire to accumulate several years of debt and then, when the price of wheat was low, pay back his seigneur in kind.

36. Pièce-sur-pièce was the most common form of log construction during the French regime, and was still widespread in the nineteenth century. Round log construction probably had entered Quebec from New England in the late eighteenth century and was widely adopted in the Shield by both French Canadians and Irish. French-Canadian and Irish houses in the Shield were often almost indistinguishable, both being essentially simple versions in wood of a Norman house, one brought from the St. Lawrence lowland, the other from southeastern Ireland. The heavily flared eaves, the porches, and the elevated ground storey, all characteristics of the vernacular French-Canadian house of the nineteenth century, often did not penetrate the Shield, presumably because of the additional work and cost associated with them.

37. In 1842 the median amount of cleared land per roture was ten arpents, and by 1861 was 19 arpents (nominal census of Petite-Nation, 1842, reel C-729).

38. See, for example, lettre de Joseph Papineau à son fils Louis-Joseph, Montréal, 28 fév. 1818, RAPQ, 1951–2, p. 182.

39. Lettre de Denis-Benjamin Papineau à son oncle Frs. Papineau, Petite-Nation, 29 fév. 1812, APQ, AP, P, 5, 29.

40. These figures are calculated from data on yields in the Nominal Census of 1861. They assume that French Canadians sowed 1½ minots of grain per arpent. A good deal of land in 1861 was still within a few years of first cultivation. Later, without a change in agricultural technology, yields would have been substantially lower.

41. This lease was arranged sometime before 1822. There is a receipt, dated 1822, for £75 ($300) for lease of the mill in the Papineau Papers (APQ, AP, P, 5, 48).

42. Lease from 1 Nov. 1833 . . . between the Hon. L-J. Papineau and the Hon. P. McGill, 20 Sept. 1834, ibid. (bundle Alanson Cooke).

43. Nominal census of Petite-Nation, 1841, reel C-1132.

44. This was a long-standing arrangement, its terms varying over the years. See, for example, D-B. Papineau à Stephen Tucker, 10 fév. 1844, APQ, AP, P, 5, 30.

45. Joseph Papineau à son fils Louis-Joseph, Montréal, 25 mars 1840, RAPQ, 1951–2, p. 299.

46. Nominal census of Petite-Nation, 1851, reels C-1131 and C-1132.

47. An exact statement would be possible only if the records of all timber concerns operating in Petite-Nation had survived. As it is, there are, apparently, no such records.

48. Nominal census of Petite-Nation, 1851. Some of the information given here is listed on the back of folio sheets and is not photographed on microfilm.

49. Ibid., 1861, reel C-1304. At this date Gilmour and Company and Stephen Tucker were the only major employers in Petite-Nation, and it can be taken that only just over 200 men worked in forest industries in the seigneurie in 1861.

50. These figures are my estimates which probably err on the side of more rather than fewer jobs. In much of the Ottawa Valley the same men were hired to cut and square timber and then to raft it to Quebec. Stephen Tucker may well have hired in this way; if so, the fifty to sixty raftsmen given in these estimates were the same men as fifty to sixty of those estimated to work in the logging camps.

51. The 1861 wages are given in the census (nominal census of Petite-Nation, 1861, reel C-1304). Wages at Hull, forty miles away, were $10 a month in 1820 and $12 a month in 1840, and there is no reason for those in Petite-Nation to have been different. See C.H. Craigie, "The Influence of the Timber Trade and Philemon Wright on the Social and Economic Development of Hull Township, 1800–1850" (MA thesis, Carleton University, 1969) p. 94.

52. My estimate, and probably too generous, based on the wage scale and inventory of jobs given above.

53. Nominal census of Petite-Nation, 1842, reel C-729.

54. Tableau d'arrérages, 1822, APQ, AP, P, 5, 48. In 1825, 46 rotures owed over 20,000 livres (ibid., 1825, APQ, AP, P, 48).

55. Etat des dettes au 11 nov. 1832, APQ, AP, P, 5, 48. By this date the 73 rotures along the Ottawa River owed approximately 40,000 livres.

56. Tableau d'arrérages, 1822, ibid.

57. There are numerous indications in the documents that the Papineaus exercised this droit de retrait. See, for example, J. Papineau à son fils Benjamin, Montréal, 7 jan. 1825, RAPQ, 1951–2, pp. 198–9.

58. Comptes entre D-B. Papineau et L-J. Papineau, 1825–37, APQ, AP, P, 5, 48.

59. At this date there was no court in the Ottawa Valley, and, as a result, minor disputes rarely reached a court. See D-B. Papineau to Philemon Wright, 14 May 1833, PAC, Wright Papers, MG24, D8, vol. 19, p. 8179.

60. Denis-Benjamin was always an easy-going seigneurial agent, often too much so for his brother's liking. Once, for example, when Louis-Joseph was determined to sue, Denis-Benjamin would go only so far as to tell the censitaires in question that they would be taken to court if their debts were not paid in three years. "Je ne scais si cela conviendra à [Louis-Joseph] Papineau," he told his father, "mais je ne pense qu'à moins de déposséder les habitants l'on puisse exiger d'avantage" (J. Papineau à son fils Louis-Joseph, St-Hyacinthe, 27 sept. 1838, RAPQ, 1951–2, pp. 291–2).

61. Although he rarely sued, Papineau did expect to be paid, and he pushed his censitaires as hard as he could short of actual eviction. During one brief visit to the seigneurie he wrote to his wife, "je vois que je n'en retirerai rien, il est trop tard, leur grains sont mangés" (Louis-Joseph Papineau à sa femme, Petite-Nation, 9 avril 1828, RAPQ, 1953–4, pp. 247–9).

62. "Oh il faudrait vivre ici pour réussir à une petite partie des améliorations que je rêve et pour forcer la rentrée des arrérages qui me permettraient de les tenter" (L-J. Papineau à Benjamin Papineau, 23 oct. 1848, APQ, AP, P, 5, 5 (folder 185).

63. Louis-Joseph Papineau à Benjamin Papineau, Montréal, 6 mai 1848, ibid. (folder 175).

64. Louis-Joseph Papineau à son fils Amédée, 28 avril 1852, APQ, AP, P, 5, 7 (folder 327).

65. Louis-Joseph Papineau à Benjamin Papineau, 12 mars 1848, APQ, AP, P, 5, 5 (folder 173). In French law the debts against land were not revealed at the time of its sale, and in this circumstance, bidders were unwilling to pay more than a pittance for rotures sold for the non-payment of dues. The seigneur could acquire them for next to nothing.

66. Chamberland, *Histoire de Montebello*, p. 165. Denis-Benjamin did not here mention Tucker by name, but other reports about him and the fact he was the only Baptist merchant in Petite-Nation leave no doubt who was being described. There is some indication that his offer was not always rejected. In the nominal census of 1851 Aureole Gravelle and his wife, both French Canadians by birth, are listed as Baptists.

67. Liste alphabétique des actes reçus par André-Benjamin Papineau, notaire à St-Martin . . . transactions en la Seigneurie de La Petite-Nation de 1837 à 1845 inclusivement, APQ, AP, P, 5.

68. Stephen Tucker to Louis-Joseph Papineau, Papineauville, 25 May 1855, APQ, AP, P, 5, 48; and also Reciprocal Discharge and acquittance from and to the Honorable Louis-Joseph Papineau and Stephen Tucker, 14 July 1858, APQ, AP, P, 5, 48. Tucker had not been paying the back dues on these rotures and in 1858 he owed approximately £900 on them.

69. L-J. Papineau to Stephen Tucker, Montebello, 27 May 1858, ibid.

70. One priest, however, reported that there was "beaucoup d'animosité" between French Canadians and Irish in Petite-Nation (lettre de M. Bourassa à Mgr Lartigue, 23 mars 1839, cited in Chamberland, *Histoire de Montebello*, p. 174). And, of course, there were many accounts in the Ottawa Valley of strife between rival gangs of French-Canadian and Irish workers.

71. One of these Protestants was a Lutheran, another, brother of the first, a Universalist, and the third, an Anabaptist.

72. This information is calculated from the nominal census of 1842.

73. Resident priests were not established in rural parishes until the 1720s, and before that time parishes were visited intermittently, as in Petite-Nation, by missionary priests.

74. Copies of all the correspondence between Joseph Raupe, the first missionary priest to visit Petite-Nation, and Joseph Papineau are preserved in the Papineau Papers (APQ, AP, P, 5, 49). Together these letters give a vivid picture of the Ottawa Valley mission in its earliest years.

75. This intricate history is treated more fully in Chamberland, *Histoire de Montebello*, chaps. 9–11.

76. Lettre de M. Brady, missionaire ambulant, à l'évêque, Petite-Nation, 4 nov. 1838; cited in Chamberland, *Histoire de Montebello*, pp. 171–3.

77. Ibid., p. 188.

78. Correspondence entre D-B. Papineau et Mgr de Guigues, Evêque de Bytown, 1850–1, APQ, AP, P, 5; see also L-J. Papineau à son fils Amédée, 21 jan. 1851, APQ, AP, P, 5, 7 (folder 299).

79. Chamberland, *Histoire de Montebello*, p. 135.

80. M. Brunet à Mgr Lartigue, 1838, cited ibid., p. 167.

81. Procès verbal d'une assemblée des habitants de la Paroisse de Notre Dame de Bonsecours, 14 juil. 1844, APQ, AP, P, 5, 46. "Cette assemblée est d'opinion qu'en payant les dîmes de patates en sus des dîmes de tout grain, tel que pourvu par la loi, la subsistance du Curé de cette paroisse serait assurée. . . ."

82. Lettre de M. Mignault à Mgr Guigues, 18 oct. 1854, cited in Chamberland, *Histoire de Montebello*, pp. 218–19.

83. Ibid., p. 155.

84. Mgr Lartigue à D-B. Papineau, Montréal, 15 juil. 1833, APQ, AP, P, 5, 28 (folder 1).

85. There are many references to drunkenness. "Il faut dire," wrote one missionary, "que

l'ivrognerie regne en maitresse . . ." (M. Bourassa à Mgr de Telenesse, 10 avril 1839, cited in Chamberland, *Histoire de Montebello*, p. 174).

86. An ordinance to prescribe and regulate the Election and Appointment of certain officers in the several Parishes and Townships in this Province . . ., 29 Dec. 1840, 4 Vic., c. 3, *Ordinances Passed by the Governor and Special Council of Lower Canada*, 1840 and 1841, pp. 9–16. See also 4 Vic., c. 4.

87. In 1833 D-B. Papineau and the priest did attempt to raise money for a school. Although they obtained over £40 in subscriptions, the project apparently collapsed (D-B. Papineau à Louis-Joseph Papineau, Petite-Nation, 17 mai 1833, APQ, AP, P, 5, 29).

88. *Ordinances Passed by the Governor and Special Council of Lower Canada*, 4–5 Vic., c. 18, 1841.

89. "Le goût de l'Education . . . n'existe pas dans le classe qui en a le plus besoin . . . plusieurs fois des parents ont été assez déraisonnables pour retirer leurs enfants de l'Ecole sans aucune juste raison de plainte contre le maître; quelquefois par animosité à cause de quelque châtiment merité infligé aux enfants; quelquefois par pique personnelle contre quelque commissaire ou Syndic; d'autres fois par un motif ignoble de vengeance, qui les portait à fair tout en leur pouvoir pour faire manquer l'Ecole" (D-B. Papineau au Gouverneur Général, Petite-Nation, 22 mai 1843, APQ, AP, P, 5, 29). "You, nor no one else not being amidst our rural population could ever conceive the extravagant notions which they entertain respecting that Great Bug Bear 'The Tax' [the school tax] and designing Scoundrels are prowling about the Country raising still more the heated minds of the Habitants . . ." (D.M. Armstrong to D-B. Papineau, 8 April 1845, APQ, AP, P, 5, 28 (folder A).

90. L-J. Papineau à D-B. Papineau, 26 Sept. 1846, Chamberland, *Histoire de Montebello*, pp. 193–4. See also letters from Denis-Benjamin to Monseigneur de Guigues, Evêque de Bytown, 18 Dec. 1850, and 1851 (more specific date not given), APQ, AP, P, 5.

91. 9 Vic., c. 27, 1846.

92. D-B. Papineau à Mgr de Guigues, Evêque de Bytown, 1851, APQ, AP, P, 5.

93. In 1843, for example, the following men were parish officials in Petite-Nation: parish clerks: J.B.N. Papineau; assessors: Thomas Schryer, Charles Cummings, and Asa Cooke; collector: Stephen Tucker; inspector of roads and bridges: Ebenezer Winters; inspector of the poor: Asa Cooke; commissioners of schools: Mr. Sterkendries (priest), Asa Cooke, Stephen Tucker, Bazile Charlebois, Charles Beautron; road viewers: Jean Lavoie, Henry Baldwin, Antoine Gauthier, François Gravelle, Elezear Frappier, Augustin Belile; fence and ditch viewers: Louis Chalifoux, Edward Thomas, Paul Sabourin, Daniel Baldwin, Antoine Couillard, Louis Beautron (Book of Proceedings of the Civil Corporation of the Seigneurie of Petite-Nation persuant of the Ordinance of the Special Council of the 4th Victoria, c. 3, APQ, AP, P, 5, 46).

94. "Et moi aussi je suis chef de colonie" (lettre de L-J. Papineau à Eugène Guillemot, ex-ministre de France au Brésil, 10 jan. 1855; printed in F. Ouellet, ed., *Papineau*, Cahiers de l'Institut d'Histoire, Université Laval, p. 99).

95. The periods of office of all the elite can best be worked out from the Book of the Civil Corporation of . . . Petite-Nation . . ., APQ, AP, P, 5, 46.

96. Louis-Joseph's wife was especially uneasy about leaving Montreal and competent medical attention. In his later years Louis-Joseph often took to task this or that member of the family for not spending more time in the seigneurie where he most loved to be.

97. L-J. Papineau à son fils Amédée, 26 juin 1848, APQ, AP, P, 5, 6 (folder 281).

98. L-J. Papineau à Mgr Guigues, 29 mars 1856; printed in Chamberland, *Histoire de Montebello*, pp. 221–2. All these names have since been changed to saints' names.

99. This characterization of Louis-Joseph hardly does justice to the complex, many-sided character of the man, although in his later years it is probably the single word which fits him best. Louis-Joseph's relationship with Petite-Nation will be looked at much more closely in another paper.

100. The tentative sketch of the social evolution of habitant Quebec that concludes this paper is based largely on work I have undertaken since the publication of *The Seigneurial System in Early Canada*. It will be given fuller treatment in subsequent essays.

101. Changes in the rate of the cens et rente after 1760 cannot be described simply. In many seigneuries they did not change, and in many others changes were spasmodic. As yet there is insufficient evidence to support the claim that English or French seigneurs, as a group, adjusted these changes in a certain way.

102. The Coutume de Paris had provided a base of civil law throughout most of the French regime, but it was a French law, evolved in conditions far different from those in early Canada, and some of its tenets were irrelevant to Canadian life for many years.

103. By the 1820s and 1830s, perhaps even earlier, the parish was undoubtedly a strong institution in rural French-Canadian life, and this image of it, as of many aspects of French-Canadian life in the early nineteenth century, has been projected back to the French regime.

FOUR

The Mennonites of Waterloo, Ontario and Hanover, Manitoba, 1890s: A Study of Household and Community

ROYDEN K. LOEWEN

The lives of middle-aged farmers David Bergey and Cornelius Plett represented two faces of the turn-of-the-century Mennonite experience in Canada. It is true that as Mennonites, both Bergey and Plett were pacifists, read centuries-old Anabaptist literature, and subscribed to the doctrine of adult, believers' baptism.[1] But Bergey was a Swiss Mennonite, whose descendants had come to Canada from Pennsylvania after the American Revolution; he spoke a south German dialect, his house was of stone construction detached from a massive wooden bank-barn, his wife wore a bonnet, and his kinship network reached into eastern United States.[2] Plett was a Dutch/North German Mennonite who had migrated from Russia to Canada in 1875; he spoke "Low German," he lived in a wooden house attached to a barn by a common ridge pole, his wife wore a kerchief, and his kinship network extended back to

Source: "The Mennonites of Waterloo, Ontario and Hanover, Manitoba, 1890s: A Study of Household and Community," *Canadian Papers in Rural History*, D.H. Akenson, ed., vol. 8 (Gananoque, ON: Langdale Press, 1990), pp. 187–209. Reprinted by permission.

Russia and into the midwestern American states.[3] Even more important than their cultural backgrounds in distinguishing their lives, however, were the different socio-economic and physical settings in which Plett and Bergey lived.[4] Bergey was from Waterloo County in southern Ontario, while Plett hailed from the rural Municipality of Hanover in Manitoba.

Waterloo and Hanover were located in starkly different regions of Canada. Historians of southern Ontario, for example, have documented the decline of the independent "yeoman" in this region. Faced with the "urban challenge" and the spread of industrial capitalism in a myriad of small cities, rural society was being threatened. Agricultural college programs, wilderness romanticization movements, and farmers' political parties were only some of the reactions to the rising urban-industrial society. In Ontario, too, a highly integrated, pluralistic society placed pressures of assimilation on non–Anglo Canadian groups.[5] Prairie historians, on the other hand, have noted how the independent farm family "made good" in an environment characterized by an abundance of land, low population densities, the wheat frontier, upward mobility from rising land values, cultural homogeneity within specific settlements, and relative isolation from the metropolis.[6]

So different were such settings as southern Ontario and the prairie west, that historians have argued that regionalism constituted a fundamental variable in Canadian history. J.M.S. Careless, for one, has rejected the search for some kind of "absolute nationalism" and emphasized instead Canada's four regions, each with its own metropolitan foci and mix of cultures. He has argued that regionalism was an important factor in leading Canadians to develop "a value system [that] has stressed the social qualities that differentiate people."[7] Immigration historians have advanced this argument by suggesting that regional differences in Canada were so great that immigrant groups that settled in more than one region failed to develop a common ethnic identity. These historians have even criticized attempts to write a pan-Canadian history of a single ethnic group. Roberto Perin, for example, has berated the *Generations* immigration history series that attempted such overviews and has cited Robert Harney's warning that such an attempt might merely be an "intellectual construct . . . rather than a reality."[8]

This essay contends that although the lives of Ontario's Bergey and Manitoba's Plett reflected distinctive regions, an inter-regional study of members of a single ethnic group may have merit. Indeed, it will be argued that the very existence of regional differences holds promise for immigration and ethnic studies. The promise of such an inter-regional study is that it may help differentiate incidental and descriptive traits of ethnic groups from what Frederick Barth has called "categories of ascriptions" of such groups — that is, their values, self-perceptions, and social interactions that undergirded those values.[9] As Anthony Giddens has argued, the essence of life for social groups must be seen in "social practices ordered across space and time" and in the very processes in which "agents reproduce the conditions that make these activities possible."[10] Bergey of Ontario and Plett of Manitoba shared similar, crucial "social practices." On the surface, regional settings appeared to have had an effect on the social behaviour of Bergey and Plett. The more highly urbanized and industrialized setting of Waterloo affected the use of English in the Bergey household, the level of interaction with the "outside" world, the educational pursuits of the Bergey children, and the household's marketing strategies. Cutting through the regional differences, however, was a common dedication to well-established "social practices" that were seen as safeguarding Mennonite culture; these practices included a life in a self-sufficient, family-oriented farm household set in a closely-knit, rural sectarian community.

These social practices, as well as the pursuits to "reproduce the conditions" to maintain these practices, comprised the common link between Bergey of Waterloo and Plett of Hanover. Thus, despite regional differences resulting in different descriptive, cultural traits, Bergey and Plett shared similar social aims. Ultimately the lives of Bergey and Plett diverged only in that they sought to procure the self-sufficient agrarian household and sectarian community in two distinctly different regions. These regional differences dictated that the Ontarians and Manitobans would sometimes develop dissimilar strategies. But because those strategies were directed to the same end there was an underlying and fundamental commonality linking Waterloo and Hanover Mennonites.

Comparing the social history of Manitoba and Ontario Mennonites is possible, of course, only with parallel sources. The 1901 Canadian census — both the nominal records and the published aggregates — provides the demographic base for this study. Tax records of Hanover and Waterloo from 1896 also provide parallel information, especially on Mennonite household economies. Parallel genealogical works enable family reconstruction. Most importantly, however, diaries kept by farmers like David Bergey and Cornelius Plett allow for a comparative study of the social dynamic in the Mennonite household. That both Bergey and Plett had neighbours who kept similar records during the 1890s enables the sketch of a wider context. David Bergey's father-in-law, Moses Bowman, in his 70s, and his acquaintances Isadore Snyder, in his 30s, and Ephraim Cressman, in his 40s, also kept diaries in the 1890s. So, too, did Plett's acquaintances Abram M. Friesen, David Stoesz, and Johann Dueck, each in his 50s, but each from a different township in Hanover.[11] While tax and census records outline the structure of the Hanover and Waterloo societies, the diaries of these eight farm householders tell of Mennonite strategies to adapt to regional constraints and opportunities.

II

If these records suggest that there was a common set of Mennonite "social practices," they also reveal the different constraints that the Ontarians and Manitobans faced in securing those practices. Clearly the Manitoba Mennonites faced fewer obstacles than did the Ontarians in the pursuit of maintaining the self-sufficient farm household and the closed sectarian community. The Municipality of Hanover, for example, had the advantage of critical mass. Indeed, Hanover was a virtual recreation of the Mennonite East Reserve, an eight-township land bloc set aside in 1873 for the exclusive settlement by Dutch–North German Mennonites from Russia.[12] Here some 2,000 Mennonites from the "Bergthaler" and "Kleine Gemeinde" congregations made permanent homes while 6,000 other Mennonites settled in the West Reserve, 100 kilometers to the west. Although the exclusivity of the East Reserve was lifted in 1891 and Ukrainian and German Lutheran settlers began entering the reserve, Hanover Municipality remained a predominantly Mennonite enclave. By 1901 the 2,373 Mennonites of Hanover still represented fully 79 percent of the municipality's 3,003 inhabitants.[13]

Waterloo County, on the other hand, had a polyglot population. In 1803, when Pennsylvania Mennonites acquired a 60,000-acre tract of land in the heart of present-day Waterloo Township, they secured the base for an almost homogeneously

Mennonite settlement. In the 1820s, when the Mennonite population reached 1,500 souls, settlements were extended westward into present-day Wilmot Township. But during this time immigration from Germany and England changed the area's ethnic composition, and by 1838, when Waterloo County was established by statute, Mennonites no longer comprised a majority.[14] By 1901 the 5,509 Mennonites of Waterloo County represented only 10.5 percent of the county's 52,594 inhabitants.[15] Adding to the difficulty of establishing a separate, agrarian Mennonite community in Waterloo County was its urban nature. Indeed, in 1901, when not a single Hanover resident lived in a town of more than 1,000 residents, almost 40 percent of Waterloo County residents lived in such towns. In 1901 Hanover's largest town was Steinbach, with 349 residents (97 percent of whom were Mennonite); in Waterloo the largest urban centre was Berlin, with 9,700 residents (of whom only 4.2 percent were Mennonite).[16]

Waterloo County was also more industrialized than Hanover. As early as 1856 Waterloo had been linked to Toronto by Grand Trunk Railroad, and in the years after 1880 steep Canadian tariffs and an aggressive Board of Trade transformed Berlin into an industrialized city. It became known for its furniture, clothing articles, leather goods, rubber products and sugar.[17] By 1910 this industrial march was crowned with a link to the Niagara Falls hydro-electricity plant. Hanover, on the other hand, produced primarily agricultural foodstuffs. They included wheat, oats, cheese, cream, eggs, vegetables and meat, mostly for consumption in Winnipeg, a full day's travel away. Timber and firewood were the only other commodities of export.[18] Although a railway skirted both the east and the west sides of Hanover by 1898, no railway was built through the heart of the municipality, and it was not till 1908 that a long-distance telephone connection was made to the outside.[19] Clearly, just as Hanover was representative of a pre-industrial, agrarian society, Waterloo County was an example of a rural community that was quickly becoming industrialized and urbanized.

Certain aspects of Mennonite social behaviour reflected these different settings. The diaries of the Manitoba and Ontario farmers, for example, record strikingly different levels of interaction with the non-Mennonite market place. The diary of Waterloo farmer David Bergey records almost daily interactions with the merchants of nearby New Dundee and those of the more distant, but larger and more vibrant, Berlin. Leaving his sons and hired hand at home to do the farm labour, Bergey undertook his visits to town for a wide variety of reasons. In a single week in January 1900 he travelled to New Dundee four times, once to cut wood at Hallman's Mill, once to obtain chicken feed at Ayr and Goldies', another time to shoe the hooves of "Lady, Fair and Ab," and the fourth time to haul in oats and attain "chopping."[20]

It was not only middle-aged Bergey who crossed the social boundaries for town. His neighbour, 70-year-old Bishop Moses Bowman, visited the outside world regularly; on one trip to Berlin in February 1890 he "paid the Pole $1.15 for mending shoes," and on another in the same month he "deposited $230 at the Bank of Commerce."[21] On the other side of the county a younger farmer, 42-year-old Ephraim Cressman, also frequently crossed Mennonite social boundaries; during 1892 he made almost daily trips to nearby Breslau and Bridgeport to purchase "choppings" and "middlings" and made weekly trips to the Saturday market in Berlin.[22] In addition to these market visits, Cressman interacted politically and socially in the wider region: during the course of 1890, for example, he attended a meeting of a "Farmers' Union" in Wilmot Township, a planning session of the Reform party in Breslau, a political debate on free trade in Berlin, the nomination meeting for county reeve at the township hall, and a "heavy stock show" in Guelph.[23]

The farmers of Hanover lived in a distinctly different world. With the exception of monthly trips to the market in Winnipeg and occasional trips to one of the French parishes bordering Hanover, most interaction off the family farm lay within the Mennonite community. Indeed, there were few trips to non-Mennonite places outside the municipality other than to Winnipeg: the only such trip noted by Cornelius Plett in 1895 was a trip to Ste. Anne des Chenes on 23 December to purchase piglets; the only trip by the Mennonite bishop-farmer David Stoesz of Bergthal in 1890 was on 23 May, when he drove to St. Pierre to fetch Dr. Harrison for David Jr., "who had been sick for a week."[24] Farmers did sometimes encounter non-Mennonites within the boundaries of Hanover, but, in most cases, they were visitors or temporary residents interested only in business. The diary of 57-year-old farmer Johann Dueck of Gruenfeld noted such a transaction on 19 January 1891, when "four Englishmen stopped in at noon and fed their horses"; he noted a similar exchange with a non-Mennonite on 20 March, when he "brought the Jew in Tannenau 4 chickens . . . [and] 10 pounds of butter for payment of what I had bought at the auction sale."[25]

Hanover Mennonites were clearly afforded a sharper concept of ethnic boundary than were the Ontarians. Trips to Winnipeg were monthly affairs, lasting three full days. And these trips were undertaken for the sale of seasonal commodities, not the purchase of daily services. When Hanover farmer Abram M. Friesen went to Winnipeg in 1895, his visits included four trips to sell potatoes, two to sell cattle, and nine to sell wheat.[26] Only occasionally did the Mennonite farmers of Hanover visit Winnipeg socially. Even when they did, there was a sense that Winnipeg lay outside of the Mennonites' social purview. Bishop David Stoesz visited Winnipeg on 27 November 1894 in order to take "brother Johann Stoesz of Minnesota . . . to see the sights and [to show him] that such a great city was to be found in this north country."[27]

That the Ontarians interacted more frequently with members of Canada's host society than did the Manitobans is also evident from census records. The census of 1901, for instance, reveals that fully 26 percent, 99 of 376 Mennonite households in the two most populated townships of Waterloo County (Waterloo and Wilmot), had a non-Mennonite servant or lodger, compared to only 6 percent of Mennonite households in Hanover.[28] The 1901 census also establishes a relatively high degree of exogamy and church abandonment among Waterloo Mennonites.[29] In fact, 29 households in Waterloo and Wilmot townships in 1901 listed the religious affiliation of one of the spouses as Mennonite, and that of the other spouse, or of one of the children or elderly parents, as either Evangelical, Lutheran, Methodist, Catholic, United Brethren, Episcopalian, or Congregational. In Hanover there were just two such households.[30]

The ability to speak English also demonstrates that Waterloo County Mennonites were more highly integrated with the wider society than were Hanover Mennonites. The 1901 Canadian census category "can speak English" allows for a close comparison. Despite the fact that most Waterloo Mennonite churches and schools still used the German language in the 1860s and that the most conservative of the Waterloo Mennonite groups opposed the learning of English, a knowledge of English was almost universal among Waterloo Mennonites by 1901.[31] In addition, at least a quarter of the Mennonite families spoke some English at home; by 1901, for example, 26.5 percent of Mennonite pre-school children between the ages of three and five spoke English. It was a different story in Hanover. Here critical mass favoured the Mennonites, and only the occasional trip to the market in Winnipeg, visits with the few Anglo-Canadian neighbours, and the teaching of English as a second language in some of the schools offered an avenue to learn the English language. Thus, by 1901, 74 percent of Hanover Mennonite men had learned some English, while only 27 percent of the women spoke the language. Moreover, not a single Hanover child between ages three and five was able to speak English in 1901.[32] Clearly, an important degree of social distance remained between the rural Mennonite household and Manitoba's wider society.

More threatening to the Mennonites' control over social boundaries than a familiarity with the language of the host society, however, were the restraints they faced as they sought to establish the farm households for the next generation. In this pursuit, the Ontarians clearly faced obstacles unfamiliar to the Manitobans. Census and tax records tell the story. By 1901, when 92 percent of Hanover Mennonite households still reported a livelihood from agriculture, only 77 percent of rural Waterloo households did so.[33]

Patterns of marriage and birth demonstrate the difficulty Waterloo families faced in accumulating the resources required to begin farming in Ontario. Mennonites, like many other European rural groups, usually allowed youth to consider marriage only when resources to establish an independent household were within sight.[34] In land-abundant Manitoba, households were clearly established by younger persons than they were in Ontario. The census records of 1901 do not record marriage dates, but they do indicate the number of unmarried adult children still living with their parents and hence hint at relative ages of marriage and household formation. The fact that twice as many (21 percent) Waterloo families had unmarried children, aged 23 or older, living at home than did Hanover families (11 percent) suggests different ages of marriage. This figure is especially significant in light of the fact that many fewer Manitoba teenaged children worked as life-cycle servants than did their Ontario counterparts; in 1901, for example, when 41 percent (156 of 379) of Waterloo Mennonite households employed unmarried youth, only 15 percent (53 of 350) of Hanover households had similar employees. These figures may reflect the more intensely cultivated Ontario farms, but they also indicate that at an age when many Ontario youth worked as servants, many Manitobans were already married.

Family size and birth rates also reflected the closing opportunities for establishing farm households in Ontario. Despite the Waterloo Mennonites' greater access to urban-based medical facilities and probable lower rates of infant mortality, their average family size in 1901 was only 5.3 persons, compared to 6.0 in Hanover.[35] The larger Hanover families, no doubt, reflected higher rates of fertility in Manitoba than in Ontario; Hanover women were relatively young when they bore their first children. Census records indicate that the average age of Hanover mothers at the birth of their first surviving child was 21.6 years, almost two years younger than the 23.5 years for the mothers of Waterloo. An even more striking statistic, revealing differing household strategies, was the percentage of households comprised of young child-bearing couples. In Hanover, 41.8 percent of the households comprised a couple in which the wife was 35 years or younger and a mother; conversely only 23.5 percent of the Wilmot and Waterloo townships were comprised of similarly defined young couples. Clearly the Ontarian youth, faced with greater restrictions in establishing separate households, married later, practiced greater fertility control, and more often left the community.

III

Despite the differences of opportunity in Waterloo and Hanover, there is evidence that Mennonites of both places actively pursued strategies to establish farm households for the rising generation and to maintain ethnic social boundaries. During the 1890s, both communities were to be successful in assuring an agrarian existence for the majority of their members. Mennonites of both places found new sources of farmland, maintained old inheritance practices, sanctioned the accumulation of land by large families, and pursued a self-sufficient household mode of production.

In the pursuit of acquiring new sources of land, the Manitobans had an easier time. Even after all the available fertile and arable homesteads in Hanover had been taken in the 1890s, farmers found new land sources within and just outside the settlement boundaries. One source of land was the 1,700 acres in each township that had been reserved as Hudson's Bay Company land and school sections. Farmer Cornelius Plett's father had purchased 480 acres of this reserved land as early as 1883, but the majority of this land was acquired during the 1890s. Another source of land became available in the 1890s, when the "open field system" in Hanover began to end and farmers began putting the old village commons to the plough. In 1894, for example, farmer Abram M. Friesen left the village of Blumenort and secured land for his children by cultivating his own individually-registered "quarter-section" on what had once been the village pasture. Other farmers found land outside of Hanover. Just to the north of Hanover lay the vacant 240-acre land parcels that had been reserved for Manitoba's Métis after the 1870 Red River uprising. Finally, there were farmers who found their land requirements in the Northwest Territory, just a day's travel by train to the west. By 1891 Bishop David Stoesz noted that he was considering "a new reserve for Mennonites" in the northwest. The significance of the emigration that followed was that Hanover remained a place where more than 90 percent of farmers cultivated their own land in 1901.

Despite the fact that Ontario Mennonites had a much more difficult time safeguarding the agricultural nature of their community, they too sought ways to ensure its survival. Urbanization and chronic land shortages made for uneasy times during the 1890s. Deep church schisms occurred as Mennonites diverged in their schemes to secure a separate ethnic identity. On one extreme, the conservative Old Order Mennonites joined their Amish neighbours in emphasizing radical social nonconformity with outward symbols such as the plain coat, the preaching table, old technologies, and plain, white meeting houses. On the other end of the spectrum, progressive Mennonite families sent their children to college in what Chad Gaffield has identified as an Ontario-wide approach to "family reproduction" within "new social and economic structures."[36]

The majority of Waterloo families, however, saw the agrarian household as the bulwark of cultural continuity. Despite the fact that the cost for land at $37 an acre in Waterloo was almost four times the $10 an acre that Manitobans were paying, the Ontario Mennonites did not waver in their search for a landed existence.[37] Well-to-do farmers simply borrowed money, leveraged their existing holdings, and purchased the high-priced developed land within Waterloo County. In 1900, for example, 55-year-old farmer David Bergey borrowed almost $7,000 and purchased another 100-acre farm, thus doubling the total farm size and enabling two of the six Bergey children eventually to own land of their own.

Poorer farmers continued to find new land sources in less developed areas outside of the two originally settled townships of Waterloo and Wilmot. Waterloo County was not like neighbouring Peel County. Here David Gagan has documented a "relentless movement of people in and out of the county at every stage of its development." Still, there was a greater emigration from Waterloo than some studies have suggested.[38] The land that David Bergey was able to purchase in 1900, for example, had been made available when owner Menno Shantz joined a Mennonite community near Didsbury, in Canada's northwest.[39] Other Ontario Mennonites joined farm communities in a dozen different American states, especially Michigan.[40] The most important source of farmland, however, was in the less fertile soil belts in Waterloo's northern townships of Wellesley and Woolwich and in the less developed areas in the neighbouring counties of Oxford, Wellington and Perth. Indeed, although the Mennonite population in the original Wilmot and Waterloo townships remained stagnant between 1881 and 1921, at just over 3,000 persons, the Mennonite population in the two new townships and the three new counties doubled from 2,506 to 5,136 persons.[41] Thus, although the number of Mennonites living in Waterloo towns had risen to 1,200 by 1921, this represented only 16 percent of Waterloo's Mennonite population. Compared to the 71 percent of Waterloo Anglo-Canadian and German residents who lived in towns, Mennonites were still clearly a rural farm-based people able to find land for the rising generation.

The degree of outmigration, however, was not the only indication that Waterloo Mennonites shared the Hanover Mennonites' commitment to reproducing the farm household. Another was the link between land accumulation and the developmental cycle of the Mennonite family. James Henretta's observation that in eighteenth-century Pennsylvania, it was the "lineal family . . . not the unattached individual, that stood at the centre of economic . . . existence" also mirrors the Canadian Mennonite experience.[42] The practice of accumulating land in order to boost the individual farmer's status, power or living standard was rare in both Waterloo and Hanover. It is true that as in most agrarian societies there were gaps between rich and poor in both Mennonite communities, with the most affluent 10 percent of Mennonites possessing about a quarter of the community's total land area, 21 percent of the land in Hanover and 23 percent in Waterloo Township. At the other extreme the poorest 10 percent of Mennonite landowners owned 2.1 percent of the total land area in Hanover and 1.4 percent in Waterloo.[43] What is significant about this wealth differentiation was its direct link to family size. In the central township of Waterloo, for example, the average family size for the wealthiest 10 percent of 229 farmers was 8.1 persons, considerably greater than the average family size of 5.9. By an accident of historical figures, the families of the top 10 percent of 109 farm families in three selected Hanover village districts was also 8.1 people, while the average family had 5.8 members.[44]

Case studies of farm families indicate that land accumulation was part of a strategy to secure generational succession; the majority of farmers in both Hanover and Waterloo, for example, engaged in a cycle of land accumulation before age 50 and then, when children came of age, of land divestiture. In Manitoba the farm of Cornelius Plett's neighbour Abram Penner was representative: he cultivated 35 acres in 1883 when he was 36 and had six small children; in 1889 at age 42 the land area had increased to 55 acres; and in 1898 when Penner was 51 and the number of children was 12 — including six unmarried sons, aged 12 to 23 — the acreage peaked at 170 cultivated acres. By 1906, when Penner reached age 59, the farm had decreased to 60 acres; in the meantime, however, six married children had been assisted onto a land area totalling 315 acres.[45] Similar patterns appear in Waterloo. Here, 55-year-old David Bergey increased his acreage to 200 acres during the same decade in which his father-in-law, Moses Bowman, succeeded in divesting the last of his 250-acre farm.[46] Such over-arching concerns with generational succession ensured that a high percentage of young Mennonite families, even in Waterloo County, would be able to establish their farms during the 1890s.

Also enabling Ontario farmers to overcome regional obstacles to land ownership was the bilateral partible inheritance system, practiced by both Dutch Mennonites in Manitoba and Swiss Mennonites in Ontario. Unlike the prevailing Anglo-Saxon system of primogeniture, in which the eldest son inherited the farm, Mennonites practiced a more egalitarian inheritance. Their aim was to establish each of the children, daughters as well as sons, on land of their own.[47] In Hanover the church-enforced inheritance by-laws, known as the "Teilungsverordnung," had been transplanted from Russia by both the Bergthaler and the Kleine Gemeinde Mennonites. These by-laws stipulated explicitly that "in order of inheritance [all] descendent children shall be first." They also outlined that in the event of the death of one of the spouses and before any remarriage, the estate should be divided in two equal parts, one part being taken by the surviving spouse, without regard to gender, and the other part held by the children. Although the children's portion could be held in trust, it was to be distributed to the heirs, in the form of capital or of land, as they turned 21. When the surviving spouse died, the remainder of the land was also to be divided equally.[48]

In Waterloo, similar centuries' old practices had been introduced from Pennsylvania. One recent study of inheritance among Waterloo Mennonites noted that "when the estate was settled all children divided the proceeds 'share and share alike.'"[49] Typical was the 1853 will of David Brenneman, which called upon his wife Barbara to "take care of my surviving children," and requested his executors to "pay his debts" and to divide "my property . . . into two portions of which my surviving widow shall have one portion and my surviving children the other portion."[50] These children, too, had their portions kept in trust until they reached the age of majority. When the surviving spouse died, the children would each again be eligible for a share of the inheritance. In his 1869 will, widower Jacob Gingerich of Wilmot, for example, ordered his executors to "divide my estate in equal portions amongst my children . . . in love and peace."[51]

The consequence of this system was not only that men and women could share similar degrees of economic power, but that a single household often had two avenues by which to accrue land. Matrilocality was evidence that men often relied on the inheritance of their wives to help establish an independent household. This was particularly true in instances in which men hailed from poorer households than their wives. A demographic analysis of the village district of Blumenort in Hanover, for example, suggests that 41 percent of the 79 marriages consummated between 1874 and 1910 involved matrilocal residence, and in 62 percent of these cases the bride came from a more well-to-do household than the groom.[52] The bride's patrimony may have been the reason why farmer Cornelius Plett's eldest son Heinrich settled in the village of his wife, Elisabeth Reimer, in 1889. Not only was Elisabeth in line to receive a 325-ruble inheritance from Russia, her father, Rev. Peter Reimer, was also one of the wealthiest men in her village.[53]

Similar examples of men relying on the inheritances of women to establish farm households are apparent in Waterloo County. Unlike Hanover women, Waterloo women sometimes remained single, but they also aided men in establishing farms. When David Bergey, for example, sought to raise the $7,300 required for the 100-acre land purchase in 1900, he turned to his spinster sister Lydia for $1,100 and to two other women for an additional $4,800, thus raising more than 80 percent of the required money from women.[54] Most often, however, women used their inheritance to help establish their own households. As in Manitoba, there were signs of this practice in matrilocal residence patterns. In 1882, for example, farmer Ephraim Cressman moved to Breslau, the home of his wife, Susannah Betzner; in the following years at least two of Cressman's brothers, Allen and Isaiah, actually moved onto farms owned by their wives' parents.[55] That there was a link between matrilocality and female inheritance is evident from the life story of farmer Henry Bear. A family history notes that after Henry Bear married Leah Bowman, the daughter of well-to-do farmer Moses Bowman, in 1868, Henry "worked out, staying away a week at a time"; later the Bears purchased a farm in neighbouring Oxford County; however, only when Leah's father stepped in with financial assistance and the Bears moved to a farm near Leah's parents did the Bear household become soundly established, with Henry rising to become a community leader.[56] Inheritance practices, like the willingness to migrate in search of land and the practice of linking land accumulation to family size, ensured that Mennonites in both Hanover and Waterloo would remain an agrarian people.

IV

Both Hanover and Waterloo Mennonites, thus, exhibited a common commitment to life on a family farm. That pursuit revealed a common cultural value. The promise of the successfully reproduced farm household was the continuity of old social networks, with people sharing common values, assumptions and self-identities. The self-sufficiency of the family farm brought all household members to identify closely with a single social unit; the rural nature of community ensured a degree of social distance from the wider society; and the pursuit of generational succession within a culture of partible inheritance provided a context in which kinship ties were allowed to take root.

Ensuring that the family farm in both Ontario and Manitoba would guarantee self-sufficiency and social distance was the farm's household mode of production. It is true that Waterloo farms were located in a region supporting a higher degree of agricultural commercialization than were Hanover farms.[57] Indeed, regional agricultural censuses indicate that Waterloo County farmers had buildings that were valued at three times those of farmers of southeastern Manitoba, $1,684 to $578, and land worth twice the amount, $3,995 to $2,180 (only in the value of machinery were the Manitobans slightly ahead).[58] True, too, the crops of Waterloo differed from those of Hanover. Agricultural historians have long documented the decline of wheat production in Ontario, and its ascendancy in western Canada.[59] Mennonite farms of Waterloo and Hanover exhibited these differences. Indeed, while the average Mennonite farmer in Waterloo Township cultivated 16.4 acres of wheat in 1896, or only 16 percent of the total average crop, the average Hanover farmer dedicated 58 percent of the household's acreage to wheat in 1891.[60] Instead of growing wheat, Waterloo farmers produced peas, corn and turnips, as well as specialty crops such as carrots and sugar beets, and orchards of apples and pears. Many of these products were used as animal feed, especially for swine and milch cows; both milk and pork were sold to local markets in Berlin or one of the neighbouring towns.[61] Hanover farmers, on the other hand, concentrated on products that could be exported to markets in Winnipeg, Ontario and overseas. Thus, besides marketing wheat and oats as cash crops, they sold milk to one of Hanover's half a dozen cheese factories.[62]

More significant than the differences of the Waterloo and Hanover crops was the fact that Waterloo and Hanover were equally geared to both self-sufficiency and the generation of capital. The farm household, self-reliant in both food and labour, both safeguarded the Mennonites' value of social distance from the wider society and guaranteed the continuation of familiar social networks.[63] Diary entries in both Waterloo and Hanover suggest a common commitment to food procurement. They speak of hog-butchering bees, large potato gardens, and butter churning in both places; they note the work of cutting logs and firewood in lush Waterloo woodlots or in the vast forest lying to the east of Hanover; they detail the process of tapping maple trees in Waterloo and picking wild fruit in Hanover.[64]

Farm diaries also record the Mennonite households' self-sufficiency in labour. True, census records note that many more farms in Waterloo employed servants than did farms in Manitoba, reflecting both the availability of labour in the east and the intensive agriculture. Still, the largest part of the Mennonite farms' labour requirement in both Hanover and Waterloo was met by family members. Younger farmers like Wilmot township's Aaron Bowman, aged 29 in 1890, could not rely on the help of his small children; he could, however, count on assistance from his retired father, Rev. Moses Bowman, his teenaged brother, Ezra, and his older married brother, Moses Jr.[65] A middle-aged farmer like 55-year-old David Bergey, on the other hand, relied almost exclusively on the labour of his children. While Bergey undertook the more public duties of running the family farm, his sons undertook the field work; typical was 5 September 1900, when Bergey noted that he was "in Dundee in P.M. . . . [while] Gilbert sowed . . . Ezra plowed and Herbert harrowed."[66]

The family labour pool also brought men and women together in a common pursuit and a joint identification with the household. Indeed, both Waterloo and Hanover Mennonites subordinated the identity of both spouses to the domestic unit. When Ontario's Moses Bowman noted in February 1890 that "we and Noahs took dinner at Aarons," or when Manitoba's Cornelius Plett noted in April 1895 that "for dinner Bernard Doerksens [visited us] . . . and after dinner Gerhard Doerksens also came," it was more than a sign of a pervading patriarchalism; it reflected a mentality that grouped each community member with a specific household.[67] In everyday life men and women strove together to ensure the survival of the household economic unit. Diaries delineate a gender division of labour, with men working the fields and women in the farmyard. However, in these days, before the full commercialization of the family farm, women's work as producers was considered crucial to the household's survival.[68]

Both Waterloo and Hanover women prepared eggs, cream, vegetables and butter for the market, as well as for household consumption. References by Manitoba's David Stoesz to "the cow stepp[ing] on [my wife's] foot while she was milking," or to "my wife . . . finishing the digging of the potatoes," refer to the work of a household producer.[69] Entries by Ontario's David Bergey noting, "at mill to pick up sorghum crop for wife," or Louisa Bowman's entries in her husband's diary recording that "cows, Topsy and Tidy calved," indicate that women's work also brought with it managerial responsibilities.[70] The differences in the work patterns of Hanover and Waterloo women reflected only the respective markets in which they operated. David Bergey's reference to "wife and I went to Berlin . . . with eggs and cheese" and Moses Bowman's note that "Mom to Dundee with . . . 19 dozen eggs . . . " are not found in Hanover. Here the market, located in distant Winnipeg, was not visited on a daily or weekly basis.[71] Nevertheless, mixed farming brought together the entire household in a common pursuit, ensuring that little outside labour would be hired, or that relatively few children would be compelled to find work in the cities.

v

Another result of the Ontario and Manitoba commitments to a rural existence was a deeply rooted communal orientation. Hanover, of course, was the epitome of a closely-knit community, bound by lines of kin and congregation and bolstered by ethnic homogeneity. Indeed, the critical mass of the Mennonite population in Hanover ensured that village councils, school boards, the fire insurance agencies, the orphans' trust organizations, the church-run credit unions, and even the municipal council would serve to strengthen a sense of ethnic community.[72] The spacious land mass of Hanover had even allowed the two main church groups, the Bergthaler and Kleine Gemeinde, to coalesce in separate townships. Hanover Mennonites did receive visitors from other Mennonite churches; in fact, in both 1890 and 1895, Jacob Y. Shantz, a leading Waterloo Mennonite, visited Hanover, on one occasion meeting with Cornelius Plett and on another with David Stoesz.[73] Most often, however, Hanover Mennonites pursued social ties within their own congregation and in their own township.[74] And most often these interactions were the informal encounters of daily life; it was when piglets were purchased, bread was borrowed, oxen rented, children hired, labour exchanged or credit extended that the community's social boundary was best articulated.[75]

Despite the pluralistic nature of Waterloo County, Mennonites here too cultivated a closely-knit community and maintained social boundaries. True, the Mennonite community here may have lacked both critical mass and the opportunity to control all community-based institutions. Yet Waterloo Mennonites also secured a high degree of "institutional completeness" that served to unite the Mennonites who were scattered within a pluralistic society. A fire insurance agency, known as the Mennonite Aid Union, was begun in 1866; an annual Bible Conference for Bible study began in 1889; an annual Sunday School Conference was first held in 1890; protracted revival meetings became an institution in 1889; a church-run "poor fund" was actively maintained throughout the 1890s.[76]

Just as in Hanover, however, it was the informal everyday interactions of rural life that safeguarded the Mennonite community in Waterloo. These informal networks shaped the community's social boundaries. Diaries indicate that Mennonite families were acutely aware of the life-cycle events of their Mennonite neighbours; births, marriages and deaths of fellow Mennonites were regularly recorded. Farmer Isadore Snyder's entry for 9 August 1892, stating that "Allan Eby and Simon Moyer killed by lightning under a tree, found dead, side by side, by their wives shortly after," was unusual only in its tragic dimension.[77] Common were entries such as Moses Bowman's for 12 January 1890, which stated: "I and Ezra to the funeral of Martin Snider's child."[78] But common too were references to interactions with fellow Mennonites in the normal course of daily life. Neighbours attended each others' sales, they exchanged goods by barter, they assisted each other in the harvest or at barn raisings, they extended credit to each other, they hired the poor or landless of their congregations, they dropped in for tea or dinner at their neighbours' on any given day, or, if they happened to be on business in a neighbouring district at nightfall, they would stay the night at a fellow Mennonite's.[79] David Bergey's diary maps the pervasiveness of these informal networks. Bergey's entry for 12 January 1900 told of a typical trip to Berlin: "Wife and I started from home at 8. A.M. . . . . Stopped at my parents on the way. . . . At Lucinda Cressman's for dinner. . . . In P.M. went to Bishop Jonas Snyders', he not being at home we went to Menno S. Webers' for supper. Then to Martin H. Bowmans' for the night."[80]

The singularly most important social network outside the household, however, was the extended kinship network that tied different households together in one intricate social unit. The abundance of land in Hanover had in fact allowed the Mennonite immigrants there to strengthen kinship networks weakened in land-tight southern Russia. Many Hanover villages were dominated by a single extended family; Cornelius Plett's 13-farmstead village of Blumenhof, for example, contained 11 farmsteads that could claim Deacon Isaak Loewen as father or grandfather.[81] Despite the fact that Cornelius Plett was a church minister, his record of daily social interactions spoke of familial coalescence. Indeed, 64 percent of his 170 visits during the first six months of 1895 were with close relatives, children, parents or siblings. On a typical Sunday, Plett and wife Helena visited the household of one of their siblings, dropped in to see Cornelius's parents, and then visited with one of their married children. During the week Plett worked closely with his relations. Within the period of one month in 1895 he drove to Steinbach to shoe a horse with brother Peter Plett; visited his elderly parents where his wife was assisting with the wash; slaughtered an ox with his daughters and sons-in-law; helped his son Heinrich butcher two pigs; visited his daughter Sara as she was "expecting a child."[82]

Waterloo County social networks also reflected the pervasiveness of kinship. Partible inheritance meant that siblings often settled in close proximity to each other.[83] Ephraim Cressman, who settled near his wife's parents' place in Breslau, made frequent mention in his diary of visitors, including "Dad Betzner, Cousin Snyder, Aunt Lydia, Cousin Eli Good, Uncle Jake."[84] It was true, however, that an increasing shortage of land in Waterloo was showing its effect on kin relationships. While nine of Cornelius Plett's eleven siblings lived within five miles of his farm, only two of David Bergey's seven siblings lived near his place. The consequence was that only 36 percent of Bergey's 32 visits during the first six months in 1900 were with close relations, a pattern also reflected in the lives of middle-aged Ephraim Cressman and the elderly Moses Bowman, whose interactions with close kin during a similar period of time represented 41 and 39 percent, respectively, of their total social interactions.[85]

These figures, however, do not necessarily reflect a weakening sense of kinship. Family historians, for example, have documented how kinship structure can change to reflect the wider social millieu.[86] Ironically, land shortages in Waterloo strengthened at least one aspect of kinship; it resulted in a relatively high number of stem families. Not only do census records indicate that twice the number of households in Waterloo as in Hanover had children older than 23 living at home, they also reveal that twice the number had elderly parents living with their children (12.6 percent compared to 6.8 percent) and five times the number had lodgers (7.2 percent compared to 1.4 percent).[87] Most significant was evidence that many more domestic units joined forces to farm in Waterloo than in Hanover. Tax records for Waterloo Township indicate that 37.6 percent of the total Mennonite land area was cultivated jointly by the households of parents and their married children; similar records for the Blumenort Township (7-6E) in Hanover indicate that only 14.8 percent of land area here was operated jointly by different households.[88] Clearly, the rural household even in times of land shortages had the flexibility to allow kin to coalesce.

VI

The lives of Cornelius Plett in Hanover Municipality and David Bergey in Waterloo County during the 1890s were different. Plett and Bergey hailed from two different Mennonite groups, they spoke different German dialects and dressed in different garb. Most importantly, their lives revealed the different regions that they inhabited; Manitoba was marked by an abundance of land and wheat frontier, while Ontario was characterized by urbanization, industrialization and cultural pluralism. Thus the Manitoba Mennonites had a well-defined sense of social boundary and recorded high rates of endogamy and linguistic retention; the Ontario Mennonites interacted almost daily with non-Mennonites, spoke more English, and more readily changed church allegiances.

Still, a common adherence to the established Mennonite values of a separated, ascetic way of life rooted in the agrarian household and sectarian community characterized the majority of Mennonites in both the Hanover and the Waterloo settlements. Both communities undertook strategies to ensure the survival of this kind of ethnic community. There were some behavioural differences that stemmed from the more intense shortage of land in Waterloo than in Hanover: the Waterloo youth waited longer before they married and formed their own households; Waterloo parents more actively sought new sources of land outside the original townships of settlement; and Waterloo Mennonites more often lived in multiple-family households. More important, however, than the lack of identical experience was that both Waterloo and Hanover Mennonites were prepared to "reproduce the conditions" required in their respective regions for the maintenance of a rural, sectarian way of life. Both were committed to the generational succession of the farm household, even when it entailed migration to new settlements or the creation of stem families. Both, too, practiced a particular system of inheritance, sanctioned a certain type of wealth stratification, and cultivated social networks that would maximize their chances of reproducing the agrarian household and hence maintain their community's social boundaries.

A comparison of a single ethnic group in two regions of Canada underlines the importance that J.M.S. Careless and Robert Harney placed in the variable of regionalism. Such a comparison indicates just how diverse the experience of any one cultural group could be within a single country. Mennonites of the prairie west and those of the urbanized east could not possibly share identical experiences or even have possessed similar descriptive traits. Still, an inter-regional comparison of minority groups such as the Mennonites suggests that common social practices could sometimes take root despite the different restraints and opportunities of particular Canadian regions. In such a circumstance the writing of a pan-Canadian experience of one group can be more than "an intellectual construct" — it can reflect a common lived "reality." For Mennonites, that reality lay within the self-sufficient household and the sectarian community. That the Mennonites of Waterloo and Hanover sometimes followed different strategies in maintaining their communities is evidence of the restraints and opportunities of their respective regions; that these strategies were geared to a similar end is evidence of the resilience of shared cultural values.

NOTES

1. For standard accounts of the history of Canadian Mennonites, see Frank Epp, *Mennonites in Canada, 1786–1920: The History of a Separate People* (Toronto: MacMillan, 1974). For sociological analyses of these communities see J. Winfield Fretz, *The Waterloo Mennonites: A Community in Paradox* (Waterloo, Ont.: Wilfrid Laurier University Press, 1989); E.K. Francis, *In Search of Utopia: The Mennonites in Manitoba* (Altona, Man.: D.W. Friesen & Sons Ltd., 1955).

2. David Bergey, diary, 1866, 1881, 1900–01, 1909, 1911, Mennonite Archives of Ontario [hereafter MAO], Waterloo, Ont.; Lorna Bergey, "Bergey Family and Farm History" (Waterloo, Ont.: Self-published, 1966); interview with Lorna Bergey, November 1990.

3. Cornelius Plett, diary, 1895, tr. Delbert Plett, Steinbach Bible College, Steinbach, Man.; Delbert Plett, *Plett Picture Book* (Steinbach, Man.: D.F. Plett Farms Ltd., 1982), pp. 53–60; Rosabel Fast, "A History of the Plett Family" (Unpublished research paper, University of Manitoba, 1978), p. 4.

4. One American historian has characterized the Dutch/Russian descendants as more aggressive materially and more inclined to "worldly involvement" than the Swiss/American Mennonites, who tended to be more soft spoken, and emphasizing a more agrarian, separate existence. See James Juhnke, *Vision, Doctrine, War: Mennonite Identity and Organization in America, 1890–1930* (Scottdale, Pa.: Herald Press, 1989), pp. 37ff. This simple differentiation does not seem to hold true for Canadian Mennonites at the turn of the century: the reason for this discrepancy may be that the Russian Mennonites who came to Canada during the 1870s were more conservative than those who migrated to the American Midwest, and the Swiss Mennonites who came to Canada from the United States during the early part of the nineteenth century may have been those who aggressively sought new sources of land.

5. See Allan Smith, "Farms, Forests and Cities: The Image of Land and the Rise of the Metropolis in Ontario, 1860–1914," *Old Ontario: Essays in Honour of J.M.S. Careless*, ed. D. Keane and C. Read (Toronto: Dundurn Press, 1990), pp. 71–94; Charles M. Johnston, "A Motley Crowd: Diversity in the Ontario Countryside in the Early Twentieth Century," *Canadian Papers in Rural History* 7 (1990), pp. 237–56; Tom Nesmith, "The Philosophy of Agriculture: The Promise of the Intellect in Ontario Farming, 1835–1914" (Ph.D. Diss., Carleton University, 1988); John English and Kenneth McLaughlin, *Kitchener: An Illustrated History* (Waterloo, Ont.: Wilfrid Laurier University Press, 1983).

6. Gerald Friesen, *The Prairies: A History* (Toronto: University of Toronto Press, 1985); Paul Voisey, *Vulcan: The Making of a Prairie Community* (Toronto: University of Toronto Press, 1988); Lyle Dick, *Farmers Making Good: The Development of Abernethy District, Saskatchewan 1880–1920* (Ottawa: Canadian Parks Service, 1989); Donald Loveridge, "The Garden of Manitoba: The Settlement and Agricultural Development of the Rock Lake District and the Municipality of Louise, 1878–1902" (Ph.D. Diss., University of Toronto, 1986).

7. J.M.S. Careless, "Limited Identities in Canada," *Canadian Historical Review* 50 (1969), p. 4. See also W.L. Morton, "Clio in Canada: The Interpretation of Canadian History," 1946, *Approaches to Canadian History*, ed. C. Berger (Toronto: University of Toronto Press, 1967), pp. 42–50.

8. Roberto Perin, "Writing About Ethnicity," *Writing About Canada*, ed. J. Schultz (Scarborough: Prentice-Hall, 1990), p. 223; Robert Harney, "Frozen Wastes: The State of Italian Canadian Studies," *Perspectives in Italian Immigration and Ethnicity*, ed. S.M. Tomasi (New York: 1977), p. 118.

9. Frederick Barth, introduction, *Ethnic Groups and Boundaries* (London: Allen and Unwin, 1969), p. 10.

10. Anthony Giddens, *The Constitution of Society: Outline of the Theory of Structuration* (Berkeley: University of California Press, 1984), p. 2.

11. Isadore Snyder, diary, 1883–1910, MAO; Ephraim Cressman, diary, 1877–92, MAO; Moses Bowman, diary, 1871, 1875, 1889, 1890, MAO; Abram Friesen, "Tagebuch," 1884–1908, Henry Friesen, Greenland, Man.: Johann Dueck, diary, tr. J. Wohlgemuth, 1887–92, Evangelical Mennonite Conference Archives, Steinbach, Man.; David Stoesz, diary, tr., n.n., 1872–96, Mennonite Heritage Centre, Winnipeg, Man.

12. For a history of Hanover see Lydia Penner, *Hanover: One Hundred Years* (Steinbach, Man.: R.M. of Hanover, 1982); Abe Warkentin, *Reflections on Our Heritage: A History of Steinbach and the R.M. of Hanover From 1874* (Steinbach, Man.: Derksen Printers, 1971); John Dyck, ed., *East Reserve Village Histories, 1874–1910* (Steinbach, Man.: Hanover Steinbach Historical Society, 1990). See also relevant sections in Francis, *In Search of Utopia*; John Warkentin, "Mennonite Settlements in Southern Manitoba: A Study in Historical Geography" (Ph.D. Diss., York University, 1961); Royden K. Loewen, *Family, Church, and Market: A Mennonite Community in the Old and the New Worlds, 1850–1930* (Toronto: University of Toronto Press, 1993); Dennis Stoesz, "A History of the Chortitzer Mennonite Church of Manitoba, 1874–1914" (M.A. Thesis, University of Manitoba, 1987).

13. Census of Canada, 1901, Table X, pp. 158–59, 218–21.

14. For histories of Waterloo County, see English and McLaughlin, *Kitchener*; Elizabeth Macnaughton, "The New Agriculture in Waterloo County" (Waterloo, Ont.: Doon Heritage Village, 1990); Fretz, *The Waterloo Mennonites*; A.G. McLellan, ed., *The Waterloo County Area: Selected Geographical Essays* (Waterloo, Ont.: Department of Geography, University of Waterloo, 1971); A.G. Hallman, *100 Years of Progress in Waterloo County, Canada* (Waterloo, Ont.: Chronicle Telegraph, 1906); Kenneth Cressman, "A Descriptive Summary and Analysis of the Changing Settlement and Occupational Patterns of the Mennonites and Amish Mennonites of Wilmot Township" (M.A. Thesis, University of Waterloo, 1988); Ezra Eby, *A Biographical History of Early Settlers and their Descendants in Waterloo Township, 1895* (Waterloo, Ont.: Eldon Weber, 1984).

15. Census of Canada, 1901, Table X.

16. Census of Canada, 1901; Hanover Municipality Tax Rolls, Rural Municipality of Hanover, Steinbach, Man. Winnipeg, possessing some 42,000 inhabitants by 1901, lay a full day's travel by horse from the centre of the municipality.

17. English and McLaughlin, *Kitchener*, pp. 53ff.

18. Royden K. Loewen, "Ethnic Farmers and the Outside World: Mennonites in Manitoba and Nebraska," *Journal of the Canadian Historical Association* 1 (1990), pp. 195–214.

19. Warkentin, *Reflections on Our Heritage*.

20. Bergey, diary.

21. Bowman, diary, 5 & 13 Feb. 1890.

22. Cressman, diary, 1890.

23. Cressman, diary, 25 and 28 Jan. 1890; 11, 12, 14 Feb. 1890; 26 & 31 May 1890; 4 & 6 June 1890; 11 & 19 Dec. 1890. Similar activity is recorded by Bergey, who attended a meeting of the Farmers' Institute on 2 May 1900 and wrote notices for a "Beef Meeting" on 31 March 1900. See Bergey, diary.

24. Plett, diary; Stoesz, diary.

25. Dueck, diary.

26. Friesen, "Tagebuch."

27. Stoesz, diary.

28. Canada Census (Nominal Records), 1901, Ontario, Waterloo North & Wilmot, Sub-districts C1–C5, H1–H6, Schedule #1, Population, Public Archives of Canada [hereafter PAC]; Canada Census (Nominal Records), 1901, Provencher, Hanover, Subdistricts D1–D6, Schedule #1, Population, PAC.

29. For other references to exogamy among Waterloo Mennonites, see Fretz, *Waterloo*, p. 124; Steiner, *Shantz*, p. 114.

30. Canada Census, 1901, Waterloo North; Wilmot; Berlin; Hanover.

31. Only after 1876, when Noah Stauffer was called to the ministry, was English first used in church work. See L.J. Burkholder, *A Brief History of the Mennonites in Ontario* (Toronto: 1935), p. 99. As late as 1890 it was an anomaly for church services to be held in English: when the American publisher John F. Funk visited Waterloo County in 1890, Ephraim Cressman noted in his diary that Funk had preached in "English." Cressman, diary, 1 June 1890.

32. Canada Census, 1901, Waterloo North; Wilmot; Hanover.

33. Ibid.

34. For a discussion of this phenomenon, see John Hajnal, "European Marriage Patterns in Perspective," *Population in History*, ed. D. Glass and D. Eversley (Chicago: 1965), pp. 101–43; Jon Gjerde, *From Peasants to Farmers: The Migration from Balestrand, Norway to the Upper Middle West* (Cambridge: Cambridge University Press, 1985).

35. Diaries of Waterloo farmers more often refer to visiting a licensed medical practitioner than do the diaries of Hanover farmers.

36. Chad Gaffield, "Children, Schooling, and Family Reproduction in Nineteenth-Century Ontario," *Canadian Historical Review* 72:2 (1991), pp. 157–91.

37. Land Title Abstracts, 7-6E, 6-6E, 5-6E (Province of Manitoba Land Titles Office, Winnipeg, Man.) and Land Title Abstracts, Township of Waterloo, Lots 51–56 & Township of Wilmot, Block A, Concession II, Lots 13–16 (Waterloo County Land Registry Office, Kitchener, Ont.) indicate these prices.

38. See David Gagan and Herbert Mays, "Historical Geography and Canadian Social History: Families and Land in Peel County, Ontario," *Canadian Historical Review* 54 (1977). Robert Dilley has suggested that in Waterloo County "migration was the exception rather than the rule." See Dilley, "Migrations and the Mennonites: Nineteenth-Century Waterloo County, Ontario," *Canadian Papers in Rural History* 4 (1984), p. 129.

39. See Burkholder, *Mennonites in Ontario*, pp. 130ff.

40. See Dilley, "Migration and the Mennonites"; Ezra Burkholder, diary, 1876, MAO; Epp, *Mennonites in Canada*, pp. 326ff.

41. Census of Canada, 1881, 1921. The county of Perth to the west of Waterloo increased its Mennonite population from 616 in 1881 to 1,335 in 1921; Oxford to the southwest saw an increase from 92 to 699; and Wellington to the north saw an increase from 221 to 508. The population of Waterloo and Wilmot townships increased from 3,048 Mennonites in 1881 only to 3,286 in 1921.

42. James Henretta, "Families and Farms: Mentalité in Pre-industrial America," *William and Mary Quarterly* 35 (1978), p. 32.

43. Hanover Municipal Tax Rolls, 7-6E, 6-6E, 5-6E, 1896; Waterloo Township Tax Rolls, 1896, Region of Waterloo [hereafter ROW], Kitchener, Ont. These gaps between rich and poor were small compared to wealth differentiation in some Canadian cities. See Michael B. Katz, "The People of a Canadian City, 1851–1852," *The Canadian City: Essays in Urban History*, ed. Gilbert A. Stetler and Alan F.J. Artibise (Toronto: 1979), p. 235. Here the wealthiest 10 percent owned 88 percent of the wealth; the poorest 40 percent earned 1 percent of the income.

44. The largest farmers in both Hanover and Waterloo seem also to have been those with the largest families. In 1896 the two largest farmers in Hanover in the three most

populated townships were Klaas Reimer and Johann Plett, who owned 640 and 520 acres respectively and who had an average of 6.5 children at home; in 1896 the two largest landowners in Waterloo Township were Joseph Fry and Moses Kraft, farming 403 and 537 acres respectively, and having an average of nine children at home. The three village districts in Hanover include Steinbach (6-6E), Blumenort (7-6E), and Gruenfeld (5-6E).

45. Hanover Tax Rolls, 7-6E, 1883, 1898, 1906; C.W. Friesen et al., *The Peter Penner Genealogy, 1816* (Steinbach, Man.: Self-published, 1973), pp. 83–140.

46. Waterloo Township Tax Rolls, 1896; Wilmot Township Tax Rolls, 1896, ROW; Eby, *Biographical History*, pp. 18, 57, 123.

47. For a discussion of the bilateral partible inheritance system in other groups, see Walter Goldsmidt and Evelyn Jacobson, "The Structure of the Peasant Family," *American Anthropologist* 73 (1971), pp. 1058–70; Sonya Salamon, "Land Ownership and Women's Power in a Midwestern Farming Community," *Journal of Marriage and the Family* 41 (1979), pp. 109–79; Ernestine Friedl, "The Position of Women: Appearance and Reality," *Anthropological Quarterly* 40 (1967), pp. 97–108.

48. *Teilungsverordnung von der Molotschna aus Russland eingewanderten Mennoniten Gemeinde in Manitoba, 1902* (Winnipeg: Molotschna Mennoniten Waissenamt, 1902); *Surrogate Court Rules for the Mennonites in the Province of Manitoba, Canada* (Schoenthal: [Manitoba Mennonite] Ministerial Association, 1903). For a more detailed discussion of this system, see Royden K. Loewen, "The Children, the Cows, My Dear Man, and My Sister: The Transplanted Lives of Mennonite Farm Women, 1874–1900," *Canadian Historical Review* 73, 3 (1992), pp. 344–73.

49. Susan Burke, "Gifts from Home: the Waterloo County Dowry," *Waterloo County Times* 5:3 (1990), p. 4. See also Jeanette Lasansky, *A Good Start: The Aussteier or Dowry* (Lewisburg, Pa.: Union County Historical Society, 1990).

50. Mae Yantzi, ed., *Family Tree of David and Barbara Brenneman* (Glen Allan, Ont.: Self-published, 1979), p. 3.

51. Clara Roth et al., "Family History and Genealogy of Jacob Gingerich and Veronica Litwiller" (Baden, Ont.: Self-published, 1975), p. 8.

52. These statistics are derived from the biographical sketches in Royden K. Loewen, *Blumenort: A Mennonite Community in Transition* (Blumenort, Man.: Blumenort Mennonite Historical Society, 1983), pp. 265–324.

53. Peter Reimer, "Rechnungsbuch, 1890–1900," Gerhard Reimer, Goshen, Ind., (not published); Hanover Tax Roll, 7-6E, 1896.

54. Bergey, diary, 1 June 1900. Bergey raised a total of $7,339.63 from eight sources, the largest amount from Susanna Zeller for $4,500 on a mortgage, another amount from Lydia Bergey for $1,100, another from Anna Bowman for $300, and the smallest from the bank for $25.00. Zeller appears to be a 50-year-old spinster from Breslau.

55. Eby, *Biographical History*, p. 123.

56. Betty Lou Eby Robbins, *The Henry Bear Family History* (Glenworth Ont.: Self-published, 1977), p. 4; interview with Lorna Shantz Bergey, 7 Aug. 1991.

57. Macnaughton, "The New Agriculture."

58. Census of Canada, 1901, Agriculture, Ontario, Waterloo; Manitoba, Provencher. The value of machinery for the average southeastern Manitoba farmer (District of Provencher) was $572, compared to $447 for the Waterloo farmer.

59. See for example Robert Ankli and Wendy Miller, "Ontario Agriculture in Transition: The Switch from Wheat to Cheese," *Journal of Economic History* 42 (1982), pp. 207–17; William Marr, "The Wheat Economy in Reverse: Ontario's Wheat Production, 1887–1917," *Canadian Journal of Economics* 14 (1981), pp. 136–45; Kenneth Kelly, "Wheat Farming in Simcoe County in the Mid-Nineteenth Century," *The Canadian Geographer* 15 (1971); J.I. Little, "The Wheat Trade and Economic Development in Upper

and Lower Canada," *Acadiensis* 11 (1981), pp. 141–51; Friesen, *Canadian Prairies*, pp. 301ff; Voisey, *Vulcan* pp. 77ff.

60. Waterloo Township Tax Rolls, 1896; Warkentin, "Mennonite Settlements," pp. 181, 188.

61. Macnaughton, "The New Agriculture"; Bergey, diary; Cressman, diary; Snyder, diary.

62. Loewen, "Ethnic Farmers." Although the Ontario farms were clearly larger, the basic animal farm inventories resembled each other — while Waterloo County farmers from Waterloo Township kept an average of 12.8 cattle, 7.6 swine and 5.3 horses, Hanover farmers from three selected townships kept an average of 13.1 cattle (7.3 cows), 5.6 swine and 3.9 horses.

63. Heinrich Balzer, "Faith and Reason: The Principles of Mennonitism Reconsidered in a Treatise of 1833," tr. and ed. Robert Friedmann, *Mennonite Quarterly Review* 22:2 (1946), p. 80. For a present-day observation of the working out of this principle, see Fretz, Waterloo, p. 183. He suggests that "farming and religious principles such as separation from the world, frugal and simple living, the ethics of love and non-violence all go well together."

64. See diaries of Plett, Friesen, Stoesz, Dueck, Snyder, Bergey, Cressman, Bowman.

65. Bowman, diary, 1 March 1890; 19 July 1890; 23 Sept. 1890.

66. Bergey, diary. Similar work patterns were evident in the Plett household in Hanover: here on 9 Sept. 1895, while son Cornelius ploughed, Cornelius Sr. "took barley to the mill" in Steinbach; and on 12 Sept., while son "dug potatoes," father "hauled oats, butter and eggs to Winnipeg." Plett, diary.

67. Bowman, diary; Plett, diary.

68. For a discussion of women in nineteenth-century agriculture see Martine Segalen, *Love and Power in the Peasant Family: Rural France in the Nineteenth Century*, tr. S. Matthews (Chicago: University of Chicago Press, 1983); Marjorie Griffin Cohen, "The Decline of Women in Canadian Dairying," *Histoire Sociale/Social History* 17 (1984), pp. 307–34; Cornelia Butler Flora and Jan L. Flora, "Structure of Agriculture and Women's Culture in the Great Plains," *Great Plains Quarterly* 8 (1988), pp. 195–206.

69. Stoesz, diary, 22 July & 17 Sept. 1891.

70. Bergey, diary, 15 Feb. 1900; 27 March 1900.

71. Bergey, diary, 30 Nov. 1900; Bowman, diary, 23 July 1890. See also Bergey, diary, 20 Feb., 16 March, 24 March, 7 April, 14 April, 25 July, 10 Nov., 4 Dec. 1900.

72. For a discussion of the operation of these various organizations see Warkentin, *Reflections on Our Heritage*, p. 70; Penner, *Hanover*, pp. 157ff; Henry Fast, "Kleine Gemeinde Brandordnung," *Pioneers and Pilgrims*, ed. D. Plett (Steinbach, Man.: 1989), pp. 269–78; Dyck, *East Reserve Villages*, pp. 125ff; Jake Peters, *The Waisenamt: A History of Mennonite Inheritance Custom* (Steinbach, Man.: Mennonite Village Museum, 1985).

73. Stoesz, diary, 16 Oct. 1890; Plett, diary, 12 Sept. 1895.

74. See Stoesz, "Chortitzer Mennonite Church": Loewen, "Family, Church, and Market."

75. See diaries of Plett, Stoesz, Friesen and Dueck.

76. Burkholder, *Mennonites in Ontario*, pp. 156ff; Bergey, diary, 12 April 1900, notes that he collected money for the church's "Poor Fund" and disbursed $30.00 of it for a Mr. Schlimm. See also Reg Good, "War As a Factor in Mennonite Economic Policy: A Case Study of Insurance Institutions Sponsored by the Ontario Conference, 1864–1954" (M.A. Thesis, University of Waterloo, 1984).

77. Snyder, diary.

78. Bowman, diary.

79. Examples of informal community interactions prevail: On 27 June 1900 David Bergey sent his son "Ezra [to] M. Bock's raising," and the next day Gilbert was sent to "Bricker's raising." On 21 June 1900 Bergey hired "Amos Bock, wife and daughter . . . to hoe turnips" (Bock was 46, owned ¼ acre and had 6 children ages 5–21). On 8 Jan. 1890, Moses Bowman collected the unpaid debt from neighbour Abram Buehler of $125 plus

interest and from his son Moses of $700. On 26 June 1900 "Gilbert [Bergey] fetched tiles in Berlin . . . and delivered to Moses Bowman those we had borrowed." On 4 April 1892, Ozias Snyder found his measure of oats, by exchanging peas at his neighbour, J.S. Betzner. On 18 Nov. 1890 Emphraim Cressman bought a hay rake out of season for $11.25 at "David Gowdy's sale." See diaries of Bergey, Cressman, Snyder, Bowman.

80. Bergey, diary. These networks also included Mennonites of other settlements. In 1900, David Bergey hosted visitors from north Dakota on 4 Jan., from Alberta on 24 Jan., from Kansas on 12 Oct. and from Michigan on 17 Dec.

81. Plett, *Plett Picture Book*, p. 22.

82. Plett, diary, Jan.–June 1895. Abram Friesen's interactions with kin represented 80 percent of his social contacts during the first six months of 1895. These figures were lower, only 34 percent, for Johann Dueck; but he may have been an exception as he had joined the progressive Holdeman church and through this network became one of the few Hanover men with a wife from Kansas who had no relations in Manitoba.

83. For other references to this link, see Tamara Hareven, "The History of the Family and the Complexity of Social Change," *American Historical Review* 96 (1992), p. 108.

84. Cressman, diary, 17 April 1890; 15 May 1890; 14 Aug. 1890; 29 Nov. 1890.

85. Bergey, diary, Jan.–June 1900; Bowman, Jan.–June, 1890; Cressman, Jan.–June, 1890.

86. Donna Gabaccia, "Kinship, Culture and Migration: A Sicilian Example," *Journal of American Ethnic History* 3 (1984), pp. 39–52; Jack Goody, "The Evolution of the Family," *Household and Family in Past Time*, ed. Peter Laslett (Cambridge: Cambridge University Press, 1972), pp. 103–24.

87. Census of Canada, 1901, Waterloo North; Wilmot; Hanover.

88. Waterloo tax records reveal that 8,669 acres of 23,054 owned by Mennonites of Waterloo Township were owned or operated jointly by parents and married children; in Manitoba's Township 7-6E, the four village districts of Blumenort, Greenland, Blumenhof and Neuanlage cultivated a total of 9,047 acres, of which 1,340 appear to be operated jointly by the households of parents and married children. Another set of figures derived from these tax records indicates that 6 of 54 (11 percent) Blumenort Township households farmed jointly, compared to 134 of 379 (35 percent) Waterloo Township households.

The Woolsey family of Quebec City. This 1809 portrait by William Berczy, Sr., is an excellent illustration of family life among the well-to-do English merchant class.

The family is the most basic of society's institutions. Despite its reputation for stability, the family is not static: its structure and functions change as society itself evolves. Over the past two decades, scholars have looked to new sources of evidence and new methods of inquiry to reconstruct family life in the past. Manuscript censuses, probate records, and parish birth, death, and marriage registers all have been used to reconstitute the patterns of family formation and household structure. Diaries and family papers, too, have been an important resource for the exploration of relationships between husbands and wives and parents and children. This research has provided considerable insight into the sexual division of labour within families and into the values and attitudes that shaped domestic relations. Legal records have been another valuable resource for family history. The examination of court records involving cases of seduction, rape, infanticide, abortion, abandonment, separation, divorce, and child custody has brought to light a great deal about societal norms and expectations and revealed that relations in the home were not always harmonious. All these new avenues of approach have enabled historians to enter the once-hidden private sphere of family life.

The nineteenth century witnessed substantial changes in the family. At the beginning of the century, the family was the locus of economic production. Husbands, wives, and children all contributed to the economic welfare of the household. The family was also the institution primarily responsible for the education of children and the care of the elderly and infirm. Many historians have argued that industrialization and the rise of the market economy changed the nature of the family essentially by separating work from the home. For the middle class, domestic industries that had employed women and children disappeared as more and more goods were produced in factories and purchased in the marketplace. The middle-class home increasingly became a place of private refuge from the trials and temptations of a competitive world. These developments significantly altered gender roles and attitudes toward children. The typically middle-class values and attitudes that shaped life in two well-to-do Victorian families, one in Red River and the other outside Charlottetown, are explored by J.M. Bumsted and Wendy Owen in Article Five. For many working-class families, however, there was no equivalent separation of home and work. In Article Six, a study based in urban Ontario, John Bullen describes the often wretched lives of working-class children who continued to fill their traditional role by making an essential contribution to the economic survival of their families.

QUESTIONS TO CONSIDER

1. How did "domesticization" and "sentimentalization" change gender roles and attitudes toward childhood in the middle-class family? How convincing is the authors' conclusion that these two families shared a common culture that transcended location and race?

2. What types of work did working-class children do, and what contributions did they make to the family economy? How did social reformers and legislators react to the problem of working children? What insights do their responses provide into middle-class values and attitudes?

SUGGESTED READINGS

Backhouse, Constance. *Petticoats and Prejudice: Women and Law in Nineteenth-Century Canada*. Toronto: University of Toronto Press, 1991.

Bradbury, Bettina. *Working Families: Age, Gender, and Daily Survival in Industrializing Montreal*. Toronto: McClelland and Stewart, 1993.

Brown, Jennifer. *Strangers in Blood: Fur Trade Company Families in Indian Country*. Vancouver: University of British Columbia Press, 1980.

Gagan, David. *Hopeful Travellers: Families, Land, and Social Change in Mid-Victorian Peel County, Canada West*. Toronto: University of Toronto Press, 1981.

Katz, Michael. *The People of Hamilton, Canada West: Family and Class in a Mid-Nineteenth-Century City*. Cambridge: Harvard University Press, 1975.

McKenna, Katherine M.J. *A Life of Propriety: Anne Murray Powell and Her Family, 1755–1849*. Montreal/Kingston: McGill-Queen's University Press, 1994.

Parr, Joy. *Labouring Children: British Immigrant Apprentices to Canada, 1869–1924*. Toronto: University of Toronto Press, 1980.

Sutherland, Neil. *Children in English-Canadian Society: Framing the Twentieth-Century Consensus*. Toronto: University of Toronto Press, 1976.

Ward, W. Peter. *Courtship, Love, and Marriage in Nineteenth-Century English Canada*. Montreal/Kingston: McGill-Queen's University Press, 1990.

FIVE

The Victorian Family in Canada in Historical Perspective: The Ross Family of Red River and the Jarvis Family of Prince Edward Island

J.M. BUMSTED AND WENDY OWEN

While a good deal has been written in recent years about the family in nineteenth-century Britain and the United States, the study of the family as an institution is in its infancy in Canada. How were families organized, what were their preoccupations and ambitions, how did their households function? Unlike Britain

Source: "The Victorian Family in Canada in Historical Perspective: The Ross Family of Red River and the Jarvis Family of Prince Edward Island," *Manitoba History* 13 (Spring 1987): 12–18. Reprinted by permission.

and the United States, Canada had precious few self-conscious literary families in the Victorian era, and so one of the most common sources for study of the individual family — private papers assiduously collected by literary scholars — simply has not existed. At the same time, substantial bodies of personal and intimate papers of articulate Canadian families, carrying sufficient detail to enable some sort of recon-struction, do survive. Two such sets of family papers are those of the Jarvis family of Prince Edward Island and the Ross family of Red River. The Jarvis Papers are in the New Brunswick Museum in Saint John, N.B., and the Ross Papers are in the Public Archives of Manitoba. A careful reading of these geographically widely-scattered doc-uments suggests the danger of approaching them as merely local records.

Some extraordinary parallels exist between the two sets of papers and the two families, although they were separated by nearly 3,500 kilometers in two relatively iso-lated colonies in British North America. In terms of the study of the nineteenth-century family, what is most striking about the parallels is how well they fit into the larger patterns of recent secondary literature on the Victorian family. The Jarvises and the Rosses were not simply unique colonial families, but very much part of a transatlantic culture. Given the facts that mama Ross was an Indian and the children "half-breeds," the similarities between the Ross and the Jarvis families suggest that we must be care-ful not to make too much either of colonial location or of racial and cultural differences.

There was a middle-class culture in the nineteenth century which transcended many theoretically exceptionalist factors. One hesitates to limit the culture to the label "Victorian," since it was equally powerful in the United States and much of Europe. Those researching the family in nineteenth-century Canada ought not, we would suggest, assume that their Canadian subjects existed in splendid isolation from general cultural developments in the western world and thus produced localized and unique patterns of behaviour. Colonial societies less often initiated than imitated, and while identifying deviations from larger patterns is crucial, one must begin with the larger patterns.

Before turning to our analysis, it might be well to introduce the two families briefly. Edward Jarvis was born in Saint John, New Brunswick, in 1789, the son of Munson Jarvis, a leading Connecticut Loyalist. Educated at King's College, Windsor, he was admitted to the New Brunswick bar in 1812 and subsequently to the bar at Inner Temple, London. He served in Malta before his appointment as Chief Justice of Prince Edward Island in 1828. In 1817 Edward married Anna Maria Boyd, the daughter of another influential Saint John family active in mercantile affairs; the Jarvis and Boyd families would intermarry frequently over the succeeding years. The couple had eight children, three of whom died in infancy and one in childhood. Those surviving to adulthood were Mary, Munson, Henry, and Amelia. Their mother — Maria, as she was known — died in 1841, and Jarvis remarried in 1843 to Elizabeth Gray of Charlottetown. This union produced three children, one of whom died in infancy. Elizabeth herself died in childbirth in 1847, and Edward a few years later in 1852. The correspondence to be discussed, mainly between members of a close-knit family writing between the Island and mainland New Brunswick, covers the period from 1828 to 1852.

Alexander Ross was born in Nairnshire, Scotland, in 1783. He emigrated to Canada as a schoolmaster, but became involved in the fur trade, joining John Jacob Astor's Astoria expedition in 1811. Ross subsequently served in the Pacific coast fur trade until his retirement to Red River in 1825. While in Oregon he had married

Sarah, the daughter of an Indian chief (an Indian princess, went the family tradition) according to the "custom of the country," and he formally remarried her in Red River in 1828. The couple had at least thirteen children, of whom the important ones for our purposes are William, Henrietta, James, and Jemima. In Red River Ross became a prominent government official — sheriff, magistrate, and member of the council of Assiniboia — as well as titular head of the Scots Presbyterian community. In his later years he authored three books describing his experiences in the fur trade and chronicling the development of Red River, a trio of works woefully neglected by Canadian literary scholars and students of Canadian historiography. The Ross family correspondence upon which we will concentrate in this study covers a shorter period of time than the Jarvis set, since only during the years 1852–1856, when young Jemmy Ross was studying at Knox College in Toronto, did the family correspond intimately and regularly.

Edward Jarvis and Alexander Ross were contemporaries, and both were important political and social figures in their respective communities. Their residential accommodation reflected their positions. Edward began planning his house in 1833, when he bought a farm on the outskirts of Charlottetown for 500 pounds. As he intended the house to be a family seat for "generations yet to come," his plans called for the use of brick, an uncommon Island building material. Most of the material was imported from England, and the construction was not completed until 1835 at enormous expense — more than "one hundred per cent upon the original estimates and contracts." Furnishing of "Mount Edward" was finished in 1836, and early in 1836 the Jarvises held a housewarming ball for 81 persons. We know considerably less about "Colony Gardens," the Ross residence in the Point Douglas area of what is now Winnipeg, but it was a large and substantial frame house, a landmark in its day. On the other hand, the later (1854) construction efforts of William Ross are discussed in the correspondence. William himself enthuses, "without boasting it is the best, the handsomest and most comfortable house on the banks of the Riviere Rouge," befitting, added his father, a "son who had stepped into the shoes of his father." The William Ross house still survives in Winnipeg, a museum open to the public as the oldest house yet in the city.

As paterfamilias, Edward Jarvis had a limited share in the day-to-day operations of his household. Like many nineteenth-century fathers he was often away — on circuit as the only judge of the Island's supreme court, on the mainland seeing to business matters in the summer months, and in England (for six months during the fatal illness of his first wife). At that, Jarvis was far more housebound than some of his contemporaries; the Earl of Dalhousie, when he returned to Britain from governing in Canada, had been away so long that he was totally unable to recognize his eighteen-year-old son. But absence aided the remoteness which most Victorian fathers liked to maintain, and Jarvis does not appear to have been especially close to his children, especially the boys, who unlike the girls were sent away to school for much of their adolescence and brought home only under financial stringency. At the same time, Jarvis did play a key role in the upbringing of his children. Major decisions were his, and many minor ones were deferred if he were absent. Jarvis did not lose sovereignty over the household, and the family, especially the women, were expected to subordinate themselves to his needs and wishes.

The Ross papers suggest that Alexander Ross was substantially closer to his children than was Edward Jarvis. In part this attitude reflected personality, in part the fact that there was nowhere to travel in remote Red River, in part probably his wife's background. Ross did make an annual hunting expedition to Shoal Lake after the harvest, but characteristically, he turned it into a family affair which became one of the high points of the year. The Ross situation was complicated by the presence of "mama" (both families called the mother "mama"), who at least by the time of the correspondence of the 1850s was no longer running the household, a position assumed by the eldest unmarried daughter. Ill health was obviously a key factor in her stepping down. Nevertheless, Ross's domination of his household was typically Victorian, the family revolving around him as it did around Jarvis. While it was true that "Ross shaped the upbringing of his half-Indian children," as Sylvia Van Kirk has emphasized, it should be noted that most middle- and upper-class Victorian fathers behaved similarly without the presence of an Indian wife. While Ross may have been less distant from his children than Jarvis, his correspondence with his absent son James demonstrated a stiffness and formality quite different from the tone of Jemmy's letters from his brothers and sisters. And like Jarvis, Ross was far more affectionate with his daughters than with his sons.

Middle-class family life in the Victorian era was characterized by two related developments. The first is generally referred to as the "domesticization" of the household, a clear separation of work-life and home-life and the withdrawal of the various household members into the privacy of the home, which became the central social unit for "the transmission of culture, the maintenance of social stability, and the pursuit of happiness." This process had been completed by the Jarvis family before the opening of the surviving correspondence in 1828, and by the Ross family by the time of the intimate letters of the 1850s and indeed probably years earlier. Closely connected with domesticization was a new attitude toward human emotion usually labelled "sentimentalization." In its Victorian context, this attitude encouraged the effusiveness of personal feelings and sentiments on certain approved topics relating to the home and the family: love, death, marriage, and "making it" in the outside world. Gone was the stoicism and terseness of earlier generations toward the vagaries of family life and relationships, replaced by open avowals of sentiment, often overstated. It should be emphasized that this openness was confined to approved topics and closely circumscribed by fairly clear and generally held ground rules of respectability. It is this new attitude of sentimentality, combined with the standards of respectability, that finds its closest parallels in the Jarvis and Ross papers.

In terms of the traditional milestones in the cycle of life — birth, education, marriage, and death — the Jarvis and Ross correspondence exhibits sentiment most openly and frequently on the subject of death. Indeed, nearly half of the Jarvis letters between 1828 and 1852 contain some reference to death: reporting one, responding to a report, or mourning the death of a loved one. The incidence is little different in the Ross letters. This emphasis is not surprising, since death and its aftermath were matters that often provoked a correspondent to take pen in hand. For the modern taste the sentiments expressed may border on the morbid and maudlin, but they filled a real need for those involved. Those familiar with either Victorian novels or the literature of Victorian piety will not be surprised, for example, to learn of the fascination of both our families with detailed descriptions of death-bed scenes.

We are given two eyewitness accounts of the final sufferings in 1841 of Maria. One, by her son, is of her last hours, and another, by her daughter, describes the terminal weeks. According to young Mary Jarvis, her mother had twice before the fatal day "called us all together to bid us farewell for ever and had recovered." A few years later Elizabeth Gray Jarvis died in childbirth, a particularly important rite of passage and a major family event, usually occurring in the home with the woman surrounded not only by the medical folk but often by friends and family as well. Spiritual preparation was important, since the risks were considerable. One gains some impression of the event and the rituals surrounding it from Munson Jarvis's description of the death of his stepmother:

> From the sudden manner of her death she must have been totally unconscious of his approach, time not even given her to bid her family farewell. Poor woman to be so suddenly summoned to appear before her Maker leaves upon us a melancholy reflection. To be promising fairly and the next moment awake in Eternity is awful. To give an idea of its suddenness, after being delivered and her little infant dandled in the arms of the nurse and kind friends around her bed and the birth announced all which took some little time, the mother called for her child and seemed most affectionately fond of it, kissing it as I was told several times, but no sooner did she resign the now Motherless babe to its nurse (but was not complaining) the Dr. was told by one in attendance that Mrs. J's feet felt cold, at once the Dr. said he was so afraid she would die, and so suddenly and apparently so easily after saying she did not feel cold had her spirit taken flight, no assistance could be rendered. . . .

Obviously the doctor had not been able to help.

Within a few months in 1856 the Ross family experienced two deaths, first that of William and then that of his father Alexander. Again, there are detailed descriptions of the last hours. Alexander Ross described William's demise to James in Toronto:

> About half an hour before his last, he called me to his bedside, clasped both my hands in his, then called for his wife and Mr. Black [Presbyterian minister of Kildonan and married to Henrietta Ross] and while he held my hands he offered up a most fervent and impressive prayer to God, asking forgiveness for all his sins, and resigning himself into the arms of his maker. "I know," said he in conclusion, "that my redeemer liveth and I know that I am going to be with him, Lord receive my spirit to everlasting rest, Amen." Then laying his head quietly on the pillow, soon expired without struggle or motion to the right or to the left.

The accounts of the death of Alexander himself were even more explicit. According to John Black:

> About daylight he called all the family around him and we were all there but poor James and gave them his parting blessing — the most affecting sight I ever saw was when he held William's poor little orphans by their little hands altogether and spoke to and blessed them. . . . Margaret received her dying grandfather's parting kiss and blessing — Willie was at home and poor Lettie was too sick to come in. All the rest of the grandchildren were present. It was like old Jacob blessing his sons and Joseph's sons.

Further details came from Jemima:

> It was 23rd before daylight he called us all around his bed one by one and shook hands with us and spoke to every one of us and blessed us and told us to be kind to one another

and not feel sorry for him, though he was going away. . . . He took all their hands and held them in his for a long time that was after breakfast and at last Mr. B said that will do now you are tiring yourself; he still held them, and all the time sitting. He asked S. to say the fifth commandment, she said it, and then they went and sat down and asked for all the C. But they were not all here W. not but the baby so he asked Mr. B. if he could let him have the pleasure of kissing his babe so he kissed the baby too.

The Ross accounts all emphasize the fortitude of the sufferer and the peace with which death was faced — not hidden from view in some distant antiseptic hospital but at home, in the immediate presence of the family circle.

They also emphasize the importance of proper spiritual preparation. As the account of the death of Elizabeth Gray Jarvis suggests, the most disturbing feature here was its suddenness. The Ross correspondence makes similar points frequently. In 1852 William Ross wrote of the death of "young James Fraser" noting "only seven days sick — what a warning for all those who are alive to prepare for death while in health for we know not the day nor the hour when the 'Knock' shall be at our door." Both Jarvis and Ross papers are full of the reminders of the constant razor-edge upon which life was balanced.

A willingness to acknowledge the trauma of the death of a loved one was also a central feature of the correspondence. The death of his first wife hit Edward Jarvis very hard, partly — one suspects — because he felt guilty about being in England for his own health while Maria was battling her fatal illness on Prince Edward Island. Daughter Mary certainly thought her father's absence, however unavoidable, contributed to her mother's demise. As Edward wrote to his wife's sister upon his return to Charlottetown late in 1841:

My own feelings have now become so nervous and sensitive that I seem to participate as much in any anxieties of my friends as if it were my own case. I cannot shake off the dreadful weight and oppression which hangs increasingly upon my spirits and the slightest exciting cause wholly overpowers me. . . . The utmost indifference to every passing event and occupation possesses me and I cannot overcome it.

Such a sense of depression was hardly surprising under the circumstances. What was different from earlier times was the openness with which Edward confessed his feelings in his correspondence for several years thereafter. Alexander Ross admitted to his son James with regard to William's death, "The event has given a severe shaking to your mother, to myself also; but we thank God that we are able to bear with it as we do. Nevertheless our position is one of pain." Such pain was now openly acknowledged.

If death and mourning were sentimentalized by the Victorians in words, they were also enshrined in new and more extreme ritualization. Mourning and commemoration of the dead took on new forms. Even the physical letter itself was part of the process. Munson Jarvis opened a letter to his Aunt Caroline with the words, "You must be aware upon seeing the border of this letter that our family has been deprived of one of its members." The first letter home of James Ross upon hearing the news of William's death was edged in black. The Jarvises were not invited to Government House on New Year evening in 1848 because "there has been a death so recently in the family" — in this case of Edward's eldest daughter Mary.

The dead were also commemorated in ways both more ostentatious and more personal. In one letter of 1842 to his sister-in-law, Edward reported ordering from England a monument to his wife ("of white marble, of the Sarcophagus shape") and added:

> I promised you a small portion of a lock of her hair — but I find there was but a very small lock preserved — and Mary is anxious to have some of it. Your sister and I therefore concluded that it would meet with your approbation that I should send you some for your locket, only in case a little could be spared after the division with Mary. I should feel very desirous to save some for you, if possible.

Burial became a matter of considerable ritualization and a symbol of the relationships of the deceased while living. Edward's parents, after an even more protracted correspondence among the family, were disinterred and placed in a family vault in the new burying ground of Saint John. John Black reported after the death of Alexander Ross, "On Monday 27th amid great concourse of people we laid him in the narrow house here at the Frog Plain — not alongside of William so that the graves are in a line — William lying at his father's feet." And although the correspondence does not show it, Edward Jarvis was buried in Elm Avenue Cemetery in Charlottetown next to his first wife, while his second wife was buried elsewhere in the same cemetery along with her family.

Another important aspect of the household was the raising of children. Expectations and training were quite different for boys and girls. Both sexes were educated at home for most of their early years by both the Rosses and the Jarvises, owing as much to the scarcity of acceptable schools as to the wishes of their parents. Neither family employed governesses or tutors. The Jarvis boys were subsequently sent off the Island to school, while it was hoped that a projected academy for young ladies on the Island would serve for the girls. When the academy did not appear, the girls were either taught at home or, after Maria's death, bundled off to relations on the mainland to learn the requisite skills. As for the Ross children, the younger boys all attended Red River Academy or its successor St. John's College, essentially a grammar school in the British tradition established by the Church of England in Red River. For James Ross to go away to university in Toronto was a considerable step for both James and his family, although others of his contemporaries from the College attended Oxford and Cambridge. Cousin Roderick Ross, Alexander Ross reported in 1854, was off to "Swell the list of Pussyites at degraded Oxford." The arrival of John Black in Red River and his subsequent marriage to Henrietta Ross opened new educational opportunities in the colony, especially for the younger Ross girls. Jemima was sent off to the manse at Kildonan in 1855 to pursue her studies, learning geography, grammar, French, and ciphering, and Henrietta Black herself "got very clever" after her marriage.

As for expectations, Edward Jarvis intended his three sons to enter the professions. Munson, the eldest, was trained for the law on the Island. Second son Henry was sent to Edinburgh to medical school, and youngest son William entered the Church. According to Edward, "I am unwilling to oppose a decided inclination in my boys for any particular profession," but it all seemed somehow to work out in fairly orthodox fashion. One suspects that Edward would have preferred the eldest to be the doctor, but Munson was not a favourite:

Munson is very studious when required to be so and has great application, but he is very idle when there is no immediate call for his exertions, he is not inclined to volunteer hard study, but pays more attention to the young ladies and driving his tandem than to more desirous matters. . . . Henry is, on the contrary, all life, activity and industry — he greatly resembles in mind as well as countenance his beloved mother. Sir Henry Huntly told me that when he first saw Henry he thought he had never seen a countenance in which were blended so much of benevolence and intelligence.

So Henry was allowed to go to Edinburgh, where he did well professionally but disappointed his father by marrying too quickly an "unhealthy" wife.

As for the Ross boys, the first-born son Alexander died early. William stepped smoothly into his father's shoes, as his father had obviously intended, and James was able to go to Toronto, where he prepared for the ministry, a career approved by the entire family. Upon the death of William, James hesitated, obviously debating whether to continue his studies or come home to assume his family responsibilities. His father wrote him a few weeks before his death that "sacrifice . . . is in my opinion a better plan for all the time we expect to live to enjoy this life, than withdraw our children from those pursuits in which their future happiness depends." After Alexander's death, James did return to Red River and assumed leadership of the family.

For the daughters there were clearly different expectations. In one letter William Ross described the Ballenden daughters as, "so far as we Red Riverians can judge perfectly accomplished ladies." He continued to list the requirements:

They can play elegantly on the Harp, guitar, piano, they sing melodiously and methodically. They can dance and waltz like true English dames, and I guess they can play the coquette too if that be any part of Ornamental Education — to tell the truth they are very nice girls.

While marriage was the ultimate goal, household management was extremely important. After the death of Maria Jarvis, Edward attempted to replace his wife as household manager with his eldest daughter. Mary escaped by marrying herself, after some agonizing over whether "I make up my mind to leave my dear Papa." Only Edward's remarriage prevented Amelia from becoming her successor. In the hiatus between Mary's marriage and his own in 1843, Edward found it difficult to continue Amelia's education, writing, "I hardly know how I can get on without her management of my household, for I shall have no one at present besides the two servant girls." After the death of his second wife, Amelia again had the responsibility for her father, but this time she had assistance from a succession of maiden aunts.

Henrietta and Jemima Ross could easily have sympathized with the problems of Mary and Amelia Jarvis. Henrietta was running the household at the time of her marriage to John Black, and Jemima was forced to step into Henrietta's shoes. Her letters to her brother indicated her problems. "I write to tell you," she announced in 1854, "that I have no time to write with Hay and harvest all are busy and I am no less busy baking and cooking for those out of doors." Mama and Isabella had gone berrying, she added. "I wanted to go too, but I had to stop and keep house." A few months later she wrote, "I suppose you have heard that Hen has left me to do for myself, . . . I am now Miss Ross Master in the house." Within a few days she commented that she was "tired with house-keeping and all its duties, for there is no end of working."

Brother William dealt perceptively with Jemima's dilemmas in a letter discussing family reactions to the annual excursion to Shoal Lake. "Sister Jem," he wrote:

> only forbodes something portentous in this trip to Shoal Lake, as mama now and then gives a hint as to who is to keep house while out — poor Jem thinks she ought to go out and finds it very hard to be made to keep house before the time, but the question comes back, whose to keep house? Papa says oh I must stay and let Jem go out, but Jem knows well that she would rather stay than her pa stay.

While Jemima was at Mr. Black's pursuing her studies, her mother's health suffered, presumably because mama was forced to take over the running of the household. After a few months she was recalled to Colony Gardens. The family "can't do rightly without her at home," William reported.

As we have been suggesting, while the household functioned around the needs of the males, it was the women who made it work. The Victorian woman's role as wife and mother ought not to obscure her onerous responsibilities as housekeeper. The role immobilized the woman and made it difficult for her to travel from the house. "I must reluctantly stay at home," wrote Maria of a projected visit by her husband to Saint John in 1837, "to take care of the establishment." To see people, especially in remote colonies, women had to expect them for long housevisits, only adding to the burden. Houseguests invited by her father were coming, reported daughter Mary reluctantly in 1843, adding, "I was very sorry for it as it will give me much more to do, . . . but I did not like to say so to Papa as he seemed to wish to have them." Maria found herself unable to report on her housewarming ball to her sister, commenting, "I was much too fatigued in mind and body to enjoy it and even the repetition is painful to me for I was obliged to force my spirits. . . . You will be astonished that I am alive," she concluded, proceeding to catalogue a herculean series of labours which ranged from supervising the slaughter of seven hogs to hanging the draperies in six public rooms. There is no evidence in either the Jarvis or the Ross papers of a direct act of defiance of male wishes by a female. The Ross and Jarvis women were not advanced thinkers; there was nothing in their upbringing to encourage notions of independence.

Both sexes had to beware of the great abyss for Victorians: the fall from respectability. This subject was a matter of considerable concern in both sets of correspondence, usually in terms of the peccadilloes of other people. When H. Wright married an illegitimate daughter of Sir H. Lowe, despite the fact that the girl "lived in his family and is very well educated," her sister's concluding comment to Maria Jarvis was "Silenzio." A young Scotch lady in Red River was "guilty of having made a faux pas," wrote William Ross to his brother, "she was delivered of a boy last week." Edward Jarvis obviously found some satisfaction when his "old antagonist" John Stewart, after burying his wife, left for England almost immediately, having "married his servant girl, 18 years of age — he is nearly 80 himself." Jarvis continued:

> The girl made him execute a will in her favor of all his property, which is to a large amount. He has commenced prosecutions against some of his acquaintances who interfered to prevent the marriage and alleged that he was insane.

Jarvis took equal satisfaction in recounting that a certain "young sprig of a parson . . . with his true orthodox spectacles upon his nose" had secretly breached the canonical law by marrying his late wife's sister. This form of "incest" remained legally forbidden in Britain, despite frequent attempts to revise the law, until well into the twentieth century. "So you see John Gunn found out by sad experience," noted William Ross with satisfaction equal to that of Edward Jarvis, "that instead of gaining by Slander he had lost by a good deal his former little respectability."

Everyone well understood the implications of breaking the codes. As Edward Jarvis wrote of the Smiths, who were "dreadfully depressed about their unfortunate brother" who had committed some unspecified offence: "well they may be — death would be far preferable to the never-ending disgrace." Fortunately, no Jarvis appears to have blotted the family name during the course of the correspondence.

While both families were conscious of the abyss, it gaped open much more widely for the Ross family, both because "mama was an Indian" and because Red River was commonly perceived as a colony of semi-civilized half-breeds. The point came out quite clearly in responses to James Ross's early success as a student in Toronto. Cousin Roderick hoped to join James at university, calling for "a mighty effort to try to make poor Red River respectable," and John Black described old Alexander's response to son-in-law George Flett at news that James had won a scholarship: "What will they say of the Brules now, Geordie?" William was already "in a fair way of becoming respectable," exulted his father, and James was not far behind, although extremely self-conscious about his origins.

All of the Ross family had to deal with racial hostility, even in Red River. Jemima was upset in 1854 at comments overheard at church about the number of "blacks" in the front pews, for example. But none of the family were more sensitive than James. John Black was forced in 1855 to give James a written lecture in response to the young man's attempts to derive a complex classical etymology for the word "halfbreed." Black observed, "Half breed is a simple natural homemade English term which we could have invented if we had known as little of Greek and Latin as we do of the Japanese." Although James was extremely proud of his father's books and literary success, he protested strenuously to the old man about his treatment of half-breeds in his writings. After the death of his father, James wrote an extremely revealing and agonizing letter to his family in Red River, in which his concerns about the abyss were clearly revealed:

> Remember, dear sisters, that we at present occupy a certain standing in the community. Owing to papa and to William — and to our connection with our worthy minister Mr. Black — I say owing to these things, we have a certain standing and respectability, and we must keep it. . . . It seems generally the case that halfbreed families dwindle into insignificance as soon as they lose their head. But why should it be so?

James would spend the remainder of his life attempting to prove that half-breeds were as good as anyone else.

But if the abyss for James Ross (and perhaps for the remainder of his siblings) was perhaps wider and the descent into it considerably shorter, we ought not to over-emphasize the differences between the Ross and the Jarvis families. The assumptions and concerns of the two families on this and other matters were, in the last analysis, remarkably similar. Both were Victorian, colonial branch. Perhaps the Jarvises were more comfortable with their status than were the Rosses, but there was considerably more common ground than one might anticipate.

SIX

....

Hidden Workers: Child Labour and the Family Economy in Late Nineteenth-Century Urban Ontario

JOHN BULLEN

The secret of a successful farm, wrote Canniff Haight in 1885, lay in "the economy, industry and moderate wants of every member of the household."[1] Haight was simply repeating the conventional wisdom of the age in his recognition that all members of a farm family, including children, contributed to the successful functioning of the household economy. Haight and many of his contemporaries, however, would not have applied the same description to families in urban-industrial centres. The movement of the focus of production from farm to factory, many social analysts believed, decreased the interdependency of the family and offered individual members a greater number of occupational choices.[2] According to this interpretation, a typical urban family relied solely on the wages of a working father and the home management of a mother for its day-to-day survival. This notion of the difference between rural and urban families survived into the twentieth century and surfaced in a number of standard historical works. As late as 1972, for example, Blair Neatby wrote: "The urban family . . . bears little resemblance to a rural family. On a family farm children can make a direct economic contribution by doing chores and helping in many of the farm activities. . . . In the city only the wage-earner brings in money; children . . . become a financial burden who add nothing to the family income."[3] Like many myths of modern civilization, these perceptions of the urban family rested primarily on outward appearances and vague unfounded suppositions.

In the past fifteen years, social historians have uncovered patterns of urban survival which indicate that many working-class families, like their counterparts on the farm, depended on "the economy, industry and moderate wants of every member of the household," including children, to meet the demands of city life. Several well known primary and secondary sources describe in graphic detail the onerous trials of youngsters as wage-earners in the manufacturing and commercial establishments of large industrial centres such as Montreal, Toronto, and Hamilton.[4] But child labour was by no means limited to factories and shops. Children also performed important economic duties in their homes and on city streets as a regular part of their contribution to the family economy. This article concentrates on youngsters between the ages of seven and fourteen who worked outside of the industrial and commercial

....

Source: "Hidden Workers: Child Labour and the Family Economy in Late Nineteenth-Century Urban Ontario," *Labour/Le Travail*, 18 (Fall 1986): 163–87. © Canadian Committee on Labour History. Reprinted by permission of the editor of *Labour/Le Travail*.

mainstream of late nineteenth-century urban Ontario, usually for no wages, but who still contributed in important ways to the day-to-day survival of their families. The latter part of the paper includes a brief examination of the special circumstances of foster children.[5] The article will describe the various types of work children performed, evaluate the contribution youngsters made to the family or household economy, determine the extent to which economic responsibilities affected a child's opportunities for personal development and social mobility, and judge the reaction working children elicited from middle- and upper-class members of society. Such an examination illuminates the social and economic structure of urban-industrial Ontario in the late nineteenth century, and casts light into the shadowy corners of urban poverty, business practices, reform mentality, and class structure.

Urbanization, like its companion, industrialization, marches to its own rhythm; it does not unfold in carefully planned and even measures. In the latter decades of the nineteenth century, Canada's urban population increased at roughly three times the rate of the general population, a pattern that struck stalwarts of agricultural society with worry and despair.[6] *The Globe* acknowledged the trend in 1894, but conceded: "The complaint about the continual movement of population from country to city is a good deal like a protest against the law of gravitation."[7] Urbanization could take several forms. Many sons and daughters of Ontario farmers, victims of land exhaustion and exclusionary inheritance customs, recognized the diminishing promise of rural life and fled to the cities in search of work and spouses with whom to begin their own families. In other instances, immigrant families, mostly from the cities and countryside of Great Britain and continental Europe, settled in Canadian cities in the hope of escaping poverty and oppression. In the latter case, fathers and older sons often emigrated first and sent for remaining family members once employment and residence had been established.

All newcomers to the city discovered an environment and value system starkly different from that of rural society. While there is no question that life on the farm rarely resembled the bucolic paradise portrayed by romantic novelists, the city's emphasis on materialism, competition, standardization, and consumption constituted virtual culture shock for many recent arrivals. Skilled and unskilled workers alike adjusted their lives to the vagaries of the factory system, the business cycle, and the seasons, in an attempt to eke out a living above the poverty line. All workers lived in fear of unemployment, which struck especially hard in winter when outdoor work was scarce and the higher costs of food and fuel could wipe out a family's modest savings. Poor families huddled together in crowded and ramshackle rental units that lacked adequate water and sanitation facilities. For some demoralized labourers, the local tavern or pool hall provided the only escape from a working life of long hours, dangerous conditions, and abysmally low wages. In the face of these oppressive conditions, workers instinctively turned to the one institution that had served their ancestors so well for generations — their families. Although old rural traditions did not survive the trip to the city completely unscarred, workers still found their most reliable and effective support system under their own roofs. Within this scheme, children played a critical role.

In most working-class homes, children assumed domestic responsibilities before they reached the age of eight.[8] Their first duties usually took the form of assisting in the daily upkeep of the home. At any hour of the day, youngsters could be found sweeping steps, washing windows, and scrubbing floors. In neighbourhoods where dirt roads, animals, wood stoves, coal furnaces, and industrial pollution were common features, keeping a home even relatively clean and liveable could require several hands and many hours of labour. In the absence of fathers whose work kept them away from home ten to fifteen hours per day, six days a week, busy mothers frequently called upon children to make minor repairs to poorly constructed houses.

Other common children's chores contributed in a more direct sense to the day-to-day survival and economic status of the family. Youngsters routinely gathered coal and wood for fuel from rail and factory yards, and fetched water from community wells for cooking and washing. To supplement the family's food supply, children cultivated gardens, and raised and slaughtered animals. What home-produced food the family did not consume itself, children could sell to neighbours or at the market for a small profit. In an age when sickness could spell disaster for a family, youngsters provided care for ill family members and sometimes offered themselves as substitute workers. It was also common for older children to assume the duties of a deceased parent, girls frequently taking up mother's responsibilities and boys stepping into father's shoes. On occasion, parents lent their children's services to neighbours in return for nominal remuneration or future favours. Although youngsters who worked in and around their homes did not normally encounter the dangers associated with industrial life, in at least one case a young Ottawa lad who was gathering wood chips outside of a lumber mill succumbed to his youthful curiosity and wandered into the plant only to meet his death on an unguarded mechanical saw.[9]

Children filled useful roles at home in at least one other crucial area — babysitting. Many working-class families found it necessary to depend on second and third wage-earners to keep themselves above the poverty line. In some cases, especially in families where children were too young for formal employment, economic need forced mothers to set aside their daytime domestic duties and take up employment outside the home. The introduction of machinery in sectors such as food processing and the textile industry created jobs for unskilled female labour, although it also depressed the general wage level and guaranteed that female earnings in particular would remain pitifully low. Such industries, along with retail stores, welcomed this cheap labour force with open arms. Wage-earning mothers, consequently, placed even greater housekeeping and other domestic responsibilities on the shoulders of their children. Most importantly, mothers enlisted older children to babysit younger siblings in their absence. In cities where day nurseries were available, even the smallest cost proved prohibitive for many working-class families.[10] These duties took on particular importance in households headed by single parents, male and female.

In most cases, children's duties around the home were divided according to sex. Girls more often babysat and attended to housekeeping matters within the confines of the home while boys commonly performed tasks outside the home. This practice was consistent with both rural traditions and the sexual discrimination characteristic of urban life. A typical example can be found in the diary of Toronto truant officer W.C. Wilkinson. Paying a call on the Stone family in 1872, Wilkinson discovered thirteen-year-old Elizabeth cleaning house with her mother while her eleven-year-old brother Thomas was busy helping their father in the garden.[11] Sexual categorization, however, was not impenetrable. Families that lacked children of both sexes simply handed chores over to the most capable and available member. In these instances, domestic necessity conquered sexual stereotyping.

The frequency and regularity with which working-class families called on their younger members to assist in a wide variety of domestic duties highlights the continuing importance of children as active contributors to the family economy. This practice also reveals that working-class families could not rely on industrial earnings alone to provide all the goods and services demanded by urban life. The entrance of mothers into the wage-earning work force undoubtedly disrupted traditional family relations. But the family responded rationally by shifting responsibilities to other members. Single-parent families adjusted in the same manner. Children's chores usually corresponded with a sexual division of labour, except in cases where this was impractical or impossible. Unfortunately, not all observers recognized the significance of youngsters' work in and around the home. Truant officer Wilkinson, for example, complained in 1873 that "in many instances children were kept at home for the most *frivolous* reasons by their parents, such as to run messages, assist in domestic duties, cut wood, and many such reasons that I am compelled to accept, although reluctantly, as the law at present only requires the[ir] attendance four months in the year."[12] (emphasis added)

Working-class parents had more pressing concerns than truancy on their minds when they kept children at home to perform important economic duties. In some cases, children's domestic responsibilities included participation in home-centred industries that formed a branch of the notorious "sweat shop" system. The term sweat shop usually described a tiny workplace, sometimes attached to a residence, where a predominantly female and child labour force toiled long hours under contract, or subcontract, producing saleable materials for large retail or wholesale outlets. A federal government inquiry in 1882 found sweat shops "sometimes being in the attic of a four-story building, at others in a low, damp basement where artificial light has to be used during the entire day."[13] The same investigation noted: "The rule, apparently which is observed by employers, is, not how many hands should occupy a certain room or building, but how many can be got into it."[14] The ready-made clothing industry, in particular, depended on sweated labour. In the simplest terms, this work extended and exploited the traditional role of women and girls as sewers for their own families. Workers discovered that they could earn a few extra dollars through this nefarious trade by fulfilling contracts in their own homes, or by bringing home after a regular shift unfinished material produced in a factory or workshop located elsewhere. In both cases, children accounted for a substantial portion of the work force.

The Globe found this to be a common practice among working-class families in Toronto as early as the 1860s:

> . . . frequently the industrious efforts of a whole family are employed to fill the orders of the employers. Often, in such instances, the child of eight or nine summers is made a source of material help in the construction of the coarser descriptions of men's garments that are now prepared for the ready-made clothing market. In the same way the female head of the house, a group of daughters, and, perhaps, the male members of the family, if no better occupation is available, turn in to assist the father in adding to their means of support.

The same article described one family that worked on clothing contracts sixteen to eighteen hours per day, six days a week.[15]

More than a decade later, in 1882, a federal government inquiry studied the conditions of 324 married female workers. The investigation revealed that 272 women performed most of their work in their own homes. The women explained that in this way they could elicit the assistance of older children and watch over infants at the same time. Of the original 324 women, 255 worked in the clothing industry.[16] Three years later, federal inspector A.H. Blackeby reported that he encountered difficulty amassing information on the wool industry specifically because so much of the work was done in private homes.[17]

In 1896, a petition from the Trades and Labour Congress moved the federal government to appoint Alexander Whyte Wright to undertake a thorough investigation of the sweating system in Canada. Wright visited factories, workshops, and private homes in Halifax, Quebec, Montreal, Ottawa, Toronto, and Hamilton. He found appalling conditions and paltry wages to be the rule in factories and shops but discovered that workers toiled longer, earned less, and suffered more in their own homes: "When a comparison is made . . . between the condition of the people who work in contractors' shops and the conditions which attend the making of garments in private homes, the advantage is, in a marked degree, in favour of the former system."[18] Wright encountered scores of children working in excess of 60 hours per week in converted bedrooms, kitchens, and living rooms. Home labourers competed with contractors for available work, thus, in Wright's words, "bringing the wages down to the lowest point at which the employees can afford to work."[19] Furthermore, most employers paid by the piece, a practice that encouraged longer hours and a faster pace of work, and discouraged regular rest periods. Wright's report also revealed that home workers occasionally needed to carry damaged materials to the employers, "frequently losing half a day because of having to make an alteration which in actual work only requires a few minutes of time. To avoid this they are often willing to submit to a fine or reduction of wages far in excess of what the making of the alteration would be worth to them."[20] Even in unionized shops where hours of labour were restricted, Wright discovered workers anxious to bring material home to accumulate some precious overtime. "The advantage of having the assistance of their families," he pointed out, "is a further inducement."[21]

Four years after Wright filed his report, a young Mackenzie King undertook a similar investigation on behalf of the postmaster-general. King found sweat shop conditions to be the norm in the carrying out of government clothing contracts: ". . . by far the greatest part of the Government clothing was made by women and girls in their homes or in the shops as the hired hands of sub-contractors. . . . In some cases the different members of the family assisted in the sewing, and in a great many cases, one, two, three or more strangers, usually young women or girls, were brought from the neighbourhood and paid a small sum for their services by the week or piece."[22] Like Wright before him, King discovered that private homes, not factories or workshops, exhibited the harshest working conditions. Children routinely assisted in the sewing process and worked as carters carrying material between home and supply houses. King also reported that home workers were required to supply their own thread, a cost which he claimed composed "a substantial fraction of the gross earnings received."[23] Many shop workers brought unfinished material home at night and completed their work with the help of their families. King concluded: "It was pretty generally conceded that, except by thus working overtime, or by the profits made by the aid of hired help, there was very little to be earned by a week's work."[24]

Home sweat shop workers received no protection from government. Although the Ontario Factories Act of 1884 and the Shops Act of 1888 restricted the age and hours of child workers in industrial and commercial establishments, both pieces of legislation specifically exempted family work from any type of regulation. Thus, in 1900, Mackenzie King could write: "When clothing has been let out to individuals to be made up in their homes, with the assistance only of the members of the household, there was absolutely no restriction as to the conditions under which the work of manufacturer had to be carried on."[25] When the Ontario government's Committee on Child Labor reported seven years later, the situation looked much the same. Wrote the commissioners: "In poor neighbourhoods in cities the practice of employing children [in private homes] is very common. The sweat shop has been termed the nursery of child labour."[26] Unlike Wright and King, these government inspectors seemed not to realize that these conditions were not the creation of cruel parents who enjoyed subjecting their children to long hours of mind-numbing work. The iniquity lay in the callousness of a competitive economic system that mercilessly squeezed workers for the last drop of their labour power while building private fortunes for retail outlet owners, such as the renowned Canadian businessman Timothy Eaton. Business practice, not family practice, underlay this widespread suffering.

The example of the residential sweat shop demonstrates that the rural tradition of family work in the home survived in the city. But new circumstances forced this old custom to undergo a severe transformation. In one sense, the image of parents and children working together invites a comparison to the shared family responsibilities characteristic of rural society. But the urban sweat shop was a long way from the country quilting-bee. Clothing contracts violated the privacy of working-class homes and subjected adults and children to strenuous conditions over which they had little influence. Long hours of tedious labour brought a minimal return. Workers danced to the demands of a consumer market while competing contractors systematically drove wages down. Middlemen turned the sweat shop system into a chain of command that featured lower wages and harder working conditions with each successive downward link. Naturally, children occupied the bottom position in the work hierarchy. Yet it is apparent from the evidence collected by Wright and King that child workers proved to be the decisive factor in the economic feasibility of many contracts. This observation exposes the cruel paradox of child workers in a competitive labour market: the more the sweating system exploited the free or cheap labour of children, the less of a chance adults faced of ever receiving a fair wage for their own work.

In other areas, working-class families used their homes as bases for personal service industries. Young children carried laundry to and from their homes while older siblings assisted in washing and ironing. In cities where young single men and working fathers temporarily separated from their families composed a significant proportion of the population, the services of room and board were always in wide demand. Family-run boarding houses daily called on children to change sheets, clean rooms, serve meals, and wash dishes. Some homes took in extra customers, or "mealers," at the dinner hour, often resulting in several sittings per day. In other instances, children prepared and carried homemade lunches to workers at their place of employment. One Hamilton woman who as a child helped her aunt and uncle operate a boarding house reminisced about her youth with telling detail: "Others were a family. We were a business. . . . I couldn't take friends home. . . . I always seemed to be so busy working that I never had time to really make friends."[27] Although these home-centred industries rose above the conditions of residential sweat shops, child workers still made significant contributions, and sacrifices, on a regular basis.

Reaching beyond the perimeters of the home, many working-class children added to the family coffers through their participation in a variety of street trades. Nineteenth-century families immensely enjoyed socializing in public, and downtown streets always bristled with activity and excitement.[28] A police survey of 1887 uncovered approximately 700 youngsters, the vast majority of them boys, who regularly performed, polished shoes, or sold newspapers, pencils, shoelaces, fruit, or other small wares on the streets of Toronto.[29] W. McVitty, chief constable of Ottawa, reported in 1890 that the streets of the capital city supported approximately 175 newsboys but very few girls.[30] Some children, under instruction from their parents, simply begged for money from passers-by.[31] There is plentiful evidence as well of teenage prostitution.[32] Collectively, these youngsters composed a unique and vibrant street culture which occasionally exhibited elements of ritual and hierarchy. Of all the young street vendors, one group stood out — the newsboys.

Newsboys were serious businessmen, not simply charity cases trying to scrape together a few pennies like the other waifs and strays common to city streets. Some of these lads lived on their own in cheap boarding houses or at the Newsboys' Lodging and Industrial Home in Toronto, or its Catholic counterpart, the St. Nicholas Home. These privately-run institutions attempted to provide independent newsboys with decent accommodation and moral and industrial training. At the Newsboys' Lodging and Industrial Home, 10¢ per day bought supper, bed, and breakfast, while $1.30 per week fetched full room and board. Many free-spirited boys, however, bristled at the home's regular curfew of 7:00 P.M., and extended curfew of 9:00 P.M. two nights a week, and sought its services only during the most desperate of the winter months. The majority of newsboys lived with their parents and pounded the streets daily as part of their contribution to the family economy. A small percentage of boys delivered door to door, but the greater number worked late into the evenings selling on the street. Some lads worked alone, while more experienced boys headed up teams of sellers. A common trick of a newsboy was to approach a customer with a single paper claiming that it was the last one he had to sell before heading home. If the unwary citizen fell for the con, the newsboy then returned to his hidden pile of papers and repeated the trick. Newsboys stationed themselves near the entrance of hotels, where they undersold the stands inside, and always stood out prominently, along with other young street traders, around the train station.[33] A passive visitor to Toronto, unable to resist the persistent overtures of the newsboys, bootblacks, and fruit vendors, would at least leave Union Station well informed, well polished, and well fed.

In some instances, the earnings of a newsboy shielded a poor family from utter destitution. When W.C. Wilkinson inquired into the absence from school of fourteen-year-old William Laughlan, the lad's mother told him: ". . . the boy was the principal support to the house, the father having been ill for a long time. The boy carried out papers morning and evening."[34] This entry from Wilkinson's diary also indicates the importance of children as substitute wage-earners. In his notebooks, newspaper reporter J.J. Kelso speculated that some newsboys, who he estimated earned between 60¢ and $1.00 a day, fully supported their parents.[35] Despite their importance as wage-earners, the vast majority of newsboys, bootblacks, and other street vendors occupied deadend jobs that promised no viable future employment. Although some business skills could be learned on the street, only a tiny percentage of enterprising newsboys managed to climb the professional ladder. Moreover, the "privation, exposure and irregular life" that characterized the street traders' existence frequently led to petty crime and permanent vagrancy.[36] In the estimation of W.H. Howland, the reform mayor of Toronto, "it was ruinous to a boy to become a newsboy, in nine hundred and ninety-nine cases out of a thousand."[37] J.J. Kelso added: "The profession of selling newspapers is in my opinion pernicious right through."[38]

Newsboys and other young street vendors attracted the attention of a new group of middle-class social reformers and self-styled child-savers. These individuals object-ed to the presence of so many roughly hewn youngsters on public streets and feared that extensive exposure to the harsher elements of city life would turn vulnerable chil-dren into vile and irresponsible adults. This, in turn, would place greater burden on the public purse through the maintenance of jails and houses of refuge. In an attempt to ameliorate this situation, J.J. Kelso and other leading philanthropists petitioned the Toronto Police Commission in 1889 to adopt measures to regulate the street traders. Kelso and his cohorts succeeded, and the resultant law, enacted in 1890, required newsboys and other vendors under the age of sixteen to apply for a licence, and for-bade boys under eight and girls of any age to participate in the street trade at all. To qualify for a badge, a boy had to maintain a clean criminal record, avoid associating with thieves, and attend school at least two hours per day. In addition to having their privileges revoked, violators could be fined or sentenced to the industrial school or common jail. Although over 500 boys applied for licences in the first year, the police failed to enforce the regulations rigorously and the law quickly fell into disuse.[39] Two years later, the Toronto Board of Education established special classes for newsboys, but met with little success. In both cases, reformers failed to recognize the enormous distance between controlled orderliness as prescribed by law and the burden of pover-ty. Irrespective of the intentions of social legislation, many working-class families depended on the contributions of children.[40] Furthermore, the arguments reformers put forward in favour of regulation revealed a deeper concern with public morality and family values than with the economic circumstances of newsboys and their fam-ilies. This attitude is especially evident in the extra restrictions placed on girls, the future wives and mothers of the nation. Susan Houston's comment on child beggars is equally applicable to newsboys and other young street vendors: ". . . it was their habits rather than their condition that roused the ire of reformers."[41]

Ironically, middle-class reformers had no farther to look than their own neigh-bourhoods if they wanted to observe the conditions of child workers. Although little information exists on the work experiences of the natural children of the middle class, there is a substantial body of material that describes the role foster children played in middle-class homes. The care of orphans and vagrant children had always posed a delicate problem for civil authorities. From the early years of Upper Canadian society, officials usually dispensed with parentless and needy youngsters by arranging appren-ticeship agreements for them. By the mid-1800s, private charitable institutions such as the Protestant Orphans' Home provided shelter and training for helpless children until placements could be found for them or until they reached an age of independ-ence. By the latter years of the nineteenth century, however, new perceptions of child welfare had emerged. Most reformers now agreed that only the natural setting of a family provided dependent children with a fair opportunity to develop proper social and moral values. Parentless youngsters and those whose natural family settings were found to be unwholesome or inadequate were now to be placed in foster homes where they would be treated as regular members of another family. In this way, reformers hoped to reduce the public cost of child welfare and at the same time prevent the creation of a future vagrant and criminal class. The primary institutional expression of this view was the Children's Aid Society (CAS), the first Canadian branch of which appeared in Toronto in 1891 as a result of the initiative of J.J. Kelso. This approach gained ground in 1893 when the Ontario government sanctioned the activities of the CAS with the passage of the Children's Protection Act and appointed Kelso as the superintendent of neglected and dependent children.[42]

Although the CAS preferred to place its charges in the countryside, in the belief that the wholesomeness and honest toil of farm life would develop moral and industrious habits, a small percentage of older children ended up in lower middle- and middle-class urban homes where they performed the normal roster of domestic duties. Despite the society's efforts to insure that each child placed out would receive elementary education and affectionate treatment, a youngster's ability to perform work around the home often proved to be the decisive factor in his or her placement. In a circular letter dated 15 September 1893, J.J. Kelso instructed CAS agents to be wary of homes that treated foster children as servants, a practice which he admitted was "altogether too common among those who apply for the care of dependent children."[43] A second letter, dated 22 April 1894, warned about parents with young children of their own who used their CAS wards as live-in nursemaids.[44] The demand for child workers also revealed itself through the report of a representative of the Girls' Home in Toronto who stated that her institution received twenty times the number of requests for girls between the ages of ten and thirteen as it did for girls five or six years old.[45]

The CAS must accept partial blame for the numerous instances in which its wards ended up as nothing better than underpaid domestic servants in comfortable urban homes. Although its members unquestionably exhibited genuine concern for the welfare of neglected youngsters, the CAS, like most childsaving agencies of the time, believed fervently that early exposure to work and discipline would guarantee the development of an upstanding and industrious citizenship. The society's literature unambiguously stated that "girls at twelve years of age, and boys at fourteen, should become self-supporting."[46] For children twelve years of age and over, the society used a special placement form that committed the child to domestic service in return for modest payment. The CAS's unbending adherence to the work ethic created a hazy atmosphere that clouded the distinction between healthy work habits and child exploitation. Even if the CAS had developed more stringent regulations pertaining to the type of work children could perform in the home, it would have been impossible to enforce them. Although the Children's Protection Act provided for the creation of local visiting committees with the authority to monitor foster homes, J.J. Kelso reported in 1894 that the province's 25 to 30 active committees represented well less than half of the needed number.[47]

Canadian households in search of cheap domestic labour could also look to any one of a dozen or more charitable institutions that specialized in the placement of British children in Canadian homes. From the time that Maria S. Rye arrived at Niagara-on-the-Lake in 1869 with a party of young orphans, the demand for British children always outpaced the supply.[48] By 1879, approximately 4,000 British youngsters were living and working with Canadian families.[49] This number would exceed 70,000 by 1919.[50] Like the Children's Aid Society, the British agencies preferred to send children to the countryside, but they also faced an overwhelming demand from city households for older girls to perform domestic work. In most cases, prospective guardians took few measures to camouflage their desire for help around the house. Moreover, correspondence and newspaper advertisements referring to available youngsters frequently emphasized the children's abilities to perform specific domestic tasks.

The best known of the child immigrants are the home children who arrived in Canada under the auspices of philanthropist Dr. Thomas John Barnardo.[51] A second group of children, which journeyed to Canada in the late 1880s and early 1890s under the watchful eye of social worker Charlotte A. Alexander, has also left useful records.[52] Alexander primarily handled girls between the ages of ten and fourteen, many of whom found places with families in urban Ontario. Some of Alexander's girls joined in home-centred industries, such as eleven-year-old Jane Busby who helped her mistress produce waistcoats.[53] The vast majority of girls, however, assumed the normal responsibilities of domestic servants or nursemaids. Although an extremely competent and hardworking girl could increase her wages from a starting salary of $2.00 a month to $9.00 after a few years' service, she still earned less than a regular domestic servant. In a letter to a friend, young Maggie Hall described a typical work day:

> I have to get my morning's work done by 12 o'clock every day to take the children for a walk then I have to get the table laid for lunch when I come in then after dinner I help to wash up then I have to give the little boy his lessons then for the rest of the afternoon I sew till it is time to get afternoon tea and shut up and light the gas then by that time it is time for our tea after which I clear away get the table ready for Miss Smith's dinner then put the little boy to bed & after Miss Smith's dinner I help wash up which does not take very long then I do what I like for the rest of the evening till half past nine when we have Prayers then I take Miss Smiths hot water & hot bottle, the basket of silver & glass of milk to her bedroom shut up & go to bed which by the time I have done all it is just ten.[54]

The letter's lack of punctuation perhaps unintentionally corresponds with the rapid pace of Maggie Hall's work day.

The letters among the Charlotte Alexander papers disclose a life of hard and tedious work that offered little in the way of security and opportunity. Alexander negotiated each placement individually, thus failing to insure that her girls would all receive the same treatment. This practice also left many girls at the mercy of particularly demanding guardians. Although Alexander obtained signed indentures for most of her placements, she had no regular visitation system which would allow for verification of the contract. Many guardians complained of the children's rough manners and poor work habits. Others unilaterally altered the terms of the agreement if the girl did not meet their expectations. Extremely dissatisfied customers simply returned unwanted girls to Alexander, or shunted them off to other residences. When children complained of unfair treatment, Alexander encouraged them to be tolerant and reminded them of how fortunate they were to have a position at all. Many children clung to their placements out of fear that another position would present even greater hardships. All girls suffered from a basic insecurity that accompanied the performance of unfamiliar duties in a strange environment. As Joy Parr has stated: "To be young, a servant and a stranger was to be unusually vulnerable, powerless and alone."[55] One letter among the Alexander papers unintentionally projects a vivid image of how onerous life could be for a working child. Lamenting the recent death of a foster child, a friend wrote to Charlotte Alexander on 29 June 1888: "Poor dear little Ada Hees passed away from this cold world — what a happy change for the dear child."[56] In the temporal sense, a more brutally frank assessment of the life of a working child would be hard to imagine.

In private homes and on public streets, children in late nineteenth-century urban Ontario routinely performed a variety of important economic duties that directly contributed to the successful functioning of the family or household economy. Youngsters not only assisted their families in this way, but in many cases provided valuable services to a demanding urban clientele. In working-class neighbourhoods, the widespread practice of child labour exposed the poverty and insecurity that plagued many families which could not rely on industrial wages alone to meet the demands of urban life. At the same time, the use of youngsters as regular or auxiliary workers denoted a family strategy that was both rational and flexible in its response to new and challenging circumstances. In the short term, working-class families could depend on children to add the last necessary ingredient to their formula for survival. In the long term, youngsters paid the price. The most significant of these costs lay in the area of education.

By the latter half of the nineteenth century, most children in Ontario enjoyed free access to primary education. But this held little promise for youngsters whose economic responsibilities at home prevented regular attendance at school. School inspectors repeatedly identified the non-enrollment and irregular attendance of working-class children as the education system's primary problem. A Toronto School Board census of 1863 revealed that of 1,632 children between the ages of five and sixteen not registered to attend school, 263, or 16.1 per cent, regularly worked at home during the day. Only full-time employment appeared more frequently on the chart as an explanation for non-attendance. This category contained 453 youngsters, or 27.7 per cent of the total. Of the remaining 7,876 registered students, only middle- and upper-class children posted a record of regular attendance.[57] Ultimately, the irregular school attendance of workers' children exposed the class bias of urban-industrial society. In Hamilton in 1871, for example, Ian Davey has shown that working-class children attended school far less regularly than did the sons and daughters of entrepreneurs. Youngsters from female-headed households occupied the bottom position.[58] Children of the working class were thus denied the full opportunity of personal development and social mobility that regular school attendance offered other youngsters. Although school attendance among working-class children improved near the end of the nineteenth century, youngsters from the middle and upper classes still enjoyed their traditional advantage. Mandatory attendance laws, first passed by the Ontario legislature in 1871 and strengthened in 1881 and 1891, affected the situation little.[59] Even when parents exhibited awareness of attendance laws, which was infrequent, such regulations proved unenforceable and irrelevant to families dependent on children's work.

This view of public education, of course, rests on the premise that working-class children had something tangible to gain by attending school. This is an arguable point in historical circles. Harvey Graff claims that for many children "the achievement of education brought no occupational rewards at all."[60] Michael Katz, Michael Doucet, and Mark Stern offer an identical assessment: "School attendance played no role in occupational mobility."[61] These authors contend that "ascriptive" conditions, such as class, ethnicity, sex, and geographic stability, exerted greater influence on social mobility than did education. This argument, however, largely depends on data drawn from the middle decades of the nineteenth century, a period when neither the public school system nor the urban-industrial labour market had advanced much beyond their formative stages. Early school promoters unquestionably placed greater emphasis on social control than they did on the creation of occupational opportunities for working-class children.[62] By the latter decades of the century, however, less obsessive school boards injected more skill-oriented programmes into the educational curriculum, such as bookkeeping and commercial arithmetic.[63] This development occurred at the same time that the urban-industrial labour market began to place a premium on these and other basic academic skills. The rapid growth of the white-collar work force sustains this argument. In 1898, Imperial Oil Canada employed only eleven white-collar workers. This number grew to 6,000 by 1919. In addition, public service employment in Canada increased from 17,000 in 1901 to 77,000 by 1911.[64] Although policies of social control and other "ascriptive" conditions remained dominant factors in late nineteenth-century society, improvements in school curriculum, coupled with the opening of new sectors in the labour market, increased the value of education for working-class children.[65] Lastly, it can be argued that if education did not provide workers' children with opportunities for upward mobility, it at least offered them lateral mobility in the form of a greater number of occupational choices within their own class.

One further dimension to the school issue warrants brief examination — the question of technical and manual training. By the 1890s, most Ontario schools offered these programmes to boys, while girls were invited to study domestic science.[66] School officials claimed that technical and manual training provided boys with practical skills and guaranteed them a secure place in the job market. Trade unionist Daniel O'Donoghue disagreed. Testifying before a royal commission in 1890, O'Donoghue declared that Ontario's labour unions were "unanimously opposed to manual training in the schools."[67] In O'Donoghue's estimation, these programmes lacked the depth and detail necessary to turn out competent workers. A careful reading of O'Donoghue's testimony, however, reveals that his real concern was that these programmes would flood an already crowded labour market, thus driving wages down and threatening the control of the workplace skilled workers had traditionally exercised through strict regulation of the apprenticeship system. Significantly, O'Donoghue did not suggest that the school board improve the quality of its programmes. Rather, he recommended that young people be sent to work on farms. Between the lines, one can detect O'Donoghue's hope that this practice would remove these children from the labour market altogether. Moreover, not all unionists shared O'Donoghue's opinion. In 1901, the secretary of the Plumbers' and Gas Fitters' Union sent a letter to the Toronto School Board commending it on its programmes of manual training.[68] This position was more consistent with the labour movement's traditional support of general primary education, as evidenced by numerous resolutions and petitions submitted to all levels of government.[69]

Discussions of the actual value of education aside, it appears that most parents believed that their children had something to gain by attending school. This is suggested by the strikingly high enrollment figures recorded by almost all urban school boards. Working-class children dutifully registered for school at the beginning of each semester, but found it impossible to maintain regular attendance in the face of economic pressures at home. In an attempt to combine economic responsibilities with educational opportunities, many working-class families sought, and received, special consideration from local school boards. Inspector James Hughes reported in 1874: "We have in Toronto a considerable number of Pupils who desire to be absent regularly for a part of each day, either as newsboys, or to perform some necessary work at home."[70] J.B. Boyle, Inspector of Public Schools in London, Ontario, reported that parents withdrew their children from school when the family economy demanded extra workers: "Sometimes they become errand boys in shops, or they sell papers, or they do what they can."[71] Lastly, children who attended school irregularly missed the full benefit of the new physical education and health programmes most schools offered by the late 1880s.[72]

Children who worked at home or on the street instead of attending school received little compensation in the form of job training. The street trades and sweat shop industries in particular exposed youngsters to elements that were both socially and physically harmful while offering no promise of occupational advancement. Although contractors often relied on the ruse of apprenticeship to encourage home workers to exploit their own children, the only opportunities associated with such labour were missed opportunities. Home-centred enterprises also deprived working-class children of the solace, privacy, and security that most middle- and upper-class youngsters enjoyed as a matter of natural right.

Social legislation and various reform movements had little immediate impact on the conditions of working children. In their attempt to make society safe for middle-class values, and at the same time guard against future costs of public welfare, reformers concentrated more on the symptoms of social maladies than on their causes. Legislation could set standards for proper social conduct, but it did little to relieve poverty. Most reformers, of course, did not view the unequal distribution of wealth and power as the root cause of social problems. In most cases, they preferred to blame the poor for their own condition. W.C. Wilkinson and the Toronto Public School Board, for example, believed that "lack of proper control by parents" was the source of irregular school attendance among working-class children.[73] Yet Wilkinson himself had recorded numerous instances of school-aged children performing important economic duties at home. Wilkinson and his cohorts might have arrived nearer to the truth had they set their sights on business élites whose hold over economic power forced many working-class families to stretch their resources to the limit simply to survive. Even trade unions exercised little influence over the conditions of many working-class families. Indeed, evidence shows that union time restrictions in clothing workshops that paid by the piece forced employees to continue their work at home with the assistance of their families.

New charitable organizations such as the Children's Aid Society unquestionably rescued numerous youngsters from the clutches of poverty and neglect by placing them in the care of benevolent and compassionate foster parents. But records left by the CAS and other child welfare agencies sadly indicate that many foster children ended up as underpaid domestic servants in middle-class homes. In addition to shouldering the burdens common to all working children, these youngsters bore the cross of class prejudice. While labouring children in working-class homes performed economic duties directly related to their family's survival, foster children provided personal service for the affluent. They were as much a symbol of a successful household as they were a component of it.

One group of historians has argued that "the family is an institution which industrialization shaped by removing the home from the site of the work-place."[74] Most others would agree in principle. Once free from the production-oriented nature of farm life, the family could devote more time to social development and material consumption. Yet for many children from lower-class families, work and home remained one, and the greater social and economic opportunities that allegedly accompanied urban life never materialized. Urban poverty forced many working-class households to apply the rural tradition of shared family responsibilities to meet the challenge of city life. But the transposition was not an easy one. Urban-industrial life provided less insular protection than the farmstead and presented workers with a greater number of competing forces. Consequently, old customs were forced to adapt to new and demanding circumstances. Despite the different pattern of social and economic relations forged by urban life, country and city still shared one common feature: in many lower-class neighbourhoods at least, work in and around the home remained a family affair.

NOTES

1. Canniff Haight, *Life in Canada Fifty Years Ago* (Toronto 1885). Cited in Michael S. Cross, ed., *The Workingman in the Nineteenth Century* (Toronto 1974), 34.

2. Late nineteenth-century writers commonly saw their society in transition from a rural-agricultural setting to an urban-industrial one. This simple dichotomy facilitated discussion of new social developments and emphasized the threat to tradition posed by emergent urban-industrial life. Modern historians, taking into account the growth of capitalism and waged labour, have offered a more complex and sophisticated analysis of social change. Michael Katz, Michael Doucet, and Mark Stern, for example, construct a three-stage paradigm which claims that "North America shifted from a peculiar variety of mercantile-peasant economy to an economy dominated by commercial capitalism to one dominated by industrial capitalism." *The Social Organization of Industrial Capitalism* (Cambridge, MA 1982), 364. Despite these more complex undercurrents of social transition, most late nineteenth-century workers identified with the rural-urban praxis. Historians develop comprehensive theories of social change over time; workers deal with the realities of life from day to day. This paper focuses on the second set of concerns.

3. Blair Neatby, *The Politics of Chaos: Canada in the Thirties* (Toronto 1972), 45. E.P. Thompson writes: "Each stage in industrial differentiation and specialisation struck also at the family economy, disturbing customary relations between man and wife, parents and children, and differentiating more sharply between 'work' and 'life.' . . . Meanwhile the family was roughly torn apart each morning by the factory bell. . . ." *The Making of the English Working Class* (New York 1963), 416.

4. See for example *Report of the Commissioners Appointed to Enquire into the Working of Mills and Factories of the Dominion, and the Labour Employed Therein*, Sessional Papers, 9, XV, no. 42, 1882; *Report of the Royal Commission on the Relations of Capital and Labour in Canada* (Ottawa 1889) [hereafter *Royal Labour Commission*]; *Annual Reports* of the Quebec Department of Labour; and *Annual Reports* of the Inspectors of Factories for the Province of Ontario. Among secondary sources, see Terry Copp, *The Anatomy of Poverty: The Condition of the Working Class in Montreal 1897–1929* (Toronto 1974); Bettina Bradbury, "The Family Economy and Work in an Industrializing City: Montreal in the 1870s," *Canadian Historical Association Historical Papers* (1979); Fernand Harvey, "Children of the Industrial Revolution in Quebec," in J. Dufresne et al., eds., *The Professions: Their Growth or Decline?* (Montreal 1979), reprinted in R. Douglas Francis and Donald B. Smith, eds., *Readings in Canadian History: Post-Confederation* (Toronto 1982); Gregory S. Kealey, *Hogtown: Working Class Toronto at the Turn of the Century* (Toronto

1974), also reprinted in Francis and Smith; Eugene Forsey, *Trade Unions in Canada 1812–1902* (Toronto 1982); Michael J. Piva, *The Condition of the Working Class in Toronto — 1900–1921* (Ottawa 1979); and Bryan D. Palmer, *A Culture in Conflict: Skilled Workers and Industrial Capitalism in Hamilton, Ontario, 1860–1914* (Montreal 1979).

5. The youngsters chosen for examination here by no means exhaust all possibilities. Children also worked in institutions such as orphanages, asylums, industrial schools, and reformatories. See Patricia T. Rooke and R.L. Schnell, *Discarding the Asylum: From Child Rescue to the Welfare State in English-Canada (1800–1950)* (Lanham 1983); Harvey G. Simmons, *From Asylum to Welfare* (Downsview 1982); Susan E. Houston, "Victorian Origins of Juvenile Delinquency: A Canadian Experience," in Michael B. Katz and Paul H. Mattingly, eds., *Education and Social Change: Themes From Ontario's Past* (New York 1975); and Susan E. Houston, "The Impetus to Reform: Urban Crime, Poverty and Ignorance in Ontario 1850–1875." (Ph.D. thesis, University of Toronto, 1974). These children have not been included as subjects of this paper on the ground that they did not belong to families or households, in the conventional sense of those terms.

6. In 1851, Ontario's rural population stood at 818,541 and its urban population at 133,463. By 1901, at 1,246,969, the rural population was still greater, but the urban population had increased dramatically to 935,978. Source: Canada, Bureau of the Census, *Report on Population*, 1 (1901). In Toronto alone the population increased from 30,775 in 1841 to 144,023 by 1891. Source: Gregory S. Kealey, *Toronto Workers Respond to Industrial Capitalism 1867–1892* (Toronto 1980), 99.

7. *The Globe*, 1 April 1894.

8. Most of the following examples are drawn from Toronto Board of Education Records, Archives and Museum [hereafter TBERAM], W.C. Wilkinson Diaries, six vols., 1872–74; TBERAM, Management Committee Minutes, 1899–1901; Hamilton Children's Aid Society, Scrapbook of Clippings, vol. 1, 1894–1961, Hamilton Public Library, Special Collections; Susan E. Houston, "The Impetus to Reform"; and Alison Prentice and Susan Houston, eds., *Family, School and Society in Nineteenth Century Canada* (Toronto 1975).

9. Testimony of John Henderson, manager for J. McLaren & Company Lumber Merchants, Ottawa, *Royal Labor Commission*, Ontario evidence, 1137–9.

10. "Annals of the Poor (The Creche)," *The Globe*, 4 January 1897.

11. TBERAM, Wilkinson Diaries, vol. 2, entry for 7 October 1872.

12. Toronto Board of Education, *Annual Report of the Local Superintendent of the Public Schools* (Toronto 1874), 45.

13. *Report of the Commissioners Appointed to Enquire into the Working of Mills and Factories*, 4.

14. Ibid., 7. See also *The Globe*, 23 September 1871, and "Toronto and the Sweating System," *The Daily Mail and Empire*, 9 October 1897 (part two).

15. "Female Labour in Toronto: Its Nature — Its Extent — Its Reward," *The Globe*, 28 October 1868.

16. *Report of the Commissioners Appointed to Enquire into the Working of Mills and Factories*, 10–1.

17. "Report of A.H. Blackeby on the State of the Manufacturing Industries of Ontario and Quebec," Sessional Papers, 10, XVIII, no. 37, 1885, 31.

18. Alexander Whyte Wright, *Report Upon the Sweating System in Canada*, Sessional Papers, 2, XXIX, no. 61, 1896, 8.

19. Ibid., 9.

20. Ibid., 11.

21. Ibid., 8.

22. W.L. Mackenzie King, *Report to the Honourable the Postmaster General of the Methods adopted in Canada in the Carrying Out of Government Clothing Contracts* (Ottawa 1900), 10.

23. Ibid., 19.

24. Ibid.

25. Ibid., 28.

26. Ontario, *Report of Committee on Child Labour 1907* (Toronto 1907), 5.

27. Interview conducted by Jane Synge. Cited in Irving Abella and David Millar, eds., *The Canadian Worker in the Twentieth Century* (Toronto 1978), 98. See also C.S. Clark, *Of Toronto the Good* (Montreal 1898), 62.

28. Conyngham Crawford Taylor, Toronto *"Called Back" From 1888 to 1847, and the Queen's Jubilee* (Toronto 1888), 189.

29. Public Archives of Canada [hereafter PAC], J.J. Kelso Papers, MG30 C97, vol. 4.

30. *Report of the Commissioners Appointed to Enquire into the Prison and Reformatory System of Ontario* (Toronto 1891), 372–3 [hereafter *Prison Reform Commission*].

31. See PAC, J.J. Kelso Papers, vol. 4; PAC, Children's Aid Society of Ottawa, MG28 184, Minutes, 1893–1906; and "Industrial Schools," *The Globe*, 4 November 1878.

32. See J.J. Kelso, *Second Report of Work Under the Children's Protection Act for the Year Ending December 31, 1894* (Toronto 1895), 12; *Hamilton Spectator*, 23 January 1894; C.S. Clark, *Of Toronto the Good*, 136; and *Prison Reform Commission*, testimony of W.H. Howland, 689, David Archibald, staff-inspector, Toronto Police Force, 701–2, and J.J. Kelso, 724.

33. These descriptions of newsboys are drawn primarily from PAC, J.J. Kelso Papers; *Prison Reform Commission*, testimony of J.J. Kelso, 723–9, and George Alfred Barnett, superintendent of the Newsboys' Home, Toronto, 729–30; Ontario *Report of Committee on Child Labour*; "The Tag System Abortive," *The Toronto World*, 22 November 1890; "The Waifs of the Street," *The Globe*, 18 April 1891; "The Industrial School," *The Telegram*, 18 April 1878; "Around Town," *Saturday Night*, 10 (21 November 1896); C.S. Clark, *Of Toronto the Good*; J.J. Kelso, *Protection of Children: Early History of the Humane and Children's Aid Movement in Ontario 1886–1893* (Toronto 1911); and Karl Baedeker, *The Dominion of Canada* (London 1900). I am indebted to David Swayze for bringing this last source to my attention.

34. TBERAM, Wilkinson Diaries, vol. 5, entry for 9 December 1873.

35. PAC, J.J. Kelso Papers, vol. 8.

36. Ontario, *Report of Committee on Child Labour*, 11.

37. *Royal Labor Commission*, Ontario evidence, 161.

38. *Prison Reform Commission*, 723. Various police chiefs across Ontario upheld the views of Howland and Kelso. See *Prison Reform Commission*, testimony of W. McVitty, chief constable of Ottawa, 372–3, and Lieut.-Col. H.J. Grasett, chief of police, Toronto, 700. See also Ontario, *Report on Compulsory Education in Canada, Great Britain, Germany and the United States* (Toronto 1891), 89.

39. "The Waifs of the Street," *The Globe*, 18 April 1891.

40. Undoubtedly, some newsboys pursued their profession as a matter of personal choice, preferring the small income and independence of the street to the demands and discipline of the school system.

41. Susan E. Houston, "Victorian Origins of Juvenile Delinquency," 86.

42. For a thorough discussion of the new approaches to child welfare, see Patricia T. Rooke and R.L. Schnell, *Discarding the Asylum*; Andrew Jones and Leonard Rutman, *In The Children's Aid: J.J. Kelso and Child Welfare in Ontario* (Toronto 1981); Neil Sutherland, *Children in English-Canadian Society: Framing the Twentieth Century Consensus* (Toronto 1976); Richard Splane, *Social Welfare in Ontario: A Study of Public Welfare Administration* (Toronto 1965); Jane-Louise K. Dawe, "The Transition from Institutional to Foster Care for Children in Ontario 1891–1921" (MSW thesis, University of Toronto, 1966); and Terrence Morrison, "The Child and Urban Social Reform in Late Nineteenth Century Ontario 1875–1900" (Ph.D. thesis, University of Toronto, 1971).

43. PAC, J.J. Kelso Papers, vol. 4. Kelso also mentioned this problem in his *First Report of Work Under the Children's Protection Act, 1893 For the Six Months Ending December 31, 1893* (Toronto 1894), 26.

44. Ibid.

45. *Proceedings of the First Ontario Conference on Child-Saving* (Toronto 1895), 59.

46. J.J. Kelso, *First Report of Work Under the Children's Protection Act,* 27.

47. *Proceedings of the First Ontario Conference on Child-Saving,* 46.

48. See Wesley Turner, "'80 Stout and Healthy Looking Girls,'" *Canada: An Historical Magazine,* 3, 2 (December 1975), and Turner, "Miss Rye's Children and the Ontario Press 1875," *Ontario History,* 68 (September 1976).

49. Ellen Agnes Bilbrough, *British Children in Canadian Homes* (Belleville 1879).

50. Neil Sutherland, *Children in English-Canadian Society,* 4.

51. A handful of informative monographs on the Barnardo children are now available. The best among them is Joy Parr, *Labouring Children: British Immigrant Apprentices to Canada 1869–1924* (Montreal 1980). For a more anecdotal approach, see Kenneth Bagnell, *The Little Immigrants: The Orphans Who Came to Canada* (Toronto 1980); Gail Corbett, *Barnardo Children in Canada* (Peterborough 1981); and Phyllis Harrison, *The Home Children: Their Personal Stories* (Winnipeg 1979).

52. PAC, Charlotte A. Alexander Papers, MG29 C58.

53. Ibid., vol. 3, Indexed Register, 1885–93.

54. Ibid., vol. 1, Maggie Hall to Miss Lowe, 13 February 1890.

55. Joy Parr, *Labouring Children,* 82.

56. PAC, Charlotte A. Alexander Papers, vol. 2, Alice Maude Johnson file, Mrs. Coyne to Charlotte Alexander, 29 June 1888.

57. Toronto Board of Education, *Annual Report of the Local Superintendent* (Toronto 1863), 43. To avoid the impression that this period lacked normal youthful playfulness, it should be noted that Toronto truant officer W.C. Wilkinson regularly discovered youngsters engaged in the usual truant shenanigans of fishing, swimming, and attending the races. See TBERAM, Wilkinson Diaries.

58. Ian E. Davey, "Educational Reform and the Working Class: School Attendance in Hamilton, Ontario, 1851–1891" (Ph.D. thesis, University of Toronto, 1975), 187.

59. The Ontario School Act of 1871 required children seven to twelve years of age to attend school four months of the year under normal circumstances. In 1881, an amendment to the act required children seven to thirteen years of age to attend school eleven weeks in each of two school terms. In 1885, another amendment reduced compulsory attendance to 100 days per year. In 1891, attendance became compulsory for the full school year for all children between eight and fourteen years of age.

60. Harvey J. Graff, *The Literacy Myth: Literacy and Social Structure in the Nineteenth-Century City* (New York 1979), 75.

61. Michael Katz, Michael Doucet, and Mark Stern, *The Social Organization of Early Industrial Capitalism,* 197.

62. For discussions of the motivations of early school officials, see Alison Prentice, *The School Promoters: Education and Social Class in Mid-Nineteenth Century Upper Canada* (Toronto 1977); Neil McDonald and Alf Chaiton, eds., *Egerton Ryerson and His Times* (Toronto 1978); and James H. Love, "Cultural Survival and Social Control: The Development of a Curriculum for Upper Canada's Common Schools in 1846," *Histoire Sociale/Social History,* 30 (November 1982).

63. See TBERAM, Management Committee Minutes, 1899–1901.

64. Gregory S. Kealey. "The Structure of Canadian Working-Class History," in W.J.C. Cherwinski and G.S. Kealey, eds., *Lectures in Canadian Labour and Working-Class History* (St. John's 1985), 28.

65. Combining "ascriptive" conditions and educational opportunities, J. Donald Wilson adds another dimension to the school question: "What happened to children in schools, how long they stayed in school, and how much they were influenced by schooling depended to a considerable extent on their ethnic and cultural background." "'The Picture of Social

Randomness': Making Sense of Ethnic History and Educational History," in David C. Jones et al., eds., *Approaches to Educational History* (Winnipeg 1981), 36.

66. Douglas A. Lawr and Robert D. Gidney, eds., *Educating Canadians: A Documentary History of Public Education* (Toronto 1973), 161, and Harvey J. Graff, *The Literacy Myth*, 210.

67. *Prison Reform Commission*, 739.

68. TBERAM, Management Committee Minutes, 14 February 1901.

69. For numerous examples see Eugene Forsey, *Trade Unions in Canada*. For a more detailed look at labour's view of technical and manual training, see T.R. Morrison, "Reform as Social Tracking: The Case of Industrial Education in Ontario 1870–1900," *The Journal of Educational Thought*, 8, 2 (August 1974), 106–7.

70. *Annual Report of the Normal, Model, Grammar and Common Schools in Ontario* (Toronto 1874), Appendix B, 84. Similar requests with positive replies can be found in TBERAM, Management Committee Minutes, 1899–1901.

71. *Royal Labour Commission*, Ontario evidence, 604–7.

72. See Neil Sutherland, *Children in English-Canadian Society*; Sutherland, "'To Create a Strong and Healthy Race': School Children in the Public Health Movement 1880–1914," in Michael B. Katz and Paul H. Mattingly, *Education and Social Change*; and Robert M. Stamp, "Urbanization and Education in Ontario and Quebec, 1867–1914," *McGill Journal of Education*, 3 (Fall 1968), 132.

73. Archives of Ontario, responses to G.W. Ross' inquiry of July 1895 regarding revisions of the Truancy Act, RG 22, Acc. 9631, Printed Circular no. 47, W.C. Wilkinson, secretary-treasurer, Toronto Public School Board, to Hon. G.W. Ross, Minister of Education, 8 October 1895. I am indebted to Terrence Campbell, formerly of the Ontario Archives, for bringing this file to my attention.

74. Russell G. Hann, Gregory S. Kealey, Linda Kealey, and Peter Warrian, "Introduction," *Primary Sources in Canadian Working Class History 1860–1930* (Kitchener 1973), 18.

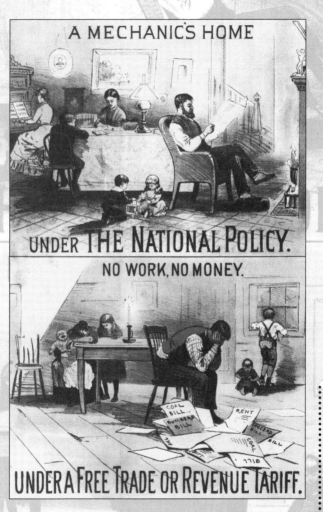

This broadside promoting the National Policy offers considerable insight into nineteenth-century gender roles and ideals.

For many years, the study of history focussed on the contributions of great men — politicians, soldiers, and entrepreneurs. During the 1960s, when feminists began to raise questions about the place of women in Canadian society, the absence of women from most historical analysis became a challenge for historians and led to the new field of women's history. At first, women's history was primarily a matter of writing women's experience and contributions into the past. As the field matured, women's history sought to depart from the framework of conventional history to offer a new narrative, different periodization, and innovative interpretative frameworks. More recently, many scholars have recognized that one cannot study the lives of women or men in isolation. The result has been the new field of gender history.

Gender is the social organization of sexual difference. Femininity and masculinity are not simply products of biology, but social constructs that change and evolve over time and the meanings of which vary across cultures and social groups. Because gender is socially constructed, its uses and meanings often reflect relationships of power and are contested. The study of gender thus provides considerable insight into the different ways in which men and women participate in society.

The shift from pre-industrial to modern industrial work patterns in the nineteenth century had a major impact on gender relations. The separation of work from the home gave rise to an ideology of separate spheres, especially among the middle class, that defined the roles and attributes of the sexes. According to this ideology, the ideal woman was characterized by piety, purity, submissiveness, and domesticity. Nevertheless, a few women did manage to pursue a career outside the home, as Jane Errington demonstrates in Article Seven, on women teachers in Upper Canada. Schoolteaching offered women an alternative to marriage or remarriage and an opportunity to enjoy a measure of financial independence and personal satisfaction. But nineteenth-century ideology had its ideal man, too, although comparatively little work has been done on the ideas, values, and practices that defined manliness. Janet Guildford helps to fill this void in Article Eight, on the construction of the ideal man in middle-class Nova Scotia women's writings.

QUESTIONS TO CONSIDER

1. How did "social norms" in Upper Canada restrict whom, where, and what women could teach? How did the curriculum offered in girls' schools reflect the emergence of the cult of true womanhood?
2. What were the characteristics of the ideal man as constructed by these Nova Scotia women writers? How did these ideals reflect the power relationships between the sexes? What are the strengths and limitations of using works of fiction as historical sources?
3. How comfortable are you with the idea that gender is an evolving social construct?

SUGGESTED READINGS

Bacchi, Carol Lee. *Liberation Deferred? The Ideas of the English-Canadian Suffragists, 1877–1918.* Toronto: University of Toronto Press, 1983.

Danylewycz, Marta. *Taking the Veil: An Alternative to Marriage, Motherhood, and Spinsterhood in Quebec, 1840–1920.* Toronto: McClelland and Stewart, 1987.

Errington, Elizabeth Jane. *Wives and Mothers, School Mistresses and Scullery Maids: Working Women in Upper Canada, 1790–1840*. Montreal/Kingston: McGill-Queen's University Press, 1995.

Guildford, Janet, and Suzanne Morton, eds. *Separate Spheres: Women's Worlds in the 19th-Century Maritimes*. Fredericton: Acadiensis Press, 1994.

Iacovetta, Franca, and Mariana Valverde, eds. *Gender Conflicts: New Essays in Women's History*. Toronto: University of Toronto Press, 1992.

Mitchinson, Wendy. *The Nature of Their Bodies: Women and Their Doctors in Victorian Canada*. Toronto: University of Toronto Press, 1991.

Parr, Joy. *The Gender of Breadwinners: Women, Men, and Change in Two Industrial Towns, 1880–1950*. Toronto: University of Toronto Press, 1990.

Strange, Carolyn. *Toronto's Girl Problem: The Perils and Pleasures of the City, 1880–1930*. Toronto: University of Toronto Press, 1995.

SEVEN

Ladies and Schoolmistresses: Educating Women in Early Nineteenth-Century Upper Canada

JANE ERRINGTON

In November 1824, a "Lady having lately arrived from England" proposed to establish "a Seminary of respectability" in Kingston. In notices distributed widely throughout the colony, she solicited "the patronage of those Ladies who [felt] disposed to place their Daughters where the most useful & polite Branches of Education are taught." "Having been accustomed to the best established methods of Tuition," she trusted that "an assiduous and unremitting attention to her Pupils and their Interests [would] ensure her success."[1]

At first glance, this brief notice is unremarkable. In Upper Canada in the first half of the nineteenth century, as in Great Britain and the United States at that time, teaching the children of others was an accepted and respectable way for a gentlewoman to earn her living.[2] Caring for and instructing children was, after all, "women's" work. As wives and mothers, almost all Upper Canadian women, at some time in their lives, had assumed the responsibilities of governess, nurse, or teacher. Exchanging those skills considered inherent in persons of their sex for a home, and/or a wage or income, was not particularly remarkable. Between 1800 and 1840, colonial newspapers

Source: "Ladies and Schoolmistresses: Educating Women in Early Nineteenth-Century Upper Canada," *Historical Studies in Education*, 6, 1 (1994): 71–96. Reprinted by permission.

frequently included notices from young girls looking for a position in a good family as a child's nurse or governess, or from older widowed women who offered to take a few children into their home and to teach them the rudiments of literacy.

The circumstances of this lady from England, however, appear to have been somewhat different. Though we do not know her name, her age, or her particular situation, or whether or not she actually opened her school, her notice suggests that she was not a young girl entering the labour market for the first time or a "poor lady obliged to work for pay."[3] This lady apparently had training and experience in "the best established method of Tuition." She aspired and, one might presume, had sufficient financial resources to establish a "Seminary of respectability." In fact, she appears to have been one of that small, though growing, number of women in Upper Canada who would have considered themselves "professional" teachers. For her and a few others in post-1815 Upper Canada, being a teacher was more than a desperate attempt to survive financially. Teaching the children of others was for these women a viable and perhaps preferable alternative to marriage or remarriage. And owning and operating one's own School or Academy for Young Ladies was a goal which promised at least the possibility of relative independence, financial security, and personal fulfilment.[4]

This is not to suggest that between 1800 and 1840 most women who taught in Upper Canada would have considered themselves or wanted to become professional teachers. As Alison Prentice notes, during this period "domestic or private teachers . . . predominated in most parts of Canada."[5] Most women who offered to teach for wages did not profess to have any specific expertise. Few claimed previous experience in a classroom. And many intended to teach only until they married, remarried, or their financial circumstances improved sufficiently to permit them to leave the labour market. But there seems little question that increasingly, Upper Canada attracted women who did look to teaching as a profession and who were able to make their living in the classroom.

In the first four decades of the nineteenth century, Upper Canada offered increasing opportunities for women to teach, and it supported a wide variety of schools, particularly schools for girls. The women who taught in the colony came from incredibly diverse backgrounds and at times had sharply differing expectations of their work. Some wanted or only had to work part-time; others never managed to own their own school. Many lady-proprietor schoolteachers were unsuccessful; a few, however, gained both fame and relative prosperity. Moreover, as the colony matured, the differences between the professional lady teacher and at least some of those who would initially have considered themselves amateurs gradually blurred. A number of widows and spinsters discovered in teaching a way to gain financial independence and personal satisfaction. And though they never professed to having professional expertise, after a number of years of owning and operating a seminary for young ladies, a few "poor ladies" inevitably acquired both the experience and the skill normally associated with a professional.

What is perhaps most ironic is that as opportunities for women to teach expanded and the number of women who earned their living in a classroom grew, schoolmistresses were increasingly circumscribed in whom they could teach, where, and what. By 1840, social norms restricted lady teachers to instructing the very young and adolescent girls, preferably within a secure domestic setting. Moreover, in response to the demands and sensibilities of middle-class patrons, women who opened "ladies' academies" were obliged to provide a curriculum that met the needs of the "true" woman of the nineteenth century — "the virtuous and discrete wife"[6] and the wise, discerning, and compassionate mother. In short, the emergence of the cult of true womanhood,[7] which established increasingly narrow standards of what was appropriate for a young girl to learn and where she could or should learn it, also promoted specialized education for girls and professionalization among some of those who taught them.

I

Colonists had been concerned about the education of their children since the arrival of the first settlers in Upper Canada in the 1780s and 1790s. The general acceptance of the need for a literate and educated citizenry was paralleled by a growing concern, particularly amongst the colonial gentry, about what type of education was appropriate for their daughters. Almost since the foundation of the colony, Upper Canadians had debated whether women could, let alone should, be formally educated. Women, after all were different from men. They were timid, feeble, and, some suggested, "their minds are not so strong and they are less capable of reasoning."[8] Others, however, emphatically defended a woman's intellectual capabilities. A brief article on "Female Education" published before the turn of the century observed that "a woman's senses are generally as quick as ours, their reason is as quick . . . and their judgement as secure and solid."[9] "It has never been proved to me that women are in any respect inferior to men," an anonymous Acetum explained to the residents of Kingston in 1812, "except in a few particulars connected with their Physical texture."[10] One young woman, vehemently replying to charges that women were intellectually weaker than men, asserted, "Believe me, Sir, the natural ability of the sexes are equal." Apparent differences, she observed, were the result of "their different education." It was the specific "purposes for which [men and women] are destined in life which accounted sufficiently for these distinctions."[11] One commentator went so far as to assert that barring women from "the privilege of ingenious education" was an inhuman tyranny.[12]

Certainly, girls, like their brothers, were expected to be able to read and write. Girls also had to be well grounded in the "domestic arts,"[13] and all those skills which they would need as future wives and mothers. As the nineteenth century unfolded, however, the skills required particularly of middle-class Upper Canadian girls expanded considerably. In Upper Canada, as in Great Britain, women, the home, and the domestic sphere were becoming important symbols of middle-class values. Increasingly, it came to be assumed that women had a special role to play in maintaining and advancing the new social order. A woman's God-given vocation, her work in life, was still to be the keeper of the hearth and wife and mother of a happy and productive family. But it was also asserted that from the security of her home, woman, as society's moral arbiter, keeper of the faith, and promoter of virtue, inevitably influenced the shape and beliefs of the wider world.[14] To properly fulfil these new responsibilities associated with the dictates of domesticity required skill and training.

"Girls . . . require much more care and attention in bringing up than parents generally suppose,"[15] articles in local newspapers frequently asserted. Mothers, who bore the primary responsibility for ensuring that girls received training appropriate to their rank and vocation, were reminded that "the education of your daughters is of the first importance," for the "very character of the country was at stake."[16] Increasingly, however, a number of Upper Canadians came to believe that home education for middle-class daughters was not sufficient. "Nothing short of the refinement of education [could] give dignity and elevation to the female character," an article in the *Farmer's Journal* explained. "Nothing can so well qualify them for participating to advantage in all pleasures desirable for mutual intercourse with the polished circles of life."[17]

It is obvious from comments in the colonial press that this conclusion met some, if not considerable, resistance, however. As a result, proponents of formal education for women went to considerable lengths to reassure opponents. Men need not "fear to lose [their] empire" over women by "thus improving their natural abilities," it was explained. Rather, "where there is most learning, sense and knowledge, there is observed to be the greatest modesty and rectitude of manners."[18] An educated woman was an asset to a discerning man, to his home, and to the future of their community. "Men of sense naturally seek companions possessing corresponding qualifications,"[19] it was asserted. An address by a teacher to her pupils printed in 1829 in the *Farmers' Journal* explained, "She whose mind has been expanded and feeling so elevated will have neatness, economy and regularity in all her domestic avocations; she will never debase herself by associating with the vulgar and the mean; she will cheerfully discern that her dwelling is the centre of her companion's happiness."[20] In short, a well-educated girl made the best wife and mother; she was in fact far more valuable to her husband than a wealthy or beautiful spouse.

Though even as late as 1840 not all Upper Canadians were convinced of the efficacy of formally educating their daughters, a growing number were. Elite families had been sending their daughters to school for some time. Increasingly, members of the middling ranks of colonial society began to believe that having their daughters attend a lady's academy was both a sign of their family's growing affluence and a way to help promote her social mobility. Moreover, many, like Anne Powell, wife of a Justice of the King's Bench, considered that sending girls to school was only practical. Not only would formal schooling educate a girl to be a good wife and mother, but the training she received there would enable her "to obtain a respectable support" if "a future emergency"[21] should arise.

The opportunities available to women to earn their living teaching in Upper Canada were directly influenced by the changing expectations middle- and upper-class families had for their daughters' education. Opportunities were also dictated by economic and social circumstances within the colony. During the first generation of settlement, Upper Canada afforded little opportunity for anyone, let alone a woman, to make her living teaching. The population was too small and there were too few families who could afford or had the inclination to send their daughters to school. After 1815, however, as the population grew, towns and villages developed, and disposable income increased, more and more women turned to teaching to help support their families and themselves. And a number consciously catered to the growing demands of middle- and upper-class parents for specialized training for their daughters, the future "true" women of Upper Canada.

II

....

In 1802, Mr. and Mrs. Tyler took "the liberty of informing" the readers of the *Niagara Herald* that they intended to open a school for young men and ladies, four years of age and older. In addition to reading, writing, and arithmetic, "the young ladies will be instructed in all that is necessary for persons of their sex, to appear decently and

be useful in the world, and of all that concerns housekeeping, either for those who wish to live in town or in country."[22] The notice for the Tylers' school provides some insight into what Upper Canadians at the turn of the century expected of their daughters' education and of the women who taught them. Practicality seemed to be the watchword. The girls' training was to be useful. And no one presumed that Mrs. Tyler had any special qualifications to teach or that she and her husband would be able to rely solely on income from the school. In fact, the notice ended with the announcement that Mrs. Tyler, "having been bred in the line of *mantua makers*," also sought work as a seamstress, and she offered "to execute her work in the neatest manner, to the satisfaction of those who may honour her with their custom."[23]

Mrs. Tyler was what one might classify as a wife-teacher. Her expertise as a teacher rested on her sex; her role in the classroom was secondary to her responsibilities as a wife. In the first half of the nineteenth century, a number of other colonial women found themselves in similar circumstances. In the post-1815 period, however, some of them, together with their husbands, consciously tried to take advantage of the growing demand for special education for the colony's daughters.

In October 1814, Mr. and Mrs. Pringle announced that they intended to open a school in Kingston for young ladies of the community. By 1820, Mr. and Mrs. Wolf of Kingston[24] and Mr. and Mrs. Roberts in Niagara[25] had established similar businesses. And over the next twenty years, a number of other couples entered the education market. In many of these family enterprises, it was clearly the husband who had experience and some expertise teaching. However, this was not always the case. When Mr. and Mrs. Maitland opened an academy in York in 1832, both apparently "had long experience in the instruction of youth."[26] In one noted instance, it was clearly the wife who was the professional teacher. The advertisement of Mrs. Twigg and her husband, who opened a girls' school in Kingston in 1825, stated openly that it was Mrs. Twigg who had both the academic credentials and "long experience" in the profession. No mention was made of Mr. Twigg's profession.[27]

In situations where it was "his" school, the presence and active involvement of the master's wife was nonetheless essential to the success of the business. When the Reverend M. Marcus opened a district school in Picton in 1833, he observed that Mrs. Marcus[28] would superintend all "the domestic arrangements," including ensuring "regularity and discipline" and providing students with "the care and comfort of a private family."[29] In those schools which accepted girls, the master's wife also taught needlework and superintended the "ladies department." And in exclusively ladies' academies, it was Mrs. Roberts, Mrs. Pringle, and Mrs. Wolfe who oversaw all the domestic arrangements of the school and taught many if not all the "ornamental" arts. Many wife-teachers probably also gave classes in other subjects, like reading and writing, where they had some particular expertise.[30]

The viability of family schools and particularly those for girls in Upper Canada is unclear. Certainly, before 1820, there was little likelihood of a woman making a career out of teaching. After the War of 1812, however, as the local population increased and the economy grew, the opportunity for aspiring schoolmistresses clearly improved. The Twiggs and the Pringles, both of Kingston, were in business for more than five years. For the Maitlands, like the Tylers, subsistence may nonetheless have been precarious. Advertisements in local newspapers suggest that most small girls' schools in Upper Canada did not survive for more than two years.[31] Moreover, most couples were unable to rely on the income they earned from their business for a living wage. Some wife-teachers were more fortunate. Their income was intended to supplement that of their husbands. While Mrs. Sturdy taught school in Port Hope in 1830, for example, her husband worked as a weaver.[32] Mary O'Brien taught in exchange for help in the house. A few women could even teach part-time, offering specialized skills to students.

The opportunity for women to tutor on a part-time basis or to teach only one of the ornamental arts was very limited, however. Most private tutors or proprietors of "specialty schools" in Upper Canada were men. Only men, for example, offered tutoring in the classics and penmanship. Male tutors also predominated in teaching dancing and French.[33] Madam Harris, who owned a dancing school in York in the late 1820s,[34] was apparently the only woman in her field. And though she offered lessons to both young ladies and gentlemen, classes were segregated and came together only once a week to practise.[35] In even the most basic of the "accomplishments" — teaching instrumental and vocal music and drawing — the number of women offering private lessons was smaller than that of men.[36] It appears that middle-class women in Upper Canada, like their sisters in Australia, were expected to acquire the ability to dance, to sing, or to play the piano. To display their talent publicly, or to offer to sell these skills openly, was not socially acceptable.[37]

The restrictions placed on what were appropriate subjects for women to teach were compounded by limitations on whom and where they could teach. Though it was acceptable for male tutors to have both boys and girls as students, women tutors usually could not. Social mores dictated, and middle- and upper-class parents determined, that wage-earning women teachers were suited, by reason of their sex and their ability, to instruct only young children and adolescent girls.[38] And it was expected that self-respecting middle-class or aspiring to middle-class women teachers preferred and should earn their living within the confines of their own home.

Thus, the few women able to trade their special skills for a part-time income were clearly fortunate. Many were obviously wives or daughters who were not totally dependent on the tuition they received for their work. Most women who wished or had to earn their own living and continue to maintain some semblance of independence were under increasing social and economic restrictions. For though the demand for formal education for Upper Canada's daughters grew in the period after the War of 1812, many prospective teachers were forced to sacrifice their privacy and open their homes to potential pupils. They also had to provide a curriculum that reflected the growing acceptance of the cult of true womanhood.

III

....

Many and perhaps most gentlewomen who turned to teaching had little choice in the matter. And many were limited in what they could offer. In 1827, Mrs. Margaret Powell, widow of Major Powell, announced to the residents of York that she was opening a school for children three to ten years old.[39] Eight years later, "the Widow of a Clergyman . . . of Belleville," Mrs. Campbell, notified local residents that she was willing to take six young ladies "into her house . . . to educate with her own children."[40] Mrs. Powell and Mrs. Campbell apparently had relatively limited means. They may well have also been somewhat hesitant about their own abilities. To resolve their financial difficulties, each proposed to open what appears to have been the equivalent of an English dame school.

Dame schools were undoubtedly a common feature in many Upper Canadian villages and towns, as they were in Great Britain and the United States.[41] It is difficult to estimate how many there were in the colony, for most widow proprietors probably did not advertise their schools. They had little need to. Students were drawn from the immediate neighbourhood and arrangements were informal. Yet dame schools may well have predominated in Upper Canada in the first half of the nineteenth century. Particularly after 1815, however, a woman with some means and some education probably preferred to take advantage of the growing demand for specialized education for girls by opening a school for young ladies. And though like Mrs. Campbell they had no special training, they and indeed many Upper Canadians assumed that their sex and life experience as gentlewomen, wives, and mothers fully qualified them to teach.

Most girls' schools established in Upper Canada before 1840 were small, and probably resembled traditional dame schools. The classroom was the proprietor's parlour; the number of students was limited and lessons may have been informal. Yet a growing number of women teachers were obviously conscious that to gain parents' approval and patronage, they had to attempt to provide the structure and formality indicative of a "real" school. As a result, Mrs. Farrand of Brockville was probably not alone in demanding the "punctual attendance of each scholar . . . during the hours of Instruction and no allowance . . . for occasional absences."[42] It is likely that many teachers tried to establish a school routine, with scheduled class time and periods of relaxation. Some teachers divided their students into primary, junior, and senior "departments."[43] Lessons in English, reading, grammar and composition, arithmetic, history, and geography were scheduled and taught by age and academic ability, with more advanced students helping the juniors. Most girls' schools in the province had very little "specialized" equipment. Texts for reading either were provided by the students or were part of the teacher's private library.[44] Though a few schools advertised that they used globes or maps in the teaching of geography, other subjects, like history or natural science, were undoubtedly taught by lecture or by having students gather local flora and fauna.[45] Many Upper Canadian parents undoubtedly considered that elaborate equipment was unnecessary. What their daughters needed was a secure environment, the company of social peers, lessons in basic literacy, and training in the "useful accomplishments."

In Upper Canada, as in Great Britain and the United States, the accomplishments, or what many termed "the ornamental branches of Female education,"[46] were emerging as "the dominant mode of education for middle-class girls."[47] This included modern languages, geography, history, and biology, subjects that would form the basis of a liberal education at the turn of the century.[48] In addition, upper- and middle-class girls in Upper Canada needed to acquire the social skills necessary for everyday life — dancing, painting, music, and needlework.

The success of a school in part depended on the ability of its proprietor to provide instruction suitable for daughters of the middle and upper classes. Certainly, plain and fancy needlework were standard subjects at all Upper Canadian girls' schools. Then, depending on the school and the skill of its mistresses or her assistants, young Upper Canadian women could also take lessons in dancing, embroidery, drawing and painting (of various kinds), instrumental and vocal music, French, Italian, German, and sometimes Latin. Many of these accomplishments were taught privately for an extra fee, or in small groups, by an assistant engaged specially for that purpose. Not every student could afford or would have the time or inclination to take more than one or two extra subjects.

Teaching many or all of the accomplishments did not guarantee a school's success, however. This also depended on the owner's financial resources, her social and business contacts, her reputation, and a number of other factors, some of which she could not control. Most girls' schools in Upper Canada appear to have been owned and operated by single proprietors.[49] Inevitably, these schools were small and enrolment was limited. To try to increase their income, a number of women teachers opened day schools,[50] and some rented rooms especially for this purpose. Teaching day students did not, however, assure the teacher a regular income. Students' attendance was often erratic, and the teacher's income fluctuated accordingly. To try to resolve this dilemma, a few teachers of day schools offered to board one or two pupils in their own homes;[51] others offered to make arrangements to have students board with neighbouring families.[52] Most women teachers taught in their own homes, however, and an increasing number aspired to the more prestigious and potentially lucrative situation of owning a boarding school.

But taking in boarders created its own problems. Not only were most Upper Canadian homes small but beds and household equipment were limited. To attempt to gain some security and predictability in the numbers of pupils, many boarding-school mistresses required that students register for at least a quarter and then provide at least a month's notice before leaving.[53] In addition, almost all colonial boarding schools required pupils to provide their own beds and linen and in some cases cutlery.[54] Taking in boarders also demanded that even the smallest school had to have a maid, or students or other household members had to assume some of the domestic responsibilities. To cope with the day-to-day operation of the school, a number of these women turned to members of their family — daughters, sisters, and mothers — or joined with friends or associates in similar circumstances, to share costs, to help with the teaching, and generally to share the many responsibilities and work related to running a school.[55] Only those schools operated by a husband and wife team, or teachers whose mothers or sisters were living-in to act as housekeepers, could hope to avoid hiring paid help.[56]

In addition to coping with the day-to-day work of teaching and housekeeping, owner/teachers of private-venture girls' schools also had to manage in an increasingly competitive academic world. Thus proprietors often felt obliged to point out those features of their schools which made them worthy of patronage. Almost all schoolmistresses offered references as to their character and respectability. Some also managed to gain and made sure to advertise that they had the public patronage and support of prominent local residents. In keeping with the sensibilities of the time, lady teachers usually also emphasized that close attention, or as Mrs. Black of St. Catharines noted, "strict regard," would be paid to students' "Moral and Religious instruction."[57] Moreover, some schoolmistresses consciously tried to make a virtue of necessity. Mrs. Marshall and her sister, Miss Davidson of Belleville, and a number of other lady teachers claimed that they were limiting the number of their students so that the instruction could be almost individual.[58] Others, like Mrs. Fraser, offered to take only a few students at her boarding school in Newmarket, so that "in point of domestic comfort, the young ladies placed under her care [could] enjoy all the privileges of home."[59]

Some teachers tried to use other factors to induce parents to patronize their establishments. Mrs. Newall announced to the residents in the eastern portion of the province in 1820 that her new location in Brockville, "in respect to health, possess[ed] superior advantages." She explained that compared with her old location in Cornwall (and, by implication, that of other local seminaries) the location of the school now "has the benefit of pure and uncontaminated air, which gives to the necessary exercise an innocent recreation of the students during the intervals of the day."[60] The Streets of Niagara Falls emphasized their proximity to two churches (a Scottish church and the Church of England) and the availability of "excellent medical advice."[61]

Whether such inducements were effective is unknown. Unfortunately, very few records remain of any of these schools. Our knowledge of colonial schoolmistresses is largely limited to their advertisements in local newspapers. But it can, I think, be presumed that, throughout the period, the majority of girls' schools were short-lived and there was little to distinguish most single or joint or family proprietor operations from the basic dame school. Most women teacher-proprietors made no claim to particular expertise. They tried to attract students on the basis of their own respectability as gentlewomen and their ability to recreate a domestic environment at their school. For many parents, such qualifications were sufficient. After 1820, however, some at least began to demand a higher standard of instruction. At the same time, a number of schoolmistresses began to offer parents the services of a professional teacher. There is no evidence that a teacher's training or experience guaranteed her financial success. Many women seemed to believe, however, that this was one important way to distinguish themselves from their competitors. And it is likely that for some it was a significant advantage.

IV

When Mrs. Twigg solicited the ladies of Kingston for their patronage in 1825, she carefully outlined the merits of her situation. "For many years," she wrote, she had "conducted a Boarding and Day School in the North of Ireland, and [had] resigned a large School in that Country"[62] to come to Upper Canada. Indeed, she observed, she had been "induced" to emigrate to Upper Canada for the purpose of opening a school.

Mrs. Twigg was not alone. Between 1820 and 1840, a growing number of professional teachers came to Upper Canada alone, or with their husbands, sisters, or mothers, with the express purpose of opening a school for girls. And many of these women, including Mrs. Hamilton of Toronto,[63] Mrs. Bickerton of Picton,[64] Mrs. Weatherstone of Kingston,[65] and Mrs. Crookshank,[66] offered testimonials of their previous teaching experience,[67] evidence of professional training, and explanations of their "philosophy of education."[68] Mrs. Grattan, who opened a school in York in 1838, for example, stated that she had "completed her studies under the guidance of the most eminent masters."[69] In 1834, Mrs. Nash, "late Teacher of the Central School in London," planned to initiate "Doctor Bell's System" in her new school in York. In particular, she informed residents, "we might produce many testimonials from some of the most eminent men of science in Europe and America, to prove the superiority of this system to the 'old way'. . . . That instruction which is brought to bear upon the mind, is superior to that by which the memory only is called into action; or that it is better to store the mind with absolute definite ideas, than to burthen the memory with unintelligible words."[70] For these women, like their sisters who immigrated to Australia, the colonies offered a viable and respectable means of earning a living and establishing a new career.[71] For some, the move to Upper Canada promised financial security; a few gained prosperity.[72]

One of the oldest and most successful girls' schools in Upper Canada was begun in York by Mrs. Goodman in September 1817.[73] With twenty years' experience teaching in England and Montreal,[74] Mrs. Goodman settled in the colonial capital apparently to take advantage of its lack of schools for girls. Initially, the boarding and day school was small and its curriculum limited to reading, writing, and grammar, and lessons in music, dancing, and fancy needlework.[75] It is likely that Mrs. Goodman taught most classes herself, though a master was engaged part-time to give lessons in dancing.[76] When she retired in the spring of 1822, her school continued, and under the direction of Mrs. Cockburn,[77] a doctor's widow from Quebec City, it became one of the premier girls' schools in the province.[78]

In 1835, an article in *The Patriot* reported that Mrs. Cockburn's Boarding School had forty pupils, drawn from the best families of York. To assist her in her work, Mrs. Cockburn employed four teachers — three women and one man; the curriculum now included instruction in painting on velvet, and flower and card work. At a public examination that year, attended among others by the Archdeacon of Toronto, the young ladies were questioned for four hours on a wide variety of subjects — reading, English grammar, composition, geography, civil history, arithmetic, etc., and "the principles of the Catechism." The result, an admiring commentator noted, "was highly pleasing and satisfactory." The girls all displayed both an "accurate knowledge of their subject" and modesty and diligence.[79] A year later, Mrs. Cockburn again increased her establishment, hiring additional assistants and expanding the boarding facilities.[80] The seminary prospered until well into the 1840s.

The Goodman-Cockburn Boarding School was not the only school of such calibre in Upper Canada. In September 1826, the Misses Purcell and Rose announced the re-opening of their girls' boarding school in York.[81] Under the patronage of the Lieutenant-Governor's wife, Lady Sarah Maitland, the York Boarding School offered twelve boarding students the subjects of French, drawing, and dancing (taught by a master) in addition to the useful and ornamental arts. Until at least 1833, Misses Purcell and Rose ensured that students were taught by the most skilled mistresses and masters.[82] In 1830 one of these assistants, Mrs. Beynon, left the school to strike out on her own.[83] And at the same time that one of the last notices for the Purcell and Rose school appeared in the local press in September 1833, Mrs. Beynon announced that she had "removed to a handsome new house" in a "fine, wholesome, airy situation" that was "well adapted for boarders."[84]

As the capital and by the mid-1830s the largest town of Upper Canada, York offered considerable scope for lady teachers. In addition to the Cockburn Seminary, the Misses Purcell and Rose, and Mrs. Beynon boarding schools, two other establishments of some note were established in the 1830s. The Misses McCord opened their girls' boarding and day school in 1831.[85] Conscious that competition in the capital was brisk, they carefully distinguished their establishment from others. "The system of teaching which they propose to follow," their initial notice in the *Christian Guardian* explained, "will be found different from the plan generally pursued, but as it is one which is now adopted in the most respectable seminaries in Great Britain and Ireland, and one by which they have always taught, they . . . feel confident that on trial it will be approved here."[86] And approved it seems to have been. For at least the next ten years, the Misses McCord "trained the minds [of young women] by intellectual

exercises, and making all the exercises of the school subservient to religion."[87] Another school which enjoyed similar success was that of the Misses Winn, "an English family of respectability and strictly moral principles" who arrived in York in 1834[88] and taught young ladies well into the 1840s.[89]

York was not the only location where professional teachers found scope for their work. Miss Leah operated a seminary for young ladies in Kingston from 1831 to at least 1840 under the patronage of the Archdeacon Stewart, while her brother (or father) was master of a commercial school in Cramache.[90] Two years earlier, Mrs. Breckenridge and Mrs. Fenwick, an English lady of "considerable experience," had opened the Niagara Seminary.[91] Their initial advertisement stated their belief that "the great object of an instructor is to inspire a taste for knowledge, and to cultivate the power of acquiring it."[92] With the patronage of "the principal families of Niagara"[93] and the help of "suitable assistants," the two women instructed students in the standard curriculum of the time and held at least annual public examinations throughout the 1830s.[94] By mid-decade, they were competing with a Miss Butler, who also offered, with her assistant, "instruction in the various branches of a polite education."[95] When Miss Butler was forced to retire due to illness in 1835, her school was assumed by Miss Christie, a former assistant, and her partner Miss Chettle.[96]

After 1815, single and married women also opened girls' schools in small towns and villages, like Cobourg, St. Catharines, Bytown, Brockville, Belleville, and Peterborough. The growing demand for "superior" education for women encouraged a few teachers to move from one community to another, either to gain a better location for their school, or to take advantage of new opportunities for employment. A case in point was Miss Radcliffe. In 1823, a brief account in the *Niagara Gleaner* described an evening "of the finest treats." "The young ladies under the tuition of Mrs. and Miss Radcliffe exhibited specimens of their industry and improvement, to an assemblage of nearly all the finest families of the Town."[97] The next month, it was announced that Mrs. and Miss Radcliffe's school would re-open.[98] Nothing more was heard of the Radcliffe school or its proprietors until 1829, when a notice in the Brockville Gazette noted that a Miss Radcliffe was now directing the Brockville Seminary.[99] It appears that at some time in the intervening years, the Niagara school had closed (and perhaps Mrs. Radcliffe had died, as there was no subsequent mention of her) and at least one of her daughters had found her way to Kingston, to teach at the high school for ladies. Then either she or her sister made her way to Brockville. The editor of the *Brockville Gazette* was clearly pleased with the community's acquisition. "We beg to congratulate the gentry of this place" on the new seminary, he wrote, particularly as Miss Radcliffe possessed "great abilities and accomplishment."[100] Two years later one of the Miss Radcliffes re-surfaced in Cobourg, where she "had undertaken a share in the direction of the Cobourg Ladies' Academy."[101]

The Misses Radcliffe, Miss Cockburn, Mrs. Breckenridge, and a growing number of women who owned and/or taught in Upper Canadian girls' schools or ladies' academies were professional teachers. They taught for a living and, given the durability of their schools, were able and expected to continue to teach throughout much of their lives. Their success was the result of a number of factors. They must have had some ability to teach, and perhaps considerable knowledge of their subjects. They also had gained a reputation, both in their local community and in some cases throughout the colony, as women of integrity, respectability, and ability. These teacher-proprietors must also have possessed some considerable skill in adminstration and management.

Like any other successful business person, they had to hire and fire employees, keep accurate accounts, establish and maintain certain routines and work schedules, and generally invest their time, energy, and financial assets wisely. Not all or even most women who began private-venture schools were so capable. And even if they had the expertise and experience, many women teachers did not have the economic resources that must have been available to Mrs. Goodman or the Misses Winn when they arrived in the colony.

Upper Canada nonetheless provided some opportunity for young, educated, and often single women teachers who arrived with sufficient capital to open their own schools. On their arrival, some found positions as a resident governess in a good family. As the number of girls' schools grew, there was an increasing demand for qualified assistants and salaried teachers. And after 1830, some young women found work as a preceptress or teacher in one of the new coeducational academies of the colony.

V

In April 1829, four trustees of a privately endowed organization announced to the public their intention of opening a new Elementary and Classical School — Grantham Academy in St. Catharines. The substantial two-storey building for the "Academick Institute" was almost complete, and the trustees now solicited applications from qualified gentlemen ("graduates of some college or university") and the services of "a competent female teacher" with "respectable references or recommendations"[102] to assume responsibilities for teaching. Eventually, a Mr. William Lewis was appointed principal and a Miss Cornelia Converse was engaged to supervise the Ladies' Department.[103] Miss Converse taught at Grantham Academy for a year; then, without explanation, she was replaced by a Miss Anderson.[104] Miss Converse returned, however, in the fall of 1831, only to lose her position two-and-a-half years later when the school failed.[105]

As advertisements attest, the curriculum offered to young women enrolled at Grantham Academy reflected the ability and expertise of their teachers. Both Miss Converse and Miss Anderson appear to have taught at least some of the basic subjects — spelling, reading, writing, arithmetic, grammar, geography, and mapping. They also provided instruction in plain and fancy needlework. In the fall of 1831, Miss Converse was acclaimed for her ability "in the higher and more useful branches of female literature."[106] While she was in residence, students could enrol in chemistry and geology, and probably history and natural philosophy. Miss Anderson's abilities were more "traditional." Considered "a young lady of ability and experience," during her tenure at the school she oversaw "the different branches which are usually taught in Female Institutions" and, particularly, gave instruction in "Musick, Drawing and Ornamental Needlework."[107]

Grantham Academy was the first of a number of coeducational private-venture day and boarding schools established in the colony in the 1830s. A professional woman teacher might find employment in the Commercial and Classical Academy[108] founded in 1833 in York, the Bay Street Academy, a day school begun by Mr. Boyd,[109] or "The Toronto Academy" established in 1837 by Mr. Scanlon.[110] All these schools maintained separate "Ladies Departments" supervised by "a Governess" or, as in the case of the Toronto Academy, the founder's wife, Mrs. Scanlon. Potential patrons were assured that the women teachers were "of unquestionable ability and respectability," and their daughters would be taught needlework and other appropriate subjects in a "separate and spacious apartment."[111]

Women willing to move out of the York area could also apply to Upper Canada Academy, a coeducational boarding school in Cobourg.[112] Sponsored and financially underwritten by donations from the Methodist Church, the Upper Canada Academy opened its doors to boarders in 1833. The school was officially non-denominational;[113] it did dedicate itself, however, to promoting "the health, morals, comfort and instruction of the children committed to its care," under a "parental government." To ensure that the students were truly regarded as "members of the same family," a preacher and his wife catered to their daily comforts. Masters and mistresses, whose duties were apparently restricted to teaching, superintended the students' education.[114] The founders of Upper Canada Academy fully accepted the belief that girls needed special and separate education. From the beginning, "young ladies from the country"[115] were afforded "Gentile accommodation," and throughout the term, "parts of the building and premises [were] assigned exclusively to the young ladies."[116] "The course of instruction prescribed for young ladies" enrolled at the Academy was, a notice explained in 1840, "as complete in all the solid and ornamental branches of female education as any in America."[117] And parents were assured in 1837 that "the young ladies were constantly under the supervision of the Preceptress" and a considerable part of their evening was spent "in the presence of an efficient monitress . . . preparing their lessons for the following day."[118]

Being a teacher at a large school in Upper Canada was considerably different from owning and operating one's own school. Miss Anderson, Miss Converse, and others in their position received a specific wage for their work, remuneration which was negotiated and did not depend on their ability to attract students or manage a business. At the same time, women hired as teachers had little independence or authority. The initial advertisement soliciting students for Grantham Academy noted that "the Female Department is visited daily by the Principal" and young ladies would be taught some "of the branches" of their education by masters.[119] Miss Converse, Miss Anderson, and others who taught for wages were undoubtedly also subject to close scrutiny in their private lives. Only women of proven and clearly evident decorum and ability could be entrusted with the care of patrons' daughters. Many of the single women who taught at one of the new coeducational schools or at one of the larger ladies' academies undoubtedly expected to marry and leave the paid work-force. Others, like Mrs. Barnes, who taught at Upper Canada Academy in 1840 and 1841, had ambitions to open their own schools and gain greater freedom of action.[120]

VI

Mrs. Tyler and her husband would have been hard-pressed to compete in the academic world of post-1815 Upper Canada. Indeed, to many colonial parents in the 1830s, Mrs. Tyler's school would have appeared hopelessly old-fashioned. Within two generations, middle-class Upper Canadians had embraced specialized education for women. It was accepted that literacy, the "domestic arts," and mastery of at least some of the accomplishments were absolutely necessary for future wives and mothers of the middle and upper classes. It is somewhat ironic that at a time when society was placing increasing importance on the cult of domesticity and prescribed that "true" women restrict their activities to the private sphere of the home, middle-class parents increasingly relied on wage-earning women to transmit these values and skills to their daughters. While continuing to perform essentially "women's" work, these wage-earners or individual proprietors provided a very strong, though often elastic, link between the public and the private worlds of Upper Canadians. Yet lady teachers were themselves often products of these new social values, and most accepted its dictates. They jealously guarded their status as gentlewomen, and carefully restricted their work and their classrooms within the domestic, private realm of home and family.

Nonetheless, a number of women teachers were implicitly challenging the basic rubric about a woman's relationship to paid labour. Many women teachers undoubtedly did expect to teach only until their financial circumstances improved. Most young women teachers did undoubtedly marry and leave the job market. Widowed women and their friends and daughters may too have hoped to remarry or to realize their husband's assets and thus regain the privacy of their homes and the rhythms of apparent leisure. A few women schoolmistresses undoubtedly found, however, that teaching provided more than a short-term solution to their financial problems. For widowed women, in particular, it offered the possibility of financial independence and personal satisfaction. And some, like Mrs. Cockburn, Miss Purcell, and the Misses McCords, imperceptively moved from the status of the "amateur" teacher to that of a professional. Though supporting and in some cases embracing in their work the "dictates of domesticity," they also seemed unwilling to give up that independence that came with working for wages.

NOTES

Short Forms:

Brockville Recorder	BR
Christian Guardian	CG
Cobourg Star	CS
Colonial Advocate	CA
Farmers' Journal	FJ
Kingston Chronicle	KC
Kingston Gazette	KGaz
Niagara Gleaner	NG
Upper Canada Gazette	UCG
Upper Canada Herald	UCH

1. *KC*, 19 Nov. 1824; *UCG*, 14 Oct. 1824; *NG*, 6 Nov. 1824; *UCH*, 22 Feb. 1825. A similar notice appeared two years earlier in the *KC*, 4 Jan. 1822.
2. See, for example, Laura Ulrich, *Good Wives: Image and Reality in Lives of Women in Northern New England, 1650–1750* (New York: Random House, 1991); Nancy Cott, *The Bonds of Womanhood* (New York: Yale University Press, 1987), 105–23; Linda Kerber, *Women of the Republic* (New York: Oxford University Press, 1989), 204; M. Jeanne Peterson, *Family, Love and Work in the Lives of Victorian Gentlewomen* (Bloomington, Ind.: Indiana University Press, 1989), 123. Philip W. Gardner notes in *The Lost Elementary Schools of Victorian England* (London: Croom Helm, 1984) that teaching "offered a source of independent remunerative employment for the woman who was progressively denied an outlet for her labour other than through its complete constriction into 'housework'" (111). For Canadian examples, see *Women Who Taught*, ed. Alison Prentice and Marjorie Theobald (Toronto: University of Toronto Press, 1991); *Gender and Education in Ontario,*

ed. Ruby Heap and Alison Prentice (Toronto: Canadian Scholar's Press, 1991); R.D. Gidney and W.P.J. Millar, *Inventing Secondary Education* (Kingston: McGill-Queen's University Press, 1990); Susan Houston and Alison Prentice, *Schooling and Scholars in Nineteenth-Century Ontario* (Toronto: University of Toronto Press, 1988).

3. Joyce Senders Pedersen, "Schoolmistresses and Headmistresses: Elites and Education in Nineteenth Century England," in *Women Who Taught*, ed. Prentice and Theobald, 39. Pedersen asserts that there were relatively sharp distinctions between these two groups of teachers. This paper suggests that this was not always the case.

4. The use of the term "professional" is quite deliberate. Though there was no "professional" training available to women during this period, many women who taught in the colony did have specific expertise and experience in the classroom. Within the context of the early nineteenth century, they considered themselves professional teachers.

5. Alison Prentice, "From Household to School House: The Emergence of the Teacher as Servant of the State," in *Gender and Education in Ontario*, ed. Heap and Prentice, 43.

6. *FJ*, 15 Dec. 1827.

7. Barbara Welter, "The Cult of True Womanhood," *American Quarterly* 18 (1968): 151–74. See also Cott, *The Bonds of Womanhood*; Leonore Davidoff, *The Best Circles: Social Etiquette and the Season* (London: Croom Helm, 1973); Peterson, *Family, Love and Work*; Deborah Gorham, *The Victorian Girl and the Feminine Ideal* (London: Croom Helm, 1982).

8. *KGaz*, 12 May 1812. This view was also reflected ibid., "Letter to the Reckoner," 16 Apr. 1811; *Gore Gazette*, 17 Nov. 1827. For further discussion of this, see Jane Errington, " 'Hidden' Women in Early Upper Canada: A Preliminary Probe," paper presented at the annual meeting of the Canadian Historical Association, 1988.

9. *UCG*, 25 Nov. 1797.

10. *KGaz*, "Letter to the Reckoner," 12 May 1812. For a discussion of how this attitude came to affect the medical profession and others throughout the nineteenth century see Barbara Maas, *Helpmate of Man: Middle Class Woman and Gender Ideology in Nineteenth Century Ontario* (Bochum: Universitätsverlag Dr. N. Brockmeyer, 1990), 46–56; Wendy Mitchinson, *The Nature of Their Bodies: Women and Their Doctors in Victorian Canada* (Toronto: University of Toronto Press, 1991).

11. *KGaz*, 18 Feb. 1812. See also ibid., 16 Apr. 1811; *UCG*, 23 Aug. 1828; *FJ*, "Respect for Females," 14 Mar. 1827.

12. *UCG*, 25 Nov. 1797.

13. *KGaz*, 3 Dec. 1811. The domestic arts were important, for among other things, they taught a girl the advantages of hard work and discipline; and as one matron noted, they prevented the nation's daughters "from forming improper attachments" as youths. See also *UCG*, 19 Oct. 1805.

14. Leonore Davidoff and Catherine Hall, *Family Fortunes: Men and Women of the English Middle Class, 1780–1850* (Chicago: University of Chicago Press, 1987), 74. Note that in Great Britain, an emerging middle class was beginning to assert a life-style and social and moral values which placed considerable emphasis on the family and the importance of women in providing "proper moral order in the amoral world of the market." This rests on the assumption that "identity is gendered" (29) and their chronicle of how middle-class women became both creators and the "bearers of status" (30). For a discussion of this as it pertains to a number of middle-class immigrant women in the nineteenth century, see Maas, *Helpmate of Man*. Maas discusses the issue of "cultural transference" of such an ideology particularly from Great Britain to Upper Canada (41–45).

15. *KGaz*, 3 Dec. 1811. See also ibid., 18 Aug. 1812; *FJ*, 26 Sept. 1827; *UCG*, 3 Aug. 1805.

16. *KGaz*, "From the Desk of Poor Robert the Scribe," 18 Aug. 1812.

17. *FJ*, "Of Female Education," 9 Apr. 1828.

18. *UCG*, "Of Female Education," 25 Nov. 1797; see also *FJ*, "The Female Character," 9 Apr. 1828; *KC*, "Why Should Females Have a Good Education," 14 Sept. 1833.

19. *FJ*, "The Female Character," 9 Apr. 1828; see also *KGaz*, "Desk of Poor Robert the Scribe," 18 Aug. 1812.

20. *FJ*, "A Woman Teacher's Address to Her Pupils," 16 Dec. 1829. See also "On the Education of Young Ladies," 26 Sept. 1827; *CG*, "From Brief Hints to Parents on the Subject of Education," 5 Feb. 1831; "Influence of Education by a Young Lady," 13 Mar. 1830; *FJ*, "The Female Character," 9 Apr. 1828. An article in the *KC*, 9 Apr. 1836, noted specifically the importance of educated women as mothers. See also *CA*, "Female Education," 28 May 1828; "Ladies Department," 22 Oct. 1831.

21. Anne Powell to George Murray, 9 July 1816, quoted in Katherine McKenna, "The Life of Anne Murray Powell, 1755–1849" (Ph.D. diss., Queen's University, 1987), 336.

22. *Niagara Herald*, 13 Feb. 1802.

23. Ibid.

24. *KC*, 10 May 1817.

25. *UCG*, 19 June 1817. After Mr. Roberts' death in 1819, Mrs. Roberts continued to teach: *Niagara Spectator*, 2 Mar. 1820. See also schools run by Mrs. MacIntosh, who started an academy with the Reverend R. Fletcher in Ernestown, *KC*, 8 Oct. 1818; Mr. and Mrs. Andrews, who opened a school in York, *UCG*, 9 Apr. 1824; and Mrs. Spilsbury, who opened a school "under the conduct of Mr. Leech" at Colborne, *CS*, 31 May 1831.

26. *CG*, 10 Oct. 1832; see also ibid., 23 Jan. 1833. The same seems to have been true of the Pringles.

27. *KC*, 8 Sept. 1826. The same may also have been the case for the Roberts.

28. *BR*, 11 Apr. 1833.

29. *Hallowell Free Press*, 30 June 1834. See also advertisements in *KGaz*, 22 Sept. 1818; *The Patriot*, 31 Mar. 1835, 30 May 1837.

30. This was specifically referred to in the case of the Tylers and Maitlands. *Gore Gazette*, 10 Oct. 1832. See also advertisement of W. Ward, *CG* 28 Mar. 1831, which noted that his wife would teach needlework.

31. Gidney and Millar, *Inventing*, 65–66. For a more detailed examination of the ephemeral nature of Upper Canadian schools, see Gidney and Millar, "From Voluntarism to State Schooling: The Creation of the Public School System in Ontario," *Canadian Historical Review* LXVI, 4 (1985): 443–73. Houston and Prentice, *Schooling and Scholars*, quite rightly question Gidney and Millar's conclusion (67–68). Given the nature of the Upper Canadian economy and of those women who taught, it is very likely that many did not advertise in local newspapers, but rather relied on word of mouth and their reputation within the community to gain pupils.

32. *CA*, 23 Sept. 1830. Mrs. Crombie and her daughters could depend, to some degree at least, on Mr. Crombie, schoolmaster of a local district school: *The Patriot*, 3 Jan. 1840.

33. The women who ran French schools included Mrs. Goodman, *UCG*, 24 Dec. 1818; Mrs. Harris, *United Empire Loyalist*, 9 Sept. 1826; Mrs. Kingman, *Niagara Spectator*, 29 Jan. 1819; Miss Merrill, *KGaz*, 3 Aug. 1816. E. Jennifer Monaghan notes in "Literacy Instruction and Gender in Colonial New England," *American Quarterly* 40, 1 (1988): 18–41, that in the early colonial period, women taught reading and men taught penmanship. "Writing," she notes, "was considered a craft" and "writing was largely a male domain" (24). Similar attitudes appear to have prevailed in Upper Canada 150 years later.

34. *UCG*, 9 Sept. 1826; *United Empire Loyalist*, 30 Aug. 1828.

35. Madam Harris, like many dancing masters, was also engaged to teach dancing at one of the local ladies' academies, Misses Purcell and Rose. She appears to have been replaced by Mr. Whale: *CA*, 10 Dec. 1829.

36. Madam Walther, *The Patriot*, 29 July 1836; Mrs. Butler, *NG*, 5 Oct. 1833; Miss Taylor, *CS*, 29 Oct. 1834; Miss Williams, *BR*, 28 June 1833; Mrs. Bickerton (also landscape painting), *KC*, 24 May 1834; an anonymous lady from England, *The Patriot*, 8 Dec.

1840, 22 May 1838. There were about a dozen schools run by men in the province, some of which, like Mr. Hill's "A Young Ladies Singing School," *KGaz*, 21 Dec. 1816, taught both boys and girls, or like Mr. Colton's, had a female assistant, *KC*, 5 July 1834.

37. McKenna notes in "The Life of Anne Murray Powell" that though Anne Powell senior was pleased that her daughter, Anne, took an active part in educating her nieces (423), William Dummer Powell refused to permit his daughter to establish a school of her own. Apparently, he claimed that she was not sufficiently educated to be a schoolteacher, and suggested that teaching was not suited to a woman of her status (432–33). See also Marjorie R. Theobald, "The Sin of Laura: A Pre-History of Women's Tertiary Education in Colonial Melbourne," *Journal of the Canadian Historical Association* 1 (1990): 257–72. One group of women did display such skills publicly: actors and performers on the Upper Canadian stage. Colonial attitudes to these women varied considerably. Most, however, believed that no self-respecting "lady" engaged in such activity.

38. Gidney and Millar, *Inventing*, 1, 19–20. They note that coeducation posed moral dangers as well as problems with the curriculum. Boys and girls needed different training and were expected to be taught separately. See also Houston and Prentice, *Schooling and Scholars*.

39. *UCG*, 11 Aug. 1827. See also advertisement of Mrs. Scott of Colborne, who opened an "infant school" for children between the ages of 2½ and 7, *CS*, 9 July 1834. Misses Savigny of Toronto offered to teach young ladies until the age of 12: *The Patriot*, 13 Nov. 1840.

40. *The Patriot*, 10 Nov. 1835.

41. See Gardner, *The Lost Elementary Schools*; J.H. Higginson, "Dame Schools," *British Journal of Educational Studies* 22, 2 (1974); Houston and Prentice, *Schooling and Scholars*, 33–35; Monaghan, "Literacy Instruction and Gender in Colonial New England."

42. *Brockville Gazette*, 27 Oct. 1831.

43. The Paris Female Seminary, *CG*, 7 Oct. 1840.

44. Both Houston and Prentice, *Schooling and Scholars*, and Gidney and Millar, *Inventing*, note the difficulty of obtaining textbooks in Upper Canada at the time.

45. See, for example, Prentice, "From Household to School House," 25–50.

46. From notice of Mrs. Fraser's school, *The Patriot*, 4 Sept. 1835.

47. Marjorie Theobald, "Mere Accomplishments? Melbourne's Early Ladies' Schools Reconsidered," in *Women Who Taught*, ed. Prentice and Theobald, 73.

48. Ibid. See also Theobald, "The Sin of Laura"; Gidney and Millar, *Inventing*, 13–19; Houston and Prentice, *Schooling and Scholars*, 77–79.

49. A cursory search of the local newspapers between 1815 and 1835 indicates that two dozen schools were opened by women on their own.

50. See, among others, the Misses Skirvings, *The Patriot*, 22, Sept. 1840; Miss Parsons, *KC*, 9 June 1832; Miss Farrand, who ran the Brockville Seminary, *Brockville Gazette*, 27 Oct. 1831; Miss Greenland, *KC*, 10 June 1825; Miss Dennison, *KC*, 14 Mar. 1833.

51. See, for example, Mrs. Hill's School in Kingston, *KGaz*, 22 Sept. 1818.

52. Miss R.A. Charlton, who ran the Paris Female Seminary, *CG*, 7 Oct. 1840. In addition to the previous references, see also Miss Currier, in Peterborough, *CS*, 13 Nov. 1833; Miss Crombie, *The Patriot*, 11 Aug. 1840; Mrs. Hamilton, *The Patriot*, 7 Jan. 1840; Miss Mary McNeighton, *British Whig*, 10 Jan. 1834; Miss Leah, in Kingston, *KC*, 17 Aug. 1833; Misses Kile, *BR*, 18 Oct. 1832; Mrs. Haines, *KC*, 25 July 1835; Mrs. Black, *FJ*, 12 Aug. 1829.

53. See, for example, Mrs. Acland of Perth, *BR*, 9 June 1831; Mrs. Scott of Sandwich, *Canadian Emigrant*, 29 Nov. 1834.

54. Miss Mossier, *NG*, 9 Mar. 1833; Mrs. Fraser, *The Patriot*, 16 Aug. 1836; Mrs. Scott, *Canadian Emigrant*, 27 Dec. 1834; Miss Acland, *BR*, 9 Jan. 1831. Even at the Upper Canada Academy, students were expected to bring linen and towels: *CG*, 29 Aug. 1838.

55. See, for example, Mrs. Haines of Kingston, who was assisted by Mrs. and Miss Johnson in 1818, *KGaz*, 15 Sept. 1815; Mrs. O'Brien's school had an assistant, in Prescott: *NG*, 21 Jan. 1831. Mrs. Roy and Mrs. Driscoll jointly announced the opening of their school in Toronto in 1839: *The Patriot*, 11 Jan. 1839.

56. Mrs. Wynne certainly had servants: *The Patriot*, 27 June 1834. Family operations were not guaranteed success. Mrs. Horton Scott and her daughters started a Young Ladies' Institute in 1834, offering young ladies "a finished education": *Canadian Freeman*, 29 Nov. 1834. Though Mrs. Scott employed "the most approved teachers" and offered a wide variety of subjects, within three months the Scotts were forced to lower their fees "on the advice of friends": *Canadian Emigrant*, 13 Dec. 1834. And there is no mention of the school in the local press after 1835: *Canadian Emigrant*, 28 Mar. 1835.

57. *UCG*, 13 Aug. 1829. See also announcement of Mrs. Bullock, *CS*, 18 Dec. 1833. School of Mrs. Marshall and Mrs. Davidson, *CS*, 6 Aug. 1834. Specific mention of this was also made by Mrs. Holland, 7 Jan. 1831; Mrs. Gibson, *Hallowell Free Press*, 14 Apr. 1834.

58. *CS*, 6 Aug. 1834. The Montjoy School, *Hallowell Free Press*, 9 Oct. 1832, took only fifteen students. See also advertisement of Mrs. Black, *UCG*, 13 Aug. 1829.

59. *The Patriot*, 16 Aug. 1836; similar sentiments were expressed by Mrs. Acland of Perth, *BR*, 1 Sept. 1831; and Mrs. Hamilton, *The Patriot*, 7 Jan. 1840.

60. *KC*, 25 Feb. 1820.

61. *CS*, 20 July 1834. The importance of location was also emphasized by Miss Savigny, *The Patriot*, 13 Nov. 1840; Mrs. Bickerton, *Hallowell Free Press*, 8 Nov. 1831; Mrs. Marshall and Miss Davidson, *CS*, 6 Aug. 1834.

62. *KC*, 18 Mar. 1825.

63. She noted that in Britain she had taught at "the principal school in the City of Limerick and afterwards one at Ambleside": *The Patriot*, 7 Jan. 1840.

64. *Hallowell Free Press*, 1 Nov. 1831.

65. *KC*, 26 July 1834 to at least 9 Apr. 1836.

66. *CG*, 30 Nov. 1836.

67. See also reference of Mrs. Croan of York, *CA*, 2 Apr. 1829 to 6 Jan. 1831; Mrs. Nash, who had previously been at the Central School of London, *British American Journal*, 13 May 1834; Mrs. Brega, whose mother, who helped her in the school, had previous experience: *CG*, 15 Oct. 1834.

68. Few women explicitly made a point of their nationality, though advertisements of a number of them included that they were "recently arrived from England" or were "British." Whether colonial parents preferred teachers from Britain over those of the United States, or those of a particular religious denomination, needs to be explored further. As Houston and Prentice note, the question of "loyalty" often arose with respect to male teachers, *Schooling and Scholars*, 41, 52, 63. See also Jane Errington, *The Lion, the Eagle and Upper Canada* (Kingston: McGill-Queen's University Press, 1987), 53, concerning the Bidwell affair in 1811. Yet throughout the first half of the century, Upper Canadian parents of some means also sent their sons and daughters south to the new republic to go to school.

69. *The Patriot*, 2 Jan. 1838.

70. *British American Journal*, 13 May 1834. Other women also stressed their system of education. See also Mrs. Weatherstone, *KC*, 26 July 1834; Mrs. Bickerton, *Hallowell Free Press*, 1 Nov. 1831; the Streets, *CS*, 2 Jan. 1833; Mrs. Butler, *NG*, 17 Aug. 1833.

71. Mrs. Weatherstone and her sister "just in from England" ran a school for girls in Kingston for at least two years in the mid-1830s: *KC*, 26 Jan. 1834.

72. See, for example, James Hammerton, *Emigrant Gentlewomen: Genteel Poverty and Female Emigration 1830–1914* (Canberra: Australian National University Press, 1979); Theobald, "The Sin of Laura" and "Mere Accomplishments?"; Houston and Prentice, *Schooling and Scholars*, note that private-venture schools were "ephemeral" at best, and the income of

their proprietors was precarious (65). The same was true of the joint-venture schools (66–69). Yet, as they note, even in the early period there were a few women who managed to prosper.

73. *UCG*, 4 Sept. 1817.
74. Gidney and Millar, *Inventing*, 48. See also McKenna, "Anne Powell," 58.
75. *UCG*, 20 Jan. 1820.
76. For example, Mr. Tobias, ibid., 30 Mar. 1820.
77. Ibid., 30 May 1822.
78. Gidney and Millar, *Inventing*, 28.
79. *The Patriot*, 21 July 1835.
80. Ibid., 23 Aug. 1836.
81. *UCG*, 26 Aug. 1826.
82. Madam Harris arrived to teach French: ibid., 30 Aug. 1828. A music master was engaged: *CA*, 12 Aug. 1830.
83. *UCG*, 11 June 1829.
84. *Canadian Freeman*, 5 Sept. 1833. The last announcement for Mrs. Beynon appeared in July 1834.
85. *CA*, 14 July 1831.
86. *CG*, 16 June 1831.
87. Ibid., 12 Aug. 1835. It should be noted that in 1840 there was a notice in *The Patriot*, 25 Aug. 1840, to re-open the school.
88. *The Patriot*, 10 June 1834.
89. Ibid., 29 Dec. 1840.
90. School opening, *KC*, 27 Aug. 1831; an announcement by brother, *CS*, 4 Oct. 1831.
91. *FJ*, 18 Mar. 1829.
92. Ibid., 6 May 1829.
93. *CG*, 27 Feb. 1833.
94. Announcements of examinations appeared in the *Niagara Herald*, 21 Jan. 1830; *NG*, 17 Dec. 1831. In 1831, 12 Feb., a Miss Fraser was hired as an assistant.
95. *NG*, 17 Aug. 1833.
96. Ibid., 23 May 1835.
97. Ibid., 28 June 1823.
98. Ibid., 3 July 1823.
99. *Brockville Gazette*, 17 July 1829.
100. Ibid., 24 July 1829. The Miss Radcliffe in Brockville was accompanied by her brother or father, who was teaching at the boys' high school: *KC*, 8 Aug. 1829, 9 Jan. 1830; *Brockville Gazette*, 24 July 1829.
101. *CS*, 24 May 1831.
102. *FJ*, 1 Apr. 1829.
103. Ibid., 5 Aug. 1829. It was also noted at this time that boarding would be arranged with families in the area.
104. Ibid., 11 Nov. 1830; 3 Jan. 1831.
105. Ibid., 16 Nov. 1831. For a time, it appears the school was financially solvent and thus the salary of its teachers assured. On 20 May 1834, the *British American Journal* announced, however, that Grantham Academy was forced to close, due to overwhelming financial difficulties. After failing to obtain a grant from the provincial government, trustees were forced in August to auction off the school building and pay off their creditors: *The Patriot*, 5 Aug. 1834; see also *British American Journal*, 5 Aug. 1834. The various public notices about the College suggest there were more than financial difficulties. In its first four years, there were four different principals and a number of male assistants. The school was revived, largely due to the efforts of William Merritt. In the 1840s, it became the St. Catharines Grammar School. See Gidney and Millar, *Inventing*, 23, 70–71.

106. *CG*, 1 Oct. 1831.
107. *FJ*, 3 Jan. 1831, 10 Nov. 1830.
108. A notice in the *CG* informed residents of York that eighty students were already enrolled, 14 Aug. 1833. For certainly the next three years, young men and women took a variety of classical and standard subjects from "qualified masters and mistresses."
109. Notice of its first public examination, *The Patriot*, 30 Aug. 1833; notice of other examinations appeared 30 Dec. 1834, 5 Jan. 1836.
110. Ibid., 14 Nov. 1837.
111. *CG*, "Concerning the Commercial and Classical School," 14 Aug. 1833. See also *CA*, 15 Aug. 1833.
112. *CG*, 20 June 1832. See Marion Royce, "Methodism and Education of Women in Nineteenth Century Ontario," *Atlantis* 3:2, Pt 1 (Spring 1978): 131–43.
113. *CG*, 29 Sept. 1830.
114. Ibid., 31 July 1839.
115. Ibid., 7 Aug. 1833.
116. Ibid., 6 May 1840.
117. Ibid., 23 Sept. 1840.
118. Ibid., 27 Dec. 1837. It was also noted that it was automatic grounds for expulsion if male students entered the girls' section of the school.
119. *FJ*, 1 Apr. 1829. Notice of annual examination, "Communications," *British Colonial Argus*, 6 Aug. 1833.
120. It was noted that Miss Barnes taught at the school: *CG*, 19 Feb. and 29 Apr. 1840. She opened her own school with Mrs. Van Norman in 1842: ibid., 4 May 1842.

EIGHT

Creating the Ideal Man: Middle-Class Women's Constructions of Masculinity in Nova Scotia, 1840–1880

JANET GUILDFORD

Middle-class women in 19th-century Nova Scotia, like their counterparts in the United States and Britain, were prolific writers. Much of what they wrote was private: letters to friends and family, or diaries written to record their daily lives and their personal spiritual journeys. Some women also wrote novels, stories, poetry, history and social and political commentary for publication. Feminist historians have established the importance of both private and published sources in understanding

Source: "Creating the Ideal Man: Middle-Class Women's Constructions of Masculinity in Nova Scotia, 1840–1880," *Acadiensis*, 14, 2 (Spring 1995): 5–23. Reprinted by permission.

the gendered dimensions of middle-class culture and identity.[1] From 19th-century women's writing we have been able to learn a great deal about how women understood themselves, their work, their sense of time and place, and their relationships with other women.[2] But their writing is also a rich source of women's ideas about men, manliness and the relationships between men and women. In fact, a study of women's writing offers an important alternative viewpoint on the history of masculinity, which has too often relied on studies of men in isolation from women, rather than in relation to them.[3]

A study of middle-class women's writing about masculinity helps us to understand more fully the process of middle-class formation. Their writing not only delineated the contours of difference between men and women, but also drew boundaries around the white Anglo-American middle class, fostering a class identity shared by both men and women. The exclusion of men who failed to conform to middle-class gender ideals, whether on the basis of their attitudes towards women or towards the monogamous heterosexual patriarchal family, is a recurrent theme.

Their writing also allows us to address a central tension in the relationship between middle-class men and women in the 19th-century, a tension fraught with considerable potential for danger to women. Middle-class women's financial, social and political status was highly dependent on the power and success of the men in their lives, while their status in the family and their safety and that of their children were dependent on the restraint of male power at home. The ideal men created by middle-class Nova Scotian women writers attempted to balance these concerns. Their ideal men were powerful and successful in the public spheres of the market and politics, but they were compassionate and companionable at home.

Through their writing, women subtly subverted and reshaped male cultural values while also reflecting them. The public and private writing of mid-19th-century middle-class Nova Scotian women both represented and constructed ideas about the proper relationship between men and women and about what they regarded as the nature of manliness. The interplay between representation and construction is complex. These women were strongly influenced by the prevailing gender ideals of their society, and by the social and literary conventions which regulated women's writing. But as they wrote to and about men they were also actively creating and modifying middle-class gender ideology.[4] Women raised sons, influenced brothers, friends, lovers and husbands, and used the power at their disposal to shape and control male behaviour in a variety of ways.

Catherine Hall, writing about English ideals of manliness, argues that the core of middle-class masculine identity was "the notion of individual integrity, freedom from subjection to the will of another."[5] She compares the lack or loss of individual autonomy to emasculation.[6] Around that central core value, however, different traits and behaviours received more or less emphasis and appreciation, and competing and overlapping versions of middle-class manliness emerged. Anthony Rotundo, in his influential study of middle-class masculinity in the northern United States, developed a chronological model of three overlapping masculine ideals.[7] His approach is a useful one because it helps to explain how and why different groups of people within the middle class might emphasize particular elements as most important in defining masculinity, and addresses the question of change over time. There is, moreover, considerable resonance between his masculine ideals and those present in the writing of Nova Scotian women and men.

Rotundo's first ideal type, the "masculine achiever," emerged in the first half of the 19th-century and was strongly shaped by economic forms. The "masculine achiever" regarded himself as active and dynamic, hard working and persistent, and he believed he should restrain his tender feelings. This ideal encouraged independence of thought and action, the core value identified by Hall.[8] Rotundo's second ideal, the "Christian gentleman," emerged after mid-century in opposition to the masculine achiever. Influenced by Evangelical Christianity, it stressed love and compassion as central male values. But the "Christian gentleman" ideal also stressed hard work and impulse control, although it discouraged excessive personal ambition and greed.[9] The areas of overlap between the "masculine achiever" and the "Christian gentleman" were substantial, and, in both, independence of thought and action retained a central place. As Catherine Hall argues, the middle-class masculine identity that emerged in Britain in the early 19th-century was located "within a rich discursive formation linking Evangelical religion, romanticism and political economy."[10]

Rotundo's third ideal, the "masculine primitive," was not part of the ideal of masculinity envisioned by any of the middle-class women writers. The "masculine primitive" emerged in the third quarter of the 19th-century, and was defined by a belief in the Darwinian notion that "all males shared primordial instincts for survival."[11] Support for the idea that physical prowess constituted a part of the middle-class masculine identity had emerged by mid-century, as evidenced by the proliferation of gymnasiums in cities like Halifax. Reflecting this ideal, P.S. Hamilton, a Nova Scotian lawyer and journalist, described himself at 35.

> I stand just under 5'11" and have been called symmetrically proportioned. I girth 42" naked around the upper part of my chest, tapering to 30" around the waist . . . I am now considered one of the first, if not the very first, in feats both of agility and strength in the Halifax gymnasium; and I understand that I have the reputation of being the best woodsman and best boxer in Halifax.[12]

It can certainly be argued that the fact that women did not idealize the "masculine primitive" reflected their ambivalence about male power and physical strength.

Although there was considerable overlap between men's and women's ideas about what constituted the ideal middle-class man, women's writing emphasized the manly qualities that were important to women in their domestic relationships, and often attributed to men values that were generally assigned to women by the gender codes of their society. Their ideal man perhaps owed most to Rotundo's "Christian gentleman," but it also contained elements of the "masculine achiever." The value placed on male tenderness and love in marriage, on male nurturance as fathers, and on men's admiration of nature and art suggests that women valued these qualities in their own lives, and wanted to promote a culture which reflected women's interests. While we must remember the class and racial specificity of the ideas about mid-19th-century women's culture developed by feminist historians in the United States such as Nancy Cott and Caroll Smith-Rosenberg and by Margaret Conrad in Atlantic Canada, the values of that culture were asserted with considerable confidence.[13] Women's confidence, nurtured by their relationships with other women and the institutions they created, was manifested in their efforts to encourage men to identify with feminine values.[14] At the same time, however, they also valued men who were successful in the public sphere of the market and politics, men who were powerful enough to support women in comfort, and to represent and protect their political interests.

Both men and women valued a harmonious domestic life. When we consider the value placed on a well-ordered domestic life by middle-class men in England and the United States, the difference between men's and women's constructions of masculinity can be understood as a difference in emphasis. John Tosh, in his study of English cleric and teacher Edward White Benson, provides compelling evidence that mid-19th-century middle-class men drew much of their male identity from their roles as husbands and fathers.[15] Like Edward Benson, Halifax lawyer and politician John S.D. Thompson was deeply concerned with his domestic life, and during his absences from home he wrote frequent letters to his wife, expressing his loneliness and his concern for the health and well-being of his wife and children.[16] Women's writing about men as fathers, husbands and lovers, as well as what they wrote about men in public life, was consonant with masculine ideals already familiar to their readers.

Women's advocacy of a masculine ideal that emphasized love, respect and trust towards women is well-represented in romantic fiction. Much romantic fiction, especially the didactic novels of manners so popular at mid-century, reads as thinly disguised advice on how to choose a husband, and it provides a useful starting point for exploring constructions of the ideal man.[17] These novels were shaped by literary conventions, but they were also works of imagination, and, as such, they provide insights into women's fantasies about ideal men in ways that are rarely so accessible in other forms of writing. As Stephen Kern suggests, "novels offered the most direct source of past ways of loving . . . [as they] render the social world and historical context of the relationships that sustain their plots."[18] They also offer sustained explorations of ideas about romantic love, which was increasingly regarded as the only right justification for middle-class marriage. Karen Lystra argues that "[r]omantic love was an intellectual and social force of premier significance in nineteenth-century America," but it was also very private.[19] Romantic fiction provides us with a public expression of ideas about it.

Choosing the right husband was a central theme in the fiction of Halifax writer Mary Eliza Herbert. As a member of a successful upwardly mobile family, Herbert had solid middle-class credentials. In addition to a literary career that included writing and publishing novels, stories and poems, and a brief stint in the early 1850s as the editor and publisher of a literary magazine, she was an active Methodist and life-long temperance advocate. She herself never married, perhaps reflecting the moral she promoted in her novels, that it was better not to marry than to marry the wrong man or for the wrong reasons.[20]

In her 1859 novel *Belinda Dalton, or Scenes in the Life of a Halifax Belle*, Herbert used an intimate late-night conversation between Belinda and her sisters as the setting for an explicit discussion of men and marriage.[21] Alice, the oldest sister, had spent the evening flirting with a foppish old bachelor, and she shocked her sisters by telling them that she would marry him if he proposed, because "a man with an income of several thousand pounds per annum is not to be despised . . . old and conceited though he be."[22] Belinda, who thought that Alice's attitude verged on the criminal, represented the correct attitude to marriage. Young, virtuous and beautiful, she had a number of suitors, and, with a little prodding from Alice, she explained why each, in turn, failed to meet her exacting standards of manliness.

William Eddington had "youth, health and good looks in his favor," but he was an egotist.

The subject of his conversation, from morning to night, is ever the same. You are continually hearing of his wonderful achievements, the dangers he has experienced, of his fearlessness and courage, and the commendations he has received for the performance of various feats. A miserable woman indeed, his wife will be, continually obliged to hear of his amiable disposition, but never beholding a proof of it.[23]

Even worse, he lacked charity, the cardinal sin in Herbert's lexicon. Belinda had seen him, just the day before, peremptorily turn away a poor woman with a baby in her arms. Edward Oliver had faults of a different kind. He was too generous and had too little respect for himself. Because he did not have "the very nicest sense of honor," he failed Belinda's test of manly independence. Henry Palmer was "young, handsome, generous, yet prudent, exceedingly fascinating in manners, unexceptionable in morals," but Belinda condemned him as a social butterfly.

He is superficial, his learning, his accomplishments, all seem to float on the surface; his affections are evanescent; like the butterfly, he is continually roving from flower to flower; there is no wellspring of generous feeling, that gush irresistibly forth, keeping the heart pure from the defiling touch of fashionable life. He is the complete "man of the world"; sentiment is on his tongue, but it never awakes noble and lofty impulses in his heart.[24]

Finally her sister Lavinia offered the possibility of Captain Alfred Elton, a young man with a flashing eye and a curling lip, who had attended a party at their house. He had neither beauty nor riches, and he had held himself aloof from Belinda all evening. But Lavinia added a story told by her maid. Captain Elton's groom had recently broken his arm and would be unfit for work for several months. With a wife and six children to support, the groom was in despair. Captain Elton, although poor by the standards of the Daltons and their circle, paid his servant's medical bills and promised to pay his full wages until he recovered. Noting Belinda's response to this story, Alice teased "[h]ow flushed your cheeks are, you really appear feverish."[25] Belinda hurried off to bed.

Through the intimate and informal late-night conversation, Herbert offered her readers some advice for identifying an ideal man as well as the signs to look for in a bad one. Drawing on her readers' familiarity with the conventions of romantic fiction, she caused her beautiful and pious heroine to flush at the mention of the poor, surly, unattractive Alfred Elton. His flashing eyes and his aloofness would already have alerted readers that this was a man to watch. And within the genre of didactic domestic fiction, Alfred Elton's sacrificial generosity to his servant was an equally important sign that the reader was meeting a romantic hero. As we learn more about Captain Elton, we discover that compassion for the less fortunate was a central pillar of his character. His aloofness from the rich and beautiful Belinda was rooted in his abhorrence at the idea of sacrificing his manly independence on the altar of Belinda's father's wealth, and in the pain caused to his tender heart by an earlier rejection. His dark brooding stance barely concealed his capacity for compassion and for passionate heterosexual love.

Captain Alfred Elton captured Belinda Dalton's heart with his benevolence to his injured groom; he kept it with one act of compassion after another. Alfred and Belinda became partners in philanthropy when they set out to rescue Belinda's impoverished, widowed school friend and her children. Alfred was deeply moved by the plight of the widow and children, and when he first encountered them in their freezing garret he had to turn his back to hide his tears. Herbert's ideal man experienced pain and heartache, especially empathetically. But he was restrained in his expression of emotion. Another male character in *Belinda Dalton* expressed the fear that his "emotions would unman" him.[26] It was manly to feel emotion, but unmanly to allow it to affect one's public performance.

Alfred Elton's compassion ultimately proved his undoing. He died after rescuing a drowning child who had fallen overboard during a transatlantic crossing. His tragic death may have served Herbert's plot, but to the modern reader it is curious and somewhat ironic. Belinda never recovered from the loss of Captain Elton; she mourned her dead hero alone for the rest of her life, and she never protested that her lover's reckless and sacrificial generosity was at the cost of her own happiness. Herbert's treatment of Elton's death supports an ideal of manliness in which a man's adherence to the dictates of his conscience was crucial, his relationship with his beloved secondary. As Hall has argued, personal autonomy is a central feature of middle-class masculinity.[27]

Herbert did, however, emphasize the importance of shared interests between lovers. Belinda and Alfred shared a love of nature. On a winter sleigh-ride Alfred listened with warmth to Belinda's praise of the beauty around her, and romantically suggested that the evergreen spruce she admired was an "emblem of constancy."[28] The association between women and nature was a powerful theme for members of the Victorian middle-class, and natural themes dominated the art, dress and decorations produced and consumed by women.[29] But Alfred's ready response reflected an enthusiasm for romanticism, with its natural themes, which was common to both men and women in the 19th-century English middle-class.[30]

A love of art and literature was another mark of Herbert's ideal man. Lawyer Levitt, the arch-villain in *Belinda Dalton*, was a selfish, cold-hearted, money-grabbing man, but we also know he fails to meet her ideal of masculinity because "the beauties of nature, the charms of poetry, and the exquisite delineations of the pencil, were objects to him, of contempt."[31] In Herbert's unpublished novel "Lucy Cameron," the heroine's dissatisfaction with her first husband was exacerbated by his disdain for art and literature; her second husband, Ralph Maynard, was devoted to literature. Of course we know that Ralph is an ideal man because during the years he and Lucy were separated by her marriage to the despicable Mr. Cameron he drowned his sorrows in helping the poor.[32]

The line Herbert drew between an appropriate emotional sensitivity to art and nature and a superficial effeminacy is a fine one, as Belinda Dalton's condemnation of Henry Palmer's flightiness and superficiality suggests. Her criticisms of all of her suitors, however, reflect a disdain for effeminacy and worldliness often present in bourgeois critiques of the aristocracy. Herbert's anti-aristocratic streak is pronounced, and her heroes and heroines all reflect the purity of heart, Christian piety and benevolent spirit which her character, Belinda Dalton, sought in a husband. In an earlier, serialized novel, "Emily Linwood, or The Promise of Bow," for example, Emily's suitor admires her simple purity and grace and rejects the rich and idle young women who clamour for his attention.[33] Anti-aristocratic sentiment is an important element in Herbert's middle-class consciousness, and her novels provide her with a vehicle for promoting it.

Herbert's emphasis on rational choice sits somewhat uncomfortably with Lystra's suggestion that love is a powerful and mysterious force which sweeps unsuspecting lovers away, sometimes against all reason.[34] But some of Herbert's characters do have a capacity for heterosexual passion. Ralph Maynard, the romantic hero of "Lucy Cameron," was haunted by his memories of Lucy with "an almost torturing intensity," and experienced rapture at their reunion.[35] "It was bliss for him to be near her" and he realized that he loved her "more deeply, more passionately, more madly than ever!"[36] Lucy responded to the meeting "with a flushed cheek and a throbbing heart."[37] The contrast with her first husband, Mr. Cameron, is clear, and underlined by the fact that Herbert does not even endow this character with the most basic prerequisite for intimacy, a first name. According to Mr. Cameron, "sensible" people did not believe in love or the "wild rhapsody of passion."[38]

The capacity for passionate love may have been a masculine ideal for some middle-class women in 19th-century Nova Scotia, but it was obviously not the only one women used in choosing a husband. The experience of two women who chose to marry Protestant ministers, one in 1823, the other in 1871, suggests the durability of other ideals. Shared religious faith, rather than romantic love, persuaded Eliza Chipman to marry a much older widower, with eight children, in 1823. "He is a beloved member of Christ and his Church, which is one particular inducement, as I always was opposed to believers and unbelievers being united."[39] Believing that God had called her to a life as a minister's wife, she was willing to take on the responsibility for eight children, one of whom opposed the marriage, and to ignore her preference for continuing to live at home with her family.[40] Romantic love also played little part in the decision of Truro teacher and missionary Mathilda Faulkner to marry George Churchill in 1871. She wrote:

> I must tell you of the great and abounding joy that has come to me this day. Mr. Churchill, who is under appointment to go to the foreign field, has written and asked me to accompany him as his companion and colabourer.[41]

It was not her enthusiasm for becoming George Churchill's wife that dominated her letter, but the opportunity to become a foreign missionary. Her ambition to be a foreign missionary had been "a burning desire" since her baptism at 14, and one which was denied to her as a single woman.[42] As was the case for Eliza Chipman's, Mathilda Churchill's husband remained a shadowy figure in her subsequent writing.[43]

Halifax writer Clotilda Jennings created a passionate love affair in her short story "The White Rose of Acadia." Although heterosexual passion is an important theme, the story's greatest value for the historian is in helping us to understand the construction of a British middle-class identity through its descriptions of ethnic difference.[44] Jennings, who often wrote under the pseudonym Alma Maude, was the daughter of dry goods merchant and municipal politician Joseph Jennings, and grew up on a comfortable suburban estate in north end Halifax. In the early 1850s she contributed poetry, and a feature called "Letters from Linden Hall," to Mary Jane Katzmann's *Provincial or Halifax Magazine*, and she continued to pursue a literary career throughout her life.[45] "The White Rose of Acadia" was written for the Industrial Exhibition of Nova Scotia and published in 1855.

Set in the Annapolis Valley in the mid-18th-century, against the backdrop of the deportation of the Acadians, "The White Rose of Acadia" is valuable for the light it sheds on the relationships among class, gender and ethnicity. The White Rose was Edith Leicester, a young English woman whose family had moved to the Gaspereaux

Valley in the early 1750s. Edith fell in love with Pierre Pontrincourt, a handsome young Acadian of noble French ancestry. The love between Edith and Pierre was as intense as any "grand passion claiming the world for its stage," but the lovers were about to become engulfed in the events leading to the deportation.[46] Jennings' portrayal of the Acadians is superficially a sympathetic one, but she did emphasize the cultural differences between French and English. The most significant difference for the plot is that Henri Pontrincourt, Pierre's father, did not trust women. That un-English and un-gentlemanly lack of trust eventually resulted in his son's death. Henri Pontrincourt sent his son on a military mission, and forbade Pierre to tell Edith why he was leaving. As a result, they were unable to reconcile before the deportation, and the night before his ship sailed Pierre slipped over the side, swam ashore, borrowed an Indian canoe, and paddled upriver to sooth Edith "with his hushed kisses . . . while she sobbed upon his breast."[47] Pierre was shot and killed by a British soldier on his return to the ship in the early morning, and Jennings clearly blamed Pierre's father for the tragedy.

Jennings' portrayal of the Acadians and their fate emphasized ethnic difference and contributed to the creation of a British middle-class Nova Scotian identity complete with deeply embedded gender codes. Jennings implied that Edith's lover Pierre could have become part of the new order, a citizen of the modern British society in Nova Scotia. But his father was a relic of the primitive past, with outdated ideas about women, ideas that cost his son's life. "The White Rose of Acadia" reflects both the romanticism of Longfellow's *Evangeline: A Tale of Acadia*, published in 1847, which presented the Acadians as a simple, devout and prosperous people, and the emerging Nova Scotian historiographical response that the deportation was justified because the Acadians were unable to compete with the more progressive and energetic race of Anglo-Americans.[48] Henri's "ungallant" view of women marked him not only as different, but as inferior. It was just this kind of difference in values among the Acadians that British Nova Scotians were using to build new justifications for their expulsion a century earlier. In Henri Pontrincourt's attitude towards women there is an implicit acknowledgement that the Acadians were fundamentally not like "us," and therefore the deportation had a moral justification.

Mary Jane Katzmann Lawson presented a similar view of the Acadians in "The Valley of the Gaspereaux," a poem she wrote in 1858. She wrote of the time when "Acadian peasants" lived in the Valley, "tilled the grassy sod" and "lifted . . . simple hearts to God."[49] Lawson published a substantial body of poetry and history in local periodicals, including *The Provincial or Halifax Monthly Magazine*, which she herself edited in the early 1850s, and much of it contributed to the construction of British middle-class masculine identity.[50] She wrote tributes to Lord Nelson, to Queen Victoria and her son, the Prince of Wales, on his 1860 visit to Halifax, to English novelist Anthony Trollope, and to Gordon at Khartoum.[51] But she is probably best remembered for her *History of the Townships of Dartmouth, Preston and Lawrencetown: Halifax County, N.S.*, which won the Nova Scotia Historical Society's Akins Prize.[52] In her chapter on Preston she discussed the immigration of African Nova Scotians, characterizing them as a "most unsatisfactory class of emigrants."[53]

Lawson's portrayal of the officers in the Maroon militia unit provides a compelling example of her racist assumption that African Nova Scotian men did not meet the standards of middle-class masculinity.[54] Although her poetry evinced an enthusiasm for imperial military men and their heroism, she characterized the Maroon officers as "vain and ambitious to be regarded as great men."[55] She wrote:

> When in the spring of 1799, Captain Solomon . . . daily mounted guard to keep in check the insubordinate Maroons, [Maroon militia officers] Montagu and Smith always appeared in blue and scarlet uniforms with high cocked-hats and gold lace, and in every way endeavored to personate the appearance and authority of the British officer.[56]

Of course, Smith and Montague were serving as British officers, but for Lawson their race disqualified them from inclusion in her version of middle-class manliness. Lawson also excluded these officers because of their failure to adhere to middle-class ideals of monogamous marriage. Thus, her tone was satiric and derogatory when she wrote that "Major Smith was the happy possessor of four wives."[57] The writing of both Jennings and Katzmann illustrates the role of Nova Scotian women in creating middle-class ideology and the need to be attentive to both its gendered elements and its ethnocentrism. The importance of men's love, trust and respect for women and their interests was a major theme in women's writing, but their vision of the masculine ideal could not accommodate different cultures or values.

Women did, however, have to accommodate the greater power and access to wealth accorded men in their own society. Law, religion and social custom all upheld male power in the family and in public life, and middle-class women had to accommodate the often conflicting needs of tempering male power in the household and promoting it in the market and in politics. Their own social status and economic well-being were highly dependent on the success of the men in their families; their political influence, too, depended on the wealth and power of their male friends and relatives. Thus the physical and emotional safety of women and their children demanded a construction of masculinity that placed a high priority on emotional tenderness, advocating the restraint of male power within the household, while supporting the carefully regulated use of it in public life. In other words, women's writing suggests a construction of masculinity which emphasized both private domestic and public political and economic roles for men.

Annie Affleck Thompson's correspondence with her husband, John Thompson, during the 1870s and 1880s provides an interesting illustration of a masculine ideal which combined both domestic and public elements.[58] Annie and John were married in 1870 and, very early in their marriage, John's legal career and, a little later, the political career that would eventually take him to the prime minister's office demanded frequent and often long absences from home. Although she missed him during his absences, Annie strongly supported John's public career. Her letters suggest that her masculine ideal included achievement and independence, but also acknowledged emotional tenderness and vulnerability. In response to this construction of masculinity she adopted a motherly role in her correspondence, nagging, cajoling and bracing her husband to withstand the separations. The letters often reflected her own emotional need for her husband, and they also had a playful and sexually suggestive tone. In 1882 Annie wrote to John in Antigonish, where he was a candidate for the Provincial Assembly.

> My poor old tired Tory
> I cannot tell you how glad I was to get your letter this afternoon. I know that you are feeling badly . . . I wish I could be with you for one ten minutes to talk square to you. You want to know how I'll feel if you are beaten well child except for you being disappointed and tired to death not one row of pins . . . except that we never gave up a fight

yet I wouldn't mind if you put on your hat and left them tomorrow[.] it is better to fight as long as you are started and be beaten than not to fight at all. So keep up your courage and I'll go part of the way to meet you coming home win or lose they can't keep you from me much longer. John is very exercised to know why they should want another man instead of pa . . .

So now my old baby you must not be such an awful awful baby until you get home and then I'll see how far you can be indulged.[59]

Annie wrote a similar letter to John in Ottawa, while he was a member of Parliament, in January 1886, in response to his complaints of loneliness.

Oh my Pet my Pet,
Can't you bully things out when I am trying to do so . . . Baby you break my heart, if you don't try to be more of a boss, and look this thing in the face and make the best of it for a little while until I can be with you.[60]

Annie's belief that a man could be weak and emotionally vulnerable in relationship to his wife is strongly reflected in her correspondence with John. Lystra found the same idea expressed in many of the love letters between 19th-century middle-class Americans.[61] John Tosh also explored this theme in his study of Edward White Benson, arguing that the "alternation of mastery and dependence" in Benson's marriage to a woman 12 years his junior "exemplified the paradox which lay at the heart of bourgeois marriage in mid-nineteenth-century England."[62] And he cites historian David Pugh's notion of the 19th-century American husband as a "patriarchal child," a concept that embraces male public power and private vulnerability, as a useful one in reconciling these apparently contradictory ideals of manliness.[63]

Fathers' relationships with their daughters revealed aspects of the patriarchal side of Pugh's characterization. In the writing of many middle-class Nova Scotian women, especially — but not exclusively — those in clergy households, fathers were accorded considerable power, and the good father emerges as one who took an active domestic role. A fatherly interest in the upbringing and education of children was an important pillar of mid-19th-century middle-class masculinity, although one often obscured by the late Victorian and Edwardian emphasis on mothering and a rigid delineation of public and private life.[64]

For some daughters, attentive fathers provided important models of masculinity. Jane Sprott, the daughter of John Sprott, a Presbyterian minister living in Musquodoboit, began keeping a diary in February 1837, when she was nine years old. The diary was, in fact, her father's idea and Jane "resolved to note down in this book any striking occurrence of any thing worthy of notice particularly to mark the goodness of God to myself and our family."[65] Many of the things she wrote about directly involved her father and her relationship with him, and others reflected John Sprott's well-publicized ideas about religion and education. Jane's mother offered her daughter a model of deep respect and love for her own father. In a letter home to her brother in 1841, she wrote:

I can never think of my father's memory but it does me good. The fond recollection of his virtue should keep us all from doing a thing mean or wicked or unworthy of him.[66]

Jane's diary is certainly infused with the spirit of her father. She wrote about his role in family fireside education, reported trips taken in his company, and copied many of his letters to family, friends and colleagues into her diary. Whether this was because she admired them, or because she was the family clerk is unclear. When she wrote statements such as "Education is an introduction abroad and a companion at home. A poor Novascotian would rather sell his garment than leave his children without education"[67] or "Fireside education is of infinite importance and it gives form and colour to every texture in life,"[68] she must have been highly influenced by her father, if not quoting him directly. Jane portrayed her father as capable of love, tenderness, laughter and hard work, and deeply interested in the spiritual and intellectual development of his children.

Shubenacadie teacher, historian and novelist Eliza Frame undoubtedly used her father as a model for the hero in her novel *The Twilight of Faith*, published in 1872. The novel describes the spiritual journey of Mary Gray, a young woman who was devastated by the death of her husband. She was led to God by the ministrations of her brother-in-law. Through long months of gentle persuasion and example he was able to bring Mary into the Christian fold, restore her to her children, and awaken in her an enthusiasm for helping others. In the story of Mary Gray, Eliza Frame expressed her gratitude to her father (who was, in contrast to Mary's brother-in-law, a farmer rather than a minister) for the spiritual instruction he had provided when she was growing up in the 1830s and 1840s. She dedicated the novel to her father, "who led me to Christ and taught me in all events to recognize the Lord Jesus."[69]

Women also created fictional father figures who were attentive to the instruction of their children. In some cases this practice served a double purpose, not only constructing an attentive and concerned father, but also lending male authority to the writers' words, especially when they were writing on subjects not generally regarded as within women's sphere. Eliza Frame, in *Descriptive Sketches of Nova Scotia in Prose and Verse*, and Miss Groves, in *Little Grace, or Scenes in Nova Scotia*, both created male voices to give authority to their work.[70] In *Little Grace*, a history of the province aimed at young readers, Grace's father and brother generously and patronizingly explain historical events. Eliza Frame created a male narrator in *Descriptive Sketches of Nova Scotia* who recounted the travels of the imaginary Andrew Urban through the province.

Women called on men to exercise their power in the public sphere in the interests of women. In the 1870s, for example, two women teachers publicly appealed to men to use their power to protect them from exploitation and oppression in their employment. Both couched their requests in terms of male chivalry. One, in a letter published in the *Journal of Education* in 1871, argued that the fact that women were paid substantially less for their work than their male counterparts, no matter how effectively that work was performed, was a "sad commentary on the chivalry and gallantry of our countrymen."[71] In 1874 a second woman teacher, whose letter was published in the *Halifax Daily Reporter and Times*, argued her case in the same terms. She complained bitterly about the lack of adequate wages and professional recognition accorded to women, and wrote that it was shocking that women were treated so badly because "one would suppose the chivalrous instincts of a *gentleman* would lead him to protect [women], not oppress [them]."[72] Whether or not these appeals were successful, they were intended to, and no doubt did, tap into the masculine ideals espoused by men. They acknowledged male power in their society and called on men to use it according to the ideals and dictates men themselves had created. By using this language, women were both criticizing men and offering them new ways of conforming to their own ideals of masculinity. For these women school teachers, the ideal man retained his power in the world but used it wisely and generously for the good of the women. It was, of course, a strategy with severe limitations for women, but it offered hope of redress in specific situations. Men, and women, familiar with the debates about the reform of married women's property law would have understood these appeals to chivalry. A number of the Nova Scotian politicians committed to legal reform were concerned with limiting the abuse of male power by men who did not accept middle-class ideals of masculinity, and therefore threatened the basis of that power as good and natural.[73]

Male power, independence and access to wealth were complex issues fraught with considerable tension for many middle-class women. A man's power, wealth and status in the world had important ramifications for the women in his life, and had to be taken seriously by women. The attainment of some degree of wealth and public respectability was a necessary prerequisite for inclusion in the emerging middle class. But women rarely endorsed the pursuit of fame and fortune as appropriate activities, and the belief that wealth, and even the pursuit of wealth, could corrupt a man emerged frequently. Mary Eliza Herbert, as was her habit, took a strong stand on this question. In "Lucy Cameron" the narrator commented:

> The trappings of wealth are very pleasant things doubtless to possess, but then if one should buy them too dearly, I am afraid it would be likely to tarnish their value.[74]

All the male characters in her novels who actively sought wealth were villains. Lawyer Levitt, who we already know had no interest in art or nature, lived only to make money at the expense of others. Lucy Cameron's husband, "a shrewd, hard business man," was another greedy ambitious villain. He speculated in gold-mining stocks, a timely activity in Nova Scotia in the 1850s, and one fraught with great symbolic resonance. Mr. Cameron dreamed of becoming a millionaire but "[m]aking haste to be rich" was Mr. Cameron's downfall, and his wealth soon "took itself wings and fled away."[75]

Herbert did not resolve the tension between the need for wealth and the evils of pursuing it. Wealth and independence came easily to her heroes, too often in the form of an unexpected legacy. In *Belinda Dalton*, the death of a distant relative provided Captain Elton with enough money to marry Belinda and to "allow her to contribute largely to the relief of her fellow creatures."[76] Belinda and her father were equally delighted with his proposal. Ralph Maynard, Lucy Cameron's second husband, had a private income whose source was never disclosed, and he supplemented it with the income from an unidentified profession. In "Emily Linwood" both of Emily's suitors inherited money.

Other women offered more complex responses to the question of wealth. In *The Twilight of Faith*, Mary Gray found her vocation in helping the young men who had come to the city in search of fame and fortune to avoid the moral temptations the city offered. Frame represented a widely held construction of masculinity that suggested another duality in the male character. Young men were vulnerable to moral temptation, but also had the capacity to resist it and to pursue pure and wholesome lives. By the early 1870s, when Frame wrote her novel, the idea of the moral mother had gained considerable currency, and Frame created, in Mary Gray, a character who embodied that role.[77] Mary invited young men to her home on Sunday evenings for hymn singing and tea drinking, and created such an attractive and welcoming atmosphere with her Christian love that many young men were delighted to abandon their previous Sunday night haunts.[78]

But Mary Gray supported her missionary enthusiasms with money she had inherited from her husband. Frame did not tell her readers the source of Edward Gray's wealth. As in Herbert's work, there is the suggestion that the morally upright are rewarded by material comfort. In her "Memoir of the Reverend James Murdoch," a pioneering Presbyterian minister and a relative, written for the Nova Scotia Historical Society, Frame argued that his life and his legacy proved "that the heritage of prayer is more enduring than the heritage of money."[79] Both Herbert and Frame sidestep some very central questions about middle-class masculinity.

They evaded questions of manly independence and worldly success that were directly addressed in the intimate and revealing memoir written by P.S. Hamilton, an ambitious Nova Scotian–born farm boy who moved to Halifax in his early 20s to make his mark as a journalist and a lawyer. Resembling Rotundo's "masculine achiever" much more closely than any of the characters created or discussed by the women writers, Hamilton strove to be regarded as *a gentleman and a man of honor*," to protect his personal independence and integrity, and to accumulate wealth and honour in the public sphere.[80] Hamilton consistently refused the help of mentors and colleagues because he feared their support would compromise his autonomy. He never found the success or the wealth he sought. His career as a lawyer and journalist brought him limited success, but his speculations in Nova Scotian gold-mining stocks, like those of Herbert's fictional Mr. Cameron, were an unmitigated disaster.[81]

Halifax journalist, lawyer and politician William Garvie, described by a contemporary as "full of bright kindly life, with a countenance betokening a man of deep thought and sympathies" and "deeply religious," had many qualities associated with the "Christian gentleman" and would have been much more acceptable to the women writers.[82] He articulated his ideas about manliness in an address to the North British Society in 1871 on "The Genius of [Sir Walter] Scott."[83] Garvie was impressed that Scott "had his whole life so regulated by a high standard of moral control, he had all his emotions so well disciplined."[84]

Garvie also admired Scott's chivalrous attitude towards women, and reminded his listeners that Scott "produced in his writings only a higher ideal of womanhood to grace his song and to sparkle forth in the pages of his romances."[85] Employing one of the standard conventions of mid-19th-century literary criticism, he contrasted the chivalrous Scott with Byron, "who turned and mutilated all the purer and all the lovelier elements in woman's nature."[86] But Garvie was also very impressed with Scott's sense of financial responsibility and independence, and told his audience about Scott's ceaseless efforts to recover from the brink of bankruptcy.[87] An honourable independence in public affairs was an important aspect of manliness to William Garvie.

Nova Scotian women writers found ways to impart special meaning to the power accorded to middle-class men in the family and in public life. Their construction of the ideal man often emphasized a protectiveness and generosity towards women that simultaneously acknowledged male power and created limits and constraints on it. Calls for male chivalry rested on an acknowledgement of male power, and enabled men to construct a masculine identity based, at least in part, on using their power for the protection of women and children. Many men, including William Garvie, found this an attractive ideal, and other historians have noted its continuing resonance for men. Carolyn Strange, for example, has examined the meaning of chivalry in the murder trials of two women in Toronto, one in 1895, another in 1907.[88]

Middle-class Nova Scotian women's writing provides us with considerable insight into their ideas about how they thought men should act towards women and children of their own class, but it also tells us a great deal about the construction of the boundaries that defined appropriate middle-class behaviour and attitudes. Mary Eliza Herbert's anti-aristocratic ideas, especially present in her condemnation of effeminate, superficial men, suggests the importance of distinguishing middle-class values from those of the aristocracy by claiming the moral high ground as belonging exclusively to the middle class. Women were active participants in creating a white Anglo-American middle-class identity, and helped to define who was "the other" through their writing. Clotilda Jennings' depiction of Henri Pontrincourt as a man who did not understand that women were to be trusted completely by men marked off the cultural differences between Anglo–Nova Scotians and Acadians. Mary Jane Katzmann Lawson's racist descriptions of African Nova Scotian men in her history of the Dartmouth area also reinforced exclusionary ideas.

We can only speculate about the influence women's writing had in shaping middle-class ideals of masculinity, although the attention historians have paid to male prescriptive literature about the nature of women demands at least equal time. Literary women's attention to the conventions of genre provided a comfortable framework for their readers to consider their ideas. The use of familiar rhetorical devices, such as calls for male chivalry, also traded on forms that readers could assimilate. Women's daily relationships with men and their power to reject unsuitable men as husbands suggest that women's ideas about masculinity would have some impact. And the power increasingly accorded to them, over the course of the 19th-century, as moral guardians gave them greater credibility when they drew social boundaries that excluded men from middle-class status for moral violations. The fact that the ideals that emerge from their writing constructed a masculinity with specific class, ethnic and racial dimensions also contributed to their persuasiveness. Their assertions about gender were more convincing because they were made in the context of an inclusive middle-class identity, attached to a cluster of ideas in a way that made their ideas about masculinity more acceptable. Women's writing provides valuable insights into the ways in which women and men together created a middle-class identity and established the moral justification for middle-class social, economic and political hegemony.

But women were denied explicit legal, economic and familial bases of power in mid-19th-century society by the gender ideals prescribed to men and women. Their constructions of a masculine ideal that emphasized compassion, love and trust for women can be understood as attempts to influence male behaviour both inside and outside the family. The fact that their ideal men had characteristics more often associated with feminine ideals suggests that women recognized the value of the traits assigned to them, and that they hoped to see these ideals permeate middle-class culture. Nova Scotian women participated actively in negotiating and constructing masculine ideals and middle-class culture.

NOTES

1. Nova Scotian women's writing has been very well served by Margaret Conrad, Toni Laid-law, Donna Smyth, eds., *No Place Like Home: Diaries and Letters of Nova Scotia Women, 1771–1938* (Halifax, 1992); Margaret Conrad, "Recording Angels: The Private Chronicles of Women from the Maritime Provinces of Canada, 1750–1959," in Diana M.A. Relke, ed., *The CRIAW Reader: Papers on Literary Productions by Canadian Women* (Ottawa, 1992), pp. 1–48; Gwendolyn Davies, "'Dearer than his Dog': Literary Women in Pre-Confederation Nova Scotia," in Gwendolyn Davies, *Studies in Maritime Literary History, 1760–1930* (Fredericton, 1991), pp. 71–87; Elizabeth Waterston, "Margaret Marshall Saunders: A Voice for the Silent," in Carrie MacMillan, Lorraine McMullen, Elizabeth Waterston, *Silenced Sextet: Six Nineteenth Century Canadian Women Novelists* (Montreal and Kingston, 1993), pp. 137–68.

2. See, for example, Margaret Conrad, "'Sundays always make me think of home': Time and Place in Canadian Women's History," in Veronica Strong-Boag and Anita Clair Fellman, *Re-Thinking Canada: The Promise of Women's History* 2nd edition (Toronto, 1991), pp. 97–112.

3. See Michael Roper and John Tosh, eds., *Manful Assertions: Masculinities in Britain Since 1800* (London, 1991), pp. 1–4; and John Tosh, "What Should Historians do with Masculinity? Reflections on Nineteenth-Century Britain," *History Workshop*, 38 (Autumn 1994), pp. 179–202.

4. See Mary Poovey, *Uneven Developments: The Ideological Work of Gender in Mid-Victorian England* (Chicago, 1988), especially Chapter One.

5. Catherine Hall, "Competing Masculinities: Thomas Carlyle, John Stuart Mill and the Case of Governor Eyre: The 1865 Riot in Morant Bay, Jamaica," in Catherine Hall, *White, Male and Middle Class: Explorations in Feminism and History* (New York, 1992), p. 257. See also Anthony Rotundo, "Learning About Manhood: Gender Ideals and the Middle-Class Family in Nineteenth-Century America," in J.A. Mangan and James Walvin, eds., *Manliness and Morality: Middle Class Masculinity in Britain and America, 1800–1940* (New York, 1987) and Clyde Griffen, "Reconstructing Masculinity from the Evangelical Revival to the Waning of Progressivism: A Speculative Synthesis," in Mark C. Carnes and Clyde Griffen, eds., *Meanings for Manhood: Constructions of Masculinity in Victorian America* (Chicago, 1990), pp. 183–204.

6. Hall, "Competing Masculinities," p. 256.

7. Rotundo, "Learning about Manhood."

8. Ibid., pp. 36–7.

9. Ibid., pp. 37–40.

10. Hall, "Competing Masculinities," p. 257.

11. Rotundo, "Learning About Manhood," p. 40–3.

12. P.S. Hamilton Diary, MG1, vol. 335, Public Archives of Nova Scotia [PANS], p. 77. This document is somewhat misleadingly listed as a diary. It is best understood as two auto-biographical fragments, the first begun in 1861, the second in 1878. In each fragment Hamilton reconstructs and interprets events in the past. For biographical information about Hamilton see William Hamilton, "P.S. Hamilton," *Dictionary of Canadian Biography*, XII (Toronto, 1990), pp. 405–7; P.B. Waite, "A Nova Scotian in Toronto, 1858," *Ontario History*, LV, 3 (1963), pp. 155–9.

13. Nancy Cott, *The Bonds of Womanhood: "Woman's Sphere" in New England, 1780–1835* (New Haven, 1977); Caroll Smith-Rosenberg, "Female World of Love and Ritual: Relations Between Women in Nineteenth-Century America," *Signs*, 1 (Autumn 1975), pp. 1–29; Conrad, "'Sundays always make me think of home.'"

14. I would like to thank Frances Early for reminding me of this important connection.

15. John Tosh, "Masculinity and Domesticity in the Victorian Middle Class Family: The Family of Edward White Benson," in Roper and Tosh, eds., *Manful Assertions*, pp. 44–73.

16. P.B. Waite, *The Man from Halifax: Sir John Thompson, Prime Minister* (Toronto, 1985).

17. Janet Eagleson Dunleavy, "Maria Edgeworth and the Novel of Manners," in Bege K. Bowers and Barbara Brothers, eds., *Reading and Writing Women's Lives: A Study of the Novel of Manners* (Ann Arbor and London, 1990), pp. 49–66.

18. Stephen Kern, *The Culture of Love: Victorians to Moderns* (Cambridge, Mass./London, 1992), p. 2.

19. Karen Lystra, *Searching the Heart: Women, Men and Romantic Love in Nineteenth-Century America* (New York and Oxford, 1989), pp. 4–6. For other discussions of romantic love see Ellen K. Rothman, *Hands and Hearts: A History of Courtship in America* (New York, 1984) and Peter Ward, *Courtship, Love and Marriage in Nineteenth-Century English Canada* (Montreal, Kingston, London, Buffalo, 1990). Unlike Ward, I argue that the emerging middle-class had developed distinctive ideas about romantic love by the middle of the 19th-century.

20. See Davies, " 'Dearer than his dog.' "

21. Mary Eliza Herbert, *Belinda Dalton, or Scenes in the Life of a Halifax Belle* (Halifax, 1859).

22. Ibid., p. 11.

23. Ibid., p. 12.

24. Ibid., p. 13.

25. Ibid., p. 14.

26. Ibid., p. 46.

27. Hall, *White, Male and Middle Class.*

28. Herbert, *Belinda Dalton*, p. 17.

29. See Sherry B. Ortner, "Is Female to Male as Nature is to Culture?" in Michelle Zimbalist Rosaldo and Louise Lamphere, eds., *Women, Culture and Society* (Stanford, 1974), pp. 67–88; Jane Leigh Cook, "Bringing the Outside In: Women and the Transformation of the Domestic Interior in Atlantic Canada, 1830–1860," *Material History Review*, 38 (Fall 1993), pp. 36–9; and Janet Guildford, "Maria Morris Miller: The Many Functions of her Art," *Atlantis*, 20, 1 (Fall/Winter 1995), pp. 113–24.

30. Leonore Davidoff and Catherine Hall, *Family Fortunes: Men and Women of the English Middle Class, 1780–1850* (London, 1987), pp. 155–79.

31. Herbert, *Belinda Dalton*, p. 29.

32. Mary Eliza Herbert, "Lucy Cameron," MS2 32, Dalhousie University Archives.

33. Mary Eliza Herbert, "Emily Linwood, or The Promise of the Bow," *The Mayflower or Ladies Acadian Newspaper*, 1, 1–6 (May–October 1851).

34. Lystra, *Searching the Heart*, p. 7.

35. Herbert, "Lucy Cameron," p. 43.

36. Ibid., p. 50.

37. Ibid., p. 51.

38. Ibid., p. 25.

39. "Eliza Ann Chipman Diary, 1823–1837," in Conrad, Laidlaw and Smythe, eds., *No Place Like Home*, p. 87.

40. Ibid., pp. 87–8.

41. "Mathilda Faulkner Churchill, Letters 1871–1879," in Conrad, Laidlaw and Smythe, eds., *No Place Like Home*, p. 122.

42. Ibid.

43. Ibid., pp. 123–33.

44. Alma Maude (Clotilda Jennings), *The White Rose in Acadia and Autumn in Nova Scotia* (Halifax, 1855).

45. Gwendolyn Davies, "Amelia Clotilda Jennings," *Dictionary of Canadian Biography*, XII (Toronto, 1990), pp. 474–5.

46. Jennings, "The White Rose of Acadia," p. 10.

47. Ibid., p. 27.

48. See M. Brook Taylor, "The Poetry and Prose of History: Evangeline and the Historians of Nova Scotia," *Journal of Canadian Studies*, 23, 1 and 2 (Spring and Summer 1988), pp. 46–67.

49. Mary Jane Katzmann Lawson, "The Gaspereaux Valley," in Harry Piers and Constance Fairbanks, eds., *Frankincense and Myrrh: Selections from the Poems of the Late Mrs. William Lawson, (M.J.K.L.)* (Halifax, 1893), p. 22.

50. For biographical information see Lois Kernahan, "'MJKL,' A Victorian Contradiction," *Nova Scotia Historical Quarterly*, 5 (1975), pp. 231–41.

51. These poems were published in the posthumous anthology of her poetry, *Frankincense and Myrrh*.

52. Mrs. William Lawson (Mary Jane Katzmann), *History of the Townships of Dartmouth, Preston and Lawrencetown: Halifax County, N.S.* (Halifax, 1893). This book was published after the author's death, and was heavily edited by Harry Piers, but most of the book was written as sketches for *The Provincial or Halifax Monthly Magazine* in the 1850s.

53. Lawson, *History of the Townships*, p. 156.

54. Suzanne Morton has argued that Lawson's treatment of African Nova Scotian women reflected the same ideas. See Suzanne Morton, "Separate Spheres in a Separate World: African–Nova Scotian Women in Late-19th-century Halifax County," *Acadiensis*, XXII, 2 (Spring 1993), pp. 61–83.

55. Lawson, *History of the Townships*, p 168.

56. Ibid., pp. 168–9.

57. Ibid., p. 168.

58. My discussion of the Thompsons' marriage is based entirely on the portions of their correspondence published in Waite, *The Man from Halifax*.

59. J.S.D. Thompson Papers, vol. 283, Annie to Thompson, 14 June 1882 from Halifax, quoted in Waite, *The Man from Halifax*, p. 112.

60. J.S.D. Thompson Papers, vol. 283, Annie to Thompson, 9 Jan. 1866, quoted in Waite, *The Man from Halifax*, pp. 157–8.

61. Lystra, *Searching the Heart*.

62. Tosh, "Domesticity and Manliness," p. 56.

63. David G. Pugh, *Sons of Liberty: The Masculine Mind in Nineteenth-Century America* (Westport, 1983), pp. 83–8, cited in Tosh, "Domesticity and Manliness," p. 56.

64. Tosh, "Domesticity and Manliness," p. 44.

65. Diary of Jane Sprott, February 1837, PANS.

66. Letter from Jane Sprott senior to Rev. Mr. Neilson, Jane Sprott Diary, 7 February 1841, PANS.

67. Jane Sprott Diary, 2 April 1838, PANS.

68. Jane Sprott Diary, 9 January 1840, PANS.

69. Elizabeth Frame, *The Twilight of Faith*, 2nd edition (Toronto, 1872).

70. Eliza Frame (writing as "A Nova Scotian"), *Descriptive Sketches of Nova Scotia in Prose and Verse* (Halifax, 1864); Miss Grove, *Little Grace, or Scenes in Nova Scotia* (Halifax, 1846).

71. "Female Teaching," *Journal of Education* (Nova Scotia), 36 (April 1871), p. 559.

72. *Halifax Daily Times and Reporter*, 12 January 1874.

73. Philip Girard and Rebecca Veinott, "Married Women's Property Law in Nova Scotia, 1850–1919," in Janet Guildford and Suzanne Morton, eds., *Separate Spheres: Women's Worlds in the 19th-Century Maritimes* (Fredericton, 1994), pp. 67–92.

74. Herbert, "Lucy Cameron," p. 3.

75. Ibid., p. 54.

76. Herbert, *Belinda Dalton*, p. 42.

77. For a discussion of this process see Poovey, *Uneven Developments*, pp. 10–11.

78. Frame, *The Twilight of Faith*.

79. Eliza Frame, "Memoir of the Reverend James Murdoch," Nova Scotia Historical Society, *Collections*, vol. II (1881).

80. P.S. Hamilton Diary, MG1, vol. 335, PANS.

81. Hamilton, "P.S. Hamilton," pp. 405–7; after some years as an itinerant journalist and newspaper editor, he died poor and alone in a Halifax boardinghouse of an overdose of laudanum. Waite, "A Nova Scotian in Toronto, 1858."

82. Biographical notes: William Garvie, *Annals of the North British Society of Halifax, Nova Scotia* (Halifax, 1905), p. 456; P.B. Waite, "William Garvie," *Dictionary of Canadian Biography*, X (Toronto, 1972), pp. 300–1.

83. William Garvie, "The Genius of Scott," *Annals of the North British Society* (1905), pp. 429–51.

84. Ibid., p. 434.

85. Ibid., p. 434.

86. Ibid. For the comparison with Byron see Ira Ferris, *The Achievement of Literary Authority: Gender, History and the Waverley Novels* (Ithaca and London, 1991), p. 243.

87. Garvie, "The Genius of Scott."

88. Carolyn Strange, "Wounded Womanhood and Dead Men: Chivalry and the Trials of Clara Ford and Carrie Davies," in Franca Iacovetta and Mariana Valverde, *Gender Conflicts: New Essays in Women's History* (Toronto, 1992), pp. 149–88.

TOPIC FIVE
The Workplace

Toronto Rolling Mills,
Mill Street, 1864.
This pastel drawing by
William Armstrong illustrates
the nature of work in an
industrial setting.

Over the course of the nineteenth century, Canada evolved from an overwhelmingly rural and pre-industrial commercial society into an increasingly urban and industrial one. This transformation resulted from a number of developments. The growth of cities and towns, technological change and innovation, immigration, an improved transportation network, reciprocity, and protective tariffs all combined to facilitate economic growth and change. The process of industrialization and urbanization dramatically altered the nature of work and the workplace.

At the beginning of the period, most work was done in small shops in or near the home by skilled craftsmen and their apprentices. Production was largely by hand, on a small scale, and for the local market. Individual craftsmen usually owned their own tools and enjoyed a high degree of autonomy in setting their own pace of work. Industrialization gradually made this artisanal system of production obsolete. The shop was replaced by the factory and a new system of manufacturing in which the pace of work was set by machines. Mechanization resulted in "deskilling," as skilled workers were replaced with semi- and unskilled workers who carried out only limited and specialized functions. The shift to the factory system also created a new type of worker, the manager or foreman, who supervised the work of others. As machinery replaced human skill, more and more capital was needed to finance manufacturing. As a result, control of industrial production passed into fewer and fewer hands, and society became increasingly divided between the capitalists, who controlled production, and the workers, who sold their labour to employers in return for a wage.

In Article Nine, Gregory Kealey analyzes the impact of these changes on the shoemakers of Toronto, a group of craftsmen who, he demonstrates, attempted to preserve their rich artisanal tradition in the face of technological innovation. In Article Ten, Robert MacIntosh explores the ways in which patriarchy and capitalism combined to create the "sweated" women needleworkers of the nineteenth-century clothing industry.

QUESTIONS TO CONSIDER

1. What were the key elements of the shoemakers' craft tradition? How did the shoemakers of Toronto respond to the introduction of new machines and the factory system?
2. What were the main characteristics of the sweating system? Why were sweated needleworkers overwhelmingly women? What type of women found themselves employed in the needle trades? Why did middle-class reformers and governments attempt to reform the sweating system?
3. Is patriarchy a necessary component of capitalism?

SUGGESTED READINGS

Cohen, Marjorie Griffin. *Women, Work, Markets, and Economic Change in Nineteenth-Century Ontario*. Toronto: University of Toronto Press, 1988.

Craven, Paul, ed. *Labouring Lives: Work and Workers in Nineteenth-Century Ontario*. Toronto: University of Toronto Press, 1995.

Heron, Craig. *Working in Steel: The Early Years in Canada, 1883–1935*. Toronto: McClelland and Stewart, 1988.

Kealey, Gregory S. *Toronto Workers Respond to Industrial Capitalism, 1867–1892*. Toronto: University of Toronto Press, 1980.

Kealey, Gregory S., and Bryan D. Palmer. *Dreaming of What Might Be: The Knights of Labor in Ontario, 1880–1900*. Toronto: New Hogtown Press, 1987.

Palmer, Bryan D. *A Culture in Conflict: Skilled Workers and Industrial Capitalism in Hamilton, Ontario, 1860–1914*. Montreal/Kingston: McGill-Queen's University Press, 1979.

Palmer, Bryan D. *Working-Class Experience: The Rise and Reconstitution of Canadian Labour, 1800–1980*. Toronto: Butterworths, 1983.

Sager, E.W. *Seafaring Labour: The Merchant Marine of Atlantic Canada, 1820–1914*. Montreal/Kingston: McGill-Queen's University Press, 1989.

NINE

···

Artisans Respond to Industrialism: Shoemakers, Shoe Factories and the Knights of St. Crispin in Toronto

GREGORY KEALEY

Cobbler, cordwainer, shoemaker — by whatever name they were of first rank in the pre-industrial world of the artisan. These "most persistent of working class intellectuals"[1] were ever present figures in the struggle for a freer and more egalitarian world. In rural England, these village radicals acted as spokesmen, organizers and ideologues in the struggles of the agricultural labourers.[2] In urban Paris they joined their brother *sans culottes* in the streets at the Bastille.[3] In London they were the main carriers of the Jacobin tradition.[4] In the United States they helped create a radical tradition of Republicanism which figured again and again in nineteenth century labour struggles.[5] In the Mackenzie Rebellion of 1837 in Upper Canada no artisan group played a more prominent role.[6] What elements in the shoemaker's craft prepared them for such prominence?

One old Lynn, Massachusetts shoemaker, reflecting on the recently lost traditions of his trade, suggested one answer:

> The peculiar nature of his business requiring of the workingman little mental concentration, allowed him to take part in discussions, or fix his attention upon any question that might engage his thoughts. His work went on mechanically, as it seemed, without needing any of that nice care which is indisposable in many of the mechanic arts. This circumstance made every workshop a school and an incipient debating club; and from this doubtless has arisen the general intelligence which is said to characterize the sons of Crispin.[7]

···

Source: "Artisans Respond to Industrialism: Shoemakers, Shoe Factories and the Knights of St. Crispin in Toronto," *Historical Papers* (1973): 137–57. Reprinted by permission.

Shoemakers were "given to deep thinking" in New England, and their shops were often visited by ministers desirous of testing their sermons before delivery. These centres of popular theological debate were considered unequipped if they did not contain a bible, a dictionary, a grammar and a weekly newspaper. Also part of every shop's standard equipment were "one or more extra seats or boxes for the accommodation of visitors" who would drop by either to read to the working journeymen or to join in listening and debating as "the best reader in the crew . . . read the news."[8] Only the pub challenged the shoe shop as a centre of popular culture, and it was often shoemakers or other artisans who ran these. Frank Foster, a printer and leader of the Knights of Labor in the United States, referred to every shoemaker's shop as a lyceum and credited the craft with "the old time front rank of comparative intelligence."[9]

Shoemakers had in addition a particularly vibrant craft tradition. Stories of St. Hugh and of Sts. Crispin and Crispianus and other types of lore provided a set of familiar and well defined customs that instilled the craftsmen with pride and solidarity.[10] On October 25, the feast of St. Crispin, cordwainers the world over marched beneath banners depicting their patron saints and engaged in drunken frolics. Shoemakers in Canada built on these traditions. This craft lore was undoubtedly carried to Canada by emigrating cobblers. These men took a prominent role in early Canadian labour organizing. Toronto shoemakers struck for higher wages and better conditions as early as 1830 and again in the 1850s. Other early shoemakers' societies are reported in Montreal, Halifax and St. John.[11] Generally in British North America, wherever shoemakers were in sufficient numbers to organize, they did.

Any understanding of the life of shoemakers in this period must start at their workplace. There can be little doubt that the artisan's relation to work was central to his identity in the pre-industrial city. Let us turn to one such city, York, Upper Canada. Shoes, as all else, were initially imported to York, but as early as 1830 shoemakers struck for an increase in their bill of prices. By 1833 a total of 68 shoemakers lived and worked in York.[12] Undoubtedly some were storekeepers, but the strike and the large number of shoemakers demonstrate that production for the local market had commenced. Thirteen years later Toronto contained 49 shoe shops, no doubt still a mixture of retailers and custom shoemakers.[13] The 1851 census reports two shoe factories in the city. While production grew slowly in Toronto, Montreal was setting the pace in Canadian shoe production. Only in the early fifties, with the advent of the sewing machine, did the artisan structure of the shoe industry come under attack.[14] The structure of the wholesale trade in Montreal until that point had involved a central shop where the cutting was done. The cut leather was first given to women working at home for binding and then to shoemakers working in small shops for bottoming. The sewing machine and ever growing markets began to change all that in the early fifties.[15]

A Montreal firm, Brown and Childs, introduced sewing machines first in that city and then in Toronto. Their Toronto branch, established in the late forties as a retail shop for Montreal goods, began to manufacture in the fifties for the western market. By 1856 two other companies had joined Brown and Childs in wholesale manufacturing in Toronto: Gilyat, Robinson and Hall and E.K. Paul and Company.[16] The new method of production involved the relocation of the female binders. The widespread use of the sewing machine in binding uppers necessitated the shift from home to factory for these women.

A rapid increase in shoe production occurred in the late fifties and early sixties. The major impetus came from the increased size of the Canadian market. Agricultural specialization and the improved transportation network allowed the new urban industries to triumph over the old village production.[17] The tariff also played an important role in the development of the shoe industry. In the 1850s, when the tariff stood at 12½%, New England goods apparently competed successfully, but the new 15% tariff combined with the dislocations of the Civil War to close off the Canadian market to American Shoes. The tariff was subsequently raised to 17½% in 1874 and to 25% in 1879 to meet manufacturers' self-interested demands.[18]

By 1860 Brown and Childs, which had become Childs and Hamilton in Toronto, employed 40 men and 15 girls in its four story establishment on Wellington Street East. These employees "were kept constantly employed in cutting, fitting and stitching, besides a number — generally over a hundred — who work in their own homes at what is termed bottoming — so that upwards of 150 hands are engaged." The company owned ten sewing machines and utilized all the other "latest appliances in labour-saving machinery." The manufactory occupied only the top two flats; the other two were given over to sales and storage.[19] The 1861 census reports seven Toronto shoe factories, but directories identify only four competitors of Childs and Hamilton in the wholesale trade. The rapid growth of Toronto shoe manufacturing was frequently described in the Toronto Board of Trade reports. In 1860 Erastus Wiman wrote of the "decrease of the manufactures of small towns over the country" and speculated that these shops would slowly become little more than cobblers' shops for the repair of city manufactures. The next year he stated that "the large shoe shops in each village where from five to ten men were wont to be employed" were a thing of the past.[20] In 1863 he reached a new eloquence in describing the industry's transformation:

> Eight years ago there was only one regular traveller from Montreal and one from Toronto who solicited orders from the country trade, and these seldom left the line of the railroad. Now it is no uncommon thing to meet from fifteen to eighteen in a single season — all keenly alive to business, and pushing into all sections of the country, remote or otherwise.

He added that "business formerly distributed over a thousand workshops in the country districts" had become "the eighteen or twenty establishments of the five cities of the provinces . . . ."[21]

Throughout the sixties the rapid growth of the Canadian market provided a further thrust toward industrialization. The perfection of the McKay machine enabled the manufacturers to bring the last remnant of outside work, bottoming, under the control of the factory. Montreal firms quickly embraced the new sole-sewing device:

> Only a year or two ago, pegged work was the kind produced; but new and improved machinery recently introduced has most materially changed the character of the articles made, a large and increasing demand now exists for sewed goods, sole-sewing machinery enabling the manufacturers to supply cheap sewed boots and shoes of all kinds thus supplanting much of the fine pegged work which had formerly been in request.[22]

In 1867 Montreal manufacturers had 250 sewing machines, 50 pegging machines, 30 closing machines, 15 sole-sewing machines, 20 sole cutters and machinery for eyeletting, punching, skiving and rolling.[23]

Toronto manufacturers quickly implemented these latest changes in production. J.M. Trout was enthusiastic in his description of the wonders of these new devices that reduced all to system:

> Childs and Hamilton's establishment is a perfect beehive of activity, and the admirable order and arrangement of the whole is as perfect as long experience and the best business tact can make it.[24]

New manufacturers emerged in Toronto in the mid-sixties. One of the quickest growing was Sessions, Carpenter and Company, which, like Childs, had started as a retailer but without Montreal connections. This firm reportedly doubled its production in 1865 and intended to redouble it in 1866. Employing 250 hands in 1867, it expanded to 400 in 1868 and then to 510 in 1870, when as Sessions, Turner and Cooper the firm opened its new Front Street factory. The description of this factory demonstrated how complete the transition to machine production was by 1870. Built at a cost of $30,000, the new three story building "utilized machinery to an extraordinary extent." The basement was used for storage, the ground floor for offices and shipping and the first floor for cutting and finishing. This floor also housed the channelling machine which shaved and cut the sole, removed strips and left the leather ready for the sewing machine. The 78 sewing machines were located on the second floor; they were operated by 119 women, who had their separate entrance and were completely segregated from the male employees on the other floors of the factory. The men's work was done on the third floor. This involved all the heavier sewing and peg work and included the larger machines used in bottoming.[25]

The 1871 census of industry demonstrates the rapidity and totality of the transformation. Of 49 boot and shoe firms in Toronto, the ten largest employed ninety per cent of the total work force and accounted for an identical proportion of the total annual product. The four largest, Sessions, Turner and Cooper (510), Childs and Hamilton (192), Damer, King and Company (191) and Paterson, Murphy and Braid (154) accounted for 66% of the workers and 64% of the production (see Tables 9.1 and 9.2.).[26] Boots and shoes had become Toronto's largest and most industrialized industry. The artisan shop of 1850 was clearly a thing of the past.

TABLE 9.1 *Boot and Shoe Industry in Toronto, Number Employed, 1871*

Size of Work Force	No. of Establishments	Total No. of Employees	% of Employees
100+	4	1047	66
50–99	4	290	19
30–49	2	79	5
10–14	5	56	4
5–9	7	41	3
2–4	14	39	3
1	13	13	1
Totals	49	1565	101

Source: Canada, Census of 1871, Industrial Mss., Toronto (R631A)

TABLE 9.2 *Largest Toronto Shoe Manufacturers, 1871*

| | No. of Employees | | | | | Production | |
| | Adult | | Children under 16 | | | | Cumulative |
Name of Firm	M	F	M	F	Total	Value of	%
Sessions, Turner	330	90	50	40	510	$300,000	
Childs & Hamilton	134	42	13	3	192	160,000	64
Damer, King	105	60	1	25	191	250,000	
Paterson, Murphy & Braid	100	50	4	—	154	160,000	
Holmes	50	24	2	7	83	100,000	
Barclay, Evans	66	8	2	4	80	75,000	85
Sanderson & Williams	50	15	3	2	70	45,000	
Dack, Forsythe & Leslie	37	20	—	—	57	60,000	
Cobley	13	30	3	3	49	35,000	90
McEntee	25	4	1	—	30	18,000	
Totals	910	343	79	84	1416		

Source: Canada, Census of 1871, Industrial Mss., Toronto (R631A)

Toronto shoe production peaked in the early seventies. After 1871 the census returns illustrate the decline of the Toronto industry. Both the 1881 and the 1891 censuses depicted a fall both in numbers employed and in the annual value produced (see Table 9.3). The growth of the Toronto industry had always been based on the production of finer quality goods than Montreal and Quebec produced. With the rapid improvements in mechanization that revolutionized the shoe trade this became as outmoded as the skill of the shoemakers themselves. Much was also said at the time about Quebec's cheaper labour supply and less organized workers, but this remains a question to be studied. Whatever the cause the Toronto fine goods trade fell before Quebec competition in the eighties and nineties.

How did the shoemakers respond to the arrival of the factory system in their lives? The effects of these changes were all-encompassing for the artisan. Formerly he had worked in a small shop; now he found himself in a factory with hundreds of other workers. Before, he alone had made the entire shoe by hand; now he worked only on parts of it with the aid of machines. In the old shops he had control over his time, his discussions, his visitors and his work; now he was subject to factory discipline like any other worker. The separation of the journeyman and his master, at one time relatively undefined, had been growing for some years, but under the shop system a certain familiarity remained. The factory created massive barriers of social distance between owner and worker. Most important, industrialization stripped the shoemaker of his most valuable possession — pride in his craft, and in his product. That the memory of both old and new was a tangible part of each shoemaker's life can be seen in a press description of one Montreal factory as late as 1885:

Indeed, there were several employees of both sexes, some of whom came to the firm as children, whose experience compasses nearly all the improvements in boot and

TABLE 9.3 *Shoe Industry in Toronto, 1871–1901*

	No. of Establishments	No. of Employees	Total Wages	Total Value of Production
1871	47	1564	$378,797	$1,334,215
1881	76	1232	345,343	1,290,392
1891	149	742	316,812	1,156,894
1901[a]	8	637	287,354	899,329

[a] 1901 CENSUS INCLUDES ONLY ESTABLISHMENTS EMPLOYING MORE THAN FIVE WORKERS.

Source: Canada, *Census, 1871–1901.*

shoe machinery . . . One old man, named Dennis Barron, who had been in their employ 43 years, remembered helping to put up the first sewing machine used on boots and shoes . . ."[27]

Shoemakers did not wait long to register their opinions of industrialization. As early as the 1850s A.J. Bray reported that in Montreal the changes initiated by Brown and Childs were "violently opposed by the shoemakers, but progress triumphed over prejudice."[28] In England the shoemakers of Northampton fought a series of strikes in the years 1857–59 in an attempt to resist the introduction of the sewing machine.[29] In Lynn, Massachusetts artisan resistance culminated in the Great Strike of 1860.[30] In Quebec City in the sixties "nos bons cordonniers . . . se liguèrent contre les petits americaines, ainsi qu'ils appelaient Messieurs Coté et Bresse et voulurent les chasser de la place . . . "[31] These phenomena were all local in nature.

The introduction of the McKay machine in the mid-sixties changed the nature of unionism in the shoe industry. The local unions quickly perceived that the new factory system demanded broader forms of organization than they had previously evolved. Ontario shoemakers met in Toronto in 1867 to form the Boot and Shoe Makers Union of the Province of Ontario only five months after the founding of the Knights of St. Crispin in Milwaukee and before that body had expanded beyond Wisconsin. Representatives were present from eight Ontario towns, and in three days of meetings they created a provincial structure for unionism in their trade. This organization probably provided the basis for the expansion of the Knights of St. Crispin into Ontario in 1869 and 1870.[32]

Newell Daniels, who had worked in the shoe industry of his native Massachusetts, founded the Knights of St. Crispin in Milwaukee in March of 1867. In the fall of 1867 the Order began to grow slowly, but in 1868 and 1869 it expanded rapidly. By April, 1870 the Order included 327 locals, and by April, 1872 around 400 lodges had been organized. The Knights entered Canada in 1868, organizing a lodge in Montreal (Lodge 122), and followed this in 1869 with lodges in Quebec, St. John (Lodge 171), Toronto (Lodge 159), Guelph (Lodge 202), Hamilton (Lodge 212), and Windsor. The next year two more Toronto lodges (315, 356) were organized, as well as lodges in Halifax, Chatham (326), Georgetown, London (242), St. Catharines (340), Stratford (233) and Barrie (353). In 1871 lodges were added in Galt (371) and Orillia (372).[33]

An analysis of the Crispin experience in Toronto demonstrates the inadequacies of much of the previous literature on the subject. To view the Order either as a pre-industrial anachronism or as a harbinger of industrial unionism has not proven particularly useful.[34] The Order took consciously from the old but always with the new situation in mind. It merged the old traditions of the wisdom and independence of the shoemaker with the new realities of factory production. The Crispins in Toronto were always far more than an economic institution. They organized excursions, balls, dinners and even a quadrille club.[35] These varied social functions probably played important roles in maintaining the old craft solidarity in the early years of the factory. The Order also provided a funeral benefit, but perhaps more important than even the financial aid thus supplied was the solemnity and dignity the attendance of one's brother Crispins lent to such an event.[36] The Order had a special funeral rite and even the death of a shoemaker became in this way an action of ritual and actual solidarity.[37] One might add that these services also proved to others the strength of the Crispin order since they involved demonstrations of large numbers of Knights.[38]

Ritual ran throughout the workings of the Order. Oaths, secret work and elaborate ceremony all can be analyzed to show the adaptation of old artisan traditions to the unprecedented situation shoemakers faced. For example, the Knights of St. Crispin initiation ode used the legend of St. Crispin in ways similar to the traditional *Histories of the Gentle Craft*, which had been given to each new shoemaker at the end of his apprenticeship in England:

> St. Crispin is the name we take;
>   May we now be inclined
> His virtues all to imitate,
>   In him a pattern find.[39]

The names and roles of the Order's officers share much in the traditions of Masonry, and in discussions about changes in the constitution in 1872 this debt was made explicit by International Grand Secretary S.G. Cummings:

> In all other orders, such as the Masons, Odd Fellows, Good Templars, and others, digests are used, and many a trouble has been amicably settled that threatened to become serious. Why should we not have one? An Order like ours, composed of such diverse elements, liable at any moment to come into collision with each other, makes a digest an imperative necessity.[40]

Cummings' second point tells us much of the uses of ritual as a device for creating solidarity.

Other parts of the Knights of St. Crispin ritual illustrated awareness of the new reality facing shoemakers:

> You well know our trade has become unreliable and fluctuating, that our wages are reduced on the slightest pretexts and that at no season of the year do we receive fair compensation for our toil; therefore we have banded ourselves togeither [sic] for the purpose of securing identity of interest, and unity of action among those of us employed on the various parts of boots and shoes.[41]

But the merging of the old and new was best described in Sir Knight's charge, which immediately preceded the initiate's solemn oath of obligation:

> Brother . . . you have wisely resolved to join this order of ours, and thus aid us in the work of rescuing our labour from its present depressed condition, and secure, through organization that degree of independence that justly belongs to us . . . .[42]

The great emphasis on ritual in the Knights of St. Crispin and later in the Knights of Labor has not received sufficient attention from historians. The study of similar patterns in England by Eric Hobsbawm and Edward Thompson has provided copious evidence of the importance of such traditions.[43] Hobsbawm's discussion of ritual in *Primitive Rebels*, however, raises many questions about the longevity of ritual in the North American labour scene. Employing a perhaps overly schematic distinction between "form" and "content," Hobsbawn writes of the triumph of the latter by the 1830s and 1840s. The tenacity of complex ritual in North American labour and its utility in new struggles have perhaps been underrated by historians, who are made uncomfortable by the presence of pre-industrial cultural traits among the emerging proletarians.

At the heart of the entire Crispin effort was the striving to regain the control that they had previously exercised over their lives. Their losses were not limited to the workplace, for they also involved the pride and self-respect they had enjoyed in their communities. When Newell Daniels visited Toronto in April of 1870 he struck on this theme again and again and ended his speech with a poem that reiterated the traditional understanding of the labour theory of value:

> Whom shall we honour as heroes?
>   To whom our praises sing?
> The pampered child of fortune?
>   The titled lord or king?
> They live by others labour,
>   Take all and nothing give.
> The noblest types of mankind
>   Are they that work to live.
> Who spans the earth with iron?
>   Who rears the palace dome?
> Who creates for the rich man
>   The comforts of his home?
> It is the patient toiler
>   All honour to him then
> The true wealth of a nation
>   Is in her workingmen![44]

In Toronto the Crispins were successful in organizing the entire male factory labour force. When they organized they accepted as members all workers presently employed in the factory, and attempted to police hiring policies only later. The timing of their organizing success is difficult to pinpoint, but from the 60 members in one lodge with which they began in January of 1869 they reached an estimated peak of around 600 in 3 or 4 lodges in December of 1870.[45] Not satisfied with organizing only the men they also made serious efforts to help create a Daughters of St. Crispin lodge in Toronto but were stymied by the manufacturers' intransigence on that issue.[46] Although unsuccessful in Toronto the Order had great success organizing women in the United States, and the Daughters of St. Crispin took their place beside Susan B. Anthony's female printers at National Labor Union meetings.[47]

A search of the Toronto directories for the personal histories of the approximately 80 members of the Knights of St. Crispin identified by name in the daily and labour press and in minutes of the Toronto Trades Assembly and the Canadian Labour Union reveals much about the composition of the Order.[48] The Order consisted solely of working shoemakers. There were no bosses or even independent shoemakers or cobblers ever mentioned as belonging to the Order. The subsequent careers of these men show how narrow were their options. The overwhelming majority of them remained shoemakers throughout. A few became proprietors of small grocery stores or saloons, a traditional sanctuary for working class leaders in the nineteenth century. One even became a labourer during the depression of the seventies, but he returned to shoemaking after a few years. The only other noticeable change was that another 4 or 5 became the proprietors of small cobbler shops, where they repaired factory shoes and perhaps did some custom work on the side. None became leaders in the industry. However, at the same time it should be noted that many of the early industrialists in this field were not practical shoemakers but entrepreneurs with available capital. The overriding impression one has of this group of Crispins is that the vast majority remained shoemakers. These workers provided considerable stability and experience to the trade union movement of the eighties. Perhaps the outstanding example among Toronto shoemakers was Michael Derham, whose career spanned the Ontario wide body of 1867, the Knights of Saint Crispin, the Knights of Labor 2211 and, finally, the Boot and Shoe Workers International Union. Two other Crispins of the seventies, James Draisey and G. Duncan, also served in the Knights of Labor Local Assembly 6250.

The Toronto manufacturers' counterattack against the Crispins started in the late fall of 1870. When the successful contract of 1869 came up for renewal the Crispins sought price increases on certain specific types of work.[49] All the manufacturers agreed to pay the increase, and peace seemed assured for another year until Hamilton refused to sign the contract, insisting that they accept his word instead. The Knights of St. Crispin refused and finally forced him to sign only by means of a short turnout at his factory. The Knights struck against him again in late December or early January after he broke the agreement by reducing the wages of some of the men. This time, however, solidarity broke down and 27 Crispins tendered their resignations and indicated they would return to work. Their resignations were refused, and when they returned and broke their oaths by revealing lodge proceedings they were expelled from the Order and the strike continued. Thus in January of 1871 Childs and Hamilton and Henry Cobley and Company published a circular attacking Crispin tyranny and closing their shops to members of the Order. They accused the Crispins of limiting their lines of manufacture, of coercing other workers into the union and in general of "arrogant and overbearing conduct." The Crispins correctly saw the assault as an attempt to destroy the union:

> Their object is of course very apparent. If they could break up the organization of the men they would be enabled to dictate terms, cut down wages to the lowest niche, make whatever objectionable rules they please, and harass their employees perpetually.[50]

The Knights of St. Crispin vowed to fight the companies and commended the other Toronto manufacturers who continued to run union shops.

This strike continued into the spring, with the companies enjoying some success in recruiting scabs, but they were not sufficient to return production to its normal level. The employers actively searched for replacements from as far away as England, where Canadian emigration agents sought 400 shoemakers for Toronto, Hamilton and London, all centres of active Crispin organization. There was even some mention of following the example of one New England manufacturer and importing Chinese labour. Labour's emerging anti-emigration policy must be studied in the context of such blatant anti-working class efforts.

The situation in Toronto took an ominous turn for the worse when the Order called a strike at a second large factory. In early April the shoemakers at Damer and King turned out. The immediate issue was the firm's refusal to fire a number of young boys who had been hired without seeking the permission of the Knights of St. Crispin. There were, however, a whole series of other issues which had been exercising the shoemakers for some time. One of these had been the company's refusal to recognize a union of the female operatives that the Knights had helped to organize. Another complaint concerned the inferior nature of the shoes being produced, which not only upset the lasters' pride but also cost them money since the uppers were so defective they took longer to work. But perhaps the final blow was management's "heaping indignities upon us, such as causing us to enter and retire from the shop by a back lane so full of dirt and slush that we could not help but wet our feet."[51] The shoemaker's pride was not something to be tampered with.

The Crispins held a demonstration April 4, when 50 of the strikers left to seek jobs in Chicago and other points west. About 400 to 500 shoemakers marched through Toronto streets, headed by the band of the Tenth Royals, a local militia company, and carrying the flags of the United States and Great Britain. On their arrival at the Great Western Depot they were addressed by H.L. Beebe, a Crispin leader, who assured them they had the support of all Toronto workers in their resistance to the bosses' unjust oppression. Tension, already high around these two strikes involving the city's largest union, was increased when *The Leader* launched an hysterical attack on the Order as a seditious and Yankee controlled threat to all things Canadian. The evidence produced was that the Stars and Stripes had been carried in the procession to the station. *The Leader* even argued that "the Mayor would have acted properly had he prevented the flag of a foreign nation being flaunted in the faces of our citizens on the public thoroughfares on such an occasion."[52] Not surprisingly, the first report of violence came only one day after *The Leader's* nonsense. Shoemakers reportedly assaulted a man at work in a Yonge Street workshop. Two men were arrested, but the details were not revealed. Late on Thursday night or in the early hours of Friday morning, April 6 and 7, the factory of Childs and Hamilton was the scene of what the *Globe* termed "a dastardly outrage." A person or persons entered the factory through a door on a back lane and proceeded to selectively destroy machines, work in progress, shoemakers' kits and, finally, the foreman's outwork records. The damaged machines included a McKay machine, battered with a sledge hammer, a channelling machine and a rounding machine. Only the areas of the factories where the scabs worked were harmed; the leather storage areas and the female operatives' workroom were untouched.

Immediately the manufacturers and the press blamed the Knights of St. Crispin. Hamilton told the press of his certainty that the Crispins were responsible. Editorially

The Telegraph argued that "under the circumstances the Knights of St. Crispin must be held responsible."[53] *The Globe* more cautiously suggested that "the appearances point strongly to members of the Society as the perpetrators of this outrage."[54] Not surprisingly the Order "repudiated any connection with it whatever" and added that the act was "not tolerated by the officers nor by the rules of the society."[55] Initially they offered a fifty dollar reward, but they withdrew it when they detected discrepancies in Hamilton's story. The owner claimed not to have discovered the outrage until late morning, but the Order claimed to have a witness who swore they had seen him there earlier. The Order then argued that the act had been committed to damage the society's reputation and went as far as to suggest that Hamilton should seek the perpetrator among his independent men.

Although police investigated the case it was never solved. The allegations of the manufacturer against the Society remained unproven. Whether or not the Knights as a body were responsible will never be known, but the evidence certainly suggests that the act was done by either members or sympathizers of the order. The attack discriminated in its targets, as did most traditional examples of "collective bargaining by riot."[56] This selectivity indicated the premises of the attack. Damage to the machines would further limit production, and the destruction of shop records and workmen's kits stood as stark warnings to strikebreakers to reconsider the magnitude of their decision. Nevertheless, in this case it was an act performed in weakness, not in strength, and represented the failure of the Order to impose its will through the new methods and techniques of collective bargaining. This recourse to pre-industrial tactics of enforcing workers' power was destined to fail against a manufacturer as large as Childs and Hamilton, who had access to far more support than did the small textile manufacturers assaulted by Ned Ludd and his followers. Again we should be cautious, for perhaps too much can be made of the traditional in this assault. Workers have continued to respond to the power of industry (reinforced when necessary by armed state power) with violence throughout the twentieth century. Also, these were unusual acts in Crispin history. John Hall found no such examples of machine breaking in Massachusetts.[57] Nevertheless, many of the assumptions of Crispin organization that we have already discussed lent themselves well to these actions. Rituals, oaths and secrecy were the constant companions of earlier uses of property damage in working class history. The very inability of the Toronto police to break the case was probably indicative of the shoemakers' collective refusal to cooperate with the investigation. One suspects that only solidarity could have protected the proponents of direct action, for the community of shoemakers was small enough that absolute secrecy within the craft seems unlikely if not impossible.

There were other incidents in this strike. Only one week after the machine breaking a striking shoemaker who either indicated his intent to scab or was too vociferous in his criticisms of the strike discovered that his kit had been destroyed by his fellow workmen, who jeered his invective over the damage. Then in mid-May the picket captain at Damer and King's factory was arrested and convicted of using threatening and abusive language to strike-breakers. A twenty dollar fine or two months imprisonment was assessed for his freedom with the word "scab." Although the two strikes seem to have continued throughout the summer, they clearly failed. In the fall the newly organized Toronto Trades Assembly took up the shoemakers' cause and attempted to arbitrate between the Order and the three non-union factories. Although the minutes record some initial success the outcome was never recorded.[58]

Crispin activity remained quite visible in Toronto and throughout Ontario despite the setbacks of 1871.[59] The Ontario Grand Lodge broke away from the International Grand Lodge in 1873, perhaps reverting easily to its earlier organizational form. Active organizing went on, and new lodges were chartered under a new numbering system which followed the old Crispin pattern, only making Lodge 159, Toronto number 1. The new lodges organized in 1873 and 1874 were Peterborough (Lodge 12), Brantford (Lodge 13), Belleville (Lodge 14), Thorold (Lodge 15), Ingersoll (Lodge 16) and Preston (Lodge 17). In 1873 strikes were fought in Orillia and Guelph. The province-wide nature of the organization was reinforced by events such as the St. Catharines excursion picnic of 1873. In late August approximately 300 Crispins and friends sailed from Toronto to St. Catharines, where they joined 200 of their Hamilton brothers and the St. Catharines Crispins. After marching with bands and banners through the main streets of the city they arrived at Montebello Gardens for games, speeches and refreshments.

The Canadian Grand Lodge met for the last time in 1876 in Hamilton, where it was noted that

> although the depressed conditions of trade had thrown many of the lodges back in point of numbers, the order on the whole was in a flourishing condition.[60]

However, this last convention also again sought international affiliation with the revived Knights of St. Crispin. For this purpose they named a delegate to the next meeting of the International Grand Lodge of the Crispins who was "to strike a basis of union." Probably nothing came of this initiative. The Lodge's disappearance at the provincial level was undoubtedly due to the dislocations of the depression. The boot and shoe industry was particularly heavily hit:

> During 1875, the manufacturing of boots and shoes received a severe check by frequent failure and because of a grossly overdone state of business. Again in subsequent years, the industry was plunged into a fearful condition of doubt and uncertainty . . . It was not until the spring of 1880 that it could be said to have before it a future which promised sound conditions.[61]

After the demise of the Provincial Grand Lodge, locals in several shoe towns retained their organization. This was certainly true in Toronto, where the Knights of St. Crispin remained on the scene until 1886, when they entered the Knights of Labor as Crispin Assembly 6250.[62] The tenacity of the Crispins in Toronto was not unique. A Crispin-led lasters' strike occurred in Montreal in 1882,[63] and Crispins marched in a St. John labour parade in 1883.[64] Just as the Knights of Labor built off a Crispin experience in the United States, they also did so in Canada.[65] In Toronto and Hamilton shoemakers were among the first Knights of Labor local assemblies organized. The Knights of Labor provided the focus for Canadian shoemakers until National Trade Assembly 216 left the order in 1889 and founded the Boot and Shoe Workers International Union, which organized its first Toronto local in 1890.[66]

The Toronto Crispins had a continuous existence until they joined the Knights of Labor, but after 1877 they ceased to be the only organization of shoemakers in Toronto. In that year a group of factory operatives, some of whom had previously belonged to the Crispins, organized the Wholesale Boot and Shoemakers' Union.[67]

The Knights of St. Crispin from this point on contained only custom shoemakers. This group of skilled shoemakers fought strikes in 1881, 1885 and 1887. In 1881 and 1887 they won pay increases, and in 1885 they successfully resisted Dack and Sons' attempt to introduce team production. The proposed teams would have consisted of five shoemakers, all working by hand, dividing the functions of custom shoemaking instead of one worker making the entire shoe.[68]

The factory operatives who joined the Knights of Labor in 1883 as Local Assembly 2212 were successful in negotiating contracts without recourse to strikes in 1879, 1881, 1882 and 1883.[69] The major strike of the eighties occurred in 1882, when the female operatives of the five major factories struck for union recognition, a uniform bill of wages and an advance. This was the first major strike of women workers in Toronto.[70] Toronto unionists provided plenty of support in this strike, which lasted three weeks. The Wholesale Boot and Shoemakers' Union lent advice, financial aid and, finally, went out on a sympathy strike with their sister shoe workers. The Knights of St. Crispin also supplied financial aid, and often Crispin leaders appeared at strike meetings to proffer support and solidarity. These strike meetings took place every afternoon, and high spirits and militancy were displayed throughout. Many of the operatives were not happy with the final settlement, and as many as a third voted to remain out on strike. The settlement won them a uniform bill in the future but no guarantee of an advance, although this remained a cloudy issue and many claimed there had been such a promise. The women who had sung the following song in April struck again in December of 1882 and November of 1883:

> We won't sew on a button,
>   Nor make a buttonhole;
> We won't stitch up a shoetop,
>   All ready for the sole,
> Until the price is raised a peg,
>   On all the shop's pay-roll.[71]

The uniform bill the bosses had promised was delivered in February of 1884, almost two years after the strike. Although there was much discontent with the new bill, no collective action was taken against its provisions.

The relative quiet in the boot and shoe industry in Toronto after 1882 was undoubtedly related to its declining economic status. Two of the largest Toronto factories failed in the mid-eighties: Damer in 1883 and Charlesworth in 1886.[72] The new Boot and Shoe Workers International Union fought and won its first strike in February 1890 against J.D. King and Company. Nevertheless, leverage against management was disappearing as the industry declined in Toronto.[73]

The history of the shoemakers' response to industrialization consists of much more than strikes and trade union organization. Indeed it is a history of the cultural adaptation of old forms to counter the new pressures of factory production. Frank Foster celebrated the old role of the shoemaker in early labour organization and looked forward to the new:

> The "blazoned banner" of St. Crispin has ever been flung out at the head of the labor column. The organization may come and the organization may go; but we may have faith that the love of right and liberty underlying all social reforms will in the future, as in the

past, give inspiration to the workmen in the gentle craft of leather. Crispin, Unionist, Knight of Labor, have all had for their ideal a better livelihood and larger possibilities for their members, and in this broadening sweep and loftier tread of labor organization lies the high hope of the days to come and children yet unborn.[74]

The transitional role of the Crispin and Knights of Labor experience can also be seen in John Hall's encounter with an old Massachusetts shoemaker:

I even found an aged laster in Lynn who claimed to have been a Crispin, though it seems clear he was confusing the Crispins with the Knights of Labor. They way he spoke of the Crispins made it unmistakable that to have been a Crispin was a proud and glorious thing. If the craftsman had to surrender his pride in his individual skills, he was no less a man of spirit. His pride henceforth would be in his loyalty to his fellow workmen and to the standards of mutual help necessary to deal with socialized and mechanized production.[75]

Never anachronistic in their response to industrialism, the shoemakers only demanded their share in the manifold gains that were constantly heralded by latter day Whigs as companions of the new order. That they did not share in the gains, or at least shared in them only to an insignificant degree, is a story for historians of the next period of the shoemakers' history. That the new Boot and Shoe Workers International Union was a strong socialist union in the United States in the first decades of its life should thus come as no surprise to those who have traced the history of the sons and daughters of St. Crispin.

NOTES

1. E.J. Hobsbawm, *Age of Revolution* (New York, 1962), p. 259.
2. E.J. Hobsbawm and George Rude, *Captain Swing* (London, 1969), pp. 18, 63–64.
3. Albert Soboul, The *Sans-Culottes* (New York, 1972).
4. E.P. Thompson, *The Making of the English Working Class* (London, 1963), p. 549.
5. Paul Faler, "Workingmen, Mechanics and Social Change: Lynn, Mass. 1800–60," unpublished PhD. thesis, University of Wisconsin, 1971, ch. 3 and conclusion.
6. Charles Lindsey, *The Life and Times of Wm. Lyon Mackenzie* (Toronto, 1862), Appendix 1.
7. David N. Johnson, *Sketches of Old Lynn* (Lynn, 1880), pp. 4–8.
8. Fred Gannon, *The Ways of a Worker a Century Ago* (Salem, 1918), p. 2 and Fred Gannon, *A Short History of American Shoemaking* (Salem, 1912), pp. 18–19. See also Herbert Gutman, "Work, Culture and Society in Industrializing America," *American Historical Review*, 78 (June, 1973), pp. 531–588.
9. George McNeill (ed.), *The Labor Movement* (Boston, 1887), p. 192.
10. Thomas Wright, *The Romance of the Shoe* (London, 1922), pp. 51–56.
11. Charles Lipton, *The Trade Union Movement of Canada* (Montreal, 1968), pp. 6, 21 and James Richard Rice, "A History of Organized Labour in St. John, New Brunswick," unpublished MA thesis, University of New Brunswick, 1968, ch. 1.
12. William Catermole, *Emigration* (London, 1831), p. 92 and Edith Firth, *The Town of York, 1815–1834* (Toronto, 1966), p. xxxiin.
13. William H. Smith, *Canadian Gazeteer* (Toronto, 1846), p. 195.
14. For a good general description of changes in the methods of shoe production see Edith Abbott, *Women in Industry* (New York, 1919), ch. 8, and for Canada see Canadian Reconstruction Association, *The Boot and Shoe Industry in Canada* (Toronto, 1920).

15. A.J. Bray, *Canada Under the National Policy* (Montreal, 1883), pp. 123–125.
16. *Toronto Directory for 1856–57* (Toronto, 1857).
17. Jean Hamelin and Yves Roby, *Histoire Economique du Québec* (Montreal, 1971), especially Part 4, ch. 2.
18. Canada, Parliament, *House of Commons Journals*, 1874, Appendix 3, pp. 63–66 and 1876, Appendix 3, pp. 90–115.
19. Toronto Board of Trade, *Annual Report for 1860* (Toronto, 1861), p. 41.
20. Ibid., p. 28 and *Report for 1861* (Toronto, 1862).
21. Toronto Board of Trade, *Report for 1863* (Toronto, 1864), p. 24.
22. William J. Patterson, *Statements Relating to Trade, Navigation, and Mining for 1867* (Montreal, 1868), p. 63.
23. Ibid.
24. Toronto Board of Trade, *Annual Report for 1865* (Toronto, 1866), pp. 39–40.
25. *Globe*, Nov. 18, 1870.
26. Canada, *Census of 1871*, Schedule 6, Industrial Census, Toronto Manuscripts, Public Archives of Canada (R631A).
27. *Globe*, Nov. 18, 1885.
28. Bray, *Canada Under the National Policy*, pp. 123–125.
29. Wright, *Romance of the Shoe*, pp. 224–226, and Alan Fox, *A History of the National Union of Boot and Shoe Operatives, 1874–1957* (Oxford, 1958), pp. 13–14.
30. Faler, *Workingmen, Mechanics and Social Change*, ch. 11.
31. *Annuaire du Commerce et de l'Industrie de Québec pour 1873* (Quebec, 1873), pp. 8–9.
32. *Globe*, Sept. 20, 1869; *Leader*, Sept. 20, 1869; *Daily Telegraph*, Sept. 20, 1869.
33. Data generated from Don Lescohier, "The Knights of St. Crispin, 1867–1874," in *Bulletin of the University of Wisconsin, Economic and Political Science Series*, VII (1910), pp. 1–102, from a perusal of the Toronto press for 1867–85, and from the *Proceedings of the International Grand Lodge of the Order of the Knights of St. Crispin*, 1869, 1870 and 1872.
34. The secondary literature on the KOSC was until recently woefully repetitive. John Commons used the experience of American shoemakers to develop his theses about the importance of market relations in the history of labour. His seminal article "American Shoemakers, 1648–1895" in *The Quarterly Journal of Economics*, 1909, was expanded on in Lescohier's Wisconsin thesis in 1910. These two works became the standard interpretation, and subsequent volumes by Blanche Hazard, *The Organization of the Boot and Shoe Industry in Mass.* (Cambridge, 1921), and Augusta Galster, *The Labor Movement in the Shoe Industry* (New York, 1924), as well as several other works, only repeated the findings of the Commons school. The work shows many of the flaws of Commons' approach: an over-emphasis on national developments, a dependence on official publications, a narrow institutional framework, and a theoretical emphasis on the centrality of market relations which deemphasizes the conflict of capital and labour. The KOSC in this view becomes an organization almost totally preoccupied with controlling the operation of machinery and closing off the factory to non-shoemakers. Conflicts thus become shoemaker versus green hand and ultimately shoemaker versus market. Struggles between workers and employers almost disappear. Only in the last twenty years has this interpretation come under attack. The first historian to question these views was John Hall, who in his thesis "The Gentle Craft: A Narrative of Yankee Shoemakers," unpublished PhD. thesis, Columbia University, 1953, discovered that in Massachusetts the Order had been far more interested in wages and hours than in green hands. Two recent theses, by Paul Faler (op. cit.) and Allan Dawley, "The Artisan Response to the Factory System: Lynn, Mass.," unpublished PhD. thesis, Harvard University, 1971, both demonstrate the weaknesses of the old view. Faler in a sensitive community study of Lynn shoemakers up to 1860 shows the development of a working class with a distinct culture

who by 1860 had moved into direct conflict with their employers. Dawley traces the Lynn story into the seventies and through a study of the membership rolls of the KOSC in Lynn finally puts to rest notions of the Crispins as a narrow labour elite of custom shoemakers fighting off other workers. Lynn Crispins represented a complete cross-section of the factory labour force and found themselves in direct conflict with their employers on a wide range of issues. Alan Fox's *History of the National Union* suggests the relative uniqueness of the Crispin success in creating a union which combined the old skilled artisans with the new factory work force. In England the machine shoeworkers split off from the old Cordwainers Society in 1873. The creation of this new union was necessitated by the inability of the old union to adjust successfully to the changes wrought by industrialization.

35. *Globe*, Nov. 28, 1868; Nov. 27, 1869; Aug. 9, 1870; Dec. 23, 1870; Feb. 11, 1871; Sept. 3, 1871; Sept. 1, 1873; *Irish Canadian*, Dec. 2, 1868; Dec. 1, 1869; *Ontario Workman*, May 9, 1872; April 24, 1873; Aug. 28, 1873.

36. For the importance of funerals see Brian Harrison, *Drink and the Victorians* (London, 1971), p. 43.

37. *Ritual of the Order of the Knights of St. Crispin* (Milwaukee, 1870), pp. 16–17.

38. For Toronto Crispin funerals see *Globe*, Dec. 15, 1873; July 5, 1881.

39. *Ritual*, p. 9.

40. Lescohier, "The Knights," pp. 93–94. On use of Masonic rites in general see Eric Hobsbawm, *Primitive Rebels* (London, 1959), ch. 9 and Noel P. Gist, "Secret Societies," *University of Missouri Studies*, XV (October, 1940).

41. *Ritual*, p. 8.

42. Ibid., p. 10. For a broader discussion of working class culture see Herbert Gutman and Gregory Kealey, *Many Pasts: Essays in US Social History*, 2 vols (Englewood Cliffs, 1973), especially the introduction.

43. Hobsbawm, *Primitive Rebels*, ch. 9 and Thompson, *Making*, especially ch. 14–15. For a discussion of these themes in Canadian history see R. Hann, L. Kealey, G. Kealey, P. Warrian, *Primary Sources in Canadian Working Class History, 1860–1930* (Kitchener, 1973).

44. *Globe*, April 13, 1870; *Daily Telegraph*, April 13, 1870.

45. *Leader*, April 10, 1871. For evidence of a fourth lodge in Toronto (366) see *Globe*, Jan. 26, 1872 and *Ontario Workman*, Feb. 20, 1873.

46. *Leader*, April 10, 1871.

47. David Montgomery, *Beyond Equality* (New York, 1967), pp. 395–399, 457–461.

48. After compiling lists of Knights of St. Crispin mentioned in the Toronto press and in the minutes of the TTA and the CLU I checked their personal biographies by following them through the Toronto directories of the seventies and eighties.

49. For detailed summaries of events see *Leader*, April 10, 1871; *Globe*, Jan. 25, 1871; Jan. 26, 1871; April 10, 1871; *Daily Telegraph*, Jan. 24, 1871. The following narrative is reconstructed from a reading of the Toronto press day by day.

50. *Globe*, Jan. 26, 1871.

51. *Leader*, April 10, 1871.

52. Ibid., April 4, 1871.

53. *Daily Telegraph*, April 8, 1871.

54. *Globe*, April 10, 1871.

55. Ibid.

56. Eric Hobsbawm, "The Machine Breakers," in *Labouring Men* (London, 1964), p. 7. On this subject see also Thompson, *Making*, ch. 14, Malcolm Thomis, *The Luddites* (New York, 1972) and Lionel Munby (ed.), *The Luddites and Other Essays* (London, 1971), pp. 33–56.

57. Hall, "The Gentle Craft," ch. 9–10.

58. Toronto Trades Assembly, *Minutes*, June 2, 1871; Oct. 20, 1871; Nov. 3, 1871; Nov. 22, 1871.

59. *Ontario Workman*, Feb. 20, 1873; March 27, 1873; June 12, 1873; Aug. 28, 1873; Nov. 27, 1873; Dec. 11, 1873; Feb. 19, 1874; March 5, 1874; *Mail*, July 26, 1873; July 21, 1875; July 22, 1875; *Leader*, Sept. 1, 1873; Feb. 12, 1874; July 22, 1875; *Globe*, Feb. 14, 1874; July 22, 1875; July 24, 1875.

60. *Globe*, July 22, 1876.

61. William Wycliffe Johnson, *Sketches of the Late Depression* (Montreal, 1882), pp. 160–162.

62. *Globe*, April 7, 1886.

63. Jean Hamelin et al., *Répertoire des Grèves dans la Province de Québec au XIXe siècle* (Montreal, 1970), p. 73.

64. Rice, *Organized Labour in St. John*, ch. 4.

65. Norman Ware, *The Labor Movement in the US 1860–1925* (New York, 1929), pp. 200–209 and Montgomery, *Beyond Equality*, pp. 199, 462–470.

66. Gerald Grob, *Workers and Utopia* (Chicago, 1961), pp. 122–124. For a local version see James Morris, "The Cincinnati Shoemakers' Lockout of 1888: A Case Study in the Demise of the Knights of Labor," *Labor History*, 13 (Fall, 1972), pp. 505–519.

67. *Globe*, Feb. 15, 1877; Oct. 21, 1879.

68. Ibid., March 11, 1885; *Telegram*, March 11, 1885.

69. *Globe*, Oct. 22, 1879; Oct. 23, 1879; Oct. 29, 1879; April 28, 1881; April 30, 1881; May 18, 1881; May 24, 1881; May 18, 1882; June 30, 1882; May 17, 1883; Nov. 17, 1883; *Mail*, Oct. 14, 1879; Oct. 21, 1879; Oct. 22, 1879; *Telegram*, April 29, 1881; May 23, 1881.

70. See *Globe, Mail, Telegram* and *News* for April and early May, 1882 for copious detail. Also see *Trades Union Advocate*, May, 1882.

71. *Trades Union Advocate*, May 4, 1882.

72. *Globe*, Jan. 13, 1883; *Labor Reformer*, Nov. 13, 1886; Dec. 25, 1886. See also Hector Charlesworth, *Candid Chronicles* (Toronto, 1925), pp. 68–70, on his father's failure.

73. *Globe*, Feb. 15, Feb. 19, Feb. 21, 1890. For the Boot and Shoe Workers International Union, especially its socialist politics, see Henry F. Bedford, *Socialism and the Workers in Massachusetts, 1886–1912* (Amherst, 1966) and John Laslett, *Labor and the Left* (New York, 1970), especially ch. 3.

74. McNeill, *Labor Movement*, p. 213.

75. Hall, "The Gentle Craft," p. 356.

TEN

Sweated Labour: Female Needleworkers in Industrializing Canada

ROBERT McINTOSH

There are "scores, hundreds, of women in this city whose only means of subsistence is by their needle. They are paid starvation wages, viz., 6 cents each for making shirts, 17 cents for making and pressing pants, 75 cents for coat and vest, etc. In the words of a skeleton living on Maitland St. with a sick girl: "I have to work with my needle until midnight to earn the money to buy bread for tomorrow. And this is my hard experience every day of the week, and every week of the year." [1]

The clothing industry emerged gradually in Canada during the 19th century, as the site of production shifted from the household (for use) to larger-scale manufacture for the market. By the end of century, the industry was one of the largest employers in manufacturing in industrial centres such as Montréal, Toronto, and Hamilton, and remained so until well into this century. [2] Unlike most contemporary manufacturing industries, the clothing trades were a major source of wage labour for women, who typically accounted for 70 to 80 per cent of all needleworkers. [3] While the clothing industry extended across the country, it was based in central Canada. By 1901 at least 7500 women in Ontario and nearly 9000 in Québec worked in their homes at garment manufacture. Many more, including more than 5500 in Ontario and nearly 1800 in Québec, worked in small contract shops. [4]

Rife with sweating by the close of the 19th century, the garment trades exhibited some of the most deplorable working conditions faced by any worker. [5] An analysis centred on the operation of the capitalist system helps to account for the grossly depressed labour standards, interminable hours of work, and wretched pay within the garment trades. It cannot explain why sweated needle workers were overwhelmingly female.

Jacques Ferland argued recently that "labour history has all too often neglected [the] wedding of capitalist oppression and patriarchal domination." [6] The terms and conditions of this wedding warrant close scrutiny. Capitalist society emerged within an existing patriarchal context, "a set of social structures and practices in which men dominate, oppress, and exploit women." [7] Capitalism and patriarchy, analytically distinct, interacted in complex, manifold, and frequently contradictory ways. Capitalist social relations adapted, used, and exploited — but never subsumed — patriarchal attitudes and practices. [8]

Source: Excerpted from "Sweated Labour: Female Needleworkers in Industrializing Canada," *Labour/Le Travail*, 32 (Fall 1993): 105–38. © Canadian Committee on Labour History. Reprinted by permission of the editor of *Labour/Le Travail*.

Historical narrative details this interaction. Women's subordinate role within the traditional household, whereby they assisted and supplemented the work of men, made them, in the context of industrial capitalist growth, of ready use to employers in search of cheaper, easily victimized, workers.[9] The initial disadvantage women faced was compounded by discrimination on the part of trade unions, which sought for decades to restrict or exclude women's wage labour as part of the struggle for the male breadwinner wage.[10]

If the interrelation between class and gender provided the context in which female sweated labour emerged, it also shaped responses to sweating. At one level, seamstresses who sweated at home were inoffensive to patriarchal norms. These women did not desert home duties and children by taking on wage labour outside the home, nor did they steal "men's" jobs. They did not toil at "rough work in hot sweaty environments in close physical proximity to unrelated men."[11]

Eventually, however, the pervasiveness of sweating came to be unsettling to patriarchal standards. Female sweating jeopardized male incomes in the clothing trades, and for this reason drew the hostility of men as wage-earners. The profound degradation associated with sweated labour threatened women's ability to perform their designated duties as homemakers and mothers. Evidence linking sweating with the emergence of slums became clearer and stronger. Chronic occupational diseases undermined women's capacity to function as mothers. The sweated trades exploited the labour of many children. Extremely poor pay, in tandem with the demoralization and degradation associated with sweating, led to the seamstress' close ties with the prostitute.[12]

Patriarchal unease intersected with concerns to mute the most destructive aspects of the capitalist system. Sweating revealed starkly how terribly damaging unchecked market forces could be. On this question a coincidence of interests emerged toward the end of the 19th century. The liberal state, concerned to "legitimize" the system, took steps to mute its most destructive aspects. On this point trade unions, on behalf of the interests of their working-class constituents, lent their support. Likewise, private and organized philanthropy, moved by humanitarian impulses, struggled to secure the legislation which some hoped would maintain what they viewed as the essential elements of their society.[13]

Consensus formed most readily concerning women. Patriarchal arguments regarding women's role and place resonated with capitalist concerns to perpetuate by timely reforms a class-based, market-driven society. If society was to be saved, reform had to begin with women.[14]

THE RISE OF SWEATING

The integrity of the traditional clothing trades had been maintained by means of formal apprenticeships. Apprentices, while subject particularly at the outset of their period of indenture to menial tasks, generally were initiated into all aspects of clothing manufacture, including the measuring and cutting of cloth, sewing, and the pressing of the completed garment.[15]

By the 1820s and 1830s, expanding markets owing to urban growth, immigration, and improved transportation (with the construction of canals, railways, and roads) brought traditional clothing manufacture under pressure.[16] Traditional garment manufacture had been largely custom work. Clothing was made to measure, manufactured on the premises, under the supervision of the master tradesman and retailed directly to the public. Increasingly, particularly in men's clothing, there was a shift from custom to readymade production, where relatively large allotments of clothing were made in standardized sizes.[17]

During this time, certain merchant tailors and dressmakers accumulated more capital, secured access to credit, left manual labour, and hired a foreman to oversee production. They began to reorganize production within their workplace. Conditions of labour deteriorated. The emergence of sweating was part and parcel of the destruction of the traditional clothing trades. Detailed research has been conducted on Montréal, the major centre for clothing manufacture in Canada throughout most of the 19th century. There, large master tailors sought to exploit expanding markets through the extension of the division of labour. As a first step, they began to take on many more than the customary one or two apprentices. Subsequently, the traditional, rounded apprenticeship was compromised as in the interest of increasing production, boys were instructed in simply one branch of clothing manufacture. The consequences of these new divisions of labour were evident even among journeymen. Because foremen took responsibility for the most demanding task of measuring and cutting cloth, journeymen tailors increasingly were called on simply to sew. The paternal aspects of the traditional craft also declined: by 1835 journeymen no longer were benefitting from the provision of room and board in the home of their masters. At the same time, employment conditions worsened: year-long contracts were giving way to shorter terms, even to payment by piece. This enabled master tailors to lay off journeymen during slack times. Finally, larger capital requirements in clothing manufacture (tied up chiefly in cloth and readymade goods) made the path to master increasingly difficult for journeymen.[18]

From in-house division of labour it was a small step to putting out parts of the work to homes (and later, to contract shops). Because most women had experience with the needle, they were brought into the clothing trades, in competition with male garment workers, by the master tailor or contractor. They were not in a position to command the pay or labour standards of journeymen: this of course encouraged their use.[19]

By the middle of the 19th century a second group had emerged as large manufacturers of readymade garments: clothing and drygoods importers, wholesalers and retailers. While they had no experience of artisanal production of clothing, they possessed the capital to profit by expanding markets for readymade clothing.[20] Moss Brothers exemplifies this second group of clothing manufacturers. They first entered the garment business in 1836, as importers of clothing. By 1856, they employed 800 men and women in Montréal.[21] Many other merchants followed this path. In 1888, it was observed that virtually no drygoods merchant in Montréal was without a workshop attached to his business.[22]

During the last half of the 19th century, a wide range of garment businesses developed. Economies in garment production were not achieved through the consolidation of machinery and labour; indeed, they were achieved through their dispersal. The industry was characterized by an increasingly advanced subdivision of labour which was often associated with extensive subcontracting. This practice had clear benefits for employers. Contractors could be dropped or underemployed as convenient. Competition among contractors exerted downward pressure on the prices they charged. Subcontracting enabled wholesale manufacturers to avoid the expense of recruiting and supervising workers. Both wholesale manufacturers and contractors were able to pass on to homeworkers many costs of production, including workspace, light, fuel, sewing machines, needles, and thread. Homework also permitted the circumvention of rudimentary state regulation of industrial standards.[23] Large manufacturers like Hollis Shorey claimed ignorance of the working conditions of these outworkers, even of the numbers employed.[24]

A handful of large wholesalers and manufacturers struggled successfully to control large portions of the market. In the middle, a variety of contract shops emerged. Some contractors were relative large, employed one or two dozen people, and specialized in certain kinds of work; they were often intermediaries between wholesalers and homeworkers. Often contractors were themselves poverty-stricken, worked out of their homes, and employed in addition to family members one or two girls from the neighbourhood. At the other extreme was the woman who laboured individually, perhaps occasionally hiring a neighbourhood girl to assist her as she struggled to meet deadlines on small consignments of clothing.

By 1900, the largest clothing manufacturers employed well over one thousand workers. Of those, only a small portion were on the manufacturer's payroll. "Inside" workers, as they were called, were employed in two (often conjoint) places: in showrooms where a small number of highly skilled tailors designed clothing and cut cloth to pattern; and in warehouses, where foremen gave out cloth to outworkers, where they inspected the completed sewing, where "trimmers" finished certain lines of goods (by hemming, for instance, by correcting mistakes, or sometimes simply by cutting off loose threads), and where pressers ironed the completed garment. In these warehouses, too, large quantities of garments were stored before shipment out. Outside workers were largely on the payroll of a subcontractor (a term used interchangeably with contractor) or working on their own account.[25]

THE SWEATING SYSTEM

The term "sweating" was introduced in Britain in the 1840s to describe the deteriorating working conditions skilled tailors had faced since the 1830s. It originally referred to the taking home of work by skilled tailors seeking to cope with falling prices, but it soon came to encompass a range of abuses including poor working conditions, irregular work, and seasonal layoffs. The expression was subsequently popularized by concerned publications like the *Morning Chronicle* and *Punch*.[26]

Sweating was soon introduced to British North America, where, we have seen, the labour standards of the artisanal workshop in Montréal were already under pressure. In 1852 Hamilton tailors too were cursing "the ill omened practice of sweating," which they defined as efforts by master tailors to "procure the utmost of labour from journeymen tailors for the smallest possible remuneration."[27] The growth of outwork and subcontracting in the late 1800s produced two new categories of sweated workers: those in small contractors' shops and those who laboured at home. In practice, there was little to choose between the two: the distinction between a shop and a home often was slight. These new categories of sweated workers, unlike the tailors who first faced the problem, consisted largely of women and girls.[28]

The sweating system, acknowledged the tailor and trade unionist Louis Gurofsky at the end of the 19th century, "work[ed] like machinery."[29] Clothing manufacturers decided to produce a line of clothing on their own account or obtained contracts from wholesalers, retailers, or the government. The cloth was bought wholesale. Designs were produced in the manufacturer's shop. Subcontracts were let. Often, responsibility for garment design and the letting of contracts was combined in the person of the shop foreman. The cutting of the cloth, button-sewing and buttonhole-making, the finishing of the garment (including pressing) might be let or done in-house, depending on the capacities of the manufacturer. Most sewing was done as outwork. It was let either to contractors or directly to women in their homes.[30]

Mackenzie King described in 1898 how some of the largest garment contracts of his day, government orders for military and Post Office uniforms, were filled. These garments were never manufactured "entirely upon the premises of the firms which were awarded the work." While all such firms cut the cloth, made buttonholes, and (often) put on buttons (the latter two jobs were done at trifling cost by machines tended by boys), most work was done off the premises by resort to one of three kinds of subcontract.[31]

The cut cloth might be sent to a contractor's shop, to a contractor's residence where workers were employed, or directly to an individual who laboured at home with the assistance of family members only (and sometimes one or two girls or young women from the neighbourhood). A hierarchy of skills was recognized. Needle work considered less skilled (where a minimum of fit was required) — trousers, vests, greatcoats — was consigned to homeworkers. Work which was deemed to call for greater skill — superior tunics, riding breeches — was sent to contractors' shops.[32]

Contractors proliferated. The barriers to entry were very low: the contractor simply needed access to clothing contracts on the one hand and to a pool of needleworkers on the other. One Ontario factory inspector wrote in 1897:

> The greatest tendency in the clothing trade appears to be against the establishment of large, sanitary workshops. The employers who own the present ones complain of their hands leaving them and taking rooms as workshops, and taking clothing to make at a lower price. The facilities offered for the hire of sewing machines and other necessary tools are so easy that a workman starting without any capital becomes an employer in the space of a week or two.[33]

Interaction between the custom and readymade sectors was not unknown: seasonal lulls in the custom trade often led custom shops to contract for readymade work.[34] Journeymen tailors, ordinarily employed in custom shops, did not scruple during the slack season to work for readymade manufacturers on their own account. Many skilled tailors displaced from custom work permanently joined the ranks of contractors.[35]

Immigrants were often found among clothing contractors. By the end of the 19th century they were often Jews, with some experience of the garment trades in the Old World.[36] The ranks of contractors included women, who might rise from individual homework to employ a number of other needleworkers.

Intense competition among contractors pushed prices down. "One contractor makes war upon the others, and the demand for cheapness is not satisfied," explained Ontario factory inspector Margaret Carlyle in 1897. "It has been told me by a contractor that they are compelled to accept the prices offered by the wholesalers; if they do not take it someone else would."[37] Contracting was both volatile and precarious: shops moved constantly, as the business changed owners or as contractors simply sought "to install themselves as cheaply as possible."[38] The ease of entry into subcontracting encouraged fly-by-night contractors and a range of associated abuses.[39] In many instances, Mackenzie King pointed out, contractors were nearly as miserable as those they employed.[40]

Lower prices, given the labour-intensiveness of clothing manufacture, necessarily meant downward pressure on wages and working conditions. "The contractor's principal concern is the cost of his labour, since he neither buys materials nor sells completed garments," explained F.R. Scott and H.M. Cassidy in 1935. "Consequently competition between contractors becomes almost entirely a question of competition in forcing down labour standards."[41]

The downward pressure on wages as a consequence of subcontracting was inexorable. Contractor underbid contractor, and, as Toronto's Mayor W.H. Howland explained to the Labour Commission in 1888, homeworker undercut homeworker.

> A sewing woman is taking shirts to make, for example, and getting so much for them. She goes in the establishment and says, "I want you to give me some work." She is told that they have plenty of workers and that they must keep their own people going; however after some conversation she asks what price they will give and they arrange to send her a lot at such a price a lower price than they have been paying. It is human nature and business nature for that to be done and it is undoubtedly done and the result is that when the regular worker comes in she has to take that price or she will not get the work.[42]

Falling wages, and persistently increasing working hours, produced a relentless probing of the limits of subsistence. "The political economists who base their calculations upon the living wage, that is to say, the smallest sum upon which human life can be sustained," wrote a late Victorian journalist, "would be surprised to find how small that sum may be."[43]

Accompanying the growth of the readymade clothing industry were increasing divisions of labour. These were of two kinds. The first respected traditional divisions of labour within the clothing trades, of which the most significant was the distinction between men's and women's wear. These divisions could be broken down further: customary subdivisions within the former included pantmaking, shirtmaking, collarmaking, and coatmaking. Within women's wear, these included dressmaking and coatmaking. These traditional subdivisions were respected by contractors who, as A.W. Wright reported in 1896, usually "confine[d] themselves as far as practicable to the making of some particular kind of garment, coats, trousers, vests, mantles or overcoats for example."[44] Contractors might further specialize in a particular quality of clothing.

The extension of readymade production led to new divisions of labour, based on stages in the manufacture of a given article. These came to include the preliminary work of patternmaking, sample-making, and cutting (often the prerogative of foremen and skilled men). The next stage, sewing (mostly done by female outworkers), could be highly specialized: individuals simply might sew sleeves, collars, or pockets, for instance. The sewing on of buttons and the making of buttonholes often were done by specialized workers.[45] Finishing or "trimming" was often in-house. It involved tasks such as hemming, repair work, and the trimming of loose threads. Garments would then be pressed. The final stage was the inspection of the completed goods by an official.

Divisions of labour undermined clothing workers' traditional skills, as garment manufacture was broken into various easily mastered components. Garments were made in assortments, cut by machinery, "and then each part of the work of making up and finishing [was] done by men, women and children skilled in doing that particular part."[46] Mackenzie King described in 1897 the extensive divisions of labour within larger contractors' shops.

> In a large shop there may be engaged in the manufacture of a single coat no less than 16 different individuals, each of whom works at a special line, and after completing one stage in the process of manufacture, passes the garment on to the next, who is skilled in his line, and so on, till the article is completed.[47]

As the readymade clothing industry grew and made increasing calls for labour, the labour it demanded was ever less skilled and ever cheaper. As a consequence, more and more women and children entered the garment trades. The division of labour in the readymade sector, A.W. Wright remarked in 1896, had "practically done away with the necessity of employing completely skilled tradesmen."[48] These basic tasks could soon be well within the competence of even young and inexperienced workers.

THE TECHNOLOGY OF GARMENT MANUFACTURE

Numerous key mechanical devices were introduced into the garment trades between 1850 and 1900. Significantly, however, these devices did not upset the prevailing division of labour in the clothing trades which allowed for outwork.[49]

Two aspects of garment manufacture remained in-house even with the emergence of extensive outwork in the 19th century. Cutting was the most highly skilled aspect of garment manufacture. The material had to be laid out on the cutting table with great care: an incorrect "stretch" would spoil the fit.[50] The introduction of expensive mechanical cutters encouraged the retention of cutting in-house. The "band knife" was introduced in the 1850s, making possible the cutting out of more than one garment at a time. During the 1870s "long knives," capable of cutting up to 18 thicknesses of cloth, were introduced, followed a decade later by steam-powered band knives, which cut up to 24 thicknesses of cloth.[51] As well, the introduction of steam presses to replace hand irons confirmed pressing as inside work.[52]

The central innovation in the garment trades was certainly the sewing machine, whose use spread rapidly from the 1850s. It revolutionized the speed at which clothing could be manufactured. By one estimate, it took 16 hours and 35 minutes to sew a frock coat by hand. The same coat took 2 hours and 38 minutes by machine.[53] The sewing machine greatly reduced the cost of producing clothing while, in the opinion of some manufacturers, improving its quality.[54] At the same time, it was *cheap* enough for the small contract workshop or home. Various other, specialized machines were invented (such as those for pocket-stitching, making buttonholes, and sewing on buttons), but a contractor could purchase one and do this work exclusively.[55]

The technical base of the industry not only allowed for extensive outwork, but encouraged it. By 1900, consequently, garment production differed from most manufacturing industries in that it was *not* becoming centralized in factories.[56] Mackenzie King estimated in 1898 that 5 per cent of men's wear [and certainly a much lower proportion of women's wear] was factory-produced.[57] Even large manufacturers like Shorey or Sanford contracted out to workers in homes or small contractors' shops, who competed fiercely among themselves for the available work. While a number of mechanical innovations had been introduced in clothing manufacture after 1850, they changed neither the industry's heavy demand for labour nor its geographical diffuseness. Into this century, Schmiechen has argued, "there was probably no industry as untouched by factory production or in which the methods of production had been standardized so little as the manufacture of clothing."[58] The industry continued to rest, as Mercedes Steedman observes, on the "systematic exploitation of a seemingly endless pool of cheap, female labour."[59]

WORKING CONDITIONS OF SWEATED NEEDLEWORKERS

Ontario factory inspector Margaret Carlyle remarked in 1899 that "most . . . garment workers in the struggle for subsistence feel obliged to accept wages that are little above subsistence."[60] In fact, wages for female needleworkers were almost uniformly below subsistence levels. One manufacturer acknowledged in 1874 that women "work very cheap."[61] For a woman without dependents, Ontario's Bureau of Industry estimated in 1889, the cost of living in Toronto was approximately $4.00 weekly.[62] Homeworkers earned nowhere near that amount. Women working in contract shops also routinely fell short of a living wage.[63]

The earliest comprehensive information on wages dates from the 1890s, when factory inspectors regularly were reporting on conditions in the needle trades, and when two federal commissions of inquiry examined sweating. Ontario factory inspector James R. Brown visited one contractor's shop which employed seven women and girls in Toronto in 1894. Some earned $1.50 weekly, some $2.00, and one, the finisher, was paid $3.00 weekly. The shop owner claimed, perhaps legitimately, that "he could not afford to pay more."[64] Louis Gurofsky testified to the Royal Commission on Sweating in 1896 that women's wages in Toronto contract shops were as low as 75 cents weekly, although $3.00 was considered a "fair" wage. The average wage failed to reach $4.00 weekly.[65] In contractors' shops in Montréal, Mackenzie King concluded in 1898, women earned between $2 and $5.30 weekly, although $3.00 was considered a good wage. Women employed in the contractor's residence earned from $1.25 to $3 weekly. As homeworkers, women could expect to earn between $1 and $2 weekly.[66]

The sweating system allowed, even encouraged, workers to exploit coworkers. Mackenzie King noted in 1898 that "[i]t was pretty generally conceded that, except by thus working overtime, or by the profits made by the aid of hired help, there was very little to be earned by a week's work."[67] He offered the examples of one woman who hired four girls to assist her at the rate of 25 cents daily (2.5 cents hourly) and another who hired five girls, some paid $2 weekly and others $1 weekly (less than 2 cents hourly).[68]

Clothing manufacturers in Montréal soon discovered that the price of subsistence was even less in outlying villages than it was in the metropolis. Québec factory inspector Joseph Lessard noted in 1897 the extension of the subcontracting network to rural areas.[69] Even Ontario contractors are reported at the turn of this century to have sent clothing to be made up in rural Québec.[70] Scott and Cassidy observed in 1935 that "a shift from town to country is a comparatively simple matter for the contractor. Cheap labour is the magnet that attracts him."[71]

Fining, the bane of homeworkers, was a further means to depress wages. A.W. Wright reported in 1896:

> When an employee in a factory or contractor's shop does imperfect work, necessitating an alteration, only the time required to make the alteration is lost. On the other hand, a person working at home must carry the goods back again, frequently losing half a day because of having to make an alteration which in actual work only requires a few minutes of time. To avoid this they are often willing to submit to a fine or reduction of wages far in excess of what the making of the alteration would be worth to them.[72]

Some warehouses made a practice of fining to reduce their wage bill. Some foremen did likewise to fatten their wallets. In either case protests from homeworkers produced a common response: "There is no more work for you."[73]

Employers' wage bills were also lowered by means of truck. Certain stores gave work only to women who purchased a sewing machine from them and accepted payment in "bons" redeemable only at the stores for which the clothing was made. In Hull, for instance, about 150 or 175 seamstresses were using sewing machines in 1901 for which they had been charged $55, payable at $2.00 monthly, or in "bons" at a rate of $2.50.[74]

The hours of labour in the needle trades were irregular. Many of these trades were highly seasonal: weeks of intense labour could be followed by weeks of idleness. Seasonality was very pronounced in custom work: in millinery, perhaps the branch where it was most evident, there might be only six months' work annually.[75] The most regular employment was found in the larger workshops and factories, where the ten-hour day and sixty-hour week were standard in Toronto and Montréal in the 1890s.[76] In some cases the working days were extended during the week to allow for a half-day holiday on Saturdays.[77]

Both the larger establishments and the smaller dressmakers', milliners', and tailors' shops were subject, however, to frequent overtime in the busy season, for which there was seldom extra payment. In the custom dress shops, this pressure arose in part from customers eager to have their new garments. For "the gratification of some few hundred of inconsiderate people" complained one factory inspector, "the health of several thousand of women and girls" was jeopardized.[78] In the larger garment establishments, legal restrictions on hours of labour were circumvented by sending workers home with garments to make up.[79] Alternatively, in contract shops, "[t]he employees eat their dinner in five minutes, and put the rest of the meal hour in at work."[80]

Homeworkers, as a matter of course, were even more victimized. Mackenzie King noted that "in private houses the time is irregular and the number of hours of work usually more." He offered the example of a woman and son sewing army greatcoats at home who grossed $4 weekly on the strength of 90 hours of work *apiece*.[81] Writing in the *Globe* a few months later, King observed that 15- or 16-hour days (at as low as $3 per week) were common for home needleworkers when employed. In practice, the working day was restricted by "no limit save that of physical endurance."[82]

To the hours of sewing by the homeworker were added the hours of waiting for work. Although work was only intermittently available, homeworkers might nonetheless be required to ask at the warehouse once or twice daily, as a condition of future work.[83] One contractor (contractors were always willing to decry the iniquities of other contractors) spoke in 1896 of one shop where he had seen women kept "waiting two hours to get half a dozen pairs [of pants]."[84] Home needleworkers' time was cheap.

However poor was the pay or however long were the hours these producers worked, factory inspectors complained most persistently about needleworkers' wretched working conditions. Workshops were overcrowded; the environment was unsanitary; the air was foul. "These [small contractors'] workshops," it was reported in 1901, "are among the worst kept. Located as best they could be in old buildings or private houses, and sometimes in basements, they lack equally in light, air and cleanliness."[85] Similar accounts continued to be heard a decade later. "One feature of industrial life that is creeping into the city," wrote another factory inspector in 1911, "is underground workshops. It is almost impossible for them to be healthy. Quite a number of these places are used as tailor shops."[86] Demands by factory inspectors that contractors improve sanitary conditions often led to the abandonment of a workshop, and a clandestine move to another.[87]

FURTHER CONSEQUENCES OF SWEATING

The very poor conditions of labour, wretched pay, and interminable hours had further consequences for the women subject to them. They demoralized workers. They led to early exploitation of children's labour. They broke women's health. They drove some women to prostitute themselves in order to survive.

Prolonged labour under grossly depressed conditions made workers timid and fearful. A.W. Wright was told in 1896 in the course of his Royal Commission that "[i]t would be as much as any man's job was worth to be found giving information."[88] Mackenzie King was struck by the fear of dismissal of the garment workers he interviewed. "The dread of their employers, entertained by men and women alike, was in many instances distressing." King did not disclose publicly the names of his informants.[89]

The sweated clothing trades were marked not simply by the exploitation of adult labour, but also by widespread use of child labour. There was strong pressure to enlist the help of children. They spared adults work in an occupation where, literally, time was money. Even five-year-old children were capable of pulling out basting: by age ten they could perform simple sewing, such as attaching buttons. Children also were employed commonly to deliver clothing bundles.[90]

Generally, children laboured within the household. A Toronto journalist recounted in 1868 that

> frequently the industrious efforts of a whole family are employed to fill the orders of the employers. Often, in such instances, the child of eight or nine summers is made a source of material help in the construction of the coarser descriptions of men's garments that are now prepared for the ready-made clothing market. In the same way the female head of the house, a group of daughters, and perhaps the male members of the family, if no better occupation is available, turn in to assist the father in adding to their means of support.[91]

Into this century children were commonly employed within the family to assist in garment manufacture. "In poor neighborhoods," the Ontario Committee on Child Labour reported in 1907, "piece work under sweat shop conditions in a room of a dwelling house . . . is very common."[92]

More viciously, children were also subject to harsh exploitation by contractors outside the family context. By the late 1800s, traditional apprenticeships had long since fallen into disuse. Children were used simply as a cheap and docile source of labour. A.W. Wright reported in 1896:

"Learners" are employed usually young girls and boys but the employer is under no obligation to teach them a trade or any part of one. Evidently such a system is capable of gross abuse and there are not wanting instances of such abuse by unscrupulous employers. I learned of one contractor, engaged in making pants and vests, who makes a practice of employing "learners" who engage to work for him without wages while they are learning the trade. These learners, usually girls, are kept at some trivial and easily mastered work, such as pulling out basting threads, sewing on buttons, or running up seams on a sewing machine, and then, when the term for which they agreed to work without wages expires, they are discharged, without having had an opportunity to learn any trade by which they can earn a livelihood, their places being filled by other "learners" who are in turn defrauded out of several months of work and time.[93]

Contractors readily acknowledged that even in the best of circumstances, young girls were hired simply because of the low wages they commanded. As a rule, they were not trained in any more than one branch of clothing manufacture. "I have twenty or twenty-five girls working for me," claimed one contractor in 1896, "and not one of them could make a coat right through."[94] That year some Toronto contractors still recalled a system of indenture, whereby girls would be apprenticed to the trade for four years, but it was no longer practised.[95]

Needleworkers were further afflicted with a distinctive set of health problems. Eye strain produced headaches, giddiness, fainting, hysteria, and occasionally even total blindness. The bent posture in which they laboured, and their lack of exercise, often led to chronic indigestion, ulcers, dysmenorrhoea, and distortion of the spine. The foul, dusty, and fluff-filled atmosphere of the workroom was linked with a variety of lung complaints, including tuberculosis.[96] Sewing machines produced a further set of problems: physical exhaustion, back and shoulder pains, pain in the legs from use of the treadle, deteriorating vision, and "the tremble," caused by the vibration of the machine.[97]

The seasonality of poverty has been extremely well described by Judith Fingard.[98] Winter posed particular hardships for clothing workers.

[I]n the dead of winter, when the trade in the retail houses is slack, and the wholesale houses keep none but their best hands on, the prospect for those who are left suddenly to their own resources is, for the time, miserable indeed. Then, the petty savings from the busy season are anxiously hoarded, and, by dint of great effort are made to last till March or April, when warmer weather, by cheapening fuel, does not so hastily deplete their scanty store, while, at the same time, the increase of work adds to the value of their labour.[99]

The seasonal patterns evident in the use of charitable agencies and public refuges almost certainly extended to prostitution.[100]

Links between needlework and prostitution were frequently drawn by contemporaries. Henry Mayhew estimated that between one-quarter and one-half of all women in readymade clothing work in London in the 1850s were forced to supplement their earnings by prostitution. In some quarters, "seamstress" almost became a euphemism for prostitute.[101]

Far too rarely was the role played by the extremely low wages women received for needle work examined. A "full-time" prostitute offered her opinion on her "seamstress sisters" in a letter to *The Times* (of London).

It is a cruel calumny to call them in mass prostitutes; and as for their virtue, they lose it as one loses his watch by a highway thief. Their virtue is the watch, and society is the thief.[102]

Canadians sensitive to needleworkers' plight made similar arguments. The *Labour Reformer* wrote in 1886:

In Toronto and other Canadian cities there are many girls employed from . . . $2 per week and up . . . Does any man suppose that girls can live respectably upon such wages? Those living with their parents may do so, but it is a lamentable fact that many of these, and more who board, increase their income in ways far from honorable, and in a manner which can only result in degrading our own and future generations.[103]

During a strike against Toronto clothing contractors in 1896, one trade unionist laid out clearly what he felt to be the crux of the issue: "These men would not care if the women prostituted their bodies at night to make a living wage."[104] Mackenzie King recorded in his diary for September 18, 1897 a visit to a needlewoman earning $1.25 weekly and "supporting herself, found she was doing so by prostitution. What a story of Hell. My mind all ablaze."[105] King subsequently hinted at more direct sexual exploitation of female needleworkers: "foremen and contractors had taken a more terrible advantage of those anxious to secure work for a living . . . too terrible to admit of publication."[106]

WHO WAS SWEATED?

Two groups of women were described by contemporaries as doing home needlework, where sweating was most evident. One group, almost certainly a minority, consisted of homeworkers whose subsistence did not depend on needlework. A Toronto journalist wrote in 1868 of women taking in sewing, "interspersing the household duties with a run at the sewing machine . . . its products . . . adding to the comforts and luxuries of their homes."[107] William Muir, a clothing contractor, echoed this view in 1874, claiming that women took in sewing "to buy finery." He continued: "These women sit down when their breakfast, dinner and supper is over, and make a garment, but are not exclusively employed at this work all day."[108] "[W]omen whose husbands are making good wages" take homework, one Toronto contractor remarked in 1896. "They want a little more money for dress and finery and compete against girls who are working for a living."[109] Home needleworkers were described in 1903 as "thrifty housewives and their just as thrifty daughters," who kept shop sewing on hand "to occupy their time in the intervals of domestic and farm work."[110]

In fact, the "typical" houseworker relied on her earnings to feed herself and her family.[111] Research focusing on the major urban centres of Montréal and Toronto has emphasized that for all but a narrow and privileged segment of the working class, the adult male's wages were inadequate to support a family — at least not until well into this century. The working-class family needed more than one breadwinner.[112] The "wives and daughters of mechanics" who are reported to have been engaged in homework in Montréal in 1874, or the "wives of labourers or mill hands" in Hull doing shop sewing in 1901, were almost certainly working to supplement a meagre family income.[113] Homework was one of the few means of earning an income available to women with children. Bettina Bradbury discovered that among the home needle-workers in St.-Jacques Ward in Montréal, 20 per cent had children under two; 45 per cent had children under five.[114] Families with older children would rely on them as secondary wage-earners; until that point in the family life-cycle, women were necessarily employed to supplement inadequate male incomes.[115] Widows, particularly those with children, were among those most dependent on home needlework. Bettina Bradbury has calculated that 40 per cent of the widows in St.-Jacques Ward and 20 per cent of those in Ste.-Anne Ward (both in Montréal) did home sewing.[116] James Munro, Sanford's foreman, acknowledged in 1888 that among Sanford's homeworkers "There are a great many widows and a great many who might as well be widows, as they provide for the whole house."[117]

The lack of alternative sources of income — coupled with pressing need — forced women into homework. No sooner had one contractor, William Muir, linked homework with pin-money, than he reported incongruously: "it makes my heart ache to have the women come crying for work."[118] In 1896, at a time of relentless price reductions in Toronto, one employer described women as "running — breaking their necks you might say — to get the work."[119] It is unlikely that these women were "breaking their necks" for pin-money.

RESPONSES TO SWEATING

However much sweating was associated with ill-lit rooms, with needleworkers huddled together out of sight in garrets and basements, its existence was evident to anyone who cared to look. Hungry-looking people, struggling under heavy loads, were commonplace in urban centres. "Every one has seen," reported one journalist in 1895, "the large numbers of women and children winding their way up or down Bay street, carrying bundles in their arms or on perambulators."[120] Trade unionist Alfred Jury lamented in 1896 "the great number of women staggering up and down with great bundles of clothing; some of the poor creatures hardly able to walk."[121] Even without their telltale bundles, needleworkers, who spent so much of their day bent over their work, often could be identified by their stooped carriage.[122]

The first to respond to sweating were its first victims, tailors. In England, London tailors found conditions in their trade deteriorated rapidly in the wake of an unsuccessful strike against outwork in 1834. By that time, as E.P. Thompson has pointed out, they no longer enjoyed the traditional protection of the Elizabethan apprenticeship statutes, repealed in 1814. The rapid growth of the "dishonourable trades" followed: wages and working conditions in the needle trades were steadily undermined by subcontracting and outwork.[123]

In British North America, as noted above, deteriorating working conditions, including outwork, were in evidence before 1850 in Montréal. In response, tailors began to form some of the earliest unions in British North America. Locals were organized in Montréal (in 1823), Toronto (1845), and Hamilton (1854) as journeymen tailors sought to maintain working standards.[124] Conflict soon followed, generally over the allied issues of pay and contracting out.[125]

The process of contracting out continued into this century, as the custom sector was eroded by relatively cheap readymade production.[126] Inside needleworkers tried, generally unsuccessfully, to prevent ever more categories of clothing from being put out.[127] In the struggle against readymade interlopers, especially in tailoring, labour

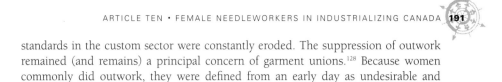

standards in the custom sector were constantly eroded. The suppression of outwork remained (and remains) a principal concern of garment unions.[128] Because women commonly did outwork, they were defined from an early day as undesirable and threatening by journeymen tailors.

By the end of the 19th century the Journeymen Tailors' Union (JTU) and the United Garment Workers (UGW) were the principal unions of clothing workers in North America. They had a precarious foothold in the custom sector, and among skilled workers in readymade manufacture.[129] Their commitment to organizing women was uncertain; their interest in — or even knowledge of — the sweated trades was questionable. Bernard Rose, head of the Montréal Journeyman Tailors, testified to the ignorance or indifference of the skilled custom tailors when, in 1901, he "emphatically assert[ed] that there exist[ed] no form of sweating, at least in the clothing industry of Montréal, at the present time."[130] A cutters' local of the UGW supported Montréal clothing manufacturer Mark Workman when an outcry arose in 1899 over his contravention of anti-sweating clauses in army uniform contracts.[131]

Early efforts to organize female needleworkers, such as those made in Toronto in 1889 (by the Knights of Labor) and in 1897, 1899, and 1900 (by the Journeymen Tailors), proved abortive.[132] It was not until the great industrial unions in ladies' wear, the International Ladies Garment Workers' Union, and in men's wear, the Amalgamated Clothing Workers of America, embarked on vigorous organizational efforts after the turn of this century that garment unions enjoyed some success in (re)establishing industrial standards.[133]

Frustrations encountered by male trade unionists in organizing women made state intervention more attractive.[134] The Trades and Labour Congress (TLC) expressed its concern respecting sweatshops from its founding conference in 1883.[135] Between 1887 and 1895 a resolution in favour of the prevailing (later union) wage on all public contracts was passed annually. In 1893, a resolution calling for the abolition of the sweating system was passed. In 1895 came a successful request for a royal commission to enquire into sweating.[136]

Certainly, collective organization on the part of sweated workers was difficult. Physically isolated, homeworkers were not necessarily acquainted with each other, even those working for the same employer. Homework pit worker against worker, as they bid against each other for work. The sweating system also held out the lure of status as an employer, which discouraged the growth of a collective sense of grievance. In contract shops, ethnic differences divided needleworkers, particularly after the turn of this century when the Jewish presence in the needle trades increased rapidly in Toronto and Montréal. The regular seasonal downturns in the clothing trades also hampered organization. Often, needleworkers were so destitute that a strike immediately meant hunger. Their low level of skill (or rather, their possession of commonly held skills) meant that any strike would be followed by an invasion of replacements. Women faced special challenges in juggling union activity with domestic responsibilities.[137]

Although sweated workers were unlikely to end sweating unassisted, individual acts of resistance occurred. Phillips Thompson offered one example in 1900:

> a poor woman took [legal] action against her employer for her wages. She was promised twenty-five cents per dozen for making boys' pants and the money was withheld on the ground that the work was not well done.[138]

There almost certainly were others, although rare and poorly documented. The sweated seamstress, while not entirely incapable of acting to limit the extent of her exploitation, was ultimately largely dependent on the actions of others.[139]

THE MIDDLE CLASS AND SWEATING

Middle-class efforts to address the problem of sweating were often spearheaded by women's organizations. In facing the problem, Canadian women had a number of American and English models. Three general ways of dealing with sweating were advocated: the organization of sweated outworkers, agitation for protective legislation, and consumer pressure (discriminatory purchasing).[140] These suggestions were not exclusive to the middle class — trade unions at various times advocated similar tactics. Underlying most calls for reform were two convictions: first, that the worker — despite the logic of the capitalist wage market — was entitled to live by his or her work. The second reflected patriarchal unease about women, particularly those with young children, who worked for wages.[141]

Canadian middle-class concern failed to produce organizations comparable to the Women's Trade Union Leagues in the United States and the United Kingdom.[142] The National Council of Women of Canada, which dedicated itself to the advancement of Canadian women (and which, nationally and locally, often demonstrated concern for working women) said of sweating in 1901: "Canada has little or no trouble with this irregular system of manufacture."[143] Ruth Frager has remarked on the gap between early 20th-century Canadian women reformers and the concerns of working-class women, "especially where ethnic differences reinforced class differences."[144] Any local anti-sweating organizations formed rested heavily on the efforts of a handful of individuals and tended to be short-lived.[145] Only with the rise of the Social Gospel movement after 1900 did the Canadian middle class develop organizations committed to a comprehensive range of social reforms.[146]

Until that time, middle-class response to sweating in Canada remained individual and episodic rather than organized and sustained. Concern was often expressed in the popular press. A Toronto journalist, for instance, wrote in 1869 of a widow

> supported by her daughter, who provides food for both, by making pants at 15 cents a pair. Let the young gentlemen who adorn King street of an afternoon, and the old gentlemen who rattle their silver in their pockets, seriously reflect on that fact.[147]

By the 1890s sweating was clearly on journalists' agenda. The Montréal *Herald* was among those newspapers which followed the sweating "question" closely. It exposed in 1897 the 75- to 80-hour work weeks in "old dark tenements" needleworkers faced.

> Occupied as they are from early morning until night, they have little time, even if they had the inclination, to give a thought to the sanitary condition of their surroundings, which are often simply vile. The combination living-room and workshop offers one of the saddest spectacles which can be sought by any humanly disposed person, who seeks light on the subject of human misery.[148]

The *Herald* endorsed in 1899 a fair wage resolution by the federal government, hoping that this measure would close the opportunities offered to "unscrupulous contractors of making large profits whilst paying starvation wages" and describing the consequences of sweating as "impaired health and a permanently broken system."[149] The *Herald* also reported the Montréal Federated Trades Council's call for the abolition of sweating, deploring that "little children of our city, who should be attending school, were being destroyed in the sweat shops."[150]

Fears about public (middle-class) health helped provoke wider concern about the sweated needle trades. Infected clothing was known to spread contagious disease, including scarlatina, diphtheria, and most ominously, smallpox. During the 1885 smallpox epidemic, for instance, many retailers boycotted goods produced in Montréal; Ontario provincial authorities insisted on inspecting and certifying readymade clothing from Montréal.[151] Individuals appalled by the plight of needleworkers saw this fear as a means to mobilize action against the practice of sweated clothing production. James Mitchell raised this worry in the first mention of sweating by a Québec factory inspector, in 1893.[152]

GOVERNMENTS AND SWEATING

The federal royal commission on sweating was appointed in autumn 1895, largely at the prodding of the Trades and Labour Congress. It was chaired by A.W. Wright, a man of broad loyalties. An erstwhile Knights of Labor stalwart, Wright had recently edited the Canadian Manufacturers' Association's *Industrial Canada*. The Canadian decision to appoint a royal commission followed major public inquiries into sweating in the United Kingdom and in the United States during the previous decade.[153]

Wright made a number of recommendations, but the federal government failed to act on any of them. An impending election may have distracted its attention. Charles Tupper pleaded "the pressure of other business."[154] In any case, clear jurisdictional problems (most of Wright's recommendations were clearly within the purview of the provinces) invariably would have produced delays.[155]

The catalyst for federal action was William Lyon Mackenzie King. He had spent winter 1896–97 doing graduate work at the University of Chicago and living at Hull House, one of North America's earliest settlement houses. There, King was first impressed by the extent of the sweated trades. Returning to Toronto the following summer, King found work as a journalist for the *Mail and Empire*, and canvassed Toronto in search of sweated workers.[156]

King soon found them, including "a poor old crippled woman who sewed night and day."[157] He discovered that many of the homeworkers with whom he was brought into contact were making letter carriers' uniforms. Years later, he described his response:

> On questioning one of the workers as to the remuneration she was receiving for sewing machine and hand work, I found that it came to a very few cents an hour. I shall never forget the feeling of pained surprise and indignation I experienced as I learned of the extent of that woman's toil from early morning till late at night, and figured out the pittance she received.

King was further astounded to discover that this homeworker was employed by no fly-by-night subcontractor: "the contracting firm was one of high repute in the city." "As I visited other homes and shops," King continued, "I found the condition of this woman's employment to be in no sense isolated, but all too common."[158] King published his discoveries in a series of newspaper articles.[159]

Mackenzie King proceeded to parlay his family's acquaintance with Postmaster General William Mulock into an appointment as a one-man commission to enquire into the conditions under which government clothing contracts were filled.[160] In his report, first published in 1898, King argued that prices were "quite disproportionate to the amount of work done" and "insufficient to constitute a living wage" for both homeworkers and needleworkers employed in the subcontractor's residence. This intensified pressure to increase the length of the working day, which might extend to 15 hours or more. Sanitary conditions were "frequently foul and noisome."[161] In short, King was able to confirm that "the 'sweating system,' with other objectionable conditions, has accompanied for many years the manufacture of uniforms [for the post office, the militia, and the Mounted Police]."[162]

King closed the report with a warning: that sweating led women to neglect their children and "the duties of the home." He emphasized "[t]he home is still the nursery of the nation."[163] Threats to the home, it was King's conviction, constituted threats to the nation.

Even before the publication of King's report Mulock had acted. He appears to have been genuinely outraged by King's disclosures to him. "Work performed at less than living prices is almost certain to be done under conditions unfavorable to good morals, health or comfort." He required that when the Post Office let contracts, a number of conditions were to be imposed.[164] Subsequently, in March 1900, Mulock introduced "The Fair Wages Resolution" in the House of Commons. This was designed to secure to workers on government contract work a level of wage generally accepted as current in the locality where the work was carried out.[165] Daniel J. O'Donoghue capped his career as a printer, workingman's advocate, and friend to the Liberal party when he was appointed the Dominion's first Fair Wages Officer in March 1900, charged with the preparation and enforcement of fair wage schedules. In the battle against sweated labour, the federal government would act as a model employer.[166]

Both Wright and King had recognized the limits to the federal government's power of action. Wright was explicit about jurisdictional problems; King was unable to offer specific recommendations to the federal government, limiting himself instead to the claim that there existed "sufficient grounds for government interference in order that future contracts may be performed in a manner free from all such objectionable features."[167] These federal commissions made clear that in future, the key legislative action against sweating was to be taken by the provinces.

Ontario and Québec, the major sites of sweating, both had passed Factory Acts during the 1880s. Factory inspectors found the needle trades particularly vexing. The conditions they encountered were deplorable and inspectors realized that the prevalence of outwork meant that there was much they failed to see. Moreover, the Factory Acts did not apply to many of the contexts of sweated labour, something subcontractors were well aware of. Louisa King recounted her frustrations in Québec in 1898 when she requested subcontractors to provide her with the addresses of homeworkers: "ils m'ont presque toujours répondu que leur ouvrage était fait dans les ateliers de famille sur lesquels l'inspecteur n'a point de contrôle."[168]

Factory inspectors were well aware of the inadequacies of the legislation they were charged to enforce.

While factory legislation tends to purify and improve the factories, it does so at an increased expenditure to the factory owners, while these other places [i.e. smaller shops and homes, outside the purview of the Factory Acts] are not subject to any such expense.[169]

Factory Acts, by stipulating basic labour standards, could only encourage manufacturers in their use of the small contract shops and homework which exhibited the most oppressive working conditions. Joseph Lessard told the Montréal *Herald* in 1897 that taxation and sanitary regulations were necessary "to force the workers out of tenements and into shop buildings, where they would be subject to the control and protection of Provincial legislation."[170] Margaret Carlyle echoed his proposal that same year, urging legislators to "drive [needleworkers] from the wretched places in which they now labor into well regulated factories and workshops."[171]

Following repeated requests by its factory inspectors, Ontario took a step toward tightening restrictions on sweating by amending its Shops Regulation Act in 1900. In future, every individual contracting out clothing was to keep a register of the names and addresses of individuals given work. Each article of clothing was to be labelled with the name of the individual who made it.[172] This legislation helped factory inspectors to locate homeworkers (and workers employed in small contractors' shops). It was, though, no solution to sweating. A legislative means to end sweating had to address the question of wages.

The first step in this direction took the form of resolutions on government purchasing policy. The federal government, as we have seen, was including fair wage clauses in some of its contracts from 1897 and passed its Fair Wage Resolution in 1900. Other governments followed. Ontario passed its Fair Wage Resolution in 1900 also.[173] In the United Kingdom, many municipal councils began to add fair wage clauses to their contracts in the 1890s.[174] In 1901, the Ottawa city council agreed to the request of its Allied Trades and Labour Association that it insist on the union label where possible in its purchases.[175] Workers soon discovered, however, that these resolutions, if inconvenient, were easily overlooked by both governments and contractors.[176]

···

The rise of sweating, it has been argued here, was conditioned by the structured inequalities of class and gender. Sweating emerged with the growth of the readymade clothing industry over the 19th century. The capitalist imperative to reduce production costs in the context of a highly competitive clothing market, in tandem with the patriarchal marginalization of women's productive labour, produced the ruthless exploitation of countless thousands of working women described here.

Class and gender also shaped responses to sweating. The social welfare programs initiated on women's behalf — and largely without their participation — were inconsequential. The impact of protective legislation such as Factory Acts, Minimum Wage Acts, and Fair Wage Acts, was slight. Only with Industrial Standards Acts did legislation begin to acquire some teeth.

Sweating's decline is primarily due to factors apart from state intervention. In Ontario, capitalist calculation of profit led to the movement of the workplace from the homes and very small shops where sweating thrived to larger workplaces, including the factory, where trade unions were to enjoy some success in enforcing minimum standards of employment. In Québec, where the movement to factory production was less pronounced, the onus to fight sweating fell more heavily on unions. In both provinces trade unions enjoyed some success between the wars in eliminating the most egregious aspects of sweating.

NOTES

1. Halifax *Morning Herald*, 20 February 1889 as cited in Judith Fingard, *The Dark Side of Victorian Halifax* (Porters Lake, N.S. 1989), 159.
2. Despite their prominence, *Labour/Le Travail*, the journal likeliest to address them, contains only two items on garment workers: Irving Abella, "Portrait of a Jewish Professional Revolutionary: The Recollections of Joshua Gershman," 2 (1977), 185–213 and a research note by Jacques Rouillard, "Les travailleurs juifs de la confection à Montréal (1910–80)," 8/9 (Autumn 1981/Spring 1982), 253–9. Ruth A. Frager, *Sweatshop Strife: Class, Ethnicity, and Gender in the Jewish Labour Movement of Toronto, 1900–1939* (Toronto 1992), stands as a noteworthy recent exception to a general neglect of needleworkers in Canadian working-class history.
3. Within the manufacturing sector, textile mills and shoe factories also made extensive use of women's labour. See *Census of Canada*, 1871–1881, Vol. III.
4. *Census of Canada*, 1901, Vol. III.
5. As defined in 1898 by one of its first Canadian students, William Lyon Mackenzie King, "sweating" described "a condition of labour in which a maximum amount of work in a given time is performed for a minimum wage, and in which the ordinary rules of health and comfort are disregarded. It is inseparably associated with contract work, and is intensified by sub-contracting in shops conducted in homes." See the *Daily Mail and Empire* (Toronto), 9 October 1897, 10.
6. Jacques Ferland, "'In Search of Unbound Prometheia': A Comparative View of Women's Activism in Two Quebec Industries, 1869–1908," *Labour/Le Travail*, 24 (Fall 1989), 12.
7. Sylvia Walby, *Theorizing Patriarchy* (Oxford 1990), 20.
8. Heidi Hartmann, "Capitalism, Patriarchy and Job Segregation by Sex," in Zillah Eisenstein, ed., *Capitalist Patriarchy and the Case for Socialist Feminism* (New York 1979), 206–47; Heidi Hartmann, "The Unhappy Marriage of Marxism and Feminism: Towards a More Progressive Union," in L. Sargent, ed., *Women and Revolution* (Montréal 1981), 1–41.
9. See Sally Alexander, "Women's Work in Nineteenth Century London: A Study of the Years 1820–1850," in Juliet Mitchell and Ann Oakley, eds., *The Rights and Wrongs of Women* (Harmondsworth 1976), 77–83. On the pre-industrial gender-based division of labour in Canada, see Marjorie Griffin Cohen, *Women's Work, Markets and Development in Nineteenth-Century Ontario* (Toronto 1988).
10. When the organization of women did occur at the end of the century other discriminatory practices were employed: lower pay rates for women, job segregation, and ghettoization were enshrined in union contracts.
11. See Wally Seccombe, "Patriarchy Stabilized: The Construction of the Male Breadwinner Wage Norm in Nineteenth-Century Britain," *Social History*, II, No. 1 (January 1986), 53–76, esp. 66–7.
12. On these points, see also Jenny Morris, *Women Workers and the Sweated Trades: The Origins of Minimum Wage Legislation* (Aldershot, Hants. 1986), 192–4.
13. See Paul Craven, *"An Impartial Umpire": Industrial Relations and the Canadian State 1900–1911* (Toronto 1980), especially Chapter 6. For a recent study of protective legislation for women, see Mary Lynn Stewart, *Women, Work, and the French State: Labour Protection and Social Patriarchy, 1879–1919* (Kingston 1989).
14. A similar convergence of forces had led to the passage of the first Factory Acts in the

United Kingdom. See Michelle Barrett and Mary McIntosh, "The 'Family Wage': Some Problems for Socialists and Feminists," *Capital and Class*, No. 11 (1980), 53.

15. Jean-Pierrre Hardy et David-Thiéry Ruddel, *Les apprentis artisans à Québec* (Montréal 1977), 119–20.

16. On the development of Canadian markets see H. Clare Pentland, *Labour and Capital in Canada 1650–1860* (Toronto 1981), Chapter V.

17. Some tailors had always kept on hand small stocks of readymade goods, generally for sale to labourers. This was a sideline, however, to their principal business of custom work. Readymade clothing was often, particularly in the early decades of its manufacture, associated with a very poor quality of workmanship and material.

18. For this paragraph I am indebted to Mary Anne Poutanen, *For the Benefit of the Master: The Montreal Needle Trades During the Transition, 1820–1842*, MA thesis, McGill University, 1985.

19. It was division of labour, not machinery, which brought women into the clothing trades in competition with men. Morris, 37. In this sense, their experience is similar to that in shoemaking, where women first came to be employed — as outworkers — by new divisions of labour. See Joanne Burgess, "L'industrie de la chaussure à Montréal: 1840–1870 — Le Passage de l'artisanat à la fabrique," *La revue de l'histoire de l'amérique française*, Vol. 31, No. 2 (septembre 1977), 187–210.

20. See Gregory L. Teal, *The Organization of Production and the Heterogeneity of the Working Class: Occupation, Gender and Ethnicity among Clothing Workers in Quebec*, PhD dissertation, McGill University, 1985, 167–9.

21. Moss Brothers also anticipated the very large Jewish presence in clothing production which emerged at the turn of this century. See Gerald Tulchinsky, " 'Said to be a very honest Jew': The R.G. Dun Credit Reports and Jewish Business Activity in Mid-19th Century Montreal," *Urban History Review*, XVIII, No. 3 (February 1990), 206.

22. Royal Commission on the Relations Between Labour and Capital [hereafter Labour Commission], *Quebec Evidence*, Part I (Ottawa 1889), 15.

23. In Québec, it also permitted avoidance of a business tax. See *Globe*, 19 November 1898, 1.

24. Canada, House of Commons, *Journals*, 1874, Vol. VIII, Appendix No. 3, "Report of the Select Committee on the Manufacturing Interests of the Dominion" [hereafter Select Committee *Report*], 23.

25. Hollis Shorey dominated the Canadian garment industry in the late 19th century. The son of a shoemaker, Shorey was apprenticed in 1839 to a tailor in Hatley. He subsequently established his own tailoring shop in Barnston, also in the Eastern Townships of Québec. In 1861 he left for Montréal, where he was employed for a number of years as a travelling salesman. At the end of 1866 he began to manufacture on his own account. By 1870 Shorey employed 305 workers, of whom 280 were women. By 1874, Shorey's business had expanded to employ from 700 to 1000 outside workers and perhaps one-tenth that number inside. In 1888 he employed 103 inside and 1450 outside. When he died in 1893 Shorey was the largest clothing manufacturer in Canada, employing 125 workers inside and 1500 outside. (Select Committee *Report*, 22–4; Labour Commission, *Quebec Evidence*, 285; Gerald Tulchinsky, "Hollis Shorey," in Francess G. Halpenny, ed., *Dictionary of Canadian Biography*, Vol. XII (1891–1900), (Toronto 1990), 968–9.

26. James A. Schmiechen, *Sweated Industries and Sweated Labor: The London Clothing Trades, 1860–1914* (Urbana 1984), 2. Similar trends were evident in contemporary Paris. See Christopher H. Johnson, "Economic Change and Artisan Discontent: The Tailors' History, 1800–1848," in Roger Price, ed., *Revolution and Reaction: 1848 and the Second French Republic* (London 1975), 87–114.

27. Hamilton *Gazette*, 28 June 1852, cited in Bryan D. Palmer, *A Culture in Conflict* (Montréal 1979), 11–2. Such abuses persisted, even in custom tailoring. See the *Labour Gazette*, February 1901, 270, on Toronto tailors and "back shops."

28. Canada, *Sessional Papers*, 1896, Vol. XXIX, No. 11 (61, 61A), *Report Upon the Sweating System in Canada* [hereafter Wright Commission], 12.
29. Wright Commission, 25.
30. *Daily Mail and Empire*, 9 October 1897, 10; *Globe*, 19 November 1898, 1.
31. William Lyon Mackenzie King, *Report to the Honourable the Postmaster General of the Methods Adopted in Canada in the Carrying Out of Government Clothing Contracts* (Ottawa 1900) [hereafter King Commission], 6–9, 18. This report was first published in 1898, and reprinted (with minor changes in pagination) in 1899 and 1900.
32. King Commission, 6–10.
33. Ontario Factory Inspector's *Report*, 1897, 19.
34. Michelle Payette-Daoust, *The Montreal Garment Industry, 1871–1901*, MA thesis, McGill University, 1986, 58.
35. Select Committee *Report*, 23.
36. On the attraction of immigrant Jews to garment-making, see Frager, op. cit. See also Robert Babcock, ed., "A Jewish Immigrant in the Maritimes: The Memoirs of Max Vanger," *Acadiensis*, Vol. XVI, No. 1 (Autumn, 1986), 136–48 and David Rome, *On Our Forefathers at Work*, New Series, No. 9 (Montréal 1978), 39–40.
37. Ontario Factory Inspector's *Report*, 1897, 23–4.
38. Ibid., 1899, 23; 1913, 49.
39. Wright Commission, 21. On such swindles, see also Ontario Factory Inspector's *Report*, 1894, 14.
40. *Daily Mail and Empire*, 9 October 1897, 10.
41. F.R. Scott and H.M. Cassidy, *Labour Conditions in the Men's Clothing Industry* (Toronto 1935), 24.
42. Labour Commission, *Ontario Evidence*, 167.
43. "Knight of Labour," "Where Labor is Not Prayer," *Walsh's Magazine* (Toronto 1895–6), 111–6, cited in Michael S. Cross, *The Workingman in the Nineteenth Century* (Toronto 1974), 153.
44. Wright Commission, 13. Montréal contractor Israel Solomon, for instance, made over-coats, employing his father and two girls. He knew nothing of the prices paid for pants or vests. Labour Commission, *Quebec Evidence*, 560.
45. This was the work undertaken by Montréal contractor Jacob Julius Rosen, who had the necessary machinery. Labour Commission, *Quebec Evidence*, 558–9.
46. Wright Commission, 13.
47. *Daily Mail and Empire*, 10 October 1897, 10.
48. Wright Commission, 11–3.
49. Even after the turn of the century, when garments for men and (a decade or two later) women became standardized, there remained a basic technical impediment to automation. Because they are made of *soft* material, garments cannot be mechanically fed into a machine; human hands are needed to hold and guide the material. See Roger D. Waldinger, *Through the Eye of the Needle: Immigrants and Enterprise in New York's Garment Trades* (New York 1986), 54–5.
50. Mercedes Steedman, "Skill and Gender in the Canadian Clothing Industry, 1890–1940," in Craig Heron and Robert Storey, eds., *On the Job: Confronting the Labour Process in Canada* (Kingston and Montréal 1986), 158.
51. Gerald Tulchinsky, "Hidden Among the Smokestacks: Toronto's Clothing Industry, 1871–1901," in David Keane and Colin Read, eds., *Old Ontario: Essays in Honour of J.M.S. Careless* (Toronto 1990), 272.
52. Ibid., 274.
53. Martha Eckmann Brant, "A Stitch in Time: The Sewing Machine Industry of Ontario, 1860–1897," *Material History Bulletin*, Vol. 10 (Spring 1980), 3.
54. See the remarks of Hollis Shorey and William Muir in the Select Committee *Report*, 24, 39.

55. Tulchinsky, "Hidden," 274.
56. Ibid., 271.
57. *Globe*, 19 November 1898.
58. Schmiechen, 26.
59. Steedman, 155–6.
60. Ontario Factory Inspector's *Report*, 1899, 26.
61. Select Committee *Report*, 36.
62. Ontario Sessional Papers, Vol. XXII, Part 7, 1890, *Annual Report of the Bureau of Industry*, 1889, Part IV, "Wages and Cost of Living," 90. The estimate given was $214.28 annually. By making provision only for board, lodging, and clothing, it identified the level of bare subsistence.
63. As a matter of course women were paid much less than men. "I don't treat the men bad," explained one Toronto clothing manufacturer, "but I even up by taking advantage of the women." *Daily Mail and Empire*, 9 October 1897, 10.
64. Ontario Factory Inspector's *Report*, 1894, 14.
65. Wright Commission, 26.
66. King Commission, 12–4.
67. Ibid., 19.
68. Ibid., 15.
69. Quebec Factory Inspector's *Report*, 1897, 39.
70. Ernest J. Chambers, ed., *The Book of Montreal: A Souvenir of Canada's Commercial Metropolis* (Montréal 1903), 171.
71. Scott and Cassidy, 24.
72. Wright Commission, 11.
73. Wright Commission, 26. On foremen demanding bribes, see Mackenzie King's article in the *Daily Mail and Empire* (Toronto), 9 October 1897, 10.
74. *Labour Gazette*, August 1901, 98; May 1901, 466.
75. Labour Commission, *Ontario Evidence*, 348, 358.
76. Wright Commission, 11; King Commission, 13.
77. Wright Commission, 24.
78. Ontario Factory Inspector's *Report*, 1899, 28.
79. Ibid.
80. Wright Commission, 24.
81. King Commission, 14–5.
82. *Globe*, 19 November 1898, 1.
83. Schmiechen, 56.
84. Wright Commission, 38.
85. Ontario Factory Inspector's *Report*, 1901, 12.
86. Ibid., 1911, 19.
87. Wright Commission, 31.
88. Wright Commission, 30.
89. King Commission, 7–8.
90. Christine Stansell, *City of Women: Sex and Class in New York, 1789–1860* (Urbana 1987), 117.
91. *Globe*, 28 October 1868.
92. Ontario, *Report of the Committee on Child Labour*, 1907, 5. See also Dr. Augusta Stowe Gullen, "Child Labour," in National Council of Women of Canada, *Report of the Fourteenth Annual Meeting* (Ottawa 1907), 105.
93. Wright Commission, 10. Mackenzie King noted too the practice of discharging girls after their period of apprenticeship at little or no pay. King Commission, 10.
94. Wright Commission, 46.
95. Ibid., 46.

96. Christina Walkley, *The Ghost in the Looking Glass: The Victorian Seamstress* (London 1981), 31–2.

97. Schmiechen, 50–1. Garment manufacture is still characterized by a distinctive set of health problems. See Susan Wortman, "The Unhealthy Business of Making Clothes," *Healthsharing*, Vol. 1, No. 1 (November 1979), 12–4.

98. Judith Fingard, "The Winter's Tale: The Seasonal Contours of Pre-Industrial Poverty in British North America, 1815–1860," Canadian Historical Association, *Historical Papers/Communications historiques* (1974), 65–94.

99. *Globe*, 28 October 1868.

100. See Ian Davey, "The Rhythm of Work and the Rhythm of School," in Neil McDonald and Alf Chaiton, eds., *Egerton Ryerson and His Times* (Toronto 1978), 221–53.

101. Cited in Schmiechen, 61. Seamstresses turned to part-time prostitution in contemporary Paris also, when their wages were inadequate. See John Wallach Scott, "Men and Women in the Parisian Garment Trades: Discussions of Family and Work in the 1830s and 1840s," in Pat Thane et al., eds., *The Power of the Past: Essays for Eric Hobsbawm* (Cambridge 1984), 83–4. The "fallen" woman depicted in a series of sketches of the underside of municipal life had been a home needleworker. See *Toronto by Gaslight: The Night Hawks of a Great City* (Toronto 1884), 61.

102. 24 February 1858, cited in Walkley, 82.

103. *Labour Reformer*, 1 December 1886, cited in Lori Rotenberg, "The Wayward Worker: Toronto's Prostitutes at the Turn of the Century," in Janice Acton et al., eds., *Women at Work: Ontario, 1850–1930* (Toronto 1974), 47.

104. Wright Commission, 42–3.

105. National Archives of Canada [NAC], W.L. Mackenzie King Diaries, MG 26, J 13, 18 September 1897.

106. *Daily Mail and Empire*, 9 October 1897. On this subject, see also Frager, 126–7.

107. *Globe*, 28 October 1868.

108. Select Committee Report, 36.

109. Wright Commission, 51.

110. Chambers, 171.

111. On this point, see also Schmiechen, 67–111; Morris, 50–79; and Lorraine Coons, *Women Home Workers in the Parisian Garment Industry, 1860–1915* (New York 1987), esp. 1–2.

112. Bettina Bradbury, "The Working-Class Family Economy, Montreal, 1861–1881," PhD dissertation, Concordia University, 1984, 84–161; Terry Copp, *The Anatomy of Poverty: The Condition of the Working Class in Montreal, 1897–1929* (Toronto 1974), 30–42; Michael J. Piva, *The Condition of the Working Class in Toronto — 1900–1921* (Ottawa 1979), 27–60. By 1928, one historian has argued, "it was possible, for the first time, for the average male manufacturing worker to raise a family on his wages alone." Bryan D. Palmer, *Working-Class Experience: The Rise and Reconstitution of Canadian Labour, 1800–1980* (Toronto 1983), 192.

113. Select Committee *Report*, 36; *Labour Gazette*, August 1901, 98.

114. Bettina Bradbury, "The Family Economy and Work in an Industrializing City: Montreal in the 1870s," Canadian Historical Association *Historical Papers/Communications historiques* (Saskatoon 1979), 87.

115. On this point, see Bettina Bradbury, "Gender at Work at Home: Family Decisions, the Labour Market and Girls' Contributions to the Family Economy," in Gregory S. Kealey and Greg Patmore, eds., *Canadian and Australian Labour History* (St. John's 1990), 119–40.

116. Bettina Bradbury, "Surviving as a Widow in 19th-Century Montreal," *Urban History Review*, XVII, No. 3 (February 1989), 151. On widows and sewing, see also Lorna R. McLean, "Single Again: Widow's Work in the Urban Family Economy, Ottawa, 1871," *Ontario History*, LXXXIII, No. 2 (June 1991), 132.

117. Labour Commission, *Ontario Evidence*, 831–2.
118. Select Committee *Report*, 39.
119. Wright Commission, 37.
120. "Knight of Labour," "Where Labor is Not Prayer," *Walsh's Magazine* (Toronto 1895–6), 111–6, cited in Cross, 157.
121. Wright Commission, 23.
122. Stansell, 113–4.
123. On the decline of the British needle trades, see Schmiechen, Chapter One; E.P. Thompson, *The Making of the English Working Class* (Harmondworth 1968), 257.
124. Jacques Rouillard, *Histoire du syndicalisme québécois: Des origines à nos jours* (Montréal 1989), 17; Eugene Forsey, *Trade Unions in Canada, 1812–1902* (Toronto 1982), 28, 17.
125. Paul Craven, "Workers' Conspiracies in Toronto, 1854–72," *Labour/Le Travail*, 14 (Fall 1984), 54; Forsey, 28.
126. Examples of the continual growth of putting-out, and efforts by inside garment workers to prevent it, include an 1896 strike against 19 custom tailor shops in Toronto when they began to put out pants (Wright Commission, 42–3); a strike in 1912 against Toronto clothmakers (*Labour Gazette*, February 1912, 784); and another Toronto strike against subcontracting in 1914 (*Labour Gazette*, June 1914, 1462).
127. Steedman, 165.
128. See, for instance, Rouillard, 256; Piva, 18; John Hample, "Workplace Conflict in Winnipeg's Custom Tailoring Trade, c.1887–1921," *Manitoba History*, No. 22 (Autumn 1991), esp. 6.
129. The Journeymen Tailors' Union of America, based in custom tailoring, arrived in Canada in 1889. It numbered only 300 in 1898. The United Garment Workers of America arrived in 1894 and focused its organizational efforts among cutters and trimmers. It peaked in strength between 1912 and 1915, when 3000 workers were organized in 24 locals. Forsey, 261, 266; Harold Logan, *Trade Unions in Canada* (Toronto 1948), 208.
130. *Canadian Journal of Fabrics*, XVIII, No. 4 (April 1901), 120.
131. *Montreal Herald*, 3 August 1899, 1.
132. See Gregory S. Kealey, *Toronto Workers Respond to Industrial Capitalism, 1867–1892* (Toronto 1980), 183; Wayne Roberts, *Honest Womanhood: Feminism, Femininity and Class Consciousness Among Toronto Working Women 1893 to 1914* (Toronto 1976), 38. The JTU had organized at least some women in Winnipeg as early as 1892. See Hample, 5, 13.
133. Logan, 210–4.
134. This was also the experience of the "new unionists" in Great Britain, who had approached the organization of women workers with enthusiasm. Their inability to organize women led them to support the push for protective legislation. Morris, 123.
135. Labour Canada Library, Trades and Labour Congress of Canada, *Annual Proceedings*, 1883, 22.
136. Forsey, 456.
137. Many of these points are made by Arthur St. Pierre, "Sweating System et Salaire minimum," in his *Le Problème social: Quelques Éléments de Solution* (Montréal 1925), 38. See also Morris, Chapter IV; Frager, 98–107.
138. Cited in Piva, 96.
139. On the question of agency, see R.B. Goheen, "Peasant Politics? Village Community and the Crown in Fifteenth-Century England," *American Historical Review*, 96 (February 1991), 42–62, esp. 60–2.
140. "[M]ore effectual than law," said Mackenzie King of discriminatory purchasing and the union label in 1897. He later changed his mind. *Daily Mail and Empire*, 10 October 1897, 10.
141. On these points, see Morris, Chap. V, and Eileen Boris, "Regulating Industrial Homework: The Triumph of 'Sacred Motherhood,'" *The Journal of American History*, 71 (March 1985), 745–63.

142. On abortive efforts to form a Canadian WTUL in 1917–18, see Frager, 140–1.

143. National Council of Women of Canada, *Women of Canada* (Montréal 1901), 105.

144. Frager, 148. On the other hand, Nellie McClung claimed to have taken Premier Rod-mond Roblin through the sweatshops of Winnipeg in 1913 as part of her campaign for the appointment of a female factory inspector in Manitoba. See Nellie L. McClung, *The Stream Runs Fast: My Own Story* (Toronto 1965), 101–6.

145. In Toronto, the Working Women's Protective Association was organized in 1893 under the dynamic leadership of Marie Joussaye. During its brief lifetime it pushed for better conditions for female workers; Roberts, 42–3. Helena Rose Gutteridge was active in Vancouver after 1911 in organizing working women and lobbying for protective legisla-tion. Alison Prentice et al., *Canadian Women: A History* (Toronto 1988), 200–1.

146. Richard Allen, *The Social Passion: Religion and Social Reform in Canada, 1914–28* (Toronto 1973).

147. *Globe*, 26 January 1869, cited in Cross, 194.

148. *Montreal Herald*, 3 February 1897, cited in Rome, 39–40.

149. *Montreal Herald*, 2 August 1899, 2, 4.

150. *Montreal Herald*, 4 August 1899, 8.

151. Michael Bliss, *Plague: A Story of Smallpox in Montreal* (Toronto 1991), 119, 142.

152. Quebec Factory Inspector's *Report*, 1893, 111; see also 1901, 166. Such concerns are echoed by A.W. Wright and Mackenzie King. See Wright Commission, 12; King Com-mission, 28–9; Globe, 19 November 1890.

153. In the United Kingdom, John Burnett conducted a major investigation into sweating in London's East End for the Board of Trade in 1887. This was followed by the striking of the "Select Committee of the House of Lords on the Sweating System," which issued five lengthy reports between 1888 and 1890. In the United States, the House of Repre-sentatives' Committee on Manufactures published its *Report* on the *Sweating System* in 1893.

154. House of Commons, *Debates*, 1 April 1896, 5052.

155. Most radically, Wright called for the extension of the Factory Acts to households "in which more than the husband and wife are employed and in which articles of any kind intended for sale are being manufactured." He further called for national standards of factory legislation. Wright also recommended that manufacturers be obliged to give fac-tory inspectors the names and addresses of all individuals to whom work was subcon-tracted. Further recommendations called for protection at law for (the often unpaid) "learners," wholesalers' responsibility for the wages of (sub)contractors' employees, the labeling of "home-produced" goods (to invite consumers to pass judgement), and the licensing of dwellings (licenses were only to be granted if dwellings met certain stan-dards of hygiene). The latter two recommendations were already law in certain Ameri-can states. (Wright Commission, 17–9).

156. William Lyon Mckenzie King, *Industry and Humanity: A Study in the Principles Underlying Industrial Reconstruction* (Toronto 1973 [1918]), 54–5.

157. NAC, King Diaries, MG 26, J 13, 18 September 1897.

158. King, *Industry and Humanity*, 55–6.

159. The first of these was "Toronto and the Sweating System," published in the *Daily Mail and Empire* on 9 October 1897.

160. King, *Industry and Humanity*, 56.

161. King Commission, 21–6.

162. Ibid., 5.

163. Ibid., 28.

164. Most importantly, subcontracting was banned (unless special permission was granted by the government, work was to be carried out on the contractor's own premises) and current wages were to be paid. If these conditions were not observed, contracts might be cancelled and/or the contractor fined. *Globe*, 30 September 1897.

165. House of Commons, *Debates*, 22 March 1900, 2466. Two and one-half years' delay indicates Mulock likely had difficulty convincing his cabinet colleagues of such a resolution. One member of the opposition declared that the resolution was simply a sop to the TLC by a government embarrassed by non-enforcement of the Alien Labour Act (2490–1). The Fair Wages Resolution formally passed on 17 July 1900 (10495–10502). The resolution did not have legal force until 1930, when the Fair Wages and Eight-Hour Day Act was passed. (21–22 Geo. V, Chap. 20, *Statutes of Canada*, 1930).

166. Doris French, *Faith, Sweat, and Politics: The Early Trade Union Years in Canada* (Toronto 1962), 132. These schedules, most commonly pertaining to public works such as wharves and post offices, regularly appear in the pages of the *Labour Gazette*. See, for instance, the issue for September 1900, 15–27. For clothing contracts, see *Labour Gazette*, October 1904, 505.

167. King Commission, 31.

168. Quebec Factory Inspector's *Report*, 1898, 80. When first passed, the Factory Acts of Québec and Ontario applied only to establishments employing more than twenty workers. Although Québec dropped this clause in 1888, it continued to exempt homework. In Ontario, although amendments in 1889 brought all establishments with at least five workers under the purview of the Factory Act, many contractors' shops escaped regulation because of their modest size. (See *Statutes of Quebec*, 1885, Chap. 32, "An Act to Protect the Life and Health of Persons Employed In Factories"; the Act was amended in 1888 [Chap. 49]. *Statutes of Ontario*, 1884, Chap. 39, "An Act for the Protection of Persons Employed in Factories"; 1889, Chap. 43, "An Act to Amend the Ontario Factories Act.").

169. Ontario Factory Inspector's *Report*, 1899, 26–7.

170. *Montreal Herald*, 3 February 1897. British Fabians had long advocated the development of "large and healthy factories." See, for instance, Beatrice Potter, *How Best to do away with the Sweating System* (Manchester 1892), 12.

171. Ontario Factory Inspector's *Report*, 1897, 24.

172. *Statutes of Ontario*, 1900, Chap. 43, "An Act to amend The Ontario Shops Regulation Act." The Act also stipulated that all dwellings where clothing was manufactured were to be certified by a health inspector, who was to set limits on the number of people to be employed on the premises. This certification was revocable at any time in the event that sanitary standards were not maintained.

173. *Labour Gazette*, September 1900, 25–6. The western provinces did not pass similar resolutions until World War One. See Bob Russell, "A Fair or Minimum Wage? Women Workers, the State, and the Origins of Wage Regulation in Western Canada," *Labour/Le Travail*, 28 (Fall 1991), 72. It was only in 1936 that Ontario gave its Fair Wage Resolution teeth by requiring by law minimum labour standards on its contracts. See *Statutes of Ontario*, 1936, Chap. 26, "The Government Contracts Hours and Wages Act, 1936."

174. Morris, 130.

175. It is unclear whether the Ottawa council had the courage of its convictions. On the first contract to be tendered after the adoption of this policy, for firemen's clothing, the sole bidder offered uniforms at $21–22 with the label, and at $16.95 without. See the *Ottawa Citizen*, 1 May 1901, 2.

176. The federal government was less than diligent in enforcing the anti-sweating clauses in its contracts. In the affair of the large clothing contract awarded Montréal manufacturer Mark Workman in 1898–99, Laurier's government winked at Workman's failure to observe anti-sweating clauses. See the House of Commons *Debates* for 1 August 1899. It was to have been applied to railway contracts. (*Debates*, 22 March 1900, 2471). Railway navvies would have been surprised to have been informed of this.

TOPIC SIX
Violence

Joseph Légaré's Burning of
the Canadian Parliament
Buildings *depicts the April
1849 riot that erupted in
Montreal following Lord
Elgin's signing of the Rebellion
Losses Bill.*

Canada has often been described as a "peaceable kingdom" free of the crime and violence of its southern neighbour. While historians have studied notable outbreaks of violence such as the 1837 rebellions in Upper and Lower Canada and the uprisings led by Louis Riel in the North West, these events are typically viewed as exceptional and not in keeping with Canadians' presumed preference for orderly and evolutionary change.

Despite the persistence of such a powerful national myth, a number of historians have discovered that violent popular disturbances were a regular occurrence in nineteenth-century Canada. One historian has identified over 400 riots between 1800 and 1850 in British North America. Political campaigns were often accompanied by violent clashes between partisan supporters. Labour disputes frequently erupted in conflict as workers fought to defend their interests or employers called in the police or militia to end a strike. Ethnic and religious rivalries could also result in violent confrontations, as Scott W. See demonstrates in Article Eleven, on the Orange Order in Saint John. See attributes the rising popularity of the Orange Order and the willingness of its members to resort to violence against Irish Catholic immigrants during the 1840s to growing nativism on the part of New Brunswickers during a period of economic uncertainty.

But violence was not confined to the public sphere, as Kathryn Harvey reveals in Article Twelve, on wife abuse in working-class Montreal during the 1870s. In her exploration of the causes of the family violence there, Harvey counters the notion of the home as a place of refuge from the brutality of the world with her picture of a very different reality for the working class. Both articles demonstrate that violence was not a rare and isolated occurrence but an everyday feature of life in nineteenth-century Canada.

QUESTIONS TO CONSIDER

1. How does See explain the rise of nativist feeling in Saint John at mid-century? Who joined the Orange Order, and what attracted them? How did the police and the courts treat the rioters? Why did the riots decline after 1849?
2. What were the immediate and the underlying causes of the family violence in working-class Montreal? How did battered women respond to their abuse? What were society's attitudes toward domestic violence?
3. To what degree was nineteenth-century Canada shaped by a "culture of violence"?

SUGGESTED READINGS

Beal, Bob, and Rod Macleod. *Prairie Fire: The 1885 North-West Rebellion*. Edmonton: Hurtig, 1984.

Bleasdale, Ruth. "Class Conflict on the Canals of Upper Canada in the 1840s." *Labour/Le Travail*, 7 (1981): 9–39.

Cross, Michael. "The Shiners' War: Social Violence in the Ottawa Valley in the 1830s." *Canadian Historical Review*, 54 (1973): 1–26.

Cross, Michael. "Stoney Monday, 1849: The Rebellion Losses Riots in Bytown." *Ontario History*, 63 (1971): 177–90.

Dubinsky, Karen. *Improper Advances: Rape and Heterosexual Conflict in Ontario, 1880–1929*. Chicago: University of Chicago Press, 1993.

Greer, Allan. *The Patriots and the People: The Rebellion of 1837 in Rural Lower Canada*. Toronto: University of Toronto Press, 1993.

See, Scott W. "Polling Crowds and Patronage: New Brunswick's 'Fighting Elections' of 1842–3." *Canadian Historical Review*, 72 (1991): 127–56.

See, Scott W. *Riots in New Brunswick: Orange Nativism and Social Violence in the 1840s*. Toronto: University of Toronto Press, 1993.

Stanley, George F.G. "The Caraquet Riots of 1875." *Acadiensis*, 2 (1972): 21–38.

Torrance, Judy. *Public Violence in Canada, 1867–1982*. Montreal/Kingston: McGill-Queen's University Press, 1986.

ELEVEN

The Orange Order and Social Violence in Mid-Nineteenth Century Saint John

SCOTT W. SEE

In March 1839, the St. Patrick's, St. George's and St. Andrew's societies held a joint meeting in Saint John, New Brunswick. Delegates noted and condemned the Protestant–Catholic confrontations that appeared to be endemic in Boston and other unfortunate American cities. In a spirit of congeniality, they applauded themselves on the good fortune of living in a British colony free of such acrimonious religious strife. Generous toasts were proposed to young Queen Victoria, Lieutenant-Governor Sir John Harvey and, most effusively, to each other.[1] A short eight years later, after Saint John and neighbouring Portland had experienced a series of bloody riots involving Protestant Orangemen and Irish Catholics, those sentiments would be recalled with bitter irony. Sarcastic comparisons would then be drawn between Saint John and New Orleans, a tumultuous city with a reputation for collective violence.[2]

What happened to shatter the calm, and why would the toasts of 1839 turn out to be so farcical in the light of events during the 1840s? Why would Saint John and Portland, relatively stable communities that escaped major incidents of social violence prior to the 1840s, become ethno-religious battlegrounds involving natives and immigrants?[3] The growth of Irish Catholic immigration to Saint John and Portland before mid-century was accompanied by the expansion of the Orange Order as an institutionalized nativist response to those unwelcome settlers. Confrontations between the two groups began with relatively mild clashes in the late 1830s and culminated in the great riots of 1847 and 1849. The Ireland-based Orange Order, fueled originally by British garrison troops and Irish Protestant immigrants, attracted significant numbers of native New Brunswickers and non-Irish immigrants because of its anti-Catholic

Source: "The Orange Order and Social Violence in Mid-Nineteenth Century Saint John," *Acadiensis*, 13, 1 (Autumn 1983): 68–92. Reprinted by permission.

and racist appeal. By mid-century it functioned as a nativist organization whose purpose was to defend Protestantism and British institutions against Irish Catholic encroachment. The clashes in Saint John and Portland were not primarily the result of transplanted rivalries between Protestant and Catholic Irish immigrants, as was commonly believed by contemporaries and historians.[4] Rather they represented both a vehement rejection of certain immigrants because of cultural and religious differences and a symbolic struggle to protect Protestant jobs against competitive Irish Catholic famine victims during a decade of severe economic hardship. Thus as Irish Catholic immigration burgeoned, so did the nativist Orange Order.

Saint John was New Brunswick's most populous city in the 19th century.[5] Settled by Loyalists in 1783 and incorporated two years later, it rapidly developed into the province's primary port for the export of staple timber goods and the import of manufactured products and foodstuffs. Lying in its northern shadow was the shipbuilding and mill town of Portland, now annexed into greater Saint John. The localities were connected by several roads, the busiest thoroughfare being a dilapidated bridge spanning an inlet on the harbour's northern extremity.[6] Both communities bustled in mid-century; along the narrow streets and wharves sailors rubbed shoulders with tradesmen, merchants, lawyers, mill workers and itinerant labourers. Moreover, both gained their economic focus almost entirely from New Brunswick's timber staple. Sawn lumber and deals were shipped to the British Isles from their wharves, while numerous sawmills and shipyards dotted their skylines. In turn, the two communities received the bulk of New Brunswick's imports, including immigrants.[7]

Despite their industriousness, Saint John and Portland had fallen on hard times in the 1840s. Indeed all of New Brunswick suffered from the worst sustained downturn since the colony's inception.[8] Several factors accounted for this. First, the colony had enjoyed decades of timber trading privileges with Great Britain due to a combination of preference subsidies and high tariffs for foreign imports. But starting in 1842, England began to shift toward a policy of free trade in an attempt to curtail its soaring deficits. Subsequently it lowered or dropped its foreign tariffs and increased colonial duties. News of England's policy change created chaos in New Brunswick. Fears of the ramifications of such a move led to a decade of lost confidence among investors and merchants. Although New Brunswick would experience a slight recovery in 1844, due primarily to speculation that Great Britain's railroad fever would stimulate the timber trade, the decade would be marked by high unemployment, rising commodity prices, commercial bankruptcies and legislative indebtedness.[9] Second, a worldwide glut of lumber and overexploitation of New Brunswick's forests caused a severe export slump.[10] Later in the decade, moreover, hundreds of workers were displaced as the province's sawmills abandoned labour-intensive operations in favor of steam-driven machinery.[11] These factors combined to create a decade of commercial distress that crippled Saint John and Portland, especially in the years 1842–3 and 1845–9.

During this decade of financial hardship, these communities experienced dramatic changes in immigrant patterns. Prior to the 1840s, both were relatively homogeneous. Indeed New Brunswick in general consisted primarily of the descendants of Loyalists and pre–Revolutionary War New England settlers, plus a moderate number of immigrants from England, Scotland and Ireland. The only significant non-Protestants were the Acadians, who populated the northern and eastern shores and the north-western interior. Moreover, the immigrant flow throughout the 1830s was strikingly consistent; for example, 1832 and 1841 differed in raw totals by only twelve.[12] This fairly uniform influx brought an increasingly large proportion of Irish, a trend that would continue to mid-century.[13]

Prior to the 1840s the majority of these Irishmen came from the Protestant northern counties. Most were of Scots or English ancestry, reflecting the British colonization of Ireland. They were artisans and tenant farmers with modest savings who sought a better life within the British colonial system. Most importantly, they shared cultural and ideological views with the native New Brunswickers and other British emigrants they encountered. They adhered to Protestantism and supported the English constitutional and political domination of Ireland. Thus they made a relatively smooth transition to their new lives in New Brunswick.[14]

During the 1830s, however, emigrant patterns within Ireland shifted and thereby profoundly altered the demographic face of New Brunswick. The more skilled, financially-solvent Protestant Irishmen from northern counties began to be replaced by more destitute Catholics from Ireland's poorer southern and western regions. The percentage of Irish Catholics who emigrated to New Brunswick before 1840 was small, yet ever-increasing. The trickle became a flood as a tragic potato famine decimated Ireland's staple crop from 1845 to 1848.[15] New Brunswick's immigration rate would increase yearly by at least 150 per cent from 1843 until 1847, when the Irish famine tide finally crested. For the mid-1840s, the province would receive virtually all of its immigrants from the Catholic districts of Ireland. For example, of the 9,765 immigrants arriving in 1846, 99.4 per cent were from Ireland. Of these, 87 per cent landed in Saint John, clearly underscoring the city's role as the province's chief immigration port. The overwhelming majority were poor Catholic agricultural labourers.[16] New Brunswick in the 1840s, and particularly Saint John, was bombarded with thousands of non-Anglo-Saxon Protestants.

The influx of Irish Catholics dramatically altered the ethno-religious faces of Saint John and Portland. Although perhaps half of the incoming Irish used the ports as temporary shelters, earning enough at manual labour along the docks for the fare on a coastal vessel heading for the United States, thousands of the poor agrarian peasants remained.[17] By mid-century, more than one-third of the residents of Saint John and Portland were born in Ireland. More profoundly, Catholicism mushroomed. Roman Catholics were as large as any Protestant sect in Saint John by the mid-1840s; when the 1861 census appeared, the first to include religious data, both localities had populations almost 40 per cent Catholic. Since the Acadians, who were New Brunswick's only other substantial Catholic population, were practically nonexistent in the Saint John region during mid-century, Irishmen accounted almost entirely for the high Catholic population.[18]

The Irish Catholics settled primarily in two sections of Saint John and Portland. They clustered in overcrowded squalor in York Point, a district of north-western Saint John bounded roughly by Union Street to the south, George's Street to the east, Portland Parish to the north and the bay to the west.[19] In Portland, they huddled in the busy wharf area on the harbour's northern shore. The two districts, connected by the "Portland Bridge," grew into twin ethno-religious ghettos during the 1840s.[20] They were so strongly identified with Irish Catholics that they would play host to virtually all of the major episodes of social violence between Orangemen and Irishmen during the decade.

The influx of thousands of Celtic Catholics into the Protestant Anglo-Saxon bastions of Saint John and Portland triggered a nativist response among the more entrenched residents. A useful paradigm for interpreting nativism was pioneered by John Higham, and while his model concerned American movements, it applies equally well for any nativist response. Higham's nativism was the "intense opposition to an internal minority on the ground of its foreign . . . connections," or a "defensive type of nationalism." Though Higham cautioned that the word "nativism," of 19th-century derivation, has become pejorative, his definition provides a valuable intellectual foundation for analyzing people's reaction to immigrants.[21] In the context of the British colonial experience, nativists tended less to focus on place of birth than to draw inspiration from the virtues of Protestantism and British institutions.[22] From this perspective, the local response to incoming Irish Catholics may clearly be considered as a nativist response. Protestants who wanted to discourage Catholic settlement and block further immigration began to channel their energies into an institutionalized counter-offensive during the 1840s. As Saint John's *Loyalist and Conservative Advocate* explained:

> The necessity . . . for Protestant organization in this Province, arose not more from the many murderous attacks committed upon quiet and unoffending Protestants, by Catholic ruffians, than from the dreary prospect which the future presented. The facts were these: several thousands of immigrants were annually landing upon our shores; they were nearly all Catholics, nearly all ignorant and bigotted, nearly all paupers, many of them depraved . . . What have we to expect but murder, rapine, and anarchy? Let us ask, then, should not Protestants unite? Should they not organize?[23]

The call to battle was dutifully answered by an organization with a history of responding to similar entreaties in Ireland and England — the Loyal Orange Order.

The Orange Order became the vanguard of nativism in mid-19th century New Brunswick, yet the organization was neither new nor unique to the province. After a violent birth in Loughgall, Ireland in 1795, Orangeism quickly spread throughout Northern Ireland and England. As a fraternal body tracing its roots to a feuding tradition between Protestant and Catholic weavers and farmers, the Orange Order paid ideological homage to the British Crown and Protestantism. Group cohesion was provided by a system of secret rituals, an internal hierarchy of five "degrees" and the public celebration of symbolic holidays such as 12 July, the anniversary of the victory of the Prince of Orange (King William III) over Catholic King James II at the Battle of the Boyne in 1690. In the early 19th century the Orange Order was firmly entrenched in the British Isles, where its members fervently combated the growth of Jacobinism and Roman Catholicism.[24]

Given the ideological foundations of the Orange Order, it transferred well within the British Empire. British garrison troops who joined the organization while stationed in Ireland carried warrants for new lodges when they transferred to new posts. Irish Protestant immigrants who settled in England and British North America also brought Orange warrants as part of their "cultural baggage." By the early 19th century, British regulars in Halifax and Montreal were holding formal Orange meetings. Lodges mushroomed as they found support among Loyalists and the swelling ranks of Irish Protestant immigrants. In 1830 a Grand Orange Lodge, headquartered in Upper Canada, obtained permission from Ireland to issue lodge warrants for all of British North America except New Brunswick.[25]

New Brunswick's organized lodges, dating from the turn of the century, clearly reflected a similar pattern of garrison troop and Irish immigrant conveyance. The earliest known lodge, formed among soldiers of the 74th Regiment in Saint John, met regularly by 1818. Six years later they obtained an official Irish warrant.[26] After several abortive efforts to establish civilian lodges in the mid-1820s, Orangeism became rooted among Saint John's Irish Protestants in 1831. Initial growth was sluggish. Fifteen local, or "primary," lodges existed by 1838, representing ten in Saint John and Portland. Membership tended to be small, with some lodges having only a handful of regular participants. Even the establishment of a provincial Grand Orange Lodge in 1837–8, under the mastership of James McNichol, failed to generate widespread growth and attract significant numbers. With the advent of the 1840s New Brunswick's Orange Lodges, particularly in Saint John and Portland, were staffed primarily by small numbers of recent Irish Protestant immigrants and British troops.[27]

A catalyst appeared in the 1840s to spur growth in the fledgling organization. The rising tide of famine immigration brought concerned Protestants to the organization's doorstep, seeking action and viable solutions to the Irish Catholic "menace." By the close of 1844, when the transition from Protestant to Catholic emigrant was well underway in Ireland, New Brunswick had 27 lodges. Of these, ten were less than a year old. As Irish Catholics arrived and filtered throughout the province, Orange Lodges burgeoned to lead the counter-offensive. Buttressed by a network of primary, county, district and provincial lodges, Orangeism swept up the St. John River Valley hard on the heels of the Catholic immigrants. Mid-century found 123 primary lodges across the province, representing a five-year growth of 455 per cent.[28] Together with its smaller Nova Scotia affiliates, New Brunswick's Orange Order boasted an estimated 10,000 members. Yet despite its impressive expansion, the Orange Order's seat of power and membership base remained firmly rooted in Saint John and Portland.[29]

The traditional membership pools did not account for the explosive growth of Orangeism. Irish Protestant immigration dropped dramatically during the 1840s, becoming negligible by mid-century. Moreover, Britain reduced its garrison troops because of budgetary constraints. What, then, explained the Orange Order's meteoric rise? How did the organization broaden its attraction to ensure its survival? The answers were to be found in the Order's ideological appeal to native New Brunswickers and non-Irish Protestant immigrants.

Evidence of Orange membership in the 1840s clearly proved that initiates came from various cultural groups and classes. While the organization may have been rooted among British garrison troops and Irish Protestant settlers, it succeeded only because it found a willing supply of Loyalist and New England descendants and non-Irish immigrants who shared its philosophical tenets. In other words, to tell the story of Orangeism in mid-19th century New Brunswick is to trace the growth of an indigenous social movement. At least half of all identified Orangemen in mid-century were born in New Brunswick. They came from all walks of life, including legislators, barristers, magistrates, doctors, ministers, farmers, artisans and unskilled labourers. Motivated primarily by locally-defined problems and prejudices, many New Brunswick natives and immigrants found the Orange Order both philosophically and socially attractive.[30]

In the Saint John region, some natives participated in Orange activities when lodges first appeared in the early 19th century. Indeed, several of the nascent city lodges drew their membership exclusively from transplanted New Englanders and Loyalists from America's mid-Atlantic and southern regions.[31] When the provincial Grand Orange Lodge organized in 1844, prestigious native Saint John residents were

there. They included W.H. Needham, a justice of the peace, H. Boyd Kinnear, a lawyer, and Thomas W. Peters, Jr., a city official. Each would assume an Orange leadership role at some point in his career.[32] During the period of intensified social violence,
in 1845–9, Saint John and Portland residents embraced the Orange Order because of
its campaign to protect Protestantism and British hegemony against the bewildering
and oftentimes frightening effects of Irish Catholic immigration.[33] For example, Portland's Wellington Lodge welcomed its largest initiate group since its inception in the
meeting following the great Orange–Catholic riot of 12 July 1849.[34]

Membership lists also illuminated the Orange Order's effective appeal to native-
born in Saint John and Portland. Data gleaned from official lodge returns, trial tran-
scripts, Orange histories and newspapers yielded the names of 84 active Orange members in the late 1840s. When matched against the available 1851 manuscript census
returns from Saint John County, they showed significant native involvement in
Orangeism: 56 per cent were not Irish-born, including 43 per cent native and 13 per
cent other Protestant immigrants.[35] Moreover, the entrenchment of Irish Protestants in
the Orange Order was evident because 80 per cent of them had emigrated to New
Brunswick prior to 1840. The occupational range already noted for provincial Orangemen was corroborated by the Saint John evidence, though a higher proportion of
members could be classified as skilled or unskilled labourers. Finally, the portrait of
Saint John Orangemen revealed a youthful organization: almost three-quarters of
those traced were less than 40 years old in 1851.[36] Clearly, the Orange Order in Saint
John and Portland in mid-century represented a mixture of native-born and Protestant immigrants.

The essential ideological glue of the Orange Order was unquestioning loyalty to
the Crown and an emphatic rejection of Roman Catholicism. With these concepts
codified in the initiation oaths, Orangeism guaranteed itself a philosophical continu-
um that transcended the divergent social appeals and emphases of individual primary lodges.[37] In New Brunswick, lodges exercised a great deal of independence. Several
accepted only temperate men; others attracted members by offering burial insurance
plans; still more touted their commitment to charitable endeavours.[38] New Brunswick's Orange Lodges had disparate social and functional appeals, and many men
gathered under the symbolic Orange banner. Except in the rare case where evidence
exists, individual motives for joining the organization are a matter for speculation.
Nevertheless, the philosophies and goals of Orangemen may be justifiably construed
from organizational rhetoric and collective behaviour.

Orange rhetoric in the 1840s strikingly resembled the propaganda campaigns
carried out by American and British nativists during the same period. New Brunswick
Orangemen charted an elaborate counter-offensive to combat Irish Catholic immigration and permanent settlement. The organization's views were stated succinctly in two
documents from the late 1840s. In a welcoming address to Lieutenant-Governor
Edmund Head, Orangemen explained:

> Our chief objects are the union of Protestants of the several denominations, to counter-
> act the encroachments of all men, sects or parties, who may at any time attempt the sub-
> version of the Constitution, or the severance of these Colonies from the British Empire;
> to bind Protestants to the strict observance of the Laws, and to strengthen the bonds of
> the local authorities, by the knowledge that there is ever a band of loyal men ready in case
> of emergency, to obey their commands, and assist them in the maintenance of order.[39]

Thomas Hill, the zealous Orange editor of the *Loyalist and Conservative Advocate*, was more direct in his appraisal of the fraternity:

> Orangeism had its origins in the *necessity* of the case; it has spread in this Province, also from *necessity*, for had not the country been infested with gangs of lawless ruffians, whose numerous riots, and murderous deeds compelled Protestants to organize for mutual defence, Orangeism would have been scarcely known. And whenever the *Cause* shall disappear, Orangeism may retrograde.[40]

Underscored in the above quotations was the unique philosophical framework which Orangemen operated within: unquestioning loyalty, exclusive Protestantism and the threat to carry out their policies with vigilante force.

New Brunswick's Orangemen, in an effort to check the Irish Catholic invasion, fought a rhetorical battle on several fronts. The overarching goal was to maintain the colony as a Protestant and British bulwark against Catholicism. The Orange Order directly appealed to all Protestants who feared that the ethno-religious supremacy enjoyed by Anglo-Saxons would be permanently undermined or destroyed by the swelling numbers of Celtic Irishmen. Orangemen even advocated the repeal of legislation giving Catholics the franchise and the right to serve in the legislature.[41]

Anti-Catholic diatribes grew in part from a papal conspiracy myth that enjoyed a North American vogue in the mid-19th century.[42] New Brunswick's Orangemen claimed the famine immigration was but a skirmish in a global battle, masterminded in the Vatican, to expunge Protestantism from the earth. A Saint John editor who supported Orangeism warned that "A great, perhaps a final, conflict is at hand between Protestant Truth and Popery leagued with Infidelity."[43] Orangemen embarked on a propaganda campaign to educate Protestants about the Pope's despotic control over Catholics — in church, in the home, in the workplace and on the hustings. Only by removing the insidious network of priests, Orangemen argued, could papal control over the "uncivilized minds" of the Irish Catholics in New Brunswick be broken.[44]

Another vital weapon in the Orangemen's arsenal rested upon the assumption that the Celtic Irish were inherently an unruly and violent race. The stereotype had a measure of truth. As a subjugated people under English rule, Irish Catholics often resorted to disruptive tactics to achieve their goals.[45] As poor Irish Catholics crowded into squalid quarters in York Point and Portland, Orangemen bandied stereotypes of the Celtic propensity for strong drink and villainy. After all, they argued, "no one can deny that the lower orders of the Roman Catholic Irish are a quarrelsome, headstrong, turbulent, fierce, vindictive people."[46] Petty crime did increase dramatically as Saint John and Portland absorbed thousands of the famine immigrants, but it is more plausible to suggest that factors such as overcrowding, poverty and hunger were more responsible for creating a crucible for crime than were cultural idiosyncrasies.[47] Tragically, Orangemen painted all Catholics with the same nativist brush. Though even the most scurrilous propagandists recognized that not all immigrants participated in this orgy of crime, they nevertheless called for Orange vigilantism in York Point and Portland. Moreover, they suggested dispersing the immigrants among loyal Protestants. The theory was that such a dilution would facilitate social control and the assimilation of those immigrants who chose to remain. For the Orangemen of mid-19th century Saint John, every Celtic Irishman was a potential criminal.[48]

New Brunswick's Orange rhetoric was also laced with racism, mirroring the contemporary British philosophy of Anglo-Saxon superiority.[49] Ethnicity was mingled with class as Orangemen railed against the "ignorant Mickie" hordes who formed a substandard "class of people." The destitution of famine immigrants as they disembarked in Saint John, and the squalor of their ghettos in York Point and Portland, appeared to corroborate Orange assertions of Celtic inferiority. Here was positive proof that the Protestant Anglo-Saxon must remain firmly in legislative and judicial control in order to assure the colony's peaceful survival.[50] The more zealous Orange propagandists, believing that assimilation was a bankrupt concept, called for the deportation of all Celtic Catholics. One might as well, they argued, "attempt to change the colour of the Leopard's spots, or to 'wash the Ethiope white,' as to attempt to tame and civilize the wild, turbulent, irritable, savage, treacherous and hardened natives of the Cities and Mountains of Connaught and Munster."[51] The editors of the *Loyalist and Conservative Advocate*, the *Weekly Chronicle* and the *Christian Visitor*, all either Orange members or openly sympathetic to the organization's policies, regularly exposed their readers to racist editorials, Irish jokes, and vignettes pointing out the sub-human proclivities of the Celtic immigrant. Through their efforts, the argument of Anglo-Saxon racial superiority fell convincingly upon the ears of native Protestants who feared the demise of peace, order and good government in New Brunswick.[52]

Yet another focal point for Orange propagandists was the tangible threat that the poor Irish Catholic immigrants represented a formidable and willing pool of cheap labourers.[53] The famine victims, thrust into the severely depressed economy of the 1840s, were greeted as pariahs by Saint John's working classes. The destitute Irish Catholics eagerly accepted the most demanding and lowest paying jobs, which in a healthy economic environment would be vacant. But during the "hungry forties," unemployed native labourers were forced to compete with the immigrants for these undesirable jobs.[54] In an attempt to combat the debilitating effects of immigrant competition, such as a general lowering of wage scales, Orangemen sounded the call for economic segregation. They suggested that Protestant merchants and employers should hire and do business only with coreligionists. By ostracizing Roman Catholic labourers, Orangemen hoped to persuade entrenched immigrants to leave, and to discourage incoming Catholics from settling in the community.[55]

While Saint John's Orangemen fought a rigorous rhetorical battle, perhaps their most effective campaigns involved physical engagements with Irish Catholics. Indeed, collective social violence grew in direct proportion to the rising levels of famine immigration and Orange membership during the 1840s. In the aftermath of each confrontation, Orangemen enjoyed even greater Protestant support from natives and immigrants alike. The number of local lodges and engorged memberships at mid-century were tributes to the Orange Order's successful appeal. The persuasive rhetorical campaigns may have won converts, but the bloody riots gave concerned Protestants tangible "proof" of the Irish Catholics' uncivilized behaviour.

The first clearly identifiable incident of collective violence between Orangemen and Catholics in Saint John occurred on 12 July 1837. Small Catholic crowds forced entry into two merchants' stores and attempted to burn them.[56] In later years such incendiarism was eclipsed by more traditional rioting. The spring of 1841 found Irish Catholics clashing with Orangemen in the streets of Saint John. At issue was an Orange commemorative arch erected to celebrate the visit of a dignitary.[57] Catholics reacted similarly the following year on 12 July, when a crowd of several hundred gathered outside a Saint John home flying the Union Jack festooned with orange ribbons. Their jeers and taunts brought Orange reinforcements from across the city; by evening a general riot prompted Mayor William Black to swear in 150 special constables. The all-Protestant volunteer squad arrested several Irish Catholics, most of whom were ultimately found guilty of rioting.[58] Although these early disturbances paled when compared to subsequent riots, they established important patterns that would be repeated throughout the decade. While Irish Catholics would be deservedly or incorrectly labelled the aggressors, the Orangemen would invariably be perceived as the defenders of Saint John's Protestant and Loyalist traditions. Moreover, an exclusively Protestant constabulary and judiciary would consistently arrest and convict only Irish Catholics for disturbing the peace.

The next three years, coinciding with the first substantial waves of Irish Catholic immigrants and the attendant surge of Orangeism, brought several important episodes of social violence. The Twelfth of July in 1843 witnessed clashes between religious crowds in Saint John and Portland, though an official Orange procession was not held.[59] A more serious incident occurred in March of the following year. Squire Manks, Worshipful Master of the recently established Wellington Orange Lodge, shot and mortally wounded a Catholic Irishman during a dispute at York Point. Angry residents poured into the streets and demanded revenge. Rather than being arrested, however, Manks was placed into protective custody and expeditiously exonerated by an examining board of city magistrates. The verdict was self-defence.[60] The year closed with sporadic riots from Christmas until after New Year's. Crowds of up to 300 Irish Catholics roamed throughout York Point and Portland's wharf district, attacking Orangemen and their property. The Orangemen enthusiastically reciprocated. Two companies of British regulars finally succeeded in quashing the disturbances, but not before one Catholic had died and dozens more from both sides had received serious injuries. Although uninvolved residents bemoaned the apparent state of anarchy, the rioting was neither indiscriminate nor uncontrolled. Catholics and Orangemen carefully picked fights only with "certain . . . obnoxious individuals."[61]

The tensions of the winter of 1844–5 culminated in a St. Patrick's Day riot that eclipsed all earlier Orange–Catholic conflicts in its violence. On 17 March 1845, Portland Orangemen fired without provocation upon a group of Catholic revellers. The incident touched off a wave of reprisals. By nightfall general rioting between Orangemen and Irish Catholics had spread throughout the wharf district and York Point. The fighting was most intense at the foot of Fort Howe Hill in Portland.[62] The rioters dispersed when British troops positioned an artillery piece near Portland's wharves. The ploy was at best symbolic, for the concentrated fighting abated in the evening when the well-armed Orangemen gained a measure of control over the streets. The riot killed at least one Catholic, although several bodies were probably secreted away for private burials. The tally of wounded was correspondingly high, with dozens of combatants being hurt seriously enough to warrant medical attention.[63] The examinations and trials in the riot's aftermath followed the patterns established in 1842. Although authorities arrested several Orangemen, including two suspected of murder, Saint John's all-Protestant Grand Jury preemptively threw out their bills before the cases could be brought to trial. Instead the jury returned bills for several Irish Catholic rioters, two of whom were ultimately found guilty and sentenced. The swift vindication of Orangemen by the Grand Jury, despite an abundance of damaging testimony, illustrated the reluctance of Protestant authorities to condemn Orange violence and their continuing propensity to convict only Irish Catholics.[64]

Saint John and Portland escaped collective social violence for the next two years, but the hiatus did nothing to diminish enmity or foster peaceful linkages between Orangemen and Irish Catholics. The latter abstained from public displays on the St. Patrick's Days of 1846 and 1847. Orangemen quietly observed 12 July in their lodges in 1845; the following year they took a steamer to Gagetown for a procession with their brethren from Queens, Kings and York Counties.[65] For 1847's Twelfth of July, when famine immigration was reaching its zenith, city Orangemen invited neighbouring brethren and staged the largest procession since the organization's inception. On 14 July a Saint John newspaper trumpeted the now familiar requiem for the Orange holiday: "Dreadful Riot! The Disaffected District [York Point] Again in Arms — Shots Fired — Several Persons Dreadfully Wounded — the Military Called Out."[66] The two-year truce had yielded only larger numbers of Catholic immigrants and nativist Orangemen, and a more sophisticated network for the combatants in both groups to utilize in battle.

The Twelfth of July started quietly enough in 1847, but as Saint John's and Portland's Orangemen began to make their way to their lodges, crowds of wary Irish Catholics spilled into the streets. One of the larger Portland lodges, probably Wellington, entertained the amateur band from the local Mechanics' Institute. All of the band members were Orangemen. In the early evening, the group led a procession of Orangemen and onlookers through the streets of Portland, across the bridge, and into the heart of the Roman Catholic ghetto at York Point.[67] The tunes they played, like most Orange favourites, were clearly offensive to Irish Catholics.[68] At the foot of Dock Street, the crowd attacked the procession with sticks and bricks, smashing many of the band's instruments and forcing the revellers to flee back across the Portland Bridge. Gathering reinforcements and firearms from their lodges and homes, the undaunted Orangemen quickly returned to their enemy's stronghold.[69]

The Irish Catholic crowd, which by now had grown to several hundred, also made use of the respite and collected weapons in the event of a reappearance of the humiliated band members and Orangemen. The buttressed Orange legions did attempt to revive the procession and music when they reached York Point. A battle was inevitable. Volleys of shots from both parties shattered the summer air, leaving scores of wounded lying in the streets along the procession route. The melee continued throughout the evening, with most of the bloodshed occurring along Dock and Mill Streets and the bridge. At midnight detachments of the 33rd Regiment, dispatched at the mayor's request, converged upon York Point only to find the streets deserted. Rather than chance an engagement with the military, both sides ceased hostilities.[70] Aided by the darkness, the Irish Catholics escaped capture and returned to their homes. The constabulary failed to make any arrests after the riot, and the Grand Jury issued no warrants.[71]

Assessment of the riot's severity is hampered due to the secretive removal of the dead and wounded by both parties, particularly the Irish Catholics. Official tallies included only one Catholic killed and several seriously wounded, but everyone involved knew that many had died during the encounter.[72] The significance of the conflict, however, emerged unclouded in the following months. Both sides were organized, well-stocked with weapons and clearly prepared to kill for their beliefs. Catholics had gathered hours before the Orange procession had entered York Point;

they were motivated by a desire to "defend" their "territory." Orangemen consciously provoked the enemy by twice marching in procession and playing obnoxious songs through the most Catholic district of Saint John. An undeniable linkage also emerged between the Orange Order and the Mechanics' Institute, which was symbolic of the nativist attraction that Orangeism had to the economically beleaguered Protestant workers facing stiff competition from famine immigrants. Finally, the riot underscored the Orange belief in vigilante justice. The procession's return to York Point represented a "heroic" action to remove a dangerous Catholic "mob" from Saint John's thoroughfares. According to Orange sympathizers, the anaemic state of the city's constabulary justified the vigilantism.[73] In retrospect, the riot of 1847 illuminated the entrenchment of social violence as a perennial method of interaction between Orangemen and Catholics.[74]

A year of bloody skirmishes was the riot's true legacy, for neither side had emerged with a clearcut victory on the Twelfth. A wave of assaults and murders swept Saint John and Portland during the weeks that followed; Orange and Catholic vengeance was the motive for all of them.[75] A sensational series of witness examinations after the murder of a suspected Orangeman in September brought religious antipathy to a fever pitch. Dozens of testimonials exposed paramilitary networks operated by militant Orangemen and Catholics. Personal revenge on a small scale appeared to be the favourite tactic of the weaker and outnumbered Catholics. Orangemen, enjoying the support of a Protestant majority, preferred a collective vigilantism whereby they dispensed extralegal justice while acting as an unofficial watchdog of the Irish lower orders.[76] By the year's end, it was apparent that the Orange–Catholic struggle had not diminished. Both sides habitually armed themselves if they ventured into unfriendly districts; each tried desperately to identify its most virulent enemies, and in many cases, both were prepared to kill for their causes.

The religious conflict of the 1840s peaked two years later in Saint John's worst riot of the 19th century. The city was quiet in 1848, much as it had been in 1846, because local Orangemen travelled to Fredericton to participate in a massive demonstration.[77] But as the Twelfth approached in 1849, Saint John's Orangemen advertised for the first time their plans for hosting provincial brethren and sponsoring an elaborate procession.[78] Motivated by vivid memories of the inconclusive 1847 conflict, Orangemen and Irish Catholics grimly prepared themselves for battle. On the eve of the holiday, Mayor Robert D. Wilmot met with local Orange officials and asked them to voluntarily abandon their plans to march. But the Orangemen, well-versed on their rights, rejected the suggestion because no provincial statute gave civilian officials the authority to ban public processions.[79] The march, they insisted, would proceed as planned.

With a measure of fatalism, Saint John prepared for the occasion. While Orangemen from Carleton, York, Kings and Queens Counties were boarding steamers and carriages for Saint John, Irish Catholics were buying arms and ammunition. Shopkeepers along Prince William Street, King Street and Market Square boarded their windows and decided to declare the day a business holiday.[80] Early on the morning of the Twelfth, hundreds of Orangemen from Saint John and Portland collected at Nethery's Hotel on Church Street and marched to a nearby wharf to greet the Carleton ferry. Among the disembarking brethren was Joseph Corum, the Senior Deputy Grand Master of the New Brunswick Grand Lodge. As the procession leader, Corum would have the honour of representing King William by riding a white horse. The Orangemen came heavily armed with pistols, muskets and sabres. After assuming a military file, they began the march to the Portland suburb of Indiantown, where they would meet the steamer bringing reinforcements from the northern counties. Their planned route would take them through both Irish Catholic bastions — York Point and Portland's wharf district.[81]

Upon reaching York Point they encountered a large pine arch, symbolically green, which spanned the foot of Mill Street. Several hundred jeering Irish Catholics clustered near the arch's supporting poles; they implored the Orangemen to continue. Outnumbered for the moment, the Orangemen accepted the humiliation and dipped their banners as they passed under the arch. While a few stones were hurled at the Orangemen, and they responded with warning shots, no fighting broke out.[82] Without further incident, the procession reached Indiantown, where it gratefully welcomed scores of reinforcements. Among the newcomers was another pivotal Orange leader. George Anderson, a Presbyterian grocer and primary lodge master, was a veteran of several disturbances in his home town of Fredericton. Anderson, bedecked with a sword that indicated his rank, assumed a position next to Corum at the column's head. The procession now numbered approximately 600 people. The men were heavily armed, the majority carrying muskets on shoulder straps. A few clutched axes that would be used to destroy the green bough when they returned to York Point. Finally, a wagon filled with weapons and supplies took up a station at the rear of the procession. As the Orangemen made their way back to York Point, Portland inhabitants observed that the procession resembled a confident army about to engage in battle.[83]

In the meantime, authorities attempted to alleviate the growing tensions with three separate plans, all of which would ultimately fail to prevent a conflict. Mayor Wilmot's first scheme was to defuse the powder keg by removing the pine arch and dispersing the Catholic crowd in York Point. Wilmot, accompanied by a magistrate and a constable, was physically rebuffed in this endeavour by a cohesive, territorially-minded crowd that chanted "Stay off our ground!" He then dispatched Jacob Allan, the Portland police magistrate, to intercept the Orangemen before they reached York Point.[84] Allan asked Corum and Anderson to bypass the Catholic district by using the longer Valley Road on their approach to Saint John. After conferring with their followers, the leaders rejected Allan's suggestion. Their men had suffered humiliation during the morning's passage under the Catholic arch; now they insisted on "Death or Victory."[85] Wilmot borrowed the third and final plan from Saint John's history of dealing with riots. At his request, 60 British soldiers stationed themselves in Market Square to prevent general rioting. While the choice of location would do nothing to prevent a conflict, for Market Square lay to the south of York Point and the Orangemen would enter from the north over the Portland Bridge, it would serve to contain the battle within the Catholic ghetto. The detachment's failure to position itself between the advancing Orangemen and the offensive arch, when it had ample time to do so, raised questions about the sincerity of the authorities' attempts to prevent bloodshed.[86]

General rioting broke out along Mill Street before the procession arrived at the bough. The Catholic crowd now numbered approximately 500, and like the Orangemen, many had armed themselves with muskets. Reports of who fired the first shots varied, but roofers working on a Mill Street building agreed that Orangemen opened fire after being met with a volley of stones and brickbats.[87] Several Catholics lay wounded or dying after the barrage, and then their guns answered the Orangemen's. A heated battle ensued. Men and women along Mill Street threw anything they could at the better-armed Orange contingent. Some engaged in fistfights with individuals they were able to pull from the Orange ranks. Corum struggled to free himself after a handful of Irishmen grabbed his horse's tether. A dozen Catholics captured the wagon filled with arms and gave its driver a sound thrashing. Hundreds of shots were fired, and at least 12 combatants lost their lives. The Irish Catholics suffered most of the casualties. After several minutes of furious fighting, the Orangemen emerged from York Point. As they headed for the safety of the troops, their procession was still intact.[88]

The British garrison, after remaining stationary in Market Square throughout the heat of the battle, went into action as soon as the Orangemen left the Irish Catholic ghetto. Without firing a shot, the soldiers marched past the procession and positioned themselves on Dock Street to seal off the Catholic district. This manoeuvre effectively doused what remained of the conflict.[89] It also gave the Orangemen the opportunity to continue their procession unmolested, for any Catholics wishing to leave York Point in pursuit would have to contend first with the soldiers. The Orangemen, heady with their successful assault on the enemy's territory, proceeded through Market and King Squares and made a circle through the city's center. Only when they entered Market Square again, with the intention of parading through York Point for the third time, were the troops commanded to impede their progress. Being satisfied with their efforts, the Orangemen agreed to disband. With the Orange threat finally removed, the Irish Catholics waiting in York Point also dispersed. The great Saint John riot of 1849 was over.[90]

The riot's judicial aftermath followed patterns well-established by 1849, although there was one notable exception. At Lieutenant-Governor Edmund Head's insistence, the Saint John Grand Jury served warrants on Orange participants as well as the Catholics. This attempt at impartiality was severely undermined, however, by a prejudiced investigative team that included the prominent Orangeman W.H. Needham.[91] Ultimately, all but five of the bills against Orangemen, including those for Corum, Anderson and 18 others, were dropped before the defendants reached trial. The five Orangemen who actually stood in the dock were swiftly declared innocent by a jury that remained seated. Much to the prosecution's dismay, the jury ignored recent provincial legislation that clearly outlawed armed public processions.[92] For the Irish Catholics, on the other hand, the judicial pattern of the 1840s remained intact. Of the 24 implicated, six were tried on assault charges, one for attempted murder and four for unlawful assembly. Two were eventually found guilty, including the alleged "ringleader" who led the defence of the green arch. John Haggerty, immigrant labourer and father of three, would spend his sixty-third birthday in the provincial penitentiary while serving his one-year sentence for assault.[93]

The 1849 riot signalled an end to collective social conflict between Orangemen and Catholics, although small skirmishes would continue for years.[94] Various factors brought about this extended truce, the most important being the hegemony established by Orangemen in Saint John and Portland. In a sense, Orangemen had won the battle of the 1840s. The Irish Catholics' attempts to check the growth of Orangeism with counter-demonstrations had failed. They undeniably suffered the most casualties in the course of the riots. Moreover, a fusion between all levels of authority and the Orange Order had taken place. Orangemen, constables and British soldiers had combined to contain every major disturbance within the Irish Catholic ghettos of York Point and Portland. The Orange Order became an acceptable accomplice for the maintenance of social control. A double standard had clearly emerged: authorities found Orange vigilantism preferable to "mob rule" by the Irish Catholic "lower orders."[95] During the 1840s Orangemen served as constables, magistrates and legislative representatives. Excepting one active magistrate in Saint John, the Irish Catholics were excluded from power. This inequity profoundly shaped law enforcement during the riots and trials. No Catholic would be allowed to sit on juries; moreover, only Irish Catholics would be found guilty of rioting offences. Even when Orangemen stood in the dock, such as after the York Point riot of 1849, they were expeditiously exonerated.[96] Ethnicity and religion targeted the Irish Catholics for suppression during the 1840s; meanwhile Orangeism developed into an unofficial arm of social control to protect the Protestant majority.

New Brunswick's improved economic environment after mid-century contributed to the demise of collective conflict by alleviating some of the fierce competition between immigrants and natives. The "Hungry Forties" had indeed been more than a historical cliché to many colonists. A sustained depression had brought scarcities of goods, food and services. Natives had competed with Irish Catholic immigrants for limited jobs, a factor that had contributed to the rapid growth of Orangeism. Economic variables alone did not cause the Orange–Green riots, but they certainly helped to account for a foundation of social tension.[97] As the province successfully weathered the English transition to free trade in the 1850s, investment capital increased and jobs became more available.[98] Thus Orangemen found one of the key elements of their rhetorical campaign against Irish Catholics undermined. Ultimately, fuller employment fostered better relations between Protestant and Catholic workers.

Another factor in the disappearance of perennial disturbances between Protestants and Catholics was the Orange Order's discontinuance of 12 July processions while it fought for provincial incorporation. Saint John and Portland Orangemen wisely decided not to risk any negative publicity that might accompany collective violence with Irish Catholics while the bill was being debated in the New Brunswick legislature. The process lasted 25 years, but eventually the trade-off of abstention for legitimacy proved fruitful.[99] Not until after the bill finally passed in 1875, in the midst of the emotional separate schools issue, would Orangemen again take to Saint John's streets to display their fervent brand of loyalty and Protestantism.[100]

Finally, a drastic reduction in the number of Irish Catholic immigrants after 1848 helped to subdue the nativist impulse. The tide of famine immigrants had dropped as precipitously as it had risen. Improving conditions in Ireland accounted for a general reduction in emigrants, especially from the poorer Catholic counties. In addition a discriminatory immigration policy, instituted at the behest of Lieutenant-Governors Sir William Colebrooke and Sir Edmund Head, curtailed Catholic immigration while it increased the number of more desirable Protestant settlers from the British Isles.[101] The results were striking: between 1851 and 1861 the percentages of Irish compared to the total immigration population dropped dramatically in both Saint John and Portland. This decrease also reflected the continuing out-migration of transient Catholics to the "Boston States" and to other British North American provinces.[102] Finally, it indicated the beginnings of a process of acculturation; the sons and daughters of Catholic and Protestant immigrants would be listed as New Brunswickers in the 1861 census. The "soldiers" of the 1840s — both Orange and Green — would be supplanted by generations to whom the violent experiences of the "Hungry Forties" would be historical anecdotes.

The Orange Order was New Brunswick's institutionalized nativist response to Irish Catholic immigration during the 1840s. Prior to this decade, the organization was a small and mostly invisible fraternal order dominated by Irish Protestant immigrants and British garrison troops. As Irish Catholic famine victims poured into Saint John and Portland during the 1840s, however, Protestant natives and non-Irish-born immigrants joined the Orange Order. Orangemen spearheaded a rhetorical campaign to combat the famine immigration, using anti-Catholic and racist propaganda to discourage the Irish from settling permanently in the city. Additionally, the Orange Order increasingly acted as a paramilitary vigilante group that freely engaged in riots with bellicose Irish Catholics. The combination of nativist rhetoric and a mutual willingness to engage in armed conflict provided a decade of collective social violence that culminated in the tragic riot of 12 July 1849. Thus Saint John and Portland, like several eastern seaboard cities in the United States, experienced a strong nativist impulse and several destructive episodes of social violence.

NOTES

1. *Weekly Chronicle* (Saint John), 22 March 1839.
2. *Morning News* (Saint John), 24 September 1847.
3. For this study, social violence is defined as "assault upon an individual or his property solely or primarily because of his membership in a social category." See Allen D. Grimshaw, "Interpreting Collective Violence: An Argument for the Importance of Social Structure," in James F. Short, Jr. and Marvin E. Wolfgang, eds., *Collective Violence* (Chicago, 1972), pp. 12, 18–20.
4. Sir Edmund Head to Lord Grey, 15 July 1849, Colonial Office Series [CO] 188, Public Record Office [PRO], London; *Royal Gazette* (Frederiction), 19 September 1849; D.R. Jack, *Centennial Prize Essay on the History of the City and County of St. John* (Saint John, 1883), pp. 136–7; Reverend J.W. Millidge, "Reminiscences of St. John from 1849 to 1860," *New Brunswick Historical Society Collections*, Vol. IV (1919), pp. 8, 127.
5. Its mid-century population stood at 23,000, making one in every 8.5 New Brunswickers a Saint John resident. Portland, with 8,500 inhabitants, was roughly one-third the size of Saint John. See New Brunswick Census, 1851, Provincial Archives of New Brunswick [PANB].
6. Presentment of the Saint John Grand Jury, 27 October 1847, Minutes, Saint John General Sessions, PANB.
7. *Morning News*, 8, 11 September 1843; Abraham Gesner, *New Brunswick; with Notes for Emigrants* (London, 1847), pp. 122–4; Reverend W.C. Atkinson, *A Historical and Statistical Account of New Brunswick, B.N.A. with Advice to Emigrants* (Edinburgh, 1844), pp. 28–9, 36–7.
8. The 1840s was a particularly depressed decade, but as Graeme Wynn eloquently pointed out, the colony was already a veteran of the 19th century boom and bust "bandalore": in 1819, 1825 and 1837, New Brunswick suffered trade depressions due to financial downturns and the erosion of speculation capital in Great Britain: *Timber Colony: A Historical Geography of Early Nineteenth Century New Brunswick* (Toronto, 1981), pp. 3–33, 43–53. See also P.D. McClelland, "The New Brunswick Economy in the Nineteenth Century," *Journal of Economic History*, XXV (December 1965), pp. 686–90.
9. W.S. MacNutt, *New Brunswick, a History, 1784–1867* (Toronto, 1963), pp. 283–4, 296; MacNutt, "New Brunswick's Age of Harmony: The Administration of Sir John Harvey," *Canadian Historical Review*, XXXII (June 1951), pp. 123–4; D.G.G. Kerr, *Sir Edmund Head: The Scholarly Governor* (Toronto, 1954), pp. 39–54; Wynn, *Timber Colony*, pp. 43–4, 51–3.

10. *Colonial Advocate* (Saint John), 14 July 1845; MacNutt, *New Brunswick*, p. 285; Wynn, *Timber Colony*, pp. 51–3.

11. *New Brunswick Reporter* (Fredericton), 13 October 1848, 24 August 1849; *Morning News*, 28 May 1849; Wynn, *Timber Colony*, pp. 150–5; MacNutt, *New Brunswick*, p. 310.

12. Immigration Returns, New Brunswick Blue Books, 1832–50, Public Archives of Canada [PAC]; "Report on Trade and Navigation," *Journal of the House of Assembly of New Brunswick*, 1866.

13. Only in 1853, after the famine abated in Ireland, would English immigrants once again become the largest group. See New Brunswick Census, 1851; "Report on Trade and Navigation," *Journal of the House of Assembly of New Brunswick*, 1866; William F. Ganong, *A Monograph of the Origins of Settlements in the Province of New Brunswick* (Ottawa, 1904), pp. 90–120.

14. Cecil Woodham-Smith, *The Great Hunger: Ireland 1845–9* (London, 1962), pp. 206–9; Lawrence J. McCaffrey, *The Irish Diaspora in America* (Bloomington, Ind., 1976), pp. 59–62; William Forbes Adams, *Ireland and Irish Emigration to the New World* (New York, 1932); Donald Akenson, ed., *Canadian Papers in Rural History*, Vol. III (Gananoque, Ont., 1981), pp. 219–21.

15. Woodham-Smith, *Great Hunger*, pp. 29, 206–13; John I. Cooper, "Irish Immigration and the Canadian Church Before the Middle of the Nineteenth Century," *Journal of the Canadian Church Historical Society*, II (May 1955), pp. 13–4; Adams, *Ireland and Irish Emigration*; McCaffrey, *Irish Diaspora*, pp. 59–62; Oliver MacDonagh, "Irish Emigration to the United States of America and the British Colonies During the Famine," in R. Dudley Edwards and T. Desmond Williams, eds., *The Great Famine: Studies in Irish History 1845–52* (Dublin, 1956), pp. 332–9.

16. Immigration Returns, New Brunswick Blue Books, PAC; M.H. Perley's Report on 1846 Emigration, in William Colebrooke to Grey, 29 December 1846, CO 188.

17. Ibid.; *Royal Gazette*, 17 March, 7 July 1847; *Saint John Herald*, 12 November 1845; James Hannay, *History of New Brunswick* (Saint John, 1909), Vol. II, p. 70: MacDonagh, "Irish Emigration," pp. 368–73; Adams, *Ireland and Irish Emigration*, p. 234; Woodham-Smith, *Great Hunger*, pp. 209–10.

18. New Brunswick Census, 1851, 1861; *Morning News*, 8, 11 September 1843; Alexander Monro, *New Brunswick; with a Brief Outline of Nova Scotia, and Prince Edward Island* (Halifax, 1855), p. 125; James S. Buckingham, *Canada, Nova Scotia, New Brunswick, and the Other British Provinces in North America* (London, 1843), pp. 409–10.

19. Kings Ward, which included all of York Point and was roughly equal in size to the other Saint John wards, had twice the population of any ward in the 1851 New Brunswick Census. For descriptions of York Point, see Grand Jury Reports, 16 December 1848, Minutes, Saint John General Sessions, PANB, and D.H. Waterbury, "Retrospective Ramble Over Historic St. John," *New Brunswick Historical Society Collections*, Vol. IV (1919), pp. 86–8.

20. Colebrooke to Grey, 28 January 1848, CO 188; Gesner, *New Brunswick*, p. 124.

21. John Higham, *Strangers in the Land: Patterns of American Nativism 1860–1925* (New Brunswick, N.J., 1955), pp. 3–4; Higham, "Another Look at Nativism," *Catholic Historical Review*, XLIV (July 1958), pp. 148–50.

22. For examples of Canadian nativist studies, see Howard Palmer, *Land of the Second Chance: A History of Ethnic Groups in Southern Alberta* (Lethbridge, 1971); Palmer, "Nativism and Ethnic Tolerance in Alberta: 1920–1972," Ph.D. thesis, York University, 1974; Simon Evans, "Spatial Bias in the Incidence of Nativism: Opposition to Hutterite Expansion in Alberta," *Canadian Ethnic Studies*, Vol. VI, Nos. 1–2 (1974), pp. 1–16.

23. *Loyalist and Conservative Advocate* (Saint John), 13 August 1847. See also issues from 20, 27 August 1847.

24. For histories of the Orange Order, see Hereward Senior, *Orangeism in Ireland and Britain 1765–1836* (London, 1966), especially pp. 4–21, 194–206; Senior, "The Early Orange

Order 1795–1870," in T. Desmond Williams, ed., *Secret Societies in Ireland* (Dublin, 1973); Peter Gibbon, "The Origins of the Orange Order and the United Irishmen," *Economy and Society*, 1 (1972), pp. 134–63.

25. Canadian Orange Order histories include Cecil Houston and W.J. Smyth, *The Sash Canada Wore: A Historical Geography of the Orange Order in Canada* (Toronto, 1980); Hereward Senior, *Orangeism: The Canadian Phase* (Toronto, 1972); Senior, "The Genesis of Canadian Orangeism," *Ontario History*, LX (June 1968), pp. 13–29.

26. James McNichol's report, *Loyal Orange Association Report, 1886* (Toronto, 1886); *Sentinel*, 3 July 1930; J. Edward Steele, comp., *History and Directory of the Provincial Grand Orange Lodge and Primary Lodges of New Brunswick* (Saint John, 1934), p. 11.

27. Miscellaneous Orange documents, courtesy of Professor Peter Toner, University of New Brunswick at Saint John; James McNichol's report, *Loyal Orange Association Report, 1886*; Steele, *History of the Orange Lodges of New Brunswick*, pp. 11, 17–21; Houston and Smyth, *The Sash Canada Wore*, pp. 69–70.

28. Lodge returns, in *Minutes of the Grand Orange Lodge of New Brunswick* [various publishers, 1846–55]; *Annual Reports of the Grand Orange Lodge of the Loyal Orange Association of B.N.A.* [various publishers, 1846–50]; *New Brunswick Reporter*, 10 May 1850; *Loyalist*, 8 June 1848; *Carleton Sentinel* (Woodstock), 15 July 1854; *Sentinel*, 3 July 1930; Steele, *History of the Orange Lodges of New Brunswick*, pp. 11–3, 37–9, 53–5, 59.

29. Because Nova Scotia's lodges, who received their warrants directly from New Brunswick, were only two years old in mid-century, the vast majority of the 10,000 members resided in New Brunswick. See "Minutes of the Grand Orange Lodge of New Brunswick and Nova Scotia," in *Weekly Chronicle*, 6 July 1849; Orange Order documents, Peter Toner; *Minutes of the Grand Orange Lodge of New Brunswick, 1846–50*; *Sentinel*, 3 July 1930.

30. Correspondence from John Earle in *Annual Report of the Grand Orange Lodge of the Loyal Orange Association of B.N.A.*, 1851; *New Brunswick Reporter*, 26 April 1850; Head to Grey, 7 September 1847, CO 188; *New Brunswick Courier* (Saint John), 25 July 1840; Steele, *History of the Orange Lodge of New Brunswick*, p. 11.

31. Houston and Smyth, *The Sash Canada Wore*, pp. 70–2; Steele, *History of the Orange Lodges of New Brunswick*, pp. 115–8.

32. "Minutes of the Organizational Meeting of the Grand Orange Lodge of New Brunswick, 1844," in Steele, *History of the Orange Lodges of New Brunswick*, p. 11; New Brunswick Census, 1851.

33. James Brown letters to *New Brunswick Reporter*, 28 April, 5, 12 May 1848; *Morning News*, 18 July 1849; John Earle's correspondence, in *Annual Report of the Grand Orange Lodge of the Loyal Orange Association of B.N.A.*, 1851.

34. Minute book, Wellington Orange Lodge, Portland, New Brunswick Museum [NBM], Saint John.

35. 1851 manuscript census returns from Saint John County are incomplete. Returns from only four of the city's wards are extant: Kings, Dukes, Sydney and Queens. Records from Portland Parish and Carleton are missing.

36. Returns for Saint John County, New Brunswick Manuscript Census, 1851, PANB; Orange documents, including dispensations and lodge returns, Peter Toner; *Minutes of the Grand Orange Lodge of New Brunswick, 1846–55*; Evidence, Saint John Riot Trials, Documents, New Brunswick Executive Council Records, PANB; New Brunswick Supreme Court Documents, PANB. The newspapers consulted were the *Loyalist, Weekly Chronicle* and *Morning News* for the 1840s, as well as the *Daily Sun* (Saint John), 13 July 1897, and Steele, *History of the Orange Lodges of New Brunswick*.

37. *Laws and Ordinances of the Orange Association of British North America* (Toronto, 1840), p. 11; *The Orange Question Treated by Sir Francis Hincks and the London "Times"* (Montreal, 1877).

38. For example, Portland's Wellington Lodge attempted to combat negative publicity after a decade of social violence by declaring itself a "benefit" organization in 1851. See Minute

Book, Wellington Orange Lodge, NBM. See also *Rules and Regulations of the Orange Institution of British North America* (Toronto, 1838), p. 5; Steele, *History of the Orange Lodges of New Brunswick*.

39. *Morning News*, 24 January 1849; *Headquarters* (Fredericton), 24 January 1849.

40. *Loyalist*, 1 October 1847.

41. *Minutes of the Grand Orange Lodge of New Brunswick*, 1852; Rev. Gilbert Spurr's address to Orangemen, in *Loyalist*, 15 October 1847; Head to Grey, 26 July 1848, CO 188; *New Brunswick Reporter*, 26 October 1849; *Carleton Sentinel*, 2 July 1850; *Weekly Chronicle*, 15 July 1842, 4 February 1848; *Christian Visitor* (Saint John), 8 March 1848; Steele, *History of the Orange Lodges of New Brunswick*, pp. 13–5, 21.

42. For discussions of the papal conspiracy theory in North America, see S.M. Lipset and Earl Raab, *The Politics of Unreason* (New York, 1970), pp. 47–59, David B. Davis, "Some Themes of Counter-Subversion: An Analysis of Anti-Masonic, Anti-Catholic, and Anti-Mormon Literature," *Mississippi Valley Historical Review*, XLVII (September 1960), pp. 205–7, Higham, *Strangers in the Land*, pp. 5–6.

43. *Church Witness* (Saint John), 21 September 1853.

44. *Minutes of the Grand Orange Lodge of New Brunswick, 1846–55*, particularly S.H. Gilbert's sermon in 1854; Grand Orange Lodge of New Brunswick's address to Queen Victoria, in Head to Grey, 28 April 1851, CO 188; *New Brunswick Reporter*, 9 April 1850; *Carleton Sentinel*, 16 July 1850; *New Brunswick Reporter*, 1 October 1847; *Weekly Chronicle*, 31 August 1849, 18 July 1851; *Loyalist*, 24 September 1847; *Church Witness*, 16 July, 13 August 1851, 6 July 1853.

45. Adams, *Ireland and Irish Emigration*, pp. 363–4; Carl Wittke, *The Irish in America* (Baton Rouge, La., 1956), pp. 46–7; Kenneth Duncan, "Irish Famine Immigration and the Social Structure of Canada West," *Canadian Review of Sociology and Anthropology*, 11 (February 1965), pp. 33, 39.

46. *Loyalist*, 6 April 1848.

47. Alexander McHarg Diary, NBM; *Morning News*, 8 January, 8 December 1841, 6 January, 14 June 1843, 5 January 1848; *Weekly Chronicle*, 5 January, 28 June 1844, 26 November 1847; Queen vs. David Nice, New Brunswick Supreme Court Documents, PANB.

48. *Loyalist*, 30 March 1848; *New Brunswick Reporter*, 20 April 1850; *New Brunswick Assembly Debates*, 8 March 1850, PANB; *Morning News*, 24 January 1849; *Loyalist*, 16 July, 15, 28 October, 4 November 1847; *New Brunswick Reporter*, 19 November 1847, 15 March 1850; *Morning News*, 11 August 1847.

49. For excellent studies of racism in the British Isles, see L.P. Curtis, Jr., *Anglo-Saxons and Celts: A Study of Anti-Irish Prejudice in Victorian England* (Bridgeport, Conn., 1968), pp. 8–9, 24–6, and *Apes and Angels: The Irishman in Victorian Caricature* (Devon, England, 1971), passim.

50. *Weekly Chronicle*, 31 August, 28 September 1849; *Loyalist*, 24 September 1847.

51. *Loyalist*, 1 October, 11 November 1847.

52. *New Brunswick Reporter*, 10 May 1850; *Loyalist*, 16 July, 17 September, 15 October 1847; *Weekly Chronicle*, 29 July 1842.

53. The theme of competition between immigrant labourers and nativists in North America is explored in Oscar Handlin, *Boston's Immigrants* (Cambridge, Mass., 1959), pp. 180–7, Higham, *Strangers in the Land*, p. 57, Adams, *Ireland and Irish Emigration*, p. 353.

54. M.H. Perley's Report on 1846 Emigration, in Colebrooke to Grey, 29 December 1846, CO 188; *Royal Gazette*, 17 March, 7 July 1847; Wynn, *Timber Colony*, pp. 155–6; Kathryn Johnston, "The History of St. John, 1837–1867: Civic and Economic," Honours thesis, Mount Allison University, 1953, pp. 24–8.

55. *Loyalist*, 24 March 1845, 17 September, 28 October, 4 November, 9, 23 December 1847; *New Brunswick Reporter*, 10 September 1847; *New Brunswick Reporter*, 19 November 1847.

56. Joseph Brown to R.F. Hazen, 11 July 1837, R.F. Hazen Papers, NBM; *Weekly Chronicle*, 14 July 1837.

57. *New Brunswick Reporter*, 26 April, 10 May 1850.

58. *Morning News*, 13 July, 5 August 1842; *Weekly Chronicle*, 15 July, 12 August 1842; *New Brunswick Courier*, 16 July, 13, 27 August 1842; Minutes, Saint John General Sessions, 9, 10, 17 December 1842, 25 March 1843, PANB; *Sentinel*, 29 October 1891.

59. *New Brunswick Reporter*, 26 April 1850.

60. Mayor Lauchlan Donaldson to Alfred Reade, 8 March 1844, New Brunswick Supreme Court Documents, PANB; McHarg Diary; *Morning News*, 5 April 1844.

61. *Weekly Chronicle*, 3 January 1845; *Morning News*, 3 January 1845; *Headquarters*, 8 January 1845; McHarg Diary.

62. Donaldson to Reade, 29 March 1845, Saint John Grand Jury to Colebrooke, 27 March 1845, "Riots and Disasters," New Brunswick Executive Council Records [Executive Council Records], PANB; *Loyalist*, 24 March 1845; *Weekly Chronicle*, 21 March 1845.

63. Minutes, New Brunswick Executive Council, 7 April 1845, PANB; Report of Doctors Robert and William Bayard, 17 March 1845, "Riots and Disasters," Executive Council Records; McHarg Diary; *Weekly Chronicle*, 21 March 1845; *Morning News*, 19 March 1845; *Observer* (Saint John), 18 March 1845; *New Brunswick Reporter*, 21 March 1845; *New Brunswick Courier*, 22 March 1845; *Loyalist*, 24 March 1845.

64. Minutes, Saint John General Sessions, 20, 22, 26 March, 14 June 1845; Donaldson to Reade, 22 March 1845, "Riots and Disasters," Executive Council Records; *New Brunswick Courier*, 5 July 1845; *Saint John Herald*, 2 July 1845.

65. *Minutes of the Grand Orange Lodge of New Brunswick*, 1847; *Weekly Chronicle*, 17 July 1846.

66. *Morning News*, 14 July 1847.

67. Orange supporters tried to disassociate the Orange Order, the Mechanics' Institute Band and the crowd that followed the procession. The *Loyalist*, 16 July 1847, claimed that the band had nothing to do with the Orange procession, while Clarence Ward made the dubious assertion that the Orange entourage consisted of "children." See "Old Times in St. John — 1847," *Saint John Globe*, 1 April 1911, p. 8. Yet an article in the *Orange Sentinel*, 29 October 1891, proudly revealed that all the band members were Orangemen.

68. For examples of these songs, see *The Sentinel Orange and Patriotic Song Book* (Toronto, 1930?), and R. McBride, ed., *The Canadian Orange Minstrel for 1860, Contains Nine New and Original Songs, Mostly All of Them Showing Some Wrong that Affects the Order or the True Course of Protestant Loyalty to the British Crown* (London, 1860). Note particularly "Croppies Lie Down," a 19th century favourite of Orangemen in Europe and North America.

69. *New Brunswick Courier*, 17 July 1847; *Morning News*, 14 July 1847; *Loyalist*, 16 July 1847; *Sentinel*, 29 October 1891; McHarg Diary.

70. *Morning News*, 14 July 1847; Colebrooke to Grey, 30 July 1847, Documents, Executive Council Records, PANB; McHarg Diary; *New Brunswick Courier*, 17 July 1847; *Loyalist*, 16 July 1847; Ward, "Old Times in St. John — 1847."

71. *New Brunswick Courier*, 7 August 1847.

72. Colebrooke to Grey, 30 July 1847, CO 188; *Morning News*, 14 July 1847.

73. *Loyalist*, 16 July 1847; Ward, "Old Times in St. John — 1847."

74. One newspaper referred to it as a "civil war": *Morning News*, 14 July 1847.

75. *New Brunswick Courier*, 24 July 1847; *Morning News*, 14, 21, 23, 28 July 1847; *Loyalist*, 23 July 1847; *Weekly Chronicle*, 30 July 1847.

76. Queen vs. Dennis McGovern, 7–17 September 1847, New Brunswick Supreme Court Documents, PANB. Note especially the testimonies of Thomas Clark, James Clark, Ezekiel Downey and Edward McDermott. See also *Morning News*, 24 January 1848; *Weekly Chronicle*, 10 September 1847; *New Brunswick Courier*, 11 September 1847; *Loyalist*, 10 September 1847; *Morning News*, 8 September 1847.

77. *Weekly Chronicle*, 14 July 1848. Fredericton's Orangemen invited provincial brethren to celebrate the anniversary of their successful 1847 battle with Irish Catholics: *New Brunswick Reporter*, 10 May 1850.

78. *Weekly Chronicle*, 6 July 1849.

79. Head to Grey, 15 July 1849, CO 188. The question of the legality of public processions, especially armed ones, would become a hotly debated topic in the House of Assembly after the riot, yet no restrictive legislation would emerge from the debate.

80. Testimonies of Thomas Paddock and Francis Jones, "Riots and Disasters," Executive Council Records; *New Brunswick Reporter*, 13 July 1848; Head to Grey, 15 July 1849, CO 188.

81. *Morning News*, 13 July 1849; *New-Brunswicker* (Saint John), 14 July 1849; *New Brunswick Courier*, 14 July 1849; Testimonies of Francis Jones, George Noble, Jacob Allan, Charles Boyd, Squire Manks and George McKelvey, "Riots and Disasters," Executive Council Records; Head to Grey, 15 July 1849, CO 188.

82. Testimonies of Josiah Wetmore, Jeremiah McCarthy, George Nobel and Jacob Allan, "Riots and Disasters," Executive Council Records; Head to Grey, 15 July 1849, CO 188; *Sentinel*, 3 July 1930.

83. Testimonies of Jacob Allan, George Mason, Samuel Dalton, Samuel Gordon and Francis Jones, "Riots and Disasters," Executive Council Records; Head to Grey, 15 July 1849, CO 188; *Weekly Chronicle*, 13 July 1849; *New Brunswicker*, 14 July 1849; *Sentinel*, 3 July 1930.

84. Head to Grey, 15 July 1849, CO 188; Testimonies of James Gilbert, Henry Gilbert, John Nixon, John Fitzpatrick, Joseph Wetmore and James Clark, "Riots and Disasters," Executive Council Records.

85. Testimonies of Jacob Allan, Francis Jones and Squire Manks, "Riots and Disasters," Executive Council Records; Head to Grey, 15 July 1849, CO 188; *Sentinel*, 29 October 1891, 3 July 1930.

86. Head to Grey, 15 July 1849, CO 188; Jacob Allan testimony, "Riots and Disasters," Executive Council Records; *Morning News*, 13 July 1849; *Temperance Telegraph* (Saint John), 19 July 1849.

87. Testimonies of James McKenzie, William Smith, Francis Wilson and Francis Jones, "Riots and Disasters," Executive Council Records; *Temperance Telegraph*, 19 July 1849; *Weekly Chronicle*, 13 July 1849; *Morning News*, 13 July 1849.

88. Testimonies of Squire Manks, James McKenzie, William Smith, Francis Wilson and Jeremiah Smith, "Riots and Disasters," Executive Council Records; *Morning News*, 13 July 1849; *Christian Visitor*, 14 July 1849; *Weekly Chronicle*, 13 July 1849.

89. Head to Grey, 15 July 1849, CO 188; Charles Boyd testimony, "Riots and Disasters," Executive Council Records; *Morning News*, 13 July 1849; *New-Brunswicker*, 14 July 1849; *Weekly Chronicle*, 13 July 1849.

90. Testimonies of Charles Boyd and Jacob Allan, "Riots and Disasters," Executive Council Records; *Morning News*, 13 July 1849; Head to Grey, 15 July 1849, CO 188.

91. Head to Grey, 15 July 1849, CO 188; *Morning News*, 23 July 1849; *New Brunswick Courier*, 21 July 1849.

92. William B. Kinnear to Head, extract, 6 September 1849, in Head to Grey, 7 September 1849, CO 188; Recognizances, July–September 1849, "Riots and Disasters," Executive Council Records; Documents, Saint John Justice Court, 1849, PANB; Inquests, 1849, New Brunswick Supreme Court Documents, PANB; 12 Victoria, c. 29, 1849, *New Brunswick Statutes*, 1849; *Morning News*, 30 July 1849; *New Brunswick Courier,* 21, 28 July 1849; *Temperance Telegraph*, 23 August 1849.

93. Documents, Saint John Justice Court, 1849; Kinnear to Head, extract, 6 September 1849, in Head to Grey, 7 September 1849, CO 188; John Haggerty petition to Head, September 1849, in Judicial Documents, Executive Council Records; *Weekly Chronicle*, 24 August 1849; *New Brunswick Courier*, 18, 25 August 1849.

94. *New Brunswick Courier*, 19 July 1851, 16, 23, 30 July, 6, 13 August 1853; *Weekly Chronicle*, 18 July 1851; *Morning News*, 15, 20 July 1853; *New Brunswick Reporter*, 15, 22 July 1853; *Freeman* (Saint John), 14 July 1855; McHarg Diary.

95. *Loyalist*, 30 March 1848; *New Brunswick Reporter*, 20 April 1850. Irish immigrants in the United States experienced a similar double standard: see Theodore M. Hammett, "Two Mobs of Jacksonian Boston: Ideology and Interest," *Journal of American History*, LXII (March 1976), pp. 866–7.

96. Documents, Saint John Justice Court, 1849; "Riots and Disasters," Executive Council Records.

97. W.W. Rostow explored the linkages between social unrest and economic downturns in *British Economy of the Nineteenth Century* (Oxford, 1948), pp. 123–5.

98. Wynn, *Timber Colony*, pp. 84–6, 166–7; MacNutt, *New Brunswick*, p. 329; James R. Rice, "A History of Organized Labour in Saint John, New Brunswick, 1813–1890," M.A. thesis, University of New Brunswick, 1968, pp. 33–4.

99. *Journal of the House of Assembly of New Brunswick*, 1850–1, 1853–4, 1857–60, 1867, 1872–5; 38 Victoria, c. 54, 1875, *Statutes of New Brunswick*, 1875.

100. Saint John's Orangemen sponsored a massive procession on the first Twelfth of July following the bill's assent. See *Freeman*, 13, 15, 18 July 1876; *Morning News*, 14, 17 July 1876.

101. Colebrooke to Grey, 30 July 1847, Head to Grey, 15 July 1849, CO 188; Colebrooke Correspondence, 1847, Head Correspondence, 1849, PANB.

102. New Brunswick Census, 1851, 1861; Immigration Returns, New Brunswick Blue Books, 1850–5, PAC; "Report on Trade and Navigation," *Journal of the House of Assembly of New Brunswick*, 1866.

TWELVE

··

To Love, Honour and Obey: Wife-Battering in Working-Class Montreal, 1869–1879

KATHRYN HARVEY

"On Thursday evening last, the twenty fourth day of July instant, my husband, the said Thomas Craven, of the said city of Montreal, Carter, came home drunk.

On the folowing [sic] morning the twenty fifth day of July instant I scolded and abused my said husband because he had come home drunk on the evening previous.

I was then in my Kitchen and he was in his bedroom and whilst I was abusing him as aforesaid, he came into the Kitchen and struck me a blow with his hands, I cannot say whether it was open or shut, in some part of the head.

··

Source: "To Love, Honour and Obey: Wife-Battering in Working-Class Montreal, 1869–1879," *Urban History Review*, 19, 2 (October 1990): 128–40. Reprinted by permission.

After I got a blow from my said husband I struck him a blow with a stick, on the arm.

He then took hold of me and shoved me out and I went back into the house and took on the stove a Kettle full of cold water and I threw it at him and he then pushed me back out of the house which is off Prince street . . . and I fell on the footwalk and in the fall I broke my right ankle.

In that scuffle I also received on the side of the left eye a wound about one inch in length, and I cannot say whether it is the result of a blow or the effect of the fall.

I cannot tell whether the said Thomas Craven intended when he so unlawfully assaulted me, to do me grevious [sic] bodily injury." [1]

These words, written in the language of the court clerk, give shape to the story of Bridget McLoughlin, one battered woman living in Montreal in the 1870s. This case, and the one that follows, was considered severe enough to merit a trial before the Court of General Sessions. Even though the injuries sustained by the wife in the second case were life-threatening and those involving Mrs Craven were not, both husbands were charged with the same offense, wounding with intent to do bodily harm.

In August 1873, Philomène Silvestre was turned out of the family home by her husband. It was not the first time. It would be the last. For 15 of the last 24 months she had lived with her brother, Félix, and his wife, who ran a hotel on Craig Street near Viger Gardens. She sought refuge there whenever she was thrown out by her husband, returning to her family when the crisis had passed.

Five months later her husband, Joseph Laporte, went to see his wife at her brother's house armed with a large pocket knife. With it he stabbed her fifteen times.[2]

Marguerite St Jean, an elderly widow, was scrubbing the stairs leading to the Silvestres' apartment at the time of the attack. She told police that "she saw the prisoner come at three different times to look in the door that opened upon the stairway and, after looking for the third time, he mounted hastily to the second storey, from whence she immediately afterwards heard cries of distress. She ran up instantly and found the accused striking violently his wife."[3]

Félix Silvestre was at home that evening of 13 January when his wife burst into their apartment crying, "Félix, ascend [sic] quickly; Joseph is murdering Philomène."[4] Silvestre, in his deposition, said that when he entered his sister's room it was too dark to see what object his brother-in-law had in his hand. On arriving, he saw Laporte strike his sister and immediately seized him and brought him outside, where he stopped a passing policeman.

At the trial, counsel for Joseph Laporte based his defense on the following arguments. The accused did not deny stabbing his wife but "alleged improper conduct on the part of Mrs. Laporte which is pretended to have driven her husband, from whom she had been for a considerable period separated, into such a phrenzy [sic] that its necessary consequence was the murderous assault in question." He also appealed to the jurors' "sympathies on the score of his children, who would lose by his conviction his care and protection." It was also pointed out that the accused "was too drunk at the time to possess any recollection of his actions."

"The jury without leaving their seats returned a verdict of guilty."[5] The prisoner was sentenced to five years for wounding with intent to do grievous bodily harm, the maximum sentence being life imprisonment.

These two cases are not cited here because they are in some way typical. The severity of the charge, intent to do grievous bodily harm, and the fact that they were seen by a higher court set them apart from the cases of assault and battery which make up the bulk of this study. What they serve to illustrate is the diversity of situations and responses.

Cases of wife-battering in nineteenth century Montreal did not follow one script, but many. The stories of Bridget McLoughlin and Philomène Silvestre that introduce this article together provide a wealth of information about wife-battering. Sometimes a wife resisted and on other occasions she did not. Police were occasionally on hand, but in the case of Bridget McLoughlin, it was her children who ran to summon the police. One attack was premeditated and involved the use of a knife. In the other, a tense situation turned violent and any weapon at hand, from fists to a kettle, expressed this anger. Both women were thrown out of their homes, a gesture that characterized many of the assaults, yet Philomène Silvestre's decision to move in with her brother was rare. The ambivalence expressed by Bridget McLoughlin over having her husband prosecuted was shared by many of the women. Although the content of the stories changed, the co-authors of these domestic tragedies remained the same: male dominance and female dependence.

This article seeks to analyse the kinds of situations in which working-class husbands in Montreal beat their wives and to examine the responses women could make. From the details of these cases of wife-battering, discovered in the newspapers and court records of Montreal, there emerges a sense of what it might have been like to be a battered woman in working-class Montreal during the 1870s.[6]

The reasons men gave for beating their wives illuminate much more than marital violence. They take us to the heart of gender relations, revealing wives' and husbands' expectations of themselves and of each other within marriage, as well as indicating the factors precipitating the violence. Prominent among the latter were drink, struggles over money, jealousy, and authority over children. The reports show, too, numerous prohibitions that prevented women from reporting this crime and underline the unequal distribution of power between men and women within marriage and within the society at large.

The analysis that knits these newspaper stories and court cases together is derived, in part, from the ideas of four historians: Nancy Tomes,[7] Ellen Ross,[8] Pat Ayers, and Jan Lambertz,[9] who have written on domestic violence in working-class London and Liverpool. In search of an answer as to why married women were beaten by their husbands in this period, they have concluded that the increased dependence of working-class wives on their husbands' wages, through their exclusion from paid labour, made women more vulnerable to male violence. The similarity of their conclusions points to their shared approach. The family economy model provides the organizing principle around which their arguments and mine revolve. Their work provides an important critique of married women's dependence and husbands' dominance where the individual and the society meet in the family.

Montreal, in the 1870s, did not provide a hospitable environment for its working-class inhabitants. Life was tempered by frequent confrontations with hunger, disease, discontinuity, and death. Scarcity took many forms. Food, clothing, a comfortable place to sleep, and a place where emotional needs could be met were all in short supply. In this context, the working-class family, in which parents and children pooled their individual earnings and resources toward a common subsistence, provided the means for survival. One of the prerequisites of a smoothly running family economy was a regular wage earned by the male head. Yet the economic conditions created by industrial capitalism could not always meet this need. Male authority and female sub-servience were being undermined by changes in the economy. Increased competition for scarce jobs and men's loss of control over the work process challenged traditional definitions of masculine authority.

Authority, opportunity, and responsibility remained unequally distributed be-tween husbands and wives, setting the stage for the violence found in the domestic disputes. This evidence shows that some women did not passively accept being beat-en by their husbands, nor did all members of society accept as legitimate a husband's right to punish his wife.

Wife-battering became an issue of public concern in Montreal in the 1870s. His-torians Margaret May and Angela Weir have pointed out that domestic violence is an issue raised during periods of active feminism.[10] In Montreal, the reasons behind this upsurge in interest in the 1870s, and the role played by women reformers and femi-nists, remain to be unravelled. The existence of newspaper accounts and court cases treating wife abuse attests to a public awareness of it as a social problem.[11] During this period, the voices of the temperance movement and middle-class law and order reformers joined in chorus to alert the public to the evils of alcohol abuse. The link made by the temperance movement between drunkenness and wife-battering fo-cussed the public's attention on a crime that remained unnamed in other periods because it had no public face. The resulting visibility in both the courts and the news-papers makes this research possible. It is to the causes, context, and contents of these domestic disputes that we now turn.

In the majority of cases, men were arrested both for being drunk and for strik-ing their wives. There seemed to be consensus among observers and those actually involved in the disputes that drink was at the root of the problem. This consensus was in part forged by the newspapers themselves. The *Montreal Star* and the *Montreal Daily Witness*, newspapers that reported crime in a similar fashion, were strong temperance supporters. John Dougall, the editor of the *Montreal Daily Witness* and one of the lead-ing advocates of temperance in Montreal, aggressively attacked the "liquor interests" from the pages of his newspaper. The police also endorsed the theory that alcohol was at the root of most crime. 'Drink and its Doings' was a much-used heading in the police court reports.[12]

For some men, wife-beating ranked as a sport that accompanied a bout with the bottle. August Guilmette, 40, shoemaker, when asked by the Recorder "if jeolousy [sic] was the cause of his malignant conduct," answered, "No, the liquor made his blood warm in his veins and he could not do without exercise."[13] Drink, the most frequently cited reason for the violence, quickly became, in the mouths of husbands, its justification. Charles Belmont came home drunk and found his wife asleep with her baby. He then emptied the red fire from his pipe on to her face to burn her. He pleaded not guilty to assault and battery.[14] A number of other men pleaded guilty to drunkenness but not guilty to assaulting their wives. They claimed that the alcohol made them violent. Joseph Laporte, too, pleaded not guilty to the stabbing of his wife Philomène Silvestre, alleging that he was too drunk at the time to possess any recol-lection of his actions.[15]

Despite middle-class reformers' efforts at controlling alcohol abuse, working-class drinking culture flourished in Montreal, to the tune of one tavern for every 143 inhabitants in 1870.[16] Peter DeLottinville's research on Joe Beef, the most famous of the tavern proprietors of this period, highlights how important tavern life was for working-class men, over and above the basic food and drink it provided.

Joe Beef's Canteen functioned as a kind of informal aid society, dispensing food and drink to the luckless and to striking canal workers, providing medicine for the sick and jobs for the unemployed. It was also a place of entertainment, gathering together those in search of pleasant diversion. Entertainment at Joe's took a variety of forms. One of the special talents of proprietor Charles McKiernan was to transform any subject into rhyming couplets for the amusement of his customers. The temperance crusader, the minister, the landlord, and the Recorder, as symbols of authority and agents of social control, were frequently the targets of Joe's poetic attacks. DeLottinville suggests that "McKiernan's humour allowed his patrons a temporary mastery over the forces which dominated their lives outside the Canteen doors."[17] One can only speculate on whether wives, in this context, came in for their share of ridicule, but it seems plausible.

According to James Snell, jokes about marriage made at the wife's expense were a popular form of humour in at least one Canadian magazine at the turn of the century. He argues "marriage humour operated as a social control mechanism, reasserting the traditional behaviour expectations and censuring 'deviant' female activity."[18]

But there was a darker side to tavern life that cast its shadow over the lives of the women and children left outside. Linda Gordon in her study of domestic violence in Boston has noted that "saloon camaraderie tended to escalate men's hostility to women, or at least consolidated and encouraged it."[19]

DeLottinville makes a convincing argument for the tavern as "a stronghold for working class culture . . . where an alternative to the individualist, competitive philosophy of the nineteenth century middle-class" was practiced.[20] Coexistent with this was the tavern as a bastion of masculinity which celebrated drunkenness, engaged in blood sports, and exercised in street brawls. It was this aspect of working-class male culture that most put women at odds with their mate. Resentment surfaced when these women were faced with a drunken husband whose leisure activities put her family's survival in jeopardy. Irate wives, attempting to retrieve drunken husbands from the reaches of the tavernkeeper, were among the cases of assault and battery seen by the Police Magistrate during this period. In one such case, the wife of the tavernkeeper, Mrs MacDonald, was charged with assaulting the wife of one of her regular customers, Mrs Farmer, who had come to collect her husband. It appeared from the evidence that Mrs Farmer, certain that her husband, a milkman, was at this tavern, where she alleged he spent a large portion of his earnings, proceeded to the barroom to induce him to return home, whereupon he resisted.[21] It might well have enraged wives to be excluded from sharing in the all important decision on how a husband's wage was to be spent.

The actual physical separation of work done by men and women, and the fact that one was waged and the other was not, helped transform both the idea and the reality of leisure. Previously, at least in many pre-industrial settings, men and women had worked and played side by side. They had pursued, in E.P. Thompson's words, "task-orientation," meaning that a worker's own sense of need and order dictated how the work would be carried out. "Social intercourse and labour are intermingled . . . the working-day lengthens or contracts according to the task — and there is no great sense of conflict between labour and 'passing the time of day.' "[22] When men left home to follow waged labour into the factories, they were made to embrace new rhythms of work and pleasure based on "time-discipline." Work was now measured in pay and pay was needed to buy both bread and pleasure at the end of the day. In this context, drinking became both the compensation and the affirmation of men's wage-earning status.

Drink now might be claimed as an inalienable right, one which men might or might not choose to share with their women. The emphasis here is on choice, for it was the men who did the choosing. John Stanton had his wife, Mary Riley, arrested for assault because he suspected her of drinking in his absence. The witness for the prosecution actually proved the husband guilty of assault. "Well surs, the man he cummed home, an' smelt the licker on her, an' shure he offered a few insults, which made her feel disagreeable about it, as no doubt, an then he strikes her just very gently on the mouth wid an axe-handle but not to excess."[23] It is interesting to note that, in her defense, Mary Riley emphatically denied interfering with her husband. Her passivity thus established her credibility as a "good wife."

Women also drank and at times to excess, but overall it seems women drank less than men. Responsibility for children, limited access or right to cash, and a work day that stretched from dawn until dusk imposed their own limits. The adage "a woman's work is never done" simply meant that the type of labour women were engaged in, the care and maintenance of the family, called for different work rhythms more akin to pre-industrial patterns of labour.[24]

A wife's leisure time was not concentrated at the end of the day. It was snatched in breaks between chores and combined with other responsibilities. Recreation for women remained inextricably bound to work. Where and how women drank confirms this. Alcohol was available to women at a variety of places, including grocery stores. Although it was illegal, some grocers sold drinks by the glass to their customers, many of whom were women out doing the daily shopping.[25]

Women who attempted to deprive men of drink by refusing to give them money or by taking it from them were chastised with violence. When the husband of Celanière Trudeau arrived home drunk, she tried to prevent him from drinking the bottle of whisky that he had brought with him. He responded by seizing the bottle and striking her on the head and abdomen.[26]

A number of wives attested to the otherwise good character of their husbands when not transformed by drink. Despite the fact that Patrick Brennan had threatened to "kill her by inches," as he had said he had done to his former wife, and then commenced to do just that, Mrs Brennan testified that he was a good husband when sober.[27] Mrs Scott "gives a sad account of the ruin and misery which has overtaken herself and children by the indulgence of her husband in drinking. When free from intoxication she admits he is a good husband but it is only seldom that he keeps steady."[28]

These women defined a good husband as one who made a regular contribution to the family purse and did not squander money on frequent visits to the tavern. It is difficult to separate the cases that involved alcohol from the struggles over money. Drinking put an intolerable strain on family budgets that were tight, even before the depression hit the Montreal economy in 1874. Men and women often had different ideas of how a man's salary should be spent. Men's drinking was clearly at odds with women's concern with feeding and clothing the family.

The sexual division of labour within the family helped create these tensions. Women's dependence on an inadequate male wage, matched with male expectations of having their physical and emotional needs met first and without fail, provided fertile ground for conflict. Men and women often had different ideas of how a man's salary should be spent.

Men who were employed occasionally, or turned their salary over to the tavern-keeper instead of to their wives, wreaked havoc with a woman's ability to make ends meet. Most labourers could not depend on steady work. Even those labourers who were employed could not always rely on being paid regularly or in cash. Women's anger mounted when their husbands' inadequacy as providers was brought home to them every time the bills were not paid and there was no food for the table. A husband's non-support added to the considerable physical burden of housework, as the conflict between Ellen Fitzgerald and her husband illustrates.

> Ellen Fitzgerald had been married to Patrick Hennessy for 28 years. He had property from which he received $11.00 per month rental. Her husband was in the habit of going on a spree and did not support the family properly. Their water rates were not paid and the water was turned off. On Saturday night she went to the neighbours for a pail of water and when she returned her husband was quarrelling with the son. She said, 'let him alone, you don't support him, you don't support yourself.' At this he grabbed her and scratched her forehead with his fist or nails.[29]

Husbands, too, were dependent, but it took different forms. Men relied on women to feed and clothe them. When a wife failed to carry out her prescribed tasks, a husband's frustration was at times measured in blows. Louis Brisson returned home one Tuesday night to find only bread and butter for supper. Brisson, a tinsmith, had been drinking hard lately and on Saturday night gave Henriette, his wife, $1.00, although he had earned $7.00 that week. He would not accept her explanations for the meal and struck her violently in the face with his fist.[30]

In many of the accounts, men drank their salary but still expected their wives to provide for them. It seems that in men's eyes, lack of payment toward the household expenses was not sufficient reason for annulling this socially sanctioned sexual contract. Some women obviously felt differently. This was one right for which they were willing to fight because they had few alternatives. Between 1874 and 1875, eight separate accusations of unlawfully and wilfully neglecting to provide for wife and children were brought by women before three separate judges from the Court of Special Sessions.[31] Not one of the petitions was successful, although it is difficult to know on what grounds they were refused. In all of the cases, the women established that they were legally married and that their husbands had stopped providing for them. Even if they had been successful, one husband's threat to leave the city rather than support his wife exposed the essential weakness of legal redress.

Yet some men felt no compunction when helping themselves to their wives' earnings and in this they were supported by the law. In Quebec, wives were not legally entitled to have an occupation different from their husbands', nor did they have the right to dispose of their salaries.[32] Some of the beatings were the result of women's trying to protect their earnings from whisky-consuming husbands.

Annie Simpson had been married to Antoine Stall for 16 years in 1876. They had had three children together, the eldest being 13 years at the time. Stall was a carter by trade, but for the last two years had given nothing toward the housekeeping expenses. He spent all of his earnings on drink. The family survived on the proceeds of washing

and a little shop kept by Simpson. Despite his lack of participation in the family economy, Stall expected his meals on the table and showed up regularly for them. He also would steal from his wife's pocketbook and threaten her life when she tried to stop him.[33]

The strategies that women used in order to get by in the absence of a dependable male wage varied depending on the age of the children and the resources they had at their disposal. Some of the following stories serve to illustrate how women coped. Henriette Brisson did what many women in her situation were forced to do: she cut costs. She began serving bread and butter for supper instead of something more substantial. In order to stretch the food supply even further, women cut back on what they ate. Evidence for this is found in the work of Peter and Patricia Ward, who linked the fall in birth weights of babies born to poor English-speaking women using the University Lying-in Hospital between 1851 and 1905 to declining nutritional standards among the working poor.[34] Bettina Bradbury in her work on the family economy in working-class Montreal argues that "the brunt of low standards of living may well have been born largely by married women and those offspring whose future life chances were largely determined before they were born. Gender combined with class position apparently made working class women, particularly married women, the least well fed and unhealthiest of Montreal's citizens."[35]

Working for a wage was one option that few married women chose. In the working-class wards of Ste Anne and St Jacques, Bradbury found that between 1861 and 1881 only one to five percent of married women reported working. There were good reasons for this. Jobs were scarce and high unemployment throughout the 1870s created fierce competition. Wages were also universally low for women, ranging anywhere from $1.50 to $5.00 a week, and less if they were employed at home sewing clothes or shoes.[36] Peddling food, rag picking, doing laundry, and child-minding were the likely means used by women to make ends meet under these circumstances. Going to court to press a claim to a husband's wages was another device, but if the years 1874–75 are any indication, it was largely an unsuccessful one. Some men did not take kindly to any criticism of their behaviour. Whether women intervened to save a child from the father's wrath or to protest a husband's infidelity, the response was often the same. For Louis Montbriant of St Paul St, violent language on the part of his wife (when she remonstrated with him for upsetting a salter) merited a clout with the bottle from which he had been drinking.[37]

Scolding behaviour on the part of the wife was considered by the husband, and in some instances by the Police Magistrate, to be a serious breach of male authority. Women convicted of abusive language were in many cases given a stiffer sentence than men convicted of assaulting their wives. The practice of punishing women more severely than men, it seems, was not limited to the crime of employing abusive language. The broader issue of unequal sentencing was first brought to public attention by The Society for the Protection of Women and Children in 1887.[38]

Jealousy was identified as the culprit in a number of the beatings. Mrs Scanlan "was felled to the ground as a butcher would an ox" by her husband on New Year's Day. A friend of the family, William Clark, had paid a call to wish them a happy New Year and had kissed Mrs Scanlan, as was the custom.[39] In Mr Scanlan's mind, what was really at stake here was his absolute control over his wife.

Leaving a husband was no guarantor of peace. Often it meant involving more people in the conflict. A number of the assaults were reported by women who already had left their husbands because of brutality and lack of financial support. Mrs Irvine's testimony echoed the sentiments of these women. "I can live better without him, your Honor, I only stand in dread of my life day after day."[40]

Social, political, economic, and legal constraints combined to limit women's responses to male violence. The formalisation of the Quebec Civil Code after 1866 changed little for women, simply rendering more clearly their inferior legal status.[41] The Civil Code re-affirmed men's superior authority within the family, that is, their power as husbands and fathers. The unequal legal status conferred on the members of the family was predicated on a married woman's legal incapacity. When a woman married, she lost her autonomy and was subject to the authority of her husband, who was legally entitled to make all decisions concerning her civil rights and her children.[42] In short, married women shared the same legal status with children and the mentally unfit.

Similar constraints were applied to women's political participation. At the beginning of the century, women were eligible to vote based on the same conditions as men. By 1849, the parliament of the Province of Canada formally abolished this right.

Women who left abusive husbands risked losing their children and their social identity. Being a woman in this period was synonymous with being a wife and mother. Leaving home stripped her of both roles. It also left her without those measures of economic protection that the family provided and without the legal autonomy of unmarried women and widows. A woman who deviated visibly from the social norm by being a single mother, a drunkard, or a prostitute automatically forfeited the right to sympathy and help afforded women who embraced the values of "true womanhood."[43]

For the majority of women, leaving their husbands for anything but a short period of time was impossible. A few certainly tried. It was more than chance that explains Philomène Gavreau's presence one week at the Recorder's Court to press charges of assault and battery against her husband and in Superior Court the following week to apply for a "Separation of bed and board." Gavreau, who ran a brothel on St Elizabeth St, could conceive of living apart from her husband by virtue of her financial independence and status as a prostitute, which had already placed her outside the bounds of respectable society.[44] In the social and economic climate of the 1870s, women alone with children faced a struggle to survive. The institution of the patriarchal family, despite its limitations, conflicts, and contradictions, remained the best survival strategy available to working-class women. Alternatives to the family, such as the convent, the brothel, or domestic service, were by and large the options only of single women. How could women have imagined autonomy, a life outside of the patriarchal family, when existing economic and social structures permitted no such configuration?

Women may have turned to their extended families as a short term solution, but the resources of the working class were quickly exhausted. Space was at a premium in most working-class housing.[45] In many instances, adding another family would have transformed a bearable living situation into an intolerable one. The sympathy offered by relatives to battered women could be limited by deeply engrained social attitudes which resisted female demands for autonomy. "To love, honour and obey" was a married woman's lot.

We can only speculate as to which institutions — other than the police and the courts — battered women turned outside the family. Annie Banks and her three year old son Edward were admitted to the home run by the Montreal Ladies Benevolent

Society in May of 1865. The reason given for accepting the Banks family was that the husband was a confirmed drunkard and Annie Banks could not live with him. Two months later she returned to her husband.[46] Whether violence was one reason behind her leaving is a matter of conjecture. Drunkenness and the death or desertion of a husband were frequently cited circumstances leading to the placement of children and women with children in this institution. Although domestic violence was never mentioned explicitly in the admittance records, drunkenness was often used in this period as a code word for domestic violence.

There were other obstacles preventing battered women from seeking immediate relief. Some women turned to the police for protection. This was not necessarily an effective option. In 1875 only 38 policemen walked the beat in Montreal.[47] In a city of 160,000 that meant one policeman for every 4,210 inhabitants. This ratio compares with the early twentieth-century idea of one constable for every 1,000 residents. The chances of a policeman in this city at this time actually intervening in a domestic quarrel were slim. During the winter months, when life was centred indoors, the possibility was even more remote. Often the law would be summoned by a relative or neighbour, but by the time help arrived the "row" was over. As one officer commented, "there was nothing to be done."[48] If a husband was also found to be drunk and/or disturbing the peace, he was arrested and charged accordingly, but the original reason for which the police had been summoned went unpunished.

In many cases, it was the woman herself who was obliged to report the crime. The procedure that the victim was obliged to follow entailed a personal appearance at the closest police station, soon after her having experienced a beating. The next step was to pay a dollar to cover the cost of a warrant for her husband's arrest. Without this dollar her complaint would be dropped. For wives who did not participate in the waged economy, a dollar was a large sum to have on hand. At a time when a policeman and many labourers earned a dollar a day, this amount must have prevented many women from seeking justice. Yet wives, as managers of the family economy, had some income at their disposal which they may have used for this purpose. Later we will see how being keeper of the family purse worked against wives, but in some contexts it might have worked to their advantage. Both the newspapers and the police remarked on wives' reluctance to prosecute their husbands. A police chief in his year-end report on crime noted that "it is difficult to obtain evidence which the wives are often unwilling to give until they are driven to it from terror of their lives."[49] It is not surprising that, of the 349 cases reported in the *Montreal Star*, at least 45 were dropped because the victim failed to substantiate the charge.

Fear kept many women away from the court room. George Scott, when arrested for assaulting his wife, threatened "to pay her off afterwards." The woman was too afraid to appear. The magistrate postponed the case to ensure Mrs Scott's presence, but to no avail. The next day she wasn't to be found.[50]

Fear and a costly judicial system that discriminated against those who were poor and did not necessarily have access to cash must have stopped many victims from procuring punishment for their abusers. For some women, having their husbands arrested was punishment enough. Once a woman paid the cost of the warrant, her husband's presence behind bars was assured until the trial. If the case was seen by the Recorder or Police Magistrate this meant a maximum stay of a few days, but in the case of the Court of Special Sessions imprisonment could be prolonged for up to a month. This delay may explain why the majority of the assault and battery cases were tried by the lower courts. Most men may have preferred to forfeit a right to trial by jury at the Court of Special Sessions in order to hasten release from the city jail.[51]

Yet this incarceration was a costly act of retribution or protection. When a woman failed to appear after laying a charge, she was still bound to pay any costs incurred by the court. When Elize Chase withdrew her assault charge against her husband, he was discharged and "the costs amounting to $4.50 fell upon the woman, and as she was a respectable but poor person, she was given 20 days to pay up."[52] Default meant a jail term for her.

When a husband was found guilty, with few exceptions he was sentenced to a fine and to payment of court costs. If these costs were not paid and the husband was jailed instead, the sources are unclear as to who assumed the costs, the wife or the courts. A few judges refused to impose a fine and recommended jail instead. They were aware that a fine was apt to punish a wife more than her husband. The ultimate irony was that, as they were keepers of the family purse, the paying of a husband's or close male relative's fine was one of the tasks that fell to women. Louis Lache was fined $2.50 or 15 days in jail. "As he was leaving the dock he turned to his wife and told her if she had the money to pay the fine he would pay her again."[53]

Many women could not afford to have their husbands jailed. They were forced to weigh the loss of his contribution to the family economy against their own physical well-being. Nowhere is women's subordination within the family clearer than in the example provided by battered wives. In many cases forfeiting their own personal safety was the price women paid for securing the family against destitution. In this situation a wife's personal survival was simultaneously both threatened and guaranteed by her place within the family. On the one hand, she was subject to the violence of her husband. On the other, being part of a family economy kept her from starvation. To protect herself against one helped undermine the other.

Interpersonal violence in working-class Montreal was not limited to wife-beating, nor was it initiated only by men. Men, women, and children often used their fists or whatever was at hand to resolve conflicts. Ellen O'Loughlin attacked Catherine Owens with a meat bone.[54] The weapon may have been original, but the act was typical of the individual's responses to conflict. Men tended to use their fists or the tools of their trade as their preferred weapons. Women's work and therefore the objects they employed differed. Emptying chamber pots "with malicious intent," and pouring kettles of boiling water on victims' heads were some of the violent gestures employed by women.

Another dimension of family violence consisted of the attacks that pitted families against neighbours, or bailiffs and policemen. In sum, families would rally to drive off outsiders who threatened family stability. The most common cases involved husbands, wives, and, in some cases, children teaming up to prevent a bailiff from seizing their property. For example, Michael Duggan and his wife, Mary Ann, both were charged with assaulting a bailiff when he visited their store in the execution of his duties.[55]

This is not to say that violent behaviour was equally distributed between the sexes. Men were clearly more violent. In 1874, of the assault and battery cases that came before the Court of Special Sessions, 138 involved acts of violence between men, 43 violence between women, 36 were attacks on women by men other than their husbands, and 7 involved women attacking men. In the cases of domestic violence, 25 husbands and 5 wives were accused of beating their spouses.[56]

This culture of violence included incidents of wife-battering despite the fact that the criminal justice system did punish perpetrators of domestic violence. The original intent of the laws restricting drunkenness and violence was to control working-class men's behaviour and not to protect women. That women may have benefitted from these laws was secondary.[57]

This claim is borne out by the type of sentences handed down to men convicted of beating their wives. In 1875, of the 31 cases that came before the Court of Special Sessions involving wife-battering, 12 were settled by the judge, meaning that the husband was not penalized and a reconciliation was imposed, and one case was dismissed because the wife failed to appear. Only one husband received the maximum sentence of six months' imprisonment with hard labour and that was because the wife almost bled to death as a result of the attack. When a woman's life was not considered to be in danger, the judge would impose a reconciliation, or a fine was demanded of the guilty party of $5.00 on average and he was ordered to pay court costs. Default on payment meant a month in the city jail.

This penalty contrasts with the punishment meted out to men and women convicted of selling liquor without a license. Most of the convictions were for small amounts of alcohol, but the sentences were the same, a $50 dollar fine plus costs or three months' imprisonment. The economy of punishment practiced by the lower courts that elevated the illegal sale of alcohol over wife abuse was completely consistent with the popularly held theory that alcohol caused most social problems, including wife-battering.

In the community, wife-beating was tolerated, within certain limits. People seemed ready to intervene and offer assistance only if the violence passed a certain threshold, or if sympathy was evoked by a victim's age or physical condition (whether she was pregnant or not), or if a weapon was involved. As the story "Affray in Wolfe St." shows, the community was willing to turn a blind eye on wife-battering until it invaded the public space and/or there was a risk of murder.

> Another of those brutal affrays which every now and then occur to alarm peaceful neighbourhoods, and render night hideous, took place last night in Wolfe St. The stillness of the evening was broken about 10 o'clock by a succession of piercing shrieks, followed almost instantly by a rush into the street from a back yard of a number of people, surrounding a woman struggling in the grasp of a man who held her by the hair, and beat her cruelly. No one interfered for some time, and the shouts and cries in mixed French and English rendered the scene exciting and painful in the extreme. The man and woman had quarrelled in their house, and it appears he had followed her into the yard, beaten her unmercifully, and in her struggles to escape, had dragged her into the street. It was some time before the spectators could separate the infuriated pair by threats of sending for the police, but at length quiet was restored before murder was done.[58]

On occasion, the fear that one day a husband would go too far and commit murder prompted a wife to take action. It was this extreme case that was most likely to receive validation, and support for it mirrored the community's own standards toward domestic violence.

Even this modicum of protection was not forthcoming in the case of a certain Mrs Franklin. Her "greatly bruised and disfigured body" was found dead upon a sofa. One cannot help but wonder if Mrs Franklin's murder by her husband, the only such murder recorded in 1869–79, could not have been averted had her neighbours applied a more stringent set of community standards to wife-battering. The fact that it is the only case of a woman beaten to death suggests that formal and informal mechanisms of control generally succeeded in preventing this most extreme form of abuse. Another possible explanation is that most attacks happened in the home and were not premeditated. In the absence of a really lethal weapon such as a gun or knife, the damage most men could inflict with their fists fell short of murder.

At the inquest into Mrs Franklin's death three people testified that they had witnessed the beatings or their aftermath.

Marie Deserault, a servant employed in a neighboring house, testified that she had noticed the prisoner beating the deceased with his fists, and had been informed by the latter that she had slept in an adjoining shed to escape ill-treatment at the hands of her husband: she had heard no noise in the house either the night before last or yesterday morning, but on calling to see the deceased on Monday last, had been told by the prisoner that she was in bed.

Albert Kay, a lad of thirteen, living with his mother in an adjoining house off St. Francois de Sales St., deposed that about three weeks since he had heard a woman sobbing in the kitchen of the house, which is nearest the lane on which it faces, and then screaming "I am killed, I am killed . . . " Some days previously, the deceased, who was at the time under the influence of liquor, had told him that she had been frequently obliged to escape the cruelty of her husband, and go sleep in his mother's shed, which was near by; he had also on occasion observed the deceased standing on the street quite red in the face, with her tongue lolling out as if she had been choked, and holding her hand to her throat.

Thomas O'Neill, aged seventy-eight, bailiff of the Court of the Queen's Bench, stated that he had known the prisoner and his wife since the year 1853; the latter had worked for his family for several years, and to whom they were all greatly attached; on the 21st the prisoner came to his house, and in answer to their enquiry said that he had left his wife in the house — also that she was probably dead; they became alarmed, and consequently, later in the day he visited the premises . . . the deceased came in by the front door; she presented a horrible appearance: the left side of her face was black, blue and swollen, and one of her eyes was in the same condition; had exclaimed "Oh Mary, what has happened to you?" She was very feeble being unable to cry, but perfectly sober, prisoner explained to account for the blackened eye, that she had fallen against the stove; she said "Oh Mr. O'Neill, I am killed!"[59]

A number of factors contributed to the murder of Mrs Franklin. It already has been mentioned that her neighbours failed to act. No community constraints bound Mr Franklin's vicious temper. The police did not intervene, quite possibly because they were never notified, and Mrs Franklin's passivity acted as poor protection. This is not to suggest that Mrs Franklin was in some way responsible for her own death, but rather to highlight how passivity and aggression were two forms of women's resistance. In this period there is evidence to show that these strategies were also subject to change.

Some women resisted their husbands physically. Evidence for this is found in the cases of marital violence in which 10 percent involved husband-beating.[60] Mrs Craven's fight with her husband was not completely one-sided. No doubt that was true of other marital conflicts. In this period, the work done by both sexes was physically demanding. Working-class women's strength and stamina were prerequisites for survival. Women did battle with store-keepers, bailiffs, children, women, and most certainly their husbands.

A distinction can be made between violence used by women and by men. Women's violence was in response to male aggression, while among men, violence was more readily used as a form of communication. A woman's willingness to assert herself in a domestic quarrel was influenced by competing notions of femininity. Middle-class ideas of proper feminine behaviour strongly condemned working-class women who fought back.[61] Passivity and dependence on patriarchal institutions for protection were considered the appropriate response. One of the conclusions Nancy Tomes drew from her research on wife-battering in working-class London between 1850 and 1890 was that as women's violence declined, shame about being beaten increased.[62]

In the last ten years, domestic violence has once again been brought to the public's attention. It has been placed on the political agenda by the feminist struggle to unite the private with the public sphere. What was once considered a family matter, and therefore private, has now been exposed to the light of public scrutiny.

Today, as in the past, public concern has been fed by the media's interest in the most brutal cases. What has changed to sustain this interest is the work done by the network of battered women's shelters that have been built from the energy unleashed by this wave of feminism. As a feminist historian concerned with domestic violence, it seems to me not only logical but essential to look at relationships between husbands and wives in the past as a potential source of insight into this present day conflict.

The conflicts that made these unions so problematic in the late nineteenth century had their sources in the unequal distribution of economic and legal power between men and women, as well as in men's almost unrestricted right to chastise their wives. In part, husbands beat their wives because they thought they could get away with it. The cases examined in this article capture the experience of that minority in the 1870s who, to a greater or lesser degree, did not.

NOTES

1. Archives Nationales de Québec à Montréal (hereafter ANQM), pré-archivage, Court of General Sessions, Montreal, August 4, 1873, #469.
2. ANQM, pré-archivage, Court of General Sessions, Montreal, January 19, 1874, #473.
3. *Montreal Star*, January 14, 1874.
4. *Montreal Star*, January 17, 1874.
5. *Montreal Star*, January 21, 1874.
6. Domestic violence does not respect class divisions. The focus on the working class was determined by the sources and not by a conviction held by this writer that wife-battering was an exclusively working-class phenomenon.

   This study is based on a sample of 349 cases of wife-battering which were brought before the Recorder's and Public Police Courts in the years between 1869 and 1879 as reported three to four times a week in the pages of the *Montreal Star*. This source was supplemented by an analysis of all cases of assault and battery involving wives and husbands seen by the Court of General and Special Sessions in Montreal for the years 1870, 1874, and 1875. The court provided the backdrop for the reporting of these cases. It was only in the criminal courts that these domestic dramas were given a public face. It was also this level of justice that was most pre-occupied with crimes committed by members of the working class.

7. Nancy Tomes, "'A Torrent of Abuse': Crimes of Violence Between Working-Class Men and Women in London 1840–1875," *Journal of Social History*, 11, 3 (1978) 328–345.

8. Ellen Ross, "Fierce Questions and Taunts: Married Life in Working-Class London, 1870–1914," *Feminist Studies* 8 (1982) 575–602.

9. Pat Ayers and Jan Lambertz, "Marriage Relations, Money and Domestic Violence in Working Class Liverpool 1919–1939" in Jane Lewis, ed. *Labour and Love: Women's Experience of Home and Family, 1850–1940* (Oxford: 1986) 195–219.

10. Angela Weir, "Battered Women: Some Perspectives and Problems" in M. Mayor, ed. *Women in the Community* (London: 1977) 109 and 113.

11. "Annual Report of the Chief of Police," *Montreal Annual Reports*, 1866–77, 1879–88. Wife-battering first appears as a separate crime in the arrest statistics found in police reports in 1866. In 1878 no statistics were tabulated for wife-battering. The following year, 13 men were charged and 8 women. It is the first time statistics on husband-battering are noted. By 1888, neither category is used in the record of arrests.

   In the *Montreal Star*, stories of wife-battering appear with much less frequency by the beginning of the 1880s. This, in part, can be explained by changes in the newspaper's format, which put less emphasis on the reporting of the activities of the Police and Recorder's Courts.

12. *Montreal Star*, July 29, 1872.

13. Ibid., October 26, 1875.

14. Ibid., February 25, 1969.

15. Ibid., January 21, 1874.

16. "Annual Report of the Chief of Police," *Montreal Annual Reports*, 1870.

17. Peter DeLottinville, "Joe Beef of Montreal: Working-Class Culture and the Tavern, 1869–1889," *Labour/Le Travailleur*, 8/9 (1981–82) 16.

18. James G. Snell, "Marriage Humour and its Social Functions, 1900–1939," *Atlantis*, 11, 2 (1986) 70.

19. Linda Gordon, *Heroes of Their Own Lives: The Politics and History of Family Violence* (New York: 1988) 265.

20. Peter DeLottinville, "Joe Beef of Montreal: Working-Class Culture and the Tavern, 1869–1889," 10–11.

21. *Montreal Star*, January 14, 1874.

22. E.P. Thompson, "Time, Work-Discipline, and Industrial Capitalism," *Past and Present*, 38 (1967) 56–59.

23. *Montreal Star*, June 27, 1871.

24. Nancy Cott, *The Bonds of Womanhood* (New Haven, Conn.: 1977) 60–61.

25. Bettina Bradbury, "The Working Class Family Economy: Montreal, 1861–1881," unpublished Ph.D. dissertation, Concordia University, 1984, 284 and ANQM, pré-archivage, Court of Special Sessions, Montreal, 1870–75.

26. *Montreal Star*, February 26, 1869.

27. Ibid., May 30, 1877.

28. Ibid., August 14, 1878.

29. Ibid., November 12, 1878.

30. Ibid., July 15, 1870.

31. ANQM, pré-archivage, Court of Special Sessions, Montreal, Nov. 6, 1874, #471, Dec. Term, #473, July 8, 1875, #447, Oct. 29, 1875, #477, Oct. 20, 1875, #477, Nov. 8, 1875, #477, July 20, 1875, #477, and Dec. 30, 1875, #478.

32. Paul-André Linteau, René Durocher, and Jean-Claude Robert, *Quebec: A History 1867–1929* (Toronto: 1983) 187–188. On the acquisition of this right in different American states see Amy Dru Stanley, "Conjugal Bonds and Wage Labour: Rights of

Contract in the Age of Emancipation," *The Journal of American History*, 75, 2 (1988) 471–500.

33. *Montreal Star*, June 2, 1876.

34. W. Peter Ward and Patricia C. Ward, "Infant Birth Weight and Nutrition in Industrializing Montreal," *American Historical Review*, 89, 2 (1984).

35. Bettina Bradbury, "The Working Class Family Economy: Montreal, 1861–1881," 462.

36. Ibid., 319.

37. *Montreal Star*, May 28, 1874.

38. National Archives of Canada, Montreal Society for the Protection of Women and Children, MG 28 I 129, Monthly Minutes and Annual Reports, 1887.

39. *Montreal Star*, January 9, 1877.

40. Ibid., February 25, 1879.

41. Paul-André Linteau et al., *Quebec: A History, 1867–1929*, 186–188.

42. Ibid., 188.

43. For a later period, see Andrée Lévesque, *La Norme déviante des femmes au Québec entre deux-guerres* (Montréal: 1989).

44. Philomène Gavreau charged her husband, Ignace Choquette, with drunkenness and assault. The case came before the Recorder March 7, 1874. See *Montreal Star*, March 19, 1874.

45. Whether the practice of doubling-up (working-class families sharing lodgings) was common in Montreal is disputed. Two different interpretations are found in the work of Bettina Bradbury, "Pigs, Cows, and Boarders: Non-Wage Forms of Survival Among Montreal Families, 1861–91," *Labour/Le Travail*, 14 (1984) 32–44 and Gilles Lauzon, "Habiter un nouveau quartier ouvrier de la banlieu de Montréal: Village Saint Augustin (Municipalité de St Henri)," M.A. thesis, history, UQAM, 1986, 75–107.

46. National Archives of Canada, The Montreal Ladies Benevolent Society, MG 28 I 388, Register of Admissions, 1865, Vol. 5.

47. *Montreal Star*, October 1874.

48. Ibid., August 9, 187?.

49. "Annual Report of the Chief of Police," *Montreal Annual Reports*, 1868.

50. *Montreal Star*, October 14, 1870.

51. Henri Elzear Taschereau, LL.D., *The Criminal Statute Law of the Dominion of Canada*, 3rd ed. (Toronto: 1893).

52. *Montreal Star*, October 14, 1870.

53. Ibid., April 24, 1873.

54. ANQM, pré-archivage, Court of Special Sessions, September 10, 1875, Box #609.

55. Ibid., May 1870, Box #459.

56. Ibid., 1874, Box #471, 472, and 473.

57. Ibid., 1875, Box #477, 478, 479, and 480.

58. *Montreal Star*, May 11, 1869.

59. Ibid., November 22, 1873.

60. ANQM, pré-archivage, Court of Special Sessions, 1870, 1873–75. Of the 87 cases of marital violence found recorded, 11 involved husband abuse.

61. Linda Gordon, *Heroes of Their Own Lives*, 276.

62. Nancy Tomes, "'A Torrent of Abuse': Crimes of Violence Between Working-Class Men and Women in London 1840–1875," 328–345.

TOPIC SEVEN

Maintaining the Social Order

Schools such as this one in the village of Adelaide, Canada West, sketched by William Elliot, played an important role in maintaining the social order in nineteenth-century Canada.

By the middle of the nineteenth century, British North America was rapidly leaving behind its pioneer past. A steadily rising population, increased immigration, the growth of towns and cities, the construction of railways and canals, the beginnings of large-scale industry, and the development of banking and the professions all provided evidence that the transition to a mature capitalist society was well under way. But although the prosperity and wealth of British North America had increased considerably, that wealth was not distributed equitably. Urbanization, industrialization, and immigration witnessed the appearance of a host of social problems such as poverty, unemployment, crime, vagrancy, and juvenile delinquency. These problems were particularly disturbing to the emerging middle classes, who advocated a variety of reforms and strategies to cope with what they feared was a growing social crisis.

One of the most important of the reforms was the creation of common schools. The movement for public schools has often been interpreted as a middle-class exercise in social control, designed to repress urban crime, train the working class in the habits of industry, and prevent the eruption of class conflict. Bruce Curtis challenges the social control interpretation in Article Thirteen, on educational reform in Upper Canada in the 1840s. Curtis argues that the creation of public schools was an attempt to construct a public out of diverse ethnic, religious, and class interests and thus was part of a larger process of state formation.

Other reforms addressed what the middle classes perceived as a breakdown of authority that could lead to social anarchy. Concern over the growing conflict between workers and owners, the spread of social misery in the cities, and the collapse of old virtues and display of new vices resulted in a concerted attempt to restore order. As Greg Marquis demonstrates in Article Fourteen, on the Saint John police establishment in the latter part of the century, many looked to the police to maintain social harmony. Although the police often acted in the interests of the commercial elite, Marquis maintains, they achieved a degree of legitimization among the working class.

QUESTIONS TO CONSIDER

1. What were the principal objectives of educational reform in Upper Canada in the 1840s? How did educational reform transform the schools into instruments of state policy?
2. How did the police and the police courts in late nineteenth-century Saint John win the support of the working classes?
3. Why do both Curtis and Marquis reject the social control model of analysis?

SUGGESTED READINGS

Beattie, J.M. *Attitudes to Crime and Punishment in Upper Canada, 1830–1850.* Toronto: Centre for Criminology, 1977.

Darroch, Gordon, and Lee Soltow. *Property and Inequality in Victorian Ontario: Structural Patterns and Cultural Communities in the 1871 Census.* Toronto: University of Toronto Press, 1994.

Fingard, Judith. *The Dark Side of Life in Victorian Halifax.* Porters Lake, Nova Scotia: Pottersfield, 1991.

Greer, Allan, and Ian Radforth, eds. *Colonial Leviathan: State Formation in Mid-Nineteenth-Century Canada.* Toronto: University of Toronto Press, 1992.

Houston, Susan E., and Alison Prentice. *Schooling and Scholars in Nineteenth-Century Ontario*. Toronto: University of Toronto Press, 1988.

Noel, Jan. *Canada Dry: Temperance Crusades before Confederation*. Toronto: University of Toronto Press, 1995.

Prentice, Alison. *The School Promoters: Education and Social Class in Mid-Nineteenth-Century Upper Canada*. Toronto: McClelland and Stewart, 1977.

Short, S.E.D. *Victorian Lunacy: Richard M. Bucke and the Practice of Late Nineteenth-Century Psychiatry*. Cambridge: Cambridge University Press, 1986.

Valverde, Mariana. *The Age of Light, Soap, and Water: Moral Reform in English Canada, 1885–1925*. Toronto: McClelland and Stewart, 1991.

THIRTEEN

Preconditions of the Canadian State: Educational Reform and the Construction of a Public in Upper Canada, 1837–1846

BRUCE CURTIS

Recent work in the social history and political economy of North American educational reform has been situated to a large extent in a "social control" paradigm. In this paradigm educational reform is treated as a response on the part of élite groups or ruling classes to the social unrest associated with industrial capitalist development. Depending upon the particular version of the "social control" thesis one encounters, educational reform is seen as an attempt to control urban poverty and crime, an attempt to repress the menace of class struggle on the part of the working class, or both.

Yet the social control thesis has tended to mystify educational development. In seeking the transformation of educational institutions in structural transformations of capitalist societies, the social control approach has tended to abstract in a misleading manner from the concrete political contexts in which actual educational reforms were made. The assumption — sometimes quite valid — that key social groups agitated for educational reform in an effort to control or repress workers has led to a failure to investigate historically the educational activities of workers themselves.[1] The view of educational reform as an essentially repressive process aimed at the control of the "poor" or the working class by an "élite" or bourgeoisie has directed attention away from both the political conflict and struggle over education, and

Source: Excerpted from "Preconditions of the Canadian State: Educational Reform and the Construction of a Public in Upper Canada, 1837–1846," *Studies in Political Economy*, 10 (Winter 1983): 99–121. Reprinted by permission.

away from an analysis of the content of educational reform. In fact, as I will argue, far from simply aiming to repress or neutralize the political activities of certain classes in society, educational reform in mid-nineteenth-century Upper Canada sought to reconstruct political rule in society by reconstructing the political subjectivity of the population. Reforms sought to do this not simply by repressing consciousness, but by developing and heightening consciousness within newly constructed state forms. Educational reform sought to build political subjects, and in so doing also constructed the state.

POLITICAL CRISIS, POLITICAL REFORM AND EDUCATION IN UPPER CANADA

The 1840s in the Province of Canada were a decade of state-building. In the wake of the rebellions of 1837–38 and Lord Durham's critical report on colonial government, the imperial state undertook to reconstruct the colonial administration. The question of the form of the Canadian state and the nature of this colonial administration dominated the political life of the Canadas for a decade. To the extent that colonial history can be read from the colonial side of the Atlantic, it can be read largely as a history of conflict and struggle over this question.

Educational reform, which also characterized the 1840s, especially in Upper Canada, was inextricably connected to questions of the form of the colonial state. All the fundamental questions concerning educational organization — who needed to be taught, who could educate them, what they needed to know, how they should learn it, who should pay for it — these and other questions were answered only by answering at the same time questions concerning the state: who would rule, how, of what would rule consist, how would it be financed. The struggle over education was at once a struggle over political rule.

Debates over educational reform in Upper Canada had characterized the political development of the colony from the first decade of the nineteenth century.[2] After the Rebellion of 1837 and the Act of Union, these educational conflicts acquired a heightened importance. To many conservative elements, especially those in the Tory Party, the Rebellion of 1837 showed that "in the bosom of this community there exists a dangerous foe."[3] The colony had been polluted by its proximity to the United Sates, "that arena for the discussion of extreme political fantasies,"[4] and by the presence of an unassimilated American population interested in democracy and republicanism. In the view of R.B. Sullivan, later president of the Legislative Council of Upper Canada, the Rebellion pointed to the existence of a crisis of government. Sullivan claimed that the existing school system had been infiltrated by American adventurers. The propagandistic activities of American tractarians had undermined the loyalties of Canadian youth to the point where their minds were

> only accessible to motives of adherence to the Government by means of terror and coercion, or through the equally base channel of personal & pecuniary advantage.[5]

In Sullivan's view — one typical of colonial conservatives — the Rebellion of 1837 was in large part the result of an educational failure. The school system and religious institutions had failed to shape the "youthful mind" of the colony adequately and to instruct people in their political duties. This meant rule could proceed only by coercion or bribery — unstable mechanisms in light of the Rebellion. The political/educational problem for conservatives was one of fixing the "good and noble sentiments" of the population on the proper objects. They were joined in this concern by the Lieutenant-Governor.[6] A major assault upon prevailing community-controlled education was launched by conservatives in the late 1830s, and this assault resulted in the production of a draft school act in 1841.

Before the Union of 1840, the Reform Party in Upper Canada had consistently championed local control in educational matters. The struggles over the state church, the colonial lands, and the powers of the elected assembly itself placed the Reform Party in a position of opposition to executive control over education and support for local autonomy.[7] After the Union, the struggles over "responsible government," struggles in which members of the Reform Party sought parliamentary autonomy for Canada within the colonial connection, also placed Reformers in a position to support decentralized, locally-directed education.

Until the political crisis of 1843–44, a version of Reform educational policy prevailed in Upper Canada. The miserably inefficient School Act of 1841 was a version of the Tory-inspired draft legislation based on the Education Commission of 1839, as amended by Reformers in committee. In 1843 under the Reform ministry of Baldwin and Lafontaine, this act was replaced by one which extended local control over educational matters while increasing the funds available. The acts of both 1841 and 1843 required localities to raise matching funds through a combination of property taxes and fees for state educational grants. The 1843 act placed the management of education in all its important aspects in the hands of school trustees elected by the parents of school children. Local trustees controlled curriculum, pedagogy, the internal management of the school, teacher evaluation and working conditions, hours of attendance, and so forth.[8] Reformers publicly vaunted the act as one which placed control over educational matters in the hands of the people directly.[9]

The School Act of 1843 was a success in practice. It increased local educational funds, legitimated local practice in educational matters, and restricted central influence over the system to one of information-gathering and coordination. Taxation for educational purposes in some instances far exceeded the legal minimum and the numbers of children enrolled in the schools increased markedly.[10] However, the Tory Party objected in principle to local control over education. The political crisis of 1843–44, which brought the Tory Party to power, led to a major reorganization of the Upper Canadian educational system.

POLITICAL CRISIS AND THE RISE OF RYERSON

Late in 1843, the Reform ministry of Baldwin and Lafontaine resigned over the reservation of the Secret Societies Bill and over the refusal of the Governor-General to distribute governmental patronage alone lines determined by the ministry. The ministry expected fresh elections, but these were not called. Instead, for several months, the colony was ruled more or less directly from the office of the Governor-General with the aid of three parliamentary ministers. A political furor ensued involving, in part, serious public agitations in favour of colonial political autonomy.[11] After some time a nominally Tory ministry was constructed by the Governor-General, and in elections held in 1844 this ministry won a small majority centered in Upper Canada. This electoral victory was in part a product of the activities of the Reverend Egerton Ryerson.[12]

An able propagandist, professional cleric, and controversial but influential leader of the moderate Wesleyan Methodist population in Upper Canada, Ryerson undertook to debate the Reformers in the press in a lengthy and much-publicized series of letters. Ryerson's political biography was a chequered one, characterized by frequent shifts in position and party alliance. A vocal opponent of executive control over education in the 1830s, Ryerson had become convinced that while a moderate degree of political liberalization in Canada was desirable, any such project demanded a reform of popular education. Ryerson supported "responsible government" in the sense of government by people educated to act responsibly. This was a matter upon which he had communicated at length with public officials.[13]

Ryerson also agreed more or less completely with the attempts by the imperial state and its first Canadian Governors-General to de-politicize the colony by replacing "factionalism" with "sound administration." This policy involved an acceptance of the legitimacy of protestant religious sects and encouraged protestant social experimentation. Protestant religion was in some ways particularly well-fitted for social reconstruction in Canada and for the continuation of British imperialism which that reconstruction implied. It put forward a vision of political universality in which social harmony, compromise, and the high moral character of social leaders would guarantee political justice.[14]

Ryerson wrote to the Governor-General as he prepared to engage the Reformers in the press that

> In the present crisis, the Government must of course first be placed upon a strong foundation, and then must the youthful mind of Canada be instructed and moulded in the way I have had the honor of stating to your Excellency, if this country is long to remain an appendage to the British Crown.[15]

After the success of the Tory Party in the elections of 1844, Ryerson was named Assistant Superintendent of Education for Upper Canada and charged with formulating a plan for educational reconstruction.

The reform of education which followed was an attempt on the part of the Tory Party to deal with a two-fold political problem in Canada: the maintenance of the colonial connection in the face of political disloyalty demonstrated by sections of the population in 1837 and again in 1843–44, and the creation of forms of rule which would work without bribery or coercion.

THE PLANNED EDUCATIONAL RECONSTRUCTION

To the Tory Party, the School Act of 1843 left control over education precisely in the hands of those most in need of instruction by the state in their political duties. In the crisis of 1843–44 and in their rather shaky response to appeals for loyalty to the Crown, sections of the rural population had shown this to be the case. Education, Ryerson wrote, had to be reorganized so as "to render the Educational System, in its various ramifications and applications, the indirect, but powerful instrument of British Constitutional Government."[16] Ryerson and the Tory administration set out to transform education into a state-directed political socialization.

To this end, Ryerson embarked upon an educational tour to collect information about educational systems in the United States and Europe. This trip produced an extensive educational report and draft school legislation which formed the basis for educational organization in Upper Canada until 1871 (if not later). Ryerson's *Report on a System of Public Elementary Instruction for Upper Canada*, printed by order of the legislature in 1847, provided the blueprint for educational reconstruction in the late 1840s.

Ryerson was by no means the first person interested in educational experimentation aimed at transforming schools into instruments of state policy. In his travels he encountered the fruits of many initiatives undertaken by members of different social classes in various countries. He also encountered, assimilated, and reproduced in his report various attempts to produce efficient and effective pedagogies and curricula. The conditions under which Ryerson's report was produced and the solutions it proposed consisted of responses to common problems faced by liberal reformers in all capitalist societies in the middle of the nineteenth century.

In general, Ryerson's *Report* suggested that the aim of education was the successful training of the forces possessed by each individual. A successful training of these forces would create habits of mind and body conducive to productive labour, Christian religion, and political order. The report was shot through with a concern for the efficient training of human energy.[17] Ryerson sought to make education *practical*, not in the sense of training people for particular occupations or teaching particular skills, but in the sense of creating habits, predispositions, and loyalties in the population which would then practically guide action. Ryerson agreed with Archbishop Whately, one of the architects of the Irish national system of education, that successful governance in representative institutions required the creation of "rationality" in the population.[18]

There were three parts to this rationality-producing education. Ryerson wrote:

> Now, education thus practical, includes religion and morality; secondly, the development to a certain extent of all our faculties; thirdly, an acquaintance with several branches of elementary education.[19]

Religion and morality were to provide the political/habitual/attitudinal content of education. The cultivation of "all the faculties" was the method of instruction, and the several branches of education were the specific contents and devices used to transmit religious and moral training. I will consider Ryerson's pedagogy before discussing the religious and moral conceptions which his reforms embraced.

INDUCTIVE EDUCATION AND PEDAGOGICAL HUMANISM

Ryerson's *Report* was in large measure a critique of a system of education common in Europe and North America in the first decades of the nineteenth century: rote learning. In the monitorial schools, common in working class districts of English cities, students were taught by rote in groups of as many as six hundred under the direction of a single teacher. Monitorial education was developed more or less simultaneously in the 1790s by Andrew Bell in Madras, India, and by Joseph Lancaster, a Quaker schoolmaster, in London. Monitorial schools were run using simple principles of the factory division of labour. The teacher was assisted by groups of child monitors, each monitor being in charge of a group of younger children. Simple bits of information passed by rote from teacher to monitor to student.

This system was extremely inexpensive to run. Also, in an age when ruling classes regarded the popularization of the ability to read with a considerable amount of political suspicion, monitorial education eliminated the need for books by having children gather around large printed cards.[20] In the first two decades of the nineteenth century, monitorial schools were quite common in England and the United States, and an attempt was made in the 1820s to introduce them into Upper Canada by the first General Board of Education.[21]

By the time Ryerson wrote, the critique of monitorial education was well developed. Spokespersons for the English workers' movement, like the Radical Ricardian William Thompson, denounced rote learning for its sacrifice of all human intellect to the memory and for its inhumanity.[22] In working class districts of English cities, monitorial schools were poorly attended and teachers were often the victims of violence.[23] The failure of monitorial education in part contributed to the development of an independent English workers' educational initiative.

To middle class school reformers — particularly the Secretary of the Massachusetts Board of Education, Horace Mann (whose writings influenced many nineteenth century reformers including Ryerson) — rote learning was rejected primarily for its inefficiency as a means of moulding the subjectivity of the student. Ryerson accepted and elaborated this criticism in his *Report*.

In this view, rote learning was seen as incapable of training the "faculties." It addressed only the memory. It did not penetrate beneath the surface of the mind to the psyche or character, and for that reason it could not form human energy in a lasting and comprehensive manner. An efficient education, on the contrary, would involve "the cultivation of all our mental, moral and physical powers."[24] An education which successfully formed human energy in a durable manner would engage as many faculties of human perception as possible:

> Our senses are so many inlets of knowledge; the more of them used in conveying instruction to the mind the better; the more of them addressed, the deeper and more permanent the impression produced.[25]

In a technical sense, one can see, Ryerson rejected rote learning for its failure to penetrate to the core of the human subject's consciousness. Ryerson's alternative to rote learning was not simply a form of ideological repression aimed at controlling or neutralizing the political energies of students. Rather, Ryerson's pedagogy sought to generate self-regulating subjects by expanding the capacity of individuals to feel and to reason within definite forms and conceptions.

In place of rote learning, Ryerson proposed the "inductive" method of education,[26] in which the emotional susceptibility of the child, as well as its simple pleasures, was enlisted in the service of instruction. This has frequently been described as "humanistic" education, and Ryerson himself drew attention to its "humanizing" result.

Inductive education proceeded by creating an emotional dependency of the child upon the teacher so that the teacher could govern the child with the utmost economy by means of looks, gestures, expressions, and qualities of voice. Once such a connection was established, once the "human" qualities of students were developed to a certain point, the teacher could, by his own mobility, deployment, and display of energy, draw out the energy of his students in a pleasing and economical manner.[27]

This pedagogy offered several advantages from the perspective of education as state-directed socialization.

In such a system, order could be maintained by the manipulation of characteristics developed by pedagogy in the student population. Violence and coercion — the physical display of brutality — would become unnecessary as elements of rule. Rather, rule would proceed through reason and sentiment. Ideally, no energy of teachers would be wasted in physical discipline. Also, no negative experiences would take place which would provide students with grounds for resisting the process of education or forming alternative grounds of self-definition. The subjectivity of the student would be completely captivated by pedagogy and his energy made readily accessible to the ends of education.[28] Rule would proceed without appearing as rule. The later consequences of this pedagogical transformation were enormous.[29]

"Humanization" was a pedagogical device which involved the development of the capacities for feeling and moral behaviour. While these capacities were ethically and aesthetically pleasing to school reformers, they were also political instruments for the development of new modes of self-regulation. The "moral" attitude which this pedagogy sought was a way of relating to others and also an ethically-founded acceptance of and affection for existing political forms.

The "humanistic" pedagogy contains, to a large degree, the key to the explanation of Ryerson's curricular reforms — especially his adamant opposition to that instrument of rote learning *par excellence*, the spelling book.[30] The thrust of pedagogy upon curriculum is perhaps nowhere more evident than in the matter of vocal music. "All men," Ryerson quoted in his argument for teaching vocal music in all the elementary schools, "have been endowed with a susceptibility to the influence of music."[31] Vocal music was an important and intrinsically pleasing avenue to the faculties. Teaching children moral songs could displace the ribald and frivolous amusements they pursued, while turning their recreation into a means of instruction. "Music," if correctly used, could "refine and humanize the pupils."[32] Ryerson approvingly quoted the English Privy Council on Education, which claimed that since the common schools of Germany had begun to teach workers to sing, "the degrading habits of intoxication" so common there had been much reduced.[33]

Ryerson's humanistic and inductive pedagogy was an instrument and tactic aimed at developing the senses so that they could be enlisted to make contact with human energy. Humanistic education was not a form of social control in any simple sense. It sought not to repress workers or students by feeding them doses of propaganda or ideology, but rather to develop their capacities for feeling and moral behaviour. Students were to become self-disciplining individuals who behaved not out of fear or because of coercion, but because their experience at school had created in them certain moral forms for which they had a positive affection. In Ryerson's pedagogy, the student would have no desire to oppose the process of education and no grounds upon which to do so. Education would be intrinsically pleasing to the student, and in consequence he or she would *become* the character sought by pedagogy. Education would produce in the population habits, dispositions, and loyalties of a sort congenial to the state and to representative government. The problem of governance faced by generations of conservative educational critics would vanish: political rule would no longer be dependent upon "social control," coercion, terror, or bribery. One would be able to appeal to the "higher sentiments" of the subject formed by education; the state would rule by appeals to the emotions and intellect of the educated population.

OUR COMMON CHRISTIANITY

Educational reform, in Ryerson's view, was "justified by considerations of economy as well as of patriotism and humanity."[34] By forming the habits and attitudes of individuals, education would eliminate poverty and crime. It would prepare individuals for their "duties and employments of life, as Christians, as persons of business, and also as members of the civil community in which they live."[35] However, the basis of the new system of education was to be what Ryerson called "our common Christianity," a subject to which his *Report* devoted thirty pages (in contrast to a few throwaway lines at the outset on poverty and crime). Ryerson repeatedly stressed the *"absolute necessity of making Christianity the basis and cement of the structure of public education."*[36] Without Christian education there would be no "Christian state," and since Canadians were Christians, their educational system should also be Christian.[37]

The question of what for Ryerson constituted "our common Christianity" is essential, then, to understanding the nature of educational reform. The development of the faculties and several branches of education were the methods and devices of a Christian education. Its content was to be found in religion and morality.

On its face, the notion of a common Christianity in Upper Canada is chimerical. Sectarian squabbling was general, and the Wesleyan Methodists were no exception. Protestants of various sects struggled against the predominance of the Church of England. Orange and green regularly smashed each other's heads in the streets. Ryerson himself belittled someone like the Reverend Robert Murray, a Presbyterian who dared to oppose the Temperance positions.[38] Absolute renunciations of Christianity were rare but certainly not unknown.[39] Despite a rather desultory replication of Archbishop Whately's list of common beliefs of all Christians, Ryerson's *Report* did not devote much energy to attempting to demonstrate that common Christianity had a real empirical content.[40]

In practice, common Christianity meant a kind of political behaviour and made reference to certain contradictory political ideals. These ideals were characteristic of an urban professional clergy attempting to articulate through Christianity a new form of social and political universality. It was through the language and discourse of protestantism in Upper Canada that the transition from social universality as membership in the state church to universality as citizenship in the political state was made. Protestantism was well-fitted for the political reconstruction being attempted in Canada during the 1840s.

At the heart of the notion of a common Christianity was a desire to create in people a predisposition to act in accordance with principles. This meant in the first place that people would accept the legitimacy of and govern themselves rationally in keeping with certain social postulates. Our common Christianity was a conception which both specified and gave divine sanction to the principles in question. These were, generally speaking, principles concerned with the relation of self to self and self to others. They involved toleration, meekness, charity, and a respect for the rights of others — including established authority. Common Christianity excluded reciprocal principles such as an eye for an eye and a tooth for a tooth, did not counsel turning the moneylenders out of the temple, and made no mention of the sanctity of struggles against slavery or debt. On the contrary, it involved turning the other cheek, meekly accepting abuses from others, being kind to those in error, and refusing to oppose actively those who caused one harm. These were principles to be posted in all the schools.[41]

Common Christianity involved, first of all, the creation of a form of social order in which subjects would willingly accept political forms, would respect political authority even if it appeared to be unjust, and would reject violent political activity. This did not exhaust the content or the efficacy of the form of rule Ryerson saw emerging from educational reorganization.

Our common Christianity and common schooling (as it was called) both expressed and embodied a limited democratic content, and much of its efficacy was based upon this content. Ryerson, following Horace Mann of Massachusetts, advocated common schooling as (in Mann's words) "the great equalizer of the conditions of men — the balance wheel of the social machinery."[42] Ryerson's reforms sought to overcome class antagonism in civil society by creating harmony and personal contact between members of all social classes at school. "Common" as an educational adjective came to mean "in common" in the 1840s rather than "elementary" or "rudimentary" as it had in the 1830s. Common schooling meant placing "the poor man on a level with the rich man."[43] It meant providing common intellectual property to members of all social classes, and in part this conception arose out of attempts in Europe and the United States to compensate the urban proletariat for its real propertylessness with a common intellectual property. In Upper Canada, this property was to be appropriated only in state institutions, and in the process of intellectual appropriation, members of all social classes would come to occupy a common position in relation to the state.

This phenomenon in Upper Canada was part of an attempt by protestant religion to create forms of civil and religious universality through educational forms of classlessness. Educational classlessness to some extent was advocated as a means to substantive classlessness, as a means of saving civil society from itself.[44] Educational reform sought to create new forms of governance. It sought to obviate the necessity of governance by the suppression of the individual will. Instead, it sought to shape and develop individual will so governance could proceed by individual self-repression, without actually being experienced as such. It sought to replace the naked exercise of coercion by the rational economy of administration.

Despite serious opposition from the Reform Party and some organs of local government (which produced alterations) the educational reforms of this alliance between the Tory Party, the imperial state, and protestant religion went forward in Upper Canada. The durability of the humanistic and classless discourses can be seen by their presence in educational training manuals well into the twentieth century.

EDUCATIONAL REFORM AND STATE-BUILDING

Educational reform cannot be seen as a process of social control, in the sense in which that term has been used in the literature, without distorting our understanding of social development. Significantly, the leading authors in the social control approach neglect almost entirely the role of the state in educational reform and the consequences for the state of this same process.

Educational reform in Upper Canada should be seen as a dialectical process in which a state educational administration was created out of conflict in civil society and in which, once created, this educational administration set about reconstructing the conflicts of which it was itself a product. The self-generation of an administrative logic can be clearly seen even in the incomplete recent histories of educational administration.[45]

There are several components to this process of the creation of an educational administration, of this process of state-building. In the most obvious sense, educational reform (to the extent that it is merely contiguous with earlier forms) embodied a new division of labour in which part of a state structure was constructed through the appropriation of functions formerly carried out communally. The state grew visibly in this process through the appropriation of a part of the social product for educational purposes, through the multiplication of individuals employed by it, and through the construction of buildings and the accumulation of other elements of educational technology.[46]

Educational reform built state knowledge as well, and in a double sense. In the first place, the school curriculum became a state property. Knowledge of and about social organization, knowledge of and about the state itself, developed under state auspices. In Canada, educational reform meant the expulsion from the elementary schools of privately produced curricula and the substitution of state curricula. Initially in Upper Canada, the curriculum after reform was comprised of books produced by the Irish National Board of Education, but increasingly after 1865 books commonly written by members of the Education Department displaced these.[47] The appropriation of state-generated knowledge came to be an important dimension of citizenship.

In the second place, the state created a new field for information-gathering in the administrative organs of education. Systematically-designed school reports had to be completed by school officials as a condition of state financing, and these reports constituted a body of knowledge about the nature and condition of the educational population, local policies, local conflicts, solutions, and so forth. This development of knowledge about the field that was to be administered was in part a condition of the legitimacy of administration itself. "Fair" and "rational" administration demanded a knowledge of "both sides" of questions, as well as a "larger view."

A detailed investigation of the processes involved in the construction of the state educational domain is beyond the scope of the present article. These are numerous and potentially illuminating for those interested in documenting the growth of the state. However, one of these processes — the complement to the construction of administrative mechanisms — must be noted. One might argue that the state grew most importantly through educational reform where it did so least visibly. Foucault has argued that political power is most effective where it vanishes.[48] Power operates most effectively, Foucault suggests, by forming the subjectivity of the ruled in such a way that rule becomes internalized. Educational reform sought to transform the subjectivity of the body politic. It sought to transform the nature of the individual's relation to himself and others such that governance could proceed by dealing with sentiments and reason. It sought to make the individual a willing participant in his own governance, giving him a "Christian character" so that there could be a "Christian nation." Insofar as this exercise succeeds, it appears to the individual only as the self he or she lives, as the elemental force of a natural law. It may not appear as a form of governance at all. This is precisely its power.

THE CONSTRUCTION OF A PUBLIC

Educational reformers in Canada and elsewhere in the initial period of reform frequently described their activity as one of "public instruction." They were somewhat mistaken. Reformers did not confront a ready-made public, a population existing on a terrain of universality and classlessness. Rather, they attempted to construct a public, to create and to extend a sphere of classlessness in which the state could rule through impartial administration.

Common schooling was to place members of all social classes in a common relation to each other and the state. Schools, scattered throughout civil society, were to be (if you will) "pure state spaces," places purged of the conflicts, struggles, and stresses of civil society. In the "republic of letters" the poor man and the rich man would be social equals.[49] Schooling would create a real commonality on a national scale.

The failure of educational reform to create substantive universality is obvious and well-documented by neo-Marxist political economy. The success and significance of this transformation of popular socialization is less well charted and indeed cannot be exhaustively treated here. Two final points can be made in this regard.

First, the educational reforms of the 1840s in Upper Canada transformed the nature of educational struggle. Very soon after the construction of a state educational administration, serious questions about the *form* of education ceased to be widely posed. The creation of a "sphere above politics," as Ryerson liked to call the school system, transformed the debate over education from one over competing and conflictual forms of education into one over the management of a state form. The construction of a public sphere transforms questions of form into questions of administration. In the process possibilities not contained in the public domain itself tend to vanish.

Secondly, with the creation of public education on a wide scale, the conception of the state and civil society as separate realms seems seriously inadequate. The social control thesis in neo-Marxism portrays the state as a repressive force located outside civil society. In fact, through educational reform the state was placed in key ways in a dialectic in which civil society and itself were reconstructed through the creation of social forms. A conception of separate spheres of state and civil society becomes difficult to sustain since the conduct of "private" activities goes forward increasingly in state forms. If the state in fact successfully shaped the subjectivity of the population as a whole (an untenable proposition at this level), in a sense all of the life of civil society would be conducted in state forms. The present article suggests at least that the relation of state and civil society is not that presented by the social control thesis, a relation of externality and repression. Rather, the state and civil society interpenetrate; the struggles and class antagonisms which are structurally based are in a crucial sense conducted in state forms. This process of what one might tentatively and hesitantly call the "colonization of civil society" demands more attention from Marxist writers.

Educational reform was part of the process of creating a domain in which the state could rule and of creating the mechanisms of rule. As such it constituted at the same time a process of state development and the preconditions for state development.

NOTES

1. This critique is extended in my Ph.D. dissertation. See Curtis, "The Political Economy of Elementary Educational Development: Comparative Perspectives on State Schooling in Upper Canada" (University of Toronto, Department of Sociology 1980), chap. 1.
2. Curtis, "Political Economy," chap. 4.
3. "Mr. Sullivan's Report on the State of the Province 1838," in *The Arthur Papers. . . .*, ed. C.R. Sanderson (Toronto 1943), pt. 1, p. 134.

4. Ibid., 134.
5. Ibid., 151.
6. Arthur to the Bishop of Montreal, 18 December 1838, in Sanderson, *The Arthur Papers*, pt. 1, p. 465. (See n. 3 above.)
7. Curtis, "Political Economy," chap. 4.
8. For the text of the Act of 1843, see J.G. Hodgins ed., *The Documentary History of Education in Upper Canada. . . .* (Toronto 1894–1910), vol. 4, pp. 251ff.
9. See Hincks's after-dinner speech in Toronto in 1843, quoted in Sir Francis Hincks, *Reminiscences of his Public Life* (Montreal 1884), 177.
10. The Midland District Council, for instance, raised over two thousand pounds by a rate on property. See Hodgins, *Documentary History*, vol. 5, p. 127. For school attendance: *Documentary History*, vol. 5, pp. 267–8. (See n. 8 above.)
11. As Dent points out in *The Last Forty Years: Canada Since the Union of 1841* (Toronto 1881), vol. 1, p. 372, the instability of the Canadian administration and the public furor over responsible government also had their echoes in the imperial parliament.
12. There is an enormous literature on the question of Egerton Ryerson's influence in the elections of 1844. See, for example, C.B. Sissons, "Ryerson and the Elections of 1844," *Canadian Historical Review* 23: 2 (June 1942), 157–76; J.M.S. Careless, *The Union of the Canadas* (Toronto 1967), 86–8; P.G. Cornell, *The Alignment of Political Groups in Canada, 1841–1867* (Toronto 1962), 14–5; Dent, *Last Forty Years*, vol. 1, p. 362 (See n. 11 above); R.D. Gidney, "The Rev. Robert Murray: Ontario's First Superintendent of Schools," *Ontario History* 63: 4 (December 1971), pp. 202–3.
13. Egerton Ryerson, *The Story of My Life*, ed. J.G. Hodgins (Toronto 1883), 284.
14. And Lord Stanley had already written to Bagot in his special instructions of October 1841: "You will give every encouragement in your power to the extension, within the Province of Religious Education, and of Secular Instruction, and you will not fail to bear in mind, that the habits & opinions of the People of Canada are, in the main, averse from the absolute predominance of any single Church." G.P. de T. Glazebrook, *Sir Charles Bagot in Canada: A Study in British Colonial Government* (Toronto 1929), 126. The connection between protestantism and the processes of the political transformation from loyalty to the state church to citizenship in the national state is little explored, relatively, and demands more attention. A useful introductory work is E.R. Norman, *The Conscience of the State in North America* (Cambridge 1968).
15. Ryerson, *Story of My Life*, 321. (See n. 13 above.)
16. Hodgins, *Documentary History*, vol. 5, p. 240.
17. I am indebted to Michel Foucault's *Discipline and Punish: The Birth of the Prison* (New York 1979).
18. Egerton Ryerson, *Report on a System of Public Elementary Instruction for Upper Canada* (Montreal 1847), 20.
19. Ibid., 22.
20. See J.M. Goldstrom, "The Content of Education and the Socialization of the Working-Class Child, 1830–1860," in *Popular Education and Socialization in the Nineteenth Century*, ed. Phillip McCann (London 1977), 93–109; Brian Simon, *The Two Nations and the Educational Structure, 1780–1870* (London 1974), 148–9. For the general question of literacy and politics, in addition to Simon, see R. Altick, *The English Common Reader* (Chicago 1963).
21. For details of the attempt, see Curtis, "Political Economy," chap. 4.
22. Brian Simon, *The Radical Tradition in Education in Britain* (London 1972), 11.
23. See Phillip McCann, "Popular Education, Socialization and Social Control: Spitalfields, 1812–1824," in McCann, *Popular Education*, 29. (See n. 20 above.)
24. Ryerson, *Report*, 57. (See n. 18 above.)
25. Ibid., 75.

26. See ibid., 131.
27. Ryerson, *Report*, 120.
28. Ibid., 168–9.
29. For instance, the general transition from the maintenance of order in the school by means, ultimately, of the physical force of the teacher to the maintenance of order backed ultimately by the administrative power of the state was one of the crucial preconditions for the successful feminization of the teaching labour force, which went forward rapidly between 1850 and 1900.
30. See the interesting exchange in Ryerson to Thomas Donnelly, Bloomfield, 21 December 1846, in Hodgins, *Documentary History*, vol. 6, p. 285.
31. Ryerson, *Report*, 129.
32. Ibid., 126.
33. Ibid., 131.
34. Ibid., 10.
35. Ibid., 11–4.
36. Ibid., 32. (Ryerson's emphasis).
37. Ibid., 50–1.
38. See Gidney, "Rev. Robert Murray." (See n. 12 above.)
39. Sanderson, *The Arthur Papers*, pt. 3, pp. 1–2.
40. Robert Gidney was kind enough to point out to me that this was a matter upon which Ryerson had elsewhere written and published a significant number of pieces.
41. See, for example, Ryerson, *Report*, pp. 44–5n.
42. Quoted in H.S. Commager, ed., *The Era of Reform*, 1830–1860 (Toronto 1960), 134.
43. Hodgins, *Documentary History*, vol. 7, p. 192.
44. Again, the role of protestant religion as a bridge leading to this conception of civil universality is crucial.
45. See the four articles by R.D. Gidney and D.A. Lawr which deal with the development of educational administration. The best is perhaps "Bureaucracy vs. Community? The Origins of Bureaucratic Procedure in the Upper Canadian School System," *Journal of Social History* 13:3 (1981), 438–57. See also "Egerton Ryerson and the Origins of the Ontario Secondary School," *Canadian Historical Review* 60:4 (1979), 442–65; "Who Ran the Schools? Local Influence on Educational Policy in Nineteenth Century Ontario," *Ontario History* 72:3 (1980), 131–43; and "The Development of an Administrative System for the Public Schools: The First Stage, 1841–50," in N. McDonald and A. Chaiton, eds., *Egerton Ryerson and His Times* (Toronto 1978), 160–84.
46. The state also grew through the physical reconstruction of the school, through the transformation of the relation of pedagogical space to the community, and, inside the schools, through the transformation of the relations of teachers and students in pedagogical space.
47. See Viola E. Parvin, *Authorization of Textbooks for the Schools of Ontario, 1846–1950* (Toronto 1965).
48. *Discipline and Punish*, 194. (See n. 17 above.)
49. Ryerson's vision was one of social harmony, a sphere of universality safe from social conflict. The teachers generally wanted reliable pay, a clear set of rules for the schools, enough schoolbooks of the same sort to go around, protection from local officials, and generally those things which would relieve the "drudges in the Republic of letters usually called Teachers of Common Schools." James Finn, London District to Murray, 29 May 1843, Public Archives of Ontario, RG 2, C-6-C.

FOURTEEN

"A Machine of Oppression under the Guise of the Law": The Saint John Police Establishment, 1860–1890

GREG MARQUIS

The coercive role of the police and the lower courts has received considerable attention. In the 1970s, revisionist criminal justice history focused almost exclusively on the police as "domestic missionaries" enforcing an "urban discipline" upon the working class. To various degrees, social control interpretations saw moral reform or "law and order" as exogenous ideologies imposed upon the masses by the middle class. American and British historians also examined the historic police role in breaking strikes and harassing trade unions.[1] These studies bequeathed a valuable contribution, namely, the thesis that police reform "aimed at reshaping popular culture as much as preventing crime."[2] One of the few Canadian articles on the development of municipal police adopts this theme, suggesting that the 19th-century Toronto police department was an instrument of middle-class hegemony or moral reform.[3]

In recent years historians have begun to examine the less-documented legitimation function of the police and courts, recognizing that the law has an ideological function. Legitimation, which should not be confused with the liberal theories of consensus that dominate official police histories, is the process by which capitalist institutions win support or at least acquiescence from the masses.[4] Without losing sight of the basic inequities of the justice system, historians, particularly in the Canadian case where police have enjoyed a degree of relative popularity, should be sensitive to the question of legitimation. To do otherwise would be to offer a one-sided view of legal order and urban government. Recent studies of the Toronto, Halifax and Hamilton police courts have displayed an awareness of the popular legitimacy of the law that has been generally ignored in social history.[5]

The present study examines the role and image of two important 19th-century institutions of criminal justice in Saint John, the police department and stipendiary magistrate's court, commonly referred to as the "police establishment." As in other Canadian cities, the close association of the lower judiciary and police blurred the distinctions between the judicial and law enforcement branches of the justice system. The focus here is on police–community relations, specifically such themes as resistance to the police, the policing of strikes, liquor licence law enforcement, the police service role and the image of the police court. The intention is not to dismiss class-conflict interpretations of the justice system, but to broaden our understanding of the

Source: "'A Machine of Oppression under the Guise of the Law': The Saint John Police Establishment, 1860–1890," *Acadiensis*, 16, 1 (Autumn 1986): 58–77. Reprinted by permission.

role of the 19th-century police establishment. It is suggested that the effectiveness of the police establishment depended largely on the tacit consent of the working class. This is not to denigrate popular hostility towards police or to characterize the working class as a faceless mass ordered by elite-controlled institutions. On the contrary, in order to gain a certain degree of acceptance the police adopted a flexible attitude towards working-class leisure activities and, together with the police court, fulfilled a number of community obligations.

The Saint John police force was formally established in 1849 in the wake of a decade of sectarian violence, criticism of local magistrates and experimentation with seasonal police, citizens' patrols and nightwatchmen. The police establishment was financed by the common council but supervised by a government-appointed permanent stipendiary magistrate, who also supplanted the mayor and aldermen in conducting the police court. In 1856 the magistrate's police duties were curtailed by a statute creating the office of chief of police, also an appointee of the provincial cabinet. The provincial government's role in Saint John was unique; other communities retained or established local control of their police. Although the civic corporation was denied direct control of the department until the early 20th century, the chief developed a working relationship with the common council's police committee, and the rank and file thought of themselves as civic employees.[6]

Between 1860 and 1890 Saint John, one of the great urban centres of British North America, experienced a relative decline in economic power and a stagnation of population. At Confederation the city was at the height of its power, dependent largely upon commerce, shipbuiding and the timber trade, and, although not an industrial centre, was experiencing economic diversification. With the annexation of the suburb of Portland in 1889 the regional metropolis contained more than 40,000 people, although the old city of Saint John had actually declined in number by several thousand since 1871.[7] In this period the police department was supervised by John R. Marshall, a Methodist and former blacksmith identified with the Liberal "Smashers" of the 1850s. Until the creation of greater Saint John, Marshall's force remained between 25 and 30 men, most of whom were the sons of New Brunswick farmers. Recruits from the country, or "bushmen," were preferred over locals, who were thought to have too many familial, fraternal and sectarian ties with the community.[8] The appointment of the police chief and stipendiary magistrate by the provincial cabinet, the preference in hiring rural New Brunswickers and the inability of police to vote in municipal and provincial elections until 1891 marked the extent to which the desire to remove police from local and popular influences had affected Saint John.[9]

Appointed to reorganize police administration in 1862, John Marshall set about improving the somewhat casual policies of his predecessor by instituting the first daily charge book and submitting monthly and annual reports to the city chamberlain and common council. As a result of the chief's increasing disenchantment with moral reform, Marshall's reports became less tempered by evangelical zeal. Arrest patterns, he noted, did not record all police activities. In 1863, for example, the force escorted home half as many intoxicated persons as it arrested for public drunkenness; in 1866 police suppressed 1,100 disturbances in private dwellings. In subsequent years these and other activities went unrecorded.[10]

Arrest statistics, however, do provide a rough indication of the department's concerns. As Table 14.1 illustrates, arrest totals peaked in the early 1860s and again in

TABLE 14.1 *Total Arrests and Arrests by Selected Categories, Saint John, 1863–1889*

		Proportion of Total Arrests by Selected Categories (%)				
	Total Arrests			*Disorderly*	*Property*	
Year	**(N)**	*Assault*	*Drunkenness*	*conduct*	*crime*	*Vagrancy*
1863	2503	11.8	30.3	9.4	8.2	3.4
1864	2256	12.9	32.9	11.4	7.2	4.4
1865	2034	12.6	43.5	3.8	7.6	4.0
1866	2459	11.1	46.1	3.1	5.8	6.7
1867	1978	—	—	—	—	—
1868	1763	—	—	—	—	—
1869	1345	—	—	—	—	—
1870	1402	12.2	63.2	2.2	6.0	2.6
1871	1512	15.0	51.6	13.2	5.2	1.0
1872	1819	16.0	54.0	5.0	3.6	0.4
1873	1891	14.4	49.0	13.4	4.2	1.6
1874	2145	12.1	58.6	2.9	4.1	0.3
1875	1304	17.3	48.0	14.2	4.4	0.7
1876	1440	15.8	49.5	12.8	9.4	1.9
1877	2092	10.6	59.7	15.4	3.0	1.3
1878	1972	8.3	73.4	3.2	4.6	7.8
1879	1232	11.0	50.3	12.7	7.6	9.4
1880	1053	11.0	45.6	11.6	8.2	14.0
1881	1224	12.1	56.5	1.5	6.9	10.1
1882	1414	10.1	47.3	11.0	3.5	10.4
1883	1272	20.7	51.0	14.0	5.4	12.0
1884	—	—	—	—	—	—
1885	1030	15.7	44.4	12.5	7.1	16.0
1886	977	11.0	47.2	10.8	6.1	15.0
1887	889	13.0	7.1	4.2	6.5	0.1
1888	865	11.3	39.3	10.1	4.2	1.7
1889	1187	8.0	62.3	16.4	3.6	1.1

Source: Compiled from Police Chief's Reports, 1863–1889. Figures for 1877 represent the last seven months of the year only. Property crime includes larceny, robbery, burglary, forgery, counterfeiting and breaking windows.

1874 and 1877–78. The average policeman made 50 arrests in 1870, 40 in 1880 and 30 in 1890. As was typical of late 19th-century North American urban police statistics, public-order offences — drunkenness and disturbing the peace — constituted on average 60 per cent of arrests. Both the police court and the police force dealt primarily with misdemeanant activity that involved problems of public order and urban regulation more than crime. Assault charges usually formed 10 to 15 per cent of arrests, offences against property 5 to 10 per cent. The marked decline in arrests during the 1880s was related in part to the increasing use of the court summons for minor offences and by-law infractions.[11]

In Victorian Saint John ethnic and sectarian tensions, if not dominating social relations, had the potential to fragment the working class. The county magistracy, the civic politicians and the police were almost exclusively Protestant, while Roman Catholics were a disproportionately high percentage of those arrested, fined and jailed. Although the population included a sizeable component of Protestant Irish, the lower ranks of the labouring class were predominantly Irish Catholic.[12] The ranks of the police and other civic departments included many members of the Loyal Orange Association, the Protestant fraternal society that dominated the province's associational activities. Rowdiness by the "bhoys" or Irish labourers was more than a police court stereotype: until the early 1870s those born in Ireland were twice as likely as natives to fall into the clutches of the police. In the early 1860s, one-quarter of the population consisted of Irish immigrants. In 1863, not accounting for transients, sailors and residents of Portland and surrounding parishes, the police arrested the equivalent of one-quarter of the Irish-born population of the city. How much of this was due to nativism or prejudice is unclear. In the early 1860s a substantial percentage of the city's young and middle-aged men, groups most likely to come into conflict with police, had been born in Ireland.[13]

As both Protestant and Catholic journalists noted in their discussions of criminality, petty offenders were typically working-class Catholics of Irish descent. In the period 1878–85, the only years in which Marshall published the religions of the arrested, Catholics, one-third of the population, contributed two-thirds of arrests.[14] Irish Catholics remained a sizeable minority, estimated in 1883 by the *Weekly Freeman*, a Catholic organ, to form two-thirds of the poorer classes. In explanation of the high incidence of Catholics in arrest records, the *Freeman* offered the widely-held Victorian theory that the legal system discriminated against immigrants and the poor: "In every city and town in the world the greater part, indeed very nearly all of those arrested belong to the labouring classes, and to the poorest and most unfortunate of those classes."[15]

By the Confederation era, the police had been accepted by the bulk of the population as a necessary, if somewhat bothersome, civic service. Resistance to the police, not uncommon at mid-century, gradually declined with the increasing domestication of the urban population. The limited size of the force meant that police patrols consisted largely of "showing the flag" in the city's several wards.[16] The police and inhabitants of poor neighbourhoods gradually reached an accommodation, the result being that constables reacted to only the most obvious examples of public disorder. In 1860 patrolmen carried cutlasses and cavalry pistols in addition to their batons, exhibiting a warlike appearance that intimidated some residents and amused others. As a veteran police sergeant recalled of the 1850s, "the masses of the people had different ideas concerning individual liberty and a considerable portion of the community were inclined to look upon the policeman as a common foe."[17] In the 1860s, following the example of unarmed English constabularies, the department abandoned its heavy arms as a good will gesture, but resistance and ridicule on the beat continued. Confrontations ranged from non-cooperation and insults to stone-throwing and the rescue of persons in custody. In 1864 beleaguered guardians of the peace were authorized by law to demand assistance from bystanders during street altercations.[18]

The unofficial use of violence was an integral part of the beat system; although the press called for more gentlemanly behaviour, summary justice continued to be dispensed in back streets and alleys. Most middle-class commentators had little sympathy for the less-than-respectable victims of police strong-arm tactics. Yet the bourgeois press universally condemned individual officers who engaged in the "unmanly" act of persecuting children, and delighted in lampooning officious or cowardly policemen. In 1874, for example, the *Daily News* noted with approval that "bonfires blazed in various parts of town" following the dismissal of an unpopular constable.[19]

A series of assaults on police finally convinced Marshall to rearm the force with revolvers in 1872. Of greater assistance to men on the beat were a series of lock-ups, crude neighbourhood holding cells designed to deter disturbers of the peace. In 1880, when the department opened a lock-up in the troublesome Lower Cove waterfront area, constables no longer had to drag belligerent disturbers of the peace several blocks to the police station. A decade later "street rows" involving police were a rarity, and the police court had experienced a noticeable decrease in assault charges. In 1890 Marshall's successor instructed his men to sheathe their batons in the English fashion rather than brandish them as clubs as was the American practice. The city, for a variety of reasons, had been pacified. Perhaps more important than the police presence, as Chief Marshall recognized, were the broader pressures of socialization. Standards of public order had changed gradually yet dramatically since mid-century; to a certain extent, the lower working class had adjusted to the concept of respectability.[20]

The use of police against trade unions was not widespread in Saint John in the period 1860–90, primarily because there were few large-scale struggles between capital and labour. Although skilled trades had begun to organize at mid-century, these were still the formative years of local labour. Strikes by shipwrights, raftsmen, navvies, riggers, millmen and stonecutters were usually brief and non-violent. Workers' associations were neither sufficiently large nor disciplined enough to engage in protracted strikes. An exception was the Labourers' Benevolent Association (LBA), formed by longshoremen who worked under the direction of stevedores. For years the Labourers' bell, still a Saint John landmark, rang out the hours of work along the waterfront. Despite the liberalization of criminal law in the early 1870s to accommodate trade unionism, employers, journalists, judges and most civic politicians remained unconvinced of the right of organized workers to prevent or dissuade non-union men from working. For the commercial elite and those who derived profits from the movement of timber and goods through the port, the role of police during strikes by the ship labourers was abundantly clear: keeping the peace on the waterfront, the hub of the city's economy, translated into preventing work stoppages.[21]

A related police service provided to employers was the rounding up of sailors who had reneged on contracted duties. As Judith Fingard details in *Jack in Port*, shipping interests faced a formidable alliance of rebellious merchant seamen and sailors' boarding-house keepers or crimps, who often enticed or assisted crewmen in leaving their vessels for the promise of more lucrative employment. The merchants and shipowners of Saint John, unlike those of Quebec, never developed a water or harbour police, and thus the city force was expected to assist captains in tracking down stray crewmen.[22] Some sailors were persuaded by police to return to their ships, others had to be forced. Between 1863 and 1889, in an average year one out of every 50 persons arrested was a mariner charged with desertion or refusing duty. Disputes between masters and seamen, including demands for back wages, were settled by the police magistrate. To minimize the influence of crimps, the magistrate often remanded deserters to jail pending the departure of their vessels. The mid-century police court register indicates that about one-tenth of the roughly 2,300 cases before the stipendiary magistrate in the period from August 1849 to the end of 1851, a considerable proportion, involved disputes between seamen and employers. The vast majority of these charges were laid by captains and mates against crewmen.[23] In Fingard's analysis the stipendiary magistrate, an important arbiter of sailors' labour disputes, particularly after 1873 changes in the law, generally favoured employers.[24]

Strike activity in the era of labour assertiveness, 1870–77, although resulting in a number of arrests and contributing to the expansion of the police department, produced no serious clashes between police and workers. The LBA was striving not only for control of the labour market but also for respectability; thus its Irish leadership, described by the *Daily News* as "ignorant and reckless men," urged restraint in dealing with "rebels" or non-union workers.[25] Three brief strikes in 1870 over the employment of "rebels" prompted a response on the part of the authorities that would become familiar: the assignment of policemen and special constables to wharves and ships and the arrest of several LBA men for fighting or assault.[26] Shipping and lumbering interests were further alarmed in 1874 when the new Millmens' Protective Union, an attempt to organize all county sawmill workers on industrial lines, sought to force a collective agreement upon employers. Sawmills were the area's most important industrial enterprises, employing hundreds of hands and providing business for shipowners, stevedores and commission agents. Millowners, dismayed at the lack of police protection against crowds of men and boys who gathered to persuade or intimidate workers into joining their cause, joined leading lumbermen and the Board of Trade in forming a Lumber Exchange. When the ship labourers began their annual campaign for workplace control and higher wages, employers discussed the possibility of hiring a special protective force. In his address to a grand jury Chief Justice W.J. Ritchie warned that "The owners of property, interfered with, will protect themselves."[27]

The size of the police force was increased as a direct result of the Labourers' Benevolent Association's 1875 strike, described by Richard Rice as the crucial New Brunswick labour struggle of the century.[28] At its peak the union claimed to represent nearly 1,500 workers but was weakened by the seasonal nature of its special work, the loading of deals. Events leading to the actual strike — fighting, intimidation and a serious attack upon a prominent shipowner — inspired the municipal authorities to hire special constables and take the unprecedented step of calling out a detachment of militia. The common council allowed the chief to hire three additional constables. Following grumbling among the rank and file that they were paid less than both strikers and "specials," the council awarded a departmental wage increase. The LBA won the support of the riggers but failed in its attempt to stage a general strike.[29] In the opinion of a prominent member of the Lumber Exchange, police protection of rebel workers was important, but "the battle with the workingman" was waged primarily with money, not force.[30]

Although no longer monopolizing the waterfront labour force after 1875, the LBA remained sufficiently strong to prevent the use of donkey engines in loading cargoes until the mid-1880s. In 1884 police protected "outsiders" working on a steamer whose captain had refused to contract with the union, and the police eventually arrested three union men for assault. In the face of considerable popular sympathy for the ship labourers, the dispute was mediated in the stipendiary magistrate's chambers. Counsel for the union, which traditionally enjoyed the support of the *Freeman*, a journal attached to Irish causes, including that of Irish labour, was Robert J. Ritchie, Liberal solicitor-general, prominent Roman Catholic and future police magistrate. The struggles of the longshoremen, in which class and sectarian factors intertwined, were in many ways typical of 19th-century New Brunswick social conflict.[31]

The use of police during strikes in the 1870s and early 1880s reflected the fact that the LBA was at the height of its power. Its membership depleted by economic downswings, outmigration and the disruptive tactics of independent stevedores, the union eventually split into rival factions. By 1890, the founding year of the local Trades and Labour Council, the vanguard of Saint John unionism was racked by internal feuds. These disputes, together with the steamship companies' strategy of bringing in outsiders to load vessels in the 1890s, meant that police vigilance on the waterfront did not abate. The labour struggles of the period did indicate that the police force served as an important guarantor of "free labour" in the commercial city. The less visible but no less important activity of securing stray sailors was a second example of police serving employers' interests. Similarly, the stipendiary magistrate's court remained an important forum for disputes between masters and crewmen.[32]

It was in dealing with leisure activity, such as the use of liquor, that the police most often came into contact — and conflict — with the working class. Indeed the single most important function of urban police was the monitoring of plebeian community life. The Saint John case, however, is an example of police failure to achieve uniform enforcement of liquor licensing laws in working-class neighbourhoods. The reasons for this were complex, but an important factor was police sensitivity to public opinion, which opposed stringent liquor law regulation. The narrow defeat of the Canada Temperance Act in an 1882 referendum indicated that a good portion of the community rejected prohibition and was satisfied with the licence system. Despite cyclical peaks in temperance strength, embodied in the election of temperance mayors, aldermen and councillors, the people of Saint John did not agree on police policy towards illegal dealers let alone the licensed trade.[33]

Historians have alluded to the 19th-century tavern as an important working-class institution, yet the place of drinking in this culture has yet to be firmly resolved. Some have noted the active role of artisans and skilled workers in temperance societies, and others have viewed liquor-licensing questions as central to working-class politics.[34] The wave of 1960s and 1970s historiography on 19th-century reform movements viewed temperance as part of a middle-class strategy to control undisciplined workers. Although employers were aware of the disciplinary potential of temperance, the 19th-century Saint John movement, in the revisionist analysis of T.W. Acheson, "cannot be easily attributed to a single social group or motivation."[35] In a broad sense temperance and prohibition were part of Victorian social reform, but they received uneven support from the elite or middle class of the port city. The divisive issue, as Acheson points out, was the question of legal coercion.

In mid-Victorian Saint John the tavern, ranging from small operations in widows' parlours to more prosperous hostelries, was a fact of city life. The diary of the young barrister Isaac Allen Jack suggests that in the early 1870s taverns were not the exclusive realm of the workingman, nor were hotels patronized solely by the middle class.[36] In practice, however, few patrons of respectable hotel bars concerned the police; it was the working class that suffered the ill effects of alcohol and arrest. Police powers in supervising legal and illegal liquor sales, limited in the 1860s, were gradually extended as a result of pressure from groups such as the Evangelical Alliance, a ministerial association, and the liquor trade itself. Between 1860 and 1890 the saloon business, the licensing of which was one of the mayor's important prerogatives, was consolidated from more than 250 establishments into less than 50.[37] Statutory and administrative restrictions of the retail trade increased police responsibilities, influenced working-class leisure activities and changed the face of neighbourhoods. The 1861 law banning Sunday sales, the 1878 amendment prohibiting liquor in grocery stores and the 1883 curtailment of Saturday night tavern hours were measures clearly aimed at the segment of the population working a six-day week. Hotel keepers, publicans, "victuallers," bootleggers and customers, however, continued to ignore provisions of the licensing laws throughout the 1870s and 1880s.[38]

Saint John police were skeptical towards the theory that moral reform could be wrought through coercive legislation. As a result, the department confined itself to picking up helpless and disorderly "drunks" and prosecuting the most blatant abusers of the liquor laws. Marshall's early reports reflected the optimism of an evangelical reformer genuinely disturbed at the social consequences of rum dens in the lower end of the city. In 1864–65 he was convinced that "the vicious classes" could be reformed through expanded police powers and a tougher licensing policy to govern working-class drinking. Frustrated by the courts' legal protection of liquor dealers, Marshall stated that the principle of "liberty of subject" so prized in British law would have to be ignored as the "honest and labourious classes" were threatened by the lazy and immoral. By the mid-1870s the chief, whose appointment had been welcomed by temperance supporters, had adopted a somewhat cynical attitude towards many expectations of moral reformers. Enforcing the liquor law, he believed, "like the law relating to murder or theft . . . does not prevent greater offence."[39] Other police spokesmen, although sympathetic with temperance principles, shared the opinion that liquor laws, particularly the Canada Temperance Act, which would have introduced local prohibition, were doomed to fail if they lacked community support.[40]

As the police authorities were to discover, public opinion and the law itself constituted formidable barriers to police action against taverns, dance halls and private dwellings suspected of violating liquor regulations. Journalists were worried that the chief's initial enthusiasm would lead to police "despotism" and "espionage" against legitimate businesses and law-abiding citizens. They also took umbrage at Marshall's blanket criticisms of the tavern business, which contributed substantial amounts to civic coffers.[41] In 1864 the right of police to enter suspected premises was seriously impeded after a dance hall operator successfully prosecuted the police chief for forcible entry and trespass. Prominent barrister David S. Kerr, involved that year in a number of cases that questioned police powers, described Marshall's force as "an arbitrary and despotic power" which together with the police court inflicted "oppression and cruelty upon the poor and unfortunate."[42] Through Kerr's instigation, two of stipendiary magistrate Humphrey T. Gilbert's decisions, one involving a publican, the second a woman convicted of vagrancy, were reversed by higher courts. In the case of the dance hall, the Supreme Court, finding the premises "utterly disgraceful" on moral grounds, awarded the proprietor token damages of one penny.[43]

The political power and spirited legal defence of Saint John liquor dealers and saloon-owners continued to frustrate the police chief and stipendiary magistrate, who were subjected to criticism from temperance interests. The readiness of prestigious barristers to represent publicans and liquor dealers also contributed to anti-lawyer feeling among temperance advocates.[44] In 1871 the legislature granted police easier access to taverns in order to enforce more stringent regulations and shorter hours of business, but hotels and saloons avoided police scrutiny through the use of back and side doors. Sunday drinking, theoretically eradicated in 1861, continued.[45]

By the late 1870s, moral reform groups demanding more effective control of the liquor traffic included the Young Men's Christian Association, the Evangelical Alliance, the Woman's Christian Temperance Union (WCTU) and the Temperance Reform Club. Similar groups, including temperance fraternal lodges, flourished in Portland, Carleton and surrounding parishes. In the Saint John case, because of the interplay of religion, ethnicity and class and the militancy of Protestant evangelicals, it is tempting to view resistance to liquor regulations as a largely Catholic phenomenon. The Catholic working- and lower-middle classes, however, were far from homogeneous. Encouraged by an often-puritanical clergy, many Irish Catholics looked with disdain upon co-religionists in the liquor business. Roman Catholic organizations, such as the Saint Aloysius and parish Total Abstinence societies, stressed moral suasion rather than legal coercion, but agreed that eradication of the liquor traffic would end much of the work of police and the stipendiary magistrate.[46]

Throughout the 1880s, moral reformers divided their time between organizing ill-fated Canada Temperance Act campaigns and pressuring police to clean up the "dance halls, gin hovels and dens of perdition" of Sheffield Street. This area, traditionally associated with garrison and waterfront life, had been described in 1862 as "the headquarters of the vilest and most infamous men and women in our City."[47] Although the families of resident tradesmen and labourers who were cultivating respectability may have shared much of the bourgeoisie's disdain for this boisterous neighbourhood, it was a favourite resort of visiting farmers, sailors and lumber workers. Its dance halls, many of which were adjacent to taverns, were reputed to be the haunt of "common prostitutes and the disorderly classes." In 1884 city authorities decided not to license the halls as licensing would provide the legal recognition and protection accorded to taverns.[48] It was not until 1891 that the common council, urged on by the WCTU and the Evangelical Alliance, backed a new police chief in closing the Sheffield Street dance halls as disorderly houses.[49]

The fact that police exercised a great amount of discretion in liquor law enforcement prompted middle-class critics, particularly those in the temperance camp, to suspect the existence of an "understanding" between the men on the beat and the men and women who dispensed alcohol. In 1863 the common council, in an attempt to professionalize the force, had removed an important incentive for police by ending the custom of awarding prosecuting officers one-half of liquor conviction fines.[50] In 1872 the News theorized that as policemen competed with one another "in taking up the biggest numbers of drunks" in order to please the chief, it was therefore in the interest of the department to tolerate illegal sales.[51] Policemen actively sought tips for small services performed for businessmen and other residents; this practice, it was feared, extended to accepting free liquor. George Day of the New Dominion speculated that half of the department had "come to the city to loaf and drink, and enjoy themselves in houses of prostitution, at public expense."[52] The most common dereliction of police duty was drunkenness, and it was tempting to suggest that the force had close ties with the disreputable parts of the city.[53]

As later investigations disclosed, many of these suspicions were valid. Men on the beat formed important and at times ambiguous relationships with tavern workers, restaurateurs, boarding-house keepers, dance hall doormen, teamsters, coachmen and even those on the underside of working-class life. This was precisely why mid-century

Toronto police reformers, in the words of Gregory Kealey, had attempted to distance police from "the plebeian milieu of which the earlier policeman had been an integral part."[54] When temperance reformers and evangelical spokesmen accused the police of collusion with rumsellers, they were commenting not only on possible corruption but also on the average policeman's strong identification with working-class community life. There were practical benefits for police in associating with the disreputable. Cartmen and hackmen, for example, helped transport the intoxicated to the lock-up. In 1890 it was revealed that an unlicensed shop in Sheffield Street had provided shelter, liquor and gifts to men on the beat in exchange for warnings about liquor raids in the area. Although taverns operated on the boundaries of the law and were often suspected of buying stolen property and aiding deserting seamen, they were also important sources of information. Most police manhunts, for example, began with a tour of the haunts of the lower end of the city.[55]

In Saint John, police reform and discipline never succeeded in isolating the men on the force from community influences. The police were not "segregated from the mainstream of working-class life" as Nicholas Rogers has suggested of the mid-Victorian Toronto force.[56] Saint John policemen were well-known residents of the ward who were often called from their dinner tables or beds to aid neighbours. They rented, bought and sold property, married into local families, joined athletic clubs, went to church and took part in fraternal orders such as the Orange Lodge. Their struggles for promotion, higher wages, benefits and better working conditions paralleled those of other civic workers. Thus the personnel of one of the most important agencies of social discipline occupied a somewhat ambiguous position in the class structure.[57]

In Saint John, as in other North American cities, the police department, largely by default, was expected to provide a number of public services not related to crime fighting. In his 1864 report Marshall suggested that the mediative and service role of the police was crucial in the work of the department: "The faithful performance of police duty, does not, in my opinion, consist in making arrests and bringing people to Court; was such the case, we might have added largely to the number. As much good, if not more, is often accompanied by quiet advice and watchfulness."[58] Before the growth of civic bureaucracies and modern welfare agencies, urban police performed a limited social service role as part of their miscellaneous duties. The American historian Eric Monkkonen has suggested that the welfare function was in part an attempt by police to control the "dangerous class" of petty criminals, transients and vagrants. Research on the early 20th-century Toronto police has revealed that its Morality Office functioned as a family complaints bureau, providing legal aid and domestic "adjustments," including the collection of support payments for deserted wives.[59] In Saint John the service orientation of the police, if less developed, was important. Patrolmen extinguished nocturnal fires and sounded the alarm for larger blazes. The police chief removed lost children from the unpleasant confines of the station to his own home. Women went to the chief to complain that spouses were violent or squandering wages needed for family necessities on gambling and drink. Parents pleaded with police to remove their sons and daughters from evil company in taverns and dance halls.[60]

An overlooked welfare service of 19th-century police departments was the provision of shelter for transients or "waifs," who were usually adult males. The police station was the last resort of indigents seeking respite from the elements or more permanent quarters in the county jail or alms house. "Protectionists" generally went to the station on their own initiative; if incapacitated they were taken by police or residents. This practice, which continued in many Canadian cities until the middle of the 20th century, was common in North American urban centres, where underdeveloped charity and welfare systems placed burdens on police bureaucracies. The station also gave emergency shelter to the mentally-ill and the injured. Between 1883 and 1890 the city provided a part-time police surgeon to tend to injured and ill policemen and prisoners, a helpful service given the condition of many lock-up inmates.[61] Taking in waifs was partly genuine charity and partly a strategy facilitating police monitoring of tramps, who were traditionally associated with crime. As with other relief activities, it was most important during the winter months and seasonal lulls that characterized Canada's labour market.[62]

Although sometimes discharged by the police chief, transients were usually paraded with the daily crowd of prisoners before the stipendiary magistrate, admonished and urged to seek employment or leave the city. In many cases the poor frankly demanded long-term incarceration or admission to the alms house for the intemperate months. Men and women who habitually asked to sleep on the police station floor were soon jailed as vagrants.[63] The significance of station shelter for both police and the homeless becomes apparent when the number of waifs is compared to the number of vagrancy arrests. During the economically-depressed 1870s, which witnessed significant outmigration and transiency, all the more complicated by the disastrous Great Fire of 1877, which levelled most of Saint John, the police harboured 1,792 waifs and laid 640 charges for vagrancy and an additional 165 charges for "lurking." The provision of police station shelter was a flexible if primitive strategy for supervising the transient poor.[64]

The characteristics of the police court as portrayed in the middle-class press were a mixture of pathos, humour and immorality. As Paul Craven has suggested in the case of the Toronto police court, press coverage was biased and had an ideological function, portraying most offenders and spectators as members of the disreputable classes, and such coverage therefore has to be handled with care.[65] In 1870 George Day described the Saint John police court audience as "unwashed Milesians, with close cropped heads and expressionless faces, with the occasional sprinkling of Africans, forming a group whose photo would not do discredit to a first-class rogues' gallery." Similarly, "Monday Morning at the Old Police Court," the frontispiece of an 1879 temperance volume, depicts a stern judge and police, batons in hand, menacing a group of derelicts. The gallery includes curious newsboys and caricatures of Irishmen.[66] Although the press considered police court spectators vulgar, the tribunal itself was held up as "the mirror of city life," a mirror that was of interest to more than middle-class moralizers.[67] The stipendiary magistrate conducted what some historians have referred to as a "people's court," an object of community curiosity and an institution resorted to by the working class with surprising frequency.[68]

Police court reporters resorted to a variety of stock characters and familiar images in their columns. Racial characteristics were important — for example, reports always noted "coloured" plaintiffs and defendants and made attempts to print testimony in Irish, Scots and Black dialect. Physical and personality irregularities were freely commented upon. A second theme, religious imagery, offers an insight into the public perception of the court. Much of this was facetious, but the portrayal of offenders as sinners at "the pew" or "penitential bench" confessing to the father-like judge was not out of place given the commentary of the magistrate. Humphrey T. Gilbert, a barrister who served as police magistrate until 1882, often spoke in religious terms, lecturing offenders as to their Christian duties. Sitting magistrates, senior aldermen who occasionally substituted for the stipendiary magistrate, resorted to similar language. Gilbert explained in 1882 that he viewed nine-tenths of the petty offenders in his court not as criminals but as children who needed firm guidance and occasional punishment.[69]

The magistrate's discretionary powers allowed for a paternalist style of justice that often gave petty offenders the benefit of the doubt. Generally, those arrested for the first time for public drunkenness were released after a night in the lock-up. Such was the case of the elderly Hiram Walker in 1860:

> He pleaded very earnestly that he was employed to go to the country, and meant to go. While engaged in getting a load ready, his employer had given him some Irish Whiskey, and not being Irish himself, this proved too much for him, but upon his soul he would go back to the country straight away, and not come back for 3 months. The Magistrate, giving him some wholesome advice, let him go.[70]

Gilbert and his assistants occasionally gave recidivists the opportunity to "take the pledge" of total abstinence in the presence of a minister and a policeman. Similarly, fines were "allowed to stand" pending the good behaviour of the defendant. As Fingard has suggested of the Halifax police court, many cases involved "magisterial arbitrations rather than formal prosecutions."[71] Parties charged with minor assaults or abusive language, two infractions that took up much of the magistrate's time, were often admonished and instructed to pay court costs. The court's combination of strictness and benevolence continued under subsequent magistrates.[72]

The court was less benevolent to perpetual offenders or those charged with violent behaviour. As a deterrent to those who engaged in tippling or rowdyism on the Sabbath, the magistrate instituted an eight-dollar fine, a considerable amount for the average working person. Gilbert held illegal rumsellers, bawdy-house operators and the lower class of taverners in contempt, yet, particularly after David Kerr's legal counter-attack of 1864, he did not allow moral sensibilities to outweigh the rule of law. When the rights of property were involved, including those of the disreputable publicans, madams and dance hall operators, the court was far from arbitrary.

Conviction rates in the Saint John court doubtless shaped community attitudes towards the stipendiary and sitting magistrates and also influenced arrest patterns. The rate of convictions, based on newspaper accounts, an admittedly incomplete source, was 67 per cent in 1860, 77 per cent in 1870 and 74 per cent in 1880, somewhat less than that of the original stipendiary magistrate's court. From August 1849 until the end of 1851 Benjamin L. Peters fined or jailed nine-tenths of those who appeared before him, a reflection of the law-and-order mandate of the new police establishment. Most of those found guilty of misdemeanours were fined. Few were sent outright to jail or penitentiary, but a considerable number were committed in default of fine payment. It is unclear how strict the court was in the collection of fines. In nearby Portland, parties were often released on the understanding that they would pay at a later date.[73]

Other than teetotallers who complained of magisterial laxity towards rumsellers and businessmen who resented the enforcement of civic by-laws, the stipendiary magistrate had few vocal critics. David Kerr, ever vigilant against the usurpation of constitutional rights, in 1865 described the court as "an astonishment among a large and enlightened British community of the 19th century," claiming that hundreds had been "illegally seized, imprisoned and convicted."[74] The assembly-line nature of the court in Kerr's view had reduced justice to "a money-making trade in snatching convictions and imposing oppressive fines and penalties for small faults."[75] Kerr was anticipating what 20th-century legal critics would see as a situation open to abuse: the close association of police and magistrate, which encouraged the latter to act more as prosecutor than impartial judge. Magisterial transgression of the procedures and etiquette of higher courts seldom concerned middle-class commentators; the press, including the *Freeman*, which was sensitive to the class and ethnic nature of justice, was more interested in the moral lessons of police court scenes. As a highly visible and somewhat flexible institution, the police court seemed to function best by ignoring the formalities deemed so essential by Kerr.[76] The court clearly had a punitive side — the imposition of fines upon the poor and friendless was a hardship that often led to imprisonment. But the magistrate's role as mediator and authority figure also responded to community needs. Binding an abusive husband to keep the peace towards his wife, for example, was hardly an imposition of bourgeois values.

For the average late-19th century urban dweller the police force and court were two of the most important institutions of the state. Longshoremen, sailors and millmen doubtless saw the police as agents of the commercial elite, but they were seldom quoted in the press. The class nature of policing and the lower courts cannot be denied; moreover, it was commented upon freely by contemporary journalists, lawyers and temperance advocates. The coercive, conservative and regulatory aspects of the police establishment and its heavy burdens upon the poor captured the attention of the *Freeman* and David Kerr, patriarch of the New Brunswick bar. Evangelical spokesmen and moral reformers, disturbed by the law's protection of the liquor traffic and punishment of its victims, resorted to a more radical critique of the police and courts. In their analysis, the police together with the courts, lawyers, civic politicians and legislators formed an unholy alliance that encouraged the degradation of working people through rum. Much of this criticism was rhetorical, but it nonetheless placed the police establishment in a bad light. Thus to further their own immediate goals — the advancement of Irish Catholics in the case of the *Freeman*, Whig liberty in the case of Kerr, and for temperance activists the defeat of the liquor traffic — bourgeois representatives adopted a class critique of the legal order.

Despite the acknowledged class biases of the administration of justice, both the police court and the police force enjoyed a measure of popular legitimacy. The police establishment had a broader mandate than keeping the peace and punishing law breakers; as an important state institution it combined coercion with a number of services, such as mediating disputes and sheltering transients.[77] The process of policing was a two-way, if uneven, street: the police had an impact upon the city, and neighbourhood feeling in turn shaped the police institution. Police reform was never as fully developed in Saint John as it was in Ontario's larger communities, where police administration was effectively removed from democratic control through the institution of commissions with a majority of appointed members. In Saint John the strong attachment of policemen to working-class community life continued to disturb middle-class critics. To credit the police with simply controlling the working class suggests a docile, defeated population and ignores the broader pressures of socialization. The theory that the police were agents of moral reform cannot be refuted by the Saint

John example, but it can be subjected to reappraisal. The legal order involved ambiguities. David Kerr had described the police establishment as "a machine of oppression under the guise of law,"[78] but as Humphrey Gilbert realized, a good dose of mercy and stern advice in the dispensation of "British justice" went a long way in fostering acceptance of the social order.[79]

NOTES

1. R. Storch, "The Policeman as Domestic Missionary: Urban Discipline and Domestic Culture in Northern England, 1850–1880," *Journal of Social History*, IX, 4 (Summer 1976), pp. 481–509; Robert Liebman and Michael Polen, "Perspectives on Policing in Nineteenth-Century America," *Social Science History*, II, 3 (Spring 1978), pp. 346–60.

2. John Field, "Police, Power and Community in a Provincial Town: Portsmouth, 1815–1875," in Victor Bailey, ed., *Policing and Punishment in Nineteenth-Century Britain* (New Brunswick, N.J., 1981), p. 50.

3. Nicholas Rogers, "Serving Toronto the Good: The Development of the City Police Force, 1834–1884," in Victor Russell, ed., *Forging a Consensus: Historical Essays on Toronto* (Toronto, 1984), pp. 135–6.

4. Eric Monkkonen, *Police in Urban America, 1860–1920* (New York, 1981); Michael Brogden, *The Police: Autonomy and Consent* (Toronto, 1982); Sidney Harring, Policing a Class Society: *The Experience of American Cities, 1860–1915* (New Brunswick, N.J., 1983); Michael Ignatieff, "State, Civil Society and Total Institutions: A Critique of Recent Social Histories of Punishment," in David Sugarman, ed., *Legality, Ideology and the State* (Toronto, 1983), pp. 183–211.

5. Paul Craven, "Law and Ideology: The Toronto Police Court, 1850–1880," in David Flaherty, ed., *Essays in the History of Canadian Law*, Volume II (Toronto, 1982), pp. 249–307; Michael Katz, M.J. Doucet and M.J. Stern, *The Social Organization of Early Industrial Capitalism* (Cambridge, 1982), pp. 201–41; Judith Fingard, "Jailbirds in Mid-Victorian Halifax," in P.B. Waite, Sandra Oxner and Thomas Barnes, eds., *Law in a Colonial Society: The Nova Scotia Experience* (Toronto, 1984), pp. 103–23.

6. T.W. Acheson, *Saint John: The Making of a Colonial Urban Community* (Toronto, 1985), pp. 214–29; G. Marquis, "The Police Force in Saint John, New Brunswick, 1860–1890," M.A. thesis, University of New Brunswick, 1982, pp. 24–33.

7. *Census of New Brunswick, 1861; Census of Canada*, 1871–91; C.M. Wallace, "Saint John, N.B., 1800–1900," *Urban History Review*, 1 (1975), pp. 18–9; Robert H. Babcock, "Economic Development in Portland (Me.) and Saint John (N.B.) During the Age of Iron and Steam, 1850–1914," *American Review of Canadian Studies*, IX, 1 (Spring, 1979), pp. 3–37.

8. The force in 1871 still included several Irish-born Protestants: Marquis, "The Police Force in Saint John," pp. 45–50; "Reports of the Chief of Police," *Reports and Accounts of the Corporation of Saint John*, 1863–90.

9. "An Act in Further Amendment to the Police Establishment in the City of Saint John," *New Brunswick Acts*, 1891, ch. LVII.

10. "Police Chief's Reports," 1863–66.

11. "Police Chief's Reports," 1863–89; Monkkonen, *Police in Urban America*, pp. 65–85; Katz et al., *The Social Organization of Early Industrial Capitalism*, p. 207; Rogers, "Serving Toronto the Good," p. 132. The patterns of police court charges for the period August 1849 to the end of 1851 are generally similar to those of later arrest records: see Police Court Record, 1849–52, Saint John Regional Public Library. This is the only surviving 19th-century police court register for the city.

12. Acheson, *Saint John*, p. 233. Throughout the period the single largest ethnic group in the "Loyalist" city were those of Irish descent.

13. "Police Chief's Reports," 1863–73. A high representation of Irish Catholics was also evident in contemporary Toronto and Hamilton police records: see Katz, *Social Organization*, p. 210 and Rogers, "Serving Toronto the Good," p. 134. Scott W. See has argued that nativism was an important force in colonial New Brunswick: "The Orange Order and Social Violence in Mid-Nineteenth Century Saint John," *Acadiensis*, XIII, 1 (Autumn 1983), pp. 68–92 [reprinted in this volume as Article Eleven, pp. 207–27].

14. "Police Chief's Reports," 1878–85.

15. *Weekly Freeman*, 3 February 1881. In its early years the *Freeman* was edited by Timothy Warren Anglin: see William M. Baker, *Timothy Warren Anglin, 1822–96: Irish Catholic Canadian* (Toronto, 1977).

16. *Daily News* (Saint John), 19 May 1874. For police divisions and deployment circa 1860, see Saint John Common Council Correspondence and Draft Minutes, 3/11, 30 July 1856, Provincial Archives of New Brunswick [PANB].

17. Scrapbook, C58, p. 222, New Brunswick Museum Archives [NBM]; *Morning Freeman*, 30 March 1860; Saint John Globe, 14 December 1901.

18. *Morning Freeman*, 2 August 1864; *Daily News*, 29 April 1872, 19 May 1874, 17 August 1875.

19. *Daily News*, 7 August 1874.

20. "Police Chief's Reports," 1863–66, 1880–89; *Daily News*, 27 December 1871, 19 October 1872; *Daily Sun*, 20 July 1880, 28 December 1884, 29 August 1890; Henry B. Young, "History of the Saint John Police Force" (typescript, 1949), pp. 4–5, NBM.

21. Richard Rice, "A History of Organized Labour in Saint John, 1813–1890," M.A. thesis, University of New Brunswick, 1968; *New Dominion and True Humourist Extra*, 1 June 1875; *Daily News*, 14 June 1870, 23 October 1871, 10 July 1872, 27 March 1874, 18 November 1875, 15 February 1877; *Morning Freeman*, 27 November 1868; Canada, *Report of the Royal Commission on the Relations of Labour and Capital, New Brunswick Evidence* (Ottawa, 1889), pp. 209–10.

22. Judith Fingard, *Jack in Port: Sailortowns of Eastern Canada* (Toronto, 1982), pp. 140–93, 220–32.

23. "Police Chief's Reports," 1863–89; Police Court Record, 1849–52. This did not include assault charges laid by masters and crew members.

24. Fingard, *Jack in Port*, p. 188.

25. *Daily News*, 6 November 1874.

26. *Daily News*, 13–15 June, 3 August 1870.

27. 1871 Manuscript Census, Saint John County; *Daily News*, 17–24 March, 24–27 April, May 1874; *Morning Freeman*, 30 April, 7 May 1874.

28. Rice, "A History of Organized Labour in Saint John," p. 71. The most violent LBA strike occurred two years later: *Daily News*, 15 February 1877.

29. Rice, "A History of Organized Labour in Saint John," p. 77; *Morning Freeman*, 27 April to 4 May 1875; *Daily News*, 2, 30 April, 5–14 May 1875.

30. *Morning Freeman*, 8 May 1875. On this occasion Chief Justice Ritchie, in his address to the circuit court's grand jury, adopted a less hostile view of strikes, questioning the wisdom of deploying special constables and militia in the face of what amounted to a peaceful withdrawal of services: *Daily News*, 12 May 1875.

31. *Daily News*, 4 May 1881, 28 April 1883; *Daily Sun*, 18 March, 24–25 April 1884. By the early 1880s the LBA was called the Ship Labourers' Association.

32. *Daily Sun*, 19 April 1887; Rice, "A History of Organized Labour in Saint John," p. 21; Saint John Trades and Labour Council, *History of Saint John Labour Unions* (Saint John, 1929); Elizabeth W. McGahan, *The Port of Saint John: From Confederation to Nationalization, 1867–1927* (Saint John, 1982), pp. 180–7; Ian McKay, "Strikes in the Maritimes, 1901–1914," *Acadiensis*, XIII, 1 (Autumn 1983), pp. 3–46.

33. *Daily Sun*, 28 January 1882; *Weekly Freeman*, 2 August 1882.

34. Lawrence T. McDonnell, "'You Are Too Sentimental': Problems and Suggestions For a New Labor History," *Journal of Social History*, XVII, 4 (Summer 1984), pp. 633–6; Bryan Palmer, *Working-Class Experience: The Rise and Reconstitution of Canadian Labour, 1800–1980* (Toronto, 1983), pp. 85, 110–1; Peter DeLottinville, "Joe Beef of Montreal: Working-Class Culture and the Tavern, 1869–1889," *Labour/Le Travailleur*, 8/9 (1981–82), pp. 9–40; Gregory Kealey, "Orangemen and the Corporation: The Politics of Class During the Union of the Canadas," in Russell, *Forging a Consensus*, p. 47.

35. Acheson, *Saint John*, pp. 138–9. See also J.K. Chapman, "The Mid-Nineteenth Century Temperance Movement in New Brunswick and Maine," *Canadian Historical Review*, XXV, 1 (March 1954), pp. 43–60.

36. I.A. Jack Diary, 1870–71, NBM.

37. *Reports and Accounts of the Corporation of Saint John, 1860–90.*

38. "An Act to Regulate the Sale of Spiritous Liquors in the City and County of Saint John," *New Brunswick Acts, 1861*; *Morning Freeman*, 29 October 1878; *Daily Sun*, 4 September 1883; Canada, Royal Commission on the Liquor Traffic, *Minutes of Evidence, I* (Ottawa, 1893), p. 489.

39. "Police Chief's Reports," 1864–66; *Daily News*, 8 October 1877.

40. Marshall never lost his interest in the problem of juvenile delinquency and continually called for a provincial reformatory. *Daily News*, 8 October 1877; *Daily Sun*, 8 February 1882; Royal Commission on the Liquor Traffic, *Evidence, I*, p. 483.

41. *Telegraph* (Saint John), 30 January 1860; *Morning Freeman*, 14 June 1864; *True Humourist*, 29 April 1865; *Morning News*, 4 December 1866.

42. *Morning Freeman*, 12 November 1864, 24 January 1865.

43. *Morning Freeman*, 24 January 1865; "Harvey vs. Marshall," in John C. Allen, ed., *New Brunswick Reports*, VI (1864–65) (Toronto, 1879), pp. 292–6.

44. *True Humourist*, 18 May, 1, 8 June 1867.

45. "An Act in Addition to an Act to Regulate the Sale of Spiritous Liquor in the City and County of Saint John," *New Brunswick Acts*, 1871, ch. 17; *Morning Freeman*, 20 February 1872; *Daily Sun*, 4 September 1883, 2 June 1885.

46. *Daily News*, 20, 21 November 1877, 18 March 1878; *Daily Sun*, 2 November 1880. The Temperance Reform Club, formed in the mid-1870s but rejuvenated by American evangelist and temperance lecturer D. Banks MacKenzie following the Great Fire, is worthy of detailed study. It enrolled large numbers of women and mechanics and became an important force in civic politics.

47. *Telegraph*, 19 December 1862; *Daily News*, 11 May 1882.

48. *Weekly Freeman*, 19 April 1884; Saint John Common Council Minutes, 28 March 1884, NBM.

49. *Daily Sun*, 2, 7 April 1891: Ernest Styles, "The Evangelical Alliance: The Story of Forty Years" (typescript, 1926), p. 7, Saint John Regional Public Library.

50. Saint John Common Council Minutes, 17 June 1863.

51. *Daily News*, 30 July 1872.

52. *New Dominion*, 16 August 1873.

53. "Police Chief's Reports," 1863; *New Dominion*, 17 July 1875; *Morning Freeman*, 22 March 1870; Daily News, 26 June 1876, 3 December 1877, 2 September 1880.

54. Kealey, "Orangemen and the Corporation," p. 74.

55. *Daily News*, 28 March 1870; *Morning Freeman*, 15 August 1878; *Daily Sun*, 2 September, 19 December 1890.

56. Rogers, "Serving Toronto the Good," p. 129.

57. Marquis, "The Police Force in Saint John," pp. 51, 60–9. The police rank and file later developed important links with the Trades and Labour Council. When a police union met opposition from civic politicians in 1918, organized labour led a successful

campaign in recalling two hostile officials: see Christopher Armstrong and H.V. Nelles, "The Great Fight For Clean Government," *Urban History Review*, 2 (1976), pp. 50–66.

58. "Police Chief's Reports," 1864.

59. Monkkonen, *Police in Urban America*, p. 150.

60. "Police Chief's Reports," 1864; *Daily Sun*, 8 February 1882, 2, 20 April 1886.

61. *Weekly Freeman*, 6 July 1883; Saint John Common Council Minutes, 15 October, 13 November 1890.

62. Monkkonen, *The Police in Urban America*, pp. 86–128. For the urban poor, see Judith Fingard, "The Winter's Tale: Contours of Poverty in British North America, 1815–1860," *Historical Papers/Communications historiques* (1974), pp. 65–94.

63. "Report of the Commissioners Appointed to Enquire into the Management of Several Public Institutions Receiving Provincial Aid," *New Brunswick Assembly Journal, 1857*, Appendix, p. 138; *News*, 24 April, 24 June 1863, 16 May 1864, 19 November 1875, 22 February 1877; *Daily Sun*, 2 June 1884.

64. "Police Chief's Reports," 1863–89.

65. Craven, "Law and Ideology," pp. 249–52.

66. *New Dominion*, 22 October 1870; Ishmail, *The Temperance Question Pro and Con from a Rational Standpoint in Connection with the Permissive Bill of 1878* (Saint John, 1870).

67. *Daily Sun*, 4 February 1882.

68. Fingard, "Jailbirds in Mid-Victorian Halifax," pp. 101–2; Katz et al., *Social Organization of Early Industrial Capitalism*, pp. 225–8, 234.

69. *Morning Freeman*, 31 January 1860, 10 March 1860; *Daily News*, 2 May 1876; *Daily Sun*, 23 July 1875, 28 January 1882; *Daily Telegraph*, 9 February 1882.

70. *Morning Freeman*, 24 January 1860.

71. Fingard, "Jailbirds," p. 101.

72. Magistrate Robert J. Ritchie, "the newsboys' friend," appointed in 1889, was active in charity organizations and established a "down and out" fund for less fortunate police court clients: *Telegraph Journal* (Saint John), 6 April 1932.

73. Police Court Record, 1849–51; *Morning Freeman*, 1860, 1870; *Daily News*, 1880; *Daily Sun*, 15 January 1889. The average rate of conviction in the Portland police court, 1871–77, was 71 per cent: *Daily News*, 1872–78.

74. *Morning Freeman*, 24 January 1865.

75. *Morning Freeman*, 12 November 1864.

76. Similar criticisms were made of the Toronto police court, where the stipendiary magistrate also served as police commissioner: Gene Homel, "Denison's Law: Criminal Justice and the Police Court in Toronto, 1877–1921," *Ontario History*, LXXIII, 3 (September 1981), pp. 171–84. Kerr's career is described in G. Marquis, "'A Hard Disciple of Blackstone': David S. Kerr, Q.C., 1809–1886," *University of New Brunswick Law Journal*, XXXV (1986), pp. 182–7.

77. Harring, *Policing a Class Society*, pp. 16–7.

78. *Morning Freeman*, 10 January 1865.

79. For insights into the prerogative of mercy in English criminal justice see Douglas Hay, "Property, Authority and the Criminal Law," in D. Hay et al., eds., *Albion's Fatal Tree: Crime and Society in Eighteenth-Century England* (London, 1974), pp. 17–63.

TOPIC EIGHT
Middle-Class Formation and Lifestyle

These civil servants, pictured outside the British Columbia legislature in 1878, were part of the new professional middle class that emerged in the late nineteenth century.

The emergence of a coherent middle class with a distinct set of values and attitudes was one of the most significant developments of the nineteenth century. The middle class, however, has proved to be a difficult and elusive group for historians to deal with, since the boundaries dividing it from the classes "above" and "below" are porous and difficult to define. The wide range of occupations, wealth, education, and training found within the "middle" group of society compounds the problem of definition and identification. Despite these difficulties, a number of historians have begun to take a new look at the formation of the middle class in the nineteenth century and the lifestyles that set it apart.

During the first half of the nineteenth century, British North Americans who belonged to what were often referred to as the "middling ranks" of society secured their status through ownership of land, success in trade and commerce, self-employment as skilled artisans, or membership in the learned professions. One's place in this diverse group was further dependent on such criteria as descent, kinship and marriage ties, and the social and political circles in which one moved. By mid-century, commercial development, increasing literacy, and growing social diversity had combined to prompt a self-conscious transformation of those groups situated between the extremes of wealth and poverty into a distinct and recognizable class. In Article Fifteen, on early Victorian Halifax, David Sutherland explores the important role played by voluntary societies in enabling their participants to forge and proclaim a class identity based on a common commitment to social stability, material progress, and moral reform.

This identity was threatened during the second half of the century by the unsettling forces of urbanization and industrialization. Many in the middle class sought new strategies for defining their position and securing their status. One such strategy was the new ideology of professionalism. In Article Sixteen, Richard A. Willie explores the development of a professional culture among Winnipeg lawyers in the last quarter of the nineteenth century. Willie looks at the informal ways in which lawyers cultivated a professional image that would set them apart as a distinct group within society.

QUESTIONS TO CONSIDER

1. Why did the number of voluntary societies in Halifax grow so dramatically during the first half of the nineteenth century? Who joined these associations? What types of activities did the societies engage in? What were the benefits of belonging to such groups?
2. What were the defining characteristics of Winnipeg lawyers' professional culture? How was this culture created and communicated?
3. What insights do these articles provide into the process of class formation?

SUGGESTED READINGS

Bliss, Michael. *A Living Profit: Studies in the Social History of Canadian Business, 1883–1911.* Toronto: University of Toronto Press, 1974.

Gidney, R.D., and W.P.J. Millar. *Professional Gentlemen: The Professions in Nineteenth-Century Ontario.* Toronto: University of Toronto Press, 1994.

Howell, Colin. "Reform and the Monopolistic Impulse: The Professionalization of Medicine in the Maritimes." *Acadiensis*, 11 (Autumn 1981): 3–22.

Millard, J. Rodney. *Master Spirit of the Age: Canadian Engineers and the Politics of Professionalism*. Toronto: University of Toronto Press, 1988.

Noel, S.J.R. *Patron, Clients, Brokers: Ontario Society and Politics, 1791–1896*. Toronto: University of Toronto Press, 1990.

Smith, Allan. "The Myth of the Self-Made Man in English Canada, 1850–1914." *Canadian Historical Review*, 59 (1979): 189–95.

FIFTEEN

Voluntary Societies and the Process of Middle-Class Formation in Early-Victorian Halifax, Nova Scotia

DAVID A. SUTHERLAND

This inquiry begins with a story, set in Halifax, Nova Scotia, in the summer of 1848. At dawn, on the morning of August 8th, a steamship named the *Unicorn* came puffing down the harbour. Packed with some four hundred men and women, it was headed for Lunenburg, on Nova Scotia's south shore. The passengers on board were members and guests of the Union Engine company, the key component of Halifax's volunteer fire-fighting establishment. Following custom, the firemen were out for a day of recreation and frivolity. When the *Unicorn* reached open water it began to pitch and toss with sufficient vigour to render many seasick. As the suffering became ever more widespread rumours spread that nausea could best be remedied with a large dose of brandy. Accordingly, at eight in the morning the steward obliged by opening the bar. Several of the passengers, along with a number of the crew, drank steadily until the vessel reached Lunenburg, at about noon.

Tumbling ashore amidst considerable mirth, the company spent the next couple of hours delighting in the hospitality offered them by residents of that friendly little outport. Then everyone trooped on board to pay a call at the neighbouring community of Chester. En route liquor was sold "as freely as at a race course," including to those in charge of navigation, with the result that the *Unicorn* grounded on her way into harbour. She broke free, however, and made it to port. There more good times were had until about dusk, when the *Unicorn*'s captain summoned all for the return journey to Halifax. On the way "drinking and drunkenness" increased such that the vessel narrowly avoided colliding with George's Island, at the centre of Halifax harbour. Tie-up occurred at midnight but festivities continued until two in the morning, when passengers finally gave a last salute and found their way home.

Source: "Voluntary Societies and the Process of Middle-Class Formation in Early-Victorian Halifax, Nova Scotia," *Journal of the Canadian Historical Association*, 5 (1994): 237–263. Reprinted by permission.

One of the first to leave was a lawyer by the name of Alexander James. At age 32, an officer in both the Mechanics' Institute and the Sons of Temperance, as well as a prominent supporter of the newly ascendant Liberal party, James was appalled by what had taken place on board the *Unicorn*. Such was his fury that on reaching home he sat up all night writing a letter of protest aimed primarily at Archibald Scott, who had kept bar on board the pleasure craft. Scott, an insurance broker, also worked for Samuel Cunard, proprietor of the *Unicorn*, as agent in charge of arranging excursion parties. In return for relatively low charter fees Scott obtained monopoly rights to sell food and drink while the vessel was on hire.

All this was perfectly legal but James, in his letter of denunciation, which appeared anonymously in Halifax's *Morning Chronicle*, insisted that Scott's behaviour violated prevailing standards of propriety. First of all, it was said that male consumption of alcohol should not have been permitted in the presence of ladies. Secondly, when drinking turned into intoxication, the bar should have been shut. Finally, Scott, an elder in St. Matthew's Presbyterian church, should not have been so flagrantly involved in such a display of gross debauchery.

Scott, aged 44, was a prominent Haligonian, sufficiently well-respected by his peers to have secured office in both the genteel Halifax Horticultural Society and the Lay Association in Support of the Church of Scotland. He also ranked as a militant supporter of the Conservatives, a party now mourning its loss in the general election of 1847, which carried Nova Scotia into the era of "responsible government." Outraged by what he saw as a slur on his character, Scott demanded, through his attorney, that the *Morning Chronicle* reveal who had written about events on board the *Unicorn*. The paper complied and when James refused to retract what he had written, Scott sued for libel. The case came to court in August 1849. A series of witnesses appeared, essentially to establish whether Scott had used undue influence to persuade men to drink. In the end it was decided that he had not. But while finding for the plaintiff the jury gave him damages of only one penny, thereby providing Alexander James with a redeeming moral victory.[1]

The firemen's excursion and the controversy it provoked occurred against a background of massive dislocation in the Nova Scotian capital. After 1815 protracted war had given way to sustained peace, forcing Halifax to look beyond its imperial military garrison to trade as the mainstay of future economic activity. But commerce proved to be a fickle friend, exposing this east coast port to a pattern of boom and bust that persisted into the 1850s. At the same time locals experienced a dizzying population upheaval, involving both large-scale growth and relatively novel ethnic and sectarian diversity, in particular that associated with a mass influx by Irish Roman Catholics. New wealth flourished alongside unprecedented concentrations of mass poverty. Technological innovation ranging from gas street lamps and harbour steamers coexisted with the dire threat of "modern" diseases such as cholera. Out of it all came an effort to transform Halifax from an eighteenth-century town into a nineteenth-century city, an effort which involved a host of reform enthusiasms ranging from evangelical religion to political liberalism. The struggle to extract progress from flux spawned a contradictory blend of ambition and anxiety among Haligonians. Their mood vacillated between boosterish claims of possessing a destiny for greatness and complaint that Halifax would forever be doomed to a "dull, stupid, phlegmatic" existence.[2]

Most outspoken in expressing both hope and fear about the future were those who belonged to what contemporaries referred to as the "middling element" of the community. Primarily made up of professionals, tradesmen, artisans and clerks, they were prime beneficiaries of Halifax's development through the second quarter of the nineteenth century. Growing in absolute numbers, increasingly literate, with ever more disposable income and leisure time, members of these strata tended to become, over time, increasingly self-conscious and ambitious. The local press, itself the creation of those with middling rank, helped foster what by the 1830s can begin to be referred to as a middle-class identity. Discussion in print of scandals involving the exercise of power by their supposed betters, along with censure of riot and arson committed by the "lower orders," transformed individual dissatisfaction into alienated public opinion. That in turn prompted bold insistence that community affairs should now be entrusted to the "self-made" men who had emerged as the true "bone and sinew" of Halifax society. Out of this potent blend of pride and prejudice came political agitation that led, in 1841, to Halifax's incorporation as a city, complete with a mayor and council elected to office by those whose success had made them ratepayers. Coinciding with and complementing that achievement was a surge of institutional activity outside the realm of government, activity which ultimately came to play a central role in the process of middle-class formation.[3]

Here the focus is on what has come to be known as "voluntary societies," formally structured private-sector organizations with a membership recruited through free choice. A few such societies had always existed in Halifax, but in the early-Victorian era their numbers grew dramatically, reaching a total of over sixty by mid-century. Simultaneously, voluntary societies became increasingly diversified in the range of their activities, moving into virtually every sector of human endeavour, from philanthropy to recreation. As well, they acquired an ever higher profile, to the point that their activities came to dominate press coverage of local news. In all of this Halifax was simply emulating a situation found elsewhere in the cities of Britain and the United States.[4]

Urbanization and the pursuit of modernization rather than the relatively narrow dynamics of industrialization seem to have provided the basic stimulus for the surge in voluntary society activity. Rapid growth, especially when associated with mass immigration, meant that many city residents found themselves isolated in a sea of strangers. For such people voluntary societies could function as a substitute for lost kinship connections. Similarly the sense of being caught up in a breakdown of traditional patterns of deference drew people to associations that promised to function as instruments of social control. Again idealism, rooted in such things as religious commitment or enthusiasms for science and technology, prompted like-minded people to set up organizations devoted to the pursuit of virtue and enlightenment. Finally, there were those who saw in associational life an opportunity to assert that their community was no longer a provincial or colonial backwater but instead had come to embrace the prevailing "spirit of the age."[5]

Analysis of the membership lists that have survived for voluntary associations in Halifax suggests that they did not attract a cross-section of the urban population.[6] Journeymen workers, unskilled labourers and common servants failed to join up, most likely because of poverty and lack of leisure time. Members of Halifax's traditional ruling elite, what might be called the "gentry," appeared relatively infrequently, probably because their privileged status meant they already possessed both self-assurance and what was needed for effective self-assertion. In contrast lawyers, doctors, clerics, retail shopkeepers, master craftsmen, manufacturers and clerks —

those occupations generally seen as being the core of the nineteenth-century middle class — demonstrated an avid enthusiasm for society life. As a result, they dominated the mainstream of associational life in Halifax, at least at the level of the general membership.[7]

In an attempt to discern more precisely why those of middle rank were drawn to voluntary societies in early-Victorian Halifax a detailed inquiry has been conducted into their activity, using both organizational records and reports in the press. Rather than look at every society, emphasis has been placed on those which placed a high value on active participation. Thus the Halifax Bible Society, which met only once a year and where most members did little more than pay subscriptions, has been neglected in favour of entities which strove to promote strong brotherhood bonds among their rank and file.[8]

Substantial information is available for several fraternal-style organizations which flourished in Halifax through the 1840s, an era of seminal importance for associational life in the Nova Scotian capital. These were the Union Engine and Axe Companies, the Freemasons, the Mechanics' Institute, the Charitable Irish Society, the North British Society, the St. George's Society and the Nova Scotia Philanthropic Society. Other organizations existed where membership brought extensive involvement, but with respect to size, durability and prominence, these seven tended to prevail.[9]

Entry into the Charitable Irish Society, for example, involved far more than offering an annual donation. Attendance at both annual and quarterly meetings was compulsory. Absenteeism, regardless of cause, rendered members vulnerable to a fine and persistent non-attendance led to expulsion. The Mechanics' Institute did not go so far as to insist on attendance at its weekly lectures, but members were pressured through press announcements to turn out on a regular basis. As for the firemen, a portion of them got together every time flames threatened the community, a phenomenon which occurred as often as forty times a year. In addition to the foregoing, all these societies sponsored an elaborate round of social gatherings. Banquets, balls, picnics, soirees and excursions became an ever larger part of the fraternal experience through the 1840s. Members were not obliged to attend these special occasions but a majority appear to have done so, perhaps because of peer pressure, but more likely in order to enjoy themselves.[10]

Individual identification with the group was further encouraged by means of welfare schemes. For example, the Union Engine Company collected 7½d. per quarter to maintain a fund "for relief of Members who may be injured at the time of duty."[11] The Nova Scotia Philanthropic Society provided members with sick benefits of up to 10s. per week. In the event of death application could be made for help in meeting funeral costs and the society would consider offering assistance to widows and orphans. The Freemasons went one step further by insisting that all members turn out in full regalia for the funeral of one of their "brethren."[12]

Rules and conventions existed within all these organizations for the purpose of stimulating friendship and co-operation among the membership. For example, the Mechanics' Institute banned discussion "on party or domestic politics, or on controverted religious topics." Moreover, the executive vigorously expressed its disapproval of the "injudicious habit," especially among young members, "of making numerous expressions of applause," lest speakers not so flattered take offence. Similarly the Freemasons of St. Andrew's Lodge insisted that "no private disputes or altercations shall be permitted during Lodge hours on any subject." Putting things somewhat more positively, the Charitable Irish Society told its rank and file they had an obliga-tion "to conduct themselves with kindness and affection," to "promote friendship and harmony" and to "aid and assist a member when in adversity or trouble"; and if a member seemed likely to suffer from "imprudent conduct," they were to intervene or seek assistance from the Society. The quest for "brotherhood" often fell short of complete attainment. Problems persistently arose over delinquency with respect to attendance at meetings and payment of dues, and on occasion meetings fell prey to what one veteran member described as "miserable political jealousy and intrigue." Periodically, executive authority had to be invoked to curb "bad language" and "disparaging remarks" among the membership.[13]

Each organization professed to have a relatively open admissions policy. Most liberal of all was the Mechanics' Institute, which welcomed anyone, male or female, who could pay an annual membership fee of 10s. All other societies excluded women from their ranks. They also insisted that applicants be at least nineteen years old and have risen beyond the rank of apprentice. Freemasons further required members to be self-employed. In order to join one of the four ethnic societies one had to have been born in either the British Isles or Nova Scotia, or be descended from someone born in those places. While religion was never formally mentioned as a criterion for admission to any of these seven organizations, the Union Engine Company had a reputation for discriminating against Roman Catholics. All societies appear to have granted their members an unrestricted right to join other organizations.[14]

Prospective members invariably had to meet formal minimum requirements with respect to affluence and popularity. Initiation fees of either 10s. or 20s. were the norm, except for the Freemasons, who charged £5 just for the privilege of applying to enter. Normally one had to be nominated by an existing member in good stand-ing. Applications were then reviewed either by a special committee or by those at-tending one of the quarterly meetings. Veto power over candidates for membership varied by organization. For example, the Charitable Irish Society required approval by two-thirds of those present and voting, while at St. Andrew's Freemasons Lodge three negative ballots translated into rejection. Only the Freemasons combined ad-mission with formal ritual, and that organization was also unique in providing for promotion through a series of ranks. Every step up the ladder cost members 40s. At each quarterly meeting those in attendance had to pay an instalment on their annual dues, along with a charge for refreshments. The cost ranged from a low of 1s.3d at one of the Masonic lodges to a high of 4s.3d at gatherings of the North British Society. Additional fees were charged for regalia and the various special events mounted by each society.[15]

Every year a few members resigned or had to be struck off the records. But these losses were more than compensated for by success in finding new recruits. For exam-ple, through the nine years after its founding in 1834, the Nova Scotia Philanthropic Society took in 398 members while losing, through death, resignation and departure from Halifax, only 71. Among the seven organizations under review individual membership, at any one time, ranged from a low of approximately 100 to a high of about 300. By mid-century they collectively held the allegiance of approximately 1300 individuals. In other words, mainstream fraternalism, as represented by these seven societies, accounted for perhaps six per cent of Halifax's overall population.[16] Scholars now suggest that those with taxable amounts of property made up no more than one-fifth of the total population. Accordingly it would appear that the fraternal portion of voluntary society activity in Halifax had come to embrace half or more of those situated between the gentry and the poor.[17]

Just because entities such as the Charitable Irish Society drew most of their rank and file from the middle ranks of urban society did not mean that their leaders also came from those strata. Studies of voluntary societies in other cities suggest that organizational leaders tended to be superior to the rank and file with respect to income and status. To some extent that was true also in Halifax, facilitated by the fact that nominations to high office tended to be controlled by committees of insiders. Moreover, some societies preferred to have the same incumbents in office year after year, especially when those officers were recruited from among Halifax's gentry. On the other hand, significant numbers of men with occupations traditionally defined as non-genteel (brewer, for example) and without kinship ties to established "old families" rose to positions of leadership in Halifax's fraternal organizations.[18]

Complete identification of those who joined up is impossible given gaps in available data, but it appears that membership began when men were in their early thirties, a time when most would be consolidating their position in terms of both career and family life. Voluntary societies proved especially attractive to those who had been born outside Halifax and who thus most likely lacked strong kinship networks within their adopted home. Protestant Dissenters and Roman Catholics as well as those of Scottish and Irish background, all of whom were deemed to be somewhat disreputable according to oligarchic convention in Halifax, flocked into fraternal organizations. In other words, entities such as the Freemasons flourished essentially because of their ability to draw in young, assertive and upwardly mobile elements of the community. Recruits were attracted by what these voluntary societies had to offer concerning conviviality, mutual support and an opportunity to develop the skills and reputation needed for advancement into the leadership ranks of Halifax society.[19]

Most of those drawn into Halifax's fraternal world led lives of quiet obscurity. But a few of their "brothers" did much better, often in ways which suggested that their success derived substantially from voluntary society activity. Consider, for example, the case of James R. DeWolf. The son of a Methodist outport merchant, DeWolf trained in Scotland for a career in medicine and then moved to Halifax in 1844, at age 26. Setting up in what had become a highly competitive profession, DeWolf sought security and connections, through both marriage and membership in various of Halifax's voluntary societies. In particular he threw himself into the Nova Scotia Philanthropic Society with such energy that he became its president in 1848, a post which allowed him, despite being a relative newcomer, to preside a year later over Halifax's centennial celebrations. Other honours followed, climaxing in 1857 with DeWolf's appointment as Superintendent of Nova Scotia's Hospital for the Insane.[20]

Another who rose to prominence largely through voluntary society activity was Lawrence O'Connor Doyle. Although born in Halifax and the son of a leading local merchant, Doyle suffered the twin disadvantages of being Irish and Roman Catholic. Opting for a career in law and politics, Doyle inserted himself into virtually every organization set up to promote the interests of Halifax's expanding Irish Roman Catholic community. In 1843 the city's Charitable Irish Society, long under the control of Protestant notables such as the Uniacke family, elected Doyle as its president at age 39. Thereafter the Charitable Irish featured in the struggle to end Protestant ascendancy in Halifax's public affairs, a struggle which in 1848 carried Doyle into the first provincial executive to function under the rules of "responsible government."[21]

Accompanying Doyle into office on that occasion was William Young, who had come from Scotland to Halifax as a youth during the war of 1812. After failure of the family business amidst Nova Scotia's postwar economic slump, Young, a Presbyterian, turned to law and then entered politics. He, too, saw fraternal activity as a means of buttressing his career. In his case it involved membership in Halifax's prestigious North British Society, an organization which by the 1840s also was in the process of being taken over by relative newcomers. In 1848, at age 49, Young ascended to its presidency, and such was his gratitude for what this organization had done to foster his career that, years later, he left it a bequest of $100,000.[22]

Another who fostered the notion that success lay through participation in voluntary societies was William Caldwell. The son of an Irish Methodist immigrant who settled in Nova Scotia's rural interior, Caldwell moved to Halifax toward the end of the 1820s. Setting up as a master blacksmith, Caldwell quickly joined the Union Engine Company. A decade later, at age 46, he became Captain of the Company. The prestige of that office, as well as the network of connections it brought, proved crucial in allowing Caldwell to be elected mayor of Halifax in 1850.[23] Much the same path was followed by Andrew Mackinlay, who came to Halifax from Scotland in the mid-1820s. Going into business as a bookseller, Mackinlay, a Presbyterian, prided himself on being an exponent of intellectual enlightenment. As such he developed an enthusiasm for the Mechanics' Institute and rose to serve as its president from 1838 to 1849. Success in discharging that office, combined with a strong enthusiasm for public service, propelled Mackinlay into politics and led to his election as mayor of Halifax in 1845 when in his mid-40s.[24]

A final example of how leadership could be forged within the fraternal world is provided by the career of Alexander Keith. Born in Scotland, and a Presbyterian by faith, Keith came to Halifax in 1817 at age 22, where he went into business as a brewer. Having joined the Freemasons prior to emigration, Keith transferred his membership to a local lodge immediately on arrival in Halifax. That affiliation proved extremely valuable as Keith struggled to develop his brewery into what eventually became one of the most successful manufactories on Halifax's waterfront. His dedication to the Freemasons, an organization then suffering considerable disarray, brought promotion, climaxing in 1840 when Keith was selected Grand Master of the Nova Scotian order. The new leader moved aggressively over the next decade to expand membership and end quarrelling among the various Masonic lodges. Successful both as a capitalist and as a lodgeman, Keith found himself co-opted into politics. After winning election as mayor of Halifax in 1843, he secured appointment to Nova Scotia's prestigious Legislative Council.[25]

The extent to which Keith or any of the others owed his advancement to voluntary society activity cannot be established with precision. It is clear, however, that fraternal leaders were in the public eye. By the 1840s local news in the Halifax press was dominated by society activities. Typical of the era was what the triweekly *Morning Post* had to say in April 1845 about a banquet put on by an elite group of Freemasons. Readers learned that some sixty gentlemen had dined starting at 7 P.M. Those at the head table appeared in regalia, and the walls of the hotel room were adorned with a host of banners and insignia. A military band played lively airs and mid-way through the proceedings a touring company of singers performed for the crowd. At 9 P.M. toasts began to be delivered, interspersed with songs and speeches. Twenty times in succession members raised their glasses in honour of everything from the spirit of Freemasonry to the fair daughters of Nova Scotia. At one in the morning the entire company proceeded out into the street "two-and-two, arm in arm, after the band, which struck up the Freemason's march." They then accompanied Grand Master Alexander Keith to his residence. Amidst deafening cheers, participants saluted their leader, first with "auld lang syne," followed by the national anthem. As the bandsmen proceeded back to barracks, playing as they went, Halifax Freemasons staggered on home, as the reporter put it, "to forget even convivial scenes in the balmy luxury of sleep."[26]

Similar festivities were put on at least once a year by most Halifax voluntary societies. Invariably held at a hotel, so as to have access to first-class catering service, attendance (male only) usually ran in the 50 to 150 range. Members came, along with invited guests, who usually included the presidents of other fraternal organizations, officers from the garrison, and leading public officials, such as the mayor. Special delight was taken when organizers managed to secure the presence of and a speech by Nova Scotia's lieutenant-governor. Typically, "mirth, fellowship, and conviviality prevailed." It was an occasion, a reporter noted, when "sectional distinctions and local prejudices are forgotten, and countrymen meet as friends." The *Morning Herald*, commenting on the combination of speeches, songs and twenty-six toasts featured in 1843 when the Charitable Irish Society met on St. Patrick's Day, observed that "a more jovial party never sat around the festive board." Protracted large-scale consumption of alcohol took its toll, however, prompting a participant in a similar affair to observe that "a few . . . yesterday morning were complaining of head-aches and nausea."[27]

The street processions which often accompanied these festive occasions heightened public awareness of voluntary society activity. For example, in June 1843 Halifax's six Masonic lodges celebrated the feast day of their patron saint beginning at 10 A.M. with a rally at city centre. The members paraded through the streets to St. Paul's Anglican cathedral church for a special service. Next came a parade to Alexander Keith's home for a salute to their leader. Attracted by colourful banners and regalia, as well as music provided by a regimental band, "thousands" of Haligonians thronged the downtown to get a glimpse of the spectacle.[28] A similar pattern of events took place at the annual meeting of the St. George's Society in 1849. Accompanied by a military band, wearing insignia, and waving banners, the members marched through town at mid-day to pay respects to their patron, the lieutenant-governor. Observed by "vast crowds," made up of both men and women, the members then proceeded back to the centre of the city to give three cheers for the Queen.[29] Much the same happened when Halifax's Charitable Irish Society celebrated St. Patrick's Day in 1850. The affair began with morning high mass presided over by the archbishop. Marching out of church in the wake of a military band, members saluted the residences of three of their leading figures and then called on the lieutenant-governor. Having affirmed their allegiance by singing "God Save the Queen," the host strolled back through town, cheering in front of the Roman Catholic cathedral before dispersing in preparation for the evening's festivities.[30]

A final example of how public display could be used both to enhance a society's morale and to make a statement to the public at large was provided by Halifax's African Abolition Society. One of three friendly societies established during the 1840s to serve the small and acutely marginalized Black population resident in the Nova Scotian capital, this organization rallied in August 1850 to commemorate the abolition of slavery throughout the British empire. After a meeting which featured such toasts as one to "Africa, the land of our Forefathers, may she . . . at last vanquish her foes," the members marched through town escorted by "half the population of the city." Preceded by a military band they made their way to Government House, there to cheer the lieutenant-governor, a gesture deliberately designed to make the point that Blacks should be recognised as full subjects of the crown.[31]

Even more effective in giving voluntary societies a high public profile were the summer excursions which, through the 1840s, became a highlight of Halifax's social season. The custom apparently began in June 1839 when the Philanthropic Society organized a picnic to commemorate Halifax's founding, ninety years earlier. Having rented one of the cross-harbour ferries, members of the Society proceeded into Bedford Basin to land at Prince's Lodge, the site of what in the 1790s had been the estate of Queen Victoria's father, the Duke of Kent. There, an "abundance of substantial viands, and lots of good liquor to moisten them" had been laid on. After lunch participants played games, walked in the woods, enjoyed a bottle of wine or listened to music provided by a military band. At dusk they came back to town, proceeded to the Grand Parade and ended by singing a song especially written for the occasion by Joseph Howe, publisher of Halifax's leading newspaper.[32]

The success of this venture proved infectious. Soon every Halifax voluntary society was holding some form of summer outing. Most popular were picnics, with the preferred site being Prince's Lodge, thanks to its bucolic charm and aristocratic connections. Over time the ceremony became ever more elaborate. For example, in 1847 when the St. George's Society held its first picnic, the affair began with a morning march through the downtown streets. Once on board their steamer, members and guests progressed around the harbour, saluting various warships with cheers and patriotic songs such as "Rule Britannia." They then moved on to the shores of Halifax's North-West Arm for an afternoon of games and dancing. Dinner was served under a massive tent pavilion while an orchestra played in the background. At dusk the whole company strolled back to town, their way lit by torches. Preceded by a military band they made their way to Masons Hall for refreshments and then danced until midnight. All this came immediately in the wake of equally extravagant outings by the Charitable Irish and North British societies. Well over one thousand people had participated in these events, many of them consisting, as one contemporary put it, of "intelligent, well dressed persons of the middling class of life."[33]

All the foregoing activity took place in the near-total absence of factional strife. The only occasion on which violence threatened to mar proceedings occurred in August 1848. Roused to bitter suspicion by news of the failure of rebellion in famine-ridden Ireland, a group of Irish "Repealers" attempted to disrupt a street parade by Halifax's North British Society to seize what they mistakenly believed to be an Orange banner. Significantly, the incident received hardly a mention in the local press, presumably because local editors feared provoking violence.[34] With this exception, private and public ceremonies put on by Halifax's voluntary societies demonstrated their growing ability to forge a sense of unity that went beyond the boundaries of a single organization. Instead of accentuating ethnic, sectarian and political fragmentation, fraternalism actually bridged those gaps, especially within the middle-rank sections of Halifax society.

At the same time, however, an undercurrent of dissatisfaction developed among certain Haligonians over the extent to which the ceremonials of fraternal life were in conflict with what they wanted as the standards of public morality. More than anything else this concern focused on prominent and heavy use of liquor to promote the bonds of brotherhood. Debate over consumption of alcohol persisted through the 1830s at a low level, but burst forth a decade later into a powerful campaign seeking not just moderation, but total abstinence and even prohibition. One consequence was a dramatic upheaval in the character of voluntary society activity in Nova Scotia's capital.[35]

Seeking both to heighten their public profile and to build internal morale, temperance leaders emulated the behaviour of other voluntary organizations. For example, in June 1842 the new St. Mary's Temperance Society, led by Lawrence O'C. Doyle, marched 1200 strong through downtown Halifax to pay their respects to the lieutenant-governor. After being received "graciously" members resumed their procession, which featured "medals, sashes, rosets, and other badges, and several splendid flags," two military bands and a troop of horsemen. A core group of 400 then went by steamer to McNab's Island, at the mouth of Halifax harbour, for a picnic complete with sports and dancing. Returning to Halifax they marched in style to St. Mary's cathedral for a salute to the Roman Catholic clergy. It all came off, one newspaper commented, with "order, comfort, and respectability."[36]

Organizations set up on such a vast scale quickly failed. They were too large to offer intimacy and also suffered from collapses in revenue when hard times prevented the poor they sought as recruits from mustering fees. Far more durable were the Sons of Temperance, which arrived from the United States in 1847 to set up a proliferation of small, highly motivated "divisions." Their weekly (later monthly) meetings gave members a chance to dress up in formal regalia, drink tea, listen to lively music and be addressed by impassioned speakers, several of whom were professional orators brought in from the American lecture circuit. In July of that year the Sons hosted a mass picnic, where participants engaged in "dancing, and singing, playing at ball, pitching quoits, and other enjoyments," all without a drop of rum, beer or wine.[37]

Exactly who joined the Sons of Temperance is difficult to establish since membership lists have not survived. But those who served as officers are known and they tended to have a lot in common with those entering non-temperance fraternal organizations. For example, the young lawyer Alexander James, who caused such a ruckus over the firemen's excursion to Lunenburg, combined membership in the Mechanics' Institute with executive office in the "Mechanics' Division" of the Sons of Temperance.

Alongside the Sons were two parallel organizations set up to cater to the special interests of two special constituencies which by the 1840s had begun to assert themselves. The first involved male youth, meaning those old enough to have joined the work force but who had not yet stepped into marriage. In 1847 activists founded the Young Men's Total Abstinence Society and within a year it boasted a membership of some two hundred. The organization's appeal derived largely from its entertainment programme. Meetings occurred monthly and through the winter featured speeches, debates and choral music. Members of the general public could attend most proceedings, on payment of a small entrance fee. Young ladies received a particular welcome and for them special events were arranged, including picnics in summer and dances in winter. Such mixed gatherings, at least one of which lasted until 3 A.M., generated complaints. But the society also won widespread approval. As a supporter observed, "we like to see the young fellows enjoy themselves, and we think those social parties, where the inebriating cup is discarded do good."[38]

Women did more than simply add life to male-organized events. As early as 1844 they had established a Female Temperance and Benevolent Society, which quickly grew to over one hundred members. Lieutenant-Governor Harvey agreed to serve as their patron, and in 1849, when the women convened a public meeting at Masons Hall, they had enough influence to secure the presence of a military band. Moreover the mayor attended, along with a gender-mixed audience described as "representing the wealth, intelligence and beauty of the city."[39]

Members of the Young Men's and the Ladies' Benevolent societies maintained a close working relationship. For example, in 1848 the women organized a fund-raising soiree to help the men in their effort to establish new meeting facilities. In return the men "rapturously passed" a vote of thanks to their sisters in the cause. Co-operation extended to include the new Sons of Temperance. Speakers were mutually shared, picnics were opened to one another, and on one celebrated occasion a committee of women appeared before a mass rally of "Sons" to present them with a new banner. In a gesture daring by the standards of the day, Mrs. Crane, president of the Ladies' Society, addressed the crowd in, as the reporter conspicuously noted, "an audible voice." In reply her committee received an oration which stressed the extent to which women had become essential for the achievement of public virtue.[40]

Temperance agitation and self-assertion by both young men and women gradually began to transform the mainstream of fraternal life in Halifax. In 1841, for example, the Charitable Irish Society inaugurated the tradition of allowing toasts at its annual banquet to be drunk using water. Five years later the Charitable Irish barred alcohol from its summer picnic, a move anticipated in 1842 by the Philanthropic Society. Similarly, organizers of the June 1847 outing put on by Dartmouth's Mechanics' Institute stressed that in order to promote "healthful and rational amusements," they would impose "the most stringent regulations . . . to prevent the sale of intoxicating liquors."[41]

As for young men, at the beginning of the 1840s both the Charitable Irish and the Philanthropic societies established youth auxiliaries. Immediately those auxiliaries began agitating for inclusion of women as guests at their public outings. After some chauvinistic grumbling about how the presence of women could compromise the spirit of true brotherhood, the elders gave in. By the end of the decade it had become an accepted custom to invite females to society outings in order to impart to the occasion "a higher tone."[42] Nevertheless, membership was not an option offered to women. They were accepted only as guests, and even then, as the firemen's controversial outing of 1848 demonstrated, their presence did not necessarily mean abandonment of "rough" forms of male celebration.

Despite lack of consensus as to how to define "respectability," especially as it pertained to alcohol, Halifax's voluntary societies became ever more confident of their ability to shape not just their own affairs but also the affairs of the larger community. This self-confidence led to increasing experimentation with events open to the general public. For example, in August 1846 the Mechanics' Institute hosted a festival on McNab's Island where people could come to see such wonders of the age as steam engines and hot air balloons. The mayor declared a holiday from business to assure a mass turnout. It was a bold move, since early-Victorian crowds had a tendency to turn rowdy, but on this occasion decorum prevailed. Emboldened by other successes fraternal leaders began to plan for the celebration of Halifax's centennial, seeing it as an ideal opportunity to present themselves as central to what it meant to be a Haligonian.[43]

Preparation for this, the largest public ceremony in the pre-Confederation history of Halifax, began in April 1849, when the Philanthropic Society sent a circular to its peer organizations asking for co-operation in staging the centennial. Next, some thirty society leaders met and decided to hand matters over to a small executive committee headed by J.R. DeWolf, president of the Philanthropic Society. Almost immediately controversy erupted, fed in large measure by the stress of hard times and political uncertainty associated with the transition to "responsible government." One disgruntled Tory newspaper asked, "with one half the population starving and the other half running away, with bankruptcy, famine, and disease rife among us, is it time to rejoice?" Nevertheless, planning went ahead, helped by the fact that DeWolf, the chief organizer, was a high profile Conservative and thus could appeal for support from those who otherwise might have seen the centennial as a partisan event put on by the new Liberal government.[44]

Festivities were scheduled for June 8th, to commemorate the entrance into Chebucto harbour of the city's founder, Lt. Col. Edward Cornwallis.[45] It would be a public holiday, with all offices and businesses closed so that citizens could become involved, as either spectators or participants. The morning dawned with sunshine. Citizens woke up to a 100-gun salute fired by Halifax's Volunteer Artillery company. Then came a "merry peel" of bells from various churches as well as the tower of the town clock. From 9 A.M. until noon soldiers of the garrison conducted military manoeuvres, climaxing in a mock attack on Citadel Hill. Meanwhile something like five thousand celebrants, all male, were forming up at the Grand Parade. At mid-day they moved out into the streets. In the words of the *Acadian Recorder*:

> The procession was upwards of a mile long, and it took nearly half an hour, from the time the van went by until the rear came up . . . It was the most imposing spectacle of the kind that was ever seen in Halifax. The City Council and Magistrates, mounted, preceded; then followed a Printing Press, and the Fire Engines, elaborately ornamented, drawn by splendid horses, and two carriages, one carrying Micmac chiefs and a moose calf, the other, a number of the oldest men in the country . . . After these came the Volunteer Artillery, N.S. Philanthropic Society, Temperance, African, St. George's, Charitable Irish, North British, and Highland Societies, Free Mason, and Truckmen mounted.[46]

Downtown Halifax was packed with both residents and visitors from the interior. Despite the numbers, decorum prevailed. According to the *British Colonist*, "the most extreme courtesy marked the crowd . . . and the most refined lady might have passed to and fro without her ear being in the slightest degree offended." Women of respectable status did appear but mostly in upper story windows, from where they could cheer on the marchers with "bright eyes and healthful cheeks, and welcome smiles."[47]

As the parade moved out onto the Commons it encountered "such a vast concourse of people as was never before witnessed in Halifax." Women turned out either on horseback, in carriages or within the security of a square formed by the marchers. At 2 P.M. the Volunteer Artillery company hailed the arrival of the lieutenant-governor by firing a 21-gun salute. After Sir John Harvey had reviewed the procession a series of speeches was given, the main one by Beamish Murdoch, long-time president of the Halifax Temperance Society. He was followed by Provincial Secretary (and former president of the Charitable Irish Society) Joseph Howe, who read a poem composed specifically for the occasion. Both speakers stressed the theme of how "mother" Halifax deserved the affection of her residents. In Murdoch's words, "other lands may boast greater wealth, other cities a more numerous population; but where can you find a city or a province whose sons and daughters love her and cling to her, as fondly, as proudly, as exclusively, as we do to Halifax, to Nova Scotia." It was Murdoch's way of telling the assembled throng that they owed a fundamental allegiance to one another as residents of a new community, one that could thrive through mobilization of a common sense of unity.[48]

That evening revolving gas lights on public buildings gave Halifax's downtown core a "mid-day splendor." Illuminated signs spelled out such patriotic words as "1749" and "VR." A shower of fireworks erupted from Citadel Hill, to be matched by half an hour of salvoes fired from a warship anchored in the harbour. Several private parties had been organized, including one by the firemen, who turned their Engine House into a ballroom and there "passed the evening right merrily." Most lively of all was the dinner/dance put on at Masons Hall by a combination of the North British and Highland societies. Attracting a numerous array of men and women drawn from "the middle classes and élite of the city and garrison," this affair went roaring on until 3:30 in the morning. Despite such *joie de vivre*, the city avoided disorder. Next morning one local editor summed up the event by saying that "the occasion passed off as peacefully, soberly, and happily as a small tea party."[49]

Civic pride prompted talk of the need for an enduring symbol of Halifax's having come of age. Discussion quickly came to focus on the building of a public hospital. As a last gesture before disbanding, the centenary committee endorsed the project. Moreover Dr. DeWolf and several other fraternal leaders who had been active in the centennial formed themselves into a lobby designed to convince government that it should fund the enterprise. The press immediately rallied in support of the idea. In the words of one editor, "something was needed to denote to posterity that so much philanthropy existed in the breasts of the generation of 1849."[50] A decade would pass before enthusiasm had been converted into institutional achievement, but the hospital issue illustrated a major shift in contemporary thinking and behaviour. By mid-century, Halifax voluntary societies had begun to assume responsibility for setting the agenda for employment of the power of the state.[51]

Of course it would be an exaggeration to suggest that Halifax had experienced an entire change of personality. Visitors to mid-Victorian Halifax repeatedly commented on what they saw as the dirt, disorder and relative stagnation of Nova Scotia's capital. For example, in 1850 a Boston editor complained that Halifax displayed "a sad want of the freshness, liveliness and cheerfulness which marks a New England town."[52] However, such acerbic observations overlooked fundamental elements of change that had taken place through the second quarter of the nineteenth century. One of the most significant of these changes involved the emergence of a Halifax middle class.

At the beginning of this era Halifax society possessed a "middling element," but it was one which lacked organizational capacity and could muster only the rudiments of collective consciousness. By the mid-1830s people in this category had begun to come together, in terms of both structure and mentality, but their actions and statements tended to be more negative than positive. Basically they had a better idea of what they were against than what they were for. Driven by a sense of victimization and vulnerability, those of modest means turned to political protest in the hope that liberal/democratic reform might improve their lot. But often that proved divisive, opening up ethnic, sectarian, and party divisions among those manoeuvring across the middle of Halifax's social hierarchy. At the same time, however, these people acquired an enthusiasm for voluntary societies, seeing them as both a shelter from adversity and an opportunity for advancement. Over time fraternalism evolved from the pursuit of individual self-help to a campaign for collective self-assertion. Societies and their members made a strategic transition from the private to the public sector. New notions of both respectability and citizenship began to be articulated, notions infused with bourgeois assumptions about the importance of work, thrift, sobriety and stewardship. In other words, by 1850 middle-class formation, as regards both structure and ideology, was well under way in Halifax.

TABLES

The following abbreviations apply throughout: CIS = Charitable Irish Society; GEO = St. George's Society; MAS = Freemasons; MI = Mechanics' Institute; NBS = North British Society; PHIL = Nova Scotia Philanthropic Society; UE/A = United Engine Company and Axe Fire Company

Occupational categories have been constructed as follows (included here are those job descriptions which appear frequently):

Artisans (ART): baker, blacksmith, block maker, butcher, carpenter; cabinet maker, carriage maker, cooper, hatter, mason, moulder, painter, plumber, printer, ropemaker, saddler, sailmaker, shipwright, shoemaker, tailor, tanner, tinsmith, watchmaker, wheelwright

Retailers (RET): bookseller, confectioner, dealer, druggist, grocer, shopkeeper, tobacconist

Merchants/Professionals (M/P): architect, auctioneer, brewer, cleric, distiller, doctor, engineer, founder, lawyer, notary public, publisher, wholesaler

Other/high (O/H): bank officer, broker, gentleman, government officer (imperial or provincial), military officer

Other/low (O/L): boarding house keeper, clerk, farmer, foreman, innkeeper, librarian, policeman, sea captain, soldier, surveyor, teacher, truckman

Unknown (U)

TABLE 15.1 *Occupational Distribution by Voluntary Society for All Members (percentages exclude the unknowns)*

	CIS		GEO		MAS		MI	
	No.	*%*	*No.*	*%*	*No.*	*%*	*No.*	*%*
ART	78	30	25	20	35	27	22	25
RET	73	28	17	14	18	14	15	17
M/P	49	19	58	46	38	29	38	44
O/H	41	16	19	15	17	13	10	13
O/L	17	7	6	5	23	17	2	1
U	192		27		115		17	
Total	450		152		246		104	

	NBS		PHIL		UE/A	
	No.	*%*	*No.*	*%*	*No.*	*%*
ART	70	37	129	42	137	77
RET	38	20	34	11	25	14
M/P	58	31	85	28	5	3
O/H	17	9	15	5	2	1
O/L	6	3	42	14	8	5
U	96		104		60	
Total	285		409		237	

Overall Distribution of the General Membership by Occupational Grouping:

	No.	*%*
ART	496	39
RET	220	17
M/P	331	26
O/H	121	10
O/L	104	8
U	611	
Total	1883	

TABLE 15.2 *Occupational Distribution by Voluntary Society for Those Serving as Officers*

	CIS		GEO		MAS		MI	
	No.	%	No.	%	No.	%	No.	%
ART	1	7	0	0	7	24	0	0
RET	4	27	2	15	4	14	2	25
M/P	9	60	8	62	10	35	4	50
O/H	1	7	3	23	6	21	2	25
O/L	0		0		2	7	0	
U	1		0		11		2	
Total	16		13		40		10	

	NBS		PHIL		UE/A	
	No.	%	No.	%	No.	%
ART	1	6	8	50	20	83
RET	8	47	1	6	2	8
M/P	7	41	6	38	0	0
O/H	1	6	1	6	1	4
O/L	0	0	0		1	4
U	1		0		4	
Total	18		16		28	

Overall Distribution of Officers by Occupational Grouping:

	No.	%
ART	37	30
RET	23	19
M/P	44	36
O/H	15	12
O/L	3	3
U	19	
Total	141	

TABLE 15.3 *Distribution of Voluntary Society Officers According to Whether They Possessed Kinship and/or Business Connections with the Inner Circle of Oligarchy*

	Insiders		Outsiders	
	No.	*%*	*No.*	*%*
CIS	5	31	11	69
GEO	12	83	2	17
MAS	11	30	26	70
MI	3	33	6	67
NBS	8	44	10	56
PHIL	6	38	10	62
UE/A	2	8	24	92

NOTES

1. A detailed report of the trial is found in Halifax *Novascotian*, 13 August 1849. See also Halifax *Sun*, 11 August 1848.

2. Halifax *Acadian Recorder*, 12 January 1850. Contemporary attitudes are explored in D.A. Sutherland, "Joseph Howe and the boosting of Halifax," in Wayne A. Hunt (ed.), *The Proceedings of the Joseph Howe Symposium* (Sackville, New Brunswick, 1984): 71–86. An overview of Halifax and the Maritime region during the second quarter of the nineteenth century is provided by P.A. Buckner and J.G. Reid (eds.), *The Atlantic Region to Confederation: A History* (Toronto and Fredericton, 1994), chs. 12–14. Also invaluable for establishing context is T.W. Acheson, *Saint John: The Making of a Colonial Urban Community* (Toronto, 1985).

3. The reform impulse in early nineteenth-century Halifax and the extent to which it involved use of the press is discussed by J.M. Beck, *Joseph Howe: Conservative Reformer, 1804–1848* (Montreal and Kingston, 1982). For shopkeeper agitation on behalf of municipal reform in Halifax, see D.A. Sutherland, "Thomas Forrester," *Dictionary of Canadian Biography* [hereafter *DCB*], VII: 307–309.

4. Developments in the United States and Britain are examined by Mary Ann Clawson, *Constructing Brotherhood: Class, Gender, and Fraternalism* (Princeton, 1989) and R.J. Morris, "Voluntary societies and British urban elites, 1780–1850: An analysis," *The Historical Journal* 26: 1 (1983): 95–118. See also Mark C. Carnes, *Secret Ritual and Manhood in Victorian America* (New Haven, 1989).

5. The linkage between urbanization and class formation is explored by Stuart M. Blumin, *The Emergence of the Middle Class: Social Experience in the American City, 1760–1900* (Cambridge, MA, 1989); Stuart M. Blumin, *The Urban Threshold: Growth and Change in a Nineteenth Century American Community* (Chicago, 1976); Mary Ryan, *Cradle of the Middle Class: The Family in Oneida County, New York, 1790–1865* (Cambridge, 1981); Paul E. Johnston, *A Shopkeeper's Millennium: Society and Revivals in Rochester, New York, 1815–1837* (New York, 1978); R.J. Morris, *Class, Sect and Party: The Making of the British Middle Class, Leeds, 1820–1850* (Manchester and New York, 1990), as well as Leonore Davidoff and Catherine Hall, *Family Fortunes: Men and Women of the English Middle Class, 1780–1850* (Chicago, 1987).

6. The following sources have provided the backbone of the information on society membership in Halifax: Charitable Irish Society (Halifax), minute books, 1834–50, Public Archives of Nova Scotia [hereafter PANS], MG20, vol. 67; St. George's Society (Halifax),

membership and dues book, 1838–67, PANS, MG20, vol. 338; North British Society (Halifax), minute books, 1768–1886, PANS, MG20, vols. 231–232; Mechanics' Institute (Halifax), minute books, 1831–46, PANS, MG20, vol. 222(A); *Rules and Constitution of the Charitable Irish Society* (Halifax, 1840 & 1854); *Rules of the St. George's Society* (Halifax, 1852); *Bye-laws of Saint Andrew's Lodge no. 137 of Free and Accepted Masons* (Halifax, 1862); *Rules and Bye-laws of the Royal Union Chapter no. 137* (Halifax, 1863); *Rules and Bye laws of Royal Sussex Lodge no. 704* (Halifax, 1851); *Bye-laws of St. John Lodge no. 161* (Halifax, 1863); *Rules of the Halifax Mechanics Institute* (Halifax, 1832); *The Constitution, Fundamental Rules and Bye laws of the Nova Scotia Philanthropic Society* (Halifax, 1843).

7. See Table 15.1.

8. *Nova Scotia Bible Society, Annual Report* (Halifax, 1847). See also Halifax *British Colonist,* 14 April 1849, 2 February 1850.

9. R.P. Harvey, "Black beans, banners and banquets: The Charitable Irish Society at two hundred," *Nova Scotia Historical Review* 6 (1986): 16–35; T.M. Punch, *Irish Halifax: The Immigrant Generation* (Halifax, 1981); J.S. Macdonald, *Annals of the North British Society* (Halifax, 1868 and 1905); R.S. Longley and R.V. Harris, *A Short History of Freemasonry in Nova Scotia, 1738–1966* (Halifax, 1966); E.T. Bliss, *Masonic Grand Masters of the Jurisdiction of Nova Scotia, 1738–1965* (Halifax, 1965); C.B. Fergusson, *Mechanics Institutes in Nova Scotia* (Halifax, 1960); D.C. Harvey, "Nova Scotia Philanthropic Society," *Dalhousie Review* 19: 3 (October 1939): 287–295; B.E.S. Rudachyk, "The most tyrannous of masters: Fire in Halifax, Nova Scotia, 1830–1850" (M.A. thesis, Dalhousie University, 1984).

10. In 1840 the Charitable Irish Society met as follows: 17 February (quarterly meeting, 125 present); 17 March (annual dinner, 106 members and guests present); 20 April (banquet to celebrate the Queen's marriage, 137 members and guests present); 18 May (quarterly meeting, 75 present); 17 August (quarterly meeting, 96 present); 2 October (special meeting to pass a motion of congratulations to the Queen for having escaped an assassination attempt, 90 present); 17 November (quarterly meeting, 114 present), Charitable Irish Society minutes, 1840, PANS, MG20, vol. 67. In 1847 the following round of activity was reported in the Halifax press: January (sleighing party by the Union Engine Company); February (ball by the same); March (St. Patrick's Day banquet by the Charitable Irish Society); April (St. George's Day banquet by the St. George's Society); June (picnic by the Philanthropic Society); August (picnic by the Charitable Irish and North British societies); September (picnic by the St. George's Society); October (opening of the Mechanics' Institute's autumn/winter lecture series); December (St. John's Day banquet by the Freemasons), as noted by the following Halifax newspapers: *Acadian Recorder, Morning Post, Sun,* and *Times.*

11. Rudachyk, "Fire in Halifax," 125.

12. The Philanthropic Society declared that its members were "unwilling to have, their indigent brethren subsisting solely on the bounty of benevolent strangers," *Constitution,* 1. During the 1840s Alexander Keith, head of the Freemasons, gave high priority to establishment of a benevolent fund; see Longley/Harris, *Short History,* 58. Attendance at funerals by Freemasons and, later, others is noted by Halifax *Morning Herald,* 8 September 1843; Halifax *Sun,* 26 October 1847; Halifax *British Colonist,* 26 October 1848; Halifax *Times,* 15 December 1848.

13. Mechanics' Institute, *Rules;* Mechanics' Institute minutes, 7 April and 10 May 1840, PANS, MG20, vol. 222(A); Saint Andrew's, *Bye-laws,* 10; Charitable Irish, *Rules,* 11; Macdonald, *Annals* (1905), 233.

14. After considerable debate over membership policy the Mechanics' Institute opted to grant admission to anyone buying an annual admission ticket. The growing presence of women at lectures was described as a "cause for congratulations" since the "ladies" would "powerfully enforce . . . the importance and delights of intellectual pursuits." See Mechanics' Institute minutes, 6 May 1840, 5 October 1841, 2 May 1842, PANS, MG20,

vol. 222(A). Allegations that the firemen practised discrimination are to be found in Halifax *Sun*, 24 April, 13 November 1846, 5/10 March 1847.

15. At mid-century common labourers in Nova Scotia earned a daily wage of 2 to 3 shillings; skilled workers made 4 shillings. See Lt. Gov. Harvey to Col. Sect. Grey, 8 May 1848, PANS, RG1, vol. 120, f. 129. The seasonality of employment and high cost of living in the colony likely meant that none but master craftsmen (what contemporaries referred to as "mechanics") could participate in fraternal life. This theme is explored by Julian Gwyn, "'A little province like this': The economy of Nova Scotia under stress, 1812–1853," in D.H. Akenson, ed., *Canadian Papers in Rural History*, vol. 6 (Gananoque, 1988): 192–225; see also Judith Fingard, "'The winter's tale': The seasonal contours of pre-industrial poverty in British North America, 1815–1860," Canadian Historical Society, *Historical Papers* (1974): 65–94.

16. Philanthropic Society, *Constitution*. While data are incomplete, membership at mid-century probably stood approximately as follows: Union Engine Company and Axe Fire Company (124), Mechanics' Institute (100), Freemasons (300), St. George's Society (140), North British Society (200), Charitable Irish Society (230), Philanthropic Society (250). In 1851 Halifax had a population just over 20,000.

17. See not only the research of Blumin and Morris cited above but also Edward Pessen (ed.), *The Many-Faceted Jacksonian Era: New Interpretations* (Westport, CT, 1977).

18. Morris, *Class, Sect and Party*, 161–203. The Halifax situation is detailed in Tables 15.2 and 15.3.

19. Biographical information on voluntary society members has been gleaned from the following: *Cunnabell's City Almanack and General Business Directory* (Halifax, 1842); *Nugent's Business Directory of the City of Halifax* (Halifax, 1858); Nova Scotia census, 1838, PANS, RG1, vol. 448; Camp Hill Cemetery burial books, PANS, MG5, microfilm; Holy Cross Cemetery burials, PANS, MG5, microfilm; Halifax County Registry of Deeds. In addition invaluable assistance in identifying obscure people has been provided by Halifax genealogist Terrence M. Punch.

20. Colin D. Howell, "James R. DeWolf," *DCB*, XIII: 272–273.

21. C.B. Fergusson, "Lawrence O'C. Doyle," *DCB*, IV: 224–227.

22. J.M. Beck, "William Young," *DCB*, XI: 943–949.

23. When Caldwell first entered municipal politics, he was assailed by Liberal opponents for being "merely" a blacksmith: see Halifax *Morning Post*, 1/4 October 1840. For the later phase of his career see Halifax *Sun*, 21 May 1847; Halifax *British Colonist*, 3 October 1850; Halifax *Novascotian*, 7 October 1850. Mention of Caldwell's family background appears in A.W.H. Eaton, *The History of Kings County* (Salem, MA, 1910), 594–595.

24. L.K. Kernaghan, "Andrew Mackinlay," DCB, IX: 510.

25. K.G. Pryke, "Alexander Keith," DCB, X: 395–396.

26. Halifax *Morning Post*, 26 April 1845. The paper's publisher/reporter was J.H. Crosskill, a Freemason who delighted in providing his readers with local colour. Thanks to his own drinking, brawling and womanizing, Crosskill personally generated a large share of news about town. See, for example, Halifax *Acadian Recorder*, 22 February 1840, 24 July 1841, 25 June 1842, 6 February 1847 and Halifax *Morning Herald*, 26 July 1841.

27. Halifax *Morning Herald*, 20 March 1843. See also ibid., 26 April 1843 and Halifax *Morning Post*, 3 December 1844.

28. Halifax *Morning Post*, 28 June 1843.

29. Halifax *Times & Courier*, 26 April 1849.

30. Halifax *Acadian Recorder*, 23 March 1850.

31. Interracial harmony on this occasion was marred by partisan political controversy over whether Joseph Howe, now the Provincial Secretary, had compromised the dignity of his office by being overly-familiar with Halifax Blacks. See Halifax *British Colonist*, 3/6 August 1850; Halifax *Novascotian*, 5/12 August 1850. Black demands for civil rights are explored

by Judith Fingard, "Race and respectability in Victorian Halifax," *Journal of Imperial and Commonwealth History* 20: 2 (May, 1992): 169–195.

32. Halifax *Novascotian*, 12 June 1839.

33. Halifax *Times*, 14 September 1847; Halifax *Acadian Recorder*, 21 August, 4 September 1847; Halifax *Sun*, 3 September 1847.

34. Macdonald, *Annals* (1905), 264–265; Halifax *British Colonist*, 17/19 August 1848. Contemporaries would have been aware of the ethnic/sectarian violence then building in neighbouring New Brunswick. Analysis of that situation is provided by Scott W. See, *Riots in New Brunswick: Orange Nativism and Social Violence in the 1840s* (Toronto, 1993).

35. For the surge of temperance activity across America see Ian R. Tyrrell, *Sobering Up: From Temperance to Prohibition in Antebellum America, 1800–1860* (Westport, CT, 1979); W.J. Rorabaugh, *The Alcoholic Republic: An American Tradition* (New York, 1979.) See also Sandra Barry, "Shades of vice and moral glory: The temperance movement in Nova Scotia, 1828–1848" (M.A. thesis, Acadia, 1986).

36. Halifax *Novascotian*, 23 June 1842; Halifax *Morning Post*, 23 June 1842.

37. Sons of Temperance activity is reported in the Halifax *Sun*, 7/11/28 February, 12 April, 28 July, 21 August, 6 October, 22/24 November 1848; Halifax *Presbyterian Witness*, 26 August 1848.

38. Items on the Young Men's Temperance Society appear in the Halifax *Morning Post*, 28 October, 31 December 1847; Halifax *Sun*, 15 September, 11 October 1847, 17 November 1848; Halifax *Presbyterian Witness*, 18 March 1848; Halifax *Novascotian*, 21 August 1848.

39. Halifax *Female Temperance and Benevolent Society* (Halifax, 1844); Halifax *Morning Chronicle*, 13 March, 20 August 1844; Halifax *Novascotian*, 19 March 1849.

40. Halifax *Presbyterian Witness*, 29 January, 8 July 1848; Halifax *Novascotian*, 10 July 1848.

41. Halifax *Acadian Recorder*, 20 March 1841; Halifax *Morning Post*, 9 June 1842; Charitable Irish Society minutes, 17 August 1846, PANS, MG20, vol. 67; Halifax *Acadian Recorder*, 12 June 1847.

42. Halifax *Morning Post*, 9/11 June 1842, 10 June, 3 August 1843, 18 August 1845, 9 June 1846; Halifax *Morning Herald*, 9 June 1843; Halifax *Morning Chronicle*, 4 June 1844; Halifax *Sun*, 11 June, 11 July 1845; Halifax *Acadian Recorder*, 21 August, 4 September 1847.

43. Halifax *Sun*, 5/10 August 1846; Halifax *Morning Post*, 4 August 1846; Halifax *Times*, 11 August 1846; Halifax *Acadian Recorder*, 7 October 1848; Halifax *British Colonist*, 3 October 1848; Halifax *New Times*, 2 October 1848; Halifax *Novascotian*, 2 October 1848.

44. Halifax *Times & Courier*, 9/17 April, 12/26 May 1849; Halifax *British Colonist*, 15 May, 2 June 1849. For context see Bonnie L. Huskins, "Public celebration in Victorian Saint John and Halifax" (Ph.d thesis, Dalhousie, 1991).

45. Cornwallis actually arrived on June 21st. But in 1839, when celebrations of the founding began, it was apparently thought that the event had occurred some two weeks earlier. See Halifax *Novascotian*, 6/12 June 1839; Halifax *Church Times*, 8 June 1849; Thomas H. Raddall, *Halifax, Warden of the North* (Toronto, 1971), 22.

46. Halifax *Acadian Recorder*, 9 June 1849.

47. Halifax *British Colonist*, 12 June 1849. On the presence of women at urban festivities, see Mary Ryan, *Women in Public: Between Banners and Ballots, 1825–1880* (Baltimore, 1980).

48. Halifax *Times & Courier*, 9 June 1849. Murdoch's career is explored by K.G. Pryke, "Beamish Murdoch", *DCB*, X: 539–540. Overlooked in that account is the fact that Murdoch died an alcoholic. See PANS, MG100, vol. 74, #29.

49. Halifax *Sun*, 13 June 1849; Halifax *Novascotian*, 18 June 1849.

50. Halifax *British Colonist*, 12/21 June 1849; Halifax *Novascotian*, 25 June 1849; *Presbyterian Witness*, 7 July 1849.

51. The transition from voluntarism to advocacy of state intervention is discussed by R.J. Morris, "Voluntary societies," 116–118.

52. Halifax *Novascotian*, 29 July 1850. See also Isabella Lucy Bird, *The Englishwoman in America* (London, 1856), 21–23.

SIXTEEN

"A Proper Ideal during Action": Fraternity, Leadership and Lifestyle in Winnipeg Lawyers' Professional Culture, 1878–1900

RICHARD A. WILLIE

Scholarly accounts of the emergence of British and American professionalism in the late nineteenth and early twentieth century usually focus on two components of that development.[1] Organized efforts by professionals to achieve monopoly control over the provision of their knowledge-based mastery and expertise, and the combined actions of autonomous individuals possessing similar professional qualifications to attain social class mobility, normally receive the most attention. This has been at least as true for studies of lawyers as for other professions.[2] The corresponding development of professional culture, as well as the ideas and approaches undergirding it, however, has been a significant component of professionalism. Yet, until recently, the subject was largely ignored or simply underdeveloped.

Professionalism grew out of the transformation of Victorian thinking concerning appropriate career paths. It involved a set of ideals for measuring occupational status and became closely tied with the emergence of middle-class society. But while professionalism emerged as the desired goal of aspirants like lawyers, it required the foundation of a professional culture with which to transmit, reinforce and develop appropriate professional attitudes. Professionalism, in the words of one author, "was a culture — a set of learned values and habitual responses — by which middle-class individuals shaped their emotional needs and measured their powers of intelligence."[3]

By the turn of the century, professional associations in Canada were seeking to rationalize more effectively the transmission of these "dominant ideas and values of professional culture,"[4] ideas which included fraternity, hierarchy and conformity. In

Source: "'A Proper Ideal During Action': Fraternity, Leadership and Lifestyle in Winnipeg Lawyers' Professional Culture, 1878–1900," *Journal of Canadian Studies*, 27, 1 (Spring 1992): 58–72. Reprinted by permission.

an increasingly complex society, universities were asked to play a far greater role in fostering and perpetuating a sense of what Paul Axelrod calls "professional consciousness," and to thereby augment the traditional formal institutional vehicles of Law Societies and Bar Associations for carrying out this function among lawyers. While exceedingly important, a focus on such visible institutional developments frequently overshadows the less formal and extra-institutional means which professional men had previously used and were continuing to use to develop and communicate "professional consciousness" to each other. The first editor of the *Manitoba Law Journal*, John S. Ewart, then a prominent Manitoba lawyer, appears to have understood this well when he aptly referred to the necessity for transmission and development of such a professional "consciousness" as the constant need for conveying "a proper ideal during action."[5]

This paper contends that the presence of aspects of male fraternity which characterized lawyer contact, certain features of leadership among lawyers and lawyer lifestyle patterns all confirm that a dynamic, inchoate and informal professional culture was in place by 1900 in Winnipeg. The formal institutional changes normally involved in the professionalization process witnessed increasing efforts by lawyers, after a permanent Law Society was formed late in 1877, to solidify their autonomous status and to protect their image.[6] Lawyers in Manitoba, especially those in Winnipeg, revealed in a variety of lawyer-generated primary sources the broader informal dimensions of their particular legal culture as well. Discovering and investigating this informal "fringe" requires an understanding that lawyers' professional culture was, as one observer claimed, diffused "in society at large."[7]

A case in point are the private letters of Colin Campbell, a Winnipeg lawyer and future attorney-general of Manitoba.[8] In 1881 he wrote to his sweetheart in Ontario about how busy he was, especially, he claimed, "when you consider the four duties upon me, social, political, professional, and literary."[9] By expressing his understanding of his lawyer calling in this way, Campbell was also revealing his personalized sense of "professional consciousness." What in fact set him apart as a lawyer in the marketplace was his highly developed sense of duty. What Campbell clearly implied was his conviction that a successful professional career obligated him daily in many professional and public social transactions, which, taken together, were purposeful interactions and opportunities to enhance and confirm his professional stature. The limits of his professional culture, in other words, extended well beyond courts and law office. Doing his duty, then, meant carrying with him in all social circumstances "a proper ideal during action."

The most obvious formal means for imparting a particular set of social attitudes and values occurred during the apprenticeship of lawyers. Legal education, writes G. Blaine Baker, gave rise to a "form of social intelligence,"[10] which informed the ways that lawyers viewed the purpose of the law, legal structures and, of course, the place of their profession in society. Lawyers coming to Winnipeg during the 1880s, principally from central Canada and mostly from Ontario, had received the bulk of their formative legal socialization into the profession through their initial law training and exposure in the east. By the following decade, however, a majority of new lawyers were Manitobans, having received their formative education and orientation experiences in the province. Determining with any degree of certainty which aspects of this professional culture were derivative and which ones were due to localized conditions would be difficult if not impossible. Nevertheless, the creation of the informal buttresses of this institutionalized legal culture began to take shape almost immediately and were still actively developing in 1900.

MALE FRATERNITY

Several factors in the socio-cultural life of lawyers were equally as important as formal regulations, the pursuit of autonomy or even legal education, in shaping professionalism. One of those factors was the male fraternity that pioneer conditions in Manitoba emphasized.[11] Youthful and unmarried, except for a few of the more senior lawyers or judicial and government appointees who enjoyed circumstances sufficiently remunerative to consider marrying and establishing households, bachelor lawyers drawn to Winnipeg's attractive economic opportunities found that the rapid pace of urban growth in Winnipeg created a difficult housing shortage. The bachelor lawyer's world included hotels and rooming houses, often shared with other men in similar circumstances.

When Campbell arrived in 1881 the city was in the midst of a feverish land-speculation boom. Finding accommodations under such conditions was not an enviable task. Another young lawyer, George William Baker, later elected the mayor of Winnipeg, commented on the problem: "Fellows are always on the hunt. It is the greatest *bête noir* of Winnipeg."[12] Finding a suitable boarding arrangement where meals could be taken at the irregular times that their work demanded presented a challenge as well. The following summer, Colin Campbell and his lawyer roommate found it necessary to seek new lodgings because, as Campbell complained, the "old maids are a little cranky so we have taken a room and will henceforth take our meals at a restaurant where they are not put out if you do not get in to dinner at 1 o'clock sharp."[13]

Bachelor lawyers spent a good deal of time together. On one typical occasion, Campbell wrote, "tonight am going to a bachelor entertainment. My old Toronto friend Isaac Campbell & Mr. Hough . . . & several other lawyers live together in Bachelor quarters and they have expected a number of us around." He added that they expected "to have a good time."[14] While lawyers could scarcely afford to restrict their social contacts to other lawyers, such opportunities were useful for the conviviality they provided, and for the crystallizing of a professional community identity in an atmosphere where common goals were articulated or simply quietly understood. As boarding house roommates, while taking meals together in restaurants, while taking baths together in the Red River during the summer heat, while attending sporting or cultural events, or as fellow members of clubs and the church and on excursions as travelling companions, or while participating in sports, young lawyers established and regularly reinforced the bonds of a professional community.

Being together allowed lawyers to size each other up. Their personalities and foibles and, therefore, their reliability could be measured. Their ability to function or thrive in the competitive conditions that prevailed after the collapse of the real estate boom in 1882, and before economic conditions settled into a saner pattern of steady economic growth, soon became known to all. As the stress of competition among this male fraternity of lawyers increased, there were both winners and losers in terms of reputation. Reminding Minnie, his fiancée, that he intended to be a winner, Campbell wrote, "to build up an honorable reputation is my great ambition in my profession."[15] Campbell clearly understood that the reputation a lawyer obtained among his professional peers was essential for being invited to form satisfactory partnerships, for winning potentially lucrative clients' accounts, for becoming known for one's special legal expertise or interests, for obtaining coveted professional referrals, for being consulted concerning business prospects and for forging necessary business links between the West and the central Canadian capital sources. Pressing this knowledge to advantage, Campbell's professional capital increased as did his practice.[16]

Lawyers believed, as did many pioneers in Manitoba, that leisure which improved individual character was worthwhile; nowhere was this more evident than in their enthusiastic endorsement of various "manly" sports. These sports, claims one author, "both nurtured . . . manly qualities and symbolically revealed that true success went to those who possessed them." Such sports, it was believed, developed and displayed "desirable mental and moral attributes, things such as decisiveness, mental vigor and clearheadedness, determination, discipline, the spirit of fair play, loyalty and integrity." When they involved team participation, the "complex rule structures," the "strategic component" and the "reaction to a constantly changing situation" such games demanded made them especially attractive for lawyers.[17] For lawyers, manly sports were a symbolic reflection of the ideals and action that their professional knowledge and skill stressed, as well as a way to promote occupational fraternity.

Shortly after taking up residence in Manitoba, Campbell reported that his overall physical prowess was improving, which he attributed to favourable climatic conditions. Endorsing manly sports, he wrote that today "I have had two baths in the Red River. Yes I am a good swimmer and beat nearly all the boys. . . . I like athletics very much boating Cricketing etc. and I intend to go in for them more." By interrupting the daily routine of the law office with "about 20 minutes exercise upon the barbells," Campbell and his partners could also ensure that their minds and body were fit. He and other lawyers also enjoyed actively participating in team sports or merely watching lacrosse and other matches as, he admitted, a way of "generally forgetting about the law."[18] Fowl shooting or angling excursions, while less strenuous perhaps, further promoted male sporting contacts among lawyers and their clients.

Marriage and aging understandably altered the full pattern of sport and recreational participation of lawyers. Lawyers like Campbell often turned to less strenuous activities like mixed croquet or lawn tennis. Organizing and patronizing athletic clubs, however, was an indirect way of supporting such worthy endeavours, and lawyers' offices often hosted organizational meetings.[19] Popular games such as curling, which encouraged easy-paced conversation, grew in importance and could bridge age barriers. In January 1887, the *Free Press* reported that "In the curling contest last evening the legal luminaries defeated the 'way backs' . . . by a score of 13 to 10."[20] John S. Ewart was skip for the lawyers, a team which combined the legal talents of two firms.

During the 1890s younger Winnipeg lawyers continued to be attracted to more active games. By this time a fairly common configuration in larger urban centres like Winnipeg was team sports with "non-sport interest groups" based upon ethnicity, religious affiliation or a recognized employment category.[21] Team sports, therefore, could link lawyers with the pride of their occupational role and had the added attraction of displaying the character and talents of those who engaged in them. Hockey, which was played by teams of seven individuals with no substitutes, frequently on poor ice surfaces, and with play often interrupted by strenuous arguments over rule interpretations, seemed tailor-made for lawyers. Hockey enjoyed enormous popularity, requiring the physical attributes of speed, strength and endurance, and, like lacrosse and rugby, was valued because it also tested the mental and moral character of players.[22] Young lawyers and student apprentices could be formidable competitive opponents on the ice as well as in the courtroom and law office.

Quasi-official ceremonial gatherings or religious ritual occasions reminded lawyers and their public of the English traditions and historic status of the profession. The official observance by the Winnipeg legal fraternity of All Saints' Day in the fall of 1879, for example, led to a sardonic editorial observation that "inconsistent as it may seem the fraternity and the saints have a wonderful affinity for each other."[23] That affinity was revealed in other ways. In 1882 the Society invited all the leading citizens to the courthouse in Winnipeg to witness the unveiling of a commissioned portrait of Chief Justice E.B. Wood. Members of the profession on such occasions appeared appropriately attired in courtroom costume. When Wood died shortly afterwards, the Society took over complete control of the funeral arrangements. With lawyers firmly in charge of the obsequies, the marshalling order of the cortege of seventy carriages and the occasion itself emphasized both the hierarchy within the profession and the profession's claims to a notable place in society.[24] Honorary banquets like the special tribute organized by the Law Students' Society in 1884 as a farewell to members about to join Lord Wolseley's Nile expedition were similarly important times to cement necessary associational links.[25]

Social gatherings like Bar dinners, which brought lawyers together in a mood of celebration and perhaps envy, were especially useful means of invoking group standards and recognizing the style among peers which spelled success. Harking back to the ancient British barrister's tradition of dining at the Inns of Court, the idea of holding an annual Bar dinner found enthusiastic support among Winnipeg lawyers in the early 1890s. On one occasion J.S. Ewart, Q.C., as master of ceremonies guided the legal gentlemen gathered at the Clarendon Hotel through an astonishingly lavish menu, numerous toasts and convivial singing. The party reportedly "broke up in the early morning." A second annual dinner was equally extravagant, the tables being "most tastefully garnished with choice exotics." Justice J.F. Bain in his remarks hoped that this annual dinner would continue because of the part it played in the "fostering and promotion of a proper *esprit de corps*."[26] It should not go unsaid that the character of this professional fraternity was unabashedly a man's world. That women might wish to enter it was simply not entertained.[27]

PERSUASIVE LEADERSHIP

In the fluid circumstances that prevailed, the particular modes of leadership which evolved in Manitoba also underlined the importance of the informal aspects of professional culture. Long recognized as an important if not essential aspect in the shaping of academic professionals in scholarly circles, mentors must certainly have played a role in the lives of Winnipeg lawyers too. Gaining favourable notice was perhaps easiest for young men with fortuitous connections, but ambition, ability, intelligence and devotion to duty could attract the counsel and notice of senior professional colleagues. Campbell came to have a very high regard for his mentor, Alfred Hoskin, a Toronto lawyer who had taken a strong interest in him, offering him crucial assistance at key points in his career. Private and unsolicited intercessions on his behalf by

Hoskin had led to strategic placements and offers of partnership in Ontario and Manitoba. Admiring the style exhibited by Hoskin, Campbell exuded that "his acts of friendship are of that quiet unostentatious way that wins your best feelings."[28] Campbell's decision to remain in Winnipeg, though he was initially anxious about his prospects there, was influenced by his mentor's advice to stay put before trying any of the country towns to hang up his shingle. The full extent of the influence of mentors like Hoskin is impossible to measure in a systematic way because only glimpses of such connections are offered by lawyers in their private correspondence. Nevertheless, it is probably fair to say that spotting, advising and assisting promising young men in the profession was becoming a significant informal feature of Manitoba's professional culture. Campbell's deliberate recognition of this in his correspondence and his favourable references to a young Isaac Pitblado, who was to become one of Manitoba's outstanding lawyers in the twentieth century and later a recruited partner in Campbell's firm, suggests that Campbell, for one, had come to understand the value of such informal mentoring and recruiting.[29]

As important perhaps for understanding the unfolding nature of the professional culture in the province at this time was the role played by informal shapers of opinion. Efforts to establish permanent professional journals to acquaint, inform and shape the opinions of readers on issues of common concern were begun in Winnipeg on two separate occasions. J.S. Ewart's opportunity came in 1883, when the Law Society undertook to publish the first issue of the *Manitoba Law Reports*, and named him editor.[30] A jointly published periodical entitled the *Manitoba Law Journal*, which was published until July 1885, provided the frequently acerbic Ewart with a regular forum for disseminating his views on acceptable professional conduct and for presenting issues as he understood them. Emphasizing the importance of this role, Ewart claimed that, without a law journal "to keep guard in this matter," some lawyers in Manitoba were lamentably operating beyond the "limits within which a lawyer may attract public attention."[31] The areas he had in mind extended beyond the normal disciplinary powers of the Society. He especially objected to the then widespread practice of advertising through the "doubtful aid of newspaper puffs" which boldly declared the recent successes and capabilities of certain politically favoured lawyers. He was especially critical of advertising legal services when the advertisement was deliberately deceiving. With an eye to how lawyers influenced the "legal spaces" where they presented themselves, Ewart used the pages of the journal in his attempt to affect the behaviour of such "transgressors of propriety."[32]

Ewart vigorously condemned what he saw as "bullying" tactics in the atmosphere of the court and other offenses against decorum, concluding that most barristers should "prefer a less prominent position with esteem and friendship of the bar and public, than leadership won by inconsiderate and indiscriminate abuse of all opponents."[33] Apparently, Chief Justice Lewis Wallbridge was finding it very difficult then to exercise discipline over several flamboyant and consistently recalcitrant barristers in his courtroom, prompting the editor to make the following plea:

> Barristers, whose manners are in other places unimpeachable, seem to forget that the rules of civility and gentlemanly demeanor are for public as well as private life, and that it is, if possible, a more gross breach of culture to shout down one who is addressing a judge than to break in upon a friend's conversation. Respect must be shown for the judge as well as the one who is addressing him.[34]

Indicating that Ewart had struck a responsive cord, a reader responded with grave concern over the effect this kind of raucous behaviour would have upon the "training which our young men" were receiving.[35]

Maintaining a proper sense of respect for traditional formal courtroom apparel and appellations and transmitting an understanding of the purposes for them also fell to opinion-setters like Ewart and his fellow editors. Rules requiring attorneys to appear for trials properly attired in wigs and gowns were being ignored because Chief Justice Wallbridge was not insisting upon the same formality his predecessor had.[36] Also occasioning comment were the unusually large number of Q.C.s awarded in 1884. Such appointments conferred the right for some lawyers to claim they were "learned in the law," as well as a traditional right of precedence in court. Ewart had many reservations about Q.C.s and, despite agreeing to receive the honorific title himself, called for its abolition, not surprisingly to little effect:

> We object to the system because it gives one barrister a fictitious importance and dignity over his fellows. If nature has endowed him with greater ability or industry, that is no reason why the Government should add to his advantages, and, if his inclinations are political rather than professional, he should look for political and not professional awards.[37]

In 1890 at the age of twenty-two, Archer Martin, a savant with wide-ranging interests, strong opinions and demonstrated erudition, established and edited the *Western Law Times.*[38] It combined up-to-date law reports, as the *Manitoba Law Journal* had before it, with witty and trenchant articles and reviews. Self-appointed and uncompromising, Martin, as might be expected from a brilliant and impatient young man, fancied himself the conservative guardian of the conscience of the profession. As with Ewart before him, Martin's strength lay in helping to influence a degree of propriety in those "fringe" areas where lawyers needed to be reminded less formally of their duty to the profession. By the 1890s most, but not all, lawyers in the province had abandoned active forms of newspaper advertising to attract clientele. Tawdry advertising occupying space in newspapers was no way for lawyers to impart a dignified image, Martin thought. The solicitations of an enterprising pamphlet advertiser who promised that subscribers from the Bar would have their portraits in a proposed publication and could receive discount prices aroused Martin's ire, and he scornfully pointed out that "the most respectable members of the profession . . . have refused to listen to his [the pamphleteer's] blandishments, having enough self-respect to prevent their stooping to this most reprehensible form of touting."[39] Such open reminders combined with stronger and often silent peer disapproval could be most effective. More sensitive than most to the unique relationship between their own behaviour and public perceptions of the profession, such opinion-setters were prompted to speak out on unsavoury practices which reflected badly on everyone yet were normally outside the realm of the formal discipline channels available to the profession.

LIFESTYLE EXAMPLE

The responsibility for passing along desirable professional characteristics or traits to others fell partly to the models embodied in the lifestyles of legal men who either had won or were awarded prominence in the legal profession.[40] The professional lifestyle developed by such lawyers was a way of rationalizing behaviour which preserved the professional and social order, which, in turn, accorded them wealth and status. Revealed in a blend of social origin, education, interests and community contact, an exemplary lifestyle was a standard of rational behaviour to which aspiring lawyers might conform. Through the not always conscious operation of such lifestyle examples, the normal standards expected of lawyers were generally invoked in the context of their social life. Cultivating a professional image through one's "life" and "style," even though individual particulars varied, could convey to fellow lawyers and the public at large that a particular lawyer was competent, erudite, learned, socially graceful, politically astute, a worthy companion, and trustworthy. Lifestyle example, combined with professional fellowship and credible, persuasive and influential direction by informal leaders, was yet another opportunity and means available for guiding a proper ideal into action.

A properly conspicuous presence could be achieved in a number of ways: demonstrated stability, leisure, learnedness and purposeful social contact. An important benchmark of stability was marriage. Contemplating this, Colin Campbell proposed to Minnie, his future wife, claiming that in the law business "you know that the same confidence is not placed in unmarried men."[41] Obviously, marriage represented an important bridge to the social world of more established and senior lawyers and the associational and lifestyle advantages they enjoyed. For aspiring professionals in Canadian society, marriage was not entered into without future "stable economic prospects"[42] firmly in place or without sufficient income to support a spouse and expected progeny. Entering into marriage and establishing a household were clearly important steps. Campbell's bachelor friends in the profession understood this; nevertheless, they reminded him that his betrothal could drag on forever if it was wholly dependent upon Campbell's feeling financially secure before marrying. Writing a humorous yet pointed factum, they argued in favour of swift nuptials to his intended, who was obviously regarded as someone with other prospects.[43]

Measured by the social respectability that it could deliver, the quest for a suitable marriage partner was a matter not taken lightly. For the Winnipeg-based lawyers who were sons of the most prominent legal families in Canada, marriages confirmed their social standing and in some instances were quite clearly undertaken to cement linkages between themselves and elite families in central and Maritime Canada. For example, J.A.M. Aikins, son of the Lieutenant Governor of Manitoba, married the daughter of the Lieutenant Governor of Nova Scotia. Hugh John Macdonald, the Prime Minster's son, was married for his second time in 1883 to Agnes Vankoughnet, whose father, Lawrence, was a highly placed civil servant in Ottawa. Marriages such as these were visible symbols of success for other less well-connected lawyers to emulate.[44]

A well-chosen wife could advance a professional career. Sharing roughly the same values and attitudes, those couples who could afford them built substantial residences situated in pleasant neighbourhoods near the Assiniboine and Red Rivers. If able, they hired maid-servants, further emphasizing their social standing and stability. Colin Campbell, for example, found it necessary at the outset of his marriage to provide a maid for his wife.[45] It would seem that neither he nor she was willing to enter matrimony without substantial indicators of their future prospects in place. Perhaps as important in the context of late Victorian polite society, having a maid freed the wives of professional men to announce and host "at homes" or to engage in "calling," which one author has called the "central leisure activity of women of this milieu."[46] For lawyers with wives capable of engaging in such social niceties there were other potential benefits. Campbell, for one, valued his wife's efforts in helping to cultivate a warm social relationship between them and the province's first and most prominent Conservative family. In 1886, while his wife was away in Ontario, Campbell was invited to play cribbage, lawn tennis and cards on several occasions with the family of Premier John Norquay. Appreciating the role that she was actively playing in fulfilling his personal aspirations in professional life, he wrote "you are very popular with the Norquays. Mrs. Campbell takes the cake with them especially the Hon John." Candidly but pragmatically, Campbell told her, "I intend to ask him for some political favors on my return and that will be a good leverage."[47]

A substantial home, travel, leisure homes, and an abundant estate to bequeath to heirs were marks of material achievement not unlike those sought by the commercial elite.[48] By the turn of the century in Winnipeg the earliest residential homes established by lawyers near the administrative and commercial hub became increasingly undesirable due to congestion, unsightliness and smells. They were gradually replaced by homes with more spacious grounds in new suburbs which promised privacy and exclusiveness in addition to a safe and healthy environment. Clustered at a remove from the city's centre and in segregated neighbourhoods, their homes set lawyers apart both physically and socially from lower socio-economic classes and non-British elements in the city. Stewart Tupper's ostentatious thirty-room castle called "Ravenscourt," situated at Armstrong's Point, was an exception.[49] Nonetheless, the residential addresses of solid if more modest homes confirm a pattern that is typical of the well-to-do middle class in industrial cities elsewhere in Canada.

Travel undertaken for leisure, self-improvement or in order to recuperate, as in the popular pristine beauty and therapeutic hotsprings of Banff, attracted lawyers by the late 1890s, as did the construction of summer resort homes. Called "rural retreats" by Archer Martin, Lake of the Woods property was the most desired by Winnipegers.[50] Of course, not all lawyers could afford either rural retreats or large homes in Winnipeg, any more than they could lavishly appoint their law offices with all the trappings of success. But the very fact that some lawyers did established a commanding standard of lifestyle.

Much has been written concerning the challenges facing all lawyers on the eve of the twentieth century.[51] They were asked to respond to urbanization, industrial growth, technological change, the growth of labour and the demands of various reform movements, each of them rendering society more complex. This telescoping of societal change was in many ways paralleled by the increasing complexity of law practice and the demands that commerce was making on the lawyer's traditional approach and independence. Lawyers had always stressed their "gentleman," "statesman," "philosopher king" roles as underpinnings of public advocacy, normally to be displayed in the "spotlight of the courtroom or assembly hall."[52] By 1900 such images were being replaced rather quickly by one in which leading lawyers avoided public forums and advised their corporate business clients in the privacy of boardrooms on how to avoid litigation or how to secure favourable legislative terms. But in the period before 1900, the evidence suggests that lawyers in Winnipeg had not completely turned their backs on the traditional literary and oratorical exploits of the generalist lawyer.

A broad literary exposure was thought to augment the lawyer's knowledge of potentially useful information. Campbell's seriousness, initiative and devotion to literary duty in professional life were evident in his reading. "The true question in reading," he wrote, "is not what we receive but what we are made to *give* from our reading

that profits."[53] Speaking in public forums, especially the courts, was a normal extension of a lawyer's work, but it was also possible to advertise oratorical skills more generally and draw attention to the rhetorical flourishes or tightly argued logic that
lawyers potentially possessed. Some senior lawyers actively cultivated speechmaking
as an avocation. J.S. Ewart, J.A.M. Aikins and others had a talent for elocution and for
delivering entertaining presentations. Ewart's interests varied and he delivered public
speeches on topics ranging from the proper use of hypnotism to the ideas of Herbert
Spencer and Edward Bellamy. Obviously from an older school that valued this form,
Ewart penned his thought on the subject, arguing that of "all speeches the worst I
think is that in which a good chain of reasoning is dismembered by interjected bursts
of rhetoric."[54] Indicating that younger men were not as convinced of the merits of such
pursuits, a contemporary central Canadian commentator noted that for lawyers to be
known as poets with "genuine oratorical talent" was useful "but not essential."[55]

Few lawyers would have argued, however, that the pattern of purposeful public
and social contacts cultivated by their senior peers was not an aspect of their professional culture worth following. An essential part of maintaining purposeful social
transactions required that political contacts not be neglected. Some lawyers saw the
practice of law as a "stepping stone" to a political career and their involvement was
intended to prepare the way for their plunge into local, provincial or national politics.[56]
Political brokering of information and support by lawyers not directly involved in
political life took many forms, but for winning political favours or patronage, keeping lines of communication open was essential. Partners in well-established firms
could make confidential requests with the calm confidence and quiet assurance that
their requests would be treated seriously. For example, J.A.M. Aikins, Q.C., of Aikins,
Culver, Patterson and McCleneghan, though a Conservative Party supporter, wrote to
Liberal Premier Thomas Greenway after his election in 1888, providing him with
unsolicited letters making recommendations for government appointments.[57] At the
opposite end of the spectrum was E.M. Wood, son of the former Chief Justice, whose
star had fallen on hard times after his leaving the province earlier as a fugitive from
justice. Few would match his obsequious approaches. Seeking to gain a sinecure on
the strength of his father's notable reputation, Wood stooped to near begging: "I . . .
most certainly think that after all my father has done for this country and the Liberal
party throughout the whole Dominion of Canada, the giving to me of a paltry little
position would be only just. . . . It means bread for my wife & children this winter."[58]

Thoughtful lawyers certainly must have struggled with the question of how
extensively they might become involved in politics. As if to answer such queries, one
commentator in 1909 argued that the day of the eminent "lawyer-politician" was
quickly coming to an end.[59] In large urban practices devotion to duty in the realm of
either law or politics diminished one's capacity in the other. The exception was the
small-town or country lawyer, who faced neither complex specialized work nor vigorous competition. The commentator's message for younger men in the profession
was clear enough. They should not expect to follow the same steps to prominence that
their seniors had when they involved themselves heavily in political life.

While church membership was an indication of religious commitment and
denominational upbringing, it also was an opportunity for social contacts with other
lawyers and potential clients. Colin Campbell joined St. Andrew's Presbyterian and
was soon reporting that he "met an old friend Mr. Irvine of the Extra Life Insurance,"
adding that "it would be an excellent place for me to spend an occasional evening."

The membership of the congregation took account of his legal skills when he was elected trustee. Campbell wrote, we "got into a very legal difficulty and it has taken some time to remove the cloud off our lands and could only be done by resignation of old trustees, election of new ones and conveyance to them."[60] Professional culture's fringe extended in this instance to the narthex and church steps and to conversations by lawyers and businessmen and other weekday associates. Unfortunately, little of what was said remains, except for a few diary and letter entries.

The lawyer's lifestyle then enveloped a wide range of experiences not exclusively confined to the courtroom, law office or legislative chambers. Memberships in the prestigious Manitoba Club or fraternal orders like the Masons with their rituals and restricted memberships, ethnic organizations, community service boards and recreational clubs, and reform efforts all drew professional men into their orbit,[61] especially by the closing decade of the century, thus shaping and constantly reshaping the nature and context of professional culture.

Lawyers in Winnipeg revealed and elaborated their informal professional culture in the context of a male fraternal experience involving bachelor-support mechanisms, numerous convivial opportunities, reputation-making and manly sports. The leadership that mentors provided and the opinion-shaping persuasiveness of professional journal editors extended far beyond the disciplining power or rules of fixed legal institutions in shaping lawyer behaviour as well. Moreover, the lifestyle examples of other lawyers characterized by demonstrated stability, leisure activity, learnedness in literary or oral pursuits and the variety of purposeful social contacts they engaged in all belonged to the realm of lawyers' professional culture — not simply because they were inherently or completely professional in nature in all cases, but because lawyers did them and would have included them in their understanding of the duties of a legal life.

Less visible than the institutional devices of legal education or the activity of law societies for imparting professional standards and expectations and for demanding conformity and discipline, the informal aspects of professional culture offer a wider perspective from which to view professionalism. A sense of "professional consciousness" or "duty" in the lawyer's pattern of extra and intraprofessional experiences was an important part of becoming a lawyer, and for those lawyers wishing to excel in their profession it was equally important for becoming prominent in the profession. A concentration on the "fringe" areas of professional culture as this admittedly cursive glance has done provides an important perspective from which to view the genesis of a professional institution and to observe these legal carriers of middle-class aspirations in English Canada. For as one author suggested recently, expanding our knowledge of the legal profession demands moving our vantage point beyond the law.[62] Similarly, gaining a fuller appreciation of the origins of the middle class in Canada requires a much closer examination of the dominant values and experiences which emerged from the lives of professional men, and later women, at the turn of the century.

NOTES

1. Magali Sarfatti Larson, *The Rise of Professionalism: A Sociological Analysis* (Berkeley: University of California Press, 1977); Harold Perkin, *The Rise of Professional Society: England Since 1880* (London: Routledge, 1989).
2. Richard L. Abel, *American Lawyers* (New York: Oxford University Press, 1989); Richard L. Abel, *Legal Profession in England and Wales* (Oxford: Blackwell, 1988); David A.A.

Stager with Harry W. Arthurs, eds., *Lawyers in Canada* (Toronto: University of Toronto Press, 1990). Canadian historians are now becoming interested in this field. Curtis Cole, "A Learned and Honorable Body: The Professionalization of the Law in Ontario, 1870–1930," Ph.D. thesis, University of Western Ontario, 1986; and Peter M. Sibenik, "'The Black Sheep': The Disciplining of Territorial and Alberta Lawyers, 1885–1928," *Canadian Journal of Law and Society* 3 (1988), pp. 109–39 suggest a similar formal institutional emphasis. W. Wesley Pue, "'Trajectories of Professionalism': Legal Professionalism After Abel," *Manitoba Law Journal* 19 (1990), pp. 384–418; and W. Wesley Pue, "Becoming 'Ethical': Lawyers' Professional Ethics in Early Twentieth Century Canada," in Dale Gibson and W. Wesley Pue, eds., *Glimpses of Canadian Legal History* (Winnipeg: Legal Research Institute of the University of Manitoba, 1991) demonstrate the shortcomings of existing perspectives.

3. Burton J. Bledstein, *The Culture of Professionalism: The Middle Class and the Development of Higher Education in America* (New York: Norton, 1978), p. x. See also Daniel Duman, "The Creation and Diffusion of a Professional Ideology in Nineteenth Century England," *The Sociological Review* 27 (1979), pp. 113–38; and Alan Smith, "The Myth of the Self-Made Man in English Canada 1850–1914," *Canadian Historical Review* 59 (June 1978), pp. 189–219.

4. Paul Axelrod, *Making a Middle Class: Student Life in English Canada During the Thirties* (Montreal and Kingston: McGill-Queen's University Press, 1990), p. 66 and Chap. 4, "Professional Culture."

5. *Manitoba Law Journal* 1 (November 1884), p. 175. For biographical details on Ewart see R.C.B. Risk, "John Skirving Ewart: The Legal Thought," *University of Toronto Law Journal* 37 (1987), pp. 335–57; and Roy St. George Stubbs, "John S. Ewart: A Great Canadian," *Manitoba Law School Journal* 1 (1962–65), pp. 3–22.

6. Lee Gibson, "A Brief History of the Law Society of Manitoba," in Cameron Harvey, ed., *The Law Society of Manitoba* (Winnipeg: Peguis, 1977).

7. Philip C. Lewis, "Comparison and Change in the Study of Legal Professions," in Richard L. Abel and Philip C. Lewis, eds., *Lawyers in Society: Comparative Theories* (Berkeley: University of California Press, 1989), p. 45.

8. W. Leland Clark, "My Dear Campbell," *Manitoba Pageant* (Winter 1974), pp. 2–11.

9. Public Archives of Manitoba [PAM], MG14C6, Minnie Campbell Papers [MCP], Box 1, Colin to Minnie, 1 March 1881.

10. "Legal Education in Upper Canada 1775–1889," in D.H. Flaherty, ed., *Essays in the History of Canadian Law* Vol. 2 (Toronto: The Osgoode Society, 1983), p. 49.

11. In using male fraternity as a descriptive device, I perhaps should note that I am not referring strictly to male fraternal organizations, which were enormously popular among middle-class North American males. See Mark C. Carnes, *Secret Ritual and Manhood in Victorian America* (New Haven: Yale University Press, 1989).

12. PAM, MG14B2, G.W. Baker Papers, Diary, p. 13 (1881).

13. PAM, MCP, Box 1, Colin to Minnie, 15 July 1882.

14. Ibid., 12 January 1884.

15. Ibid., 15 June 1883.

16. An account of his strategy for developing a precorporate general practice is found in Richard A. Willie, "'It is Every Man for Himself': Winnipeg Lawyers and the Law Business, 1870 to 1903," in Carol Wilton, ed., *Beyond the Law: Lawyers and Business in Canada 1830 to 1930* (Toronto: The Osgoode Society, 1990), pp. 263–97.

17. Morris Mott, "The British Protestant Pioneers and the Establishment of Manly Sports in Manitoba, 1870–1886," *Journal of Sport History* 7 (1980), pp. 28, 29.

18. PAM, MCP, Box 1, Colin to Minnie, 14 July, 8 and 10 September 1883.

19. Notices such as one announcing a meeting of the Winnipeg Cricket Club to be held in the offices of Ewart, Fisher and Wilson were common. *Manitoba Free Press*, 9 January 1886.

20. *Manitoba Free Press*, 27 January 1887.
21. See Carl Betke, "The Social Significance of Sport in the City of Edmonton in the 1920's," in A.R. McCormack and Ian MacPherson, eds., *Cities in the West* (Ottawa: National Museums of Canada, 1975).
22. Morris Mott, "Flawed Games, Splendid Ceremonies: The Hockey Matches of the Winnipeg Vics, 1890–1903," *Prairie Forum* 10 (1985), pp. 169–87 emphasizes this point.
23. *Manitoba Free Press*, 1 November 1879.
24. Ibid., 15 July and 11 October 1882.
25. Ibid., 5 and 6 September 1884; see also Roy MacLaren, *Canadians on the Nile, 1882–1898* (Vancouver: University of British Columbia Press, 1978), chap. 5.
26. *Western Law Times* 2 (1891), p. 12; ibid., 3 (1892), p. 10. A copy of the elaborate four-page menu is located in PAM, MG14B21, Colin Campbell Papers, Box 2, 1892 folder.
27. The single exception to this arose when solicitor Clara Martin was admitted to the Ontario bar in 1897. See Constance Backhouse, "To Open the Way for Others of My Sex: Clara Brett Martin's Career as Canada's First Woman Lawyer," *Canadian Journal of Women and Law* (1985), pp. 1–41. The first application for admission by a female student in Manitoba was not submitted until Melrose Sissons did so in 1911. See Cameron Harvey, "Women in Law in Canada," *Manitoba Law Journal* 4 (1970), pp. 9–38.
28. PAM, MCP, Box 1, Colin to Minnie, 13 April 1882.
29. PAM, RG3A1, Attorney General Papers, Colin Campbell, Letterbook 3, 463, Campbell to Alfred Hoskin, 18 September 1903.
30. Archives of Western Canadian Legal History, A2793, Law Society Minutes, 5 and 13 October 1882. The *Reports* represented the first opportunity for the legal profession of Manitoba to enhance their legitimacy by exporting a tangible item of their legal culture. G. Blaine Baker, "The Reconstitution of Upper Canadian Legal Thought in the Late-Victorian Empire," *Law and History Review* 3 (1985), pp. 219–92 underlines that such exports were a mark of legal maturity.
31. *Manitoba Law Journal* 1 (April 1884), p. 63.
32. Ibid., (May 1884), p. 79 and "Rows in Court," p. 71.
33. Ibid., "Bullying Barristers" (May 1884), p. 67.
34. Ibid., (April 1884), p. 57.
35. Ibid., (May 1884), pp. 79–80.
36. Ibid.
37. Ibid., (December 1884), p. 178.
38. He edited the *Times* until 1894, when he moved to Victoria on his appointment to the Supreme Court of British Columbia, trial division. He was the author of *The Hudson's Bay Company Land Tenures* (1898).
39. *Western Law Times* 3 (1891), p. 103.
40. See William R. Johnson, "Education and Professional Life Styles: Law and Medicine in the Nineteenth Century," *History of Education Quarterly* (Summer 1974), pp. 185–207.
41. PAM, MCP, Box 1, Colin to Minnie, 28 June 1883.
42. See Peter Ward, Courtship, *Love and Marriage in Nineteenth Century English Canada* (Montreal and Kingston: McGill-Queen's University Press, 1990), p. 153.
43. PAM, MG14B21, Colin Campbell Papers, Box 1, Bodwell to Campbell, 6 October 1883.
44. These men were among the "newcomers" discussed in Richard A. Willie, "'These Legal Gentlemen': Becoming Prominent in Manitoba, 1870–1900," Ph.D. thesis, University of Alberta, 1989.
45. PAM, MCP, Box 1, Contract, 11 August 1884.
46. Sarah Carter, "The Woman's Sphere: Domestic Life at Riel House and Dalvernet," *Manitoba History* 11 (Spring 1986), p. 59.
47. PAM, MCP, Box 2, Colin to Minnie, n.d. June 1886; 20, 24 and 27 July 1886.

48. See Alan Artibise, *Winnipeg: A Social History of Urban Growth 1874–1914* (Montreal: McGill-Queen's University Press, 1975), chap. 2. The information contained in probated wills is also especially useful, when available, for viewing accumulated estate assets.

49. See Sarah Carter, "Armstrong's Point: Victorian Suburb in the Heart of Winnipeg," *NeWest Review* 13 (March 1988), pp. 4–5.

50. *Western Law Times* 3 (1892), p. 84; W.L. Morton, *Manitoba: A History* (Toronto: University of Toronto Press, 1957), p. 266. *Manitoba Free Press*, 30 July 1898 devoted a feature article to such leisure time pursuits.

51. A very good presentation of these themes is Gerald W. Gawalt, ed., *The New High Priests: Lawyers in Post–Civil War America* (Westport, CT: Greenwood, 1984).

52. James Forbes Newman, "Reaction and Change: A Study of the Ontario Bar 1880–1920," *University of Toronto Faculty Law Review* 32 (1974), pp. 55–56.

53. PAM, MCP, Box 1, Colin to Minnie, 29 October 1881.

54. *Manitoba Free Press*, 16 November 1897; PAM, MG14C22, J.S. Ewart Papers, Box 1, Letterbook 1, Ewart to H.W. Darling, 29 March 1889.

55. "Law and Lawyers from a Student's Point of View," *The Barrister* 2 (January 1896), p. 25. A most useful explanation for the demise of this once cultivated skill is Donald M. Scott, "The Vanished Profession: Public Lecturing in Mid-Nineteenth Century America," in Gerald L. Giesen, ed., *Professions and Professional Ideologies in America* (Chapel Hill: University of South Carolina Press, 1983).

56. J.R. Mallory, "The Lawyer in Politics," *Dalhousie Review* 30 (October 1950), pp. 229–36; T.H. Marshall, "The Recent History of Professionalism in Relation to Social Structures and Social Policy," *The Canadian Journal of Economics and Political Science* 5 (August 1939), pp. 325–40; W.H. Trueman, "Lawyers in Public Life in Western Canada," *Canada Law Times* 35 (1915), pp. 200–07.

57. PAM, MG13E1, Greenway Papers, 2, 325, J.A.M. Aikins to Honorable Thomas Greenway, 21 October 1889.

58. Ibid., 1, 158, E.M. Wood to Greenway, Private, 22 October 1888.

59. A.B. Morine, "The Place of the Bar in the Public Life of the Dominion," *Canada Law Times* 29 (1909), p. 155.

60. PAM, MCP, Box 1, Colin to Minnie, 22 February 1882, 18 January 1884.

61. Hugh J. Macdonald and J.A.M. Aikins, both temperance supporters, gave speeches to the Humane Society of Winnipeg in 1896. W.R. Mullock, a prominent lawyer in the temperance movement, was elected president of the Manitoba Temperance Society in 1892.

62. Wilton, ed., *Beyond the Law*.

TOPIC NINE
Popular Pastimes

The Canadian lacrosse champions of 1869, from Kahnawake. Sport became an important expression of local pride, class, and ethnic identity in the nineteenth century.

One of the greatest recent contributions of social history has been a rediscovery of the pastimes and amusements that formed an important part of popular culture. For many years, historians regarded the recreational and leisure activities of ordinary people as trivial and unworthy of serious examination. This perspective stemmed in part from a tendency to equate culture with refinement, the high arts, and the activities of the mind. Such an approach made culture the preserve of an educated and well-to-do elite. But in the 1960s and 1970s, social historians began to redefine culture to include all those activities and ideas that make up a way of life. Culture, they argued, was not limited to any particular type of activity or group but rather consisted of the many symbolic forms and everyday practices through which people express and experience meaning. Within this definition, previously neglected subjects such as public celebrations and sport acquired new significance.

The articles that follow clearly demonstrate that the study of popular pastimes and amusements provides a great deal of insight into the construction and maintenance of class, gender, and ethnic identities and the relations that exist between different social groups. In Article Seventeen, Bonnie Huskins examines the ways in which different types of public feasting reflected the structure of society in early Victorian Halifax and Saint John. Huskins maintains that the rituals associated with these events played an important role in expressing the participants' identity, position, and status. In Article Eighteen, on lacrosse in small-town Ontario in the late nineteenth century, Nancy B. Bouchier explores the use of sport by middle-class social reformers to control the behaviour of working-class youth and establish their own cultural hegemony. Both essays highlight the degree to which popular culture involves a struggle between subordinate and dominant groups in society.

QUESTIONS TO CONSIDER

1. If feasting and drinking was a mode of social communication, what meanings were conveyed by the different types of feasts in Halifax and Saint John? How did the rituals surrounding feasting and drinking help to define social boundaries? How does Huskins explain the gradual "gentrification" of such events?

2. In what ways did lacrosse as it was "reinvented" and organized embody middle-class assumptions about class, race, and gender in the late nineteenth century? How successful were middle-class reformers in using sport to assert their cultural hegemony?

3. Is popular culture better understood as something that is generated by "the people" or as something that is imposed on them from above?

SUGGESTED READINGS

DeLottinville, Peter. "Joe Beef of Montreal: Working-Class Culture and the Tavern, 1869–1889." *Labour/Le Travailleur*, 8/9 (1981–82): 9–40.

Francis, Daniel. *The Imaginary Indian: The Image of the Indian in Canadian Culture*. Vancouver: Arsenal, 1992.

Gerson, Carole. *A Purer Taste: The Writing and Reading of Fiction in English in Nineteenth-Century Canada*. Toronto: University of Toronto Press, 1989.

Howell, Colin. *Northern Sandlots: A Social History of Maritime Baseball*. Toronto: University of Toronto Press, 1995.

Jasen, Patricia. *Wild Things: Nature, Culture, and Tourism in Ontario, 1790–1914.* Toronto: University of Toronto Press, 1995.

Marks, Lynne. *Revivals and Roller Rinks: Religion, Leisure, and Identity in Late-Nineteenth-Century Small-Town Ontario.* Toronto: University of Toronto Press, 1996.

Metcalfe, Alan. *Canada Learns to Play: The Emergence of Organized Sport, 1807–1914.* Toronto: McClelland and Stewart, 1987.

Walden, Keith. "Respectable Hooligans: Male Toronto College Students Celebrate Hallowe'en, 1884–1910." *Canadian Historical Review,* 68 (March 1987): 1–34.

SEVENTEEN

From Haute Cuisine to Ox Roasts: Public Feasting and the Negotiation of Class in Mid-19th-Century Saint John and Halifax

BONNIE HUSKINS

We ought to have had our guns charged — Ay, and our glasses too, in readiness — so that the moment of the joyful event should reach the city — we would have nothing to do but "let go and haul."

(Saint John *Morning News*, 3 April 1840)

INTRODUCTION

One of the most popular and universal forms of celebration is feasting and drinking. Despite its popularity and universality, the public feast has not received sufficient scholarly attention from historians. Most of the historical studies on feasting focus on the role of the feast in medieval or early modern Europe.[1] The literature on the Victorian era tends to chronicle changing manners and eating habits in a rather antiquarian fashion.[2] An exception is Harvey Levenstein's *Revolution at the Table: The Transformation of the American Diet*, which examines "why and how [people in the 19th and early 20th centuries] change or do not change their food habits."[3] In the Canadian historiography, much of the recent literature centres on drink and responses

Source: "From *Haute Cuisine* to Ox Roasts: Public Feasting and the Negotiation of Class in Mid-19th-Century Saint John and Halifax," *Labour/Le Travail*, 37 (Spring 1996): 9–36. © Canadian Committee on Labour History. Reprinted by permission of the editor of *Labour/Le Travail*.

to drinking, in the form of the temperance and prohibition movements.[4] While the experience of drinking in the Victorian era is currently being dissected by scholars such as Judith Fingard, who graphically portrays the consequences of alcoholism on recidivists in *The Dark Side of Life in Victorian Halifax*, James Sturgis, who describes the Rennie family's battle with alcohol in 19th-century Canada, and Cheryl Krasnick Warsh, who examines the "drinking woman" at the turn of the century,[5] more emphasis needs to be placed on "what lay behind . . . the fervid advocacy of temperance" and moral reform.[6] We also need more analyses of the experience of eating (as well as drinking) in 19th-century Canada. Thus, the primary objective of this paper is to delineate a typology or hierarchy of public feasts in mid-19th-century Saint John and Halifax, which will provide us with an alternate lens through which to view class and culture. Joseph Gusfield has commented that "what is eaten and how it is eaten constitute a mode of communication and can be read as a cultural object, embodying the attributes of social organization or general culture."[7] In the popular bestseller *Much Depends on Dinner*, Margaret Visser similarly notes: "Food — what is chosen from the possibilities available, how it is presented, how it is eaten, with whom and when, and how much time is allotted to cooking and eating it — is one of the means by which a society creates itself and acts out its aims and fantasies."[8] While an analysis of feasting and drinking can provide many insights into the nature of society, this paper will focus on how we can use food and drink as markers of class and as instruments in the process of class formation. This emphasis on food, drink, and social relations is borrowed from structuralists like anthropologist Mary Douglas and sociologist Pierre Bourdieu, who argue that "food categories encode social events, as . . . they express hierarchy, inclusion and exclusion, boundaries, and transactions across boundaries."[9] Mary Douglas has noted that "we need to stop thinking of food as something that people desire and use apart from social relations . . . It is disingenuous to pretend that food is not one of the media of social exclusion."[10] Did feasting and drinking in mid-19th-century Saint John and Halifax help to define the boundaries of inclusion and exclusion, as suggested by these social scientists?

In order to answer this question, it will be necessary to explore the various meanings and uses of public feasts. Why did people in different classes partake of "victuals" and "spirits"? How does this reflect their different priorities and social practises at mid-century? Mary Douglas argues that "the ordinary consuming public in modern industrial society works hard to invest its food with moral, social, and aesthetic meanings." If we do not seek out these meanings, "festivities [will be] treated as illegitimate demands on the world's productive system, the source of social inequalities and ultimately responsible for the maldistribution of food," clearly an incomplete and misleading understanding of such events.[11] In this paper I will systematically explore the meanings of the public feast for the middle-class and working-class inhabitants of mid-Victorian Saint John and Halifax. Emphasis will be placed on public secular feasts — that is, the banquet, ox roast, institutional repast, and tea and coffee soirée — which were held to commemorate royal and patriotic anniversaries. The most notable celebrations in this analysis include the observance of Queen Victoria's coronation in 1838 and her marriage in 1840, the birth of the Prince of Wales in 1841, and the celebration of his visit in 1860 and his marriage in 1863. This is by no means meant to be a comprehensive analysis of feasts or celebrations. The focus here is on public secular feasting — I will not be dealing with religious feasting or the private dinner. It is only through these local micro-studies that we can effectively "get at" the meanings associated with food and drink. As Mary Douglas notes: "The meanings of food need to be studies in small-scale exemplars."[12]

What role did drinking and feasting play in the creation and dramatization of class distinctions in mid-Victorian Saint John and Halifax? All classes dined and imbibed at mid-century; it was a "heavy-eating, hard-drinking age."[13] Residents could choose from a wide variety of taverns and saloons. In 1830, Saint John issued 206 tavern licenses and 29 retail licenses, which meant that 1 citizen in 50 held a liquor seller's license. Halifax contained 200–300 drinking houses and shops by the 1860s, approximately 1 drinking establishment for every 100 inhabitants, including women and children.[14] Many working-class recreations "centred on the tavern," and liquor had also become an "integral part of the work culture." Respectable men and women largely confined their drinking to the home or to more exclusive venues. Eliza Donkin, a young Victorian woman from Saint John, noted the "habitual use of liquor in the family circles."[15] National societies often celebrated their anniversaries with annual banquets.[16] Celebrants also dined in observance of certain *rites de passage*, Christmas, and other high days and holy days, as well as during commemorative celebrations. Although all classes drank and feasted, did they do so in the same way and for the same purpose? Indeed, it is the argument of this paper that different forms of feasting reflected and reinforced contemporary class divisions. Middle-class and elite residents, for example, drew their social circles tighter by partaking of exclusive indoor banquets.

BANQUET

The banquet, a frequent accompaniment to the grand ball, was one of the most long standing and popular elite entertainments. Judith Fingard mentions the ball (and banquet) as one of the leisure activities which united the "well-to-do" in the winter months in pre-industrial Canada.[17] Private citizens, provincial and civic officials, and voluntary organizations usually orchestrated the entertainments. Saint John's common council hosted a "corporation dinner" in honour of Queen Victoria's coronation in 1838.[18] Two years later, the lieutenant governor of Nova Scotia marked Queen Victoria's marriage by holding a ball and banquet, as did members of the North British Society, Highland Society, and St. George's Society.[19] In Saint John, similar entertainments were given by the "Victoria Club," a volunteer company, and the Freemasons.[20] A committee of private citizens and government officials organized the dinner and dance held in honour of the visit of the Prince of Wales to Halifax in 1860.

Balls and banquets promoted exclusivity by restricting attendance to a clique of local, provincial, imperial, and military dignitaries, and by charging a relatively high subscription or admission price for everyone else. A perusal of the guest list for Saint John's "corporation" banquet in 1838 shows that it mainly consisted of civic and provincial officials, military and militia officers, and commercial and mercantile elites (see Table 17.1). One local correspondent complained:

> a dinner to fifty persons, including the corporate body is not in form or intent a public festival, but merely a private concern apparently to answer some party, and to gratify a few persons at the expense of the public.[21]

"A Bluenose" requested that the idea of an exclusive ball and banquet be abandoned for Halifax's coronation celebration, and that the day be

TABLE 17.1 *List of Guests for Corporation Dinner at Coronation, Saint John, 1838*

Mayor	Robert F. Hazen
Recorder	William B. Kinnear
6 Aldermen —	Henry Porter, John Humbert, Thomas Harding, Gregory Van Horne, Robert Salter, George Bond
6 Assistants —	John Knollin, Lewis W. Durant, Wm Haggerty, Ewan Cameron, Thomas Coram, Joseph Beatteay
Common Clerk	James Peters, Jr.
Dy Common Clerk	James William Boyd
Sheriff	James White
Coroner	James T. Hanford
Hon. William Black	Legislative Council
Hon. Hugh Johnson	Executive Council
Hon. Charles Simonds	Executive Council
Mr. Barlow	Thomas, House of Assembly, Saint John City
Mr. Woodward	Isaac, House of Assembly for Saint John City
Mr. Partelow	John R., House of Assembly, St. John County
Mr. Jordan	John, House of Assembly, St. John County
Lt. Col. Benjamin L. Peters	Saint John City Militia, 1st Batt.
Lt. Col. Charles Ward	Saint John City Militia, Rifle Batt.
Lt. Col. George Anderson	St. John County Regt.
President of the Bank of N.B.	Solomon Nichols
President of the City Bank	Thomas Leavitt
President of the Whaling Co.	Thomas Nisbet
President of the Water Co.	Lauchlan Donaldson
Chief Justice	Hon. Ward Chipman
Judge Parker	Robert, Supreme Court
Coll. of Her Maj's Customs	Henry Bowyer Smith
Master of the Rolls	Hon. Neville Parker
President of St. George's Soc. John V. Thurgar	
President of St. Andrew's Soc. John Robertson	
President of St. Patrick's Soc. Thomas L. Nicholson	
Rev. B.G. Gray	Benjamin G., Rector of Saint John, Anglican
Rev. Mr. Gray	I.W.D.?, AM, Asst. Missionary at Saint John
Rev. Mr. Coster	Ven. George, AM, Archdeacon, Church of England or Frederick, Rector of Carleton
Rev. Robert Wilson	Church of Scotland, Saint John
Rev. Enoch Wood	Wesleyan, head for Saint John Station
Rev. Stephen Bamford	Wesleyan, Supernumerary
Re. Mr. Dunphy	James, Catholic, Saint John
Treasurer B. Robinson	
Judge of Probate	Henry Swymmer, surrogate, Saint John
Attorney General	Hon. Charles Jeffrey Peters
President of St. John Marine Ins., J. Kirk	

TABLE 17.1 *(continued)*

....

President of St. John Bridge Co., W.H. Street[a]	
Col. Goldie	C. Leigh, CB, 11th Regt., Army
Col. Bishop	Lt. Col., Commandant, 11th
Col. Mercer, R.A.	
Commissary W.H. Robinson	William, Asst. Commissary General
Commissary Goldsmith	Oliver, Asst. Commissary General
Cap. Whinyates	Frederick W., Commanding Royal Engineers
Cap. Evans, RA	Mark
Cap. Armstrong, RA	
Lt. Gordon, RA	
Serg Major Shombray	
Cap. Richmond	M., 11th
Cap. Richardson	I., 11th
Lt. Moore	E. Adjutant, 11th
Lt. Gould	Goold, James, 11th
Lt. Colburn	Cockburn, Alexander, 11th
Lt. Boyd	Lewis, A., 11th
Lt. Brown	Browne, Alexander, 11th
Paymaster Boyd	Alexander H., 11th
Quarter Master Worsley	
Ensign Cox	Symes, 11th
Town Major John Gallagher	
Mr. Frith, Ordnance	Frederick C., Ordnance Dept., Store Keeper and Barrack Master, Army
Hon. E. Botsford	Amos E., Executive and Legislative Councils
Col. Otty	Allen, Commandant, Saint John Sea Fencibles
Mr. Grant, Coll., St. Andrews	Alexander, Collector, Port of St. Andrews
John Ward, Sr., Esq.	Merchant (timber), Shipowner[b]
George Harding, Esq.	Merchant[c]
Daniel Ansley, Esq.	Tanner[d]
Craven Calvary, Esq.	Victualler[e]
Isaac Olive, Esq.	Shipbuilder[f]
Mr. John Clark, Sr.	Baker[g]
Benjamin Stanton, Esq.	Blacksmith/Shoemaker[h]

[a] IN THE *ALMANACK*, 1838, HE IS A DIRECTOR; JOHN ROBERTSON IS THE PRESIDENT.

[b] ACHESON, *SAINT JOHN*, 52, 63.

[c] CARD CATALOGUE, UNDER "HARDING, GEORGE," SJRL.

[d] REGISTER OF VOTERS, 1809, SHELF 46, SJRL.

[e] REGISTER OF VOTERS, 1785–1862, SHELF 46, 13, SJRL.

[f] WARD SCRAPBOOK, 2ND LOT, SHELF 19, 356, 357, SJRL.

[g] D.R. JACK, *NEW BRUNSWICK FAMILIES, ESPECIALLY OF LOYALIST DESCENT*, VOL. 1, 220–1, SJRL.

[h] REGISTER OF VOTERS, 1795, SHELF 46, SJRL.

....

Source: The information in the left column was transcribed from "List of Guests for Corporation Dinner at Coronation, 1838," in Robert F. Hazen Papers, Box 2 Shelf 36, File 15, #29 [NBM]. The information in the right column was collected from the *New Brunswick Almanack* (Saint John 1838, 1839), except where noted.

spent in a manner in which all could enjoy themselves; — the halls of our Provincial Building have been desecrated enough already. This cannot be the case with a public ball [and banquet], which, make it as public as you please, will not be attended by the generality of the community. It would be more highly prized, (as I doubt not they will also think), if His Excellency, the Army, the Navy, and those in high rank among our civilians, would for this occasion, unbend as much of their exclusiveness as would be proper, and encourage and patronise such amusements as all without exception, high and low, rich and poor, may participate in with exultant satisfaction.[22]

Organizers of the ball and banquet held for the Prince of Wales in Halifax in 1860 restricted admission to 250 invitations and 1000 tickets, priced at a restrictive two sovereigns for a man and one sovereign for a woman. According to the *Evening Express*, these prices kept the attraction "a rather more aristocratic affair than it otherwise would have been."[23]

Such events provided an opportunity for the display of respectability, breeding, and refinement. Thorstein Veblen has remarked that "conspicuous consumption" is *prima facie* evidence of one's "pecuniary success" and "social worth."[24] "A Bluenose" described the typical ball and banquet as an event at which

Tom, Dick, and Harry, tag, rag, and bobtail, might have an opportunity of displaying their breeding before the wives and daughters of the big wigs; and the wives and daughters of the little wigs an opportunity of being laughed at by Tom, Dick, and Harry, by Lord Somebody, and the honble [sic]. Mr. Nobody, or the red-coat and blue-coat schools. No such thing Mr. Editor — by the powers! — this is not the way the Coronation of Her Majesty should be observed in any of her dominions — at home or beyond the seas.[25]

The dinners served at these events were notable for the "strict rules" governing the "presentation of food, the varieties permitted at a given occasion, and rules of precedence and combination."[26] The menu for the Prince of Wales' marriage feast at the Halifax Hotel in 1863 is an example of 19th-century *haute cuisine*. Many of the dishes featured in the bill of fare are French in origin. Indeed, culinary respectability has been associated with French (and Italian) cooking since the exchange of cooks and recipes among the "courtly strata" in the Middle Ages.[27] However, the 19th century witnessed the "full establishment of a French international culinary hegemony," not only in Europe, but in North America as well, as the great French chefs fled from their aristocratic employers after the Revolution, and set up their own restaurants, and wrote cooking manuals, which disseminated their culinary arts.[28] Most of these French dishes were rather "fussy" items, noted for their sauces. Some of the simpler English dishes did survive the French culinary onslaught, particularly the basic meat items. The caterer of the Halifax banquet undoubtedly consulted one of the cooking manuals written by these French chefs, for many chefs like Alexis Soyer specialized in organizing and catering grand banquets, like the one in Halifax.[29]

The courses served at the Prince of Wales' marriage feast resemble those associated with "service à la française." "Service à la française" was a tradition of serving dinner dating back to the Middle Ages, and was characterized by three set courses and dessert. Soup and/or fish comprised the first course. The second course consisted of the meat dishes, divided into "entrées" (fancy side dishes, usually of French origin) and "relevés" (larger and plainer items, usually English in origin). The third course was usually game and/or shellfish, followed by dessert (sometimes divided between "relevés" and "entremets"). Proponents of "service à la française," as evident in this menu, also offered a number of options in each course, and served them all simultaneously, like a modern buffet.[30]

In the 1860s, "service à la russe" made its appearance in England and France, although it was not universally followed until the 1870s–1890s. The main difference between "service à la française" and "service à la russe" was that, in the latter, the servants carved and portioned the meal, and served the dishes in pairs or sets of alternatives. Dishes were passed around and not laid on the table; also, menus were distributed.[31] This gave the hosts more time to entertain their guests and "drew attention to the quality and sophistication of individual dishes."[32] The Prince of Wales' marriage feast in Halifax reflects "service à la russe" in that menus were evidently printed, and courses listed as sets of alternatives in the bill of fare. However, it is not known whether or not the dishes were served this way by the servants; also, the courses themselves still reflect "service à la française." Regardless, Haligonians evidently found it important to structure their banquets according to typical middle-class rules of etiquette. This structure undoubtedly helped to define the banquet as "one of the weapons in the social armory" of respectability and exclusivity.[33]

The nature of the wines served at such events also expressed class identity. Mary Douglas reminds us: "We must take note of the exclusionary potential represented by the serried ranks of vintage and lesser wines . . ."[34] For the banquet held in Halifax in 1860 in celebration of the visit of the Prince of Wales, the organizing committee selected 12 dozen sherries, 31 dozen high quality champagnes, including 23 dozen of "Mumm's," and 28 dozen of the cheaper wines.[35]

Banquets also reinforced middle-class masculinity. Although the ball was one of the only celebratory activities in the mid-Victorian period in which middle-class women could actively participate,[36] they usually retired from the banquet table before the toasts began because public drinking was primarily a male ritual. The men often raised their glasses in honour of the women, but such "accolades" were only "minor and perfunctory exercises."[37] According to Levenstein, women were also expected to show greater "gastronomic restraint."[38]

The list of toasts at such affairs acknowledged the hierarchy of colonial society. Royal occasions particularly paid tribute to the lieutenant governor, as the Queen's representative. At Saint John's corporation dinner in 1838, those present acknowledged Lieutenant Governor Sir John Harvey and his actions in the recent border war with the United States.[39] Toasts were also customarily extended to Queen Victoria and the royal family, the colonial secretary, the governor general, the British officers and the army and navy, the provincial administration, the sister colonies, the lieutenant governor's wife and the "fair daughters" of the colonies, and other special guests.[40]

Thus, the balls and banquets held during public celebrations in the early-to-mid 19th century promoted exclusivity and respectability by restricting attendance, encouraging displays of opulence and finery, serving *haute cuisine* and fine wines, and toasting and thereby reinforcing the status quo, including the inequalities of class and gender.

OX ROAST

Celebratory regalement was not confined to the middle and upper classes. The general public also partook of "great outdoor feasts where massive quantities of meat, game, and liquor were consumed."[41] The Nova Scotia Philanthropic Society inaugurated the custom of having an annual picnic to celebrate the founding of Halifax.[42] The first natal day picnic at the Prince's Lodge in 1839 consisted of an "abundance of viands and lots of good liquor to moisten them." Similarly, approximately 300 people enjoyed a feast of "fish, flesh, and fowl" during the 1845 picnic.[43]

Larger outdoor feasts were also held in the public squares and commons. It is significant that the feasts provided for the general public and the poor took place out of doors. One reason was pure logistics. Organizers did not have the facilities sufficient to accommodate large crowds. But the "out of doors" also conveyed images of democracy and freedom which suited the mass demonstration. In a letter to the editor of the *Morning Journal*, a Haligonian admitted that the "Codfish Aristocracy" had every right to hold a ball and banquet for the Prince's visit in 1860, and to set the admission so high that "plebeians" could not attend, but it was not so with outdoor demonstrations, which "ought to be every person's business, and every person's privilege to share in."[44] The *Acadian Recorder* also described the out of doors as "the proper field for a full and unrestrained feast of enjoyment."[45]

In 18th- and early 19th-century England, public outdoor feasts functioned as instruments of paternalism organized by the British gentry, well-to-do farmers, and members of the local government, on such occasions as the completion of the harvest, and historical and patriotic anniversaries.[46] In mid-Victorian New Brunswick, ruling merchants in single industry towns provided similar feasts, as in Chatham, where Joseph Cunard provided free food and drink for the working-class inhabitants dependent on his sawmills and mercantile enterprises.[47]

Providers of outdoor feasts in the more complex urban centres of Saint John and Halifax also wished to gratify the masses and ensure their own popularity. In Saint John, the onus for such meals lay primarily with the mayor, aldermen, and assistants, who were primarily artisanal in makeup.[48] Most of the common council's appropriation for Queen Victoria's coronation and marriage festivities in 1838 and 1840 went toward the provision of outdoor feasts for the public. In 1838, the council allocated £332/16s/3d for the public "repast" (compared to only £115 for the corporation banquet and £7/10s for a supper in the city jail).[49] Of the £250 earmarked for the marriage celebration in 1840, £210 was expended on outdoor feasts, £30 for dinners in the charitable and penal institutions, and £10 for gun powder for the militia.[50] During the coronation festivities, two aldermen and assistant aldermen cut up and distributed the food in their constituency on the west side (Carleton), symbolizing the central role of the common council in providing "victuals."[51] Since Halifax was not incorporated until 1841, private citizens and provincial and imperial officials organized and financed the events in 1838 and 1840. In addition, the Nova Scotia Philanthropic Society sponsored outdoor feasts for the Mi'kmaqs in 1840 and during the Halifax centenary in 1849. During its first year, the Halifax city council conformed to the Saint John practice by superintending a spread for the poor.[52]

The provision of these feasts was based on the premise that a full stomach ensured favourable and loyal sentiments. "A Looker On" observed that Carleton's coronation feast in 1838 produced "an effect on the people, calculated to call forth the best feelings toward the parent state and our youthful and maiden Queen." By the same token, the lieutenant governor of New Brunswick thought that the Queen's marriage celebration in Saint John should involve the poor, and thus "promote a happy spirit of social union, harmony, and loyalty among them."[53]

Gratuitous feasts can also be understood as an expression of philanthropy. The well-to-do were "goaded by tender consciences and insistent churches" to provide for the poor as a "christian duty." Many believed the maxim that the rich man's "wealth is a talent, for the employment of which he must hereafter render an account."[54] Providers also responded to popular demand; the public expected good deeds during such occasions, just as the English gentry were "obliged by custom to make disbursements for recreations."[55] The *Acadian Recorder* saw the voluntary offerings of the elite during Halifax's coronation celebration in 1838 as

> the contribution of all, whom fortune has blessed, with the means of bestowing happiness to others, and testify to the whole world how highly Nova Scotians value the privilege and honour of belonging to the British empire, having a direct interest and concern in the grand constitutional ceremony which consecrates VICTORIA our Queen.[56]

The public feast also had great ritual significance. The selection of the ox as the favoured entrée for these public feasts can be explained partially by its capacity to feed a large number of people, but also by its symbolism. Feasts were based on "mythical or historical events" which were "re-enacted . . . through symbols and allegories."[57] According to Hugh Cunningham, roast beef, plum pudding, and ale revived images of John Bull and Merrie England, and were considered part of the English "birthright." In the latter half of the 19th century, Victorians adopted these staples as "sacraments" in a "continuing mythology of national superiority and class identity."[58] Ritual significance also accompanied the practice of roasting the ox. In proposing an ox roast for the poor on the Grand Parade in Halifax in 1838, a correspondent referred to it as "an imitation of good old English hospitality."[59] The ox roast also had pagan roots and, as such, exhibited ritualistic behaviours and traits developed through custom and precedents.[60] Before the barbecue, participants adorned the ox with ribbons in imitation of "sacrificial garlands," and processed with the animal as during pagan sacrificial rituals.[61] In Saint John in 1838, the ox was led on its cortege by a black man named Jim Brown, probably a butcher, for later he carved the ox after it had been slaughtered and roasted. Butchers often marched with oxen during trades processions, afterwards slaughtering them and distributing the meat as alms.[62]

The class makeup of those who attended these events is difficult to determine. It is clear that the providers were primarily artisanal (in the case of Saint John), and middle class (in the case of Halifax). It is also clear that these providers intended the repasts primarily for the working class and the poor. While the "rich" could "partake [of public feasts] if they pleased," Alderman John Porter of Saint John contended, the "poor should be especially invited."[63] Some middle-class feasters did attend, often distancing themselves from the crowds in private marquees and tents. During the Halifax coronation celebration, an exclusive clientele patronized a private marquee on the common, where "Her Majesty's health was drunk with the utmost possible enthusiasm." The Charitable Irish Society of Halifax erected a "hospitality tent" during the coronation celebration and the centenary in 1849, where "members could refresh themselves . . . and dance."[64] It is probable, however, that most of the people who attended ox roasts were working-class in origin, given the increasingly non-respectable image and reputation of such events.

What did outdoor repasts mean to the working-class participants who partook of them? First and foremost, the public feast was a source of free food and drink. As in

18th-century America, ceremonial occasions and holidays determined the type of meal to be eaten by the "lower orders."[65] The public dined not only on ox meat, but on other foodstuffs as well. In 1838, Saint John's common council provided barrels of bread baked into small half-pound loaves, plum pudding, and two hogsheads of ale. During the Queen's marriage celebration in Saint John in 1840, the people on Saint John's east side consumed 36 hams, 35 rounds of boiled corned beef, and a large quantity of cheese, as well as 8 roasted sirloins, 1250 pounds of bread, and 120 gallons of wine and ale. In King Square, servers also cut up and distributed a large wedding cake.[66] The prevalence of large fatty joints and sweets, and the paucity of vegetables and fruits, reflects the general nature of the working-class diet in 19th-century America.[67]

Although a Saint John newspaper congratulated the citizens in 1840 for "not having outraged *all* decency," a little "irregularity" was observed, which suggests that some tried to commandeer more than their fair share, a reflection of the tendency of the poor in pre-industrial Canada to "feast and be merry" during seasons of plenty.[68] Saint John's *Morning News* satirized the public's perception of the Queen's marriage feast as an opportunity for gluttony, in the form of a "letter" written by a "servant" named "Dorothy Prim":

> Tables are to be spread in King and Queen square for the poor people to stuff themselves at; and Sam says I shall have a cut of roast beef, and whatever else is goin. I do hate this livin on Gaspereau all one's life.[69]

Although this letter was undoubtedly a satirical creation of the editor, it still reflects actual sentiments among the working-class inhabitants of Saint John and Halifax, for they did complain about having to rely on fish.[70] Thus, in this context, the ox roast can be seen as a diversification of the regional working-class diet.

Homeless children also enjoyed the feast organized in honour of Queen Victoria's marriage in 1840:

> Ragged urchins about the streets, were upon the alert much earlier than usual, and strained their treble pipes more outrageously than ever to testify their joyful anticipation of roast beef and cake.[71]

Roast beef and cake were also anticipated by those who found themselves in poor houses and public carceral facilities during public celebrations.

INSTITUTIONAL REPAST

— let the poor in the jails forget their sorrows in rejoicing over the entertainment we prepare for them, and let the poor in the poor-house dance for joy and gladness on that day (Cheers).[72]

(Michael Tobin, Halifax, 1838)

Public feasts served not only to differentiate working-class recipients from respectable artisans and middle-class providers and participants, but also to distinguish the "deserving" from the "undeserving" poor. Victorian middle-class philanthropists portrayed the "deserving" poor as honest and enterprising citizens victimized by illness or misfortune, while the "undeserving" poor were characterized as lazy, profligate, and even criminal.[73] Organizers of public feasts wished to ensure that only the "deserving" poor received victuals, but at public distributions it was difficult to identify the deserving recipients.[74] During a public meeting to consider the celebration of the birth of the Prince of Wales in Halifax in 1841, Samuel G.W. Archibald, the attorney general of Nova Scotia, referred to the disorder of the coronation feast in 1838, which interfered with the orderly distribution of the food.[75] A correspondent of the *New Brunswick Courier* believed that very few poor deserved a feast in honour of the Queen's marriage in 1840 because in Saint John he perceived "very little suffering from poverty, unless it be where poverty and vice are united."[76]

The distribution of food could be more readily monitored by institutionalizing the public feast. The fragmentation of public feasts into individual dinners for the poor in penal and charitable institutions made them much easier to control than outdoor ox roasts.[77] Thus, provisions for the poor and unfortunate during special occasions frequently took the form of "repasts" in the poor asylums and public carceral facilities. Halifax's committee for the celebration of Queen Victoria's coronation in 1838 organized special dinners for inmates of the poor house, the city gaol, and the Bridewell. Similarly, the Saint John common council organized a dinner in the gaol and, in 1840, distributed provisions to the almshouse, hospital, asylum, gaol, and workhouse in commemoration of Victoria's marriage. In Halifax during the nuptial celebration, Nova Scotia's lieutenant governor, Sir Colin Campbell, donated a supply of beef, bread, and beer to the inmates of the poor asylum and the prisoners in the gaol, and the Charitable Irish Society raised subscriptions for dinners in the poor asylum, the gaol, and the Bridewell. When the Charitable Irish Society entered the poor asylum, they found the "old ranged round the room, children in the centre, and tables 'literally groaning' under a profusion of substantial fare."[78]

Poor houses and penal institutions also marked the Prince of Wales' *rites de passage* with special feasts and entertainments. The inmates of the asylum, gaol, and Bridewell in Halifax enjoyed special dinners as part of the celebration of the birth of the Prince of Wales in 1841. The Prince of Wales' visit nineteen years later was observed with a gaol dinner in Saint John and an entertainment in Halifax's poor asylum. The lieutenant governor of New Brunswick donated provisions to several poor asylums in the province in honour of the Prince's wedding in 1863, and the Nova Scotia treasury also paid for a dinner at the poor asylum.[79]

Who attended the feasts in these institutions and what functions did they play? The institutions catered to a wide spectrum of working-class inhabitants, ranging from the "under-class" recidivists described by Judith Fingard, to the elderly poor, homeless children, and otherwise well-established artisans who had fallen on hard times. Indeed, poor asylums have been described as "catch-all" institutions.[80] A reporter described the different categories of recipients who sat down to a repast in the Saint John asylum in 1863:

> . . . such inmates as were able to move sat down to the sumptuous repast provided for them. The sight was truly interesting. At one table might be seen the poor, decrepid old man, at another the child of misfortune; at one table the emaciated youth, at another, the enfeebled woman.[81]

Judith Fingard has discovered that some poor inhabitants arranged to enter the poor house and the prison in order to take advantage of special dinners, as well as for protection and security.[82] The poor debtors in the gaols who did not have the re- sources to buy bread and had to rely on rations from other prisoners, undoubtedly welcomed these celebratory meals.[83] Institutional feasts were also significant for those who were used to a more substantial diet. An inmate of the Saint John poor house, who had recently fallen from relative respectability as an artisan, commented that "the victuals here is bad and the allowance not half enough for anyone in health."[84]

Regardless of need, inmates expected to be treated "properly" during these din- ners in the institutions.[85] The gaol commissioners in Saint John prepared a special meal for the prisoners during the Prince of Wales' visit in 1860, consisting of salmon, roast beef, vegetables, plum pudding, and a keg of ale. However, two or three "turbulent spirits" led by an elderly debtor named Barney O'Brien managed to convince the other prisoners in the upper hall not to attend the dinner because they were not being treat- ed like *gentlemen*. They contended that it would not be "dignified" to sit down to a feast unless one of the gaol committee or at least the high sheriff presided at the table as chairman. Participation would also be considered if they were provided with the "proper appendage" — a gallon of whiskey. Unfortunately, their protest came to naught, and the next day their share was fed to the prisoners in the lower hall.[86]

Thus, the organization of special feasts for the inmates of the poor relief and pe- nal institutions can be understood as a more rational and controlled means of pro- viding for the poor during public celebrations. Inmates utilized these feasts as sources of much-needed "victuals," and Barney O'Brien and his conspirators even attempted to use the repast as a vehicle for the attainment of working-class respectability.

TEA AND COFFEE SOIRÉE

For another segment of the population, none of these forms of feasting sufficed. They provided an alternative — the tea and coffee soirée.

Why would people turn away from the customary feast and search for an al- ternative? Changing palates may have led to a gradual shift in eating patterns and preferences. Among the articulate, the popularity of roast beef and plum pudding waned by the late 1840s. One commentator commented in 1849 that "John Bull . . . has taken uncommonly to eating turkey and potatoes [two American dishes] for his Christmas dinner, although he continues to swear by roast beef and plum pudding before strangers." He went on to suggest that

> we Nova Scotians should adopt the fare so liberally awarded to us for our national dish,
> and serve it up as a *pièce de résistance* for the benefit of those who may drop in upon us
> with the laudable desire to write a book about "the manners and customs of the Nova
> Scotians."[87]

The change in palate of the residents was accompanied by a growing concern over the manner in which the ox was cooked, primarily the waste involved in roasting the whole animal, and the aesthetics of the practice.[88] In 1838, the *Novascotian* thought that the "days of ox-roasting may as well go after the days of chivalry."[89] As ox roasts became more sporadic, the knowledge of how to cook the animals proper- ly gradually disappeared. The Charitable Irish Society tried to roast an ox in Halifax during the coronation in 1838, but it was eventually disposed of, probably due to over-cooking.[90]

The effects of urbanization also help to explain the erosion of public feasts. Ox roasts were initially a product of pre-Victorian times, when Saint John (and Halifax) resembled a "collection of small market villages."[91] But the "village atmosphere" which had generated communal feasts was changing in the 19th century. One of the most obvious victims of urban growth was the ward system of civic government and, by extension, many of the ox roasts which had been organized by the common council and held in the individual wards. In 1863, the Saint John common council declined the suggestion made by Alderman Robinson to provide each ward with a grant toward "furnishing the poor of the ward with dinner at public expense" in celebration of the Prince of Wales' nuptials. Instead, Alderman Robinson personally provided food and drink for the poor of his Sydney ward and other wards as well.[92] Despite this isolated display of paternalism, communal ward activities like ox roasts were being superseded by city-wide spectacles organized by a more impersonal civic administration.

Public feasting also suffered from the effects of 19th-century moral reformism. Beginning in the 1820s, Halifax and Saint John experienced the emergence of evangelical, temperance, and rational recreation movements. While these causes found support at all social levels, abstinence and prohibition were taken up in force by the evangelical elements of the lower middle and respectable working classes. Besides an array of temperance organizations, a reformist clique called the "puritan liberals" emerged on the Saint John common council who were committed to temperance and purity in public life. The Halifax city council also demonstrated a growing commitment to the bourgeois ideals of efficiency and progress.[93]

Reformers displayed a variety of responses to public feasting and drinking. Some reformers had no use at all for public festivities, particularly when they functioned as gratuitous charities. The emerging bourgeoisie in Victorian England experienced considerable tension between work and leisure, accentuated for those with the evangelical convictions of the "Protestant work ethic." Public entertainments such as feasts were considered to be frivolous and irreconcilable with the "dignity of labour." Indeed, a familiar maxim advised that the "truest charity is to find employment that will give food; and not food without employment." The feast tended to induce idleness, drinking, and other slothful qualities.[94]

Some reformers reconciled the tension between this demoralizing frivolity and the sanctity of work by attempting to either modify or change existing celebrations, or by providing alternative rational recreations. Temperance and abstinence reformers centred on drink as the primary concern. Some moderates advocated a simple reduction in the amount of liquor consumed, while other "distinguished patricians" of the temperance cause in Saint John, such as Charles Simonds and John Gray, moved for a restriction of the type of alcohol served, finding nothing wrong with ale and wine, but drawing the line at hard liquors.[95]

The arrival in the 1840s of the American fraternal temperance organization called the Sons of Temperance facilitated the movement toward abstinence as a form of social control. These abstainers thought that public celebrations should be changed into more rational and orderly events by prohibiting the use of alcohol. The *Morning Sun* spoke of the influence of temperance on public recreations:

> The general effect which "Temperance principles" have on some of these occasions, and
> perhaps on all of them to some extent, go far to remove old objections to such modes
> of recreation. The great blame of festive occasions, was that of the miserable cup of

intoxication; — prohibit that, and man enjoys himself, generally as a respectable creature.[96]

Alderman Salter, a puritan liberal on Saint John's common council, objected to the availability of intoxicating beverages at the marriage celebration in Saint John in 1840. He believed that the common council would not be setting a good example for their constituents by encouraging intemperance in this way. He saw drunkenness at the ox roast in Carleton in 1838 and had no doubt that again many would go away "gloriously drunk." He advocated a more "rational and consistent" celebration which avoided unnecessary noise, confusion, and intemperance: "Englishmen might not get drunk on ale, because they were accustomed to it; but Bluenoses might, and the temptation might be very dangerous." He did not approve of the loyalty of the bottle, but preferred "sober, honest" loyalty.[97] However, fellow puritan liberals Aldermen Porter and John Humbert, and "populist conservatives" such as Gregory Vanhorne, Thomas Harding, and Assistant Aldermen William Hagarty and Ewan Cameron, spoke out in favour of the feast.[98] Alderman Porter saw little drunkenness at the coronation. He "would let the poor have a good glass of ale if they wished it," and did not think it would do them any harm. Indeed, the majority of the aldermen voted in favour of a conventional feast for the celebration of Queen Victoria's marriage in 1840.[99]

Other proponents of temperance and abstinence suggested offering more rational alternative events, such as temperance soirées. These attractions offered not merely free food and entertainment, but also instruction and thereby respectability.[100] Offended by the drunkenness during public celebrations, the St. John Temperance Society organized a tea and coffee soirée during Queen Victoria's coronation celebration in Saint John in 1838, as did the Provincial Temperance Society and the St. John Auxiliary to the New Brunswick Foreign Temperance Society in 1840 to celebrate the Queen's nuptials.[101] The programs were pseudo-religious and instructive, incorporating hymns, band music, and discourses on themes ranging from temperance to "Our Laws" and the "British Constitution." The messages of many of these speeches reinforced middle-class family values and separate spheres ideology. During the soirée in celebration of the Queen's marriage, Captain O'Halloran delivered an oration on "Matrimony" in which he urged those who had not yet been "tyed by Hymen" to follow the illustrious example of their Queen and Prince Consort.[102] These temperance entertainments were attended by a number of women, who also joined the ranks of the temperance organizations. In 1840, Sir John Harvey congratulated the tea and coffee meeting for the large proportion of women present. He echoed the sentiments of the "cult of true womanhood," referring to women as "the good angels of the other sex sent to win them back to the ways of Purity and Peace."[103]

The food served at the temperance soirées was a lighter fare than that associated with ox roasts, banquets, and institutional repasts, with tea and coffee as the only liquid refreshments, perhaps reflecting the influence of American food reformers as well as temperance advocates.[104] Although organized by temperance societies, the events were probably attended by abstainers as well, for temperance supporters had no qualms about using ale.[105] One guest contended that the atmosphere did not suffer because of the lack of alcohol: "we may safely defy Port or Madeira to impart to their votaries more genuine hilarity and social feelings than were inspired by these fragrant productions of the East." Instead of a drunken display, the coronation meeting was a source of "rational intercourse" and a "feast of reason for the soul." The guest concluded: "long live Victoria to share the affections of such a loyal people, and long live the Temperance Cause to suggest so rational a mode of expressing those feelings." The success of the temperance soirées in 1838 and 1840 ensured its continuation as a "regular feature of temperance life" in Saint John.[106]

Moral reformers in the temperance and abstinence camps were not entirely successful in regulating popular behaviour during celebrations. The inherent class bias of their organizations posed one of the most serious problems. While reformers condemned the nature of public feasts and tried to change them in an effort to contribute to the improvement and elevation of the general public, their efforts at individual reformation, and the provision of alternative forms of celebrating, catered more to people of their "own kind," that is, the middle class and particularly the respectable working class. William Baird contended that the "more important work for the members of the Division [Sons of Temperance] seemed to be the reformation of talented and influential men, whose example was producing a most damaging effect."[107] The restriction of attendance at the soirées reflected this class bias, as tickets were first offered to members of the temperance societies and then to the general public.[108] An "insistence upon certain prerequisites of conduct and appearance" at the events further excluded "the unscrubbed." At a time of heightened social extremes, attempts to ameliorate and elevate the lower orders were jeopardised by many middle-class citizens, who were concerned with reinforcing not reducing social distance.[109]

CONCLUSION

Public feasting and drinking in Saint John and Halifax obviously reflected and reinforced the more general pattern of mid-Victorian diversity and class differentiation. In the first place, each type of feasting supported a very different class of recipient: the banquet was attended largely by the middle class, the ox roast by the general public (particularly the working class), the institutional repast by the "institutionalized poor" (representing a wide spectrum of working-class citizens), and the temperance soirée by the lower middle and upper working classes.

The food, drink, and attendant ritualism of these different types of public feasts also expressed hierarchy and defined the boundaries of inclusion and exclusion. The structure and content of French *haute cuisine* and the drinking and toasting rituals at middle-class banquets symbolized the respectability and exclusivity of the dinners. The ox roast, on the other hand, revived images of Merrie England and John Bull paternalism. There is evidence, however, that the working-class recipients interpreted the ox roast in a more pragmatic utilitarian fashion: as a source of free food and drink, and as a vehicle of respectability. Finally, the soirée's juxtaposition of tea, coffee, and instruction against the alcohol, heavier fare, and drunkenness of the banquet, ox roast, and institutional repast permitted respectable working-class temperance advocates to separate themselves from the gluttony of the "gentry" and the vulgarity of the "masses."

Social distance was also reinforced by accessibility; middle-class participants could attend just about any form of festivity they wished (indeed, they organized most of the ox roasts and institutional repasts). The lower classes, however, were blocked from attending the balls and banquets, the temperance soirées, and institutional repasts, as organizers instituted various forms of "screening," such as high ticket prices and availability, codes of dress and etiquette, and evidence of deservedness.

This desire for social distance intensified by the 1860s, as middle-class and respectable working-class organizers began appropriating more of the celebration budgets for their own exclusive banquets. In other words, they transformed "feasts of participation" into "feasts of representation."[110] You will recall that £210 of a total £250 appropriated for the celebration of the Queen's marriage in Saint John in 1840 was expended on outdoor feasts for the poor; however, by 1860, the organizing committee for the Prince of Wales' visit to Halifax spent over half of their £4579/13s/1d on the grand ball and banquet.[111] The *St. John Globe* of 1863 commented on the changing priorities of celebration committees:

> A provision to give a good dinner to the poor was voted down, that two or three hundred of the elite, including the Common Council, may be able to enjoy a dance. Was there ever anything more heartless or cruel?[112]

The end result of this "gentrification" of public celebrations was that, by the late 19th century, few alternatives save private picnics and treats remained for the general public and poor, who "measured improvement" by the "bellyful."[113]

NOTES

1. Bridget Ann Henisch, *Fast and Feast Food in Medieval Society* (University Park and London. 1976). Feasting and drinking were some of the primary functions of festivals in the early modern period (*Carnaval* in Southern Europe and autumn feast days in Britain), Peter Burke, *Popular Culture in Early Modern Europe* (London 1978), 178, 183, 186, 193, 195, 196. "Sustenance" as well as "sociability" were important components of public celebrations in 18th-century America, Barbara Karsky, "Sustenance and sociability: Eating habits in eighteenth-century America," *Annales*, 40 (September–October 1985), 51–2. By the time of King George III's jubilee in 1809, the British expected a "free meal" during celebrations. See Linda Colley, "The apotheosis of George III: Loyalty, royalty, and the British nation, 1760–1820," *Past and Present*, 102 (February 1984), 119.
2. Sarah Freeman, *Mutton and Oysters: The Victorians and Their Food* (London 1989); Jean Latham, *The Pleasure of Your Company: A History of Manners and Meals* (London 1972); Gerard Brett, *Dinner is Served: A History of Dining in England, 1400–1900* (London 1968).
3. Harvey A. Levenstein, *Revolution at the Table: The Transformation of the American Diet* (New York 1988). For the subsequent volume, see Levenstein, *Paradox of Plenty: A Social History of Eating in Modern America* (New York 1993).
4. A by no means complete list of studies on the 19th-century temperance movement: see Ernest J. Dick, "From temperance to prohibition in 19th century Nova Scotia," *Dalhousie Review*, 61 (Autumn 1981), 530–52; J.K. Chapman, "The mid-nineteenth-century temperance movements in New Brunswick and Maine," *Canadian Historical Review*, 35 (1954), 43–60; T.W. Acheson, *Saint John: The Making of a Colonial Urban Community* (Toronto 1985), ch. 7; Gail G. Campbell, "Disenfranchised but not quiescent: Women petitioners in New Brunswick in the mid-19th century," *Acadiensis*, 18 (Spring 1989), 22–54; Gary Hartlen, "'From a torrent to a trickle': A case study of rum imports and the temperance movement in Liverpool, Nova Scotia," in James H. Morrison and James Moreira, eds., *Tempered by Rum: Rum in the History of the Maritime Provinces* (Porters Lake 1988), 62–75; Cheryl Krasnick Warsh, "'John Barleycorn must die': An introduction to the social history of alcohol," in Cheryl Krasnick Warsh, ed., *Drink in Canada* (Montréal 1993), 3–26; Jan Noel, "Dry patriotism: The Chiniquy crusade," in Warsh, *Drink in Canada*, 27–42; Glenn J. Lockwood, "Temperance in Upper Canada as ethnic subterfuge,"

in Warsh, *Drink in Canada*, 43–69; Jacques Paul Couturier, "Prohibition or regulation? The enforcement of the Canada Temperance Act in Moncton, 1881–1896," in Warsh, *Drink in Canada*, 144–65.

5. James L. Sturgis, "'The spectre of a drunkard's grave': One family's battle with alcohol in late nineteenth-century Canada," in Warsh, *Drink in Canada*, 115–43; Cheryl Krasnick Warsh, "'Oh, Lord, pour a cordial in her wounded heart': The drinking woman in Victorian and Edwardian Canada," in Warsh, *Drink in Canada*, 70–91.

6. Sturgis, "'The spectre of a drunkard's grave,'" 115.

7. Joseph Gusfield, "Passage to play: Rituals of drinking time in American society," in Mary Douglas, ed., *Constructive Drinking: Perspectives on Drink from Anthropology* (Cambridge 1987), 76. This comment is an explanation of the structuralist perspective.

8. Margaret Visser, *Much Depends on Dinner* (Toronto 1986), 12.

9. Stephen Mennell, *All Manners of Food* (Oxford 1985), 11. Mennell is discussing the contributions of the structuralists; Mary Douglas, "A distinctive anthropological perspective," in Douglas, *Constructive Drinking*, 8.

10. Mary Douglas, "Standard social uses of food: Introduction," in Mary Douglas, ed., *Food in the Social Order: Studies of Food and Festivities in Three American Communities* (New York 1984), 36.

11. Douglas, "Standard social uses of food," 5–6.

12. Ibid., 8.

13. J. Murray Beck, "James Boyle Uniacke," *Dictionary of Canadian Biography*, VIII, 903.

14. Acheson, *Saint John*, 140; Judith Fingard, "'A great big rum shop': The drink trade in Victorian Halifax," in Morrison and Moreira, *Tempered by Rum*, 90.

15. Acheson, *Saint John*, 142; Reminiscences of Eliza Donkin, collected and compiled by Morley, Scott, 33, New Brunswick Museum [NBM].

16. I. Allen Jack, *History of St. Andrew's Society of St. John New Brunswick, 1798–1903* (Saint John 1903); D.C. Harvey, "N.S. Philanthropic Society," *Dalhousie Review*, 19 (October 1939), 287–95; Robert P. Harvey, "Black beans, banners, and banquets: The Charitable Irish Society of Halifax at two hundred," *Nova Scotia Historical Review*, 6 (1986), 16–35.

17. Judith Fingard, "The poor in winter: Seasonality and society in pre-industrial Canada," in Michael S. Cross and Gregory S. Kealey, eds., *Pre-Industrial Canada, 1760–1849* (Toronto 1985), 63–4.

18. D., "Corporation Dinner, alias Humbug!" in Saint John *Weekly Chronicle*, 22 June 1838, also 29 June 1838.

19. Halifax *Acadian Recorder*, 11 April 1840; Halifax *Times*, 14 April 1840.

20. "An Infant," Saint John *Commercial News and General Advertiser*, 27 March 1840 (shortly after renamed *Morning News*); Saint John *Morning News*, 29 May 1840; *New Brunswick Courier*, 28 March 1840, 4 April 1840, 30 May 1840.

21. "Corporation Dinner, alias Humbug!" Saint John *Weekly Chronicle*, 22 June 1838. An old man in Thomas Hardy, *The Mayor of Casterbridge* (London 1962), 39, describes a similar corporation dinner: "'tis a great public dinner of the gentle-people and such like leading volk — wi' the Mayor in the chair. As we plainer fellows bain't invited, they leave the winder-shutters open that we may get jist a sense o't out here."

22. "A Bluenose," Halifax *Times*, 22 May 1838.

23. Meeting of the Acting Committee, 21 June 1860, in Minutes of the Meetings of the Committee for the Reception of H.R.H. the Prince of Wales, 1860, MG1, 312A, Public Archives of Nova Scotia [PANS]; Halifax *Evening Express*, 3 August 1860.

24. Thorstein Veblen, *The Theory of the Leisure Class* (New York 1934), 127.

25. "A Bluenose," Halifax *Times*, 22 May 1838.

26. Douglas, "Standard social uses of food," 15.

27. Mennell, *All Manners of Food*, 60, 102.

28. Ibid., 135, 136.

29. Ibid., 102, 147, 150–1.

30. Freeman, *Mutton and Oysters*, 184–91; Mennell, *All Manners of Food*, 79, 150.

31. Mennell, *All Manners of Food*, 150; Freeman, *Mutton and Oysters*, 184–91.

32. Levenstein, *Revolution at the Table*, 16.

33. Ibid., *Revolution at the Table*, 14.

34. Douglas, "A distinctive and anthropological perspective," 9.

35. Meeting of the Acting Committee, 10 July 1860, in Minutes of the Meetings of the Committee for the Reception of H.R.H. the Prince of Wales, 1860, MG1, 312A, PANS.

36. Halifax *Morning Sun*, 27 July 1860.

37. Halifax *Sun*, 11 June 1845; Halifax *Novascotian*, 20 August 1860. In San Francisco in 1855, women were invited to observe the elaborate preparations for a banquet, but were then expected to leave "demurely." See Mary P. Ryan, *Women in Public: Between Banners and Ballots, 1825–1880* (Baltimore 1990), 18; men raising their glasses, see Ryan, *Women in Public*, 135. In court circles, Queen Victoria tried to avert excessive drunkenness by insisting that gentlemen not be left on their own for too long, see Alan Delago, *Victorian Entertainments* (London 1971), 12. Cheryl Krasnick Warsh notes that the drinking woman in Victorian Canada was viewed as a form of "bastardized masculinity," see Warsh, " 'Oh lord, pour a cordial in her wounded heart,' " 89.

38. Levenstein, *Revolution at the Table*, 12.

39. *New Brunswick Courier*, 30 June 1838.

40. For a customary list of toasts, see Halifax *Times*, 3 July 1838, 28 April 1840.

41. Karsky, "Sustenance and sociability," 61.

42. Harvey, "N.S. Philanthropic Society," 292. The Charitable Irish Society had their first picnic in 1846, see Harvey, "Black beans, banners, and banquets," 22–3.

43. *Novascotian*, 12 June 1839; Halifax *Sun*, 6 and 11 June 1845.

44. "A Right Loyal Citizen," Halifax *Morning Journal*, 30 May 1860.

45. Halifax *Acadian Recorder*, 18 April 1863.

46. Robert W. Malcolmson, *Popular Recreations in English Society, 1700–1850* (Cambridge 1973), 59–65; G.S. Metraux, "Of feasts and carnivals," *Cultures*, 3 (1976), 8. For a description of a harvest supper in rural England in the early 19th century, see Thomas Hardy, *Far From the Madding Crowd* (London 1967), 240–6.

47. Graeme Wynn, *Timber Colony: A Historical Geography of Early Nineteenth-Century New Brunswick* (Toronto 1981), 135–7, 167.

48. Acheson, *Saint John*, ch. 2.

49. Saint John Common Council Minutes, 7, 15 June 1838, 5 July 1838, 12 March 1840, microfilm, NBM; excerpt in the Saint John *Daily Sun*, 12 April 1887.

50. Saint John Common Council Minutes, 13 May 1840, 19 March 1842, NBM; *New Brunswick Courier*, 16 May 1840; excerpt in Saint John *Daily Sun*, 12 April 1887. The corporation was congratulated in 1840 for their "liberality." See Saint John *Morning News*, 25 May 1840.

51. "A Looker On," *New Brunswick Courier*, 7 July 1838; Saint John *Daily Sun*, 18 June 1887.

52. Halifax *Acadian Recorder*, 25 April 1840, 2 May 1840; Halifax *Times*, 5 May 1840; Halifax *Times and Courier*, 7 June 1849; Halifax *Times*, 21 December 1841.

53. "A Looker On," *New Brunswick Courier*, 7 July 1838; *New Brunswick Courier*, 9 May 1840.

54. Judith Fingard, "The relief of the unemployed poor in Saint John, Halifax, and St. John's, 1815–1860," *Acadiensis*, 5 (Autumn 1975); Judith Fingard, "Attitudes towards the education of the poor in colonial Halifax," *Acadiensis*, 2 (Spring 1973), 19; Gwenyth Andrews, "The establishment of institutional care in the mid-nineteenth century," Honours essay, Dalhousie University, 1974, 2.

55. Malcolmson, *Popular Recreations*, 56, 66.

56. Halifax *Acadian Recorder*, 2 June 1838.

57. Metraux, "Of feasts and carnivals," 7.

58. Hugh Cunningham, "The language of patriotism, 1750–1914," *History Workshop*, 11 (1981), 11, 18, 21; for images of John Bull, see Patrick Joyce, *Culture, Society, and Politics* (London 1981), 286–7, 295; Peter Bailey, *Leisure and Class in Victorian England: Rational Recreation and the Contest for Control, 1830–1885* (Toronto 1978), 89.

59. Halifax *Times*, 29 May 1838. The Halifax *Times*, 28 April 1840 commented re a dinner and dance given by the St. George's Society: "For once John Bull forgot to grumble, and did his best to honour his Patron by proving the strength and tension of his digestive faculties, qualities in the composition of Englishmen, which, where roast beef and plum pudding are concerned, are said to be of no mean order."

60. Metraux, "Of feasts and carnivals," 8.

61. Saint John *Daily Telegraph*, 21 April 1883.

62. Saint John *Daily Telegraph*, 21 April 1883; excerpt in Saint John *Daily Sun*, 18 June 1887; Susan G. Davis, *Parades and Power: Street Theatre in Nineteenth Century Philadelphia* (Philadelphia 1986), 121. I am unsure whether the meat was distributed cooked or uncooked.

63. *New Brunswick Courier*, 23 May 1840.

64. Excerpt in Halifax *Acadian Recorder*, 30 June 1887; Charitable Irish Society Minute Book, 25 May 1849, 8 June 1849, PANS; Harvey, "Black beans, banners, and banquets," 21, 23. For description of such a tent, see Hardy, *The Mayor of Casterbridge*, 109–11.

65. Karsky, "Sustenance and sociability," 59.

66. *New Brunswick Courier*, 30 June 1838; Saint John *Weekly Chronicle*, 29 June 1838; Saint John Common Council Minutes, 7, 15 June 1838, NBM; reminiscence in Saint John *Daily Sun*, 18 June 1887; Saint John *Morning News*, 25 May 1840; *New Brunswick Courier*, 30 May 1840. In Carleton also, a great deal of food was eaten.

67. Levenstein, *Revolution at the Table*, 4–5.

68. Saint John *Morning News*, 25 May 1840 (emphasis is mine); Fingard, "The poor in winter," 76.

69. "Dorothy Prim," Saint John *Morning News*, 22 May 1840.

70. See Rev. Dr. Cochran in W.M. Brown, "Recollections of Old Halifax," Nova Scotia Historical Society, *Collections*, 13 (1908), 89.

71. Saint John *Morning News*, 25 May 1840.

72. Extract in Halifax *Acadian Recorder*, 20 June 1887.

73. Fingard, "The relief of the unemployed poor," 38–9.

74. Andrews, "The establishment," 4.

75. *Novascotian*, 16 December 1841. Also recall the "irregularities" during the marriage feast in Saint John. See Saint John *Morning News*, 25 May 1840. In 1897 the Halifax *Herald* described a feast for the poor as an "indiscriminate and unintelligent" form of alms-giving. See *Herald*, 5 July 1897.

76. Letter to editor in *New Brunswick Courier*, 18 April 1840.

77. Institutional repasts were also a function of the "discovery of the asylum" as an accepted mode of dealing with poverty and other social problems. See Andrews, "The establishment," 2, 89; James M. Whalen, "Social welfare in New Brunswick, 1784–1900," *Acadiensis*, 2 (Autumn 1972), 55–6. However, Francis does not think that the Lunatic Asylum was a humane method. See Daniel Francis, "The development of the lunatic asylum in the Maritime provinces," *Acadiensis*, 6 (Spring 1977), 23–38.

78. For Halifax coronation, see Halifax *Acadian Recorder*, 11 August 1838; for Saint John coronation, see excerpt in Saint John *Daily Sun*, 12 April 1887; for Saint John marriage, see Saint John Common Council Minutes, 14 May 1840, NBM; *New Brunswick Courier*, 16 May 1840; Saint John *Weekly Chronicle*, 29 May 1840; for Halifax marriage, see Halifax *Acadian Recorder*, 11 April 1840; for Charitable Irish Society, see *Novascotian*, 23 April 1840; Halifax *Times*, 21 April 1840; Halifax *Acadian Recorder*, 25 April 1840; Charitable Irish Society Minutes, 9, 27 April 1840, 18 May 1840, PANS.

79. For birth, see *Novascotian*, 16 and 30 December 1841; Halifax *Acadian Recorder*, 25 December 1841; for visit, see Saint John *Morning Sun*, 23 July 1860. Also see entry for a dinner in the poor asylum on the occasion of the Prince's visit to Nova Scotia in 1860 in Halifax's Poor Asylum Account Book, August 1860, RG 35-102, 33 B.1, PANS; for wedding, see *St. John Globe*, 11 March 1863; Saint John *Morning News*, 18 March 1863; Halifax's Poor Asylum Account Book, May 1863. Inmates of the charitable and penal institutions continued to receive special meals during the celebrations of Queen Victoria's jubilees in the late Victorian era. See Halifax *Acadian Recorder*, 20 June 1887; Saint John *Daily Echo*, 14 May 1897; Halifax *Herald*, 25 June 1897.

80. Whalen, "Social welfare," 60; Judith Fingard defends her use of the term "under class" in the introduction to her *The Dark Side of Life in Victorian Halifax* (Porters Lake 1989).

81. *New Brunswick Courier*, 14 March 1863.

82. Fingard, *The Dark Side of Life*, 52, 54–5, 57.

83. John Smith to Mayor Robert Hazen, 17 April 1838, in Robert F. Hazen papers, Box 1, Shelf 36, Packet 2, #15, NBM.

84. James Thompson to the North British Society, 16 November 1838, in Records of the North British Society, MG 20, vol. 253, no. 185A, PANS.

85. Fingard, *The Dark Side of Life*, 51.

86. Report of Justice Balloch to a meeting of the sessions in Saint John *Morning News*, 5 September 1860; Saint John *Freeman*, 6 September 1860.

87. "Ventriloquus," Halifax *British Colonist*, 24 May 1849. Similarly, another Hallgonian contended that the "youngsters" of the late Victorian age would "turn their noses up" at the barrels of gingerbread (plum pudding) which were served during the coronation celebration in 1838. See "Doesticks," Halifax *Acadian Recorder*, 10 July 1897.

88. See the mayor's comments in *New Brunswick Courier*, 28 March 1840, and Alderman Porter's remarks in 23 May 1840. There was also concern about the waste and excess of festivals in early modern Europe. See Burke, *Popular Culture*, 213.

89. *Novascotian*, 5 July 1838.

90. Halifax *Times*, 3 July 1838.

91. Acheson, *Saint John*, 5. An ox was roasted in many pre-Victorian celebrations in Saint John, including the defeat of Napoleon in May 1814, the coronation of George IV in October 1821, and the ascension of William IV. See J.V. Saunders, "Early New Brunswick celebrations," *New Brunswick Historical Society Newsletter*, 24 (November 1987), 3–4; *New Brunswick Courier*, 13 October 1821. In this sense they resembled the roasts held during village fairs and festivals. See Malcolmson, *Popular Recreations*, 59–64.

92. Saint John Common Council Minutes, 7 March 1863, NBM; compare this to the 50th anniversary of the landing of the loyalists in Saint John in 1833, when the mayor provided a special feast for the poor at his own expense. See Saint John *City Gazette*, 16 and 23 May 1833; For Alderman Porter, see *St. John Globe*, 11 March 1863; *New Brunswick Courier*, 14 March 1863.

93. For puritan liberals, see Acheson, *Saint John*, 181–2; for Halifax city council, see Janet Guildford, "Public school reform and the Halifax middle class, 1850–1870," Ph.D. thesis, Dalhousie University, 1990.

94. For Protestant work ethic, see Bailey, *Leisure and Class*, 5; Fingard, "The relief of the unemployed poor," 36. A correspondent of the Halifax *Herald* opposed holding a feast for the poor during Queen Victoria's diamond jubilee celebration in 1897 because it undermined the "pride and spirit of self-reliance" of the deserving poor. See *Herald*, 5 July 1897.

95. The *Novascotian*, 10 December 1840, commented regarding the reduction of whiskey consumed at a fair in Ireland: "How much of confusion, and quarrelling, of profane swearing, and loss of time, and of evils, was avoided by leaving the difference between 8 gallons and 8 puncheons unswallowed"; for selective policy, see Acheson, *Saint John*, 146.

96. Halifax *Morning Sun*, 20 July 1846, as quoted in David Francis Howell, "A history of horse racing in Halifax, N.S., 1749–1867," M.Sc. thesis, Dalhousie University, 1972, 44.

97. This connection between drunkenness and loyalty can be traced back to at least 1809, when the press commented regarding King George III's jubilee: "It is not amidst intoxication . . . that we are to look for that steady or enthusiastic loyalty which is at once the pledge and test of popular allegiance." See Colley, "The apotheosis of George III," 117.

98. For a discussion of these aldermen, see Acheson, *Saint John*, 181–2.

99. For debate, see *New Brunswick Courier*, 23 May 1840.

100. Bailey, *Leisure and Class*, 39, 42; Acheson, *Saint John*, 159.

101. Although there were no soirées in Halifax for the public celebrations in question, they were becoming popular events there as well. The *Novascotian*, 9 December 1841, recommended a soirée as an event for the celebration of the birth of the Prince of Wales.

102. Saint John *Morning News*, 27 May 1840.

103. In Saint John, women served as members of the "Saint John Total Abstinence Society." They composed 40 per cent of the organization before 1835, less than 25 per cent after that date, and edged up to 30 per cent in 1840. See Acheson, *Saint John*, 144. Women also formed their own "Ladies' Total Abstinence Society for the City and County of Saint John," which submitted a temperance petition to the legislature in 1847. See Campbell, "Disenfranchised but not quiescent," 37; *New Brunswick Courier*, 30 May 1840.

104. Levenstein, *The Revolution at the Table*, ch. 4.

105. Acheson, *Saint John*, 145.

106. "A Guest," *New Brunswick Courier*, 30 June 1838; for temperance life, see Acheson, *Saint John*, 146.

107. William I. Baird, *Seventy Years of New Brunswick Life* (Saint John 1890), 162, Saint John Regional Library [SJRL]; Reminiscence of Eliza Donkin, NBM.

108. *New Brunswick Courier*, 23 June 1838, 18 April 1840, 22, 25 May 1840.

109. For prerequisites, see Bailey, *Leisure and Class*, 105; because of "mischievous conduct," no youths were permitted at the temperance meetings in Halifax in 1843 unless accompanied by a parent or guardian, or signed in by a member. See Halifax *Morning Herald*, 31 May 1843; for social distance, see Malcolmson, *Popular Recreations*, 164.

110. Metraux, "Of feasts and carnivals," 8–9.

111. A sum of £2530/17s/9d was expended on the ball and banquet — Financial account at the end of the Minutes of the Meetings of the Committee for the Reception of H.R.H. the Prince of Wales, 1860, MG1, 312A, PANS.

112. *St. John Globe*, 7 March 1863. In the column "Things Talked Of in Halifax," the *Halifax Reporter*, 11 April 1863, had a similar "beef":

> The provincial funds, the peoples' money, the public chest must be freely bled to give a few (who least deserve it) a luncheon, a jollification, a swig at a champagne glass, while the same amount spent in providing comforts for the many needy and poor persons in the city, would be the means of bringing gladness and joy to the hearts of those who are in want.

113. Bailey, *Leisure and Class*, 89.

EIGHTEEN

Idealized Middle-Class Sport for a Young Nation: Lacrosse in Nineteenth-Century Ontario Towns, 1871–1891

NANCY B. BOUCHIER

During the late nineteenth century, social groups attempting to establish a cultural hegemony used sport as a site for their struggles over culture.[1] Although the coalition of interests best denoted as the respectable Victorian middle class won this battle, the victory was neither complete nor truly coherent. Thus, a study of the local adoption of amateur lacrosse in Ingersoll, and its nearby archrival Woodstock, Ontario[2] provides a way of exploring how social groups in small localities used sport to experience, and contribute to, the formulation of a hegemonic culture.[3]

One outcome of this late nineteenth-century process is a most enduring legacy. It is the notion that games somehow build character, and, by extension, that sport is a potent vehicle for achieving and reinforcing certain social goals, and rectifying the physical and moral ills of society. Perhaps best known through the phrase "muscular Christianity,"[4] this notion deeply pervaded the amateur sport movement that created the institutional framework necessary for sport competition to thrive during the last century, and for the acceptance of sport as an integral aspect of our educational system today.[5]

In their quest to project their world view of respectability through team sport, sport reformers approached it from a rational, utilitarian perspective.[6] Their claims about sport's character-building qualities and the sporting performances choreographed to buttress these claims constitute the stories that Canadian sport reformers were telling about themselves and their world.[7] By doing so, they rendered sport an arena for the acting out of the hegemonic process. Since in the process the voices of those whom they deemed to be their opponents have been muted, not recorded, or suppressed through time, detractors remain a hazy group. Thus, we are left mainly with the legacy of those who held the dominant agenda for sport. However, we do have some clues to the identity, actions, and perhaps beliefs of those who resisted their efforts.

Amateur lacrosse is a particularly ripe sport in which to study the phenomenon of sport as a site for an emerging hegemony. It advanced the popular, late nineteenth-century notion that games build character, and it bore a particular "Canadian" stamp. It provides a fascinating example of the larger sport-reform phenomenon during the era of Canada's birth as a nation and a particular vision of how sport could cultivate

Source: "Idealized Middle-Class Sport for a Young Nation: Lacrosse in Nineteenth-Century Ontario Towns, 1871–1891," *Journal of Canadian Studies*, 29, 2 (Summer 1994): 89–110. Reprinted by permission.

"Canadian character." Although lacrosse had origins in Indian religion, tradition, and society, white urban men with a specific social agenda devised its organized form.[8] These men took the Indian game and "reinvented" it in the effort to create a version of a Canadian sporting culture that projected their particular vision of reality and belief system (that was class-bound, racist, and gender-specific).[9] Lacrosse was conceived by them as a vehicle for cultivating Canadian nationalism, manliness, and respectability in male youth, and to keep the leisure activities of males in check. Projecting lacrosse as a quintessentially Canadian sport, lacrosse propagandists, like propagandists for other popular sports of the day, received support from social reformers, religious leaders, and educators.[10] They maintained that such sports cultivated and contributed to the emerging urban-industrial Canadian nation.

This research addresses several interrelated issues in the use of sport in hegemonic struggles over culture through an examination of the development of lacrosse in the two towns during the sport's heyday, between 1871 and 1891. It first identifies certain social themes embraced both locally and nationally by the organized lacrosse movement, particularly nationalism, manliness, and youth reform through rational recreation. These themes mark lacrosse as a sport with a social agenda based upon a particular vision. Then, using demographic data on the Ingersoll and Woodstock clubs, it identifies the organizers and players who masterminded and carried out this process of reforming local sport. The research also shows that middle-class reformers were keenly aware of harmful diversions (such as swearing, drinking, gambling, immorality) that surrounded sport, and were concerned about the acceptability of certain sports themselves (such as horseracing, dog and cockfighting, bull and bear baits, and pugilism).[11] The reformers sought to monopolize the forms and meanings that local sport was to take. By the late 1880s, town councils allowed these men, who were connected to an evolving cult of respectability, to organize annual community civic holidays through their local Amateur Athletic Associations (AAAs), which regulated community sport. Finally, the research shows the ways in which sport reformers infused urban boosterism into their social agenda for lacrosse.

AAA efforts to define legitimate activities for others, like similar efforts to sublimate and marginalize unacceptable traditions, remained ongoing in the hegemonic process. While they did manage to systematize and rationalize some familiar sports and to remove others from the athletic grounds while promoting utilitarian, respectable, and representative team sports such as lacrosse, the social agenda of sport reformers met with resistance.[12] Ironically, boosterism fuelled playing field violence during intense competition as well as rowdiness in the stands. Such responses caused problems for idealistic visions of sport, prompting middle-class sport reformers to make concessions in order to maintain their hegemony.

....

Like other social thinkers concerned with physical health, youth, and Canadian society, the headmaster of Woodstock College, J.E. Wells, believed that physical development played an essential role in the shaping of a national character in Canadian youth. Some seven years after Confederation, he wrote in the *Canadian Monthly and National Review* that physically well-developed youth were needed for young Canada to assume "the attitudes and tones, and to some extent the responsibilities of, nationality." Wells believed that Canadians possessed certain inheritable qualities, which, tempered by climatic conditions, would "prove most favourable to mental as well as physical development." The latter was viewed as the key to national development: "bone and muscle and nerve fibre must be necessary antecedents of brain power."[13] This, in turn, undergirded nation-building. Like other educational institutions, Wells's Woodstock College, which later became McMaster University, sought to stimulate the mental and physical development of youth through "a rational program of gymnasium work and outdoor sports featuring lacrosse."[14]

Wells was not alone in his concerns and efforts. Proselytizers for lacrosse throughout Canada shared this nationalist orientation and, through it, hoped to create a culture of purposeful sport.[15] For example, Dr. William George Beers, the Montreal dentist credited with facilitating the early development of the Canadian Dental Association, spearheaded the creation of the National Lacrosse Association in 1867, advocating that lacrosse could shape boys into manly Canadian nationalists.[16] With an almost evangelical fervour his *Lacrosse: The National Game of Canada* (1869) proposes a nationalist agenda for his vision of sport.[17] Beers pushed his point as far as he could:

> It may seem frivolous, at first consideration, to associate this feeling of nationality with a field game, but history proves it to be a strong and important influence. If the Republic of Greece was indebted to the Olympian games; if England has cause to bless the name of cricket, so may Canada be proud of Lacrosse. It has raised a young manhood throughout the Dominion to active, healthy exercise; it has originated a popular feeling in favour of physical exercise and has, perhaps, done more than anything else to invoke the sentiment of patriotism among young men in Canada; and if this sentiment is desirable abroad, surely it is at home.[18]

Despite such claims lacrosse is not our national sport: we simply do not have one. Still, the myth persists. It was initiated in the nineteenth century by men such as Beers, and W.K. McNaught, author of *Lacrosse and how to play it* (1873), who commended lacrosse as having "a nationalizing influence upon all who come in contact with it, and, for this reason alone, if for no other, it ought to be encouraged." More recently, Canadian sport historian Don Morrow has argued that the notion that lacrosse is our national sport continues to be supported through "a kind of consensual validity: if something is claimed to be true enough times, it is often accepted as truth — then and now."[19]

Part of the lacrosse myth's success can be attributed to late nineteenth-century efforts to point to the aboriginal origins of the game in order to vindicate and justify the sport as a national symbol. In his writings Beers made all of the necessary connections. For example, he romanticized Indians as noble savages, themselves a feature of the rugged Canadian northern landscape, which white men were successfully conquering through their nation-building pursuits.[20] By extension, he believed that the Indian game could be used toward nationalist ends. Beers was certainly not alone in this effort. In "The Northern Character: Theme and Sport in Nineteenth Century Canada," Canadian sport historian David Brown traces the blending of the northern theme with Victorian beliefs in muscular Christianity.[21] He points out that Beers developed and fused the themes of northern character and national sport in *Lacrosse: The National Game*, at the same time that R.G. Haliburton published *The Men of the North and their Place in History*. Beers's approach, Brown argues, "provided Canadian nationalists with another medium through which they could promote their country and its benefits vigorously on both a national and international scale."[22]

Lacrosse promoters credited the physical robustness that they believed Indians had (but which white urban males, who were doomed to sedentary occupations, lacked) to the vigorous demands that lacrosse made on their physiques. They linked this attribute to their ability to conquer the Canadian wilderness by reshaping it to suit middle-class, white-male, urban culture. It would produce "the greatest combination of physical and mental activity white man can sustain." They believed that they significantly elevated the moral tone of lacrosse. Beers bluntly claimed his version of lacrosse was as "much superior to the original as civilization is to barbarism."[23]

Repeated themes — "nation-building," "boyish sport," and "young manhood" — were central to the promotion of lacrosse as a rational recreation aimed primarily at Canadian male youth. The concern of social and sport reformers with the "problem" of urban youth helped to fuel lacrosse's reform agenda. As high school enrolments increased (nearly doubling in Ontario between 1875 and 1895), and as the apprenticeship system declined, middle-class males were dependent on their families for longer periods of time than had previously been the case.[24] With children and adolescents increasingly under female scrutiny — in schools and in the home — some social observers feared that boys were becoming increasingly feminized and were lacking in male role models.[25] Many argued that, unchecked, this situation would result in males becoming physically weak and, therefore, powerless. Keenly concerned about this, parents and social reformers sought appropriate spare-time activities to occupy young males. Through these activities they hoped to expose them to masculine role models and to teach them the importance of manly physical activity in an increasingly sedentary world.

In both Ingersoll and Woodstock clergymen repeatedly stressed the relationship between manliness and the leisure habits of male youth. Sermon titles reveal their preoccupations: "How Does Physical Welfare Affect Moral Conduct?"; "Young Man's Leisure"; "Where Do You Spend Your Time?"; "True Manhood"; and "A Manly Man."[26] As Ingersoll's Rev. P. Wright asserted in 1872, the lack of a conception of true manhood was a "fruitful source of failures in young men." He determined that, with a grasp of this concept, "evil has no chances for young men." Simply cultivating brute strength and courage in youth was not sufficient for the pursuit of manliness: each element had to be "suitably controlled."[27]

To Canadian social and sport reformers lacrosse was one solution to the problem of urban male youth. Lacrosse was a means to the end of cultivating manliness in youth and developing character so that young men would remain on the path of righteousness. Its newness appealed to the reform-minded since it was socially insulated from taverns and other unsavoury institutions where illegal and publicly castigated sports, such as pugilism and cockfighting, thrived in an environment of alcohol and gambling. As George Beers put it, lacrosse did not have "debasing accompaniments such as the bar room association" that plagued other sports.[28] When responding to the *Commission Appointed to Enquire into the Prison and Reformatory System* about potential cures for youth idleness, Woodstock's gaoler offered: "I would keep children employed at something or other," for example, "good honest play, a game of lacrosse or similar amusement."[29] Presumably, similar efforts to keep boys on the right path led to the granting of the title "Tzar" of the Beavers Lacrosse Club to Woodstock's Chief Constable T.W. McKee.[30]

Lacrosse superbly embodied the notion that games build character, a key ingredient in nineteenth-century conceptions of muscular Christianity.[31] Historians J.A.

Mangan, David Brown, and other scholars have shown how this powerful ideology of sport was a class-bound phenomenon rooted in British mid nineteenth-century public school reform.[32] Public school sports played under the watchful eye of men such as Dr. Thomas Arnold at the Rugby school aimed to instill valued character traits such as team-work, self-sacrifice, courage, manliness, and achievement. School masters believed that these traits were transferable to other real-life situations. Popular novels by English authors Charles Kingsley and Thomas Hughes, and writings by American Thomas Wentworth Higginson, among others, brought these beliefs to life.[33] They projected sport as a means of character-building and not an end in itself.

Such arguments undercut prevailing ascetic-pietist objections to sports as useless, immoral, and socially improper.[34] Protestant clergymen, educators, and social observers had, until this time, encouraged moderate forms of physical activity simply to keep people's bodies and minds refreshed and fit for work, but they still held deep suspicions of the fun and frivolity surrounding sporting activities.[35] Higher motives for sport were thus needed to transform rowdy, idle diversion into a morally uplifting, socially sanctioned activity appropriate to the social and physical changes of an increasingly industrialized society. According to Canadian sport historian Gerald Redmond, muscular Christianity's social construction attempted "to reconcile the centuries-old Christian faith with the new realities of the modern world to the apparent satisfaction of Victorian and Edwardian consciences."[36] It met with a considerable degree of success: its rise marked the evolution from a tradition of ascetic Protestantism to one of a moral athleticism. Church leaders and religious institutions emerged as patrons, rather than critics, of sport.[37] After the turn of the century, such support lent credibility to incorporating sport into the public school curriculum as a means of providing for the social and moral education of students, while at the same time physically educating their bodies.

Amateur lacrosse upheld muscular Christian principles. In fact, the National Lacrosse Association received its most prestigious award, the Claxton Flags, from a charter member and sometime president of North America's first Young Men's Christian Association.[38] The deed of gift records Montreal millionaire, philanthropist, and social reformer James T. Claxton's desire to "promote by every means in his power the fostering of clean, amateur athletics amongst the youth of Canada."[39] This occurred long before the YMCA embraced sport as a means of cultivating the spiritual, social, and physical dimensions of man.[40]

The muscular Christian influence on lacrosse resulted in demands that players develop a rational, educated strength: speed and agility were to be carefully circumscribed by an idea of right action.[41] To this end, the rules of lacrosse restricted what players were to do, both physically and socially.[42] Bruises, cuts, scrapes, and broken bones were likely to occur if 24 players on the field, sticks in hand, were simply to charge after a single ball. A "scientific" approach aimed to eliminate violence and injury by de-emphasizing physical contact for the presumed higher social skills believed to be obtained through the activity.[43] This system of beliefs relegated brute force to the status of being inherently unmanly. Organized clubs aimed to reinforce learning experiences through the creation of a sporting "freemasonry" of those similarly indoctrinated.[44]

Expressions of manly camaraderie were commonplace: lacrosse club members shared grief in their losses and celebrated their accomplishments.[45] For example, local merchant Edward W. Nesbitt, secretary of Woodstock's Beavers, received an exquisite silver tea service from the club at a testimonial to him honouring his forthcoming marriage in 1879. A beautiful parchment scroll, elaborately detailed in gold, accompanied the gift. Its inscription with its echoes of the Sermon on the Mount speaks volumes about the club's social and moral goals:

> We feel it is no empty boast when we say that it is an honour to belong to the Beaver Lacrosse Club of Woodstock. The Young men who organized this Club nine years ago have retired and now occupy positions of trust and honour in our community leaving their places in the Club to be filled by other and younger men who bid fair to follow in the footsteps of their predecessors. At home and abroad the name of the Beaver Lacrosse Club has been and is now a synonym of honesty, uprightness, and fair dealing. Taking defeat in the same good natured and gentlemanly manner that they have scored victories, and on all occasions, recognizing the golden rule *To do to others as they wished to be done by*.[46]

In 1871, some four years after the creation of the National Lacrosse Association, Ingersoll and Woodstock sportsmen turned their attentions to cultivating this stylized approach to sport. Their involvement in lacrosse coincided with local baseball clubs losing their single-handed dominance of the towns' interurban, amateur team competition.[47] Not surprisingly they had turned first to baseball, a likely candidate for their reform efforts, since it was a highly familiar and popular activity amongst children and youth.

In 1864 Woodstock's first known sports club for young men, the Young Canadian baseball club, created the Silver Ball award (which came to be popularly known as the emblem of the Canadian Baseball Championship), to stimulate interurban, challenge-match competition.[48] Over the next five years Woodstock's home team defended its Canadian championship title, with a home field advantage, against rivals from Ingersoll, Guelph, and other Ontario towns. The *New York Clipper*, the premier sporting journal of the day, kept North American readers abreast of Woodstock and Ingersoll team activities.[49]

By the late 1860s and early 1870s, however, a growing emphasis upon winning had begun to undercut organized baseball's early social orientation and to tarnish its clean image. With rowdyism, gambling, and professionalism on the rise in amateur baseball, local reformers began to promote lacrosse as *the* organized sport of the day. It was precisely at the point when intense competition and pressure to win resulted in the Woodstock Young Canadians losing their Canadian championship to their archrival, the Guelph Maple Leafs, that matters worsened. Associations between baseball and rowdyism surfaced among players and fans, illustrating the difficulties reformers faced in eradicating alternate traditions. At an 1868 Silver Ball match between the Young Canadians and the Maple Leafs, fights broke out as toughs roamed the stands, "no one" daring "to interfere with them in their nefarious work."[50]

According to sport reformers, baseball's respectability wavered because teams paid players under the table and heated competition sparked lively betting.[51] Baseball reformers repeatedly sought new solutions to these dilemmas — creating new leagues to reaffirm their intention, requiring amateur documentation from players to limit the involvement of itinerant professional athletes, having amateur sponsoring agencies fund team expenses through gate receipts to lessen the impact of money on the game. Yet the behaviours of players, fans, and others ensured that the plague persisted. In

1884, the Woodstock amateur club presented their strongly worded view of the matter: "we have no sympathy whatever with 'professional sport,' as it is now carried on in the interests of speculators and gamblers . . . the result of a professional baseball match has no more interest for us than the result of a fight between two ownerless street curs."[52]

In the midst of such controversy, local sport reformers turned their focus upon lacrosse, packaging it as a purer, and a particularly Canadian, team sport. They were confident in the ability of the existing national-level regulatory agency (the NLA) to oversee the sport locally. Demographic data on Ingersoll and Woodstock club organizers and players reveals the identities of the people who masterminded and carried out this reforming of local sport. The organizers of Ingersoll and Woodstock lacrosse clubs are readily found in local historical records. The names of the men who ran local lacrosse clubs between 1871 and 1890 read like a local social register; indeed, their names are still present on local buildings, street signs, and memorials.[53]

Seventy-two Ingersoll and Woodstock men who organized local lacrosse between 1871 and 1890 show striking demographic similarities, and while the data includes a considerable range of affluence and power (especially regarding occupation), some important conclusions can be drawn. For example, they operated within an exclusively male network. Presumably they never officially prohibited females from involvement because existing social and cultural constraints had already done this work.[54] And, with only three exceptions, for almost 20 years group members were exclusively Protestants.[55] Beyond this, their shared social background united the reformers and differentiated them from other local males. If one applies a taxonomy to census data and uses it as a proxy for class, that data reveals that, as a group, these men had a very different occupational pattern than the overall local workforce (see Table 18.1).[56]

Only a very small group of manual workers, drawn from labour's small aristocracy of skilled artisans, were lacrosse organizers. Middle-class men (holding non-manual occupations in banks, law offices, mercantile establishments, and publishing offices) dominated lacrosse organizations. As such, they vastly over-represented their segment of the local workforce hierarchy.

Their local voluntary association and political involvement also afford highly suggestive glimpses into the social similarities and shared values of these sport reformers. To summarize the data in Table 18.2, lacrosse organizers engaged in remarkably similar voluntary activities. At least two-thirds of them were officers in more than one

TABLE 18.1 *Occupational Characteristics of Ingersoll and Woodstock Lacrosse Executives Compared to Local Male Workforces, 1871–1890*[a]

Occupational Categories	Lacrosse Organizers	Male Workforce[b]
Non-manual	94%	26%
Manual skilled	6%	48%
Manual unskilled	0%	26%
Total number	72	2883

[a] IN ROUNDED FIGURES.

[b] COMBINED, INGERSOLL AND WOODSTOCK MALE WORKFORCES OVER 16 YEARS DERIVED FROM 1881 MANUSCRIPT CENSUSES.

TABLE 18.2 *Voluntary Organization Profiles of Ingersoll and Woodstock Lacrosse Club Executives, 1871–1890*[a]

| | % Involved | |
Type of Organization	*One organization*	*More than two*
Sport clubs	100%	66%
Social/fraternal orders	44%	24%
Town council	32%[b]	—
Board of trade	15%	—
Total number	72	

[a] IN ROUNDED FIGURES.

[b] SIX HELD THE OFFICE OF MAYOR OR REEVE.

sports club, and slightly less than one-half of them held offices in reform-based societies and other fraternities. Beyond this, one in three sat on the local town council, while roughly one in six sat on the board of trade.

Through exclusively male sport clubs, reform societies (for example, Royal Templars of Temperance), and fraternal lodges (for example, the Independent Order of Odd Fellows), these men created environments in which notions of respectability could be formulated, and then promoted. The ritual, literature, and social practices of their various organizations emphasized certain key ingredients that they deemed to be essential to their cause: responsibility, sobriety, honesty, thrift, support for the dominant religion, and personal and sexual morality. Christopher Anstead has shown how, with their policing of individual members' behaviour, these groups spread the ideology of respectability to a wider audience.[57] Other voluntary activities, such as membership in the board of trade and election to the town council, provided avenues for other commitments, such as boosting their town's economic development through supporting aspects of industrial growth.

Because lacrosse clubs drew members from different social backgrounds than club organizers, there was a need for co-operation, presumably based in consent, from certain members of the subordinated classes. Between 1880 and 1889, three-quarters of club members were between 15 and 21 years of age — a small cohort drawn from what was only 14 percent of the local male population. Their membership was touted by the press as a matter of social prestige and envy for other boys.[58] As seen in Table 18.3, the youth in these clubs came from more socially diverse backgrounds than club organizers. Proportionately more lacrosse players came from a home where the household head worked with his hands than did lacrosse organizers. Still, no players came from the homes of unskilled workers.

In short, amateur lacrosse in Ingersoll and Woodstock was a class-based phenomenon like the amateur movement itself. Lacrosse reformers, like reformers for other sports, wished to restructure local sport along carefully circumscribed social lines, and they appear to have elicited support through working-class youth involvement. Just as sport organizers in both towns adopted lacrosse as a vehicle for their reform agenda, they also envisioned creating a local institution to carry out their agenda for sport on a grander scale. One way to achieve this agenda was through the creation of a multi-sport amateur agency which aimed to regulate all local sport.

TABLE 18.3 *Occupational Characteristics of Ingersoll and Woodstock Lacrosse Players Compared to Male Workforces, 1880–1889*[a]

Occupational Categories	Lacrosse Players	Male Workforce[b]
Non-manual	46%	26%
Manual skilled	54%	50%
Manual unskilled	0%	24%
Total number	147	2883

[a] IN ROUNDED FIGURES FOR OCCUPATION OF HOUSEHOLD HEAD.

[b] COMBINED, INGERSOLL AND WOODSTOCK MALE WORKFORCES OVER 16 YEARS ESTIMATED FOR 1885, DERIVED FROM 1881 AND 1891 MANUSCRIPT CENSUSES.

In April 1884, Woodstock's Beaver lacrosse club, together with the local amateur baseball and bicycle clubs, organized a local multi-sport regulatory agency, the Woodstock Amateur Athletic Association (WAAA). Two years later Ingersoll sports reformers, including leaders of the Dufferin lacrosse club, followed suit and created the Ingersoll Amateur Athletic Association (IAAA), which was incorporated in 1889.[59] In both cases these umbrella organizations for sports clubs (notably for lacrosse, baseball, cycling, and tennis) were designed to encourage and regulate amateur sports. The respective town councils also authorized their AAAs to be responsible for creating community sporting and social entertainments for the Queen's Birthday and Dominion Day civic holidays.[60] This "stamp" of approval from local government ensured sport reformers important opportunities to display and disseminate their version of sport.

Under AAA governance local sport was structured in ways that middle-class sport reformers preferred; these preferences were institutionalized and their underlying rationales were articulated through exclusive gentlemen's clubs.[61] AAA constitutions asserted their reform orientation through the mandate "the encouragement of athletic sports, the promotion of physical and mental culture among, and the providing of rational amusements for members."[62] Like other middle-class voluntary associations, the AAAs had strict rules carefully circumscribing the conduct of members. Club rooms prohibited all drink, gambling, betting, lotteries, and profane language. Those defying the rules of "gentlemanly conduct" were expelled.[63]

Modelling their own associations on the exclusive and powerful Montreal Amateur Athletic Association (1881), IAAA and WAAA organizers sought to suppress all but carefully restricted amateur sports which bore the mark of muscular Christianity.[64] Stressing what they called morality and justice in sport, they emphasized efficiency and organization, and denigrated any alternative in order to elevate their own vision for sport. Determined to establish amateur sport as *the* natural and only legitimate version of sport, they strove to marginalize other practices. To this end, local AAA officials attempted to suppress certain sports by eliminating them from the landscape of community sport, especially holiday competitions, and by limiting which sports were granted AAA club affiliation. Amateur regulations demanding that athletes be "carded" in order to compete, while limiting club membership, also worked toward this goal.

Local AAA sport reformers and town councillors alike believed that socially exclusive amateur sports would enhance their town's physical and moral greatness.

Yet the AAAs were joint-stock ventures capitalized through membership fees — and one had to first pass a blackballing to enter AAA ranks. Socially exclusive, they were nevertheless designated by town councils to represent the town. Thus the AAAs upheld the façade, though not the substance, of democracy.[65]

The social fabric of a group of 103 Ingersoll and Woodstock AAA executives similarly belies any notion of democracy. The AAA officials, while individually possessing a considerable range of affluence and power, exhibited certain social traits as a group that sharply set them apart from the local populace. Like the lacrosse executive, they almost all held non-manual occupations of a professional, commercial, or administrative nature (see Table 18.4).

Like sport reformers generally, IAAA and WAAA organizers tended to be engaged in other voluntary and fraternal activities by which they shaped and reflected their world view of respectability and capitalism (see Table 18.5). The intricate ties between the amateur clubs and the agendas of social reform and boosterism promoted by their organizers can also be seen in interurban lacrosse competition and in the ways in which it was supported locally.[66] By infusing sporting events with their vision, they aimed to reinforce their appearance as natural social and political leaders.

From the early 1870s club organizers and town councillors had featured lacrosse matches on Dominion Day holidays.[67] Thousands flocked into town to view these events. After noon-time parades, speeches from local dignitaries, and picnics, the afternoon sport performance began. The profits derived from 10 cent admission fees to holiday matches alone could support a club's expenses for the entire season. To ensure successful holiday–sport events, Woodstock clubs, like clubs from Montreal and Toronto, arranged exhibition matches against Indian teams from nearby reserves.[68] The war-painted Indians also performed war dances and concerts after the matches. Appropriately costumed, they played their tightly choreographed role, though whatever they themselves thought of that role remains unknown. There is no doubt, however, that the lacrosse propagandists created the extravanganzas to symbolize and celebrate what Canada as a young nation had become. The productions aimed to fortify and celebrate one version of pride in locality and Canadian nation, while evoking images of the sport's distant origins in aboriginal culture.[69]

One sketch published in the 1893 Dominion Day edition of the *Sentinel* gave the desired effect of reinforcing what lacrosse propagandists saw as the intimate connection between lacrosse and the Canadian nation. The sketch consisted of a crest with

TABLE 18.4 *Occupational Characteristics of IAAA and WAAA Executives and Local Male Workforces, 1884–1896*[a]

Occupational Category	AAA Executives	Male Workforce[b] 1891
Non-manual	95%	26%
Manual skilled	5%	51%
Manual unskilled	0%	23%
Total number	103	4400

[a] IN ROUNDED FIGURES.

[b] FOR OCCUPATION OF HOUSEHOLD HEAD IN THE WORKFORCE OF MALES OVER 16 YEARS. COMBINED AND AVERAGED BETWEEN 1891 INGERSOLL AND WOODSTOCK MANUSCRIPT CENSUSES.

TABLE 18.5 *Voluntary Profiles of IAAA and WAAA Executives, 1884–1896*[a]

Type of Organization	Organization Executives % Involved
Amateur sports clubs executives	100%
Fraternal order executives[b]	63%
Town council	23%
Board of trade	16%
Total number	103

[a] IN ROUNDED FIGURES.

[b] DATA ON SOCIAL AND FRATERNAL ORDER MEMBERSHIP KINDLY SUPPLIED BY CHRISTOPHER ANSTEAD.

symbols for each province surrounded by scenes of Canadian wilderness. A well-placed lacrosse stick in the diagram gave the illusion that lacrosse, geography, and climate worked together to unite the Canadian nation.[70]

To sport reformers lacrosse offered all sorts of possibilities for creating and maintaining a cultural hegemony. Lacrosse teams, seen by local government to be legitimate agents of local boosterism, were projected to represent the town's merit, and were themselves considered capable of cultivating high civic standards. Throughout the year citizens followed Ingersoll and Woodstock teams through NLA divisional competition. Club victories often prompted community-wide celebrations; for example, in 1888 Ingersoll citizens petitioned the mayor to declare a half-holiday so they could celebrate the advancement of the Dufferins to the southern district championship. In 1901, on the occasion of Woodstock's birth as a city, the *Sentinel* proclaimed that the Beavers had given Woodstock "an enviable reputation in the realm of sport."[71] This reputation, it implied, was both a symptom and an emblem of the type of drive and determination that had nurtured the town's rise to city status. Team uniforms, themselves symbols of order and respectability, and team names reinforced ties to the home town, providing myth-makers with opportunities to tell stories about themselves and their reality; in such narratives sports fields became symbolic battlegrounds.[72]

Community organizations, mayors, local professional men, and merchants strongly supported club efforts. As early as 1871 even Woodstock's Ladies' Benevolent Society publicly offered their support. They graced the Beavers with a $15 donation and embroidered goal flags, "worked in gold [and] surmounted by a Beaver." Like the Claxton Flags, which were the emblem of the Canadian championship, they were a treasure to behold. Individuals also handed out rewards to club players for their social and sporting skills.[73] In keeping with the thrust of amateurism, the awards were symbolic rather than monetary. In 1874 Dr. Turquand, sometime executive of the Royal Arcanum, 10-year town council veteran, and sometime mayor, donated a silver cup for Woodstock's best all-round player. In 1880 Samuel Woodroofe, local jeweller, sometime WAAA executive, and executive of the local bicycle and football clubs, donated a silver medal for a club running competition. He shrewdly placed it in his store window for a week, thus calling attention to the team and drawing in curious customers. In 1888, sometime president of the WAAA and newly elected president of the Canadian Lacrosse Association, local grocer E.W. Nesbitt donated a diamond pin for the best all-round player who showed punctual attendance.[74]

Yet the residual element of a displaced rowdiness could be found within the connection between team and town that was fostered by capitalist boosterism, and shaped by the hand of middle-class businessmen. With its growing popularity in the late 1870s and 1880s and with the increasing associations between lacrosse teams and the corporate community, the gap between what sport reformers hoped to achieve through lacrosse, and what actually happened, widened significantly.[75] Pressures for victory, coupled with intense fan and player identifications with the home team, undermined reformers' efforts.[76] So, too, did greater player commitment to winning for the glory of the team and the honour of the town. Of course, rewards for proper conduct and punctual attendance would have been needless if individual players had been behaving in desired ways.

Despite prohibitions, frequent newspaper reports of money won and lost showed that fans still bet on sport competition, especially when their home team was involved. In 1879 Simcoe's team and their backers arrived for a match in Woodstock "supplied with heaps of wealth," which Beaver supporters "readily took up."[77] It was only a short step from betting to game fixing and under-the-table payments to amateur players. In July 1887 the Brantford Brants had courted Beaver players Kennedy, Kelly, and Laird with offers of jobs that guaranteed a sizable $20 per week salary during seasonal play. One week later certain Brantford fans reportedly offered Beaver player (and Patterson Factory worker) Ed Kennedy $20 to throw a game. The local press decried the action and praised Kennedy's refusal to take part in the schemes. The *Sentinel* claimed: "this is the sort of thing that is ruining lacrosse, it is the betting spirit that leads to such attempts at fraud. Unless betting and the influence of betting men is stamped out, amateur lacrosse is dead — in fact it don't deserve to live."[78]

Efforts to eradicate betting and other prohibited behaviours at local playing grounds were to no avail. Obviously, many resisted. Some flatly refused to behave in prescribed ways while at games. Others simply refused to participate in the community event. They found nearby spots — the cemetery hill overlooking the WAAA grounds, for example — where they could sit on tombstones and watch the performances *gratis*. Resisting the WAAA social agenda, such hill-sitters garnered the best of both worlds. They had the pleasure of watching an afternoon's sport on their own terms: segregated from those who would presume to tell them how to behave, they could enjoy a good drink, a cuss, and a bet amongst like-minded people while watching a game of lacrosse. Better yet, they were physically distanced from, but quite visible to, frustrated WAAA executives. Abhorred by the recalcitrants "flaunting" their disdain for the WAAA agenda and its visions of what was appropriate personal behaviour, the frustrated WAAA officials appeared flabbergasted that their appeals to honour and decency fell on deaf ears: the hill-sitters were unmoved by WAAA threats to publish the names of "sneaks" and to photograph them in the act.[79]

Lacrosse organizers also had difficulty constraining other forms of resistance, like violent behaviour on the field. Tremendous player commitment to winning stretched the limits of rules on the playing field. The emphasis of lacrosse increasingly shifted from the process of character-building to the goal of mere victory. Lacrosse play also shifted from cultivating and displaying an educated strength toward exhibiting unrestrained brutality. Like hockey today, the sport bred player violence during emotion-packed competition. This, of course, ironically enhanced the sport's appeal to those inclined toward unsavoury, or brutal, sport.

During one visit to Ingersoll in 1888, for example, Woodstock players found themselves under attack in the heavily charged environment of lacrosse competition.[80] During the match (refereed by what the Woodstock press referred to as "daisy" umpires), one Woodstonian player checked his opponent. Hundreds of Ingersoll fans responded by mobbing him and his teammates. The melee lasted 15 minutes. After the field cleared and play recommenced, one obscenity-screaming spectator (who just happened to be the local police chief) chased down a rough Woodstock player and, catching him by the throat, thrashed him.

Lovers of the sport throughout southwestern Ontario knew well the antipathy between the two towns that was prompted by playing-field battles. Commenting on this state of affairs an Embro *Courier* editorial pointed a harsh finger at overzealous fans: "if the spectators of these two towns would keep quiet and not interfere so, much of the bad feeling between the boys would die out." The Tillsonburg *Liberal* similarly blamed the spectators, who, it maintained, should "keep their mouths shut and not interfere with the players disputes which occur on the field." The *Chronicle* responded to the indictment, acknowledging the displaced rowdiness inherent in intense interurban competition: "if you expect the spectators in rival towns to keep quiet you make great big mistake." Fan behaviour at lacrosse competition, encouraged by boosterism, thus undercut images of respectability, especially with fans howling "like maniacs."[81] And while this rowdiness was mostly in the stands, rather than at the centre of public display, it was still problematic for sport reformers since it was far from invisible.

Often the local press, an instrument of persuasion in the hegemonic process, stepped into the battle, admonishing locals to be "gentlemanly." But even the papers exhibited elements of displaced rowdyism when, for example, after the Woodstock match in question, the *Chronicle* suggested that "had the spectators stepped in and hammered some of them and maimed them for life the punishment would be no less than they deserve."[82]

This situation, although testifying to lacrosse's immense popularity as a form of action-packed competition and entertainment, undercut attempts to reform the sport. With its rising popularity, by the 1890s lacrosse increasingly became an antithesis to the vision of Canadian youth and sport first expounded by middle-class sport reformers. As the gap between ideation and behaviour widened, lacrosse clearly did not live up to expectations of it as a truly national game that united social groupings under the leadership of a small, select group of men.

The social reform agenda for sport, and the search for sport forms that appeared to solve the social, physical, and moral ills of society, are resilient legacies from the sports-conscious decades of the last century. So, too, is the manipulation of sport to buttress a certain vision of reality. In the case of lacrosse, middle-class reformers aimed to make their (racist, class- and gender-bound) reality credible, and, in so doing, to legitimize their role as the natural leaders of society. With working-class youth filling lacrosse clubs, they appear to have enlisted some co-operation and support from subordinated groups. Even so, their hegemony was never complete, nor truly coherent. The notions of building character through wholesomely Canadian amateur team sport and of playing for the honour of the town, institution, or country one represented just did not comfortably fit, and residual elements — violence, and rowdyism in particular — remained. Yet at the same time the notions upon which the amateur lacrosse movement was built laid a general foundation for organized sport to assume its prominent role in Canadian culture today. The contradictions in the belief that games build character and, at the same time, that sport competition says something about the competitors and, more importantly, the places or institutions they represent, thrives today in Canadian sporting culture.

NOTES

1. For a discussion of a hegemonic struggle, see Keith Walden, "Speaking Modern: Language, Culture, and Hegemony in Grocery Window Display, 1887–1920," *Canadian Historical Review* LXX.3 (1989): 285–310. A now dated discussion of the trend of Gramscian-influenced historical research is found in T.J. Jackson Lears, "The Concept of Cultural Hegemony: Problems and Possibilities," *American Historical Review* 90.3 (June 1985): 567–93.

2. For the history of both towns, see Brian Daw, *Old Oxford is Wide Awake! Pioneer Settlers and Politics in Oxford County 1793–1855* (Woodstock: John Deyell Co., 1980); and Colin Read, *The Rising in Western Upper Canada 1837–1838* (Toronto: University of Toronto Press, 1982). On Ingersoll, see James Sinclair, *A History of the Town of Ingersoll* (Ingersoll, c.1924); George N. Emery, "Adam Oliver, Ingersoll and Thunder Bay District," *Ontario History* LXVIII.1 (1976): 25–44; Ronald Adair Shier, "Some Aspects of the Historical Geography of the Town of Ingersoll" (B.A. thesis, University of Western Ontario, 1967). On Woodstock, see Marjorie Cropp, "Beachville the Birthplace of Oxford" (reprint Beachville Centennial Committee, 1967); and John Ireland (pseud.), "Andrew Drew and the Founding of Woodstock," *Ontario History* 60 (1968): 231–33.

3. See Mark Dyreson, "America's Athletic Missionaries: Political Performance, Olympic Spectacle, and the Quest for an American National Culture, 1896–1912," *Olympika* 1 (1992): 70–90 for a good analysis of America's professionalising middle class's attempts to engineer a cultural hegemony through sport and the making of an American national culture in the context of progressive-era modernity.

4. On masculine Christianity, see Peter McIntosh, *Sport and Society* (London: C.A. Watts, 1963) 69–79; Gerald Redmond, "The First Tom Brown's Schooldays and Others: Origins of Muscular Christianity in Children's Literature," *Quest* 30 (Summer 1978): 4–18; Guy Lewis, "The Muscular Christianity Movement," *Journal of Health, Physical Education and Recreation* (May 1966): 27–30; J.A. Mangan, *Athleticism in the Victorian and Edwardian Public School: The Emergence and Consolidation of an Educational Ideology* (Cambridge: Cambridge University Press, 1981); Idem, *The Games Ethic and Imperialism: Aspects of the Diffusion of an Ideal* (Markham: Viking Press, 1986); David Brown, "Athleticism in Selected Canadian Private Schools for Boys to 1918" (Ph.D. dissertation, University of Alberta, 1984).

5. For a survey of the rise of organized sport in Canada, see Don Morrow et al., *A Concise History of Sport in Canada* (Toronto: Oxford University Press, 1989) and Idem, "Canadian Sport History: A Critical Essay," *Journal of Sport History* 10.1 (September 1983) 67–79; Other related works include Alan Metcalfe, *Canada Learns to Play: The Emergence of Organized Sport 1807–1914* (Toronto: McClelland & Stewart, 1987); Richard Gruneau, *Class, Sports and Social Development* (Amherst: University of Massachusetts Press, 1983); Morris Mott, ed. *Sports in Canada: Historical Readings* (Toronto: Copp Clark, 1989); Sid Wise, "Sport and Class Values in Old Ontario and Quebec," *His Own Man: Essays in Honour of A.R.M. Lower* ed. W.H. Heick and Roger Graham (Montreal: McGill-Queen's University Press, 1974) 93–117.

6. Peter Bailey, *Leisure and Class in Victorian England: Rational Recreation and the Quest for Control, 1830–1885* (Toronto: University of Toronto Press, 1966); and Chris Waters, "'All Sorts and Any Quantity of Outlandish Recreations': History, Sociology, and the Study of Leisure in England, 1820–1870," *Canadian Historical Association Historical Papers* (1981): 8–33.

7. Clifford Geertz, "Notes on the Balinese Cockfight," *The Interpretation of Cultures* (New York: Basic Books, 1973) 417.

8. I use the term Indian because the lacrosse writers of the era used this term. Their ethno-centrism limited their ability to see aboriginal peoples as having any "culture." For a view of the game from the Indian oral tradition, see *Tewaarathon (Lacrosse): Akwesasne's Story of Our National Game* (North American Indian Travelling College, 1978). On Euro-pean interpretations of lacrosse in Indian cultures, see Stewart Culin, "Games of the North American Indians," *Twenty-fourth Annual Report of the Bureau of American Ethnology* (Washington: Government Printing Office, 1907); George Catlin, *Letters and Notes on the Manners, Customs and Condition of the North American Indians* vol. 2 (London: The Egypt-ian Hall, 1871); and Michael A. Salter, "The Effect of Acculturation on the Game of Lacrosse and on its Role as an Agent of Indian Survival," *Canadian Journal of the History of Sport and Physical Education* 3.1 (May 1972): 28–43.

9. On organized lacrosse, see Don Morrow, "The Institutionalization of Sport: A Case Study of Canadian Lacrosse," *International Journal of History of Sport* 9.2 (August 1992): 236–51. See also Robert W. Henderson, *Ball, Bat and Bishop* (New York: Rockport Press, 1947); Alexander M. Weyand and M.R. Roberts, *The Story of Lacrosse* (Baltimore: H & A Herman, 1965); T.G. Vellathottam and Kevin G. Jones, "Highlights in the Development of Canadian Lacrosse to 1931," *Canadian Journal of the History of Sport and Physical Edu-cation* 5.2 (December 1974): 37; Christina A. Burr, "The Process of Evolution of a Com-petitive Sport: A Study of Lacrosse in Canada, 1844 to 1914" (M.A. thesis, University of Western Ontario, 1986); and Metcalfe, *Canada Learns to Play* 181–218.

10. See Kevin G. Jones and T. George Vellathottam, "The Myth of Canada's National Sport," *CAPHER Journal* (September–October 1974): 33–36; *Globe and Mail* 20 December 1868; Morrow, *A Concise History of Sport* 53–54.

11. For example, the activities found in Edwin C. Guillet, *Pioneer Days in Upper Canada* (Toronto: University of Toronto Press, 1979), especially Chapters IX and X. For a good social analysis of a particularly castigated sport, see Elliot J. Gorn, "'Gouge and Bite, Pull Hair and Scratch': The Social Significance of Fighting in the Southern Backcountry," *American Historical Review* 90.1 (February 1985): 18–43.

12. For an extended discussion, see Christopher J. Anstead and Nancy B. Bouchier, "From Greased Pigs to Sheepskin Aprons: Rowdiness and Respectability in Victorian Ingersoll's Civic Holidays," unpublished manuscript, 1993.

13. J.E. Wells, "Canadian Culture," *Canadian Monthly and National Review* (1875): 459–67.

14. See *Sentinel-Review Express Industrial Edition* February 1906; *Woodstock College Memorial Book* (Woodstock: Woodstock College Alumni Association, 1951). On physical education and sports programs in Canadian schools, see Frank Cosentino and Maxwell L. Howell, *A History of Physical Education in Canada* (Toronto: General Publishing Co., 1971); M.L. Van Vliet, *Physical Education in Canada* (Scarborough: Prentice-Hall, 1965); Brown, "Ath-leticism in Selected Canadian Private Schools"; Jean Barman, *Growing Up in British Columbia: Boys in Private School* (Vancouver: University of British Columbia Press, 1984), Chapter Four; G.G. Watson, "Sports and Games in Ontario Private Schools: 1830–1930" (M.A. thesis, University of Alberta, 1970).

15. Nationalism through sport thrived elsewhere, too. See Donald Mrozek, *Sport and Ameri-can Mentality, 1880–1910* (Knoxville: University of Tennessee Press, 1983); Peter Levine, *A.G. Spalding and the Rise of Baseball* (New York: Oxford University Press, 1985). On cul-tural motifs and nationalism, see Eric Hobsbawm, *Nations and Nationalism Since 1780: Programme, Myth, Reality* (New York: Cambridge University Press, 1990).

16. Peter Lindsay, "George Beers and the National Game Concept: A Behavioral Approach," *Proceedings of the 2nd Canadian Symposium on the History of Sport and Physical Education* (Windsor: University of Windsor, 1972) 27–44. On the Canadian nationalist theme in sport, see Morrow, "Lacrosse as the National Game," in *A Concise History of Sport,* 45–68; Alan Metcalfe, "Towards an Understanding of Nationalism in Mid-Nineteenth Century

Canada — A Marxian Interpretation," *Proceedings of the 2nd Canadian Symposium on the History of Sport and Physical Education* 7–14; R. Gerald Glassford, "Sport and Emerging Nationalism in Mid-Nineteenth Century Canada," ibid. 15–26.

17. George Beers, *Lacrosse: The National Game of Canada*. His other lacrosse-related publications include "Canadian Sports," *Century Magazine* 14 (May–October 1879): 506–27; Goal Keeper (pseud.), *The Game of Lacrosse* (Montreal: The Montreal Gazette Steam Press, 1860); "The Ocean Travels of Lacrosse," *Athletic Leaves* (September 1888): 42; "A Rival to Cricket," *Chambers Journal* 18 (December 1862): 366–68.

18. Beers, *Lacrosse: The National Game* 59.

19. W.K. McNaught, *Lacrosse and how to play it* (Toronto: Robert Marshall, 1873) 21. Morrow, *A Concise History of Sport* 54.

20. Beers, "Canadian Sports" 506–27; "Canada in Winter," *British American Magazine* 2 (1864): 166–71; "Check," *Canadian Monthly* 11 (1872): 256–62; "Canada as a Winter Resort," *Century* (1854–55): 514–29.

21. David Brown, "The Northern Character Theme and Sport in Nineteenth Century Canada," *Canadian Journal of History of Sport* XX.1 (May 1989): 52. See also Carl Berger, "True North Strong and Free," *Nationalism in Canada* ed. Peter Russell (Toronto: McGraw-Hill, 1966), 3–26; Idem, *The Sense of Power: Studies in the Ideas of Canadian Imperialism 1867–1914* (Toronto: University of Toronto Press, 1970) 128–53.

22. Brown, "The Northern Character Theme," 47–48, 52.

23. Beers, *Lacrosse: The National Game* 32, 33. The comparison continues "or [as] a pretty Canadian girl to any uncultivated squaw."

24. M.C. Urquhart and K.A.H. Buckley, *Historical Statistics of Canada* (Toronto: Macmillan, 1965) 591. On schools and reform, see Susan E. Houston, "Politics, Schools, and Social Change in Upper Canada," *Canadian Historical Review* 53 (September 1972): 249–71; Idem, "Victorian Origins of Juvenile Delinquency: A Canadian Experience," *History of Education Quarterly* 20 (Fall 1972): 254–80; Houston and Alison L. Prentice, *Schools and Scholars in Nineteenth Century Ontario* (Toronto: University of Toronto Press, 1988); and Alison L. Prentice, *The School Promoters, Education and Social Class in Mid-Nineteenth Century Upper Canada* (Toronto: McClelland and Stewart, 1977).

25. This point has recently been a focus of sport history scholarship; see Steven A. Riess, "Sport and the Redefinition of Middle Class Masculinity," *International Journal of the History of Sport* 8.1 (May 1991): 5–27; J.A. Mangan and James Walvin eds., *Manliness and Morality: Middle Class Masculinity in Britain and Americas, 1800–1940* (Manchester: Manchester University Press, 1987). See also E. Anthony Rotundo, "Body and Soul: Changing Ideals of Middle Class Manhood," *Journal of Social History* 14 (1983): 23–38; Joseph Maguire, "Images of Manliness and Competing Ways of Living in Late Victorian and Edwardian Britain," *British Journal of Sports History* 3.3 (December 1986): 265–87; David Howell and Peter Lindsay, "The Social Gospel and the Young Boy Problem, 1895–1925," *Canadian Journal of History of Sport* 17.1 (May 1986): 79–87; David I. MacLeod, "A Live Vaccine: The Y.M.C.A. and Male Adolescence in the United States and Canada," *Social History/Histoire Sociale* 11.21 (1978): 55–64.

26. Reprints of Sermons, in whole or part, found in *Woodstock Sentinel* 20 November 1887; *Woodstock Herald* 14 March 1845; *Ingersoll Chronicle* 25 October 1888, 30 January 1868.

27. *Chronicle* 7 November 1872.

28. Beers, *Lacrosse: The National Game* 35.

29. Ontario, *Report of the Commissioners Appointed to enquire into the Prison and Reformatory System Sessional Papers* XXIII Part III (No. 7), 1891, 529. Thanks to Susan Houston for bringing this item to my attention.

30. *Sentinel* 19 April 1880.

31. McIntosh, *Sport and Society* 69–79; Lewis, "The Muscular Christianity Movement"; Redmond, "The First Tom Brown's Schooldays and Others."

32. Mangan, *Athleticism in the Victorian and Edwardian Public School*; Idem, *The Games Ethic and Imperialism*; Brown, "Athleticism in Selected Canadian Private Schools"; Watson, "Sports and Games in Ontario Private Schools"; Gruneau, *Class, Sports and Social Development* 101–3; Eric Dunning, "Industrialization and the Incipient Modernization of Football," *Stadion* 1.1 (1975): 103–39.

33. This is best exemplified in Thomas Hughes's widely read classic *Tom Brown's Schooldays* (1857), in the fiction of Charles Kingsley, and in Thomas Wentworth Higginson's "Saints and their Bodies." The writings of Canadian novelist Ralph Connor are also reminiscent of this approach. See Bruce Haley, "Sport and the Victorian World," *Western Humanities Review* 22 (Spring 1968): 115–25; Idem, *The Healthy Body and Victorian Culture* (Cambridge: Cambridge University Press, 1978).

34. On the ascetic-pietist legacy and sport, see Barbara Schrodt, "Sabbatarianism and Sport in Canada Society," *Journal of Sport History* 4.1 (Spring 1977): 22–23; Dennis Brailsford, "Puritanism and Sport in Seventeenth Century England," *Stadion* 1.2 (1975): 316–30; Peter Wagner, "Puritan Attitudes Towards Physical Recreation in 17th Century New England," *Journal of Sport History* 3 (Summer 1976): 139–51; Nancy Struna, "Puritans and Sports: The Irretrievable Tide of Change," *Journal of Sport History* 4 (Spring 1977) 1–21.

35. Gerald Redmond, "Some Aspects of Organized Sport and Leisure in Nineteenth Century Canada," *Sports in Canada: Historical Readings* ed. Morris Mott (Toronto: Copp Clark, 1989) 97–98.

36. Ibid., 98.

37. Howell and Lindsay, "The Social Gospel and the Young Boy Problem, 1895–1925"; C.H. Hopkins, *History of the YMCA in North America* (New York: Associated Press, 1951). Also see Diane Pederson, "Keeping Our Good Girls Good," *Canadian Women Studies* 7.4 (1986): 20–24.

38. On early formation of the National Lacrosse Association, see Peter Lindsay, "A History of Sport in Canada, 1807–1867" (Ph.D. dissertation, University of Alberta, 1969) 114–32.

39. Claxton's obituary from *Sunday World*, 1908, as cited in Harold Clark Cross, *One Hundred Years of Service with Youth: The Story of the Montreal YMCA* (Montreal: Southam Press, 1951) 144.

40. These dimensions were to become symbolized through the association's hallmark, the triangle. See Cross, *One Hundred Years of Service with Youth*. On Woodstock's YMCA, see W. Stewart Lavell, *All This Was Yesterday: The Story of the YMCA in Woodstock, Ontario, 1868–1972* (Woodstock: Talbot Communications, 1972).

41. John Weiler, "The Idea of Sport in Late Victorian Canada," *The Workingman in the Nineteenth Century* ed. Michael Cross (Toronto: University of Toronto Press, 1974) 228–31.

42. On rational recreation, see Bailey, *Leisure and Class in Victorian England*; Idem, "'A Mingled Mass of Perfectly Legitimate Pleasures': The Victorian Middle Class and the Problem of Leisure," *Victorian Studies* 21.2 (Winter 1978): 7–28.

43. Beers, *Lacrosse: The National Game of Canada* 51–56. Burr analyses the evolution of the science of the game in "The Process of Evolution of a Competitive Sport."

44. Beers, *Lacrosse: The National Game* 50. On fraternal societies see Christopher J. Anstead, "Fraternalism in Victorian Ontario: Secret Societies and Cultural Hegemony" (Ph.D. dissertation, University of Western Ontario, 1992); J.S. Gilkeson, *Middle Class Providence, 1820–1940* (Princeton: Princeton University Press, 1986).

45. The Beavers, for example, paid for the funeral of their mascot, little Jimmy Kinsella, who died in an accident at Karn's Organ Factory, *Sentinel* 22 January 1887. On club celebrations for individuals, see *Chronicle* 7 July 1887, *Sentinel* 30 June 1887.

46. "Testimonial to Edward W. Nesbitt. Woodstock 26 November 1879." Woodstock Museum (my italics).

47. On 16 June 1871 the *Sentinel* reports, "with the loss of the late lamented Silver Ball lacrosse seems to be the favoured game this season." Journalist Henry Roxborough

argues that because of baseball's immense popularity in the area, the adoption of lacrosse generally lagged in southwestern Ontario. Henry Roxborough, *One Hundred Not Out: The Story of Nineteenth Century Canadian Sport* (Toronto: Ryerson Press, 1966) 40. On the Guelph–Woodstock rivalry that led to the Woodstonians' dethroning, see *Guelph Evening Mercury* 5 August 1868; *Guelph Evening Telegram* 27 September 1923; and William Humber, *Cheering for the Home Team: The Story of Baseball in Canada* (Erin: The Boston Mills Press, 1983).

48. *Hamilton Spectator* 11 August 1864; *Chronicle* 13 and 20 July, 21 and 26 August 1869. This earliest attempt to create a Canadian "national" baseball association in 1864, led by Woodstock's Young Canadian Club, relied almost completely on the American model of the National Association of Baseball Players (NABBP). The Canadian association, like most baseball ventures throughout the period between 1860 and 1885, structured competition on a challenge-match, or exhibition, basis. See Hamilton *Times* 24 August 1864 and *Spectator* 11 and 24 August 1864; Ingersoll *Chronicle* 26 August, 7 October 1864; *The New York Clipper* 14 September 1864.

49. *The New York Clipper* 14 September 1864, 1 October 1864, 27 June 1868, 19 and 26 June, 17 July 1869, 28 May 1871.

50. *Guelph Evening Mercury* 5 August 1868.

51. See Humber, *Cheering for the Home Team* 27–37; Metcalfe, *Canada Learns to Play* 85–98 and 164–66. Metcalfe rightly notes that baseball was alienated from the mainstream of the amateur sport movement and that it was "significantly different from the other [amateur] sports in that its movement toward league competition came at a slower rate" (88). Baseball lacked well-rooted protectionist agencies (a sporting press, a "national" baseball association, or an institutional tradition) in the face of the American professional model, especially after 1871.

52. On the 1876 Canadian League, see *The New York Clipper* 22 April, 6 May 1876; Bryce's 1876 *Canadian Baseball Guide* (London, Ontario, 1876); *Canadian Gentleman's Journal of Sporting Times* 28 April 1876; George Sleeman Collection, Regional Collections, File 4065, D.B. Weldon Library, University of Western Ontario; *Star Weekly* 19 July 1924.

53. The names of sport players and executives were extracted from reports in local newspapers and Canadian and American sport periodicals, team photographs, various local history sources, and sport-related collections. They were hand-linked to corresponding manuscript census rolls for the urban populations of Ingersoll and Woodstock. Demographic data (age, place of birth, religion, marital status, occupation, and the name and occupation of household head) were derived from the record linkage. Occupation information was corroborated, supplemented, and verified through town directories, tax assessment rolls, local histories, and local genealogies. Data on social and fraternal orders kindly supplied by Christopher Anstead.

54. On the sporting activities of females and social constraints impinging on them, see Patricia Vertinsky, *The Eternally Wounded Woman: Women, Exercise and Doctors in the Late Nineteenth Century* (Manchester, England: Manchester University Press, 1990): Helen Lenskyj, *Out of Bounds: Women, Sport, and Sexuality* (Toronto: The Women's Press, 1986); and Michael Smith, "Graceful Athleticism or Robust Womanhood: The Sporting Culture of Women in Victorian Nova Scotia, 1870–1914," *Journal of Canadian Studies* 23.1/2 (Spring/Summer 1988): 120–37.

55. Religion itself played a significant role in community social-class formation. A systematic relationship exists between the religious and social-class background distributions in the populations. For a statistical analysis of this phenomenon, see Nancy B. Bouchier, "'For the Love of the Game and the Honour of the Town': Organized Sport, Local Culture and Middle Class Hegemony in Two Ontario Towns, 1838–1895" (Ph.D. dissertation, University of Western Ontario, 1990) 90–92.

56. The occupational classification is based upon Gerard Bouchard and Christian Pouyez, "Les Categories Socio-Professionelles: Une Nouvelle Grille de Classement," *Labour/Le Travail* 15 (Spring 1985): 145–63.

57. This understanding of fraternal orders is the central argument of Anstead, "Fraternalism in Victorian Ontario." See also Mary Ann Clawson, *Constructing Brotherhood: Class, Gender and Fraternalism* (Princeton, 1989); Brian Greenberg, "Workers and Community: Fraternal Orders in Albany, New York, 1845–1885," *The Maryland Historian* (1977).

58. *Sentinel* 20 June 1887.

59. *Sentinel* 4, 11, 18 April 1884; *Chronicle* 3 and 10 June 1886; *Woodstock Amateur Athletic Association Constitution and Bylaws* (Woodstock: Sentinel-Review Co. Printers, 1908). This followed resolution of difficulties over obtaining acceptable playing field space. *Sentinel* 4, 11, 18 April 1884; *Chronicle* 3 and 10 June 1886, 29 March 1889, 1 April, 30 May 1890; *Ingersoll Amateur Athletic Association Constitution and Bylaws* (Ingersoll, 1889).

60. Nancy B. Bouchier, "'The 24th of May is the Queen's Birthday': Civic Holidays and the Rise of Amateurism in Nineteenth Century Canadian Towns," *International Journal of the History of Sport* 10.2 (August 1993): 159–92. Sport clubs often hosted some form of sports events during the Queen's Birthday and Dominion Day holidays. For example, the Montreal Lacrosse Club organized matches against teams from the St. Regis and Caugnawaga Reserves (*Gazette* 23 May 1884, 22 May 1885).

61. On gentlemen's clubs see Gilkeson, *Middle Class Providence*, especially Chapter 4, "The Club Idea." On clubs, sport, and Toronto's interlocking social elite, see R. Wayne Simpson, "The Elite and Sport Club Membership, Toronto, 1827–1881" (Ph.D. dissertation, University of Alberta, 1987). On the social-class background of other sports clubs, see Bouchier, "'For the Love of the Game and the Honour of the Town,'" especially Chapter 4.

62. WAAA, *Constitution and Consolidated Bylaws* (Woodstock: Sentinel-Review Company Printers, 1908), Article II; *IAAA Constitution and Bylaws* (Ingersoll, 1889), Article II.

63. See Mangan, *Athleticism in the Victorian and Edwardian Public School*; Brown, "Athleticism in Selected Canadian Private Schools"; Gruneau, *Class, Sports and Social Development* 101–3; Dunning, "Industrialization and the Incipient Modernization of Football"; WAAA, *Constitution and Consolidated Bylaws*, Article IX; IAAA *Constitution and Bylaws*, Article IX.

64. See Don Morrow, "The Powerhouse of Canadian Sport: The Montreal Amateur Athletic Association, Inception to 1909," *Journal of Sport History* VIII.3 (Winter 1981): 20–39; Idem, *A Sporting Evolution*; Metcalfe, *Canada Learns to Play*; Charles Ballem, *Abegweit Dynasty, 1899–1954: The Story of the Abegweit Amateur Athletic Association* (Charlottetown, 1986); Gerald Redmond, "Some Aspects of Organized Sport and Leisure in Nineteenth Century Canada," *Sports in Canada: Historical Readings* ed. Mott, 81–106; Wise, "Sport and Class Values."

65. WAAA, *Constitution and Consolidated Bylaws*, Article VI; *IAAA Constitution and Bylaws*, Article VI. On the socially exclusive nature of amateurism, see Alan Metcalfe, "The Growth of Organized Sport and the Development of Amateurism in Canada, 1807–1914," *Not Just a Game: Essays in Canadian Sport Sociology* ed. Jean Harvey and Hart Cantelon (Ottawa, 1988) 33–50.

66. Anstead and Bouchier, "From Greased Pigs to Sheepskin Aprons."

67. Between 1871 and 1890, Ingersoll featured lacrosse on eight Dominion Day holidays, whilst Woodstock did so on 11 holidays.

68. In 1871 the Beavers paid the Grand River Indians $60 to compete against them in the 24 May match. Ten cent admissions covered this outlay and brought a $159 profit to the club (*Sentinel* 7 July 1871). Other Indian teams were the Tuscaroras, Onondagas, Muncitown, Sioux, and Six Nations. *Sentinel* 7 July 1871, 31 May, 23 August 1872, 26 June 1874, 23 May, 4 July 1879, 30 April 1880, 23 June 1882, 25 May 1887; *Chronicle* 9 May 1877. George Gray, a Woodstonian, recorded his observations about two such matches

in his diary 3 July 1871 and 24 May 1872. Woodstock Museum, George A. Gray Diaries, 1857–1878.

69. This is very much in keeping with the dominant theme of the 1876 and 1883 Canadian lacrosse tours to Britain. Don Morrow, "The Canadian Image Abroad: The Great Lacrosse Tours of 1876 and 1883," *Proceedings of the 5th Canadian Symposium on the History of Sport and Physical Education* (Toronto: University of Toronto Press, 1982), 17. On sporting tours and empire, see David W. Brown, "Canadian Imperialism and Sporting Exchanges: The Nineteenth Century Cultural Experience of Cricket and Lacrosse," *Canadian Journal of History of Sport* XVIII.1 (May 1987): 55–66.

70. *Sentinel-Review* 1 July 1893.

71. *Chronicle* 14 September 1888; *Sentinel* "Birth of the Industrial City," 9 July 1901.

72. On the relationship between team and town, see Morris Mott, "One Town's Team: Souris and its Lacrosse Club, 1887–1906," *Manitoba History* 1.1 (1980): 10–16; Carl Betke, "Sports Promotion in the Western Canadian City: The Example of Early Edmonton," *Urban History Review* 12.2 (1983): 47–56.

73. *Sentinel* 7 July 1871; *Chronicle* 13 July 1871, 30 June 1885, 19 May 1887, 10 May 1888.

74. *Sentinel* 1 April 1874, 21 May 1880, 21 November 1884, 16 May 1888.

75. On escalating violence and rowdyism in lacrosse, see Metcalfe *Canada Learns to Play* 181–218; Idem, "Sport and Athletics: A Case Study of Lacrosse in Canada, 1840–1889," *Journal of Sport History* 3.1 (Spring 1976): 1–19; Burr, "The Process of Evolution."

76. Barbara S. Pinto, " 'Ain't Misbehavin': The Montreal Shamrock Lacrosse Club Fans 1868 to 1884." Paper presented to the North American Society for Sport History (Banff, Alberta, 1990).

77. *Sentinel* 22 and 29 August 1879, 25 August 1882, 15 September 1886, 28 and 30 June 1887; *Chronicle* 23 June 1887.

78. *Sentinel* 20 July 1878; *Chronicle* 23 June 1887; *Sentinel* 30 July 1887.

79. *Sentinel* 3 July 1885.

80. *Sentinel* 6 September 1888.

81. Reported in *Sentinel* 7 August 1885. Related to the incident *Sentinel* 7 and 14 August 1885; *Chronicle* 6 August 1885. Sentinel 30 July 1887. *Tillsonburg Liberal* editorial reprinted with comments Chronicle 28 June 1888.

82. *Sentinel* 30 July 1887.

TOPIC TEN
Religious Life and Culture

The devotional revolution of the nineteenth century significantly increased the role of both lay women and female religious orders, such as the nuns of Quebec City's Hôtel-Dieu Hospital, pictured here, in the Roman Catholic church.

Religion occupied an important place in the lives of Canadians during the nineteenth century. Most Canadians looked to the church and the clergy as the foremost moral authority. Religion also played a central role in defining one's social identity: it dictated whom one married and associated with, shaped one's secular values and attitudes, and influenced one's politics and leisure activities. But despite its obvious importance, few historians have studied the influence of religion in people's lives. Most studies of religion in Canada have concentrated on the development of denominations and institutions, the relationship between church and state, and the evolution of religious thought. As a result, the history of religion has tended to focus on the messengers and the message rather than on the people in the pews.

The two articles that follow are a welcome departure from this traditional approach, in that both demonstrate the important ways in which religion shaped and was shaped by everyday life and culture. In Article Nineteen, Brian Clarke examines the influence on Irish immigrants in Toronto of the new devotional practices introduced into the Roman Catholic church with ultramontanism, a movement stressing conformity and uniformity in dogma and discipline. Clarke is particularly concerned with the ways in which these practices and the lay associations promoting them helped to mould and define gender roles as well as social relations within the parish and the community. In Article Twenty, David Marshall explores how changing social and material conditions as well as the spirit of doubt accompanying scientific developments and a new secularism altered Protestant attitudes toward death in the late nineteenth century.

QUESTIONS TO CONSIDER

1. How did Catholic piety change in the nineteenth century? What did church leaders hope to achieve through the "devotional revolution"? What attracted women to the new confraternities?
2. How and why did the attitudes and rituals surrounding death change in Protestant culture in the nineteenth century?
3. What resources can one use to recover the place of religion in the lives of ordinary people?

SUGGESTED READINGS

Airhart, Phyllis D. *Serving the Present Age: Revivalism, Progressivism, and the Methodist Tradition in Canada.* Montreal/Kingston: McGill-Queen's University Press, 1992.

Brouwer, Ruth Compton. *New Women for God: Canadian Presbyterian Women and India Missions, 1876–1914.* Toronto: University of Toronto Press, 1990.

Clarke, Brian P. *Piety and Nationalism: Lay Voluntary Associations and the Creation of an Irish-Catholic Community in Toronto, 1850–1895.* Montreal and Kingston: McGill-Queen's University Press, 1993.

Cook, Ramsay. *The Regenerators: Social Criticism in Late Victorian English Canada.* Toronto: University of Toronto Press, 1985.

Cook, Sharon Anne. "Through Sunshine and Shadow": *The Woman's Christian Temperance Union, Evangelicalism, and Reform in Ontario, 1874–1930.* Montreal/Kingston: McGill-Queen's University Press, 1995.

Gagan, Rosemary R. *A Sensitive Independence: Canadian Methodist Women Missionaries in Canada and the Orient.* Montreal/Kingston: McGill-Queen's University Press, 1991.

Grant, John Webster. *A Profusion of Spires: Religion in Nineteenth-Century Ontario.* Toronto: University of Toronto Press, 1988.

Marshall, David. *Secularizing the Faith: Canadian Protestant Clergy and the Crisis of Belief, 1850–1940.* Toronto: University of Toronto Press, 1992.

Westfall, William. *Two Worlds: The Protestant Culture of Nineteenth-Century Ontario.* Montreal/Kingston: McGill-Queen's University Press, 1989.

NINETEEN

The Parish and the Hearth: Women's Confraternities and the Devotional Revolution among the Irish Catholics of Toronto, 1850–1885

BRIAN CLARKE

Any attempt to understand the religious life of Catholic immigrants to Canada must begin with a knowledge of the religious situation in their country of origin at the time of their departure. The religious background of Irish Catholic immigrants, such as those who poured into Toronto in the wake of the Great Famine, has been expanded by historians like Emmet Larkin who have examined the impact of the Ultramontane revival on the religious practice of the laity. These historians have pointed out that the Ultramontanes were dedicated to effecting a far-reaching program of religious renewal. In addition to regularizing the laity's observance of canonical duties, such as attendance at Sunday Mass, the Ultramontanes sought to extend the range of lay piety. Devotions newly authorized by the papacy, paraliturgical rituals such as the rosary and the benediction of the Blessed Sacrament, were to become part of the everyday piety of the laity.

Historians of Irish Catholic immigrants, in both Britain and the United States, have observed that women were far more likely than men to attend church and to embrace the wide range of piety advocated by Ultramontane reformers.[1] Nevertheless, women's devotional organizations, or confraternities as contemporaries called them, have not as yet been examined in any depth. This lacuna is all the more puzzling since

Source: *Creed and Culture: The Place of English-Speaking Catholics in Canadian Society, 1750–1930,* Terrence Murphy and Gerald Stortz, eds. (Montreal/Kingston: McGill-Queen's University Press, 1993), pp. 185–203. Reprinted by permission of McGill-Queen's University Press.

it is often assumed that women's predominance in these organizations is directly related to their high level of devotional practice. One of the reasons why these confraternities have been overlooked is that historians have generally disregarded the role of the laity in the parish. All too often when the laity and their parochial organizations are examined, they are viewed as extensions of the clergy. Consequently, lay activism, especially that of women, is largely ignored.

Since the Catholics of Ireland are today a church-going people with one of the highest rates of attendance in the world, it is often assumed that they have always been so. In his pioneering article "The Devotional Revolution in Ireland," Larkin maintained that before the Great Famine of 1845–9 Irish Catholics were not noted for their religious observance, at least when measured by the usual official indices of church attendance.[2] Rather, he argued, the Catholics only became a church-going people in what he characterized as a devotional revolution during the quarter-century following the famine. Larkin's essay has provoked much discussion and debate among historians of Ireland. Some scholars, most notably S.J. Connolly, have argued that the revolution in lay religious observance was almost exclusively a post-famine phenomenon.[3] Others, especially Patrick Corish and K.T. Hoppen, have maintained that there was marked continuity in the growth of religious practice among the Irish before and after the famine.[4] Before the famine, church attendance had reached about 40 per cent, which means that by any measure a considerable proportion of the population were practising Catholics. As Larkin has subsequently pointed out, while the devotional revolution had made greater headway before the famine than he had originally allowed, its diffusion was still largely limited to the prosperous social classes and, in general, to the English-language regions of the country.[5] A devotional nucleus did exist in pre-famine Ireland, but even in areas such as the southeast, where the devotional revolution had made progress, religious observance had not yet reached anything like the universal level it was to gain in the three decades after the famine. Nor did devotional practice match the intensity and quality that marked that of post-famine Ireland. Even though the devotional revolution began before the famine, it was consolidated in the following generation, when an extraordinarily high level of religious observance became all but universal.[6]

The debates of Irish historians over the timing and scope of the devotional revolution in Ireland have an important bearing in determining the religious background of those Irish Catholics who came to Toronto. The Catholic population of Toronto was largely composed of immigrants who arrived in Canada during or shortly after the Great Famine of 1845–9. In 1841 there were some 2400 Irish Catholics in the city; by 1851 the Irish Catholic population had jumped to 7940 people, a more than three-fold increase over one decade.[7] What exposure would these immigrants have had to the beliefs and practices of the Catholic church in their home counties before departing for North America? Religious practice in pre-famine Ireland was differentiated along both class and regional lines. Substantial farmers and their families were the most likely to attend church and, as a class, were the backbone of the devotional revolution. While substantial farmers did not emigrate to North America in large numbers in this period, agricultural labourers were the mainstay of Irish Catholic emigration to Canada.[8] Official Catholicism had made few inroads among this population, who tended to stay away from church on Sundays as at any other time.[9] Other Irish Catholic immigrants to Toronto, albeit a minority, came from modest backgrounds either in small-scale farming or in the trades.[10] The exposure of these immigrants to the official teachings and rituals of the Roman Catholic church would vary according to where they grew up in Ireland.

Information on the regional origin of Irish Catholic immigrants is exceedingly rare. Fortunately, parochial marriage records make it possible to paint a regional profile of young adult immigrants married in Toronto between 1850 and 1859.[11] The vast majority of these immigrants, nearly one-half of the total, were from Munster. Those from Leinster came in a distant second, comprising a little over one-quarter of the sample. Immigrants from Connaught and Ulster together made up the remaining quarter. Of all these immigrants, only a handful came from cities, where in almost all regions church attendance was generally high, somewhere in the range between 60 and 70 per cent.[12]

In rural Ireland the Catholic church was weakest in Ulster and, above all, in Connaught. In these two provinces, the population far outstripped the institutional resources and personnel of the church, and, as a consequence, the majority of people did not attend church regularly. The situation was a good deal better in Munster, but even here the people's contact with the church was mixed. In County Clare, the leading county of origin for immigrants from the province, the church was an exceptionally vibrant institution. Nevertheless, in many parts of Munster, including areas in Counties Limerick, Tipperary, and Cork, which ranked consecutively after Clare in the number of immigrants recorded in the parochial marriage registers of Toronto, the church's parochial network was greatly overextended. Only in Leinster, with the exception of the Diocese of Meath, was the church a vibrant religious institution capable of reaching the laity in the region, and as a result church attendance was uniformly high in the province. Given their class backgrounds and their regional origins, many of those who emigrated to Toronto could hardly have had extensive exposure to the official beliefs and practices of the Catholic church before leaving for North America.[13]

During the 1850s the majority of Irish Catholic immigrants in Toronto stayed away from church on Sundays and continued to ignore the canonical injunctions of the church, much as they had done in Ireland. When Armand de Charbonnel assumed his duties as the second Roman Catholic bishop of Toronto in 1850, only two churches served the entire Catholic population. Although these churches were reasonably well filled on Sundays, only two-fifths of those Catholics who were required to attend church could have actually done so, a rate that compares favourably to the national pattern found in Britain at the time.[14] While the ecclesiastical authorities could have reasonably taken solace in the Roman Catholic turnout on Sundays, they saw things differently.

As dedicated reformers, Bishop Charbonnel and his clergy judged lay religious practice from a standard far more exacting than that of their predecessors. The clergy could only view the laity's religious behaviour with shock and horror. "I have everywhere met a great deal of ignorance," Charbonnel sadly admitted.[15] Besides ignoring the religious obligations of canonical Catholicism, too many Irish Catholic immigrants, Charbonnel believed, were totally ignorant of the essentials of their faith, such as how to say the Hail Mary, to hear Mass, and to make their confession.[16] In response to this situation, the clergy not only sought to elevate the standard of religious practice, but also endeavoured to extend the range of Catholic piety. The laity were to discharge their canonical obligations of attendance at Sunday Mass as well as the fulfilment of Easter duties and, in addition to this canonical minimum, to perform a wide variety of devotions. Instructed in the ideals of Ultramontanism, the clergy of Toronto in effect redefined what it was to be a practising Catholic.

The clergy were also deeply disturbed by the social behaviour of the Irish Catholic immigrants. Drunkenness and idleness, Charbonnel complained, were far too common among the Irish, and he was certain that the dissolute pastimes of the Irish were responsible for their indifferent religious observance. The moral reform of the laity, he concluded, was essential to effect their spiritual renewal. The Roman Catholic clergy, like their evangelical counterparts, set out to reform popular recreation: dancing, drinking, parties, and other amusements were denounced as "immediate occasions of sin alike to those who indulge in them and to willing spectacles [sic]."[17] What was at stake was nothing less than a way of life. The traditional work rhythm of the Irish, with its intense activity followed often by equally intense festivities and drinking, was incompatible with the demands of canonical Catholicism, which stressed the necessity of a well-regulated life. Self-discipline, punctuality, and the tenets of Catholicism were mutually reinforcing. The rationalization of social life and the promotion of the regular discharge of religious duties went together.

With only two churches, both located in the east end of the city, and with little in the way of social institutions, the Catholic church at the time of Charbonnel's arrival in 1850 was in a poor position to influence either the religious or the social behaviour of the laity. One obvious response to the situation was to make the church more accessible to the laity. Over the next eight years Charbonnel built three more churches to give Roman Catholicism an institutional presence throughout the city. It was one thing to provide adequate accommodation for the Catholic population, quite another to attract people who were not in the habit of going to church to attend Mass.

Parish missions, the Catholic version of the revival meeting, were one method by which the church sought to awaken the lukewarm. During services held morning and evening over several days, mission preachers would impress upon the laity how perilous their spiritual state was on account of sin, a condition that could be redeemed only by a conversion sealed by the sacraments of the church. The high point of the parish mission was the call to the confessional, followed by the reception of communion.[18] By stressing the immediate necessity of conversion, the mission fostered an experiential and personal form of piety. Yet the sporadic and episodic character of these services meant that the church had to turn to other means to sustain the laity's commitment to the church. In order to realize the church's twin mission of moral and spiritual renewal, the parish had to become the social and religious centre of the Irish Catholic community. The most effective means to achieve that end were parochial voluntary organizations that offered the laity a religiously informed alternative to the pastimes available outside of the church. Through its network of parish-based voluntary associations, which occupied the laity's leisure time, the church sought to influence both the social and the religious behaviour of the laity.

Parochial organizations were of many types — social service, recreational, and devotional — but confraternities were the linchpin in the clergy's campaign for spiritual renewal. Charbonnel began founding parochial confraternities in the early 1850s. By the early 1860s two of the largest confraternities, the Sodality of the Blessed Virgin Mary and the Children of Mary, were well established in the city's parishes. The Apostleship of Prayer or League of the Sacred Heart was introduced to the city by Charbonnel's successor, Bishop John Joseph Lynch, during the mid 1860s and, by the following decade, its parochial branches had become a fixture. The one significant latecomer, the Archconfraternity of the Holy Family, was not generally organized in the parishes until the early 1880s.[19] These devotional associations for adults, with the significant exception of the St. Vincent de Paul Society, which Charbonnel introduced to the diocese in 1850, were supported almost exclusively by women, even though most confraternities were open to men.

Most of the devotions promoted by the confraternities — the devotions to Mary, to the Blessed Sacrament or eucharist, to the Sacred Heart of Jesus and the way of the cross — were not new. Nevertheless, Catholic piety underwent a dramatic change in both style and content during the nineteenth century. The papacy's adoption of particular devotions by granting papal authorization and indulgences served to standardize these devotions according to Roman norms and usage.[20] Moreover, the papacy's energetic promotion of these devotions resulted in Catholic piety being recast into a complex of devotions that were articulated to one another, so much so that this form of Catholicism can be aptly termed devotional Catholicism. Catholic piety became characterized by the repeated performance of ritualistic actions that were to inspire the devotion of the faithful, as for example in the rosary.

All Catholic devotions sought to induce the faithful to forge a personal and familiar bond with Jesus, Mary, or one or another saint.[21] By entering into a relationship with these supernatural beings through the various devotions of the church, the believer could participate in the communion of the saints and share in the salvific economy of prayer and merit mediated by the Roman Catholic church. Through Mary, the Mother of God, the manual for the Archconfraternity of the Holy Family assured the faithful, "we have the most certain means of obtaining [the] inestimable gift of divine love, since she has been appointed by her Son, the Treasurer and Dispenser of all graces, and is therefore our most compassionate intercessor and advocate with God."[22] Devotions provided a highly ritualized entry into this redemptive universe. It is through these devotions that the religious world of Irish Catholic women is revealed.

Among the devotions promoted by the confraternities, it is perhaps the resurgence of Marian piety that most clearly illuminates the development of devotional piety among Irish Catholic women in Toronto. All the parish religious societies — the Association of the Children of Mary, the Sodality of the Blessed Virgin Mary, the Archconfraternity of the Holy Family, the Apostleship of Prayer also known as the League of the Sacred Heart — promoted devotions to Mary, especially the saying of the rosary. The rosary was a series of prayers, usually counted on a string of beads, in which the faithful recited fifteen decades of the Hail Mary, with each decade preceded by an Our Father and followed by a Glory Be to the Father. Associated with each decade was a meditation on the life of Mary and Jesus that linked Mary's purity and maternal solicitude with the salvific work of Jesus.

The rosary could be easily performed both in the church and in the home. Consequently, the rosary became an intensely private devotion. During the celebration of the Mass, the attention of many women was usually directed towards saying the rosary.[23] Few could understand Latin, and Catholic prayer books, because of Pius IX's prohibition of translations of the liturgy, usually provided only "Mass devotions and meditations" rather than liturgical texts.[24] Individually as well as collectively, these devotions imparted the distinctive doctrines of the Roman Catholic church. The rosary, like other Catholic devotions, was the prism through which the laity interpreted the Mass. Far from isolating its devotees, the rosary inevitably led to communal affirmation through the reception of the sacraments.

The purpose of the rosary, Charbonnel explained, "is to unite ourselves, in the course of our daily actions and sufferings [sic] to the Blessed Virgin Mary, to Her thoughts, Her Judgments, Her feelings, Her conversations, so that we may live and die as she did for God alone."[25] Mary's devotion to Jesus provided lay women with a model of true piety and maternal solicitude. As the Mother of God and a divine mediator, Mary was the spiritual mother of the faithful. Her graces and spiritual favours, purchased through her sacrifice and suffering, led her devotees to Christ crucified.[26] In the meditations the laity were encouraged to engage in while reciting the rosary, the sufferings of Mary were associated with Christ's sacrifice and his loving offer of salvation given up in the Mass. The Passion was thus central to the rosary, as it was to all other devotions. Marian devotionalism bridged the seemingly infinite gulf between the sacred and profane and made the sacraments much more accessible to the laity. By establishing such an intimate relationship with Mary, a relationship rooted in Christ's passion, the rosary inspired Irish Catholic women to receive the sacraments and so unite themselves with Christ. Without the sanctifying grace conveyed by the sacraments, Archbishop Lynch warned, "we can make no progress towards eternal life."[27] When informed by the sacraments, "the most indifferent works become eminently meritorious and of truly apostolic efficacy."[28]

The rosary fostered a personal quest for holiness that centred on the sacraments of the parish church. As a result, all women's confraternities advocated the frequent — monthly — reception of the sacraments.[29] As this piety was a form of sacramental nurture, it was firmly rooted in the collective affirmation of the Roman Catholic faith, the sacrifice of the Mass. By stressing the sacramental foundation of Catholic piety, the confraternities made an essential contribution to the establishment of parochial piety. Not only did they encourage the performance of private devotions at Mass and the regular reception of the sacraments, as the mark of a practising Catholic, but they also provided an important impetus for the public celebration of parochial devotions, such as the benediction of the Blessed Sacrament. In the interval between the reception of the sacraments, the performance of these devotions served to reinforce the sacramental relationship between the faithful and the divine forged in the sacrifice of the Mass offered up in the parish church. At the same time that the devotion to Mary led lay women to the altar, it was designed to suffuse day-to-day life with the sacraments.[30] The rosary, like all devotions, fostered a distinctive way of life for Irish Catholic women.

Both in style and in content, Marian devotions were a microcosm of the piety favoured by the Ultramontanes. All devotions — the way of the cross, the forty-hours devotion, the devotions to the Sacred Heart of Jesus — had the same ultimate aim and followed the same general pattern as the rosary. As schools of piety, confraternities played a leading role in popularizing these devotions. Besides promoting the saying of the rosary, women's confraternities encouraged daily prayers, usually the reciting of the Our Father and Hail Mary, as well as the use of other devotional aids: the crucifix with or without the miniature *Via Crucis*, the *Agnus Dei*, scapulars, medals, and prayer cards. One confraternity, that of the Holy Family, went so far as to advocate lotteries of such devotional aids as a means of encouraging their use. These portable aids fostered the practice of private home devotions among Irish Catholic women.[31] The day of a confraternity member was punctuated by short devotions such as the litany of the Blessed Virgin Mary, short exclamatory prayers ("My dear Jesus, I love you"), and, if possible, a visit to the Blessed Sacrament or a statue of the Blessed Virgin in the parish church.[32] As with the rosary, the purpose of these devotions and devotional aids was to integrate the grace communicated by the sacraments into the daily lives of members of the parish societies.

Although some devotions could be performed almost anywhere, their emphasis on the sacraments meant that they were church-centred forms of piety. Yet, as the proponents of the confraternities understood, such piety was best imparted and sustained in intimate groups rather than in the general anonymity of the larger congregation. Through their regular weekly meetings and collective devotions, confraternities created a social setting in which women could practise Catholic piety and appropriate its way of life. Most confraternities had a special room for their meetings where the members could engage in various religious exercises and in the business of formal meetings. These rooms were also used by the smaller devotional circles into which most confraternities were divided, where they could meet without the usual comings and goings of the parish church. In the privacy of these smaller meetings, each member was encouraged to participate and contribute to the group's activities. Not only did the repeated performance of the devotions cement the members' commitment to the Catholic church, but these exercises enabled members to get to know each other better and to form new friendships.[33] By providing mutual support, parochial devotional organizations sustained their members in the practice of piety and enabled them to integrate these devotions into their daily lives.[34]

The purpose of the confraternities was to popularize the devotions of the church. Yet how many Catholic women in fact joined these parish organizations? Unfortunately, complete and detailed reports on parish confraternities are extremely rare; only one full parish report, from St. Mary's parish in 1881, has survived in Toronto. In this parish of 5000, there were 1620 confraternity members or almost a third of the total Catholic population. This figure apparently includes 570 school children, which if deducted from the total membership leaves 1050 or roughly a quarter of the remaining parish population.[35] This large enrolment was not at all unusual. At about the same time, the Apostleship of Prayer in St. Paul's parish alone had some eight hundred members. While a substantial segment of the parish population joined confraternities, the available figures from St. Mary's do not indicate where the true strength of these organizations lay. In the city-wide Saint Joseph's Society, for example, men accounted for only a tenth of the membership, three-fifths of whom were married to women who had previously joined the society.[36] Membership in some of the parish confraternities for adults was limited to women only, but even those that were open to men, such as the Archconfraternity of the Holy Family or the Apostleship of Prayer, failed to attract significant male support.[37] St. Paul's parish, the leadership of the two main confraternities, the Apostleship of Prayer and the Archconfraternity of the Holy Family, was wholly composed of women, a good indication that their adult membership was almost entirely female.[38] Contemporary newspaper accounts confirm that women in other parishes made up the vast majority of the confraternities' adult membership.[39] The sex-specific membership of the confraternities is significant in establishing their impact on Irish Catholic women in general. How great an influence the parish confraternities had can be seen when the enrolment statistics from St. Mary's are examined more closely. If it is assumed that women made up about half of the parish's adult population and nine-tenths of the confraternities' membership in the parish, then some 42 per cent of all women in that parish belonged to one or another of the parish confraternities.[40]

Even these figures probably discount the full impact of the parish confraternities on the female population. The Saint Joseph's Society, for example, had an average membership of 158, yet over ten years some 336 people, the vast majority of them women, at one time or another belonged to the society.[41] This membership turnover indicates that static membership figures underestimate women's involvement in the parish confraternities. St. Mary's may not have been a typical parish, but it is clear that confraternities enjoyed extensive support among Irish Catholic women. By contrast, very few men joined confraternities. Although it is likely that more men took up devotions than their membership in confraternities would suggest, there was a marked difference between men's and women's religious behaviour. Not only did women attend church more regularly than men, but they were also far more involved in its devotional life. The correspondence between the world view of the devotions and the social role of women, particularly in the family, provides the answer.

The general expectation, certainly one encouraged by the church, was that women would marry, unless they were destined for a religious life. While the evidence is admittedly scanty, it would appear that the vast majority of Irish Catholic women eventually did marry.[42] After marriage, most Irish Catholic women worked in the home rather than outside.[43] Industrialization resulted in the growing separation between the home and men's place of work, a development that led many women to regard their homes as their distinct sphere. At the same time, industrialization sharpened the distinction between the paid work done by men in the workplace and the unpaid work women performed in the home.[44] Even though the work women did in the home was essential to their families' survival, they were economically dependent on their husbands, whose wages were the household's main source of income. Such dependence undercut the ability of women to exercise authority in the home, a situation that inevitably led to many a domestic quarrel.

Catholicism, however, developed a cult of domesticity that through its devotional observances sacralized the home as well as women in their capacity as the preservers and defenders of the home's sanctity. This process is especially apparent in the devotions to Mary, for the Virgin Mary represented feminine attributes raised to a supernatural level. Her divine qualities of maternal solicitude and service to others were precisely those that women were expected to fulfil, albeit on a more mundane level. Further, these qualities were not mere attributes, but virtues. If the Virgin Mary represented the sum total of feminine qualities, she also embodied virtue tout court. Nor was this combination of femininity with virtue in the person of Mary coincidental, for the two were seen as synonymous. In this sense, the Virgin Mary personified the idealization of womanhood, and a particular type of womanhood at that: woman as the repository and embodiment of self-sacrificing virtue, purity, and motherhood.[45] At the same time that Catholic piety validated the domestic role of women, it legitimized their authority in the home.

Devotional Catholicism also drew a sharp contrast between the home and the world: the home was a moral haven in a materialistic and immoral world.[46] According to this cult of domesticity, when at leisure the man's place was in the home, shielded from the dangers of the world, especially those of the tavern, by the comforting and virtuous influence of his wife. Women were to protect the sanctity of the home, and it was their responsibility to encourage the religious observance of their husbands.[47] In this way, confraternities bestowed upon women a moral power and influence over those on whom they were dependent.

If the devotions of the church encouraged women to exercise initiative in the privacy of the home, what role did the members of confraternities play in the parish church? It is not clear who the activists in the confraternities were and what went on in the confraternity meetings. Catholic newspapers generally took little notice of parish confraternities and their leaders, except when they were raising funds for the church. Even then, newspapers tended to emphasize the contributions of the wives of well-known Irish Catholic laymen. The others were referred to by their last name only, if they were noticed at all. This usual anonymity of confraternity activists shows that confraternities, like women's work in general, were undervalued in the male power structures of the church and of the Irish Catholic community. Yet confraternities required a large number of leaders, activists who were willing to commit their time and talent to the confraternity week in and week out. Most confraternities, such as the Apostleship of Prayer or the Archconfraternity of the Holy Family, were divided into prayer circles with no more than twenty-five members, each with its own leader. A large parish confraternity would depend upon some forty circle leaders to conduct its monthly or biweekly meetings.[48]

The composite structure of the confraternities had important consequences for lay leadership among Irish Catholic women. Most confraternities had plenary sessions as well as assemblies of the individual circles. The plenary meetings were usually of a set format and often required the presence of the parish priests to offer instruction, initiate new members, or perform the benediction of the Blessed Sacrament. In contrast to the plenary sessions presided over by the clergy, there were so many separate meetings of the confraternity circles that an overworked clergy must have left the circle leaders to their own devices. Parish confraternities thereby provided a limited outlet for lay leadership. Circle prefects would lead their members through a set round of devotions, but they were also expected to offer a short instruction and demonstrate ingenuity in making the meetings both lively and entertaining. Each circle leader was responsible for the general administration and well-being of her circle: she was to collect fees, console sick members, reassure the faint hearted, and recruit new members.[49]

As members of confraternities, women also exercised leadership in the parish at large. The women's confraternities were the most successful parish fund-raisers. While men, usually members of the St. Vincent de Paul Society, sat on the committee of management to supervise financial arrangements, it was the women who prepared the food, decorated the hall, made articles to be sold or auctioned off, and above all persuaded the public to contribute their mite.[50] The fund-raising of the confraternities was essential not only for the continuing operation of the church's social institutions and parishes, but also for the construction of new buildings. By 1872 Catholic church buildings and social institutions were valued at more than half a million dollars, far outstripping any other denomination in Toronto, an impressive achievement for a largely lower-working-class denomination.[51] In addition to fund-raising, a few women's confraternities were directly involved in charity work through their auxiliaries, popularly known as sewing societies, whose members visited the sick and provided warm clothing for the poor in winter.[52] When fund-raising, staging of parish socials and entertainments, conducting of confraternity meetings, organization of volunteers for various parish projects, holding of various sewing and baking bees, and operation of the benevolent societies are added up, it becomes clear that parish confraternities offered Irish Catholic women an opportunity to demonstrate their administrative ingenuity as well as to exercise leadership.[53]

Nonetheless, the field for lay leadership open to women, even to middle-class women, was restricted. The parish priests' authority was "always supreme" in the confraternities, and lay leaders were to concern themselves solely with "material administration."[54] In contrast to parochial organizations for men, where elections for the executive prevailed, the parish clergy usually appointed lay leaders from among the prominent ladies of the parish. The confraternities' leadership reflected the social hierarchy of the parish.[55] The manner in which the clergy directed these societies and appointed their leadership was unmistakably paternalistic. Women were frequently relegated to a position of service and subordination. The founding of the Society of Our Lady of Perpetual Help, a women's benevolent society in St. Michael's parish, illustrates how women dealt with this paternalism. The wives of some of the wealthiest laymen in the parish respectfully requested Archbishop Lynch to call a meeting so that the society, which now had numerous members, could be "properly organized." They further asked that the archbishop "speak in favorable terms of it in the Cathedral."[56] The society was already organized, but its leaders recognized that a proper show of deference was necessary to obtain the necessary ecclesiastical sanction. These women obviously knew what they wanted and how to get it, but this petition also demonstrates that they usually depended on the good will of others to achieve their goals. Power remained firmly in the hands of the clergy.

Yet for many women the religious and social life of the parish confraternity was attractive. For one thing, the Roman Catholic church provided one of the few forms of respectable recreation available to Irish Catholic women outside the home. Then, too, in the confraternities, women could find much needed moral support and receive assurance they were living up to the new and demanding role of the angel in the home. Perhaps of greater significance was the opportunity confraternities offered to their members to associate with other women and engage in corporate action with them. Many of the social relations that circumscribed women's social life were prescribed either by traditional ties, as in the case of kin, or by an accident of geography, as in the case of neighbours. In the parish confraternity women could form close friendships and collaborate with other women of their own choosing who shared their interests and ideals.

The influence of the confraternities extended far beyond their largely female membership. Confraternities played a critical role in the development of the public performance of devotions in the parish church, such as vespers, the benediction of the Blessed Sacrament, and the forty-hours devotion.[57] When these parish-centred devotions were first introduced, the confraternity members were their most fervent practitioners. The observance of these rituals by the members of the confraternities galvanized the parish and acted as a leaven, encouraging others to participate in these devotions of the church. Confraternities also played an important role in changing the ethos of the parish and the tone of Catholic worship. In rural, pre-famine Ireland, Catholic services were frequently punctuated by the continual traffic of the congregation as they entered or left the church, the yelping of dogs, and the loud conversations of parishioners. After Toronto's devotional revolution, contemporary observers frequently commented on the reverential behaviour of the laity when in church: while the priest said Mass, save for the occasional protest of an infant in arms, only the whispers of the faithful telling their beads and rustling of the congregation as they knelt and rose could be heard.[58]

Confraternities reinforced the parish as the locus of piety, but confraternity members also exercised their influence in a much more informal and personal way. Many sons and daughters, not to mention husbands, were introduced to the devotions and teachings of the church by women belonging to the confraternities. As a result, few families could escape contact with Catholic values and rituals. The appeals of these women in the privacy of their homes are now unfortunately beyond the reach of the historian, but they were effective. Reliable figures on church attendance are hard to obtain, but an enumeration of Sunday services by the *Globe* in 1882 reveals that slightly over 70 per cent of all Catholics of canonical age attended Sunday Mass. Women were still more likely to attend church, but this figure indicates that many men, perhaps a bare majority, now assisted at Mass. Yet if men increasingly discharged their canonical obligations, they still lagged behind in taking up devotions. The predominance of women in the parish confraternities underlines the uneven diffusion of devotional Catholicism in Toronto. By the late 1880s the Roman Catholic church finally managed after many failed attempts to establish parish societies for men on a secure footing, but these organizations emphasized recreational pursuits rather than devotional observances. Only after the turn of the century did confraternities gain a large following among Catholic men.[59]

According to the clergy, as Jay Dolan has remarked, the laity were to pray, obey, and, of course, pay the bills.[60] In practice, the laity, women in particular, did much more than that. Women's confraternities were a major agency for popularizing devotional piety. As result of their efforts, the practice of devotions became common among Irish Catholic women. Confraternities offered Irish Catholic women an associational life in the parish that wedded female sociability to devotional Catholicism and its world view. This form of piety imparted to its practitioners a social and a religious identity that were mutually reinforcing. Confraternities offered women the opportunity to create a religious and social world. Within the male-dominated power structures of the Roman Catholic church they could not make that world in any way that they chose to, but they successfully claimed a social vocation both in the home and in the parish as their own.

NOTES

1. Lynn Hollen Lees, *Exiles of Erin: Irish Migrants in Victorian London* (Ithaca, New York: Cornell University Press 1979), 184–5; and Ann Taves, *The Household of Faith: Roman Catholic Devotions in Mid-Nineteenth-Century America* (Notre Dame: University of Notre Dame Press 1986), 18 and 87.
2. Emmet Larkin, "The Devotional Revolution in Ireland, 1850–75," *American Historical Review* 77 (June 1972): 625–52; reprinted in Emmet Larkin, *The Historical Dimensions of Irish Catholicism* (Washington: Catholic University of America Press 1984).
3. S.J. Connolly, *Priests and People in Pre-Famine Ireland: 1780–1845* (London and New York: Gill and MacMillan and St. Martin's Press 1982).
4. Patrick J. Corish, *The Irish Catholic Experience: A Historical Survey* (New York: Michael Glazier 1985), 232; K.T. Hoppen, *Elections, Politics and Society in Ireland* (Oxford: The Clarendon Press 1984), 197–224; Desmond J. Keenan, *The Catholic Church in Nineteenth-Century Ireland: A Sociological Survey* (London: Gill and Macmillan 1983), 242–5.
5. Larkin, *Historical Dimensions of Irish Catholicism*, 8.
6. Ibid., 5–9.

7. *Journals of the Legislative Assembly of Canada*, 1842, appendix M, and *Census of Canada*, 1851–2, 1, 30–1 and 66–7.

8. Cecil J. Houston and William J. Smyth, *Irish Emigration and Irish Settlement: Patterns, Links, and Letters* (Toronto: University of Toronto Press 1990), 57–63; S.H. Cousens, "Emigration and Demographic Change in Ireland, 1851–1861," *Economic History Review*, series 2, 14 (1961): 275–7.

9. Connolly, *Priests and People*, 277–8; Archives of the Roman Catholic Archdiocese of Toronto (ARCAT), Lynch Papers, "The Evils of Wholesale and Improvident Emigration From Ireland."

10. S.H. Cousens, "The Regional Pattern of Emigration during the Great Famine," Institute of British Geographers, *Transactions and Papers* 28 (1960): 128–33; ARCAT, J.M. Jamot, "Census of City Wards," c. early 1860s.

11. ARCAT, St. Paul's Parish, Marriage Register, 1850–9; St. Michael's Cathedral, Marriage Register, 1852–9; St. Mary's Parish, Marriage Register, 1857–9.

12. David Miller, "Irish Catholicism and the Great Famine," *Journal of Social History* 9 (1975): 87.

13. Corish, Irish Catholic Experience, 174, 176, 181–2, 184, and 208–9; Miller, "Irish Catholicism and the Great Famine," 85–8; Connolly, *Priests and People*, 91–2 and 94–5.

14. ARCAT, Charbonnel Papers, Bishop Armand Charbonnel to Cardinal Giacomo Fransoni, 26 May 1851; W.S.E. Pickering, "The 1851 Religious Census — A Useless Experiment?" *British Journal of Sociology* 18 (1967): 382–407.

15. Charbonnel Papers, Bishop Charbonnel to M. de Merode, 12 July 1852 (my translation).

16. Ibid., Bishop Charbonnel to Cardinal Fransoni, 30 May 1852, and Bishop Charbonnel to John Wardy, 1 Dec. 1854.

17. Ibid., pastoral 1856, pastoral 1858, and "Regulations for the Retreat preceding St. Patrick's Feast," 1859.

18. Jay P. Dolan, *Catholic Revivalism: The American Experience: 1830–1900* (Notre Dame: University of Notre Dame Press 1978), 77–8, 83–4, 95–6, and 112.

19. *Mirror*, 15 Sept. 1854; Charbonnel papers, Saint Paul's Parish Report, c. 1859; Lynch Papers, St. Michael's Cathedral Report, c. 1861, and J.C. Pouxel to Bishop John Joseph Lunch, 23 Nov. 1863; *Canadian Freeman*, 1 June 1865; *Irish Canadian*, 31 May 1883.

20. Taves, *Household of Faith*, 27 and 94–6.

21. Ibid., 48–51, 81, and 83–8.

22. *Manual of the Archconfraternity of the Holy Family* (np, nd), 2.

23. Charbonnel Papers, Rev. M. O'Shea to Bishop Charbonnel, 15 Jan. 1858, and Rev. E. Rooney to Bishop Charbonnel, 1858; Edward Kelly, *The Story of St. Paul's Parish* (Toronto: Private 1922), 252.

24. See *Rules of the Society of St. Vincent of Paul* (Toronto 1861), 53–123.

25. Charbonnel Papers, pastoral, 2 Feb. 1855.

26. *Catholic Weekly Review*, 12 May 1887; *Exercise of the Via Crucis* (Rome: Sacred Congregation de Propaganda Fide 1834), 30–1.

27. *Irish Canadian*, 1 March 1876; *Third Glorious Mystery, Fourth Glorious Mystery, Fifth Sorrowful Mystery*, and *Fifth Joyful Mystery* (Montreal: D. and J. Sadlier, nd).

28. *Apostleship of Prayer — Ticket of Admission*.

29. Ibid.; ARCAT, St. Michael's Cathedral, Book of Announcements, Third Sunday after Lent, 1882, and Second Sunday after Easter, 1884.

30. H. Ramière, *The Apostleship of Prayer: Explanation and Practical Instruction* (Baltimore: John Murphy 1864), 6; *Bulletin of the Society of St. Vincent of Paul* (Bulletin), Sept. 1872, 218, and June 1879, 173.

31. Lynch Papers, Archbishop Lynch to Rev. T. Wardy, 9 Dec. 1862, pastoral, Aug. 1869, and J.M. Jamot, "Confraternity of the Scapulary of Mt. Carmel"; *Bulletin*, Sept. 1872, 298; *Manual of the Archconfraternity of the Holy Family*, 106–12.

32. *Manual of the Archconfraternity of the Holy Family*, 9–10 and 127–9.

33. *Apostleship of Prayer — Ticket of Admission*; Ramière, *Apostleship of Prayer: Explanation*, 6; *Bulletin*, April 1872, 126; *Work of the Holy Agony of Our Lord Jesus Christ* (np 1863); Kelly, *St. Paul's Parish*, 254–63; Mary Hoskins, *History of St. Basil's Parish, St. Joseph Street* (Toronto: Catholic Register and Canadian Extension 1912), 63–6, 81–2, and 92.

34. *Apostleship of Prayer — Ticket of Admission*; Ramière, *Apostleship of Prayer: Explanation*, 6; *Bulletin*, April 1872, 126; *Work of the Holy Agony of Our Lord Jesus Christ*.

35. Lynch Papers, St. Mary's Parish Report, 15 Aug. 1881.

36. ARCAT, "Register of the Saint Joseph's 'Bona Mors' Society," 1863–73.

37. St. Michael's Cathedral, Book of Announcements, Twenty-Fifth Sunday after Pentecost, 1882, and Second Sunday after Pentecost, 1883.

38. Kelly, *St. Paul's Parish*, 251–64.

39. *Globe*, 20 June 1881 and 1 June 1883; *Catholic Weekly Review*, 14 June 1890; *Irish Canadian*, 5 June 1872 and 17 May 1888.

40. These calculations are based on the sex ratio found in *Census of Canada, 1880–81*, 1, 73.

41. "Register of the Saint Joseph's 'Bona Mors' Society," 1863–73.

42. *Canadian Freeman*, 23 March 1871; *Irish Canadian*, 22 Jan. 1879; "Register of the Saint Joseph's 'Bona Mors' Society," 1863–73.

43. Jamot, "Census of City Wards," c. early 1860s; Hazier Diner, *Erin's Daughters in America: Irish Immigrant Women in the Nineteenth Century* (Baltimore: Johns Hopkins University Press 1983), 51–2.

44. Joan W. Scott and Louise A. Tilly, "Women's Work and Family in Nineteenth-Century Europe," *Comparative Studies in Society and History* 17 (1975): 52–3; Nancy F. Cott, *"Bonds of Womanhood": Women's Sphere in New England, 1780–1835* (New Haven: Yale University Press 1977), 61–2 and 69; Alison Prentice, Paula Bourne, Gail Cuthbert Brandt, Beth Light, Wendy Mitchinson, and Naomi Black, *Canadian Women: A History* (Toronto: Harcourt Brace Jovanovich 1988), 121–2.

45. Charbonnel Papers, pastoral 1854; Ramière, *Apostleship of Prayer: Explanation*, 5.

46. *Irish Canadian*, 20 March 1870.

47. John Francis Maguire, *The Irish in America* (New York: Sadlier 1873), 123.

48. *Archconfraternity of the Holy Family; Apostleship of Prayer — Ticket of Admission*; Kelly, *St. Paul's Parish*, 263.

49. *Bulletin*, April 1882, 126; Lynch Papers, St. Mary's Parish Report, 15 Aug. 1881; *Catholic Weekly Review*, 14 June 1890.

50. *Irish Canadian*, 7 July 1869, 13 Dec. 1870, 10 Sept. 1873, and 18 Nov. 1886; *Canadian Freeman*, 29 Dec. 1864, 6 June 1867, 4 June 1868, and 17 Feb. 1870; ARCAT, St. Paul's Parish, Book of Announcements, First Sunday in September, 1872, Sixteenth Sunday after Pentecost, 1875, Second Sunday after Advent, 1875, and Fourth Sunday after Easter, 1876; St. Michael's Cathedral, Book of Announcements, Twelfth Sunday after Pentecost, 1881, Third Sunday after Easter, 1882, and Fifth Sunday after Easter, 1882; *Globe*, 28 Oct. 1880.

51. *Globe*, 16 May 1872.

52. *Irish Canadian*, 7 Nov. 1877, 20 Nov. 1878, and 19 Nov. 1879; *Catholic Weekly Review*, 19 Nov. 1887, 21 April 1888, and 28 March, 4 and 25 April 1891; Lynch Papers, Helen Crawford et al. to Archbishop Lynch, 8 Dec. 1874.

53. *Manual of the Archconfraternity of the Holy Family*, 11–17; *Bulletin*, May 1873, 152; Lynch Papers, St. Mary's Report, 15 Aug. 1881; St. Paul's Parish, Book of Announcements, Second Sunday after Easter 1871, 2 July 1871, Palm Sunday 1873, Twenty-second Sunday after Pentecost 1873, Fourteenth Sunday after Pentecost 1874, Second Sunday after Advent 1875, Sexagesima Sunday 1876, Sixth Sunday after Pentecost 1876, Twentieth Sunday after Pentecost 1876; St. Michael's Cathedral, Book of Announcements, Seventeenth Sunday after Pentecost 1881, Twentieth Sunday after Pentecost 1881, and Septuagesima Sunday 1882.

54. *Archconfraternity of the Holy Family; Bulletin*, April 1872, 125 and June 1879, 173.

55. *Archconfraternity of the Holy Family; Canadian Freeman*, 28 Nov. 1861, 23 Jan. 1862, 1 Jan. 1863, and 1 June 1865; *Irish Canadian*, 16 June 1869, 16 Feb. 1870, 19 July 1871, 4 Feb. 1874, 20 Nov. 1878, 4 Oct. 1883, 29 July 1886, and 6 Sept. 1888; *Globe*, 8 Oct. 1874, 28 Oct. 1880, and 18 Nov. 1884; *Catholic Weekly Review*, 19 Nov. 1887, 1 Feb. 1890, and 18 April 1891; Hoskins, *St. Basil's Parish*, 96–8; Lynch Papers, Archbishop Lynch to Miss Banks and the Children of Mary, nd, and Helen M. Crawford et al. to Archbishop Lynch, 8 Dec. 1874.

56. Lynch Papers, Helen M. Crawford et al. to Archbishop Lynch, 8 Dec. 1874.

57. *Canadian Freeman*, 22 June 1865 and 22 June 1871; *Irish Canadian*, 21 Sept. 1875; *Globe*, 7 Feb. 1882.

58. John Ross Robertson, *Landmarks of Toronto*, 6 vols. (Toronto: Toronto Telegram 1914), 4, 324–5.

59. *Globe*, 7 Feb. 1882. My calculations have been based on *Census of Canada, 1880–81*, I, 174–5, and II, 100–1, and have been adjusted to reflect population growth over one year. Almost 27 per cent of the city population was under the age of twelve, the usual age among Catholics for first communion and confirmation. I have used this figure to calculate the rate of attendance of Irish Catholics.

60. Jay P. Dolan, *The Immigrant Church: New York's Irish and German Catholics, 1815–1865* (Baltimore: Johns Hopkins University Press 1973), 165.

TWENTY

"Death Abolished": Changing Attitudes to Death and the Afterlife in Nineteenth-Century Canadian Protestantism

DAVID MARSHALL

On 26 February 1889, George Paxton Young, the eminent moral philosopher from the University of Toronto, died. In most respects Young's funeral was typical of practicing Christians of high station in late Victorian Canada.[1] His body lay in Convocation Hall at the University of Toronto. There was little hint of funeral gloom as everything was designed to beautify the surroundings. The walnut casket was mounted on massive silver ornaments and was lined with white cashmere. It was open and on Dr. Young's breast lay a cluster of palm leaves signifying victory, Easter lilies symbolizing everlasting life, and lilies of the valley indicating purity. According to the reporter for the *Toronto Mail*, "the features of the dead man looked much the same as they did in life, and were it not for the pallor one might think him sleeping, so placid

Source: An earlier version of "'Death Abolished': Changing Attitudes to Death and the Afterlife in Nineteenth Century Canadian Protestantism" was presented at the Canadian Historical Association in Victoria, 1990. Reprinted by permission of the author.

was the expression of his countenance." Surrounding the coffin were the numerous wreaths and floral arrangements that had been sent by mourners. At the funeral service, the Rev. D.J. Macdonnell offered prayer, and Daniel Wilson, the President of the University of Toronto, delivered the address on the mysteries of death. Then a large procession of over four hundred, including the academic staff of the university, students and former students, and prominent Ontario politicians, marched through Queen's Park and then northward to Mount Pleasant Cemetery at the boundary of the city, where Young was laid to rest.[2]

On the following Sunday, D.J. Macdonnell delivered a funeral sermon with the provocative title "Death Abolished," during which he reflected on the significance of George Paxton Young's life. Macdonnell was known as a passionate, forthright, and bold preacher. Over a decade earlier, he had been charged with heresy for wondering whether the Presbyterian doctrine of everlasting punishment of the wicked might be inconsistent with God's loving and merciful nature.[3] In "Death Abolished," Macdonnell confidently stated his beliefs regarding death and the afterlife. He outlined how *"the abolition of death"* had been accomplished by Christ. There was "physical death"; but it was, he emphasized "a beginning rather than an ending, a process of life rather than of death. . . . It is the shuffling off of the mortal coil of flesh that the life within may have room to expand and may receive from God a *'spiritual body'* which may be a fit organ for the renewed spirit." According to Macdonnell, Christ robbed death of its terror "by bringing the blessedness of the future home of the soul so prominently into view that the soul is content to leave its earthly tabernacle."[4] These thoughts clearly minimized the gloomy and menacing aspects of death and virtually denied the presence of divine judgement, punishment for sinfulness, and hell. There was little sense of finality or of death being an end to life. Macdonnell was assured of the presence of a God of infinite mercy and the prospect of life everlasting. These views were consistent with the sentimental and romantic attitude toward death that Philippe Aries has suggested emerged in late nineteenth century European culture. The most dramatic indication of the age of "beautiful death," he has written, was the "retreat of evil" and the "end of hell."[5]

Robert Weir, a concerned layman, decided to review "Death Abolished" in order to point out that Macdonnell had confined his commentary to the "sunny side" of the question. He was reluctant to debate Macdonnell for he felt it inappropriate to make a funeral sermon the subject of controversy. Nevertheless, he charged that the sermon was contrary to Christ's own teaching and experience because it indicated that life was somehow "unbroken" and there was no death. The concept of "Death Abolished" seemed to compromise the central events of historic Christianity: Christ's death on the cross, burial in the tomb, and resurrection. These events were interrelated, Weir argued, and if any one of them was questioned then the whole edifice of Christianity would crumble. For the more orthodox, the attempt by some clergymen to remove death's sting by ignoring the fact that death was indeed a separation, an ending, and an occasion that was accompanied by God's judgement was dangerous since it undermined God's moral government, thereby potentially encouraging a drift away from Christian faith.[6] In the view of conservative social critics, there was little to halt a precipitous decline in morality if apprehension of divine judgement and the everlasting punishment of the wicked disappeared. Here juxtaposed were the two opposing views of death that dominated Victorian thought. Clearly, in theological literature and in church circles the understanding of death had become a highly contested issue.

It is important to stress that religious beliefs did not have a monopoly on the attitudes and rituals surrounding death. They were mixed with many folk customs and beliefs, such as visitation of the body and funeral wakes, both designed to help keep evil spirits away.[7] Moreover, during the later nineteenth century in Canada, death was surrounded by ever increasing commercialization, especially among the respectable middle classes. Special mourning clothes and jewellery, elaborate decorations and plumes, black crepe, black bordered writing paper, durable and sometimes ornate and expensive coffins, and large headstones with pious epigraphs became integral to the rituals of death.[8] Funeral processions, in particular, were highly public occasions for families to stage their wealth, respectability, and status. In this atmosphere, death was not the great leveller but rather a key moment for the ranks and divisions of the social hierarchy to be demonstrated.[9]

Nevertheless, the rituals surrounding death were public events full of Christian imagery and meaning. With the possible exception of the physician and the undertaker, there were few in society who dealt with death on a more constant and intimate basis than the clergy. They were frequently at the deathbed and they were an integral part of the ritual process, which was designed to ease the passage from the deathbed to burial in the grave. Many people found support and meaning in the rituals and teaching of Christianity as they struggled to cope with either the death of a loved one or the apparently inexplicable death of someone very young. Rituals were designed by the churches to impress the public with the cardinal truths of Christianity: the mortality of the earthly body and life everlasting of the redeemed soul in heaven.

One of the most important rituals surrounding death in the nineteenth century were funeral sermons. They were frequently published in the local newspaper or as a pamphlet. They were designed as a memorial to the deceased person's life and an explanation for his or her death. Pastors often celebrated the faith and works of the deceased, hoping that his or her life would serve as an inspiration for others to lead a Christian life. Clergy also preached more generally on the Christian understanding of death to the broader community. Funeral sermons, therefore, expressed attitudes toward death. They are an important barometer for tracing changing attitudes.

Christian teaching about death has always been full of paradox or ambiguity. On the one hand, death was something to be feared. It was a terrible calamity, the result of sin and the enduring presence in the world. It represented a loss and the end of earthly life. On the other hand, death was a blessing, a merciful deliverance from the miseries of this world into the hands of a loving and sympathetic God. It marked a rebirth or beginning of life everlasting. In no period has one view absolutely dominated.[10]

In the early part of the nineteenth century, there was great fear and uncertainty surrounding the mystery of death. The more foreboding aspects of death were an integral part of the clergyman's message. In many funeral orations, clergy issued dire warnings that unless the unregenerate converted immediately, they would surely be cast into hell forever. The occasion and circumstances of anyone's death were believed to be providential and the concept of divine judgement was stressed in commentaries about death. Around mid-century, the delicate balance in attitudes toward death began to shift away from anxiety over the circumstances and meaning of death to some assurance that death was not to be feared. References to divine judgement and eternal damnation in hell waned. By the late Victorian period, there was much greater emphasis on the Christian hope of life everlasting, which made possible the celebration of death as a passage to perfect happiness and fulfilment in a heavenly paradise. Reflecting the optimistic mood of the late Victorian period, the clergy's central message became one of consolation and hope.

In comparing the attitudes toward death and the afterlife of the early and late nineteenth century, the change seems dramatic. But over the course of the century, these changes were often subtle. There was no one event, discovery, or trend that was responsible for the changes. There was not a clear turning point. The shift in understanding death and the afterlife was a long, slow process and largely one of emphasis or degree. One view did not completely replace the other, as the controversy between Macdonnell and Weir indicates. Moreover, the differing views of death were variations of attitudes deeply rooted within Christianity. It is the purpose of this study to explore the changing religious attitudes toward death and the afterlife in Victorian Canada and to suggest reasons for the shift in emphasis within Christian understanding.[11]

....

In the Victorian era, death was an ever present reality or an obvious companion of life. Due to the perils of giving birth, the incidence of infant diseases, numerous outbreaks of infectious epidemics, and the dangers involved in many workplaces, life expectancy was terribly uncertain and often short. Few families were able to avoid the tragedy of someone being struck down well before old age, whether it be in infancy or in the prime of life.[12] Before attempts by governments in Canada to register vital statistics were initiated in the 1860s, people had their own crude but effective manner of calculating death rates. In an 1847 sermon on the certainty of death, the Rev. John Irvine discussed the fifty four deaths in his Saint John parish over the past year. People of all ages, from four months to seventy one years, had passed away. Some died from a sudden and unexpected accident, some "wasted away by the pining hand of insidious consumption," some had "fallen amid the flames of a violent fever," and some had "gradually sunk amid the flight of years." He suggested that if the current rate of deaths in the parish was sustained, then by the end of 1848, one sixteenth of those sitting in the pews "must be in heaven or hell!"[13] The massive number of deaths resulting from an outbreak of an infectious disease, such as cholera or smallpox, often created a general sense of panic at all levels of society.[14] Everyone was susceptible and moreover felt helpless in the face of disease and other threats to life. Medicine was largely ineffective before the scourge of disease, and until the introduction of antisepsis in the late 1860s, medical procedures were extremely perilous. Death was not something that could be easily ignored or thrust into the background of life.

It is doubtful that questions of death and dying always occupied people in their daily lives. But it would be difficult, indeed, for people to avoid the mysterious and disturbing questions relating to death when they were sick, mourning the death of a loved one, worrying about the outbreak of disease, or taking notice of a catastrophe or tragic accident. Coping with death was not a mere matter of intellectual curiosity or adherence to church doctrine. As numerous clergy pointed out, it was a matter of "the heart's deep instincts" to ask whether one ceases to exist or "takes up a new residence." Does the soul, one cleric speculated for his congregation, "continue in a cold cheerless separation — hovering over the remains of its former companion, waiting and longing for a happy reunion? . . . Shall we together be all happy or miserable hereafter? Or shall we be solitary in our woe — divided in our bliss?" In 1833, the Rev. John Smith of Kingston, Upper Canada, captured the anxiety people experienced when confronted by a death. "This widowhood of the affections — this desolation of the heart — this wilderness of grief which the death of those we love creates, is rendered still more distressing by the fearful doubts, which overhang their invisible state, and the equally impenetrable incertitude of our own."[15]

In the early nineteenth century, death was referred to as the "enemy" by many clergy. A great deal of the terror that surrounded death was associated with the fact that, too often, "the young, full of promise and big with hope," were "prematurely snatched away."[16] Because significant numbers died long before they reached old age, death often seemed unnatural. In October of 1860, soon after the death of Peter Mc-Gill, the Rev. William Snodgrass reminded his Montreal congregation that the "wise Creator" was the "king of terrors," who "ceaselessly plies his cruel work, driving right and left his well-aimed, fatal shafts, sparing neither youth nor beauty, dignity nor wealth, usefulness nor honour, but hurrying away the subjects of resistless power and universal dominion, . . . to replenish the dark but spacious storehouse of the tomb."[17] Death was an ominous event which exhibited the absolute sovereignty of God and the powerlessness of humans.

The uncertainty of life was constantly referred to in funeral orations. Whenever a young person died, clergy stated that the death could strike at any time and no one should postpone the decision for immediate conversion. Everyone had to be prepared. In 1847, when Mary Sophia Whitehead died at the age of twenty, the local preacher pressed those at the funeral service to "seek the Lord; and wait not till the freshness of youth is gone, as if it were ever too early to secure the blessings." Otherwise life will be full of "sorrow and disappointment"; there will be "days of evil and bitterness."[18] Concern with the precariousness of life allowed clergy to exhort backsliders and shore up people's faith. The imperative of immediate conversion was stressed for the unregenerate. Death was always nearby. The Rev. Robert Irvine raised macabre, haunting images to warn his Saint John congregation that "there is a voice issuing from every open grave, from every dying bed, and from every mourning family, which speaks in admonitory language, and warns you and me, that we have not a single moment to lose; yet although these are admonitions which are daily, I might say hourly, falling upon our ears, still we seem to pass them by unheeded and unheard."[19]

Moral meaning was attached to death. God's purpose in bringing about death, many believed, was to correct sin and to strengthen faith. Death of a loved one was regarded as a test of faith. Eliza Chipman was the wife of the Baptist minister William Chipman. Her life was rooted in the strongly evangelical ethos of the Maritime Baptist church. She felt "safe in saying that . . . I passed through what is generally termed a sound conversion." When confronted by difficult decisions or situations, she hoped that she was "in the presence of Almighty God, and can make free surrender of soul and body, all into his blessed hands, to lead, to guide, to defend me through the thorny maze." She lost her first born child in 1830 and then another four years later. Eliza regarded the death of her children as a punishment and test. "God," she confided to her diary, "has seen fit in his wisdom to hand me the cup of affliction to drink of, . . . I know my dear Redeemer has chastened me for my profit." In deep despair, she trusted that God would fairly judge her daughter, and for herself, she sought "the supporting grace of God." Eliza Chipman sought comfort in the saviour "who art the restorer of the breach"; but she was also deeply moved by the conviction that the death of her daughters was the result of divine judgement.[20]

Deadly diseases, in particular, were thought to be a punishment from God and a means to bring about spiritual regeneration and moral righteousness. Many thought that the cholera outbreak of 1832–1834 was divinely imposed. Thomas Webster, a London area yeoman who later became a Methodist preacher, concluded that the "disease was most fatal among the intemperate."[21] The Rev. Anson Green, a Methodist saddle bag preacher, was convinced that his bout with cholera was a trial. Many years after the attack, he wrote:

> Severe as was the ordeal through which I passed, this visitation did me good. . . . I had always entertained gloomy thoughts of death, and doubts concerning my final triumph over the grim monster. Not that I doubted my acceptance with God. I was clear in my experience of sins forgiven; but I feared that when I went down into the chilly floods of Jordan my faith might fail, and I might be left to sink in those cold billows at last, with- out hope and without comfort. May the Lord pardon these fears. They were ungrateful, if not sinful. When I sank down to the very verge of death, heavily pressed with a mal- ady the most dangerous and revolting, I was serene and happy. Not a doubt to trouble me; not a cloud to obscure the spiritual horizon. But I found that He who gives grace to live by will surely give grace to die by. Dying grace for a dying hour.

Although numerous home remedies were applied by the family caring for him, Green thought that he was saved by God and that this threat of death marked an important turning point in his spiritual life. His doubts about life everlasting disappeared and he became more hopeful about the future as a result of this crucial experience.[22] Cholera was only the most virulent of many diseases which seemed to demonstrate that death was a means of God's moral government over fallen humanity.

The Rev. Alexander Sutherland, one of the most prominent preachers within Ca- nadian Methodism, drew a stark picture of death as a punishment for sinfulness. He entreated his congregation to "imagine yourself in some vast prison, where the cells are as numerous as the mounds in the graveyard and each cell with its chained pris- oner, and so would you not think at once: 'Here must be a vast amount of guilt to fill these cells.'" Sutherland completed this commentary on sin and punishment by pointing out that "just as the graveyard is God's prisonhouse, so the graves are cells where he has confined so many prisoners."[23] This troubling imagery of a stern God and a dark prison-like afterlife was designed to shock people into repentance.

The occasion of anyone's death was regarded as an opportunity for religious ed- ification by the clergy. Lessons were to be learned from the circumstances of death. The Rev. William Robertson of the small community of Chesterfield, Ontario, was particularly harsh about the death of the local physician in an 1873 railway accident. The purpose of his sermon was to outline the solemn lessons that were contained in the tragedy. He found this "peculiarly difficult," for Dr. Corson was "greatly esteemed for his skill . . . and faithful attention to the duties of his profession." Many in the community had witnessed his tenderness, or experienced his sympathy in the "cham- bers of sorrow," when he was dealing with suffering or someone's death. Since the railway accident occurred on a Sunday, it seemed clear to Robertson that Corson's death contained a divine lesson and warning. The Almighty was demonstrating his displeasure with the recklessness of Sabbath breakers. "Visitations of sudden deaths," Robertson reminded his parishioners, "are eminently fitted, by their severity as well as singularity, to arrest the attention and impress the hearts of men."[24] The tragic accident was treated as an occasion for a stern argument for the strictest Sabbath Observance; it was intended to fortify the existing moral code and church sanctioned community standards.

The problem with funeral sermons that used the occasion of someone's death as an opportunity to bring about conversion was that it did not offer any immediate solace. Mourners were not consoled by preaching that emphasized damnation and hell. Such notions were distant from the pain and sense of separation the grieving experienced. In 1850, Margaret Dickie Michener's husband died while away from home. While recovering from the shock, Margaret confessed in her diary: "I find consolation in prayer. I cannot say I feel resigned." She struggled with the concept that her husband's death was somehow a judgement from God. The local minister's funeral sermon was from the text "Be ye also ready." It failed to move Margaret. During the sermon she could only think of how much better it would be if her husband's body was laid out before her. What consoled this grieving widow was "scribbling" in her diary and visiting friends. In deep mourning, she was comforted by the "many promises in scripture," not the dire warnings about everlasting suffering and the necessity for everyone to repent.[25] Many clergy appreciated that if they were to have an effective role in helping people cope with death then their message had to be comforting and consoling. There were practical reasons prompting many clergy to turn away from the doctrine of hell and divine punishment.

....

One way that people consoled themselves was to observe how their loved ones actually died. Margaret Michener was denied this opportunity since her husband did not die by her side. Perhaps this is why words of consolation were so extremely important to her. Nevertheless, death was frequently a household event in the nineteenth century. The dying were not removed to an institution away from the home; rather they remained an integral part of family life. The dying were the centre of attention and activity. There was great anxiety about the nature of a loved one's death. The deathbed was considered God's last court, and how the dying faced up to this final trial both determined and was a sign of one's fate. "Death must be the subject of awe," one minister reminded his congregation in 1851, for "*immediately after death there is judgement* — the judgement in which there can be neither change nor termination."[26] This judgement, many believed, was completely dependent on one's faith.[27] Death, therefore, was the most important event in anyone's life.

The Rev. Robert Irvine suggested to his congregation that if they witnessed the death of someone who was "unsanctified by the Spirit of God," they would "see those eyes which are growing dim with the shadows of mortality, and behold that countenance which betrays the inward workings of remorse, and you see a fearful picture of bondage by which the ungodly man is enslaved." The soul of the dying sinner is "tormented with the terror of death."[28] These experiences, however, rarely came to light. As Alexander Sutherland pointed out, "friends hide" these painful trials "and wish them forgotten."[29]

Nevertheless, clergymen claimed that those who were unsure about their immortality approached death with fear and loathing. The Rev. Smith was very explicit about the final moments in the life of Barnabas Bidwell, the controversial Upper Canadian reform politician. He indicated how Bidwell laboured under considerable doubt and depression during his illness. He had confessed himself to be a sinner, but did not feel the "comforts of the gospel." Consequently, according to Smith, a "feeling of uncertainty deepened painfully" as Bidwell "felt certain that life was drawing to a close." In the funeral oration, Smith outlined what he considered to be Bidwell's deathbed conversion.

> But prayer was offered up for him, and it was heard, for on the forenoon of the evening in which he died the cloud was removed; he was enabled to look away from himself as a guilty creature, and to look to Jesus as the author and finisher of his faith. Then, so far from fearing death, he longed for its approach; and when specially asked if he felt that it would be a relief, he plainly intimated his confidence that it would, and prayed "Even so come Lord Jesus come quickly." [30]

Prayer and devotion at the deathbed had helped Bidwell overcome his terror, and he died the "good death." Bidwell's final trial explains why there was such anxiety about sudden deaths in the nineteenth century. They deprived the victim of the opportunity to prepare for death, and more importantly, to make a final restitution or a deathbed conversion.

On the other hand, it was thought that those with a conviction of God's abiding presence faced death with a sense of confidence. During the "good death," the dying put their temporal and spiritual life in order.[31] Typically, final arrangements were outlined and worldly goods were distributed. It was deemed important that the dying attempt to console those grieving around them by proclaiming that they felt God's saving presence nearby. Eliza Tremain, a devout Baptist church member from Halifax, had a long bout of consumption. The minister who was with her the night before she died reported that she uttered the following last words: "I expected to be *supported* by my Saviour when I came to this hour — but I have been *comforted* — *It is lovely to die.*" Apparently, Eliza's death had an edifying and uplifting effect on the witnesses at her deathbed. One wrote to a friend that Eliza bore her suffering with a "most enviable Christian serenity, assurance, and resignation, and but waits the expected moment, that shall change suffering humanity into blissful spirituality." Another attendant observed that Eliza "exchanged her probation of extreme suffering for the blissful abode of redeemed spirits, affording to the last moment the encouraging and convincing evidence of the precious truths of our most holy religion."[32]

According to many accounts, the devout were given the strength and fortitude by God to endure the greatest suffering and pain with calm and piety. In 1864, James Hervey, a loyal member of Saint Andrew's Presbyterian Church in Montreal, was struck down with a "disease that generally prostrates every mental faculty as well as every physical energy." But according to the Rev. Mathieson of Montreal, "God was mercifully pleased to preserve his consciousness almost to the last moment." This divine act enabled Hervey to leave "with his sorrowing friends a token of his firm faith in Christ Jesus, to console them, . . . and stir them up to secure the same comforting hopes for their dying hour."[33] The image of the graceful, peaceful deathbed, in which the dying person, surrounded by family and friends, dispensed words of consolation, dominated Victorian literature. Such accounts may have been designed to conform with convention; but they were also necessary. With the belief that the unregenerate would suffer in hell forever, it was important to the bereaving to witness their loved ones experiencing a "good death," since that was a clear sign of redemption and life everlasting. The alternative of everlasting punishment was too much to bear.

Despite the constant references to the prospect of eternal punishment for the unregenerate in early nineteenth century sermons and funeral orations, the hope of life everlasting was always suggested as a real possibility. John Jennings, the minister at Bay Street Presbyterian Church in Toronto, argued that it was incorrect "to read our fate only in the language of death." The gospel, he emphasized in an 1868 sermon, "places a lamp of living hope in the coffin, . . . and by its light we read with joy that we shall rise again."[34] Such imagery temporized the dark, menacing aspects of death that were very much a part of the evangelical preachers' message. A belief in future life, in which the human soul cast off its earthly body at death and had a separate spiritual existence, was the foundation for Christian based consolation. The gospel of the risen Christ, one clergyman explained, "soothe[s] our pain and abate[s] our instinctive dread [so] that we may never be afraid to die."[35] To overcome the tremendous sense of loss and grief that most experienced when a loved one or friend died, ministers stressed that

> such mournful occasions are far from being unmitigated afflictions. To such friends themselves it is a blessed release from sorrow, suffering, trial, and care, and the beginning of the complete fulfilment and fruition of that lively hope to which they have been begotten again, by the resurrection of Jesus Christ from the dead; and to us who remain behind, as stricken mourners, in this vestibule of the grave, it is surely far more than a sufficient compensation to know that their spirits have been conveyed to the region of the celestial light.[36]

The compelling need for consolation on the part of the grieving prompted the clergy to stress the reassuring doctrine of future life. During the later half of the nineteenth century, there was less emphasis on death being the final court of divine judgement, and fewer references to damnation and hell. Instead there was growing assurance that there was, indeed, everlasting and better life after death. The horrifying and gloomy images surrounding death were being replaced by images of tranquillity and beauty. Romantic notions of death and the afterlife became paramount in popular culture.

Pastoral imagery dominated funeral services and consolation literature. For example, while Charles Gordon was serving as a student missionary in southern Manitoba in the summer of 1885, he was startled by some chilling news. On the morning of a community picnic, a two year old boy drowned in the stream that ran beside the family home. Gordon struggled to console the grieving parents by suggesting that their son was being embraced by Jesus in heaven. "We try and speak of the other home, the better country, where Jesus is, who used to take the children of Judea in his arms, and the tears come in quiet weeping, and the saviour comforts. . . . We read the words about the New Heaven and the New Earth, and sing together the children's hymn 'Safe in the Arms of Jesus.'" Gordon emphasized the continuities between life on earth and in heaven. The little boy was not lost; he was safe. At the burial service, Gordon pointed out that the "little grave" was surrounded by the "sun-kissed" hills and flowers of the open prairie. In pointing to these pastoral surroundings, Gordon made reference to the regenerative powers of nature. He reminded the mourners that every day the "sun died," only to rise again the next morning.[37] Typically, clergy drew on the awe-inspiring yet visual changes in nature to convey the mysterious transformation that occurs at death. There is always rebirth or resurrection. This analogy between nature and the revealed truths of Scripture was suggested to console people that death was natural, beautiful, and most importantly, a new beginning.

....

The parallels being drawn between death and nature were highly significant, since they reflected the growing conviction that death was the result of natural causes. As death was being considered a natural event instead of a supernatural one, the idea that humans could somehow conquer death was becoming more current. It seemed that other aspects of nature were being conquered through technological innovation, advances in engineering, or scientific and medical breakthroughs. There was a growing conviction that somehow humans could shape the character and perhaps the timing of someone's death. Medical intervention was allowed to contribute significantly to the realization of a "beautiful death." At the very least, medicine could make death a less painful, if not peaceful, passage. Consequently, the physician began to compete with the clergyman in the management of the deathbed.[38]

A fascinating glimpse of the growing determination to secure a beautiful death through medical intervention is provided in the last days of Mary Houstoun Cochrane. She was suddenly taken ill in late December of 1870. The pain was excruciating and she frequently "uttered a loud scream." Her husband, the Rev. William Cochrane of Brantford, Ontario, was overcome, for "her sufferings continued without abatement." He called the local physicians. But they did not merely give a diagnosis and suggest that final preparations be made. Instead they intervened to reduce the pain and suffering by administering drugs. The "sleeping draught" allowed her to rest much easier. "To the watchers by her bed," Cochrane reported, "it seemed a more natural and refreshing sleep." The view of the "good death" had changed. It came to be seen as a gentle, peaceful, and quiet passage to a better home, not as the supreme test of Christian fortitude. Despite the attendance of the physicians and the application of numerous medical treatments, "there was no help." When death was near, Cochrane noted that suddenly "her eyes grew bright and lustrous as if she caught a glimpse of glory as the spirit enters the veil." In the end, Cochrane believed that God took his wife, but during the last painful days he was willing to allow the physicians to intervene to slow down the process, help take the pain away, and in the very final hours, revive her with some stimulants so that she "might once more speak, if only to give a blessing to the sobbing ones around her deathbed."[39]

This willingness to intervene in the process of death rests at the foundation of changing attitudes toward death. The supernatural view, in which death was considered an act of Providence, was emphasized less as death was increasingly regarded as the result of natural causes.[40] This demystification of death opened the door to greater human intervention. Perhaps death could be controlled or tamed by medicine. It seemed within the grasp of human capacity to remove the dark, ominous, and painful aspects of death. Advances in scientific medicine probably fuelled the expectation that death could be painless and "beautiful." There was no sense of spiritual trial during Mary Cochrane's death, and there was significant effort to reduce her physical pain. Her death was designed to be a gentle release or passage to a better life. Since death was considered a natural event, intervention in the process of dying was now possible without fear that the inscrutable will of God was being somehow transgressed. Furthermore, the growing emphasis on a loving and merciful God contributed to this belief that human intervention did not defy God's moral government. Indeed God was being increasingly consigned to the background in many people's thoughts and actions surrounding death. Some of death's most terrifying mysteries were lifted with the decline in the belief that humans had no choice but to accept the final trial meted out by an exacting, judgemental God.

....

Another indicator of changing attitudes toward death was the theological debate over the question of the eternal punishment of the wicked.[41] This controversy began in the 1830s in Canada. The debate was particularly spirited in Halifax because a Universalist church was established there. The doctrine of everlasting punishment was dismissed by Universalists as a pagan superstition, and instead universal salvation was emphasized.[42] The more conservative or traditional clergy and laity valiantly defended the orthodox evangelical view that the reprobate state was fixed and future punishment was everlasting.[43] The most staunch defenders of this view insisted that the wicked would be punished, and "the penalty of the law of God . . . is eternal conscious suffering." They argued that Scripture, in the plainest language, declared that "the final doom of Satan will be *endless torment*, and that the wicked will share the same."[44] The Rev. William Cochrane was convinced that this was a question of substantial public interest, and so he collected many of the writings expressing the various views in a lengthy volume, *Future Punishment; Or Does Death End Probation?*, published in 1868. In selecting the essays, Cochrane tried "not to misrepresent the views held by those at variance with the Evangelical Creed," but the underlying message of the collection was a defence of orthodoxy.[45] This debate was at its height in Canada between the 1850s and 1870s and did not subside until the late 1880s.

For many, the idea of a punishing, judgemental God who consigned individuals to eternal damnation was morally unacceptable. The Rev. John Paul's 1883 tract was typical of what many clergy and lay persons were arguing. He explained that orthodox doctrines concerning the everlasting punishment of the wicked had caused himself and many others to react against Christianity and hope for a better gospel.

> This awful doctrine has cast a shadow over my whole life. In the days of my childhood and youth, I was made miserable by the terrific preaching of men who seemed to take pleasure in dwelling vehemently upon it. The thought that . . . the tens and hundreds of thousands of the "unconverted" around us, including some of our own friends and relatives were hastening onward to a life of hopeless and endless suffering, so oppressed me that I was almost in continual sorrow. My deep sympathy for suffering humanity around me as I worked and walked through life combined with the sad thought (as we have been taught to believe) that these myriads of mankind were constantly dropping into an everlasting hell of pain, was often more than my spirit could bear.

After much reading and study, he dismissed the doctrine of the eternal punishment of the wicked "as an odious night-mare of medieval ignorance and superstition." Paul settled on a more "comforting . . . cheering and hopeful" outlook regarding God's moral government and the ultimate destiny of humankind which suggested that the wicked were not consigned to hell but to everlasting death.[46] Many who had moved beyond orthodox doctrine, however, could not dismiss the notion of some form of punishment for human sinfulness. Instead they altered their understanding of the form of punishment. Alexander Sutherland's teaching remained rooted in evangelical

Christianity, and he argued that sinfulness resulted in banishment from God.[47] The concept of everlasting physical torment in hell had largely disappeared.[48]

As clergy made fewer references to hell and punishment in their funeral orations, they paid more attention to the nature of heaven and life in the hereafter. Up to the 1870s, most clergymen rarely speculated on the nature of heaven. "We cannot penetrate the veil of eternity; we cannot follow the released spirit to the secret abode, or tell the manner of its existence, or the measure of its beatitude," the Rev. William Bulloch noted.[49] But with the decline of the image of a judgemental God and the emergence of the image of a merciful and loving God, there was growing confidence that God could somehow be more clearly appreciated and understood. Accompanying this changing image of God was a changing image of the nature of the afterlife in heaven. It was thought that Christians "should seek to gain definite and well defined ideas regarding our Heavenly inheritance."[50] No longer was heaven considered to be beyond human comprehension or view. As the mystery of heaven was removed, a sense of the afterlife was brought into clear focus.

Heaven was regarded in physical as opposed to supernatural terms. The dominant early nineteenth century image of heaven as a remote place of "celestial light" where a transcendent God reigned was replaced by idyllic pastoral or domestic images. In many of the popular gospel tunes of the late nineteenth century, the image of heaven as a home or domestic bliss was constantly repeated.[51] It was thought that the redeemed would have "material bodies preserving their individual identity," and consequently, earthly human personality would be sustained and memory would be an "undying possession." During the afterlife, intimate family relationships and friendships would be renewed and perpetuated.[52]

The possibility of being reunited with loved ones became the central note sounded in consolation literature. When the Rev. E.H. Dewart's son suddenly died on 9 January 1877 at the age of five, Dewart wrote a poem as a memorial and an outlet for his grief. The poem reflected the many stages typical of the grieving process. Dewart opened sounding the notes of denial. "I reel beneath the sudden blow / . . . my heart cannot believe its woe — / I cannot think him dead." He described how he was haunted by the sounds of his son at play and how much joy and sorrow accompanied any memories of Albert's "loving presence." It was difficult for Dewart to escape the piercing and dark vision that his son "lies cold and silent with the dead." Consolation for Dewart rested in the belief that his son had been delivered from the miseries of the world and had been received into God's merciful arms. "No storm can break thy tranquil rest. / No sin thy spirit stain; / No sigh no grief — no tears shall flow / for ills that darken life below." Nothing tested faith in the abiding presence of God more than the death of a child, and Dewart prayed for understanding. "Shed light upon my darksome path, / Breathe hope into my heart; / And teach me, though it seems like wrath, / How merciful Thou art." The ultimate hope Dewart derived "from [the] bitter seeds of grief and gloom" was the belief that if he trusted in God then "in the world above / Where Death can never blight" he would "meet my darling boy again."[53] Belief that he would be re-united with his son in the afterlife was the only hope that could console this grieving father.

Even greater hopes than intimate personal fulfilment and family reunion were attached to the afterlife in the late nineteenth century. According to the author of one tract on the nature of heaven, most people "fondly hope" that their "cherished desires" will be fulfilled in heaven. "To the poor it will be a place of plenty. To the sick it will be a place of health. To the sorrowful and despondent it will be a place of joy." Heaven was not a place of prayers and contemplation before an awe-inspiring saviour, but a place of great activity. In heaven, there would be perpetual spiritual, moral, and social fulfilment.[54] In the age of Darwin, everlasting life in the hereafter was regarded as an evolutionary process. This image of heaven as a place where human society was ultimately perfected was consistent with the aspirations of the social gospel. Progressive clergymen and reformers were confident that the Kingdom of God could be created on earth. Such lofty aspirations seemed to be within the grasp of Christian societies, especially when heaven was understood in these very human and material terms. As McDannell and Lang suggest in their history of heaven: "Once heaven becomes the stage of human activity, and God recedes into the background, belief in that God is less crucial."[55] There were strong secular undercurrents in these more romantic views of death and the afterlife.

....

It is tempting to attribute these changing views of death to improving mortality rates. Perhaps death was becoming less threatening. With increased life expectancy, improving health, and fewer contagious diseases to rob people of a full life, death could be consigned to the background of life. Demographic research indicates that mortality conditions in Canada improved gradually but steadily throughout the latter half of the nineteenth century.[56] A complex array of factors, such as better sanitation and hygiene, an improved standard of living and diet, advances in medicine and medical services, and public health reform, contributed to the improvement in life expectancy. This improvement, however, was not universal. In the overcrowded and unsanitary districts of Canada's burgeoning cities, infant and maternal mortality remained strikingly high and there were numerous outbreaks of life threatening infectious diseases.[57] High mortality rates persisted into the twentieth century.[58]

Change in attitudes to something as mysterious and elemental as death and the afterlife, therefore, defy strict materialistic explanations. Other factors, such as expanding scientific and medical knowledge, the rise of a romantic sensibility, changing understanding of human destiny, and an ongoing spiritual quest to reach a fuller appreciation of God, also played an important role. None of these factors were necessarily rooted in improved material conditions. In the case of changing attitudes toward death, the root of the change was as much cultural, intellectual, and religious as it was demographic, economic, or material.

There were certain aspects of the modern attitude toward death which reflected the atmosphere of spiritual doubt that had crept into the late nineteenth century.[59] Reflecting the growing uncertainty in specific doctrines such as the Last Judgement and the everlasting punishment of the wicked, there was, in funeral orations, a growing emphasis on consolation instead of on preaching the need for immediate conversion. By emphasizing consolation, in effect, the clergy were focusing their attention on the mourners and how they might cope in this world. The real "sting" of death hit those left behind on earth and not the departed. More significant than the challenge to certain doctrines was the declining confidence in the presence of the spiritual and the power of the supernatural. Death was increasingly regarded as a natural rather than a providential event. The afterlife in heaven was imagined in more this-worldly terms. It was considered to be a place dominated by human activity and material or worldly aspirations, not a spiritual place of absolute devotion and worship of God.

Perhaps Robert Weir's rebuttal of "Death Abolished" was a defence against these more secular undercurrents that were influencing the attitudes and rituals surrounding death in the late nineteenth century. His critique reflected concern that traditional Christian beliefs were being replaced by a modern view which relegated God to the background of this most mysterious drama in life. Religious beliefs were still deeply ingrained in the modern outlook. While Macdonnell's "Death Abolished" boldly repudiated any dark or menacing concepts of death, it clearly expressed supreme confidence in the Christian promise of life everlasting. What seemed apparent to Weir was that one of the foundations of the Christian world view and discipline was being weakened in the outpouring of sentimentality that was surrounding death. The very concept of death was being avoided, if not denied.

This romantic perspective, which all but dismissed the reality and finality of death, was clearly evident in a devotional pamphlet written by the Rev. Charles W. Gordon in 1900.

Death . . . is an empty thing, simply a shade that crosses our heart. The realities are beyond. He has arrived, and we feel the pull of His immortality upon our spirits. . . . So when death comes, we push it aside. We make our passage through with comfort, held and drawn by our great hope. When death arrives at our home, knocks at our door and tries to throw his excluding shade over the faces of those we love, we resent his impertinence, and say to him, "O death, where is thy sting? O grave, where is thy victory?" We are not losing our true life or anything else worth having, we are about to gain everything because of our immortal hope in Jesus Christ.[60]

Death was neither a radical break from life nor a mysterious event to be feared. Instead it was a journey to a recognizable but better "home." Gordon's homily captured perfectly the late century confidence that somehow death could be conquered because it was indeed an easy passage to a better life. Death had indeed lost its "sting"; it was being denied. As the reporter at George Paxton Young's funeral observed, Young somehow did not appear to be dead, for he "looked much the same as . . . in life . . . one might think him sleeping." In taking away the fears surrounding death, the clergy may have lessened the impulse for people to follow the Christian precepts concerning death. Clearly, in the more secular atmosphere of the late nineteenth century, heaven was being made to look like life on earth and the dead were being made to look like the living.

NOTES

1. R.D. Gidney, "George Paxton Young," *Dictionary of Canadian Biography*, Vol. XI (Toronto 1982).
2. *Toronto Mail*, 2 March 1889.
3. J.F. McCurdy, *Life and Work of D.J. Macdonnell* (Toronto 1897), 88–154 and David B. Marshall, *Secularizing the Faith: Canadian Protestant Clergy and the Crisis of Belief, 1850–1940* (Toronto 1992).
4. D.J. Macdonnell, "Death Abolished: A Sermon Preached in St. Andrew's Church, Toronto on Sunday, 3rd March 1889 In Connection With the Death of George Paxton Young, LL.D." (Toronto 1899).
5. Philippe Aries, *The Hour of Our Death* (London 1981), 473–4. In his discussion of attitudes toward death in the United States in the nineteenth century, James Farrell refers to

similar developments as evidence of the "death of dying." See *Inventing the American Way of Death, 1830–1920* (Philadelphia 1980), 5–12, 74–89.

6. Archives of Ontario, Robert S. Weir, "Review of Rev. D.J. Macdonnell's Sermon Entitled Death Abolished" (np, nd), 1–32.

7. For a superb discussion of the mix of Christian and folklore beliefs surrounding death in early nineteenth century England, see Ruth Richardson, *Death, Dissection and the Destitute* (London 1987), 3–29. See also Bertram Puckle, *Funeral Customs: Their Origin and Development* (London 1926).

8. These aspects of the rituals of mourning and remembrance are explored in J.G. Curl, *The Victorian Celebration of Death* (London 1972) and J. Morley, *Death, Heaven, and the Victorians* (London 1971).

9. On the role of parades and processions in general, see Susan Davis, *Parades and Power: Street Theatre in Nineteenth Century Philadelphia* (Philadelphia 1986) and Mary Ryan, "The American Parade: Representations of the Nineteenth Century Social Order," in Lyn Hunt, ed., *The New Cultural History* (Los Angeles 1989). For the Canadian context, see Bonnie Huskins, "The Ceremonial Space of Women: Public Processions in Victorian Saint John and Halifax," in Janet Guildford and Suzanne Morton, eds., *Separate Spheres: Women's Worlds in the 19th Century Maritimes* (Fredericton 1994).

10. See Arnold Toynbee and others, *Man's Concern with Death* (New York 1968), 116–44.

11. The historical investigation of attitudes toward death was initiated by Philippe Aries in *Western Attitudes toward Death: From the Middle Ages to the Present* (Baltimore 1974). Recently Aries' work has been criticized for over dramatizing the change in attitudes and not being sensitive to differing national experiences. See J. McManners, "Death and the French Historians," in J. Whaley, ed., *Mirrors of Mortality: Studies in the Social History of Death* (London 1981). Other significant studies include David Stannard, ed., *Death in America* (University of Pennsylvania 1975); David Stannard, *The Puritan Way of Death: A Study in Religion, Culture and Social Change* (Oxford 1977); Clare Gittings, *Death, Burial and the Individual in Early Modern England* (London 1984); R. Houlbrooke, ed., *Death, Ritual, and Bereavement* (London 1989); Sylvia Barnard, *"To Prove I'm Not Forgot": Living and Dying in a Victorian City* (Manchester 1992). A study of death in Canada is Serge Gagnon, *Mourir hier et aujourd'hui: De la mort chrétienne dans la campagne québécoise au XIXe siècle à la mort technicisée dans la cité sans Dieu* (Quebec City 1987). See also Michael Cross and Robert Fraser, "'The Waste That Lies before Me': The Public and Private Worlds of Robert Baldwin," *Canadian Historical Association Historical Papers*, 1983.

12. Pioneering studies of the life cycle and life expectancy emphasize the persistence of high mortality rates throughout the nineteenth century. See Michael Katz, *The People of Hamilton, Canada West: Family and Class in a Mid-Nineteenth Century City* (Cambridge, Mass. 1975), 33; David Gagan, *Hopeful Travellers: Families, Land and Social Change in Mid-Victorian Peel County, Canada West* (Toronto 1981), 89–93; Bettina Bradbury, "The Fragmented Family: Strategies in the Face of Death, Illness, and Poverty in Montreal, 1860–1885," in Joy Parr, ed., *Childhood and Family in Canadian History* (Toronto 1982), 109–28; and Jean-Claude Robert, "The City of Wealth and Death: Urban Mortality in Montreal, 1821–1871," in Wendy Mitchinson and Janice Dickin McGinnis, eds., *Essays in the History of Canadian Medicine* (Toronto 1988), 18–38.

13. Robert Irvine, "The Certainty of Death and the Preparation Necessary for Meeting It: A Sermon Preached in the Saint John Presbyterian Church on the last Sabbath of 1847" (Saint John 1848), 11.

14. Geoffrey Bilson, *A Darkened House: Cholera in Nineteenth Century Canada* (Toronto 1980); Michael Bliss, *Plague: A Story of Smallpox in Montreal* (Toronto 1991).

15. J. Smith, "Immortality: A Sermon Occasioned by the Death of Barnabas Bidwell, Esq." (Kingston 1833), 3–5. See also William Jackson, *Immortality Versus Annihilation: An Enquiry Concerning the Nature and Destiny of the Human Soul* (Montreal 1872), 53–4;

Goldwin Smith, "The Immortality of the Soul," *Canadian Monthly and National Review*, May 1876.

16. John Barclay, "A Sermon Preached in St. Andrew's Church, Toronto, On the Occasion of the Lamented Death of One of the Elders of the Church, The Late Hon. Archibald McLean, President of Her Majesties Court of Error and Appeal for Upper Canada" (Toronto 1865), 10–13.

17. William Snodgrass, "The Night of Death; A Sermon, Preached on the 7th Oct., 1860, Being the First Sabbath after the Funeral of the Honourable Peter McGill" (Montreal 1860), 8–13.

18. Jonathan Shortt, " 'Peace in Believing': Exemplified in the Case of the Late Mary Anne Sophia Whitehead, Who Fell Asleep in Jesus on Sunday, the 7th March 1847, in the 29th Year of Her Age" (Toronto 1847), 14–15, 22–5.

19. Robert Irvine, "The Certainty of Death," 11–12.

20. "Memoir of Mrs. Eliza Chipman" (Wolfville 1835), reprinted in Margaret Conrad et al., eds., *No Place Like Home: Diaries and Letters of Nova Scotia Women, 1771–1938* (Halifax 1988). The excerpts quoted are from 26 Dec. 1830 and 6 May 1834. For a broader study, see Nancy Dye and Daniel Blake, "Mother Love and Infant Death, 1750–1920," *Journal of American History*, Vol. 73, No. 2, Sept. 1986.

21. United Church Archives, Thomas Webster Papers, "My Memoirs: A Story of Early Pioneer Life in Canada West," 1871, 61–2.

22. Anson Green, *The Life and Times of the Rev. Anson Green* (Toronto 1877), 186–9. This theme of Providence and the 1832 cholera epidemic is explored in Charles Rosenberg, *The Cholera Years: The United States in 1832, 1849, 1866* (Chicago 1962), 40–54.

23. United Church Archives, Alexander Sutherland Papers, File 13, Sermons "1 Corinthians 15: 6–7," nd.

24. William Robertson, "The Ministry of Sudden Death" (Woodstock 1873), 6–8, 16–17. See also Walter Roach, "Sermon Preached in the Scotch Church Beauharnois . . . On occasion of the Deaths By Drowning of Messers F. Cowan and C.J. Chard" (Montreal 1845), 19–23.

25. Excerpts of Michener's diary are reprinted in Conrad et al., eds., *No Place Like Home*, 110–14.

26. William Bulloch, "The Ruler's Daughter Raised: Funeral Discourse Preached at the Chapel of Ease, Halifax, March 16th, 1851" (Halifax 1851), 5.

27. John McCaul, "Emigration to a Better Country: A Sermon Preached in the Cathedral of Saint James, Toronto, on Saint Patrick's Day, 1842" (Toronto 1842), 5–6, 13.

28. Robert Irvine, "The Certainty of Death," 14.

29. A. Sutherland, "1 Corinthians 15: 6–7."

30. J. Smith, " 'Immortality': A Sermon Occasioned by the Death of Barnabas Bidwell, Esq.," 17–18.

31. For an account, see Agnes Machar, *Faithful Unto Death: A Memorial of John Anderson, Late Janitor of Queen's College, Kingston, C.W.* (Kingston 1859), 46–54.

32. E.A. Crawley, "The Righteous Shall Be In Everlasting Remembrance: A Sermon Preached in Granville Street Baptist Chapel, Halifax, N.S. March 27, 1837, On the Occasion of the Decease of Mrs. Eliza Tremain, A Member of the Baptist Church Worshipping in that Place" (Halifax 1837), 11, 17.

33. Alexander Mathieson, "The Vanity of Earthly Objects of Attachment. A Sermon Preached in St. Andrew's Church, Montreal on the Occasion of the Death of James Hervey, Esq." (Montreal 1864), 24–6. See also "A Sermon Preached in the Cathedral Church of St. James, Toronto, Canada on the 15th Day of May 1842, by the Honourable and Right Reverend The Lord Bishop of Toronto, on the Death of Elizabeth Emily, Wife of Mr. Justice Hagerman" (Toronto 1842), 11; and D.H. MacVicar, "In Memoriam. A Sermon Preached in the Canada Presbyterian Church, Cote Street Montreal, on Sabbath,

March 14th, 1889, On the Occasion of the Death of John Redpath Esq." (Montreal 1869), especially the "Obituary Part," 20–9.

34. John Jennings, "In Memorium. A Sermon on the Death of Miss Margaret Macdonald" (Toronto 1868), 8–9.

35. George Whitaker, "A Sermon, Preached at the Church of St. John the Evangelist, Toronto," nd, 6.

36. William Snodgrass, "The Night of Death," 26.

37. C.W. G[ordon], "Jottings from a Missionary Diary," *Knox College Monthly*, Vol. IV, No. 1, Nov. 1885. For a general discussion of consolation literature, see Ann Douglas, "Heaven Our Home: Consolation Literature in the Northern United States, 1830–1860," in David Stannard, ed., *Death in America*, 49–68.

38. On the rise of the medical profession in Upper Canada/Ontario, see R.D. Gidney and W.P.J. Millar, *Professional Gentleman: The Professions in Nineteenth-century Ontario* (Toronto 1994), passim; and Colin Howell, "Elite Doctors and the Development of Scientific Medicine: The Halifax Medical Establishment and the 19th Century Medical Profession," in Charles G. Roland ed., *Health, Disease and Medicine: Essays in Canadian History* (Hannah Institute of Medicine 1982), 69–95, 105–22.

39. This account is based on William Cochrane's Diary, Archives of Ontario, William Cochrane Papers, Series B-6, Diary 27 Dec. 1870 to 8 Jan. 1871; and William Cochrane, *A Quiet and Gentle Life. In Memorium: Mary Neilson Houstoun Cochrane* (Brantford 1871), 45–6. On the growing division between the medical and the religious world view, see S.E.D. Shortt, "Physicians and Psychics: The Anglo-American Medical Response to Spiritualism, 1870–1890," *Journal of American Medicine and Allied Sciences*, Vol. 39, 350–4.

40. The rise of the natural understanding of death is outlined in Farrell, *Inventing the American Way of Death*, 44–68.

41. This debate dominated much of the theological discussion about death in Victorian Canada and elsewhere. See Geoffrey Rowell, *Hell and the Victorians: A Study of the Nineteenth-century Theological Controversies Concerning Eternal Punishment and the Future Life* (Oxford 1974).

42. N. Gunnison, "The Coming of Christ, End of the World and Everlasting Punishment: A Sermon Preached in Halifax, Nova Scotia, 27 June 1858 . . . and Commended to the Attention of All Believers in the Dogma of Endless Misery!" (Halifax 1858), 10–13; N. Gunnison, "A Sermon on the Life and Death of Samuel C. West, Preached in the Universalist Church, Halifax, N.S. Nov. 21, 1858" (Halifax 1858). For a direct attack on the preaching in the Halifax Universalist church, see "Remarks on a Discourse, Preached and Published By the Rev. D.M. Knappen, Pastor of the Universalist Church, Halifax. By a Layman" (Halifax 1845). On the Halifax Universalist Church and universalism in nineteenth century Maritime society, see Phillip Hewett, *Unitarians in Canada* (Toronto 1978), 79–84.

43. J. Lenfest, "What Will Become of the Wicked?" (Halifax 1861); John G. Marshall, "Scriptural Answer to a Late Pamphlet on the Teaching of the Universalist Church" (Halifax 1874); John Campbell, "A Sermon on the Doctrine of Everlasting Punishment, Preached at St Andrew's Scotch National Church" (Halifax 1875); G. Field, "Sermon on the Subject of Everlasting Punishment, Delivered at the new Jerusalem Temple, Toronto, May 7, 1876" (Toronto 1876); John G. Marshall, "Testimony of the Bible Concerning Everlasting Punishment: Comments on Canon Farrar's 'Eternal Hope' and How to Obtain Everlasting Happiness" (Halifax 1878); William Shaw, "Eternal Punishment: A Lecture Delivered Before the Theological Union of Victoria University, May 5, 1833" (Toronto 1884).

44. G.A. Hartley, "Immortality Versus Annihilation" (Saint John 1867), 50–1; William Jackson, *Immortality Versus Annihilation: An Inquiry Concerning the Nature and Destiny of the Human Soul* (Montreal 1872), 179ff.

45. William Cochrane, *Future Punishment; Or Does Death End Probation?* (Brantford 1868), preface.

46. John Paul, "A Tract for the Times. 'A Burning Question!' Future Punishment Will It Be Endless Suffering?" (Montreal 1883), 8, 12, 17–19.

47. Alexander Sutherland, "The Final Outcome of Sin: A Homiletical Monograph" (Toronto 1886), 18–23.

48. Hell became secularized by the late nineteenth century. It was no longer a place where the wicked would be tormented in their afterlife. Instead the concept of hell was applied to this world, and especially to appalling social conditions, such as slums, factories, and the industrial city. See Michael Wheeler, *Death and the Future Life in Victorian Literature and Theology* (Cambridge 1990), 196–218.

49. William Bulloch, "The Ruler's Daughter Raised," 8.

50. D. Stewart, "The Heavenly Inheritance, or Reasonable and Scriptural Thoughts Regarding Heaven and the State and Condition of the Redeemed" (Seaforth, Ont., 1900).

51. See, for example, Hugh T. Crossley, *Songs of Salvation As Used By Crossley and Hunter in Evangelistic Meetings and Adapted for the Church*, Grace, School, Choir, and Home (Toronto 1887).

52. See J.E. Hopper, *Life in the Hereafter World, or "Shall We Know Each Other There?"* (Saint John 1894) 17–18; and W.L. Magee, "Shall We Know Each Other There?" (Ottawa 1882), 15. On the relationship between spiritualism and traditional Christian views of the hereafter, see Ramsay Cook, "Spiritualism, Science of the Earthly Paradise," *Canadian Historical Review*, 65, March 1984, 4–27.

53. E.H. Dewart, "Our Dear Dead Boy. In loving Memory of Albert Ernest Dewart, Who Died Suddenly on the 9th of January 1877, Aged 5 Years and 12 Days," in E.H. Dewart, *Additional Poems* (Toronto 1892).

54. D. Stewart, "The Heavenly Inheritance," 10, 22–3.

55. Colleen McDannell & Bernhard Lang, *Heaven: A History* (New Haven 1988), 305–15, 332–5.

56. Kevin McQuillan, "Ontario Mortality Patterns, 1861–1921," *Canadian Population Studies*, Vol. 12, No. 1, 1985, 31–45. On the thorny problem of constructing an accurate record of mortality rates, see George Emery, *Facts of Life: The Social Construction of Vital Statistics, Ontario 1869–1952* (Montreal 1993).

57. See Terry Copp, *The Anatomy of Poverty: The Condition of the Working Class in Montreal, 1897–1929* (Toronto 1974), 88–105; and Alan F.J. Artibise, *Winnipeg: A Social History of Urban Growth, 1874–1914* (Montreal 1975), 223–38. For a moving and graphic account of the 1885 smallpox outbreak in Montreal, see Michael Bliss, *Plague: A Story of Smallpox in Montreal.*

58. Rosemary Gagan, "Mortality Patterns and Public Health in Hamilton, Canada, 1900–14," *Urban History Review*, Vol. XVII, No. 3, Feb. 1989, 161–75.

59. Marshall, *Secularizing the Faith*, passim.

60. Ralph Connor, "Christian Hope" (Toronto nd) 29–30.

Photo Credits

TOPIC ONE
F.G. Claudet/British Columbia Archives and Records Service/HP-9326.

TOPIC TWO
National Gallery of Canada, No. 2036. Gift of Gordon C. Edwards in memory of Senator and Mrs. W.C. Edwards.

TOPIC THREE
National Gallery of Canada, No. 5875. Gift of Major Edgar C. Woolsey, Ottawa, 1952.

TOPIC FOUR
National Archives of Canada/C-95466.

TOPIC FIVE
Metropolitan Toronto Reference Library/T 10914.

TOPIC SIX
McCord Museum of Canadian History, Montreal.

TOPIC SEVEN
John Ross Robertson Collection, Metropolitan Toronto Reference Library/T 16581.

TOPIC EIGHT
British Columbia Archives and Record Service/HP-17826.

TOPIC NINE
Lee Pritzker Collection, National Archives of Canada/C-1959.

TOPIC TEN
Louis-Prudent Valle, National Archives of Canada/PA-139146.

READER REPLY CARD
....

We are interested in your reaction to *Age of Transition: Readings in Canadian Social History, 1800–1900,* by Norman Knowles. You can help us to improve this book in future editions by completing this questionnaire.

1. What was your reason for using this book?

   ❏ university course   ❏ continuing education course   ❏ personal interest

   ❏ college course   ❏ professional development   ❏ other _____

2. If you are a student, please identify your school and the course in which you used this book.

3. Which chapters or parts of this book did you use? Which did you omit?

4. What did you like best about this book?

5. What did you like least about this book?

6. Please identify any topics you think should be added to future editions.

7. Please add any comments or suggestions.

8. May we contact you for further information?

Name: _____

Address: _____

_____

Phone: _____

(fold here and tape shut)

0116870399-M8Z4X6-BR01

Larry Gillevet
Director of Product Development
HARCOURT BRACE & COMPANY, CANADA
55 HORNER AVENUE
TORONTO, ONTARIO
M8Z 9Z9